Myanmar
(Burma)

Michael Clark
Joe Cummings

LONELY PLANET PUBLICATIONS
Melbourne • Oakland • London • Paris

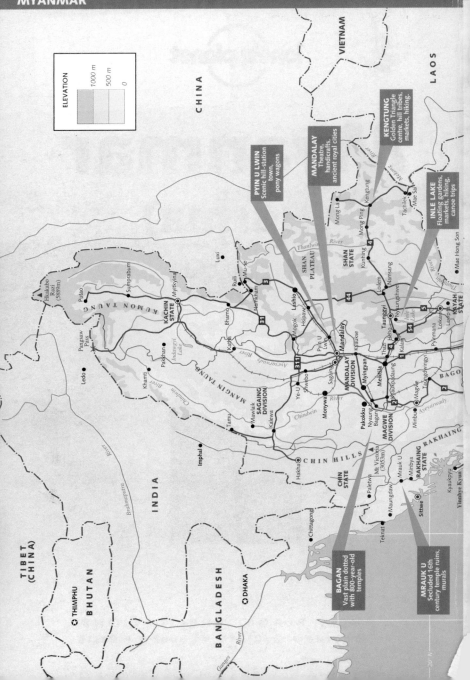

ELEVATION

1000 m
500 m
0

VIETNAM

LAOS

CHINA

TIBET (CHINA)

INDIA

BANGLADESH

BHUTAN

☸ THIMPHU

☸ DHAKA

PYIN U LWIN
Scenic hill-station town, pony wagons

MANDALAY
Theatre, handicrafts, ancient royal cities

KENGTUNG
Golden Triangle centre, hill tribes, markets, hiking.

INLE LAKE
Floating gardens, markets, hiking, canoe trips

BAGAN
Vast plain dotted with 800-year-old temples

MRAUK U
Secluded 16th century temple ruins, murals

KACHIN STATE

KUMON TAUNG

MANGIN TAUNG

SHAN PLATEAU

SHAN STATE

KAYAH STATE

SAGAING DIVISION

MANDALAY DIVISION

MAGWE DIVISION

BAGO

CHIN HILLS

CHIN STATE

RAKHAING STATE

RAKHAING

Hkakabo Razi (5889m)

Mt Victoria (3053m)

Putao

Sumprabum

Luxi

Myitkyina

Bhamo

Katha

Pangsaw Pass

Ledo

Khamti

Pakhan

Indawgyi Lake

Tamu

Mawlaik

Kalewa

Ye-U

Shwebo

Monywa

Imphal

Hakha

Paletwa

Maungdaw

Teknaf

Chittagong

Sittwe

Minbya

Mrauk U

Minbu

Magwe

Kyaukpyu

Yinbye Kyun

Pakokku

Nyaung U

Bagan

Yenangyaung

Taungdwingyi

Pyay

Pyinmana

Mu-se

Ruili

Namhkam

Lashio

Hsipaw

Mogok

Mong Yu

Pyin U Lwin

Mandalay

Kyaukse

Myingyan

Meiktila

Kyaukpadaung

Sagaing

Thazi

Kalaw

Pindaya

Taunggyi

Nyaungshwe

Inle Lake

Loikaw

Loilem

Kunhing

Namsang

Mong Ping

Mong La

Kengtung

Tachilek

Mae Sai

Mae Hong Son

Thanlwin River

Salween River

Mekong River

Irrawaddy River

Ayeyarwady River

Chindwin River

Brahmaputra River

Ganges River

Gulf of Martaban

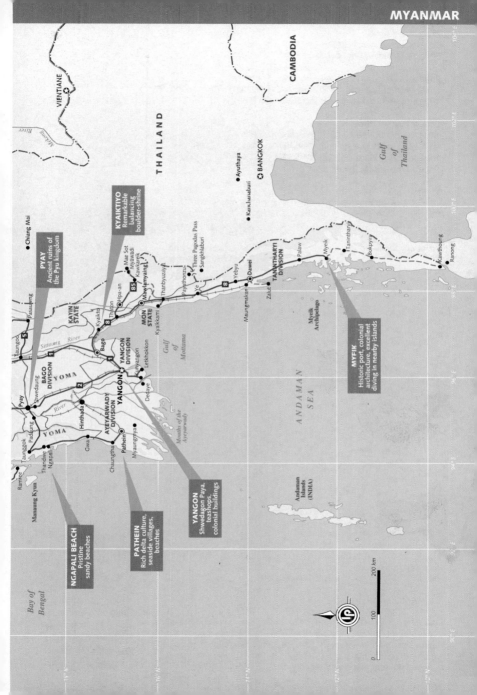

Myanmar (Burma)
7th edition – January 2000
First published – December 1979

Published by
Lonely Planet Publications Pty Ltd A.C.N. 005 607 983
192 Burwood Rd, Hawthorn, Victoria 3122, Australia

Lonely Planet Offices
Australia PO Box 617, Hawthorn, Victoria 3122
USA 150 Linden St, Oakland, CA 94607
UK 10a Spring Place, London NW5 3BH
France 1 rue du Dahomey, 75011 Paris

Photographs
All of the images in this guide are available for licensing from
Lonely Planet Images.
email: lpi@lonelyplanet.com.au

Front cover photograph
Plying a *chaung* (canal) in Nyaungshwe, Shan State (Sara-Jane Cleland)

ISBN 0 86442 703 4

text & maps © Lonely Planet 2000
photos © photographers as indicated 2000

Printed by Colorcraft Ltd, Hong Kong

Contents – Text

AROUND MANDALAY 263

BAGAN REGION 290

NORTH-EASTERN MYANMAR 347

SOUTH-EASTERN MYANMAR 398

WESTERN MYANMAR 425

LANGUAGE 449

GLOSSARY 462

ACKNOWLEDGMENTS 466

INDEX 475

MAP LEGEND back page

METRIC CONVERSION inside back cover

Contents – Maps

3

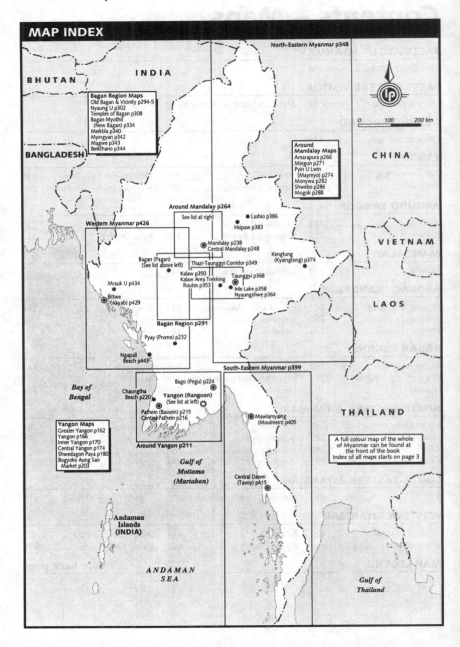

MAP INDEX

North-Eastern Myanmar p348

BHUTAN

INDIA

Bagan Region Maps
Old Bagan & Vicinity p294-5
Nyaung U p302
Temples of Bagan p308
Bagan Myothit
  (New Bagan) p334
Meiktila p340
Myingyan p342
Magwe p343
Beikthano p344

BANGLADESH

**Around
Mandalay Maps**
Amarapura p266
Mingun p271
Pyin U Lwin
  (Maymyo) p274
Monywa p282
Shwebo p286
Mogok p288

CHINA

0   100   200 km

Around Mandalay p264

See list at right

Western Myanmar p426

Lashio p386

Hsipaw p383

VIETNAM

Mandalay p238
Central Mandalay p248

Kengtung
(Kyaingtong) p374

Bagan (Pagan)
(See list above left)

Thazi-Taunggyi Corridor p349

Mrauk U p434

Kalaw p350
Kalaw Area Trekking
Routes p353

Taunggyi p368

Sittwe
(Akyab) p429

Inle Lake p358
Nyaungshwe p364

LAOS

Bagan Region p291

Pyay (Prome) p232

Ngapali
Beach p443

South-Eastern Myanmar p399

Bago (Pegu) p224

Bay of
Bengal

Chaungtha
Beach p220

Yangon (Rangoon)
(See list at left)

Pathein (Bassein) p215
Central Pathein p216

Mawlamyaing
(Moulmein) p405

THAILAND

Yangon Maps
Greater Yangon p162
Yangon p166
Inner Yangon p170
Central Yangon p174
Shwedagon Paya p180
Bogyoke Aung San
Market p203

Around Yangon p211

A full colour map of the whole
of Myanmar can be found at
the front of the book
Index of all maps starts on page 3

Gulf of
Mottama
(Martaban)

Central Dawei
(Tavoy) p415

Andaman
Islands
(INDIA)

ANDAMAN
SEA

Gulf of
Thailand

The Authors

Michael Clark

Michael first visited Myanmar in 1987, while working in Malaysia as a university lecturer. His overseas travels began with a summer job in the merchant marine, followed by a hitch-hiking trip to Greece, and then a two year stint in Malawi as a US Peace Corps volunteer. Graduate work in Hawaii and a teaching job in Japan followed. When not on the road, Michael teaches English to international students in Berkeley, California, where he lives with his wife Janet, and kids Melina and Alexander. He has written for the *San Francisco Examiner* and is a co-author of Lonely Planet's *New York, New Jersey, & Pennsylvania* guidebook, and he updated the Myanmar chapter of *South-East Asia on a shoestring*.

Joe Cummings

Joe has been travelling and working in South-East Asia since the 1970s, enjoying stints as a translator-interpreter, movie extra, English teacher and freelance writer. He has written over 30 original guidebooks, photographic books, phrasebooks and atlases for countries in Asia and North America and has recently co-written *Myanmar Style* and edited a book-length biography of Bogyoke Aung San. For Lonely Planet, he has authored the *Thai* and *Lao* phrasebooks, as well as guides to *Thailand*, *Bangkok*, *Thailand's Islands & Beaches* and *Laos*, parts of *South-East Asia on a shoestring* and *World Food: Thailand*. Joe has also published articles on culture, politics and travel in many print and online periodicals, including *Ambassador*, *Asia Magazine*, *Asian Wall Street Journal*, *Bangkok Post*, *Expedia*, *Fables*, *Geographical*, *The Nation*, *Outside*, *San Francisco Examiner* and *South China Morning Post*.

FROM THE AUTHORS
From Michael

My thanks to the many Burmese people who informed, inspired and sustained me during my travels through Myanmar – Ko Zaw Tun, Hsipaw's Mr Book; Zin Mi Tan and the Moustache Brothers family; Ma New Ni of the Royal Guest House; Yin Yin and Htay Htay Myint of the Four Sisters in Nyaungshwe; Marie Min and family who provided food for thought; Percy, Dien, Moe and Khaing of Santa Maria Travel & Tours; William of Tour Mandalay; U Ba Kyi of the Bagan Bookshop; and to artist Ma Thanegi for reality checks. Among the many travellers who provided invaluable help, special thanks to Marc Escobosa for insights and upbeat travel tips; road jesters Richard Ellert and daring Andrea for gold-leaf stories; Claude Charroneau for the sidestreets of Yangon;

Anke Rosa for humour and kindness, along with Jennifer Bartlett, Aru Santhiran, Julius and Kirstin, Lani and Roy, and true trekkers Simon Wills and Ben McCormack; Tom and Michelle for 50th St candlelight refuge; and Kristin and Sally at Lonely Planet's Melbourne office for their steady support through it all, along with Janet, Melina and Alex at home.

From Joe
Thanks to U Lu Maw and the Moustache Brothers family – U Nyo Than, Ko Shwe Bo, Daw Yei Waing, Ma Win Mar, Ma Ni Ni Lin, Ma Taik Kyi and Ma Cho Tu – for their Mandalay hospitality and inspiration. In Yangon, Percy Win Swe of Santa Maria Travel & Tours was helpful as always, while the Three Seasons Hotel's Mie Mie was and is every traveller's dream hotel manager.

In Dawei I thank DeGaulle for putting up with all the tricky questions and showing me a side of Dawei I would never have otherwise known, and in Myeik thanks to John for similar assistance. I'm indebted to Luca Tettoni for illuminating moments in Bangkok, Yangon and Mandalay, and for pointing out the *yethi* (antique) in Mandalay that now keeps watch over my sitting room in Chiang Mai.

Conversations with Ma Thanegi were, as always, both enlightening and encouraging. Rick Heizman's Shanachie CDs of dreamy Burmese music provided the perfect work soundtrack. Vicky Bowman takes sash and crown for her linguistic, cartographic and cultural insights.

Dedication
We dedicate the 7th edition of Myanmar to U Par Par Lay, in prison since January 1996 for inciting people to laugh at the present regime.

This Book

From the Publisher

The 7th edition of Myanmar (Burma) was produced in Lonely Planet's Melbourne office by coordinators Sally O'Brien (editorial) and Glenn Beanland (mapping and design). Sally was assisted with proofing by Joanne Newell, Martin Heng and Kristin Odijk, while Glenn was assisted with mapping by Tim Fitzgerald, Chris Love and Jack Gavran. Layout checks and assistance were provided by Tim Fitzgerald, Chris Love, Martin Heng and Kristin Odijk. The illustrations by Mick Weldon were coordinated by Matt King, and the photographs were supplied by Valerie Tellini and Fiona Croyden of Lonely Planet Images. Thanks to Chris Lee Ack for technical support, Leonie Mugavin for research assistance, Tim Uden for Quark wizardry, Quentin Frayne for the Language chapter, Guillaume Roux for the cover, Tamsin Wilson for design advice and front pages, and Lara Morcombe for the Index. Special thanks to Vicki Bowman, Michael Clark and the extraordinary Joe Cummings for all their hard work and patience.

THANKS

Many thanks to the travellers who used the last edition and wrote to us with helpful hints, advice and interesting anecdotes. Your names appear in the back of this book.

Foreword

ABOUT LONELY PLANET GUIDEBOOKS

The story begins with a classic travel adventure: Tony and Maureen Wheeler's 1972 journey across Europe and Asia to Australia. Useful information about the overland trail did not exist at that time, so Tony and Maureen published the first Lonely Planet guidebook to meet a growing need.

From a kitchen table, then from a tiny office in Melbourne (Australia), Lonely Planet has become the largest independent travel publisher in the world, an international company with offices in Melbourne, Oakland (USA), London (UK) and Paris (France).

Today Lonely Planet guidebooks cover the globe. There is an ever-growing list of books and there's information in a variety of forms and media. Some things haven't changed. The main aim is still to help make it possible for adventurous travellers to get out there – to explore and better understand the world.

At Lonely Planet we believe travellers can make a positive contribution to the countries they visit – if they respect their host communities and spend their money wisely. Since 1986 a percentage of the income from each book has been donated to aid projects and human rights campaigns.

Updates Lonely Planet thoroughly updates each guidebook as often as possible. This usually means there are around two years between editions, although for more unusual or more stable destinations the gap can be longer. Check the imprint page (following the colour map at the beginning of the book) for publication dates.

Between editions up-to-date information is available in two free newsletters – the paper *Planet Talk* and email *Comet* (to subscribe, contact any Lonely Planet office) – and on our Web site at www.lonelyplanet.com. The *Upgrades* section of the Web site covers a number of important and volatile destinations and is regularly updated by Lonely Planet authors. *Scoop* covers news and current affairs relevant to travellers. And, lastly, the *Thorn Tree* bulletin board and *Postcards* section of the site carry unverified, but fascinating, reports from travellers.

Correspondence The process of creating new editions begins with the letters, postcards and emails received from travellers. This correspondence often includes suggestions, criticisms and comments about the current editions. Interesting excerpts are immediately passed on via newsletters and the Web site, and everything goes to our authors to be verified when they're researching on the road. We're keen to get more feedback from organisations or individuals who represent communities visited by travellers.

Lonely Planet gathers information for everyone who's curious about the planet – and especially for those who explore it first-hand. Through guidebooks, phrasebooks, activity guides, maps, literature, newsletters, image library, TV series and Web site we act as an information exchange for a worldwide community of travellers.

Research Authors aim to gather sufficient practical information to enable travellers to make informed choices and to make the mechanics of a journey run smoothly. They also research historical and cultural background to help enrich the travel experience and allow travellers to understand and respond appropriately to cultural and environmental issues.

Authors don't stay in every hotel because that would mean spending a couple of months in each medium-sized city and, no, they don't eat at every restaurant because that would mean stretching belts beyond capacity. They do visit hotels and restaurants to check standards and prices, but feedback based on readers' direct experiences can be very helpful.

Many of our authors work undercover, others aren't so secretive. None of them accept freebies in exchange for positive write-ups. And none of our guidebooks contain any advertising.

Production Authors submit their raw manuscripts and maps to offices in Australia, USA, UK or France. Editors and cartographers – all experienced travellers themselves – then begin the process of assembling the pieces. When the book finally hits the shops, some things are already out of date, we start getting feedback from readers and the process begins again ...

WARNING & REQUEST

Things change – prices go up, schedules change, good places go bad and bad places go bankrupt – nothing stays the same. So, if you find things better or worse, recently opened or long since closed, please tell us and help make the next edition even more accurate and useful. We genuinely value all the feedback we receive. Julie Young coordinates a well travelled team that reads and acknowledges every letter, postcard and email and ensures that every morsel of information finds its way to the appropriate authors, editors and cartographers for verification.

Everyone who writes to us will find their name in the next edition of the appropriate guidebook. They will also receive the latest issue of *Planet Talk*, our quarterly printed newsletter, or *Comet* our monthly email newsletter. Subscriptions to both newsletters are free. The very best contributions will be rewarded with a free guidebook.

Excerpts from your correspondence may appear in new editions of Lonely Planet guidebooks, the Lonely Planet Web site, *Planet Talk* or *Comet*, so please let us know if you *don't* want your letter published or your name acknowledged.

Send all correspondence to the Lonely Planet office closest to you:

Australia: PO Box 617, Hawthorn, Victoria 3122
USA: 150 Linden St, Oakland, CA 94607
UK: 10A Spring Place, London NW5 3BH
France: 1 rue du Dahomey, 75011 Paris

Or email us at: talk2us@lonelyplanet.com.au

For news, views and updates see our Web site: www.lonelyplanet.com

HOW TO USE A LONELY PLANET GUIDEBOOK

The best way to use a Lonely Planet guidebook is any way you choose. At Lonely Planet we believe the most memorable travel experiences are often those that are unexpected, and the finest discoveries are those you make yourself. Guidebooks are not intended to be used as if they provide a detailed set of infallible instructions!

Contents All Lonely Planet guidebooks follow roughly the same format. The Facts about the Destination chapters or sections give background information ranging from history to weather. Facts for the Visitor gives practical information on issues like visas and health. Getting There & Away gives a brief starting point for researching travel to and from the destination. Getting Around gives an overview of the transport options when you arrive.

The peculiar demands of each destination determine how subsequent chapters are broken up, but some things remain constant. We always start with background, then proceed to sights, places to stay, places to eat, entertainment, getting there and away, and getting around information – in that order.

Heading Hierarchy Lonely Planet headings are used in a strict hierarchical structure that can be visualised as a set of Russian dolls. Each heading (and its following text) is encompassed by any preceding heading that is higher on the hierarchical ladder.

Entry Points We do not assume guidebooks will be read from beginning to end, but that people will dip into them. The traditional entry points are the list of contents and the index. In addition, however, some books have a complete list of maps and an index map illustrating map coverage.

There may also be a colour map that shows highlights. These highlights are dealt with in greater detail in the Facts for the Visitor chapter, along with planning questions and suggested itineraries. Each chapter covering a geographical region usually begins with a locator map and another list of highlights. Once you find something of interest in a list of highlights, turn to the index.

Maps Maps play a crucial role in Lonely Planet guidebooks and include a huge amount of information. A legend is printed on the back page. We seek to have complete consistency between maps and text, and to have every important place in the text captured on a map. Map key numbers usually start in the top left corner.

> Although inclusion in a guidebook usually implies a recommendation we cannot list every good place. Exclusion does not necessarily imply criticism. In fact there are a number of reasons why we might exclude a place – sometimes it is simply inappropriate to encourage an influx of travellers.

Introduction

Then, a golden mystery upheaved itself on the horizon – a beautiful, winking wonder that blazed in the sun, of a shape that was neither Muslim dome nor Hindu temple spire. 'There's the old Shwedagon', said my companion. The golden dome said, 'This is Burma, and it will be quite unlike any land you know about.'

Rudyard Kipling Letters from the East (1898)

To those who know it, Myanmar (formerly Burma) is a land of mystifying contradictions, a country with two names whose spirited people have withstood centuries of oppression, from Kublai Khan to King George VI to the present military regime. Today grinding poverty is evident, even as much of urban Myanmar puts on a modern face. At the same time, elegant remnants of past grandeur can transport the attentive visitor to the dynasties of 11th century Bagan (Pagan) along the Ayeyarwady (Irrawaddy) River.

Though not immune to western influences, Myanmar remains insular and intriguing. The nation was virtually sealed off from the outside world in 1962, when a military junta took control of the government and methodically transformed the country from the world's leading rice exporter into an economic dependent of its largest neighbour, China. Myanmar has come under increasing international scrutiny following a popular uprising in 1988 and the military government's refusal to relinquish power following national elections in 1990. Efforts by the junta to attract tourism have done nothing to lessen international criticism of its harsh policies.

This is a nation at odds with itself and the international community. Its most famous prisoner of conscience, Nobel Peace Prize recipient Aung San Suu Kyi, refuses easy exile, and its citizens are confronted daily with Orwellian billboards claiming to express 'The People's Desire'. Humourless slogans urge citizens to 'Crush all internal

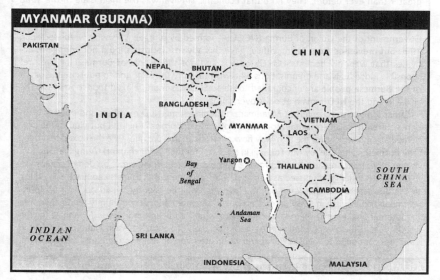

MYANMAR (BURMA)

PAKISTAN

CHINA

NEPAL BHUTAN

BANGLADESH

INDIA

MYANMAR

VIETNAM

LAOS

Yangon

Bay
of
Bengal

THAILAND

SOUTH
CHINA
SEA

CAMBODIA

Andaman
Sea

INDIAN
OCEAN

SRI LANKA

INDONESIA

MALAYSIA

Should You Visit Myanmar?

The question of whether informed tourism helps or hinders the restoration of democracy and human rights in Myanmar is the subject of ongoing debate both in and out of the country.

Myanmar remains under tight military rule. Dissent of any sort is suppressed, and political prisoners are jailed for expressing their opinions publicly. Crimes have ranged from telling jokes to owning unregistered fax machines. Several people have died in custody. The practice of *corvée* (draft labour, or involuntary civilian service to the state) is still practised in Myanmar. It is not uncommon in small towns and on isolated roads to see gangs of teenage girls and boys doing road work in 10 hour shifts for nothing more than meal money.

The State Law & Order Restoration Council (SLORC), the abominable military junta that has run Myanmar since 1962, recently changed its name to the less catchy State Peace & Development Council (SPDC). But most observers of the political scene are reluctant to give up the nasty-sounding SLORC acronym, and its use is still common.

Because of the Burmese government's poor human-rights record, several activist groups outside Myanmar advocate boycotting all forms of travel to the country, as a means of isolating the government and forcing reform. Inside Myanmar, there are a number of people who support such a policy, including pro-democracy leader and former National League for Democracy (NLD) secretary-general Aung San Suu Kyi. This pro-boycott group argues that much of the money from tourism goes directly into the pockets of the very generals who continue to deny Burmese citizens the most basic civil rights.

However, others involved with Burmese politics, including many members of the NLD, feel that a travel boycott of Myanmar is counterproductive, arguing that socially responsible travel in Myanmar can be of benefit both to the Burmese and to the international community. The pro-travel group points out that since socialism was banned in 1989, the lot of the average Burmese has improved and the potential for the general populace to benefit from tourism is greater than ever before. They note that economic survival was the main issue of the 1988 riots that resulted in over 3000 deaths.

During the government's feeble 1997 Visit Myanmar campaign, the National Coalition Government of the Union of Burma (NCGUB), formed by refugee MPs who were elected in 1990 but prevented from taking office, gave this advice: 'Tourists should not engage in activities that will only benefit SLORC's coffers and not the people of Burma. However, responsible individuals and organisations who wish to verify the facts and to publicise the plight of the Burmese people are encouraged to utilise SLORC's more relaxed tourist policies'. The NCGUB and the NLD remain at odds over this issue.

Other long-time observers in Myanmar – including some NLD members and political dissidents currently in jail – maintain tourism is not only economically helpful but vital to the pro-democracy movement for the two-way flow of information it provides (see the boxed text titled 'The Burmese Fairy Tale' by Ma Thanegi in the Facts for the Visitor chapter). Aung San Suu Kyi, on the other hand, regards tourism for the purpose of exchanging views on democracy as virtually useless. She has dismissed as patronising the argument that tourists can teach something to the Burmese about their own plight. However, until the country began opening up to investment and tourism in 1989, almost no one in the international community (certainly not in the international media) seemed to care about what had been going on in Myanmar for the last 35 years. Myanmar's admission to the Association of Southeast Asian Nations (ASEAN) in 1997 has continued to focus regional and world attention on its investment and trade policies.

Should You Visit Myanmar?

Advocates of a travel boycott have found it is not without cost. Myanmar has already experienced the resulting isolation and, as the NCGUB has observed: 'The military in Burma first seized power in 1962. It expropriated all private businesses, drove out all foreigners and isolated the country from the outside world. In three decades, the military transformed a prosperous and peaceful country into a strife-torn Least Developed Country'.

Since the package tour requirement was waived in 1993, many Burmese citizens believe the potential for ordinary people to benefit from tourism has increased. Many more believe that keeping the Burmese isolated from international witnesses to the internal oppression may only cement the government's ability to rule by fear. Draft labour was used during the restoration of the Mandalay Palace before its completion in 1997, but discontinued shortly after foreign visitors began reporting the practice to the outside world.

Anyone contemplating a visit to Myanmar should realise there are no clear-cut answers. It is possible that any contribution made to the nation's economy may allow Myanmar's repressive government to stay in power a bit longer. The issue is further complicated by the fact that many new business enterprises are 'joint ventures' between the Burmese government and private firms. Privatisation of the tourist industry is no exception.

However, tourism remains one of the only industries to which ordinary people have access. Any reduction in tourism automatically means a reduction in local income earning opportunities. For this reason alone, we continue to believe that the positives of travel to Myanmar outweigh the negatives. Many Burmese citizens eke out a living from tourism, however small.

Our editorial belief is that if people decide to visit Myanmar, they should support non-government-sponsored tourism, and they should go with as much advance information as possible, travelling with their eyes and ears open. If you'd like to maximise the positive effects of a visit among the general populace, while minimising support of the government, follow these simple tactics:

- Stay at private, locally owned hotels and guesthouses, rather than in government-owned hotels.

- Avoid package tours connected with Myanmar Travel & Tours (MTT, the state tourist agency). Many independent tour agencies are available in Yangon.

- Avoid MTT-sponsored modes of transport, such as the Yangon-Mandalay Express trains, the MTT ferry between Mandalay and Bagan, and Myanma Airways (MA) flights.

- Use ordinary public transport (including some private trains and many fights).

- Buy handicrafts directly from the artisans, rather than from government shops.

- Avoid patronising companies involved with military-owned Myanmar Economic Holdings. Companies with solid links to the Tatmadaw (armed forces) are often called Myawadi or Myawaddy.

- Bring a few popular (but not politically sensitive) paperback books or recent magazines to give to Burmese people. Books and magazines are often expensive or hard to find in cash-poor Myanmar, and this simple act will be much appreciated.

- Write to the Myanmar government and to the Myanmar embassy in your country expressing your views about the human-rights situation there.

and external destructive elements as the common enemy'. Yet there are places here that testify to an ecstasy of the spirit, from sparkling Shwedagon Paya in Yangon (Rangoon) to the golden domes of Mandalay Hill, which seem to float above a harsher reality.

The visitor to Myanmar is likely to find a people ever-proud of their 'Burmeseness' – spiritual, compassionate and soft-spoken, but struggling to survive the contradictory whims of a military dictatorship. This nation is certain to surprise with its vast ruins that span a millennium of triumph and suffering, and its indelible images of a resourceful people living in a land of both abundance and poverty. Myanmar promises the visitor a new and uneasy awareness of a country seesawing between a hard history and a state of grace.

Facts about Myanmar

HISTORY
Early Pyu & Mon Kingdoms

Virtually nothing is known of Myanmar's prehistoric inhabitants, though archaeological evidence suggests the area has been inhabited since at least 2500 BC. It may originally have been sparsely populated by Negritos or proto-Malays who are thought to have inhabited the lowland and coastal areas of Myanmar (Burma), Thailand and Malaysia. The remnants of this race appear today in only a few isolated pockets in the interior of the Thai-Malay Peninsula and on a sprinkling of islands in the Andaman Sea. If these Negritos were indeed Myanmar's original inhabitants, one theory holds that they were displaced by peoples who migrated into the area from other parts of South-East Asia. At any rate, Myanmar's nation-building history really begins with the struggle for supremacy between the various peoples who inhabited different regions of the country around a thousand years ago.

A group known as the Pyu – possibly hailing from the Tibeto-Burman plateau or from India – created city-states in Central Myanmar at Beikthano, Hanlin and Thayekhittaya (Sri Ksetra) during the second Christian millennium. Little is known about these people; the art and architecture they left behind indicate they practised Theravada and Mahayana Buddhism mixed with Hinduism, and that they had their own alphabet. The Pyu were dispersed or enslaved by Yunnanese invaders during the 10th century AD, leaving Central Myanmar without any clear political succession.

Around the 6th century the Mon – who may have originated in eastern India or who may have been indigenous to mainland South-East Asia – settled the fertile lowlands stretching from the Ayeyarwady (Irrawaddy) River delta across Thailand (then Siam) to Western Cambodia. Inscriptions left behind by the civilisation they developed referred to this area as Suvannabhumi (Golden Land). According to official Burmese history, the Mon capital occupied the area around Thaton in present-day Myanmar, though outside scholars argue more convincingly that Suvannabhumi was centred in Thailand's Nakhon Pathom.

Enter the Bamar, or Burmans, who came south into Myanmar from somewhere in the eastern Himalayas around the 8th or 9th century. Once the Pyu were vanquished by the Yunnanese, the Bamar supplanted the Pyu in Central Myanmar, a region that has since been the true cultural heartland of Myanmar. Shortly after they took over the central region, the Bamar came into conflict with the Mon in a long and complicated struggle for control of the whole country. By the time the Bamar had irrevocably ended up on top, the Mon had largely merged with Bamar culture or, bearing in mind how much Mon culture the Bamar had absorbed, vice versa.

Great Kings of Bagan (Pagan)

It is thought that Bagan (Pagan) was actually founded on the banks of the Ayeyarwady River in 849, but it entered its golden period 200 years later when Anawrahta ascended the throne in 1044. Anawrahta consolidated the kingdom, drawing several regions around it into satellite or vassal status and creating the first centralised government the country now called Myanmar had ever known. Virtually all written history pertaining to Myanmar begins with this era; legendary Bagan kings from the 2nd century AD are probably no more than invented personages.

Initially animists, the Bamar had picked up a hybrid form of Buddhism – part Tantric, part Mahayana – in their migration to Myanmar. When the Mon king Manuha of Thaton, to the south, would not cooperate willingly with Anawrahta's request for their *Tripitaka* (the holy canon of Theravada

Myanmar's Capitals & Ruling Chronology

It's difficult to create a precise summary of the different historical periods in Myanmar due to the general lack of accurate historical records. The only clearly documented eras are those which have been considered 'Burmese' by Burmese historians: that is, the Rakhaing, Pyu, Mon and Bamar kingdoms. Periods of Shan or Siamese rule – even when power extended well into Central Myanmar – aren't counted.

Rakhaing

Dhanyawady	? to 6th C
Wethali	4th to 8th or 9th C
Mrauk U	13th to 18th C

Pyu

Beikthano	? to 5th C
Hanlin	3rd to 9th C
Thayekhittaya	3rd to 10th C

Mon

Thaton (Dvaravati)	? to 10th C
Hanthawady	10th to 16th C

Bamar

Bagan	11th to 14th C
Sagaing	1315 to 1364
Inwa	1364 to 1555
	1629 to 1752
	1765 to 1783
	1823 to 1837
Taungoo	1486 to 1573
Shwebo	1758 to 1765
Konbaung	1783 to 1823
	1837 to 1857
Mandalay (Yadanapon)	1857 to 1885

British

Sittwe & Mawlamyaing	1826 to 1852
Mandalay	1852 to 1886
Yangon	1886 to 1947

Buddhism), Anawrahta marched south and conquered Thaton in 1057. He took back not just the Buddhist scriptures, but also the king and most of his court. This injection of Mon culture inspired a phenomenal burst of energy from the Bamar. Bagan quickly became a city of glorious temples and the capital of the first Burmese kingdom to encompass virtually all of present-day Myanmar. What we today identify as 'Burmese' is really a fusion of Mon and Bamar cultures that came about at the height of the Bagan era.

Anawrahta was accidentally killed by a wild buffalo in 1077. None of his successors had his vision or energy, and Bagan's power declined slowly but steadily. Kyanzittha (1084-1113) attempted to unify Myanmar's disparate peoples, and later kings like Alaungsithu and Htilominlo built beautiful shrines, but essentially Bagan reached its peak with Anawrahta.

Bagan's decline coincided with the rise to power of Kublai Khan and his Tartars in the north. They invaded Myanmar from Yunnan in China in 1287 and Bagan's rule collapsed before the onslaught. Shan tribes from the hills to the east – closely related to the Siamese – took the opportunity to attack and grab a piece of the low country, while in the south the Mon broke free of Bamar control to establish their own kingdom once again.

New States Arise

For the next 250 years Myanmar remained in chaos. In the south the Mon kingdom remained relatively stable, but in the north there was continuous strife. Between the two, a weaker Bamar kingdom was established at Taungoo, east of Pyay (Prome), and it retained its independence by playing off one major power against the other.

At first the Mon established their new capital close to the present Thai border at Mottama (Martaban) near Mawlamyaing (Moulmein), but after a series of skirmishes with the Siamese it was shifted to Bago (Pegu), near Yangon (Rangoon) and the Mon country became known as the Kingdom of Hanthawady. Around this time Myanmar received its first known European visitor, Venetian trader Nicolo di Conti, who travelled along the coast in 1435 and left behind brief accounts of Tanintharyi (Tenasserim) and Rakhaing (Arakan).

In 1472 Dhammazedi, considered the greatest of the Bago kings, came to the throne. A major Buddhist revival took place and the first diplomatic contact with Europeans was made. During this time the great Shwedagon Paya in Yangon began to assume its present form.

Meanwhile the Shan took over Upper Myanmar once again and founded the Kingdom of Inwa (mistakenly called Ava by the British) near present-day Mandalay in 1364. Along the western coast the Rakhaing (a people living near the Indian border) established Mrauk U (Myohaung), a Buddhist kingdom with fields of temples to rival Bagan. Surprisingly, it was not the establishment of Bago, Inwa or Mrauk U that was to prove the catalyst for the reunification of Myanmar, but tiny Taungoo, which had been founded by Bamar refugees from the new Shan kingdoms.

In the 16th century a series of Taungoo kings extended their power north, nearly to Inwa, then south, taking the Mon kingdom and shifting their own capital to Bago. This hold was initially fragile, but in 1550 Bayinnaung came to the throne, reunified all of Myanmar and defeated the neighbouring Siamese so convincingly that it was many years before the long-running friction between the Burmese and Siamese re-emerged. Burmese historians sometimes refer to this era as the Second Burmese Empire.

With Bayinnaung's death in 1581, this new Burmese kingdom immediately went into decline; and when, in 1636, the capital was shifted north from Bago to Inwa, the idea of a kingdom taking in all of Myanmar was effectively renounced. Inwa was the capital of Myanmar, but it was a long way from the sea, so it was effectively cut off from communication with the outside world. This isolation eventually contributed to the conflict with the British.

Final Kings of Mandalay

In the 18th century the decline became serious as hill tribes once more started to raid Central Myanmar, and the Mon again broke away and established their own kingdom in Bago. In 1752 the Mon took Inwa, but in the same year Alaungpaya came to power in Shwebo, 80km north of Inwa, and spent the next eight years rushing back and forth across Myanmar – conquering, defeating and destroying all who opposed him. He was the founder of the last Burmese dynasty and it was his near-invincibility that later deluded the Burmese into thinking they could take on the British.

Alaungpaya's son, Hsinbyushin, charged into Thailand for good measure, and so thoroughly levelled the capital of Ayuthaya that the Siamese were forced to move south to their present capital of Bangkok. Bodawpaya, who came to power in 1782, was also a son of Alaungpaya and managed to bring Rakhaing (Arakan) back under Bamar control. This was to be the direct cause of the first Anglo-Burmese conflict.

Rakhaing, the eastern coastal region of the Bay of Bengal, had long been a border region between Myanmar and India; its people were a blend of Bamar and Indian races. Refugees from Rakhaing fled into British India and from there planned to recapture their country. This so irritated the Burmese that they, in return, mounted raids across the border into British territory. This did not make the officials of the British Raj very happy.

At this time the British, Dutch and French were all vying for power in the East, and all had established at least some sort of contact with the Burmese. However, the Burmese showed little interest in dealing with European foreigners commercially. The British, increasingly worried about the threat posed by French interests in the region, sought to shore up their possessions in India by gaining some sort of control or influence of the eastern side of the Bay of Bengal. Border incidents in Rakhaing and Assam soon gave the British the excuse they needed.

In 1819 Bagyidaw came to the throne in Myanmar. A hot pursuit across the Assam border by Burmese troops led to a declaration of war by the British. The increasing isolation of the Burmese court at Inwa contributed to this disastrous (for the Burmese) war; but there is little doubt that the British were more motivated by geopolitical considerations than by concern for Assamese refugees. After an inept, mismanaged campaign lasting two years, the British finally forced the Burmese to surrender, and imposed the Treaty of Yadanabon upon them. Under its terms, Britain gained control of Rakhaing (Arakan) and Taninthayi (Tenasserim), and Myanmar had to pay a large reparation in silver to the British and accept a British 'resident' at Inwa. Within a few years, however, several British residents managed to form reasonable relations with Bagyidaw.

Unfortunately, Bagyidaw was followed by the much less reasonable Tharawaddy Min, and he in turn by his even crazier son, Bagan Min. It had long been the custom for a new king to massacre all possible pretenders to the throne, but Bagan Min took this policy to new extremes. In the first two years of his reign 6000 people were executed. The British resident had been forced to withdraw during Tharawaddy's brief reign, and frontier incidents began to flare up again. The British seized upon an extortion incident in Yangon in 1852, during which two British ship captains had allegedly been kidnapped by Burmese government officials, in order to open hostilities in the Second Anglo-Burmese War.

In fact, it's possible that this incident never actually took place, and that the British were again motivated by the necessity of protecting their Indian possessions. In any case, most historians agree that this war was started on the basis of a grossly exaggerated pretext by the British. It's more likely that they realised what a bad deal they had made in taking over Rakhaing and Taninthayi, which were of little practical or commercial use. Rather, they sought the use of a suitable port, such as Yangon.

The British quickly took over Yangon, Mottama and Pathein (Bassein), and marched north to Pyay. Unlike the first war, the British conducted this campaign with stern efficiency, and met little opposition from the ill-equipped and disorganised Burmese forces. After a series of skirmishes and one-sided battles, the war was over – this time, the British annexed all of Lower Myanmar, which became a province of India.

Bagan Min, now extremely unpopular, was deposed and Mindon Min became king of Myanmar, or at least what remained of it, in 1853. Mindon proved to be a wise realist who eventually came to amicable terms with the British, yet cleverly balanced their influence with that of other European (and American) powers. During this period the industrial revolution came to full flower in Europe, and Lower Myanmar became an important and profitable part of the British Empire due to its enormous teak resources and vast potential for growing rice.

Unhappily for the Burmese, Mindon made one important mistake – he did not adequately provide for a successor. When he died in 1878, the new king, Thibaw Min, was propelled into power by his ruthless wife and scheming mother-in-law. Thibaw was so far down the list of possible successors that the 'massacre of kinsmen' reached unheard-of heights, and in the new age of the telegraph and steamship, the news soon reached Europe in lurid detail. Thus European and British attitudes towards the new king were tarnished from the start.

Thibaw proved to be a totally ineffective ruler. Upper Myanmar soon became a sorry scene as armed gangs and ruthless officials vied with each other to extort money from the hapless peasants. Enormous numbers of Burmese fled to the stability of British Lower Myanmar, where there also happened to be a great demand for labour for the new rice trade.

Finally, in 1885, another Anglo-Burmese conflict flared up. The British resident had again withdrawn from Mandalay, and a petty dispute over the exploits of the Bombay Burmah Trading Company was the excuse the British needed to send gunboats north to Mandalay. In two weeks it was all over: the money Thibaw had thought was going into defence had actually gone into corrupt officials' pockets and the British took Mandalay after only the most token resistance.

In order to stamp their authority upon Upper Myanmar, the British undertook a brutal two year military campaign throughout the region. Similar in execution to the Highland Clearances of Scotland approximately a century earlier, British forces ruthlessly crushed any signs of opposition, killing many innocent civilians and destroying numerous villages.

British Period

Once again Myanmar was united, but this time with the British as masters. To the British, Myanmar was just another chunk of Asia that now had the good fortune to be part of the Raj. To the Burmese, the situation was not nearly so pleasant: Upper Myanmar may have been only part of the whole country, but it was the heartland of Myanmar; Thibaw might have been a bad king, but he was a Burmese king.

Now Myanmar was just a part of British India – and what was worse, Indians, whom the Burmese had traditionally looked down on, came flooding in with the British. As the swampy delta of the south was turned into rice paddies, it was the Indians who supplied the money to improve the land, and those same Indians who came to own it when the less commercially experienced Burmese proved unable to make it pay or to pay for it. By 1930 half of Yangon's population was Indian. As Myanmar's national income grew, the country became increasingly dependent upon imports, and the profits from rice cultivation were whisked out of the country to pay for more and more imported goods.

The British applied direct rule only to the areas in which Bamar were the majority – Central Myanmar, Rakhaing and Tanintharyi. The 'hill states' belonging to the Chin, Kachin, Shan, Kayin and Kayah were permitted to remain largely autonomous,

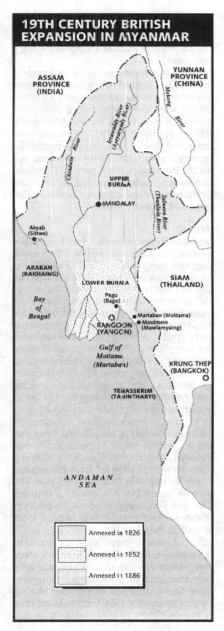

19TH CENTURY BRITISH EXPANSION IN MYANMAR

ASSAM PROVINCE (INDIA)

YUNNAN PROVINCE (CHINA)

Irrawaddy River (Ayeyarwadi River)

Chindwin River

Mekong River

UPPER BURMA

Salween River (Thanlwin River)

MANDALAY

Akyab (Sittwe)

ARAKAN (RAKHAING)

LOWER BURMA

SIAM (THAILAND)

Bay of Bengal

Pegu (Bago)

Martaban (Mottama)
Moulmein (Mawlamyaing)

RANGOON (YANGON)

Gulf of Mottama (Martaban)

KRUNG THEP (BANGKOK)

TENASSERIM (TANINTHARYI)

ANDAMAN SEA

Annexed in 1826

Annexed in 1852

Annexed in 1886

though officially part of the Raj. This difference between direct and indirect rule has haunted Myanmar's political history ever since.

Burmese nationalism grew, although it remained a shadow of the movement in India, and in the 1920s and 1930s the British were eventually forced to make a number of concessions towards Myanmar's self-government. In 1937 Myanmar was separated from India, but internally the country was torn by a struggle between opposing Burmese political parties. There had also been a peasants' uprising earlier in the 1930s and sporadic outbursts of anti-Indian and anti-Chinese violence.

WWII

Japanese-Burmese contact had been made well before Japan entered WWII. Indeed Bogyoke Aung San, who had first made his name through university-level political action and was later to become the 'father figure' of independent Burma, had fled to the Japanese in 1940, following his arrest for participation in the Burmese Communist Party (BCP). Aided by the Burmese Independence Army (BIA), the Japanese army marched into Myanmar within weeks of Pearl Harbor and by mid-1942 had driven the retreating British-Indian forces, along with the Chinese Kuomintang (KMT) forces (which had come to their aid), out of most of Myanmar. Japan declared Myanmar an independent country and allowed Aung San and his '30 comrades' to create the Burma National Army (BNA). One of the 30 was a Sino-Burmese native of Paungdale (near Pyay) named Shu Maung, who took the nom de guerre Ne Win, meaning Brilliant Like The Sun. Aung San took the position of defence minister; Ne Win became chief of staff of the BNA.

The Japanese were able to maintain Burmese political support for only a short time before their harsh and arrogant conduct managed to alienate the Burmese. Aung San expressed his bitterness during his stay at Japan's 15th Army headquarters in Maymyo (now Pyin U Lwin):

> I went to Japan to save my people who were struggling like bullocks under the British. But, now we are treated like dogs. We are far from our hope of reaching the human stage, and even to get back to the bullock stage we need to struggle more.

The imaginative 'Chindit' anti-Japanese operation, mounted by the Allies with air-supplied troops behind enemy lines, also encouraged further anti-Japanese feeling. Soon an internal resistance movement sprang up, and towards the end of the war the BNA hastily switched sides to the British. The Allies prevailed at a cost of approximately 27,000 casualties; nearly 200,000 Japanese perished in the fierce, protracted battles.

Independence

That Myanmar was heading rapidly towards independence after the war was all too clear, but who should manage this process was a different question. On 27 January 1947 British Prime Minister Clement Attlee and General Aung San signed an agreement on behalf of the UK and Burma respectively. The Aung San-Attlee agreement stipulated that a constituent assembly would be elected in April by, and consisting of, Burma nationals only; that certain matters which had previously been formally reserved for the British governor would in future be brought before an executive council that would function as an interim government; that the Burmese army would come under the control of the interim government; and that Burma would receive an interest-free loan of approximately 8 million pounds sterling from the UK.

The executive council in consultation with non-Bamar representatives, was to nominate a Frontier Areas Committee composed of an equal number of members from Ministerial Burma (British-dominated Burma) and the border states which had had some degree of autonomy under the British. This committee would determine ways for frontier peoples to participate in the drafting of a constitution.

In February 1947 Aung San met with leaders from the Shan, Chin and Kachin communities in Panglong, a township in the Shan State. Together, they signed the famous Panglong Agreement, guaranteeing Burma's ethnic minorities the freedom to choose their own political destiny. Although representatives from the Kayin, Kayah, Mon, Rakhaing and many other ethnicities were noticeably absent from the meeting, the agreement was broadly interpreted to mean that it would apply to all ethnic communities in what the British called the Frontier Areas.

When elections for a constituent assembly were held on 9 April 1947, Aung San's Anit-Fascist People's Freedom League (AFPFL) won an overwhelming 172 seats out of 255. The BCP took seven seats, while the Bamar opposition led by U Saw took three seats. Twenty-four seats were allotted to the Kayin community, four seats to the Anglo-Burman community and 45 seats to the Frontier Areas.

The British wanted a gradual transition, allowing time to rebuild the shattered economy and political system before the handover. Bogyoke Aung San wanted independence immediately, because if given time, other political parties could gain ground on his strong position at the close of the war. He also wanted to establish a democratic, civilian government:

> We must make democracy the popular creed. We must try to build up a free Burma in accordance with such a creed. If we should fail to do this, our people are bound to suffer. If democracy should fail the world cannot stand back and just look on, and therefore Burma would one day, like Japan and Germany, be despised. Democracy is the only ideology which is consistent with freedom. It is also an ideology that promotes and strengthens peace. It is therefore the only ideology we should aim for.

However, Aung San's incredibly prophetic views didn't win over his political opponents, and in late 1945 he made another prediction:

> How long do national heroes last? Not long in this country; I do not give myself more than another eighteen months of life.

Eighteen months and six days later, in July 1947, 32-year-old Aung San and six of his assistants were assassinated in a plot ascribed to U Saw, a pre-war political leader who had refused to sign the Aung San-Attlee agreement that was to usher in Burmese independence. A few conspiracy theorists speculate that General Ne Win may have ordered the assassination, due to Aung San's plans to demilitarise the government. However, Aung San's main source of political support had been the BNA and Ne Win, and U Saw – who favoured British-style capitalism and Bamar domination rather than the national socialism and ethnic autonomy espoused by Aung San – had more motive than anyone else in the ongoing power conflict between Aung San and his various political opponents. U Saw apparently believed that his position as prime minister in pre-WWII Myanmar would be reinstated if Aung San and the AFPFL could be successfully thwarted.

MICK WELDON

Bogyoke Aung San, the famous father of both Myanmar's independence movement and Aung San Suu Kyi, was assassinated in 1947 and is regarded as a martyr.

While the world mourned a hero's death, Prime Minister Attlee and Aung San's protégé U Nu signed an agreement for the transfer of power in October 1947. On 4 January 1948, at an auspicious middle-of-the-night hour, Myanmar became independent and left the British Commonwealth. As Aung San had promised, the national presidency was given to a representative from an ethnic minority group, and Sao Shwe Thaike, a Shan leader, became the first president of the Union of Burma.

Almost immediately, the new government was faced with the complete disintegration of Myanmar. The hill tribe people, who had supported the British and fought against the Japanese throughout the war, were distrustful of the Bamar majority and went into armed opposition. The communists withdrew from the government and attacked it. Muslims from the Rakhaing area also opposed the new government. The Mon, long thought to be totally integrated with the Burmese, revolted. Assorted factions, private armies, WWII resistance groups and plain mutineers further confused the picture.

In early 1949 almost the entire country was in the hands of one rebel group or another, and even Yangon suffered fighting in its suburbs. At one stage the government was on the point of surrendering to the communist forces, but gradually, and with particularly valuable assistance from loyal hill tribe contingents, the government fought back, and through 1950 and 1951 regained much of the country.

Although much of Myanmar was now at least tenuously under government control, a new problem sprang up for the battered Burmese. With the collapse of Chiang Kai-Shek's KMT forces before Mao Zedong, the tattered remnants of his army withdrew into Myanmar and mounted raids from Northern Myanmar into Yunnan, the bordering Chinese province. Being no match for the Chinese communists, the KMT decided to carve their own little fiefdom out of Burmese territory. The Burmese government now found itself fighting not only a

mixed bag of rebels, communists, and gangs of out-and-out brigands and *dacoits* (highwaymen), but also a US-supported, anticommunist Chinese army. Amazing as it may seem, while operating an embassy in Yangon and espousing friendly relations with the new Burmese government, the USA was also flying in supplies to the Chinese forces encamped within Myanmar's borders; forces whose main source of income was the cultivation of opium poppies for the production of heroin!

Burmese Road to Socialism

In the mid-1950s, although the central government strengthened its hold on the country, the economic situation went from bad to worse. A number of grandiose development projects succeeded only in making foreign 'advisors' rather wealthy, and in 1953 the Burmese bravely announced that aid or assistance from the USA were no longer welcome, as long as US-supplied Chinese nationalist forces were at large within Myanmar. Despite the sickly economy, U Nu managed to remain in power until 1958 when, with political turmoil about to become armed chaos yet again and the KMT problem still unresolved, he voluntarily handed the reins over to a military government under General Ne Win.

Freed from the 'democratic' responsibilities inherent in a civilian government, Ne Win was able to make some excellent progress during the 15 months his military government operated. A degree of law and order was restored, rebel activity was reduced and Yangon was given a massive and much-needed cleanup.

In early 1960 elections were held and U Nu came back to power with a much improved majority, but once again political turmoil developed. His party threatened to break up into opposing groups and in early 1962 Ne Win assumed power again and abolished the parliament. He established his own 17-member Revolutionary Council, announcing that the country would 'march toward socialism in our own Burmese way'. This time U Nu did not hand over power voluntarily, and along with his main ministers was bundled into prison, where he remained until forced into exile in 1966. He later ineffectively opposed the Ne Win government from abroad. In 1980 U Nu returned from exile under an amnesty program for political offenders and devoted himself to translating Buddhist scriptures, except for a brief period of political involvement in 1988. U Nu died of a heart attack at age 88 in Yangon in February 1995.

Soon after coming to power in 1962, Ne Win announced the new path Myanmar would follow: 'The Burmese Road to Socialism'. It was a steadily downhill path. Nationalisation policies were extended right down to the retail shop level in 1966 when it was announced that a long list of items would only be available from 'Peoples' Shops'. The net result was frightening: many everyday commodities immediately became available only on the black market, and vast numbers of people were thrown out of work by the closure of retail outlets.

A disingenuous 'sock the rich' measure demonetised the largest banknotes (K50 and K100); anybody so unfortunate as to have these notes found them to be worthless. Many of the retail traders who became unemployed following the nationalisation of retail trade were Indians and Chinese, and they were hustled out of the country with Draconian thoroughness. No compensation was paid for their expropriated businesses, and each adult was allowed to depart with only K75 to his or her name plus K250 in gold – even a woman's jewellery in excess of that amount was to be confiscated. As many as a quarter of a million people of Indian and Chinese descent left Myanmar during the 1960s. Anti-Chinese riots in Yangon in 1967 – spurred by fears that the Chinese were about to 'import' China's Cultural Revolution – resulted in hundreds of Chinese deaths.

In late 1974 there were serious student disturbances over the burial of former United Nations (UN) secretary-general and longtime Ne Win political foe, U Thant, yet overall the government appeared firmly in control and determined to continue its strange progress towards a Burmese Utopia. In late 1981 Ne Win retired as president of the republic (retaining his position as chair of the Burmese Socialist Programme Party, the country's only legal political party at the time), but his successor was more or less hand-picked and the government remained guided very much by Ne Win's political will.

1988 Anti-Government Uprising

As Myanmar's economy stagnated, the country's standard of living slid downhill year after year. Finally, in 1987 and 1988, the long-suffering Burmese people decided they had had enough of their incompetent and arrogant government and packed the streets in huge demonstrations, insisting that Ne Win go.

Ne Win voluntarily retired in July 1988, but it was too late to halt the agitation of the people. The massive pro-democracy demonstrations, spurred by the further demonetisation of large notes and a prophecy that Burma would become a 'free country' on the auspicious date of 8-8-88, were brutally crushed, with at least 3000 deaths over a six week period.

Ne Win's National Unity Party (NUP; formerly the Burmese Socialist Programme Party) was far from ready to give up control, and the public protests continued as two wholly unacceptable Ne Win stooges succeeded him. The third Ne Win successor came to power after a military coup in September 1988, which, it is generally believed, was organised by Ne Win.

A newly formed State Law & Order Restoration Council (SLORC) established martial law under the leadership of General Saw Maung, commander in chief of the armed forces, and promised to hold democratic National Assembly elections in May 1989. The SLORC also changed the country's official name from the Union of Burma to the Union of Myanmar, claiming that 'Burma' was a vestige of European colonialism.

The opposition quickly formed a coalition party called the National League for

Democracy (NLD) and campaigned for all they were worth. U Nu tried to declare a parallel government based on the 1945 constitution, but the long-suppressed Burmese population rallied around charismatic NLD spokesperson Aung San Suu Kyi, daughter of national hero Bogyoke Aung San. Suu Kyi, conversant in Burmese, Japanese, French and English, and married to an Oxford University professor, brought a hitherto unseen sophistication to Burmese politics.

Nervous, the SLORC tried to appease the masses with new roads and paint jobs in Yangon, and then attempted to interfere in the electoral process by shifting villages from one part of the country to another and by postponing the election. Perhaps the biggest surprise came with the announcement that the government was abandoning socialism in favour of a capitalist economy in all but a few industries.

In July 1989 Aung San Suu Kyi was placed under house arrest.

MICK WELDON

Nobel laureate Aung San Suu Kyi spent almost six years under house arrest in Yangon, thanks to the SLORC (now SPDC) regime.

1990 Free Election & the Lionisation of Aung San Suu Kyi

Once the government was confident it had effectively reduced the opposition, in May 1990 it allowed the country's first free election in 30 years. In spite of all preventive measures, the NUP lost the election to the NLD, which took 392 of the 485 contested seats. The SLORC barred the elected members of parliament from assuming power, however, decreeing that a state-approved constitution had to be passed by national referendum first. In October 1990 the military raided NLD offices and arrested key leaders. Many were subsequently released, though since that time over a hundred elected parliamentarians have been disqualified, imprisoned, exiled or killed.

Before her arrest in 1989, Suu Kyi had been appointed secretary general of the party. The main NLD candidates in line for any potential premiership that might have occurred if the 1990 election of MPs had been recognised by the current regime were U Aung Shwe, U Tin Oo and U Kyi Maung, all ex-officers. It was widely acknowledged, even back in 1990, that the SLORC would never allow a person of Aung San Suu Kyi's background (ex-resident of Myanmar, and married to a Briton) to run for office; it was equally acknowledged that the candidates who stood best chance of acceptance by the military dictatorship were those with a military background. It turned out that even this was not enough to make the ruling junta relinquish control.

Had the NLD been installed in government, Suu Kyi may have been given a high position (although the suspended constitution would have to have been rewritten, since it contained a clause forbidding those married to foreigners from holding high public office – a clause supported by Suu Kyi's late father, Aung San), but as long as the NLD remains a besieged opposition, we'll never know.

After the events of 1988-89, the world press at first gave amazingly little coverage to politics in Myanmar. In January 1991 Suu Kyi was awarded the Sakharov Prize for freedom of thought by the European Parliament, and in October of the same year she was honoured with the Nobel Peace Prize; both awards were issued as tributes to her selfless leadership in Myanmar's pro-democracy movement. Yet another international honour came her way in June 1992 when the United Nations Educational, Scientific, and Cultural Organization (UNESCO) awarded Suu Kyi the Simon Bolivar Prize for action contributing to 'freedom, independence and dignity of peoples and to the strengthening of a new international economic, social and cultural order'.

Suu Kyi was honoured with a fourth international award in May 1995 when India presented the leader, in absentia, with the Jawaharlal Nehru Award for International Understanding, citing her as 'brave, non-violent and unyielding'. Much to the joy of the Burmese people and her supporters abroad, the government finally released Suu Kyi from house arrest in July 1995 after nearly six years. Suu Kyi's detention was the most potent symbol of government repression and the biggest magnet for international attention, but many other high-level dissidents, including the NLD's Tin U and Kyi Maung, were also released – not from house arrest, but from prison. For the remainder of 1995 and early 1996, these opposition leaders held optimistic discussions amongst themselves and with the ruling regime for the first time since 1988. The content of such dialogues was encouraging enough to stave off the most virulent official criticism from other countries, yet vague enough that it promised little in terms of substantial change.

Although western pressure on the government to release Aung San Suu Kyi and to instate the elected government steadily increased during the early 1990s, leaders of the ASEAN countries (Thailand, Malaysia, Singapore Brunei, Indonesia and the Philippines) rejected a US bid to participate in economic sanctions against Myanmar, saying they preferred a policy of 'constructive engagement'. As Singapore Prime Minister Goh put it: 'The policy of isolating Myanmar in our view has not worked because it has chosen to be isolated for many years. To further isolate it will not bring results'.

Thailand halted its timber and mineral deals with the Burmese, however, following border skirmishes between Thai and Burmese forces. The Burmese have repeatedly shelled Thai territory since 1992, while attacking pro-democracy and Karen insurgent armies in eastern Myanmar. In April 1995 Burmese and Christian Karen troops marched across the Thai border, raided five refugee camps, torched several hundred homes and repatriated Karen refugees to Myanmar at gunpoint. This did not sit well with the Thai government, which has begun to rethink its Myanmar policy and now openly advocates a more critical approach within ASEAN.

Following Yangon's continued persecution of Rohingya Muslims in Myanmar's Rakhaing State, Indonesia and Malaysia began withdrawing their limited support of the Myanmar government. An estimated 200,000 Muslim refugees fled to Bangladesh in 1992 to avoid military repression, in a situation that alienated the Muslim community around the world. Under the auspices of the UN High Commissioner for Refugees, all but 21,000 had returned to Myanmar by the end of 1997.

Political & Economic Expansion

However reprehensible the repudiation of the 1990 election, Burmese politics has stabilised considerably since the events of 1988 to 1991. Truces with 15 different insurgent groups, along with major military victories against the Karen and Mon rebels along the Thai border, have consolidated Yangon's rule. More significantly, economic liberalisation raised the overall standard of living, at least before the South-East Asian currency/credit crisis of 1997 set back all economies in the region.

Prompted in part by the stagnant economy, top SLORC officials decided to clean house within its own ranks in November 1997, relieving several corrupt ministers of their positions and replacing the 21-member SLORC with a 19-member group calling

Name Changes

One of the cursory changes instituted by the government since the 1988 uprising has been a long list of roman spelling changes for geographic names, in a further effort to purge the country of its colonial past. In most of the name changes, the new romanised versions bring the names phonetically closer to the everyday Burmese pronunciation.

Myanmar versus Burma

In 1989 the official English name of the country was changed from the Union of Burma to the Union of Myanmar, to conform to Burmese usage. There has been no change in the Burmese name for the country. Myanmar has, in fact, been the official name since at least the time of Marco Polo's 13th-century writings; the first Burmese-language newspaper, published in 1868, was called *Myanmar Thandawzin*, translated by the British as Burma Herald. In the country's 1947 Constitution, the Burmese version reads Myanmar, the English version Burma.

In Burmese literary contexts, the name Myanmar refers to the whole country, Bamar (from whence the English got Burma) refers to Burman ethnicity, or to the Burman language. In everyday parlance, Bamar-pyi (Land of the Burmans) may also be used to refer to the country. The new government position finds Myanmar more equitable, since it doesn't identify the nation with any one ethnic group. If the current military regime releases control of the government to the National League for Democracy, however, there's always the possibility all the names could revert back to their colonial versions.

Linguistically speaking, the change is quite reasonable, but it has become something of a political football between the opposition and the government. The official United Nations designation is now Myanmar, and Amnesty International uses this name as well; some English-language periodicals – such as *Asiaweek* – recognise the change, while others (eg *Time*) don't.

The 'r' at the end of Myanmar is merely a British English device used to lengthen the preceding 'a' vowel; it is not pronounced. State enterprises that use Myanmar in their titles typically spell the word without an 'r', eg Myanma Airways, Myanma Five Star Line, Myanma Timber Enterprise and so on.

---

itself the State Peace & Development Council (SPDC). Although this may temporarily have relieved the government of some leakage of public funds, it did very little to improve the government's image either at home or abroad. Mostly, it was business as usual.

Despite the government's human rights record, a number of foreign investors – most of them Asian – continue to plough huge amounts of foreign currency into private development projects, especially in the central Yangon to Mandalay corridor. Singaporean and Japanese companies hold significant investments in the country, while China remains the junta's biggest military supporter.

The land border between Myanmar and China stands wide open for legal and illegal trade, and acts as the main supply line for millions of dollars worth of Chinese weaponry destined for Myanmar's military, along with another estimated billion US dollars in consumer goods annually. Beijing considers Yangon a seaport for Western China, conveniently linked to Yunnan Province by the WWII-era Burma Road. A 1994 visit to Yangon by Chinese Premier Li Peng – the man who ordered the Tiananmen Square massacre one year after Myanmar's bloody 1988 putdown – reaffirmed China's firm approval of SLORC rule. The US renewal of 'Most Favoured Nation'

Name Changes

Myanmar versus Burmese

Officially in post-1989 Myanmar, the word now used to mean Burmese – referring either to a citizen of Myanmar or the language, or to any attribute of the country as a single entity (cuisine, culture etc) – is Myanmar. In other words, it's Myanmar people (or Myanmars), Myanmar language and Myanmar customs, as in Berber people or Magyar language. Because of the lack of familiarity with the use of Myanmar as an adjective however, Lonely Planet is staying with the word Burmese for references to the people and language, just as most mid-20th century literature on Thailand continued to use the term Siamese, even after the name of the country had been officially changed (by a dictatorship) from Siam to Thailand in 1949. Bamar will be used to refer to the Burman ethnic group and to the cuisine.

colonial name	burmese name	colonial name	burmese name
Akyab	Sittwe	Moulmein	Mawlamyaing or
Amherst	Kyaikkami		Mawlamyine
Arakan	Rakhaing or	Myohaung	Mrauk U
	Rakhine	Pagan	Bagan
Ava	Inwa	Pegu	Bago
Bassein	Pathein	Prome	Pyay or Pyi
Burma	Myanmar	Rangoon	Yangon
Chindwin River	(no change)	Salween River	Thanlwin River
Irrawaddy River	Ayeyarwady River	Sandoway	Thandwe
Mandalay	(no change)	Sittang River	Sittoung River
Martaban	Mottama	Syriam	Thanlyin
Maymyo	Pyin U Lwin	Taunggyi	(no change)
Mergui	Myeik (or Beik, in	Tavoy	Dawei
	spoken language)	Tenasserim	Tanintharyi

trade status for China was received with delight in Yangon. In fact, as long as China remains a major foreign-trade hub in Asia, Myanmar's government believes it need not fear potential trade sanctions from other nations.

Meanwhile the repression of free speech and other human rights continues under SPDC leadership. A report commissioned by the International Commission of Jurists (ICJ) in Geneva describes systematic human rights violations, including arbitrary arrests of anyone opposed to the junta, torture of detainees, severe media restrictions, forced relocation of half a million urban dwellers, and forced conscription of civilians to serve

as porters and human mine sweepers for the military. The government also often requests 'volunteer beautification' labour from city, town and village residents, requiring them to paint their houses, dig drainage ditches, build walls and weed the roadside.

The last practice, however, appears to be on the wane. In 1996 the government began using military personnel rather than unpaid civilians for many public works projects. According to the US Department of State's 1998 review of human rights practices in Myanmar, this new policy and the increasing use of heavy construction equipment resulted in a decline in the use of unpaid labour on physical infrastructure during 1996-97, especially for irrigation projects and railroad building. By the end of 1998 green-uniformed soldiers, rather than civilians, were more commonly seen carrying out such tasks as road building and construction work.

According to Amnesty International's 1998 report:

> More than 1200 political prisoners arrested in previous years, including 89 prisoners of conscience and hundreds of possible prisoners of conscience, remained in prison throughout the year. Hundreds of people were arrested for political reasons; although most were released, 31 – five of them prisoners of conscience – were sentenced to long terms of imprisonment after unfair trials. Political prisoners were ill-treated and held in conditions that amounted to cruel, inhuman or degrading treatment. Members of ethnic minorities continued to suffer human rights violations, including extrajudicial executions and ill-treatment during forced labour and portering, and forcible relocations. Two people were sentenced to death.

Still, it must be said that those Burmese who don't openly express dissent, and who have the wherewithal to participate in Myanmar's limited economic growth, remain more satisfied with the government now than at any time since the 1970s. In the larger cities at least, a genuine middle class, however small, has appeared. The government, for its part, seems to believe the general citizenry won't risk relative political stability and prosperity by open revolt and so it is a little more likely to loosen further the restrictions enacted during the standoff of 1988-90.

Recent political upheaval in Malaysia and especially Indonesia, on the other hand, may frighten the government into taking increasingly repressive measures for reasons of internal security. Whether the population at large is encouraged by events such as the deposal of Indonesia's President Soeharto or whether it is indifferent to them – or perhaps incapable of any optimism during the current regional economic crisis – is very difficult to gauge at this point.

Western Responses

Pressure from western countries ebbs and flows. Although the European Union (EU) enacted a withdrawal of military attachés, an arms embargo and a suspension of non-humanitarian aid in 1992, Europe had become one of Myanmar's largest trading partners by the mid-1990s. Australia, too, restored military relations in 1994 after a three year moratorium over Myanmar's human rights record.

In 1995 the British parliament's House of Lords discussed and then ruled out possible sanctions against Myanmar. By 1996 the UK and France were the nation's first and second largest investor countries. Individual western companies, however, have taken direct action to discontinue doing business in Myanmar. Big American retailers Levi Strauss, Macy's and Liz Claiborne each halted imports of textiles from Myanmar in 1996, while manufacturers Pepsi, Carlsberg and Heineken all pulled out of joint ventures with the government.

The US government stopped all aid to Myanmar in 1997. In one of the bolder western initiatives, in October 1998 the EU extended a ban on the granting of entry or transit visas for members of the SLORC/SPDC to include other senior members of the military and their families as well as anyone 'who formulates or benefits from the regime's policies inhibiting the transition to democracy'. To make the ban more difficult to evade, the names of the individuals on the EU's visa blacklist are not made public.

Many observers comment that the only way to hurt Myanmar's junta diplomatically would be to put pressure on the government's two strongest allies in Asia. According to this line of thought, if the EU and the US would dare to ban visas and/or trade with Singaporean leaders and Chinese dictators they might actually make a difference in Myanmar. However, since both the EU and the US engage in substantial trade with Singapore and China, they aren't likely to make the kind of empty gestures they've made concerning Myanmar.

In August 1998 the SPDC detained 18 foreign activists – all of whom had arrived in Myanmar on tourist visas – for distributing business cards bearing the message (in English and Burmese) 'We are your friends. We support your hopes for human rights and democracy. 8-8-88 – Don't forget – Don't give up'. Although sentenced to five years of hard labour for attempting to incite unrest, the protestors were pardoned and deported after spending nearly a week in relatively comfortable police guesthouses. The leaflets had no immediately discernible effect on activism in Myanmar, other than making ordinary Burmese citizens more paranoid about associating with foreigners.

In December 1998 Myanmar's government announced that no member of the British government involved in implementing policies toward Myanmar, or their families, would henceforth be issued a visa to enter Myanmar.

Stalemate?

Meanwhile, the NLD membership at large has lost much strength. Only a handful of NLD leaders remain free, and none are permitted to leave Yangon. Although Suu Kyi can move about Yangon, every time she has tried to leave the capital to visit the countryside, she has found her way blocked by the military. Government propaganda labels Suu Kyi an 'opportunist' and 'genocidal prostitute', while state newspaper cartoons portray her as a witch or as a marionette dancing to strings pulled by her husband, Oxford professor Michael Aris. Dr Aris, who hadn't seen his wife since January 1996, died of cancer on his 53rd birthday in 1999, shortly after Yangon denied him a visa to see Suu Kyi one last time in Myanmar. Fearing that she would be refused re-entry to Myanmar, Suu Kyi herself ignored the government's suggestion that she leave the country to visit her husband's deathbed in England.

To some in the west Suu Kyi has become a figure who seems destined to move from arrest to political office, like South Africa's Nelson Mandela or South Korea's Kim Young Sam. Among the rank and file in Myanmar today, however, many citizens no long consider either her or the NLD viable alternatives to the much-hated government or even ideologically relevant to daily life in Myanmar. A palpable resignation has set in, so complete has the government's chokehold on dissent become. In particular Burmese students, whose universities have been closed since the early 1990s, have grown restless with regard to the situation, including the NLD. They would like to hear a more lucid message from Suu Kyi and the NLD, who continue to declare target dates for parliamentary or constitutional conventions yet never follow through, since the junta is easily able to block their every move. Some citizens hope The Lady (one of Suu Kyi's nicknames) or the party will call a general strike that would immobilise the government and force the SPDC's hand. Many secretly debate why Suu Kyi, if she is so determined to dislodge the military regime, hasn't already called for such action. Perhaps with the economy growing but still not strong, most people fear a major disruption in the current balance of power would effect a near-complete economic collapse.

Independent Myanmar observers have noted that neither side appears to want substantive dialogue, despite claims to the contrary. The military is happy with the status quo, observing that support for the NLD and for Suu Kyi is on the wane, and knowing that they are winning the war of attrition, at least in the short term. The NLD, for its part, seems unwilling to agree to any sharing of power with the military, stubbornly refusing to accept the fact that those in power might never recognise the 1990 election results. It also believes that any move to cooperate with the military – the only available political solution at this time – would bestow legitimacy upon the regime.

In mid-1998 NLD chairman U Aung Shwe met with Lt Gen Khin Nyunt (1st secretary of the SPDC), who agreed to release all NLD members detained at that

The Burmese Fairy Tale

Like many Burmese, I am tired of living in a fairy tale. For years, outsiders portrayed the troubles of my country as a morality play: good against evil, with no shade of grey in between – a simplistic picture, but one the world believes. The response of the west has been equally simplistic: it wages a moral crusade against evil, using such magic wands as sanctions and boycotts.

But for us, Myanmar is no fairy-tale land with a simple solution to its problems. We were isolated for 26 years under socialism and we continue to lack a modern economy. We are tired of wasting time. If we are to move forward, to modernise, then we need everyone to face facts.

That may sound like pro-government propaganda, but I haven't changed since I joined the democracy movement in August 1988. I have lived most of my life under the 1962-88 socialist regime – another fairy tale, this one of isolation. In 1988 we knew it was time to join the world. Thousands of us took to the streets, and I joined the National League for Democracy (NLD) and worked as an aide to Aung San Suu Kyi.

I worked closely with Ma Suu, as we all called her, for nearly a year. I campaigned with her until 20 July 1989, when she was put under house arrest and I was sent to Insein Prison in Rangoon, where I spent nearly three years.

I have no regrets about going to jail and blame no one for it. It was a price we knew we might have to pay. But my fellow former political prisoners and I are beginning to wonder if our sacrifices have been worthwhile. Almost a decade after it all began, we are concerned that the work we started has been squandered and the momentum wasted.

In my time with Ma Suu, I came to love her deeply. I still do. We had hoped that when she was released from house arrest in 1995 that the country would move forward again. So much was needed – proper housing and food and adequate health care, to begin with. That was what the democracy movement was really about – helping people.

Ma Suu could have changed our lives dramatically. With her influence and prestige, she could have asked major aid donors such as the USA and Japan for help. She could have encouraged responsible companies to invest here, creating jobs and helping build a stable economy. She could have struck up a constructive dialogue with the government and laid the groundwork for a sustainable democracy.

Instead, she chose the opposite, putting pressure on the government by telling foreign investors to stay away and asking foreign governments to withhold aid. Many of us cautioned her that this was counterproductive. Why couldn't economic development and political

time. Before the release could be made, however, the NLD announced it would unilaterally call a meeting of its parliament; Khin Nyunt immediately rescinded the offer. The NLD was bluffing, as it never convened the parliament – both sides appear to have been playing out a charade of cooperation.

For the moment, the SPDC remains the only game in town and will remain so unless, or until, the military leadership decides

to relinquish control. Many Burmese say they expect major political changes to occur only after Ne Win (88 years old in 1999) dies. A revolt among progressive officers in the military is seen as one possible, but unlikely, alternative to the current political situation. Another is that the generals will actually hand over the reigns to a civilian government, as promised, if the new constitution is ever completed and ratified (see The Constitution in the Government &

The Burmese Fairy Tale

improvement grow side by side? People need jobs to put food on the table, which may not sound grand and noble, but it is a basic truth we face every day.

Ma Suu's approach has been highly moral and uncompromising, catching the imagination of the outside world. Unfortunately, it has come at a real price for the rest of us. Sanctions have increased tensions with the government and cost jobs. But they haven't accomplished anything positive.

I know that human-rights groups think they are helping us, but they are thinking with their hearts and not their heads. They say foreign investment merely props up the government and doesn't help ordinary people. That's not true. The country survived for almost 30 years without any investment. Moreover, the USA, Japan and others cut off aid in 1988, and the USA imposed sanctions in May 1997. Yet all that has done nothing except send a hollow 'moral message'.

Two westerners – one a prominent academic and the other a diplomat – once suggested to me that if sanctions and boycotts undermined the economy, people would have less to lose and would be willing to start a revolution. They seemed very pleased with this idea – a revolution to watch from the safety of their own country.

This naive romanticism angers many of us here in Myanmar. You would deliberately make us poor to force us to fight a revolution? American college students play at being freedom fighters and politicians stand up and proclaim that they are striking a blow for democracy with sanctions. But it is we Burmese who pay the price for these empty heroics. Many of us now wonder: is it for this that we went to jail?

Unfortunately, the Burmese fairy tale is so widely accepted it now seems almost impossible to call for pragmatism. Political correctness has grown so fanatical that any public criticism of the NLD or its leadership is instantly met with accusations of treachery: to simply call for realism is to be labelled pro-military or worse.

But when realism becomes a dirty word, progress becomes impossible. So put away the magic wand and think about us as a real, poor country. Myanmar has many problems, largely the result of almost 30 years of isolationism. More isolation won't fix the problems and sanctions push us backward, not forward. We need jobs. We need to modernise. We need to be a part of the world. Don't close the door on us in the name of democracy. Surely fairy tales in the west don't end so badly.

Ma Thanegi, a pro-democracy activist and former political prisoner, lives in Yangon.

Politics section later in this chapter). More likely, the best-case scenario will imitate the ill-fated Indonesian model, in which the military is guaranteed a certain number of seats in the national legislature. (See The Constitution in the Government & Politics section later in this chapter for details on how this game is being played out.) An old Burmese proverb continues to sum up the current prevailing attitude: 'Water flows, fish follow'.

GEOGRAPHY
Size & Shape
Myanmar covers an area of 671,000 sq km, sandwiched between Thailand and Laos to the east and Bangladesh to the west with India and China bordering country to the north. The country extends from approximately 28°N to 10°N latitude; the Tropic of Cancer crosses the country just above Mogok in the Mandalay Division and also intersects the Chin, Kachin and Shan states.

The shape has been likened to a parrot facing west, with the beak touching Sittwe (Akyab), the claws gripping Yangon, the tail extending down the Tanintharyi peninsula, and outstretched wings forming the three northernmost states. Its greatest length from north to south is approximately 2000km, while the widest east to west distance is around 1000km.

The Bay of Bengal and the Andaman Sea form the southern boundaries of the country. The central part of the country is marked by expansive plains and wide rivers emptying into the Bay of Bengal and the Gulf of Martaban (the upper Andaman Sea). Mountains rise to the east along the Thai border and to the north, where you find the easternmost end of the Himalayas (highest elevations around 6000m).

Rivers

Most of the country's agriculture is centred along the floodplains of the 2000km Ayeyarwady River (spelt Irrawaddy in former times), which flows south from its source (actually the confluence of two rivers), 27km north of Myitkyina, to a vast delta region along the Gulf of Martaban south-west of Yangon. Navigable year-round for at least 1500km, the Ayeyarwady has played a major role in domestic transport and communications for centuries. At the height of British rule, as many as nine million passengers a year were carried along this huge river by the colonial Irrawaddy Flotilla Company. The company even operated a class of luxury paddle wheelers fitted with polished brass-and-wood trim.

Other major rivers are the Chindwin (navigable for 792km), which joins the Ayeyarwady between Mandalay and Bagan; the Kaladan (navigable for 177km), which flows from Paletwa in the southern Chin State to the Bay of Bengal at Sittwe; the Sittoung (formerly Sittang; non-navigable due to strong currents), which flows through Taungoo and meets the sea between Bago and Mawlamyaing; and the Thanlwin (formerly Salween; navigable for just 89km),

which has its headwaters in China, and for some distance forms the border between Myanmar and Thailand before eventually reaching the sea at Mawlamyaing. The Mekong River forms the border between Myanmar and Laos.

Mountains

The Himalayas rise in the north of Myanmar, and Hkakabo Razi, right on the border between Myanmar and Tibet, is the highest mountain in South-East Asia at 5889m. Gamlang Razi is only slightly lower at 5835m. West of Bagan towards Rakhaing, Mt Victoria rises to 3053m. A wide expanse of comparatively dry plain stretches north of Yangon, but hill ranges running north-south separate the central plain from Myanmar's neighbours.

Coastline

Myanmar's coastline extends 2832km from the mouth of the Naaf River near Bangladesh to the southern tip of Tanintharyi Division near Ranong, Thailand. Coastal barrier and delta islands are common in the estuarial areas stretching from the Rakhaing State to Mawlamyaing. Off peninsular Myanmar, farther south, over a thousand continental islands dot the littoral sea, forming a mostly uninhabited island group sometimes called the Mergui Archipelago.

Resources

Myanmar is fortunate in possessing huge stands of teak and other hardwoods. According to the most recent World Development Report put out by the UN, Myanmar has an estimated natural forest area of 43%, down 12% from 10 years ago, and is ranked 33rd among the world's top 100 countries (ahead of the USA, Australia and most European countries). The Bago Yoma (*yoma* means mountain range in Burmese), extending between the Ayeyarwady and Sittoung river valleys, is the most heavily forested area and the source of most of the country's teak.

The most valued woods are teak and *padauk* (cherrywood). Timber concessions (and smuggling) to India, China, Japan, Thailand and other Asian countries slowed considerably during the Asian economic crisis of 1997-98. State-owned Myanma Timber Enterprise (MTE) accounts for most of the logging undertaken throughout the country. Reportedly the company follows a sustainable 'selective tender' system devised by the British in 1356 to maintain forest cover. Timber extraction has in fact decreased rather than increased yearly since 1994. The latest government plan calls for the complete elimination of all log exports, figuring that the greatest potential revenue comes from processed wood products rather than raw timber. If this plan is carried out, cutting should slow even further. Unfortunately illegal logging in areas of the country controlled by insurgent armies – particularly in the Shan and Kayin states – is not controlled. These areas – rather than the MTE – are the greatest source of timber smuggled to neighbouring countries. China is currently the biggest buyer of Burmese timber, followed by Singapore, India, Thailand and Japan.

The country's lengthy coastline provides a wealth of saltwater fisheries. Until recently, all fisheries were state-owned, but since 1991 several private domestic and foreign companies have begun large-scale processing of marine products along the coast. The harvesting of shrimp in particular – estimated at a potential 13,000 tonnes per year – is a major source of national revenue.

The country is also rich in gems, oil, natural gas and mineral deposits, which, like timber, serve as direct sources of foreign currency for the Tatmadaw (armed forces).

CLIMATE

Myanmar undergoes an annual three season cycle that follows the classic 'dry and wet monsoon climate' pattern common to other parts of mainland South-East Asia. The south-west monsoon starts between mid-May and mid-June, bringing frequent rains that continue into late October. The rain tends to fall mainly in the afternoons and evenings. Although it takes the edge off the

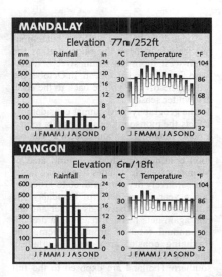

intense heat, it does tend to make things unpleasantly humid. Generally speaking, travelling in the rainy season is not particularly difficult, though unpaved roads may occasionally be impassable. In Central Myanmar it rains most during August and September, when occasional floods may occur.

The November to May dry period that follows begins with lower relative temperatures because of the influences of Asia's north-east monsoon. This second monsoon bypasses all but the south-easternmost reaches of Myanmar below Myeik (Mergui) but results in cool breezes throughout the country. As a result, during December and January the temperature can drop to near freezing at night in the highlands of the Kalaw-Taunggyi area.

In February the temperatures start to rise, and during March, April and May it can be unpleasantly hot. In Yangon the temperature often tops 40°C and in Mandalay and Bagan – part of the 'dry zone' lying in the rain shadow of the Rakhaing Yoma (Arakan Range) – it gets even hotter. The annual water festival, when people douse each other with cold water, takes place in April at the height of the hot season.

Dry season rains known as 'mango showers' occasionally bring welcome but temporary relief. In May the rains start as the south-west monsoon again sweeps northward from the Indian Ocean. In October the rain tapers off and you're back to the cool, dry winter season.

The geography of Myanmar considerably affects the monsoon rains. The delta region around Yangon gets about 250cm a year, but the rainfall rapidly diminishes as the monsoon continues north; the central area of Myanmar (which includes Bagan) is a large, comparatively dry zone with 60 to 110cm of rain a year. Then, north of Mandalay, the hill ranges force the winds higher and the rain again gets heavier, reaching a drenching annual total of around 350cm. The Rakhaing coastal area near Bangladesh and the Tanintharyi coastal strip beside southern Thailand are exposed to the full force of the south-west monsoon rains, which are often held over the region by the mountain ranges inland. Thus these coastal areas get very heavy rainfall; Sittwe receives over 500cm a year, Mawlamyaing around 440cm, most of which falls during the south-west monsoon.

ECOLOGY & ENVIRONMENT

From the snow-capped Himalayas in the north to the coral-fringed Myeik Archipelago in the south, Myanmar's 2000km length crosses three distinct ecological regions within the vast Indo-Malay biogeographic realm: the Indian subregion along the Bangladesh and India borders; the Indo-Chinese subregion in the north bordering Laos and China; and the Sundaic subregion bordering peninsular Thailand. Together these regions produce what is quite likely the richest biodiversity in South-East Asia.

Very little natural history research has been carried out in Myanmar due to the country's self-imposed isolation from the rest of the world since independence. Most of the studies available date to the British colonial era and are not reliable by today's standards. Tertiary education in the country, which has never approached the levels of

other countries, has further declined in quality since the 1970s, hence local research is even more scant. Myanmar's new openness to tourism and foreign investment has only recently extended to the reception of trained wildlife researchers. In 1998, the Smithsonian Institute was invited to conduct limited flora and fauna surveys in the country. Additionally, a recent memorandum of agreement cosigned by the Wildlife Conservation Society (WCS) and Myanmar's Ministry of Forestry may further open the country to contemporary natural historians.

FLORA

As in the rest of tropical Asia, most indigenous vegetation in Myanmar is associated with two basic types of tropical forest: monsoon forest (with a distinctive dry season of three months or more) and rainforest (where rain falls more than nine months per year).

Monsoon forests are marked by deciduous tree varieties, which shed their leaves during the dry season to conserve water; rainforests are typically evergreen. The area stretching from Yangon to Myitkyina contains mainly monsoon forests, while peninsular Myanmar south of Mawlamyaing is predominantly a rainforest zone. There is much overlapping of the two – some forest zones support a mix of monsoon forest and rainforest vegetation.

In the mountainous Himalayan region above the Tropic of Cancer, Myanmar's flora is characterised by subtropical broadleaf evergreen forest up to 2000m; temperate semi-deciduous broadleaf rainforest from 2000m to 3000m; and evergreen coniferous and subalpine snow forest passing into alpine scrub above 3000m.

Along the Rakhaing and Tanintharyi coasts, tidal forests occur in river estuaries, lagoons, tidal creeks and along low islands. Such woodlands are characterised by mangrove and other coastal trees that grow in mud and are resistant to sea water. Beach and dune forests, which grow along these same coasts above the high-tide line, consist of palms, hibiscus, casuarinas and other

Environmental Consciousness

At the moment, Myanmar lacks the legal structure for a viable national park system and there are virtually no organised environmental movements as yet. Most Burmese recycle non-biodegradable materials as a matter of course; unlike in wealthier countries, disposability is still considered a luxury reserved for the rich. Rubbish isn't yet a serious problem in Myanmar due to this thrifty recycling ethic. However, as the country develops economically its natural resources and environmental purity will come under increasing pressure.

What can the average visitor to Myanmar do to minimise the impact of tourism on the environment?

In outdoor areas where rubbish has accumulated, consider organising an impromptu cleanup crew to collect plastic, styrofoam and other nonbiodegradables for delivery to a regular rubbish pickup point. If there isn't a pickup somewhere nearby, inquire about the location of the nearest collection point and deliver the refuse yourself.

By expressing your desire to use environmentally friendly materials – and by taking direct action to avoid the use and indiscriminate disposal of nonbiodegradables – you can provide an example of environmental consciousness not only for the Burmese but for other international visitors.

Visitors might also avoid all restaurants serving 'exotic' wildlife species (eg barking deer, pangolin, bear). The main patrons of this type of cuisine are wealthy Burmese, along with visiting Chinese from Singapore, Hong Kong and Taiwan.

When using hired boats in the vicinity of coral reefs, insist that boat operators avoid lowering their anchors onto coral formations. Likewise, volunteer to collect (and later dispose of) rubbish if it's obvious that the usual mode is to throw everything overboard.

Naturally, you should refrain from purchasing coral or items made from coral while in Myanmar. In Chaungtha many souvenir stalls offer coral clusters; although talking to the vendors won't get you anywhere, try expressing your concern to the village officials who may take action if they receive enough complaints. Burmese sensitive to western paternalism are quick to point out that on a global scale the so-called 'developed' countries contribute far more environmental damage than do the poorer countries of South-East Asia; for example, per capita greenhouse emissions for Australia, Canada or the USA average over five tonnes each, while the South-East Asian countries contribute less than 0.5 tonnes per capita.

Hence in making complaints or suggestions to the Burmese employed in the tourist industry, it's important to emphasise that you want to work *with* them, rather than against them, in improving environmental standards.

Joe Cummings

tree varieties which can withstand high winds and occasional storm-sent waves.

The country's most famous flora includes an incredible array of fruit trees (see the Food section in the Facts for the Visitor chapter), over 25,000 flowering species, a variety of tropical hardwoods, and bamboo. Of the last, considered one of Asia's more renewable plant resources, Myanmar may possibly contain more species than any country outside China. One pure stand of bamboo in Rakhaing State extends over 7770 sq km. Cane and rattan are also plentiful.

As mentioned earlier, Myanmar currently boasts natural forest cover of 43%. Another 31% of the land surface is covered by secondary forest, most of which is subject to shifting 'slash-and-burn' cultivation.

Myanmar holds 75% of the world's reserves of *Tectona grandis*; better known as teak to English speakers, and *kyun* to the Burmese. This dense, long-wearing, highly prized hardwood is one of Myanmar's most important exports, for which the biggest consumers are China, Singapore and India.

FAUNA

When Marco Polo wrote about Myanmar in the 13th century, he described 'vast jungles teeming with elephants, unicorns and other wild beasts'. Though Myanmar's natural biodiversity has no doubt altered considerably since that time, it's difficult to say just how much.

The most comprehensive wildlife survey available at the time of writing was undertaken by the Bombay Natural History Society between 1912 and 1921 and published as the *Mammal Survey of India, Burma and Ceylon*. In Myanmar *The Wild Animals of Burma*, published in 1967, is the most recent work available and even this volume simply contains extracts from various surveys carried out by the British between 1912 and 1941, with a few observations dating to 1961.

As with flora, the variation in Myanmar's wildlife is closely associated with the country's geographic and climatic differences. Hence the indigenous fauna of the country's northern half is mostly of Indo-Chinese origin while that of the south is generally Sundaic (ie typical of Malaysia, Sumatra, Borneo and Java). In the Himalayan region north of the Tropic of Cancer, fauna shares the Indian biogeographical realm with areas of North-Eastern India. The large overlap area between zoogeographical and vegetative zones – extending from around Myitkyina in the north to Bago Yoma in the central region – means that much of Myanmar is a potential habitat for plants and animals from all three zones.

Myanmar is rich in bird life, with an estimated 1000 resident and migrating species. Coastal and inland waterways of the delta and southern peninsula are especially important habitats for South-East Asian waterfowl.

Burmese Tuskers

The *Elephas maximus* plays such an important role in montane Myanmar that the Burmese use different names for male elephants according to tusk characteristics:

with two tusks	*sweh-zoun*
with one tusk	*hte*
without tusks	*hain*
widely spread, curving tusks	*sweh-ga*
straight, downward-curving tusks	*sweh-zaiq*
short, stumpy tusks	*sweh-touq*
stumpy tusks shaped like banana buds	*ngapyaw-bu*

According to a 1955 edition of the *Journal of the Bombay Natural History Society*, the old rule of thumb that an Asian elephant's shoulder height is about twice the circumference of one of its forefeet is accurate more than 95% of the time.

Joe Cummings

Distinctive mammals – found in dwindling numbers within the more heavily forested areas of Myanmar – include leopards, jungle cats, fishing cats, civets, Indian mongooses, crab-eating mongooses, Himalayan bears, Asiatic black bears, Malayan sun bears, gaur (Indian bison), banteng (wild cattle), serow (an Asiatic mountain goat), wild boars, sambar, barking deer, mouse deer, tapirs, pangolin, gibbons, macaques. Sea mammals include dolphins and dugongs.

An estimated 2000 tigers are thought to inhabit the primary forests, about four times as many as in neighbouring Thailand. Around 10,000 Asiatic elephants – roughly a third of all those on the planet – are widely distributed on Myanmar. Among these are 6000 pachyderms that make up the world's largest herd of working elephants, most of which are used in logging and agriculture. It's encouraging that this number exceeds by a thousand that tallied by English scholar FT Morehead in his 1944 treatise *The Forests of Burma*.

Both the one-horned (Javan) rhinoceros and the Asiatic two-horned (Sumatran) rhinoceros are believed to survive in very small numbers near the Thai border in the Kayin State. The rare red panda (or cat bear) was last sighted in northern Myanmar in the early 1960s but is still thought to live in Kachin State forests above 2000m.

Herpetofauna include four sea turtle species along with numerous snake varieties, of which an astounding 52 are venomous. These include the common cobra, king cobra (hamadryad), banded krait, Malayan viper, green viper and Russell's pit viper.

Endangered Species

Myanmar is not a signatory to the UN Convention on International Trade in Endangered Species of Wild Flora & Fauna (CITES), and neither the International Union for Conservation of Nature & Natural Resources (IUCN) nor the WCS have reliable figures of the status of any species that might be threatened or endangered.

At the moment, deforestation by the timber industry poses the greatest threat to wildlife habitats. In areas where habitat loss isn't a problem, hunting threatens to wipe out the rarer animal species. Even in the nation's nominally protected lands, wildlife laws are seldom enforced due to corruption and a general lack of manpower. While many animals are hunted for food, tigers and rhinos are killed for the lucrative overseas Chinese pharmaceutical market. Among the Chinese, the ingestion of tiger penis and bone are thought to have curative effects. Taipei, where at least two-thirds of the pharmacies deal in tiger parts (in spite of the fact that such trade is contrary to Taiwanese law), is the world centre for Burmese tiger consumption.

Marine resources are threatened by a lack of long-range conservation goals. For the moment, Myanmar's lack of industrialisation means the release of pollutants into the seas is relatively low, but overfishing, especially in the delta regions, is a growing problem. The country must also deal with illegal encroachment on national fisheries by Bangladeshi, Thai and Malaysian fishing boats.

National Parks

Myanmar claims to have three national parks and 17 wildlife sanctuaries (including two marine and three wetland environments), which together protect about 1% of the nation's total land surface. Compared to international averages, this is very low coverage (Thailand, by comparison, has 12% coverage); the government reports that it has plans to raise protection to 5% by the end of the century. None of these protected areas features any facilities for researchers or visitors of any kind, and most are in fact off-limits to foreigners. Exceptions are the Lampi Island Wildlife Preserve, off the coast of Tanintharyi Division, which can be visited with permission from the regional authorities (best obtained via a travel agency in Yangon), and the more accessible Mt Popa National Park near Bagan.

GOVERNMENT & POLITICS
The System

The Tatmadaw and their political junta, the SPDC, continue to rule Myanmar with an iron fist. The Pyithu Hluttaw (People's Assembly) last convened in May 1990, while the Council of People's Justices was dissolved following the events of 1988. In effect Myanmar is centrally ruled by one executive branch, which is controlled by the military.

The military's NUP, founded by General Ne Win, is the only party with real political power at the moment, though it is clearly symbolic rather than substantive since there is no pretence that the country functions via party politics. The NLD has been effectively isolated, while another 'opposition' party, the Union Solidarity & Development Association (USDA), is simply a national front for the SPDC. The USDA has become increasingly important as a way of mobilising mass support for SPDC policies – through a blend of reward and coercion – and as a potential future mechanism for managing the transition from military to civilian rule.

The true centre of control, the SPDC, is made up of four government heads and military commanders from various regions around the country. Some observers say the 1997 changeover from SLORC to SPDC is merely a case of old wine in new bottles, while others speculate it could signal a change in military policies. At the top, however, sit the same four generals: SPDC chairman and Ne Win's appointed successor, General Than Shwe; vice-chairman General Maung Aye; first secretary (and head of military intelligence), Lt General Khin Nyunt; and second secretary General Tin Oo. Attached to the SPDC are a 14 member cabinet and a separate 14 member advisory board.

Than Shwe and Khin Nyunt seem moderate compared to their predecessor, General Saw Maung, who headed the party from 1988 until his nervous breakdown in late 1991, during which he made rambling speeches on such mystical topics as Jesus' supposed sojourn in Tibet. It is widely believed that Khin Nyunt, 'secretary one' (also 'S-1'), is the most powerful man in the government simply because he is the favourite of the retired Ne Win. In 1992 Khin Nyunt reportedly foiled an attempt by mainstream field commanders to remove him from government office. This internal element allegedly opposed his close links with China, which they associate with the now-defunct BCP, once their most troublesome frontier opponent.

Behind the scenes, some say that real control has remained in the hands of postal clerk-turned-dictator Ne Win (commonly spoken of as 'the Old Man') since 1962. Ne Win is said to be obsessed with astrology and numerology to the extent that virtually every major tactical decision at the national level is based on consultations with horoscopes and obscure number charts. One result was the introduction of K45 and K90 banknotes in the late 1980s. Ne Win reveres the number nine; both 45 and 90 are multiples of nine, and the digits of both numbers add up to nine. He has been married seven times, his wealth is said to rival that of the late Ferdinand Marcos, and he owns property in England, Germany and Japan. Recently his health has been poor and he has spent much time undergoing medical treatment in Singapore, where he is often hosted by Singapore's ex-prime minister, Lee Kuan Yew. Some observers disagree with the assessment that Ne Win still wields any real power, speculating instead that although his advice is occasionally sought and respected, the SPDC Cabinet follows its own dictates and no one else's. Only two people – Ne Win and Khin Nyunt – know for certain what their relationship truly signifies.

Following the repression of the 1990 election results, many successfully elected NLD candidates fled to Burmese refugee camps just over the eastern Myanmar border in Thailand, where they formed a National Coalition Government of the Union of Burma (NCGUB) in December 1990. However the NLD central executive committee in Yangon, no doubt under pressure from the Tatmadaw, disavowed any connection with the NCGUB immediately and to this day refuses to recognise the 'government in exile'.

Myanmar's government is one of the least efficient tax collectors in the world, with tax revenues estimated at a mere 2% of gross domestic product (GDP). In addition to the difficulty inherent in collecting cash from large sectors of the populace living on a subsistence level, in a mostly non-cash economy, tax offices are easily bribed to turn a blind eye. Another factor is the long-running Burmese tradition of corvée, or draft labour, in which the average citizen is expected to contribute manual labour to public works projects – such as road widening or landscaping – a few days each year. Those who have the means may pay a tax instead of working.

Political Freedom

While Burmese citizens have relative economic freedom in all but state-owned trade spheres (naturally these are the big ones, like timber and oil), their political freedom is strictly curtailed. Peaceful political assembly is banned and citizens are forbidden to talk to foreigners about politics. All government workers in Myanmar, from mail carriers to university professors, must sign a pledge not to discuss the government among themselves, at risk of losing their jobs. In everyday practice, plenty of Burmese talk to foreigners about political issues as ong as they can be sure no Burmese are listening, voicing such common laments as 'our government is run by a bunch of idiots'.

The opposition movement that began in 1988 appears to be quelled now, with many leaders and spokespersons under arrest and the military in firm control. Student demonstrations in late 1996 were considerably smaller than those in 1988 and 1990 – both in number and in geographical scope. They were limited to Yangon and Mandalay and mostly consisted of street sit-ins rather than marches. In all cases demonstrators moved quickly when security forces turned up. It is no coincidence that public universities in Myanmar have been closed since 1996. Although public gatherings in front of Suu Kyi's Yangon home have been prevented since 1996, the NLD continues to hold regular meetings, albeit only with prior permission. As *Asiaweek* recently pointed out, open meetings of any similar opposition party would be impossible in North Korea, Vietnam, Laos or Brunei.

George Orwell (who wrote *Animal Farm* and *1984* and who once served with the British colonial police in Burma) could hardly envision a more Orwellian regime than that currently held in place by the Tatmadaw. It has turned friend against friend and family member against family member in a web of mutual suspicion. The military employs a large network of informers, who circulate in cinemas, teashops, offices and private homes to ferret out 'minions of colonialism' – anyone who voices opposition to the government. A national dress code requires all citizens to dress in 'proper' Burmese attire; trousers (for men or women), for example, are frowned upon unless necessary in one's occupation. For-

eign music (ie any music with foreign lyrics) is banned from the radio.

Among the most visible signs of the government's current strategy are the prominent red-and-white signboards posted in public areas of all Myanmar's major cities. They carry slogans, in Burmese (and occasionally in English), such as these:

- Only when there is discipline will there be progress.
- The strength of the nation lies only within.
- Beware of aboveground and underground destructive elements.
- Observance of discipline leads to safety.
- Anyone who is riotous, destructive and unruly is our enemy.
- The Tatmadaw shall never betray the national cause.

In addition, virtually all government publications carry the following list headed 'People's Desire':

- Oppose those relying on external elements, acting as stooges, holding negative views.
- Oppose those trying to jeopardise stability of the State and progress of the nation.
- Oppose foreign nations interfering in internal affairs of the State.
- Crush all internal and external destructive elements as the common enemy.

Of course the Tatmadaw never explains how it is they have discerned what the 'national cause' or the 'People's Desire' really might be, since without elected representatives in the government they couldn't possibly know!

Cynics say that the opposition never stood a chance and that the 1990 election was either a small tactical error on the part of the military or simply a way of identifying the opposition (reportedly, anybody who ran for election against the NUP was immediately put on the arrest list). Some even contend that had the opposition taken over, Myanmar would now be in a state of anarchy. Many younger Burmese, however, still harbour hopes that some day they will be able to wrest control of the country from the feared and hated Tatmadaw.

Political Imprisonment & Execution

Although detention of suspected dissidents is common, most are released after a few days or weeks of questioning. The government also makes a big show of releasing prisoners at regular intervals each year – an age-old South-East Asian practice that is supposed to confer merit upon the rulership and, rather ironically, demonstrate Buddhist compassion. On 27 March (Armed Forces Day) 1995, the government released 31 high-profile political prisoners, including Tin U, cofounder of the original NLD and former army chief of staff. Another bone to the opposition was the 1995 state-sponsored public funeral of U Nu – the only democratically elected prime minister Myanmar has ever known. In the same year, the government also reduced by one-third the prison terms of 23,000 convicts who had participated in construction projects around the country. Similar releases were made in 1996 and 1997.

The government has carried out only four official executions in the last 25 years, none of which involved prisoners of conscience. Two more prisoners were sentenced in death in 1997, though neither sentence has yet been carried out. Of course these low figures do not include extrajudicial killings – mostly in frontier areas – anecdotally documented or semi-documented by various international human rights groups. Compared to China, which officially and publicly executes over 2000 people a year in addition to carrying out an unknown number of extrajudicial killings, Myanmar's government appears relatively less bloodthirsty.

The Constitution

Myanmar has had three constitutions since gaining independence from the British in 1948, the most recent of which was suspended by the SLORC in 1989. In 1993 after four years of snail-like progress, a short-lived attempt to hold a national convention ended with an NLD walkout. In 1995 the government finally organised a second national convention, consisting of 702 delegates who were given the task of drafting a new national charter. Most delegates were selected by the junta; less than 15% hailed from the NLD, which has largely been coopted by the NUP.

The delegates were instructed in no uncertain terms to draft a charter giving the military leadership special 'emergency powers' that included the right to suspend ordinary government procedures. The parameters also dictated that the charter disqualified anyone married to a foreigner from holding high public office (a clause also favoured by the late Aung San). The SLORC/SPDC has repeatedly promised that once the constitution is ratified – whether by public referendum or by other means yet to be decided – civilian rule will come. As trade minister Lt General Tun Kyi told international reporters in 1994: 'When the constitution is completed, democracy will be restored'.

The beleaguered NLD delegates walked out of the national convention in November 1995 to protest the non-elective delegate selection as well as the lack of democratic administrative protocol. Two days afterwards, the government officially expelled the NLD from the convention for being absent without permission, and the entire proceedings were adjourned in March 1996. Although the chartering body hasn't since reconvened, the military government appears determined to draft a constitution that will ensure a dominant role for the military services in the country's future political structure, based on the Indonesian model. How long it will take is anyone's guess; after six years the charter is less than half-finished.

Administrative Divisions

For administrative purposes, Myanmar is divided into seven *tain* (divisions) where Bamar are in the majority (Yangon, Ayeyarwady, Bago, Magwe, Mandalay, Sagaing, Tanintharyi); and into seven *pyi* (states) where non-Bamar are in the majority (Shan, Kachin, Chin, Rakhaing, Kayah, Kayin, Mon).

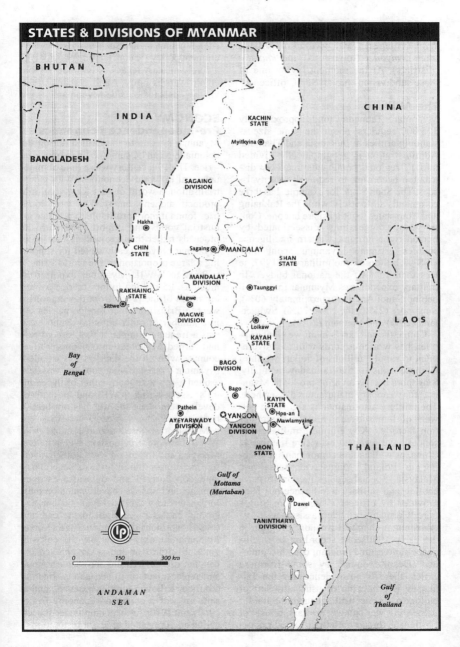

STATES & DIVISIONS OF MYANMAR

BHUTAN

CHINA

INDIA

BANGLADESH

KACHIN STATE

Myitkyina

SAGAING DIVISION

Hakha

CHIN STATE

Sagaing MANDALAY

SHAN STATE

MANDALAY DIVISION

Taunggyi

RAKHAING STATE

Magwe

MAGWE DIVISION

Sittwe

Loikaw

KAYAH STATE

LAOS

Bay of Bengal

BAGO DIVISION

Bago

KAYIN STATE

Pathein

Hpa-an

AYEYARWADY DIVISION

YANGON

Mawlamyaing

YANGON DIVISION

MON STATE

THAILAND

Gulf of Mottama (Martaban)

Dawei

TANINTHARYI DIVISION

0   150   300 km

ANDAMAN SEA

Gulf of Thailand

Each state and division is subdivided into *kyay* (villages), *kyay ywa oksu* (village tracts), *myonei* (townships) and *khayain* (districts). At the moment, every one of these subdivisions has an SPDC office.

The Military

Myanmar's Tatmadaw totals approximately 325,000 regulars, about the same size as standing armies in Indonesia and Thailand. Administration is geographically divided into 12 regional commands unevenly distributed according to regional security issues. The Shan State, for example, has three commands all to itself, while the Rakhaing and Chin states together share but one. Contrary to exaggerations disseminated by human rights groups, western intelligence sources estimate Myanmar spent only US$1.7 billion on the military in 1997, ie less than 15% of the national budget. In military expenditures Myanmar ranks well behind Saudi Arabia (approximately 60%), Singapore (25%), the USA (20%), Switzerland (20%) and Vietnam (20%).

China, the military's main weapons supplier, has written accords with the government to supply millions of dollars worth of Chinese arms to the Tatmadaw annually. Singapore acts as an arms broker to Myanmar for weaponry manufactured elsewhere. The military also maintains a growing network of domestic small arms and ammunition factories. Key Burmese military personnel have received extensive training in China, as well as less comprehensive training in Poland, Yugoslavia, India and Malaysia. Specialised instruction in parachuting and military intelligence has been provided by officers visiting from Singapore. Germany provided assistance in establishing a chemical weapons program in the early 1980s but according to intelligence sources this program been discontinued. Despite claims by some Burmese exiles, there is no evidence that the Tatmadaw is producing or using any sort of biological or chemical agents in the field.

In civil war zones, military abuse of civilians – forced portering, forced reloca-

tions and extrajudicial executions – appears rife. Whether or not such abuses are government policy (ie considered genocidal) or a purely military legacy of half-century-old ethnic wars is hotly – and perhaps irrelevantly – debated outside Myanmar.

ECONOMY
Pre-Independence Economics

Myanmar's value to the British during the colonial era can be summed up in one word – rice. The 19th century was a time of major upheaval in world economies. With industrialisation, a world market for agricultural products suddenly emerged as some countries found it more profitable to produce industrial goods and import food with the proceeds rather than grow their own food. Myanmar proved ideally suited for supplying a large proportion of the world's rice.

Prior to WWII, Myanmar exported as much as 3.5 million tonnes of rice a year, but much of the profit from this enterprise went to British or other foreign parties. As in a number of other colonial countries, it was a frequent complaint that foreign rule had turned Myanmar into a one-product country, with all the dangers this entailed. Myanmar's rice-growing potential was devastated along with many other of the country's assets during WWII, and the path of development since the war has not been a happy one.

Myanmar suffered major damage from WWII, far more than most of its neighbours: Malaysia and Indonesia were quickly overrun and thus suffered little damage; Thailand collaborated and thus also escaped damage; and war was never waged on most Indian territory. Yet in Myanmar, air and ground battles raged right to the end and caused enormous destruction. Furthermore, Myanmar quickly threw off the colonial yoke after the war and never enjoyed the benefits of overseas aid for reconstruction and replacement of ruined assets. Internal conflicts following independence, and a shift towards a command economy in the 1960s and 1970s further complicated the situation and prevented efficient restoration.

Under Military Rule

For a time, Myanmar remained dependent upon rice as a major source of foreign earnings even though its efficiency as a rice producer was steadily declining. Despite the worldwide advances in agriculture – miracle rice, fertilisers, etc – Burmese were managing to produce less per hectare even two decades after independence than before. By the mid-1960s, the area used for rice production was slightly above pre-war levels but the actual output was somewhat lower. Yet the population had increased by over 50% compared to pre-war levels and by now is probably double what it was. The upshot is that after WWII there was little rice to export and barely enough to feed the country. By 1987, Myanmar was considered one of the 10 poorest countries in the world.

Since the government's abandonment of socialism in 1989, the economy has changed rapidly. By 1995 the economy was growing at a rate of 6.4% per year, the highest since before Ne Win took power in the early 1960s. As of late 1998 this had slowed to 4% or 5%, still one of the highest rates in crisis-beleaguered South-East Asia, largely due to the nation's limited use of international credit. Myanmar ranks sixth in world rice exports behind Thailand, the USA, Pakistan, China and Australia. Processing and manufacturing have tripled over the last 10 years and now provide more of the country's GDP than agriculture, although in terms of employment, agriculture still outranks all other sectors. Nominal per capita income is US$765, but when adjusted for purchasing power parity this amounts to US$753, the second lowest figure in Asia after Afghanistan (US$720).

Inflation runs at an estimated 30% per annum when adjusted for dollar usage and purchasing power parity – more like 70% if judged by a *kyat* (Burmese currency) index alone.

The country carries a modest foreign debt of US$4.3 billion, less than one tenth that of Thailand's and the lowest Myanmar has seen since 1994. Hard-currency reserves stand at US$50 to US$70 million, up from US$30 million three years ago. Despite this comparatively solid position, the government has refused to discuss loan servicing with the World Bank, to whom it owes US$700 million. In September 1998 the World Bank responded by assigning Myanmar 'non-accrual' status, a distinction it shares with countries such as North Korea.

Certain key commodities and services remain in government control or are fully state-owned. One of the most profitable state corporations is Myanma Oil & Gas Enterprise, whose production of crude oil almost doubled between 1996-97 and 1997-98. Myanma Gems Enterprise, Myanma Timber Enterprise and Myanmar Fisheries Enterprise are also extremely profitable.

Continued domination of such state-owned enterprises (SEEs) may be on the wane. In September 1998 Myanmar transferred the Ywama Steel Mill, the largest SEE leased out since privatisation began, to local private entrepreneurs. In January 1999 the government announced the privatisation of 68 more SEEs, including four factories, seven rice mills and 57 cinemas.

Despite ongoing privatisation, solid growth and low debt, all is not rosy with the economy. Merchants and entrepreneurs prosper while farmers and workers are barely able to scrape by. The retail price of rice multiplied nine times between 1984 and 1993; the wholesale price increased 21 times. Between this guidebook edition and the previous one, many consumer prices tripled, although for rice and other staples, for which the price is government-controlled, prices rose only 13% to 18%. The maximum government salary of US$15 per month hasn't changed this decade; Burmese citizens must typically spend around 65% of their monthly income on food. This leaves little to spend on consumer goods, so most Burmese, for example, rely on discarded, second-hand clothes imported by ship from Singapore, Malaysia and Japan in huge bales. Most of the clothes you see hanging in upcountry markets are 'bale' clothing, which fetch around K160 to K200 per piece for shirt or blouse, just K400 for a used denim jacket.

International Trade

Since 1990 the government has moved to-wards more economic involvement with the outside world and has a number of major foreign-aided projects under way, along with many joint ventures with foreign-owned companies. Under new investment laws, even wholly owned foreign enterprises are now permitted in certain sectors. Over 25 foreign banks have branches in Yangon.

Between 1989 and 1993, the number of exporters and importers registered in Myanmar increased from 986 to 4813. By 1998, as a result of the South-East Asian economic crisis, this number had reached a plateau though it had yet to decline; reduced incomes in neighbouring countries have made Myanmar's cheap exports even more attractive. The nation's main export revenues come from forest products, pulses, rice, gems and pearls, followed by much lesser incomes from maize, rubber, cotton, jute, minerals and marine products.

By far the largest importers of Burmese commodities are Singapore and India (about a billion kyat each in 1996-97), followed at some distance by Thailand, Hong Kong, China, Malaysia and the European Union. In the reverse direction, most imports to Myanmar originate from Singapore, Japan, Thailand, China, North America, Malaysia and India.

When it comes to direct foreign investment in Myanmar, the single largest players are Singapore and the UK, each investing around US$1 billion in 1996-97, the last year for which figures are available. Singapore's presence in Yangon has become so great that many Burmese complain that the city has become a Singaporean economic colony. Some distance behind the UK march France (US$465 million), Malaysia (US$436 million), Thailand (US$425 million), the USA (US$243 million) and the Netherlands (US$237 million).

The government continues to control all legal foreign trade in timber, minerals, gems, oil and gas – although foreign companies have been contracted for the exploration and extraction of some minerals and petroleum. These and other large, private ventures – such as international hotels – must be underwritten or sponsored by someone in the government. Ministers typically take a piece of every project that requires their approval, often as much as 5% of the project's estimated value. Tatmadaw officers thus enriched live in colonial-style villas in Yangon's best suburbs and are chauffeured about in the latest-model Japanese cars. Most conduct multiple business affairs that assure a comfortable retirement.

Many Chinese who fled Myanmar following nationalisation in the 1960s are now returning to participate in the liberalised economy. Those who can speak Burmese are able to get national ID cards even though they aren't Burmese citizens; this permits overseas Chinese to use kyat to purchase goods and services that usually require US dollars, enabling them to enjoy lifestyles that are obscenely extravagant by ordinary Burmese standards.

Underground Economy

Although the black market is no longer the only game in town, it still plays a major role in Myanmar's economy. Many Burmese with civil service jobs hang up their coats at the office, then leave to do business elsewhere for the rest of the day, buying and selling a variety of home-grown commodities and smuggled consumer goods. Without income earned (and goods purchased) on the black market, virtually no civil servant in present-day Myanmar could survive.

Beyond simple subsistence, the objective of most black-market traders is to stockpile as many US dollars as they can as hedges against inflation and the vagaries of Burmese currency. The difference between the official exchange rate for kyat and the free-market rate is enormous: in 1998 it was around K6 per US$1 at the official rate versus K350 per US$1 on the free market.

In northern Myanmar, rural cash economies revolve around the opium and heroin trade, which forms the largest single component of Myanmar's underground economy. In a typical year over 3000 tonnes of raw opium are produced; reportedly, more than half the heroin sold in North America is refined from opium grown in Myanmar. Although the government has an explicit anti-narcotics policy and there appears to be no direct political connection with opium/heroin producers, a certain military complicity at local levels is undeniable. On top of this, drug trafficking profits are allowed to circulate freely in Myanmar's laissez faire economy. Practically all large, privately managed businesses have been invaded, from banks to airlines to hotels. As *Jane's Intelligence Review* summed up the situation in its March 1998 issue:

> To date there is no hard evidence to support the contention that military involvement in the trade has been orchestrated from Yangon as a matter of policy. However, the repatriation and laundering of narco-profits as well as the impunity enjoyed by the barons has clearly become institutionalised: a 'don't-ask' policy over the source of funds used by Burma's new generation of narco-capitalists has been adopted at the highest level of government.

In the final analysis, the quiet takeover of Myanmar's private-sector economy by narco-barons and their associates allows for one charitable interpretation: the junta is prepared to turn a blind eye to the process in the overriding interest of securing peace, integrating insurgent-held areas into the national mainstream and promoting economic development – if necessary with dirty money.

Some analysts, prepared to credit the junta with a long-term narcotics strategy, argue that the government may even hope that over time today's drug lords, attracted by the prospect of making real money legally, may mellow into legitimate business tycoons. One senior Yangon-based diplomat puts it this way:

> Just as the government wants to deal with opium cultivators by showing them a different way to make a living, eg crop substitution, so it is trying to deal with leaders by showing them too there's a different way of making a living – 'We'll let you go "legit", if you stop your refining and trafficking'.

In 1997 a government minister tried to blacklist a company fronting for the United Wa State Army (which controls much of the drug trade in the northern Shan State) for allegedly 'submitting false accounts'. The minister, General David Abel, was promptly removed from his post and no further action was taken against the company.

Tourism

Tourism, an obvious source of hard currency, came to a temporary halt following the 1988 uprising, but quickly recovered after 1992, as a result of liberalised visa regulations and an expanding tourist infrastructure.

Pre-1988 tourism peaked in 1986-87 at 41,000 arrivals per year. During the restrictive 1990-92 period the incoming stream slowed to around 4000 per annum. By 1992-93 it was back up to 22,000 and in 1994-95 around 60,000 people reportedly visited Myanmar.

In 1996-97 the government mounted a feeble Visit Myanmar Year campaign – and despite their efforts to encourage tourism, visitor numbers peaked at 180,000, far short of the hoped-for half a million. Since 1996 visits to Myanmar appear to have dropped back to perhaps as few as 100,000 to 120,000, mainly due to steep declines in intra-Asia travel influenced by economic considerations. French, German, Italian, Japanese and American tourists top the list, though no one nationality has sent more than 1500 tourists in any year. Yearly receipts earned via tourism so far amount to less than US$1 million, much of which is spent by business travellers.

Tourism growth is hampered by a number of factors, including the deficiency of hotel, restaurant and transportation infrastructure outside the Yangon-Mandalay-Bagan-Inle Lake quadrangle. Other significant factors include the lack of repeat visits due to the offensive two-tiered pricing system for hotels and the high admission fees to historic and religious sites. The country's poor human rights image record also acts as a deterrent to tourism.

POPULATION & PEOPLE
Population
Since the government does not control the entire country, a complete census has not been possible since the British days. As of 1998 the population is estimated to be about 48.8 million according to international sources (but 46.4 million according to the Myanmar government), with an annual growth rate of around 2.1%. Approximately 74% live in rural areas.

The largest cities, in declining order, are Yangon, Mandalay, Pathein, Mawlamyaing, Taunggyi and Sittwe. Population statistics for each of these cities have not been made public since 1973, and local estimates vary wildly depending on whom you ask; Yangon appears to have 3 or 4 million people, Mandalay around 800,000, the remainder 300,000 or fewer.

People
Myanmar's population can be divided into four main ethnological groups – Tibeto-Burman, Mon-Khmer, Austro-Thai and Karennic. Tibeto-Burman speakers encompass 78% of the population and include the majority Bamar plus over 30 smaller tribal groups including the Rakhaing, Chin, Kachin, Lisu, Lahu and Akha. Most of the Mon-Khmer are Mon living in the Gulf of Martaban area, along with smaller groups in the north such as the Intha, Wa and Palaung. Most of the Austro-Thais are Shan living in the north; 'Shan' in fact comes from the same Austro-Thai root as 'Siam', both meaning 'free'. The Karennic groups include the numerous Kayin (Karen) and Kayah (known to the British as the Karenni) tribes living along or near the central Thai-Burmese border. There are also around 6000 Hmong-Mien peoples scattered around the north and north-east.

Although ethnologists have identified 111 different ethnolinguistic groups in Myanmar, the government recognises 67, officially clustered by language origin into just eight 'national races': Bamar, Shan, Mon, Kayin, Kayah, Chin, Kachin and Rakhaing.

The exact percentage belonging to each group is a hotly debated topic both inside and outside Myanmar. In the absence of any scientifically conducted census, no one can claim to know the true ethnic breakdown. Best estimates run as follows: Bamar 65%, Shan 10%, Kayin 7%, Rakhaing 4%, and Chin, Kachin and Mon around 2.3% each. Chinese, Indian, Assamese and other minorities comprise less than 1% each.

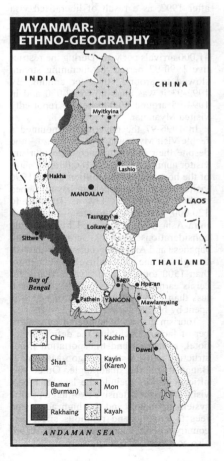

MYANMAR: ETHNO-GEOGRAPHY

INDIA

CHINA

Myitkyina

Hakha

Lashio

MANDALAY

LAOS

Taunggyi
Loikaw

Sittwe

THAILAND

Bay of Bengal

Bago   Hpa-an

Pathein   YANGON   Mawlamyaing

Chin   Kachin

Shan   Kayin (Karen)

Bamar (Burman)   Mon

Rakhaing   Kayah

Dawei

ANDAMAN SEA

continued on page 51

Insurgency

Independent Myanmar has been plagued by rebellion since its inception in 1948. By the early 1990s, outside observers estimated there were as many as 35 insurgent factions operating inside the country, including national or ethnic liberation parties, 'warlord organisations' and Kuomintang (KMT) remnants. The estimated numbers in these individual groups range from as few as 50 (the on-again, off-again Tai National Army, Palaung State Liberation Organisation, Kayah New Land Revolution Council) to the tens of thousands, eg Mong Tai Army (MTA) and the Shan United Army (SUA). Most have formed loose affiliations among themselves, while some are splinter groups or factions vying for local supremacy (Ma Ha San faction of the Wa National Army, or WNA; Karenni People's United Liberation Front versus the Karenni Liberation Army). Others are tactical wings for political parties, such as the Karen National Liberation Army (KNLA), for the Karen National Union (KNU).

The names can be quite confusing. One group may have more than one title (ie the United Pa-O Organisation and the Pa-O Shan State Independence Party), while different, unaffiliated groups may have similar names, such as the Shan State Army (SSA; ethnic Shans – member of the National Democratic Front or NDF), the Shan United Revolutionary Army (ethnic Shans; once allies of the Third Chinese Irregular Forces – a remnant of the 93rd Nationalist Chinese Army) and the SUA, a 'warlord' group of ethnic Shans, Chinese and other minorities, under the former leadership of the infamous Khun Sa, who is also known as Chang Chifu and Sao Mong Khawn. In 1985 the SUA merged with the Mong Tai Army under the Tai-land Revolutionary Council (Tai is what the Shan call themselves).

These groups operate primarily in the various states of outer Myanmar, where Bamar are in the minority, as opposed to 'Myanmar proper', where the Yangon government has control. They occasionally cause mischief outside their own territory; the Karen have attacked Bamar strongholds in Bago, Dawei and Kyaikto, and were responsible for bombings in the delta area near Yangon, and the primarily Karen suburb of Insein, on the outskirts of the capital in the 1980s. In early 1992 a band of Karen rebels were routed by the Myanmar army just south of Yangon.

The situation is complicated by the fact that insurgency in the 'Golden Triangle' area is, in many cases, linked to the thriving opium and heroin trade there. Because of this, some foreign opponents of the trade, which is largely controlled by the Shan, Wa and Kokang, have expressed qualified support of Burmese efforts to eradicate insurgency in the north-east. Thus, the opium trade has helped to splinter foreign attitudes toward Yangon; governments that might otherwise support anti-Yangon movements have been forced to tolerate the ruling regime in the name of the 'war on drugs'. Yangon, in turn, exploits foreign ambivalence to the full, identifying all insurgency with the opium trade.

Among these insurgent groups, the most significant government opponent has been the NDF, an alliance of nine non-communist insurgent groups formed in 1976. The avowed purpose of the NDF was to provide military assistance to members under government attack and to work towards common political ends on a national level, while retaining local independence. The nine or 10 member groups may share a combined force of over 25,000 soldiers, though it's doubtful they could ever rally together for a truly unified offensive.

During the mid-1980s, the NDF sought to enter into negotiations with the Burmese government in order to come to a peaceful resolution of the age-old majority-minority conflict. Meetings arranged and conducted by the Burmese proved unsuccessful and since the 1988

Insurgency

Yangon uprising, the NDF has refused to talk again until representatives of both parties can meet outside Myanmar under a neutral chairmanship. Following the truces of 1989-94 and the 1995 Burmese military victories against the KNU (once the backbone of the NDF), any bilateral settlement is highly unlikely to occur in the near future.

Until 1989 the most conspicuous nonparticipant in the NDF was the Burmese Communist Party (BCP), a seasoned group that reached peak numbers (12,000 to 15,000 troops) in the late 1970s and early 1980s. The BCP became increasingly isolated due to changes in attitude in China dating to 1979, when Beijing began distancing itself from the heavily Maoist BCP. In contrast, Chinese relations with the Burmese government have improved greatly since the end of the Chinese Cultural Revolution – Ne Win finally paid a visit to Beijing in 1985, just one month after China stopped broadcasting the Voice of the People of Burma from across the border.

Other nonethnic opposition groups include the Democratic Alliance of Burma (DAB), the National League for Democracy in Liberated Areas, the National Coalition Government of the Union of Burma (NCGUB) and the All Burma Students' Democratic Front (ABSDF). Most of the latter groups operate from refugee camps along the Thai-Burmese border or in KNU-protected villages in eastern Myanmar. None field their own armies and, although they meet endlessly and produce stacks of bold declarations and mission statements, they have very little real power.

Karen National Union

The half-century-old KNU has offered armed resistance against the Burmese government ever since independence, claiming that the autonomy promised them in the Panglong Agreement of 1947 was never honoured by the Burmese. Until recently, the KNU and its tactical arm, the KNLA, controlled most of the Kayin State, home to perhaps a million Karen. Their independent territory, called Kawthoolei by the Karen, was long headquartered in Manerplaw, located across the Thanlwin River from Tha Song Yang, Thailand, close to the Thai-Burmese border.

Manerplaw also served as headquarters for the DAB, an alliance of a dozen rebel groups fighting for regional autonomy. It was also the seat of the National Coalition Government of the Union of Burma (NCGUB), a 'parallel government' established by a group of disaffected National League for Democracy (NLD) members who won parliamentary seats in the ill-fated May 1990 national elections. The prime minister of the parallel government is Dr Sein Win, cousin to Aung San Suu Kyi and son of U Ba Win (who along with his brother Aung San was assassinated in 1947). Along with the exiled MPs, the coalition included an alliance of ethnic insurgent groups led by Karen general Bo Mya and Kachin leader Brang Seng. The NCGUB was severely weakened by the departure of many of its ethnic partner groups to take advantage of government truces.

In January 1992 the Burmese army's 22nd and 44th divisions along with part of the 66th Light Infantry Battalion – a combined strength of 20,000 troops – advanced on Manerplaw from the west, but suffered heavy casualties. Outmaneuvered by the KNLA, the government declared a unilateral ceasefire.

After a rift between Christian and Buddhist Karen caused the KNU to split into two hostile factions, the Burmese army violated the ceasefire in January 1995 to offer support to the

Insurgency

Buddhist faction, the Democratic Karen Buddhist Organisation (DKBO); this time around they were able to take Manerplaw. The KNU leadership headed south, but lost their second capital, Kawmoora (opposite Sai Yok, Thailand), at the end of February 1995.

Up until now the Yangon policy has been one of containment, but this now seems to have changed to 'exterminate them once and for all'. Fighting with the KNLA is now concentrated close to a proposed underground gas pipeline from the Gulf of Martaban to Thailand. After eight Burmese petroleum engineers were killed by the KNLA near Dawei in 1995, the government immediately pulled all engineers out of the field and began heavy military operations in the area.

From all recent accounts, the once-mighty KNLA has been greatly damaged by the Buddhist-Christian split and the loss of their Manerplaw headquarters. They now operate in reduced numbers from an area just inside Myanmar, opposite Um Phang District in Thailand's Tak Province. Joe Cummings recently visited the KNLA camp and interviewed the KNLA's second-in-command, General Taw Hla. According to Joe, the camp situation appeared bleak – more like a lower echelon hospital then a tactical headquarters. When asked about Aung San Suu Kyi and the NLD, General Taw Hla said the KNU leadership mistrusted the NLD's intentions with regard to ethnic minorities.

Shan & Wa Rebels

If the Burmese government is able to vanquish the KNU – an outcome not by any means assured at this point – its final, and perhaps most powerful, remaining adversaries are the Shan. Although opium warlord Khun Sa 'surrendered' to Yangon in January 1995 (and in so doing negotiated a rather comfortable retirement for himself), his SUA remains very powerful in southern Shan State. Shan rebels consider their homeland an independent Shan state called 'Tai-land' and command over 20,000 troops. The SUA is probably the second largest and most well-equipped ethnic army in Myanmar, with an arsenal that includes Russian SAM-7 anti-aircraft missiles. In conjunction with the allied Shan State Army and Mong Tai Army, the SUA operate their own military academy, where cadets begin training as young as age 12.

Shan insurgency has been considerably weakened by the splintering of the 2000 troop Shan United Revolutionary Army (SURA), under Major Yawt Soek, following Khun Sa's 1996 surrender.

MICK WELDON

Insurgency

Some observers speculate that the Burmese military won't make too much of an effort to defeat the Shan because of mutual benefits obtained via the opium trade. The infamous Lo Hsing-han, a Shan warlord who once competed with Khun Sa for control over the narcotics trade, has been seen playing golf with Burmese army officers near Bago. The Shan, along with the Wa and Kokang in north-eastern Shan State, have recently begun manufacturing and transporting amphetamines for the Thai and Chinese markets.

With the Shan and Karen splits, the 10,000 member United Wa State Army (UWSA) in north-eastern Shan State has emerged as the largest and most powerful rebel army in Myanmar today. Described by the US State Department as 'the world's biggest armed narcotics trafficking organisation', the UWSA is heavily involved in the production and trade of amphetamines as well as opiates. For all intents and purposes, the Wa army runs its own independent state in northern Shan, free from Myanmar government interference, along with a smaller region on the Thai border, directly opposite Fang.

Truces

Over the last 10 years the anti-Yangon insurgency has weakened considerably. In 1989 the ethnic rank and file of the BCP – many of them Wa troops – revolted against their Bamar leadership and eliminated the 41-year-old BCP in one fell swoop during the so-called 'Pangsang Mutiny'. Bamar communist leaders fled to China, and BCP territory passed on to the UWSA, who quickly negotiated a truce with Yangon that same year.

Next came a similar truce with the Kachin Independence Organisation (KIO), one of the best armed and most organised of the insurgent armies. The KIO truce was followed by similar agreements with the Kayah and the White Pa-O, also major players in the insurgency game. In June 1995 the New Mon State Party (NMSP) and its Mon National Liberation Front (MNLF), who had been fighting the government since 1949, signed a ceasefire with the Burmese military. This raised the total of signed truces with ethnic insurgent groups to 15. In some cases, especially among the Wa, Pa-O and Kokang, such agreements mean turning a blind eye toward opium and heroin trafficking. In many such instances, the Burmese army is thought to be actively cooperating in the narcotics trade – like rival Mafia dons who've agreed to end hostilities in order to share criminal profits.

The only armies of significance still fighting belong to the Karen (KNU/KNLA) and Shan (MTA/Shan State Progress Party, allied with the SSA, and the separate Shan United Revolutionary State Army, or SURSA). The Karen rebels were hit hard during a succession of Burmese offensives in 1994 and 1995. The much feared SSA lost its foremost military and political leader, the widely admired Sao Sai Lek, who died in early 1995.

On the political front, Yangon has taken a lesson from the Thai battle against insurgency during the 1970s and early 1980s by declaring amnesty for all groups except the Shan, and by building hospitals, schools and roads in frontier areas in an effort to win villagers away from rebel leadership.

None of these political and military successes mean that insurgency in Myanmar has been defeated. But a steady movement towards peace, if not total reconciliation, seems obvious. Meanwhile, military leadership in Yangon uses the widespread insurgency as an excuse for continuing human-rights abuses and as an explanation for draining public funds into military confrontations with rebel forces.

continued from page 46

Obviously the Burmese are not a homogeneous people, a fact which has caused the country many problems over the years. For centuries, Myanmar was torn by the struggle for supremacy between the Bamar and the Mon, which eventually ended with the Bamar in control, only to be overwhelmed by the British and the long arm of the Raj. The British gave a certain amount of autonomy to the Shan and Kayin states, later guaranteed in the Burmese constitution but disregarded by Ne Win and subsequent regimes.

Since independence the internal instabilities have shown themselves again, and today sizeable tracts of the country are only nominally under government control. The main opposition comes from ethnic minorities living along the Thai and Chinese borders. These groups were long distrustful of the lowland Burmese, and with British 'protection' gone, their distrust grew into armed resistance, which the central government has taken many years to mollify or overcome.

Under the British many other nationalities also came into Myanmar – particularly Indians and Chinese. Prior to independence, Yangon was much more an Indian city than a Burmese one, as Indians were generally preferred by British employers. A large proportion of the Indian population has been expelled since independence, although there are still many people of Indian descent in Myanmar. The Chinese have got equally short shrift from time to time – particularly during the Cultural Revolution in China, when many Chinese found themselves very unpopular in Myanmar. During the wholesale nationalisation of the economy in the 1960s and 1970s, many Indian and Chinese business-owners fled overseas; some are returning now that socialism has become sufficiently diluted.

Development

The 1998 UN Human Development Report (UNHDR) ranks Myanmar 134 out of 174 countries with regard to overall human development, with a human development index (HDI) rating of 0.481 (on a scale of 10). The HDI ranks countries according to statistics collected with regard to life expectancy, adult literacy, school enrolment ratios, real GDP per capita (PPP) and adjusted real GDP per capita. In the 1970s and 1980s Myanmar's development status placed it among the world's 10 poorest countries; it is now the highest-ranked in the UN's 'low human development' category, with 19 countries placed below it on the index. Asian countries with lower HDIs than Myanmar include Laos, Pakistan, India, Cambodia, Bangladesh, Nepal and Bhutan; the remainder of the nations in this category are in Africa or the Caribbean.

The country has an infant mortality rate of 79 per 1000 and an average life expectancy of 60 years. The average citizen consumes 2448 calories per day; in Asia only Afghanistan, Nepal and Cambodia have lower calorie intakes. For the percentage of daily calories accounted for by rice consumption, Myanmar ranks first worldwide. Doctors number only three per 10,000 citizens. According to the UNHDR, 74% of Burmese citizens have access to safe drinking water, a 252% increase since 1980.

EDUCATION

Despite an overall national literacy rate of 83.1%, only an estimated 27% of the general population completes primary school. Primary schools outnumber middle schools more than 10 to one, and there are twice as many middle schools as high schools. Around 1500 monasteries around the country offer free primary education. The shortage of trained teachers is critical, with only 19 teacher training schools and institutes in the entire country. Since 1997 UNESCO and UNDP have helped administer special primary programs for the very poor.

There are nine public universities and 21 colleges, most of them in Yangon and all of them closed since 1996, due to the government's fear that students will organise antigovernment protests or start riots. Those few students whose families can afford the tuition fees may attend small private institutes specialising in business, computer science or foreign languages. A few post-graduate programs at Yangon University, the Yangon Institute of Technology and the Mandalay Institute of Technology have also been permitted to operate. A new, free Buddhist university in Yangon has become an important source of general higher education for students who would otherwise have nowhere to study.

ARTS

Burmese culture, at the court level, has not had an easy time since the collapse of the last kingdom – architecture and art were both royal activities which, without royal support, have floundered and faded. On the other hand, at the street level, Burmese culture is vibrant and thriving, as you'll see at the first *pwe* (show) you visit.

Dance & Drama

Myanmar's truly indigenous dance forms are those that pay homage to the *nats* (spirits*)*. In special nat pwe, one or more nats is invited to possess the body and mind of a medium; sometimes members of the audience are possessed instead, an event greatly feared by most Burmese. Nat dancing styles are very fluid and adaptable, and are handed down from older pwe dancers to their offspring or apprentices.

In contrast, few of Myanmar's classical dance-drama styles are entirely indigenous. Most arrived from Thailand during periods of Burmese conquest of Thai kingdoms. Today the dances most obviously taken from Thailand are known as *yodaya zat* (Ayuthaya theatre), as taught to the Burmese by Thai theatrical artists taken as war captives from Ayuthaya by King Hsinbyushin in the late 18th century. So thorough is the public perception that Thailand was the primary source for all court arts that the term *yodaya* can be applied loosely to describe any 'elite' art form even today. Around this same period Zinme pannatha (Chiang Mai plays) were translated into Burmese, providing the text for another entire dance-drama genre.

The most Burmese dances feature solo performances by female dancers who wear dresses with long white trains, which they kick into the air with their heels during the foot movements – some outside observers see a Chinese influence in these movements (they do seem to resemble certain aspects of Chinese opera). A *zat pwe* involves a recreation of an ancient legend or Buddhist *jataka* (life story of the Buddha) while the *yamazat* picks a tale from the Indian epic *Ramayana*. The arm and head movements often seek to mimic those of Burmese marionette theatre. Burmese dance scholars have catalogued around 2000 dance movements, including 13 head movements, 28 eye movements, nine neck movements, 24 ways of moving only one hand plus 23 using both hands, 38 leg movements, eight body postures and 10 walking movements.

Classical dance-drama is currently enjoying a revival in Myanmar and is occasionally performed at the National Theatre in Yangon, where around a dozen amateur theatre groups regularly practice and perform yamazat. Traditional yamazat can also be seen in Mandalay, Amarapura and Sagaing. In Mandalay, yamazat performers even have their own shrine, where masks of the principal *Ramayana* characters receive offerings of fruit and flowers. Shorter, excerpted performances may be seen at large banquet-style restaurants in Yangon and Mandalay. Since Burmese classical dancing emphasises pose rather than movement, and solo rather than ensemble performances, it can soon become a little boring for TV-hyped western tastes. By contrast the less common, but more lively, *yein pwe* features singing and dancing performed by a chorus or ensemble.

Most popular of all is the *a-nyeint pwe*, a traditional-variety pwe somewhat akin to early American vaudeville or Thai likay; see the boxed text 'A-Nyeint Pwe – From Slapstick to Satire' in the Mandalay chapter for details. One of the easiest ways to tell a-nyeint pwe from zat pwe or yamazat is that in both of the latter the musical instruments sit on the floor (or on the ground in an outdoor performance), while in a-nyeint pwe the instruments are placed on a stage with the dancers and actors.

Marionette Theatre

Youq-the pwe (Burmese marionette theatre) presents colourful puppets up to a metre high in a spectacle that many aesthetes consider the most expressive of all the Burmese arts. Developed during the reign of King Bagyidaw in the Konbaung period, it was so influential that it became the forerunner to zat pwe as later performed by actors rather than marionettes. As with dance-drama, the genre's 'golden age' began with the Mandalay kingdoms of the late 18th century and ran through to the advent of cinema in the 1930s.

The Burmese have great respect for an expert puppeteer; indeed a youq-the pwe is thought to demand a more skilled and artistic performance than a zat pwe. Some marionettes may be manipulated by a dozen or more strings; certain nats may sport up to 60 strings, including one for each eyebrow. The marionette master's standard repertoire requires a troupe of 28 puppets including Thagyamin (king of the gods); a Burmese king, queen, prince and princess; a regent; two court pages; an old man and an old woman; a villain; a hermit; four ministers; two clowns; one good and one evil nat; a Brahmin astrologer; two ogres; a *zawgyi* (alchemist); a horse; a monkey; a *makara* (mythical sea serpent); and an elephant. These figures bring together the talents of singers, puppeteers, musicians, woodcarvers, embroiderers and set designers.

Marionette theatre declined following WWII and is now mostly confined to tourist venues in Yangon, Mandalay and Bagan. Rather less frequently it appears at pwes sponsored by wealthy patrons.

Music

Burmese music, which features strongly in any pwe, can be rather hard for unaccustomed western ears to enjoy. As with other Asian music, it is very short on the harmony so important in western music and tends to sound 'harsh, tinkly and repetitive', as one early observer described it. The perceived harshness is probably due to the fact that Burmese scales are not 'tempered' as western scales have been since Bach. As in western music, the Burmese diatonic scale has seven tones, but they are arranged equidistantly within the octave, and there is no tempering or retuning of the 4th and 7th intervals as with western scales.

Traditional Burmese music is primarily two dimensional in the sense that rhythm and melody provide much of the musical structure, while repetition is a key element in developing this structure. Subtle shifts in rhythm and tonality provide the modulation usually supplied by the harmonic dimension in western music. These techniques have been 'rediscovered' in western musical trends, as in the minimalism of Steve Reich, Philip Glass, Terry Riley and Brian Eno. There is also a significant amount of improvisation in live performance, an element traditional Burmese music shares with jazz.

Classical Music The original inspiration for much of Myanmar's current musical tradition came from Thailand (then Siam) during the reign of King Hsinbyushin, particularly after the second conquest of Thailand in 1767. During this period, Siamese court musicians, dancers and entertainers from Ayuthaya were brought to Myanmar by the hundreds in order to effect 'cultural augmentation'. Myanmar's kings were very good at 'capturing' culture (the same was done with Mon culture from Thaton). Burmese classical music as played today was codified by Po Sein, a colonial-era musician, composer and drummer who also designed the *hsaing waing* (the circle of tuned drums, also known as *paq waing*) and formalised classical dancing styles. Such music is meant to be played as an accompaniment to classical dance-dramas which enact scenes from the jatakas or from the Indian epic *Ramayana*

Musical instruments are predominantly percussive, but even the hsaing waing may carry the melody. These drums are tuned by placing a wad of *paq-sa* (drum food) – made from a kneaded paste of rice and wood-ash – onto the centre of the drum head, then adding or subtracting a pinch at a time till the desired drum tone is attained. By the use of multiple hand and stick strokes, Burmese percussionists can create melodic and chordal patterns on the large banks of drums employed in a typical performance.

In addition to the hsaing waing, the traditional *hsaing* (Burmese ensemble) of seven to 10 musicians will usually play: the *kye-naung* (a circle of tuned brass gongs); the *saung gauq* (a boat-shaped harp with 13 strings); the *pattala* (a sort of xylophone); the *hneh* (an oboe-type instrument related to the Indian *shanai*); the *pa-lwe* (a bamboo flute); the *mi-gyaung* (crocodile lute); the *paq-ma* (a bass drum); and the *yagwin* (small cymbals) and *wa-leq-hkouq* (bamboo clappers), which are purely rhythmic in nature and are often played by Burmese vocalists. It is also common to see a violin or two in a hsaing, and even the Dobro (an American acoustic slide guitar played on the lap) is occasionally used. Solo piano music has also become part of the traditional Burmese musical repertoire. At the National Museum in Yangon you can view an exhibit of Burmese musical instruments, including old Mon violins, the use of which may predate that of violins in Europe.

An older performance mode features duets of two female musicians playing Burmese harp and crocodile lute. This style of playing originated during the reign of King Badomintara in the late 18th century, when court maidens were trained on these instruments.

A 1997 CD entitled *White Elephants & Golden Ducks*, recorded in Myanmar using a DAT recorder and issued on the Shanachie label, offers a good sampler of traditional Burmese instrumental and vocal music. A 1998 follow-up CD, *Pat Waing: The Magic Drum Circle of Burma*, does a beautiful job of rendering the hard-to-reproduce paq waing drum sounds. To hear how the Burmese have been translating their tradi-

tional music into piano performance for the last hundred years or so, listen to the equally high-quality *Sandaya: The Spellbinding Piano of Burma* (Shanachie, 1998). Shanachie has plans to release two more CDs of digitally recorded Burmese music, one devoted to the saung gauq and another to western stringed instruments played in Myanmar – slide guitar, mandolin, zither, banjo and violin.

Folk & Pop Older still is an enchanting vocal folk music tradition still heard in rural areas where the Burmese may sing without instrumental accompaniment while working. Such folk songs set the work cadence and provide a distraction from the physical strain and monotony of pounding rice, clearing fields, weaving and so on. You'll hear this most readily in the Ayeyarwady Delta between Twante and Pathein. Myanmar's urban ears are fed via radio and cassette tapes by a huge pop music industry based in Yangon. The older generation prefer a pop sound created in the 1950s and 1960s by combining traditional Burmese melodies and rhythms with western instrumental settings. Younger Burmese listen to heavily western-influenced sounds – the pervasive power of rock music has penetrated even the government prohibition on western music (except for lyrics, which must always be sung in Burmese).

Modern Burmese pop borrows from many sources – Burmese folk melodies and old Scottish reels, as well as modern tunes taken directly from international pop hits. Burmese heavy metal groups with names like Iron Cross, Wild Ones and Emperor have become very successful in recent years. Other than bans on non-Burmese lyrics, headbangers are restricted by the regulation (not very well enforced) that hair not fall below the shoulders.

Architecture

Traditional temple architecture brings together all the *pan seh myo* (ten types of flower), the traditional Burmese arts schemata:

- Gold and silversmithing *(ba-dein)*
- Blacksmithing *(ba-beh)*
- Bronze, copper and brass casting *(ba-daing)*
- Woodcarving *(ba-bu)*
- Lathe-work *(pan-buq)*
- Painting *(ba-ji)*
- Lacquerware *(pan-yun)*
- Stucco work *(pan-daw)*
- Stone carving *(pan-ta-maw)*
- Masonry *(pa-yan)* and stone-cutting *(pan-yweh)*

It is in architecture that one sees the strongest evidence of Burmese artistic skill and accomplishment. Myanmar is a country of stupas, or Buddhist reliquaries, often called 'pagodas' in English. The Burmese seem unable to see a hilltop without wanting to put a religious monument on top of it. Wherever you are – boating down the river, driving through the hills, even flying above the plains – there always seems to be a stupa

in view. It is in Bagan that you see the most dramatic results of this national enthusiasm for religious monuments: for over two centuries a massive construction program resulted in thousands of shrines, stupas, monasteries and other sacred buildings.

The Paya The *Paya* (pa-YAH), the most common Burmese equivalent to the often misleading English term pagoda, literally means holy one and can refer to people, deities and places associated with religion. For the most part it's a generic term for what students of Hindu-Buddhist architecture call a stupa. There are basically two kinds of paya: the solid, bell-shaped *zedi* and the hollow square or rectangular *pahto*. A zedi or stupa is usually thought to contain 'relics' – either objects taken from the Buddha himself (especially pieces of bone,

Burmese Iconography

Buddhist architecture in Myanmar – whether old or new – tends to employ a set of common decorative motifs taken from Hindu-Buddhist mythology. These may appear as free-standing sculptures, often placed near gates and doorways; as bas relief on the exterior walls of *theins* (ordination halls) or *pahtos* (temples or shrines); or as gold-leaf paintings or woodcarvings on doors. Each motif symbolises a particular positive quality associated with the religion and is meant to confer that quality upon the place as well as the people who enter the place.

motif	burmese	pali/sanskrit	meaning
half-lion/half-dragon	chinthe	singa	courage, royalty
goose (Brahminy duck)	hintha	hamsa	unity
human from the waist up, ostrich-like bird waist down	keinnayi (male) keinnaya (female)	kinnari kinnara	love
sphinx-like, half lion, half human	manouq-thiha	manussingha	security
eagle-like bird	galoun	garuda	strength
legless dragon	naga	naga	peace, prosperity
ogre	bilu	yaksha	protection
sea serpent	magan	makara	blessing
earth goddess	wathoundaye	vasundhara	maternal protection
peacock	daun	–	sun or patriotism
rabbit	youn	–	moon or peace
crowned Buddha-like figure holding a lotus flower	lokanat	lokanatha or avalokitesvara	world peace, future brotherhood

teeth or hair) or certain holy materials such as Buddha images and other religious objects blessed by a famous *sayadaw* (Burmese Buddhist master, usually chief abbot). Both zedis and pahtos are often associated with *kyaung* (Buddhist monasteries).

The term pahto is sometimes translated as temple, though shrine would perhaps be more accurate since priests or monks are not necessarily in attendance. The so-called Mon-style pahto is a large cube with small windows and ground-level passageways; this type is also known as a *ku* or *gu* (from the Pali-Sanskrit *guha*, or cave). In later Bagan structures, indoor passages led to outside terraces on several levels, a style usually ascribed to the Bamar rather than the Mon. The overall Bamar concept is similar to that of the Mayan and Aztec pyramids of Mesoamerica; both architectural styles are designed so that worshippers climb a symbolic mountain while viewing religious reliefs and frescoes along the way.

If all this seems too confusing, just remember that the generic Burmese term for all these structures is paya. The famous Mon zedi in Yangon is called Shwedagon Paya, and Bagan's greatest pahto is known as Ananda Paya.

Payas function basically as a focus for meditation or contemplation. In the case of solid payas (zedis), if there is a need for some sheltered gathering place or a place to house images or other paraphernalia, then this will usually be an ancillary building to the paya. There may be small shrines, pavilions, covered walkways or other such places all around a major paya. These are often more heavily ornamented than the zedis themselves. *Hman-si-shwe-cha*, which describes the combination of giltwork with coloured glass mosaic, is one of the most popular types of ornamentation in Mon and Bamar temples.

Zedi Styles Zedis go under different names in other Buddhist countries; they may be called *dagobas* in Sri Lanka, *chedis* or *jedis* in Thailand, *stupas* or *chaityas* in India, but basically they all refer to the same idea. Although at first glance all zedis may look alike, you'll soon realise there have been many, often subtle, design changes over the years. Early zedis were usually hemispherical (the Kaunghmudaw at Sagaing near Mandalay) or bulbous (the Bupaya in Bagan), while the more modern style is much more graceful – a curvaceous lower bell merging into a soaring spire, such as the Shwedagon Paya in Yangon. Style is not always a good indicator of a zedi's original age since Myanmar is earthquake-prone and many have been rebuilt over and again, gradually changing their design through the centuries.

One thing many zedis seem to have in quantity is an air of tranquillity. Even when it's noisy around a zedi, when some sort of festival or ceremony is going on, the atmosphere is still charged with that tranquil magic that seems to pervade everything around it. High above you can hear the wind bells tinkling from the *hti*, the decorative metal 'umbrella' that tops the structure. Around the base, people are meditating, strolling around, or simply chatting. Zedis have a warmth; an easygoing feeling of friendliness that is quite unmatched by any other religious building.

Other Buildings Traditionally, only the zedi, gu and pahto have been made of permanent materials; until quite recently all secular buildings – and most monasteries – were constructed of wood and thus there are few old wooden buildings to be seen. Even the great palaces were made of wood, and with the destruction of Mandalay Palace during WWII there is no remaining wooden Burm-ese palace. There are only a few reminders of these beautifully carved buildings remaining in Myanmar, and even these are deteriorating today, due to lack of protection.

Although so little remains of the old wooden architectural skills, there are still many excellent wooden buildings to be seen. The Burmese continue to use teak with great skill, and a fine country home can be a very pleasing structure indeed. Unhappily, the Burmese have proved far less adept with more modern materials, and Myanmar boasts some appalling corrugated-iron-roofed buildings and concrete monstrosities. Even with finer, older buildings the emphasis has always been more on quantity than quality – Myanmar boasts no great buildings of meticulous artistry like India's Taj Mahal. But when it comes to location – balancing a delicate stupa on a towering hilltop or perching one on the side of a sheer precipice – the Burmese have no match.

Although historical monuments in the Bamar-majority areas are fairly well preserved, elsewhere in Myanmar this is sadly not the case. An extraordinarily beautiful, 100-year-old Shan-style palace in Kengtung (Kyaingtong) was razed to build a 14 storey hotel on the new Thailand-China route. Other palaces in this area are also in line to be demolished.

Buildings erected during the British colonial period feature a variety of styles and materials, from the rustic wood-and-plaster Tudor villas of Pyin U Lwin to the thick-walled, brick-and-plaster, colonnaded mansions and shophouses of Yangon, Mawlamyaing and Myeik. Much of the ornamentation found on these old colonial dames was inspired by local architecture, replacing, for example, the 'gingerbread' typical of British Victorian rooflines with the Burmese equivalent found on Buddhist monastery buildings. Until recently scant attention was paid to preserving colonial architecture – for political as well as economic reasons – but nowadays many are being restored.

Buddhist Sculpture

Remarkably little research has been carried out on the topic of Burmese religious sculpture other than that from the Bagan and Mandalay eras. A rich Buddhist sculptural tradition in wood, bronze, stone and marble existed among the Shan, Mon and Rakhaing peoples but these have received short shrift from both Bamar and foreign scholars.

Even Bamar sculpture is hard to come by in the country.

Compared to the inhabitants of neighbouring countries, the Burmese have had a difficult time preserving historical, non-architectural art. Seldom does one come across any Buddha images older than 100 years in Burmese payas or kyaungs – after a few weeks of looking one gets the definite impression that most such sculptures have been sold or stolen. This may be partially due to the Burmese belief that images from old kyaungs or payas may be unlucky, so why collect them? Mandalay's Mahamuni Buddha image, a Rakhaing sculpture, is just about the only famous image of any age – probably because it's too heavy to steal! Unfortunately the years of war and poverty have taken their toll on the arts and you'll easily find more Burmese religious sculpture on display in Hong Kong, San Francisco and London than in Myanmar.

Painting

Early Burmese art was always a part of religious architecture – paintings were something done on the walls of temples, sculpture something to be placed inside them. Since the decline of temple-building, the old painting skills have deteriorated considerably. Modern Burmese paintings in the western style reflect only a pale shadow of the former skill, and the one painter of any renown, U Ba Kyi, paints murals and canvases commissioned for the larger hotels and government offices. Many contemporary artists in Yangon and Mandalay work in modern international styles, even when painting traditional subjects.

Woodcarving

Burmese woodcarving was reserved mainly for royal palaces, which were always made of timber and became showpieces for the skilful woodcarver. When royal palaces ceased to be built, woodcarving skills rapidly declined, although the new construction boom has brought about a small but growing woodcarving renaissance – again mostly seen in hotels.

Shapes of the Buddha

Despite stylistic variations, Buddha images in Myanmar are remarkably similar in overall shape and form. This is because sculptors are traditionally bound by certain iconographical parameters that specify the hand and body positions the Buddha may assume, as well as the physical characteristics which the sculptor is required to depict. The way the monastic robes drape over the body, the direction in which the hair curls, the proportions for each body part – all are to some degree canonised by these texts. The tradition does leave room for innovation, however, allowing the various 'schools' of Buddhist art to distinguish themselves over the centuries.

One aspect of the tradition that almost never varies is the posture of the Buddha image. Four basic postures (Pali: asana) are portrayed: standing, sitting, walking and reclining. The first three postures are associated with the daily activities of the Buddha, namely: teaching; meditating; and offering refuge to his disciples, which can be accomplished in any of these three asanas. The reclining position represents the Buddha's dying moments when he attained *parinibbana* (ultimate nirvana). Another key iconographical element is the figure's *mudra* (hand position).

Bhumisparsa (touching the earth) In this classic sitting posture the right hand touches the ground while the left rests in the lap. This hand position symbolises the point in the Buddha's legendary life story when he sat in meditation beneath the legendary banyan tree in Bodh Gaya, India, and vowed not to budge from the spot until he gained enlightenment. Mara, the Buddhist equivalent of Satan, tried to interrupt the Buddha's meditation by invoking a series of distractions (including tempests, floods, feasts and nubile young maidens) – the Buddha's response was to touch the earth, thus calling on nature to witness his resolve. The bhumisparsa mudra is one of the most common mudras seen in Buddhist sculpture; it's also known as the *maravijaya* (victory over Mara) mudra.

Dhyana (meditation) Both hands rest palms-up on the Buddha's lap, with the right hand on top, signifying meditation. This mudra is always accompanied by a sitting posture.

Vitarka or Dhammachakka (exposition, or turning of the wheel of dharma) When the thumb and forefinger of one hand (vitarka) or both hands (dhammachakka) form a circle with the other fingers curving outward (similar to the western OK gesture), the mudra evokes the first public discourse on Buddhist doctrine. A sitting posture is most common with these mudras, though it's occasionally seen in standing images.

Abhaya (no fear) In this posture, one or both hands extend forward, with palms out and fingers pointing upward, to symbolise the Buddha's offer of protection or freedom from fear to his followers. This mudra is most commonly seen in conjunction with standing or walking Buddhas, and occasionally with sitting images.

Bhumisparsa

Shapes of the Buddha

Dhyana

Vitarka

Dana (giving, or offering) Either one or both hands extend forward in this posture, with palms up and parallel to the ground, to signify the offering of *dhamma* (Buddhist teachings) to the world. Rarely seen in seated images, this is almost always accompanied by a standing posture.

Physical Characteristics

According to the Mahapacana Sutta of the Pali canon, there are 32 body marks whereby one can recognise a Buddha. Most of these can easily be seen on any Burmese Buddha image:

1 Well-planted feet
2 Wheel marks on the base of the feet
3 Projecting heels
4 Long fingers
5 Soft, delicate hands and feet
6 Hands and feet covered with a network of lines
7 Arched feet
8 Antelope limbs
9 Hands that can reach to the knees without bending
10 Private member in a sheath
11 Golden complexion
12 Delicate skin
13 One hair for every pore
14 Body hairs standing straight up
15 Upright limbs
16 Protuberances on the hands, feet and shoulders
17 Lion chest
18 Full shoulders
19 Rotundity of a banyan tree
20 Well-rounded branching of the trunk
21 Superior delicacy of taste
22 Lion jaw
23 Forty teeth
24 Even teeth
25 Teeth without gaps
26 Very white teeth
27 Large and thin tongue
28 Brahman voice
29 Dark eyes
30 Ox-like lashes
31 White tuft between the eyebrows
32 Protuberance on the crown of the head

Literature

Religious texts inscribed onto Myanmar's famous *kammawas* (lacquered scriptures) and *parabaiks* (folding manuscripts) were the first literature as such, and began appearing in the 12th century. Until the 1800s, the only other works of 'literature' available were royal genealogies, poetry and law texts. A Burmese version of the Indian epic *Ramayana* – called *Yama Thagyin* or *Yama Yagan* in Burmese – was first written in 1775 by poet U Aung Pyo. The first printed books in the country were produced by missionaries; the American Baptist Mission was responsible for virtually all publishing until the late 19th century, when the first Burmese-owned press began printing a Burmese-language newspaper.

Today the Burmese are great readers, as you'll realise from the piles of books in the street at every night market. Because of the heavy restrictions placed on verbal expression by the military government, topics are greatly circumscribed. Of the 3660 books published in Myanmar in 1993 (the last year for which such statistics are available), 1171 had to do with arts and culture, 713 pertained to religion and only 129 to language and literature. A paltry 22 titles came out in the fields of political and social sciences.

SOCIETY & CONDUCT
Traditional Culture

The social ideal for most Burmese citizens – no matter what their ethnic background – is a standard of behaviour commonly termed *bama hsan-jin* or Burmese-ness.

The hallmarks of bama hsan-jin include: an acquaintance with Buddhist scriptures (and the ability to recite at least a few classic verses); the ability to speak idiomatic Burmese; showing respect for elders; dressing modestly; showing discretion in behaviour towards members of the opposite sex; and most importantly, exhibiting modes of expression and comportment that value the quiet, subtle and indirect rather than the loud, obvious and direct.

The degree to which a Burmese can conform to these ideals matches the degree of respect he or she will receive from associates. Although high rank – civil, military or clerical – will exempt certain individuals from chastisement by social inferiors, it doesn't exempt them from the way they are perceived by other Burmese. This goes for foreigners as well, even though most first-time visitors can hardly be expected to speak idiomatic Burmese or recite Buddhist scripture. Nowadays one also hears the term *myanma hsan-jin* although clearly the cultural norms themselves originally derive from Bamar *(bama)* and/or Mon culture.

Dos & Don'ts

The usual Asian rules of conduct apply in Myanmar, plus there are a few specially Burmese ones. As with elsewhere in Asia it is unseemly to show too much emotion – losing your temper over problems and delays gets you nowhere, it just amazes people. Stay calm and collected at all times. The Burmese frown on such displays of anger just as much as they frown on too open a display of affection.

As in other Buddhist countries the head is the highest part of the body – spiritually as well as literally. You should never deliberately touch somebody else on the head or pat a child on the head. Equally, the feet are the lowest part of the body – don't point your feet at somebody.

Buddha images are sacred objects, so don't pose in front of them for pictures and definitely do not sit or climb upon them.

A couple of rules apply specifically to women. Women should never ride on the roofs of vehicles or boats, which would be a cultural insult to any male passengers below. Those males who weren't gravely offended might take the roof-sitting as licence to harass such 'loose women'.

Monks are not supposed to touch or be touched by women. If a woman wants to hand something to a monk, the object should be placed within reach of the monk, not handed directly to him.

Dress One should dress neatly (no shorts or skimpy tank tops) when visiting religious sites. Most important of all in Myanmar, remember to take off your shoes and socks before entering the grounds of any Theravada Buddhist shrine, zedi, temple, paya or monastery. Even at the most dilapidated, run-down, ruined paya in Bagan the 'no footwearing' rule still applies. You must go barefoot in every part of a Buddhist compound, not just in the shrine buildings as in neighbouring Buddhist countries. In the middle of the day going barefoot can get a little painful as the paved area around a paya often becomes very hot. At major payas there will often be a mat walkway around the platform.

At one time this restriction caused quite a stir between the Burmese and the British. As part of the growing surge of nationalism between the wars, and as a neat way to put the British in their place, the Burmese decided to rigidly enforce the no-footwear rules, from which the Europeans had previously been exempted. Signs also suddenly appeared announcing that there was to be 'no umbrellaring' – in case you've never seen anyone do this, it means using an umbrella to point things out!

Shoes – but not necessarily socks – are also taken off before entering private homes. Actually the Burmese very rarely wear socks. You'll find it easier to deal with temples and private homes if you follow their example and go sockless. Or take it a step further and wear slip-on sandals – the most convenient footwear for travelling in Myanmar – like the locals do.

Beach attire or sloppy lounge clothes are not considered appropriate for walking around town. The attitude of 'this is how I dress at home and no one is going to stop me' gains nothing but disrespect or even disgust from the Burmese. Men should try to keep their shoulders covered except at the beach or when bathing. Likewise long trousers, *longyis* (sarong-style garment) or skirts are considered more appropriate than shorts in all situations except at the beach. Women can wear sleeveless blouses, but should try to avoid tight or breast-baring tank tops.

Treatment of Animals
All non-human animal life is considered potential protein in Myanmar. The keeping of pets is considered rather eccentric behaviour, and for the most part dogs and cats are considered mere scavengers living off the crumbs of human society. Some Chinese restaurants keep caged live animals – from fish to small bears – both as advertising and as potential dishes from the menu (though this practice is nowhere near as common as in China, Taiwan or Singapore).

RELIGION
Around 87% of Burmese are Buddhist. During the U Nu period Buddhism functioned as a state religion of sorts – as embodied in such catch-phrases as 'the Socialist Way to Nibbana'. Nowadays there is complete freedom of religion, though within the government Buddhists tend to attain higher rank more easily than non-Buddhists, simply because Buddhism is considered a key element in bama hsan-jin.

An appreciation of Buddhism and its history in Myanmar is a prerequisite for outsiders wishing to better understand the Burmese mind.

Burmese Buddhism
Early Buddhism & Theravada Reform
The Mon were the first people in Myanmar to practice Theravada Buddhism, called the Southern School since it took the southern route from India, its place of origin. King Asoka, the great Indian emperor and devout Buddhist convert, is known to have sent missions during the 3rd century BC to Suvannabhumi, or the Golden Land – an area taken to be the fertile river deltas of what are today Myanmar, Thailand and Cambodia. A second wave is thought to have arrived in South-East Asia via Sinhalese missionaries from present-day Sri Lanka, sometime between the 6th and 10th centuries.

By the 9th century the Pyu of Upper Myanmar were combining Theravada with elements of Mahayana and Tantric Buddhism brought with them from their homelands on or near the Tibetan Plateau. When the Bamar of Bagan supplanted the Pyu they inherited this amalgamated form.

During the early Bagan era (11th century), Bamar king Anawrahta decided that the Buddhism practised in his realm should be 'purified' of all non-Theravada elements, a task he set for Mon monks captured by his armies in Thaton, Lower Myanmar. Although Burmese Buddhism was never totally rid of Mahayana, Tantric, Hindu and animist elements, his efforts were remarkably successful in bringing the Burmese around to a predominantly Theravada world-view.

History & Tenets Strictly speaking, Theravada Buddhism is not a theism like Hinduism, Judaism, Islam or Christianity, since it is not centred around a god or gods, but rather is based on a psychophilosophical system. Today it covers a wide range of interpretations of the basic beliefs, which all start from the enlightenment of Siddhartha Gautama, a prince-turned-ascetic, in northern India around 2500 years ago. Gautama was not the first Buddha, nor is he expected to be the last.

Neither Buddha (The Enlightened) nor his immediate pupils ever wrote the *dhamma* (Buddhist teachings) down, so a schism developed a thousand years after Gautama's death and today there are two major schools of Buddhism. The Theravada (doctrine of the elders) school holds that to achieve *nibbana* (nirvana), the eventual aim of every Buddhist, you must 'work out your own salvation with diligence'. In other words it is up to each individual to work out his or her own fate.

The Mahayana (large vehicle) school holds that individuals should forego the experience of nibbana until all humankind is ready for salvation. The goal is to become a Bodhisattva (Buddha-to-be), rather than a fully enlightened Buddha. From this perspective, no one can enter nibbana without the intervention of a Bodhisattva.

The Mahayana school have not rejected the other school, but claim they have extended it. Hence Mahayanists often refer to Theravada as Hinayana (small vehicle) Buddhism. The Theravadins, on the other hand, see Mahayana as a misinterpretation of the Buddha's original teachings. To those who would choose, Mahayana offers the 'soft option' (have faith and all will be well), while the Theravada is more austere and ascetic, and, some might say, harder to practise.

In the Buddhist world today, Theravada Buddhism is followed in countries such as Sri Lanka, Laos, Cambodia, Thailand and Myanmar. Mahayana Buddhism is practised in Vietnam, Japan, China, Taiwan and Singapore. There is also a variety of more esoteric divisions of Buddhism such as the Hindu-influenced Tantric Buddhism of Tibet and Nepal, and the Zen Buddhism of Japan, all of which are forms of Mahayana in general principle, since they adhere to the Bodhisattva ideal.

Today the majority of Buddhists in Myanmar belong to the Theravada sect; those who profess Mahayana Buddhism comprise fewer than 1%, virtually all of whom are of Chinese descent.

Buddha taught that the world is primarily characterised by *dukkha* (unsatisfactoriness, infelicity), *anicca* (impermanence) and *anatta* (insubstantiality), and that even our happiest moments are only temporary, empty and unsatisfactory.

The ultrapragmatic Buddhist perception of cause and effect – *kamma* in Pali, *karma* in Sanskrit, *kan* in Burmese – holds that birth inevitably leads to sickness, old age and death, hence every life is insecure and subject to dukkha. Through rebirth, the cycle of *thanthaya* (Pali: *samsara*) repeats itself endlessly as long as ignorance and craving – the remote and proximate causes of birth – remain.

Only by reaching a state of complete wisdom and nondesire can one attain true happiness. To achieve wisdom and eliminate craving one must turn inward and master one's own mind through meditation, most commonly known to the Burmese as *bhavana* or *kammahtan*.

Buddha preached four noble truths:

1. Life is dukkha.
2. Dukkha comes from *tanha* (selfish desire).
3. When one forsakes selfish desire, suffering will be extinguished.
4. The 'eightfold path' is the way to eliminate selfish desire.

The eightfold path is divided into three stages: *sila* (morality), *samadhi* (concentration), and *pañña* (wisdom and insight). The eightfold path consists of:

1. Right speech
2. Right action
3. Right livelihood
4. Right exertion
5. Right attentiveness
6. Right concentration
7. Right thought
8. Right understanding

This is an evolutionary process through many states of spiritual development until the ultimate goal is reached – death, no further rebirths, entry to nibbana. To the western mind this often seems a little strange – for most westerners death is the end, not something to be looked forward to but something to be feared.

In addition to the four noble truths and the eightfold path, devout Burmese Buddhists adhere to five lay precepts, or moral rules (*thila* in Burmese, *sila* in Pali), which require abstinence from:

1. Killing
2. Stealing
3. Unchastity (usually interpreted among laypeople as adultery)
4. Lying
5. Intoxicating substances.

Along with the moral and philosophical tenets outlined above, Buddhism emphasises love, compassion, nonviolence and tolerance of other belief systems. This tolerance has often resulted in its assimilation into other religions, as eventually happened in India with Hinduism, or in its absorption of already extant beliefs, as happened with the Burmese nats. The personal experience one has of Buddhism remains similar from country to country despite local adaptations, changes, amalgamations and inclusions: an overriding impression of warmth and gentleness, and a religion practised by sympathetic people who are always eager to explain their beliefs.

Rebirth vs Reincarnation In Myanmar the Buddhist concept of rebirth has been corrupted over the years into a common belief in reincarnation. If you're good, some say, 'women can be reborn as men, poor men as rich men, non-Burmese as Burmese – it's all very logical'. Actually Buddha taught that there is no part of a person that can be called the soul, and that rebirth is the continuation of a mental or physical process rather than the transfer of a spiritual entity from one life rank to another.

Nibbana – liberation from the mundane world of mental and physical bondage – is the only goal worth pursuing, since all lives, rich or poor, beautiful or ugly, are forever subject to suffering, impermanence and lack of meaning. Effectively, nibbana is an end to the cycle of rebirths (both moment to moment and life to life) that define existence.

Kan is central to the doctrine of rebirth, but it's not fate, as sometimes described, but rather the ultimate law of causation. Not only does rebirth result from actions we have committed in a previous life, but each moment in our lives is the result of previous moments – during each of which we made conscious or unconscious choices that determined our current lot. At each and every moment one has the opportunity to improve one's kan; thus, in Theravada Buddhism each person alone is responsible for his or her destiny, not only from life to life but from moment to moment. Buddha did not claim that his way was the only way, simply that no one can escape the natural laws of causation.

In spite of these obviously profound truths, the most common Burmese approach is to try for a better future life by feeding monks, giving donations to temples and performing regular worship at the local paya. For the average Burmese, everything revolves around the *kutho* (merit), from the Pali *kusala* (wholesome), one is able to accumulate through such deeds. One of the more typical rituals performed by individuals visiting a stupa is to pour water over the Buddha image at their astrological post (determined by the day of the week they were born) – one glassful for every year of their current age plus one extra to ensure a long life. Asked what they want in their next life, most Burmese will put forth such seemingly mundane and materialistic values as beauty and wealth – or rebirth somewhere beyond the reach of the military regime.

Monks & Nuns Socially, every Burmese male is expected to take up temporary monastic residence twice in his life: once as a *samanera* (novice monk between the ages of 5 and 15) and again as a *pongyi* (fully ordained monk, sometime after age 20). Almost all men or boys under 20 years of age participate in the *shinpyu* (novitiation ceremony) – quite a common event since a family earns great merit when one of its sons takes robe and bowl. A samanera adheres to 10 precepts or vows, which include the usual prohibitions against stealing, lying, killing, intoxication and sexual involvement, along with ones forbidding: eating after noon; listening to music or dancing; wearing jewellery, garlands or perfume; sleeping on high beds; and accepting money for personal use. A novice usually lasts a week or two – nine days is an auspicious number.

Later in life a male should spend three months as a hpongyi at a monastery during Waso (the Buddhist Lent), which begins in July and coincides with the rainy season. For many men the post-rice harvest, hot-season hiatus between January and April is a more convenient time. Some men spend as little as three to nine days to accrue merit as monks. Others may enter the monkhood a third time, since three is considered an especially lucky number.

There are currently an estimated 250,000 monks in Myanmar; this number includes the many monks who have ordained for life as well as those undergoing temporary ordination. Of these a significant percentage become scholars and teachers, while some specialise in healing, folk magic or nat exorcism.

All things possessed by a monk must be offered by the lay community. Upon ordination a new monk is typically offered a set of three robes (lower, inner and outer), costing around K2000 for a standard grade cloth of cotton or dacron, a bit more for the thick acrylic robes worn during the cool season. Bright red robes are usually reserved for novices under 15, darker colours for older, fully ordained monks. Other possessions he is permitted include a razor, a cup, a filter (for keeping insects out of drinking water), an umbrella and an alms bowl. The latter are usually plain black lacquer bowls made in Inwa or Sagaing; monks carry them to gather their daily food from householders in their monastery precincts.

At one time the Theravada Buddhist world had a separate Buddhist monastic lineage for females, who called themselves *bhikkhuni* and observed more vows than monks did – 311 precepts as opposed to the 227 followed by monks. Started in Sri Lanka around two centuries after the Buddha's lifetime by the daughter of King Asoka, the bhikkhuni tradition in Sri Lanka eventually died out and was unfortunately never restored.

In Myanmar, the modern equivalent are women who live the monastic life as *dasasila* ('Ten-Precept' nuns), often called *thilashin* (possessor of morality) in Burmese. Burmese nuns shave their heads, wear pink robes, and take vows in an ordination procedure similar to that undergone by monks. Burmese nuns don't go out on daily alms-food rounds but they do collect dry food provisions every 15 days in most locales, or as often as once a week in some places.

continued on page 68

Nat Worship

The widespread adoption of Buddhism in Myanmar suppressed, but never replaced, the pre-Buddhist practice of *nat* (spirit) worship. Originally animistic – associated with hills, trees, lakes and other natural features – the Burmese nat has evolved into a spirit that may hold dominion over a place (natural or human-made), person, or field of experience. Orthographically, the written Burmese word nat is derived from the Pali-Sanskrit *natha* (lord or guardian), though this spelling may have overlaid an existing indigenous term. Despite the continued efforts of some Buddhist leaders to downgrade the nat cult, it remains an important dimension of everyday Burmese life.

Before King Anawrahta came to power in Bagan in the 11th century, it was common for the Burmese to build small shrines or spirit houses dedicated to land nats who were displaced by the construction of houses, monasteries or other buildings, or by the planting of rice and other crops. The owners or tenants of the buildings made daily offerings of food, incense and flowers at the shrines to placate these 'guardian' nats. Unpropitiated, such nats might cause misfortune to befall the land's human tenants.

Separate, larger shrines were built for a higher class of nats, descended from actual historic personages (including previous Thai and Bamar kings) who had died violent, unjust deaths. These suprahuman nats, when correctly propitiated, could aid worshippers in accomplishing important tasks, vanquishing enemies and so on. A few Hindu *devas* (spirit-beings) and Mahayana Buddhist *bodhisattvas* – each with its own magicoreligious function – also participated in the nat pantheon.

In his push to make Theravada Buddhism the national faith, King Anawrahta tried to ban nat worship in Bagan, which was (and still is) the strongest bastion of spirit worship in Myanmar. As part of his antinat campaign, he ordered the destruction of all nat shrines in the kingdom, and banished all Hindu images to a desecrated Vishnu temple renamed Nathlaung Kyaung (Monastery of the Prisoner Nats). He also forbade the practice of animal sacrifice at nearby Mt Popa, a volcanic outcropping considered the abode of the 36 most powerful human nats in the Bamar spirit pantheon. Instead of abandoning their belief in nats, however, the Bamar merely took their practices underground, rebuilding the guardian nat shrines in their homes.

Realizing he was turning the people away from Buddhism, rather than destroying their faith in the nats, the king rescinded his total ban and allowed nat images and shrines on *paya* (pagoda) grounds. He himself led the way by placing images of the 36 nats from Mt Popa at the base of the sacred *zedi* (stupa) of Shwezigon. To these universally recognised 36, Anawrahta added a 37th, Thagyamin, a Hindu deity based on Indra, who he crowned 'king of the nats'. Thagyamin thus outranked the previous nat king, Mahagiri-nat (Lord of the Great Hill, a reference to Mt Popa). Since, in traditional Buddhist mythology, Indra paid homage to Buddha on behalf of the Hindu pantheon, this theistic insertion effectively made all nats subordinate to Buddhism.

Anawrahta's scheme worked, and today the commonly believed cosmology places Buddha and his teachings at the top, with the Hindu and Bamar nats at second and third place. In spite of the nats' lower position in the hierarchy, the Burmese nat cult is nearly as strong as ever. The Burmese merely divide their devotions and offerings according to the sphere of influence: Buddha for future lives, and the nats – both Hindu and Bamar – for problems in this life. A misdeed, for example, might be redressed by offerings made to Thagyamin, who once a year records the names of those who perform good deeds in a book made of gold leaves, those who do evil deeds in a book made of dogskin. Offerings to Thurathati (Sanskrit: Saraswati), a nat in charge of education, may help a student pass a tough exam.

Nat Worship

Since the Bagan era, the house guardian nat has stayed indoors and merged with Mahagiri to form Eindwin-Min Mahagiri (Lord of the Great Mountain (who is) in the House). In most homes, this dual nat is represented by a large, unhusked coconut which is dressed with a red *gaung baung* (turban), perfumed, and hung from a pillar or post somewhere in the house. This nat must receive daily offerings from the house's inhabitants; for many Burmese, this is the only nat worshipped on a regular basis. Other nats, particularly in Bamar-dominated central Myanmar, have shrines in paya or monastery grounds which receive occasional offerings only during pilgrimages, or bimonthly full/new moon visits.

Some of the more animistic guardian nats remain outside home and paya. A tree spirit shrine, for example, may be erected beneath a particularly venerated old tree, thought to wield power over the immediate vicinity. These are especially common beneath larger banyan trees *(Ficus religiosa)*, as this tree is revered as a symbol of Buddha's enlightenment; an offering made to a banyan nat conveniently doubles as a Buddhist offering. A village may well have a nat shrine in a wooded corner for the propitiation of the village guardian spirit. Such tree and village shrines are simple dollhouse-like structures of wood or bamboo; their proper placement is divined by a local *saya* (teacher or shaman), trained in spirit lore.

Knowledge of the complex nat world is fading fast among the younger Burmese generation, many of whom pay respect only to the coconut-head house guardian. Red and white are widely known to be nat colours; drivers young and old tie red and white strips of cloth onto the side-view mirrors and hood ornaments of their vehicles for protection from the nats. Those with a general fear of nats will avoid eating pork, which is thought to be offensive to the spirit world. The main fear is not simply that spirits will wreak havoc on your daily affairs, but rather that one may enter your mind and body, then force you to perform unconscionable acts in public – acts that would cause other Burmese to shun you. Spirit possession – whether psychologically induced or metaphysical – is a real phenomenon in Myanmar.

Staunch Burmese Buddhists claim to pay no attention to the nats, as if the nats didn't exist. On close questioning, however, they will usually admit this is only because they 'outrank' nats due to their adherence to Buddhism, and thus they have no reason to fear them. It is commonly believed that Buddhists can stay out of the nats' reach as long as they keep the five lay precepts against lying, stealing, killing, harmful sexual behaviour and intoxication. In particular, drunkenness is considered an invitation to spirit possession.

Nat Festivals

On certain occasions, the nat cult goes behind simple propitiation of the spirits (via offerings) and steps into the realm of spirit invocation. Most commonly, this is accomplished through *nat pwes* (spirit festivals), special musical performances designed to attract nats to the performance venue. Virtually all indigenous Burmese music is designed for this purpose; the 'classical' forms seen in tourist restaurants came relatively late in the country's music history. When enough money is available, a nat pwe may be hosted the night before a *shinpyu* (Buddhist novitiation ceremony) as a way of receiving the nats' blessings – perhaps, on some level, even asking the nats' permission for the novice ordination. Often the nat pwe is part of a variety of musical, dramatic and comedic performances that last from dusk till dawn; those spectators who object to nat pwes (or are fearful of the nat world) can then leave during the nat pwe and return later for the rest of the show.

Nat Worship

The nats like loud and colourful music, so nat pwe musicians bang away at full volume on their gongs, drums and xylophones, producing what sounds like some ancient form of rock and roll. Such music lures the nats to the vicinity of the pwe, but it still takes a spirit medium, or *nat-gadaw* (literally, nat wife), to make one materialise. Most nat-gadaws are either women or male transvestites who sing and perform special dances that invite specific nats to possess them. Once possessed they continue to sing and dance while in trance, often performing various feats that 'prove' a spirit has taken them over – such as dancing with a large bowl of water balanced on their heads or bending over backwards to snatch an offered k50 bill with their mouths. The highly entertaining androgyny displayed by some nat-gadaws brings the spectacle even closer to rock and roll, à la Mick Jagger or David Bowie at their most outrageous.

Every nat pwe is accompanied by a risk that the invited spirit may choose to enter, not the body of the medium, but one of the spectators. One of the most commonly summoned spirits at nat pwes is Ko Gyi Kyaw (Big Brother Kyaw), a drunkard nat who responds to offerings of liquor imbibed by the nat-gadaw. When he enters someone's body, he's given to lascivious dancing, so a chance possession by Ko Gyi Kyaw is especially embarrassing. During one of his visits to Bagan, Joe attended a nat pwe near Lawkananda Paya, in which Ko Gyi Kyaw possessed a 14-year-old girl in the audience. Her family was mortified when she began dancing drunkenly around the tent, her longyi flapping away immodestly to show her legs.

Once possessed by a nat, the only way one can be sure the spirit won't return again and again is to employ the services of an older Buddhist monk skilled at exorcism – a process that can take days, if not weeks. Without undergoing such a procedure, anyone who has been spirit-possessed may carry the nat stigma the rest of their lives. Girls who have been so entered are considered unmarriageable unless satisfactorily exorcised. Nat-gadaws who choose to devote their minds and bodies to nat possession, and thus live on the fringe of normal Burmese society, usually have a history of involuntary nat trance. By the time they become spirit mediums, they're considered strong enough to handle such trance states.

Though nat pwes are commonly held as an adjunct to festivals throughout Bamar Myanmar, the grandest of all occur during the annual nat festival in Taungbyone, about 20km north of Mandalay. Held each August (more specifically for six days up to, and including, the full moon of Wagaung) since Anawrahta's reign, the Taungbyone festival honours the so-called Muslim Brothers, Byat-wi and Byat-ta, two of the most famous nats from the Bagan era. Nat-gadaws and nat devotees from all over Myanmar convene in a Woodstock-like collection of tents for a week of drinking, wild music and nat possession. Another nat festival, rather smaller than the one at Taungbyone, follows immediately afterwards at Yadana-gu, a paya south of Amarapura. This one revolves around the ritual bathing of nat images on the banks of the Ayeyarwady (Irrawaddy) River; many festival-goers arrive by sampan from Amarapura.

MICK WELDON

continued from page 64

Generally speaking, nunhood isn't considered as 'prestigious' as monkhood. The average Burmese Buddhist makes a great show of offering new robes and household items to the monks at their local kyaung but pay much less attention to the nuns. This is mainly due to the fact that nuns generally don't perform ceremonies on behalf of laypeople, so there is often less incentive for self-interested laypeople to make offerings to them. Furthermore, many Burmese equate the number of precepts observed with the total Buddhist merit achieved, hence nunhood is seen as less 'meritorious' than monkhood since nuns keep only ten precepts – the same number observed by male novices.

This difference in prestige represents social Buddhism, however, and is not how those with a serious interest in Buddhist practice regard the nuns. Nuns engage in the same fundamental eremitic activities – meditation and dhamma study – as monks do, activities that are the core of monastic life. When more than a few nuns reside at one temple, it's usually a sign that the teachings there are particularly strong. In Sagaing alone there are 145 nunneries housing over 2000 thilashin.

Monasteries Monastic communities are called *kyaungtaik, pongyi-kyaung,* or simply kyaung for short. The most important structure on the monastery grounds is the *thein* (Pali: *sema,* a consecrated hall where monastic ordinations are held). Kyaungs may also be associated with one or more zedis or pahtos. An open-sided resthouse or *zayat* may be available for gatherings of laypeople during festivals or pilgrimages.

Non-Theravada Elements in Burmese Buddhism The Theravada Buddhism practised by the Burmese is no more a 'pure' form of the belief system than Mexican Catholicism is 'pure' Roman Catholicism. In everyday life it is blended with bits of spirit worship, Hinduism and Mahayana Buddhism. The nat cult in particular plays an important role in the religious life of most Burmese, who, it is said, 'love the Buddha, but fear the nats'. See the boxed text on Nat Worship in this chapter for more detail on this fascinating aspect of Burmese metaphysical life.

Mahayana elements survive in the worship of at least two *arahats* (enlightened disciples) of the Buddha, whose images are often encountered at Burmese payas. In Mahayana Buddhism these would be considered Bodhisattvas. The monk Sivali (Shin Thiwali in Burmese) is shown holding a walking staff and fan; he is believed to bring prosperity and good fortune to those who make offerings or pay homage to him, especially in preparation for travel. Upagupta (Shin Upagot) sits crosslegged on a lotus raft in the middle of the ocean with a begging bowl and appears to anyone who faces physical danger. Offerings to Shin Upagot ensure that the monk will save the devotee's life in instances of mortal danger; others pray to Upagot for good weather. Burmese Buddhists also worship Lokanatha, otherwise known as Avalokitesvara, a Mahayana deity who is thought to be protecting the world between the passing of the last Buddha and the coming of the next. The crowned Lokanatha sits on a lotus pedestal, with his left thigh parallel to the pedestal and his right knee upright, while holding a lotus flower in his right hand. Almost all major payas in Central Myanmar feature separate shrines to these three figures somewhere in the grounds.

Hinduism survives mainly in the form of Burmese astrology, which is based on the Indian system of naming the zodiacal planets for Hindu deities and is very important for deciding the proper dates for weddings, funerals, ordinations and other life-cycle ceremonies. A cabalistic ritual called Paya-kozu (Nine Gods), held on behalf of those who have fallen ill or have experienced serious misfortune, similarly invokes Hindu deities. A *ponna* (or Brahman priest) – usually but not always of Indian descent – often officiates at rituals such as these and may also divine the most auspicious moment for significant occasions.

Ne Win's infamous fascination with numerology is shared by many Burmese Buddhists. Nearly everyone in Myanmar reveres the number nine, thought to have an inherent mystic significance. In Burmese the word *ko* (nine) also means 'to seek protection from the gods'; *nat-ko* signifies propitiation of the nats, and offerings are often made in nines, eg nine candles, nine kinds of food, nine cups of tea and so on.

Recommended Reading If you're interested in learning more about Buddhism, the following books are recommended (publisher supplied when difficult to find):

Buddhism, Imperialism, and War, by Trevor Ling
Buddhist Dictionary, by Mahathera Nyanatiloka
Essential Themes of Buddhist Lectures Given by Ashin Thittila, Department of Religious Affairs, Yangon
The Buddhist World of Southeast Asia, by Donald K Swearer
In This Very Life: The Liberation Teachings of the Buddha, by Sayadaw U Pandita
The Initiation of Novicehood and the Ordination of Monkhood in the Burmese Buddhist Culture, by Sao Htun Hmat Win, DRA, Yangon
Living Dharma: Teachings of Twelve Buddhist Masters, ed Jack Kornfield
The Long View: An Excursion into Buddhist Perspectives, by Suratano Bhikkhu (T Magness)
The Mind and the Way, by Ajaan Sumedho
Things as They Are, by Maha Boowa Nyanasampanno
Religion and Legitimation of Power in Thailand, Laos, Burma, ed Bardwell L Smith
Theravada Buddhism in Southeast Asia, by Robert C Lester
What the Buddha Taught, by Walpola Rahula

Two good sources of publications on Theravada Buddhism are the Buddhist Publication Society, PO Box 61, 54 Sangharaja Mawatha, Kandy, Sri Lanka, and the Barre Center for Buddhist Studies, Lockwood Rd, Barre, MA 01005, USA.

On the Internet, an excellent source is Access to Insight – Readings in Theravada Buddhism (world.std.com/~metta/index.html), from which you can freely download many publications (including the complete English version of the Pali canon), all cross-indexed by subject, title, author, proper names and even Buddhist similes. Two other recommended Internet sites with lots of material on Theravada Buddhism include Buddha Net (www.buddhanet.net) and DharmaNet Electronic Files Archive (sunsite.unc.edu/pub/academic/religious_studies/Buddhism/DEFA/Theravada).

See Meditation Study in the Facts for the Visitor chapter for a discussion of monasteries and meditation centres in Myanmar where foreigners may study *satipatthana vipassana*, a highly systematic style of Buddhist meditation.

Other Religions

Among non-Buddhist Burmese citizens, 5% are animist, 4.5% Christian, 4% Muslim and 1.5% are Hindu. Most Muslims and Hindus, as well as many Christians, are of Indian descent and live in the larger towns and cities.

Most other Christians in Myanmar are found among the tribal minorities, though the majority of the tribal people remain animist. Christian missionaries have been active in Myanmar for over 150 years. The American Baptists were first on the scene, but apart from certain hill tribes, especially the Kayin, they have had little success with the Burmese. The Church of Myanmar – formerly the Church of England – has about 30,000 members and a large cathedral in Yangon.

Facts for the Visitor

SUGGESTED ITINERARIES

With the exception of the Myeik Peninsula from Mawlamyaing (Moulmein) to Kawthoung, Myanmar's asymmetric shape doesn't lend itself to simple, linear north-south or east-west routes. Depending on your interests and available time you might pick from the following circuits or combine parts of several to create your own travel route.

The standard tourist visa is valid for 28 days, though only a relatively small percentage of visitors stay that long. This validity usually suffices for most people but you can receive two extensions of 14 days each, for an additional 28 days, if you so desire. Simpler yet is to pay US$3 for every day that you overstay your visa. Still want to see more of Myanmar? Fly back to Bangkok and get a new visa – there is no mandatory waiting period between visas.

The following suggested itineraries assume you want to see as much of the country as possible within a given interval. Another approach would be to spend more time in a few places rather than less time in many. Depending on your inclinations, you might decide to spend a full two weeks or even more just exploring the Mandalay – Bagan (Pagan) area. If you're into mountains and minority cultures, several weeks spent in the Shan State could be very rewarding. Unlike in neighbouring Thailand, where people may reside on one beach for weeks at a time, few visitors in Myanmar choose to hole up in one place for their entire stay.

The vast majority of visitors begin their journeys in Yangon (Rangoon). Depending on how much time they have available, some people decide to save their Yangon explorations until after they've seen other parts of the country. On the other hand, upcountry Myanmar will probably seem less overwhelming if you spend some time acculturating in Yangon first.

We hope there's enough information and evaluation in this guide for you to make up your own mind about where to go during your sojourn in Myanmar. However, if you're unsure of how and where to allot your time, the suggestions below may be of some assistance. Keep in mind one major caveat for all Myanmar travel: transport delays are entirely normal throughout the country, so always be prepared to alter your itinerary in the face of unforeseen events such as railway repairs, road washouts, cancelled flights and bad weather.

One Week

Yangon, Mandalay & Bagan For a short Myanmar sampler, start with a two day taste of Yangon's heavily gilded *payas* (pagodas) and urban intensity, then travel to the former royal capital of Mandalay by bus or plane (skip the train, as it's not time efficient) to take in the city's historic Mahamuni temples. The several smaller royal cities surrounding Mandalay are must-sees as well. Two days in Mandalay will suffice for people in a hurry. From Mandalay you can then shift to Bagan by plane, bus, boat or chartered car to revel in Myanmar's greatest archaeological site, a wide plain studded with *pahtos* (temples or shrines) and *zedis* (Buddhist stupa) dating from the 10th to 14th centuries. After one or two nights in Bagan, it's back to Yangon to catch your return or onward flight. If you intend to spend two nights in Bagan, you'll have to fly to Yangon to complete this circuit in a week.

Yangon, Bago & Kyaiktiyo A somewhat less touristy and less hurried alternative to the Yangon-Mandalay-Bagan circuit would be to head east from Yangon to Bago (Pegu) – home to a huge reclining Buddha and one of the more important zedis in the country – and onward to the famous 'golden rock' mountaintop shrine at Kyaiktiyo. One night each will suffice for Bago and Kyaiktiyo, thus leaving more time for Yangon at the beginning and end of the trip. All travel along this circuit must be done by road, whether using public or private transport.

A more ambitious eastern route would continue on from Kyaiktiyo to Mawlamyaing, once colonial Burma's most important teak port and an engaging Lower Myanmar city of Mon-style payas, historic mosques and moss-trimmed colonial architecture.

Two Weeks

With two weeks at your disposal you could accomplish both of the previously described one-week circuits back-to-back or spend more time in either Bagan or Mandalay (perhaps adding the hill station of Pyin U Lwin (Maymyo) north-east of Mandalay). Or choose one of the week-long suggestions and add one of the following.

Delta & Western Beaches After completing one of the aforementioned circuits, start again in Yangon and head west into the huge Ayeyarwady Delta. The scenic overnight boat trip to Pathein (Bassein) is highly recommended, and after a night in Pathein you can reach Chaungtha by road in a couple of hours. Staying there one or two nights will leave you enough time to continue north along the coast to Ngapali for another couple of days' beach time before catching a flight back to Yangon. Or do the trip in reverse, starting in Ngapali and working your way down the coast and through the delta. During the rainy season parts of this road may be washed out.

Another way to visit these areas would be to plan a road circuit from Yangon to Pyay (Prome), then Pyay to Ngapali, down to Chaungtha and Pathein, and back to Yangon. This saves the cost of a flight between Ngapali and Yangon, and allows you to fit in Pyay since it's considerably faster to travel between Pathein and Yangon by road than by boat. You could also proceed in the other direction, from Yangon to Pathein and around to Pyay, instead.

Meiktila or Thazi to Inle After doing Mandalay or Bagan, double back to Meik-tila or Thazi by road, and then take a week to cover the eastern road out to Inle. Stop at the former British hill station of Kalaw and the Pindaya caves along the way. From Inle you can either fly back to Yangon (via the nearby market town of Heho) or schedule an extra day for the long bus ride(s).

Pyin U Lwin, Hsipaw & Lashio If you want to get a little more off the beaten track in the Shan State, skip Inle and spend a few days in and around Hsipaw, a charming centre for Shan culture, with a side trip to the Shan/Chinese market town of Lashio. Road travel is the most efficient way to reach Hsipaw and Lashio, but railroad bridge buffs may want to sacrifice travel time to ride the rails across the historic Gokteik Viaduct. On the way out of Mandalay, a stopover in the quirky former 'hill station' of Pyin U Lwin is worthwhile.

If the road from Lashio south to Loilem, then west to Taunggyi, ever opens up to foreign visitors, one could make a very interesting and efficient loop from Mandalay to Lashio, then to Inle and back to the centre via Kalaw and Pindaya.

Mrauk U or Pyay The archaeologically minded could skip the beaches, lakes and hill stations and spend their second week at Myanmar's second greatest Buddhist ruins site, Mrauk U (Myohaung). At the moment this area is only accessible to tourists via flights to Sittwe (Akyab) from Yangon, but it's probably only a matter of time before existing road links between Sittwe and Taungup and between Sittwe and Minbu (opposite Magwe) are upgraded and opened to foreign visitors. Flights between Bagan and Mrauk U are also a future possibility, and this would save having to backtrack to Yangon before hopping on the flight to Sittwe.

If you don't want to spend an entire week in Mrauk U and Sittwe, add more time to your first week in Bagan, perhaps including the smaller ruins site at Salay. Or take a one night trip from Yangon to Pyay and visit the archaeological site at Thayekhittaya.

One Month

Ruins, Hill Stations & Beaches In a month you can sample many of Myanmar's major highlights. After a few days in Yangon (or leave the capital for the end), take a bus or car north with a stopover in Taungoo or Pyinmana, then on to Mandalay, Pyin U Lwin and Bagan. Then head east into the Shan State to experience either the Inle circuit or the Pyin U Lwin – Lashio route. Of course you could do this route in reverse.

With roughly a week left in your itinerary, fly to Ngapali, enjoy a few days at the beach, and then work your way down the western coast through Chaungtha and Pathein back to Yangon.

Want more ruins? Skip Chaungtha and Pathein, and spend your fourth week on the Mrauk U/Pyay circuit described previously. Of course, this would require more internal flights.

East by South-East If beach resorts don't matter much to you, go for a major intake of culture by starting with the aforementioned Bago and Kyaiktiyo circuit, then continue eastward to Mawlamyaing's captivating blend of colonial, Indian, Kayin and Mon influences. From Mawlamyaing, continue by road or rail to the old tin port of Dawei (Tavoy), assuming the road is open (it was iffy at the time of writing). While in Dawei, don't miss Myanmar's largest reclining Buddha, and Maungmagan, perhaps Myanmar's longest undeveloped beach. From Dawei you can catch a flight farther south to Myeik (Mergui), one of South-East Asia's most historic ports. After seeing Myeik you can either fly back to Yangon to finish your trip, or continue on another plane to Kawthoung at Myanmar's southeasternmost tip. Although Kawthoung has little of any interest to offer the traveller, you can exit Myanmar and enter Thailand by boat here, thus avoiding any backtracking to Yangon.

Two Months

In two months you can combine several of these itineraries to link different regions in Myanmar. If Kachin culture interests you, add Bhamo and Myitkyina in northern Myanmar's Kachin State. Neither of these towns is of huge intrinsic interest, unless you manage to arrive during a *manao* (Kachin festival). However, the train trip from Mandalay to Myitkyina or the boat trip from Mandalay to Bhamo are unparalleled in Myanmar in terms of stimulating experiences. Both trips are possibly time-consuming; flights are available from Mandalay, but if you fly you'll miss what could be the best parts of these trips.

PLANNING
When to Go

Climate-wise, the best season for visiting most of Myanmar falls between November and February – during these months it rains least and is not so hot.

The cool hill stations of the Shan State or the wind-swept Rakhaing (Arakan) State or Tanintharyi (Tenasserim) Division coasts are best visited when the rest of Myanmar is miserably hot, from March to May. Bagan, Mandalay and the rest of the 'dry zone' in central Upper Myanmar can be nearly intolerable during these months. During the height of the monsoon season, from July to September, the dry zone gets less rain and humidity than the rest of the country, while roads along the delta region south-west of Yangon, as well as anywhere along the coast, can become impassable.

The peak months for tourist arrivals are December, February, July and August. The least crowded months – though as yet Myanmar never actually seems to be over-crowded – are May, June and September.

Where You Can Go

Travel anywhere in the standard tourist circuit – Yangon, Mandalay, Bagan, Inle, Taunggyi and to any points between or near these destinations – is freely allowed for anyone holding a valid passport and tourist visa. This includes places just off the main linking routes, such as Bago, Pyay, Shwebo, Magwe, Monywa, Taungoo and Pyinmana – basically any place in Central Myanmar between the Shan Yoma (mountain range) to the east and the Ayeyarwady (Irrawaddy) River to the west – plus most places in the Ayeyarwady Delta region (Pathein, Twante, Thanlyin (Syriam) and Letkhokkon).

Several other places farther off the beaten path that used to require travel permits no longer require them. These include Bhamo, Myitkyina, Kyaiktiyo, Mawlamyaing, Dawei and Myeik, all of which required permits as recently as three years ago.

Travel to certain other places in Myanmar requires a permit – actually a typed letter stamped with various government seals – issued by the Ministry of Hotels & Tourism (MHT) and approved by the Ministry of Defence. Such permits are available directly from Myanmar Travels & Tours (MTT) in Yangon or through many Yangon travel agencies. There's no charge for the travel permit itself but the catch is that a permit won't be issued unless you arrange for the services of a paid guide. Travel agencies work similarly; you must contract the services of a guide or driver before they'll arrange for a permit.

In March 1997 the government finally published an official list of places that are open only to 'package' travel and places open to 'foreign independent travellers' (FITs). This list remains unchanged at the time of writing, but there's no way to know how or when it might change in the near future. Most places in the country are now open to individual, nonpackage travellers. Mogok is one obvious exception – visiting there requires a guide and purchase of a US$500 package. See the Mogok section in the Around Mandalay chapter for details. Other places open only to people who purchase package tours include Muse, Namkham, Kyu Kok and Kunlon in the northern Shan State. All of these areas are Myanmar-China border crossings and are for the most part used by Chinese tourists, although in theory any nationality may arrange to travel in these districts.

Only two states – Kayah and Chin – are entirely off-limits for all tourists, with or without a permit or whether on tours or

alone. Certain parts of the Shan State, Kayin State, Mon Division and Tanintharyi Division are also off-limits – usually those areas with active ethnic insurgency or banditry, or where travel conditions are so bad that the government fears for Myanmar's international reputation as a potential tourist destination. Parts of the Shan State, Mon State and Tanintharyi Division fit all three of these criteria.

It's obvious that the most touchy destinations are in frontier areas where the headquarters of ethnic insurgencies are based. In some of these areas – for example, between Taunggyi and Kengtung in the Shan State – military checkpoints placed at close intervals along every government-controlled road leading into these areas catch anyone who tries to enter from either end.

For specific information see Dangers & Annoyances later in this chapter as well as the relevant destination chapters later in this book.

Even *with* a permit, there's no guarantee the local authorities won't give you the boot – as happened to several visitors to Myitkyina in 1995. That year MTT was issuing permits to Myitkyina with the caveat that upon your arrival, the Myitkyina authorities could arbitrarily refuse entry. For other places, like Mawlamyaing (Moulmein), permits would be easy to get one week and impossible the next, depending on the level of rebel activity in the area. Although visiting either of these places no longer requires a permit, the same principle may still apply in places that do require them.

Once you arrive, permit in hand, at your destination, there are other papers to be filled in. Since these places also require the services of a guide, your guide should take care of these procedures.

Any or all of this could change overnight, especially as Myanmar's frontier areas become more 'secure' following cease-fire agreements with insurgent groups and military victories over those groups who won't negotiate. By the time you read this, travel restrictions may have loosened considerably – or things could have gone the other way. Most likely the constant passport checking will persist as long as the ruling junta maintains its warlord mentality – a centuries-old legacy in Myanmar.

Confusing? Welcome to Myanmar!

Maps

Country Maps Good, up-to-date maps of Myanmar are difficult to find outside Myanmar. In Yangon you can pick up the full-colour, folded *Myanmar Tourist Map*, published on coated stock by Design Printing Services (DPS), from many hotels and bookshops. Sometimes it's free, sometimes it costs up to K500. All major towns, cities and roadways are clearly marked on this map, and it's relatively up-to-date. The Myanmar government's Survey Dept publishes a very good paper sheet map of the country, simply entitled *Myanmar*, with a scale of 1:2,000,000. Although the latter map is a little large to carry around in a daypack and the noncoated paper decays rapidly, it's good for general reference. You'll occasionally find it for sale from the footpath book vendors on Pansodan Lan in Yangon.

We've seen proofs of Periplus Editions' new *Myanmar Travel Map*, a similar folded map that looks better in terms of detail, accuracy and consistency, and will be available worldwide in shops selling maps.

The inferior and more costly Nelles' *Myanmar*, a folded map on coated stock, contains many errors but does have the advantage of being easily available outside Myanmar so that you can play with it before you arrive.

Myanmar's Survey Department also publishes a multipage 1997 *Myanmar Atlas*, complete with colour relief but labelled in Bamar language only. This atlas provides the most up-to-date and detailed set of maps available. You may find it for sale among the Pansodan Lan book vendors.

The much-touted *Tactical Pilotage Charts* published by the US Department of Defence are, by comparison, almost worthless.

City Maps DPS publishes very useful and fairly detailed city maps of Yangon, Man-

dalay and Bagan. As with their *Myanmar Tourist Map*, these city maps are printed on durable coated stock and are available from various hotels and bookshops in Yangon, and to a lesser degree in Mandalay and Bagan. If you anticipate spending a lot of time in the capital, look for a new DPS bilingual atlas, *The Map of Yangon*, a detailed street and place directory.

MTT also prints city maps oriented towards tourists, but they tend to be out-of-date and less detailed. These maps are available from the MTT office in Yangon on Sule Paya Lan, or from individual MTT offices in these respective cities.

What to Bring

Even at the height of the cool season you'll rarely need anything more than a sweater while on the plains – and probably only for the nights in Bagan, where it can get a little chilly. It can get rather cold up in the hill country, so if you're going to Pyin U Lwin (Maymyo) or Inle bring a warm sweater or light jacket. A light sleeping bag might also be useful in other parts of the Shan State, especially in Kalaw and Taunggyi where the one or two blankets per person supplied by guesthouses is not always enough during the cool season.

Otherwise it's normal tropical gear – lightweight, but 'decent', clothes. Myanmar is a prim, conservative country; shorts (particularly when worn by women) or short skirts are inappropriate.

When travelling in Myanmar, we strongly advise that you wear sturdy sandals or thongs rather than shoes – simply because you take them off and put them on so often when visiting temples and payas. Remember that the sunlight is intense in Myanmar – protect your head in open places like Bagan, or when out on Inle Lake. Mosquitoes can be a major irritant, so bring protection in the form of insect repellent, mosquito coils or even a mosquito net.

Bring any items you feel may not be available in Myanmar – mosquito repellent, film, batteries and medicines are the most likely examples. Simple toiletries like soap, toothpaste or toilet paper are readily available; in fact toilet paper is much easier to find and is cheaper than in India. Remember that anything western that is difficult to find in Myanmar will have an absurdly high value. Western clothes (interesting T-shirts), electronic gadgets, calendars, disposable lighters, ballpoint pens, lipstick and make-up are all items many Burmese would love to have. They have to be name brands though, something from the USA or Europe, not any old Asian product! You can always use them to barter for handicrafts, bribe sluggish bureaucrats or simply give away and make people happy.

An unsewn *longyi* (sarong-style garment) can be a very handy item; it can be used to sleep on or as a light bedspread (many guesthouses don't supply top sheets or bedspreads), as a makeshift 'shopping bag', as a turban/scarf to keep off the sun and absorb perspiration, as a towel and as a small hammock – to name just a few of its many functions.

If you plan to wash your own clothes, bring a along universal sink plug, a few plastic clothes pegs, and plastic hangers or 3m of plastic cord for hanging wet clothes on.

A small but strong padlock is useful for locking your room door in small upcountry guesthouses where locks aren't provided.

Burmese women don't use tampons, and they are almost impossible to find even in Yangon. If you use them, bring them with you. If you're coming through Bangkok, the more upscale pharmacies there may carry Tampax brand tampons. Sanitary napkins are widely available from minimarts and supermarkets in Thailand, but not in Myanmar.

Many women have found that the Keeper menstrual cap – a reusable natural rubber device that is inserted to catch menstrual flow – is a convenient and environmentally friendly alternative to disposable tampons or pads.

TOURIST OFFICES
Local Tourist Offices

MTT, formerly known as Tourist Burma, is part of the MHT – the official government tourism organ in Myanmar. Its main office

(☎ 01-275328, 278386, fax 282535) is at 77/91 Sule Paya Lan in Yangon, beside the Sule Paya.

MTT has little in the way of brochures or leaflets, unlike most other South-East Asian tourist offices. Its main function, in fact, appears to be to sell tours and transport at premium rates and to keep tabs on foreign visitors.

Apart from the main Yangon office there are also MTT desks in Mandalay, Bagan, Nyaungshwe (Yaunghwe) and Taunggyi. Until the early 1990s it was the only travel agency in the country; nowadays it competes with over 100 private travel agencies.

With the privatisation of the tourist industry, it's no longer difficult to avoid MTT while travelling round Myanmar. Two of its remaining monopolies are express train tickets between Yangon and Mandalay and express boat tickets between Mandalay and Bagan, neither of which can be purchased by a foreigner except through MTT (or its representatives at the station/pier). But in both cases there are alternatives to using MTT transport, so even here you can bypass the bureaucrats.

In areas where, until 1995, your only choice for a place to stay was a hotel owned by the MHT (eg Mawlamyaing), there are now plenty of private hotels or guesthouses. This time around we didn't find any place in the country where you had to stay in an MHT-owned hotel. Even in little-visited Dawei and Myeik, none of the foreigner-approved accommodations were government-run or government-owned. See the Accommodation section later in this chapter for more information on where to stay.

Just as the MHT has so d off almost all its hotel properties, there are rumours it may dissolve MTT in the face of competition from better-run travel agencies. In all honesty it must be mentioned that MTT actually has some very charming, very experienced guides, each of whom was trained at the long-running MHT school opposite what was the Baiyoke Kandawgyi Hotel (now known as the Kandawgyi Palace Hotel) in Yangon. Many of the better private agencies in Yangon employ former MTT guides; some agencies are even owned by former MTT guides.

Tourist Offices Abroad

Myanmar maintains no branches of the MTT abroad, although most Myanmar embassies and consulates around the world disseminate limited tourist information to anyone interested.

VISAS & DOCUMENTS
Passport

Entry into Myanmar requires a passport valid for at least six months from the time of entry. If you anticipate your passport ex-

piring while you're in the country, you should obtain a new one before arrival or inquire from your government whether your embassy in Myanmar (if one exists – see the list of foreign embassies later in this chapter) can issue a new one after arrival.

Visas

The Myanmar government issues 12 types of visitor visas and border permits, including such quaint-sounding ones as 'caravan trader permit', 'seasonal mahjis permit' and 'frontier visa'. Leisure travellers are issued the tourist visa, which is now valid for four weeks (28 days) and is readily available through most Myanmar embassies or consulates abroad. At the embassy in Bangkok you can usually receive a visa the same day you apply for it. The simple application process requires three passport-size photos and around US$10 to US$18 for the visa fee.

For part of the 1960s the doors into Myanmar were firmly shut, then they slowly reopened. Twenty-four-hour stays were permitted at first, then along came the seven day visa. In 1988 civil disturbances closed the doors again for about six months. By the end of 1990, 14-day tourist visas were being issued with regularity, but only if you came as part of a package tour. Towards the end of 1992 Myanmar began to reintroduce FIT visas, which, although still limited to 14 days, allowed much more freedom to plan things yourself. In March 1994 the tourist visa was lengthened to 28 days, making it now possible to see a good bit of the country at a comfortable pace.

The only fly in the ointment is that you have to exchange a nonrefundable minimum of US$300 upon arrival into Foreign Exchange Certificates (FECs; this requirement is waived for package-tour visa holders). For most visitors this isn't much of a problem since the FECs may be used to pay for hotels as well as train and plane tickets; the average individual easily spends this much when staying three weeks or more. FECs may also be exchanged for *kyat*, the national currency, at the free-market rate – see the Money section later in this chapter for details.

What's My Line?

Ever since 18 foreign activists were arrested in Yangon for distributing anti-government leaflets, Myanmar's embassies/consulates abroad have been more scrupulous in checking out the backgrounds of anyone applying for a tourist visa. In particular, writers and journalists may have a difficult time obtaining visas. Therefore it is probably not a good idea to list your occupation as any of the following: journalist; photographer; editor; publisher; motion picture director or producer; cameraperson; videographer; or writer. Of course plenty of journalists and photographers do get into the country – by declaring a different profession on the visa application.

Myanmar foreign missions may also be suspicious of anyone whose passport shows two or more previous visits to Myanmar in the same five year period. Obviously the government can't believe anyone would want to visit Myanmar more than once or twice! In cases like these you'll need more of a reason than simply 'tourism' for receiving another visa. We won't suggest any alternatives here, but we encourage you to be creative.

Joe Cummings

Towards the end of 1998 we heard from reliable sources in Yangon that the FEC requirement might soon be rescinded.

Beware of travel agents in Bangkok (especially on Thanon Khao San) who will try to sell you a 'special visa' (often said to be a business visa) or other type of visa that would exempt you from the US$300/300FEC exchange requirement. Only holders of tourist visas bearing the stamp 'package tour EVT' are exempt from the FEC requirement. Yes, some agencies are able to obtain this type of visa – but don't pay any extra charges till you see the visa first.

Visa Extensions Although some Myanmar embassies abroad will say tourist visa extensions aren't permitted, once in Myanmar you can usually extend your visa up to 28 days beyond the original 28 day validity – at the discretion of the Department of Immigration & Manpower. The usual procedure requires five photos plus payment of a US$36 fee, but this can vary from office to office. If you're refused at one office, try again at another location – in low-tech Myanmar there are no computer checks or other easily communicated record of visa extension applications. Some offices are slower than others; allow two or three days for the extension to go through. In Yangon it tends to be a more complicated and drawn-out procedure than in Mandalay.

The type of permit issued for such extensions is called a 'stay permit'. To be granted an extension, your passport must be valid for six months after the end of your planned stay in Myanmar. Of late the normal extension granted has been valid for only 14 days, after which you may be granted another 14 day extension. In such cases, each 14 day extension will cost US$36.

If you overstay your visa by a day or two due to unavoidable transport difficulties, there's usually little hassle at Yangon international airport if immigration authorities can verify your story. If not, be prepared to part with some cash for a short-term extension. The usual fine (or fee) is US$3 per day; obviously if you plan to stay fewer

Paper Games

Wherever you go in Myanmar, your passport is likely to be checked frequently. In fact every airport arrival, anywhere in the country, requires a passport-and-visa check and the filling in of some papers with your name, passport number and visa number. Hotel staff also check passports and visas. At the airport in Sittwe we once had our passports checked by no ess than five different persons, each of whom wrote our names, passport numbers and visa numbers in ledgers or on little scraps of paper! The scraps of paper were just the corners torn from a plain sheet of paper.

At some point in your Myanmar travels, you come to realise that the country is still run like a loose-knit collection of warlord states. Even when you're just moving from one Bamar-majority div sion to another, your papers are checked. On top of this, every time you enter a small town or village by car, someone appears to exact a tribute from the driver in the form of a 'road tax'. The same happens for Burmese road travellers.

Joe Cummings

than 12 days beyond the original 28 allotted by your visa, it's less expensive – and simpler – to pay the overstay fine than to file for a visa extension.

Onward Tickets
Myanmar immigration does not seem very concerned with whether or not you arrive with proof of onward travel. Legally speaking all holders of tourist visas are *supposed* to carry such proof. In over 20 years of frequent travel in and out of Myanmar, our onward travel documents haven't been checked once.

Travel Insurance
A travel insurance policy to cover theft, loss and medical problems is a wise idea. There are a wide variety of policies and your

travel agent will have recommendations. The international travel policies handled by STA Travel and other student travel organisations are usually good value. Some policies offer lower and higher medical expenses options but the higher ones are chiefly for countries, like the USA, which have extremely high medical costs.

Driving Licence & Permits
Myanmar does not allow tourists to drive motorised vehicles, so you won't need a driving licence.

Student Cards
Several readers have reported receiving discounted entry fees for monuments in Myanmar upon presentation of the International Student Identity Card (ISIC). Sample comments included:

After showing our ISIC cards we were granted free access. Students must ask – some officials may be reluctant, though some were even willing to refund our prior paid admissions.

Although your book did not mention it, the ISIC card was very useful in Myanmar when I visited in January 1997; I could use it very easily even if no sign indicated a discount for students. I always showed it and asked if a discount was available – this worked quite well, netting at least a 50% discount most of the time, occasionally free. When I visited Kyaiktiyo, I flashed my card and the guard only wanted half of the US$10 fee. When I insisted a bit more he reduced it to one third, then finally let me pass for free.

It's possible to get in free to a lot of the attractions in Myanmar using a student card. It didn't work at the Shwedagon or in Bagan, but it did at lots of other attractions.

We've never heard of anyone receiving a discount for any other type of student or youth card. We predict that as more foreign visitors try to receive discounted entry fees with ISIC cards, the government will be forced to formulate policy regarding student discounts. In which direction they will go – either allowing such discounts or

declaring the cards invalid for Myanmar – remains to be seen.

Hostel & Seniors' Cards
Myanmar recognises neither of these cards for discounts.

International Health Card
These are no longer recognised by many countries and, in fact, medical authorities in some western countries no longer issue them. In Myanmar the authorities no longer ask to see them at the airport, although visitors from African countries may be asked to show a certificate of yellow fever vaccination. These need not appear on the World Health Organization's (WHO) yellow card; any hospital or clinic stationery will do.

Photocopies
It's a good idea to keep photocopies of all vital documents – passport data page, credit card numbers, airline tickets, travellers cheque serial numbers and so on – in a separate place from the originals. In case you lose the originals, replacement will be much easier to arrange if you can provide issuing agencies with copies. You might consider leaving extra copies of these documents with someone at home or in a safe place in Yangon or another point of entry.

EMBASSIES & CONSULATES
Myanmar Embassies & Consulates
Addresses of Myanmar's relevant embassies and consulates include:

Australia
    (☎ 02-6273 3811)
    22 Arkana St, Yarralumla, ACT 2600
Bangladesh
    (☎ 02-60 1915)
    89B Rd No 4, Banani, Dhaka
Canada
    (☎ 613-232 6434/6446)
    Apt 902-903, 85 Range Rd,
    The Sandringham, Ottawa, Ontario K1N 8J6
China
    (☎ 010-532 1584/1425)
    6 Dong Zhi Men Wai St, Chaoyang District, Beijing

France
  (☎ 01-42 25 56 95)
  60 rue de Courcelles, 75008 Paris
Germany
  (☎ 0228-21 0091)
  Schumannstrasse 112, 53113 Bonn 1
Hong Kong
  (☎ 02-2827 7929/9843)
  Room 2424, Sun Hung Kai Centre, 30
  Harbour Rd, Wanchai
India
  (☎ 11-600 251/252)
  No 3/50F Nyaya Marg, Chanakyapuri,
  New Delhi 110021
Indonesia
  (☎ 021-327 684, 314 040)
  109 Jalan Haji Agus Salim, Jakarta Pusat
Israel
  (☎ 03-540 0948)
  12 Zalman Schneor St, Ramat Hasharon
  47239, Tel Aviv
Italy
  (☎ 06-854 9374)
  Via Vincenzo Bellini 20m Interno 1,
  00198 Rome
Japan
  (☎ 03-3441 9291)
  8-26, 4-chome, Kita-Shinagawa,
  Shinagawa-ku, Tokyo 140
Laos
  (☎ 21-314910)
  Thanon Sok Pa Luang, PO Box 11,
  Vientiane
Malaysia
  (☎ 03-242 4085)
  5 Taman U Thant Satu,
  55000 Kuala Lumpur
Nepal
  (☎ 01-521 788)
  Chakupat, Patan Gate, Lalitpur,
  Kathmandu
Philippines
  (☎ 632-817 2373/fax 817 5895)
  4th floor, Basic Petroleum Building, 104
  Carlos Palancar St, Legaspi Village,
  Makati, Manila
Singapore
  (☎ 65-338 1073)
  B & N Bldg No 05-04, 133 Middle Rd
  Singapore 0718
Switzerland
  (☎ 022-731 7540)
  47 Ave Blanc, 1202 Geneva
Thailand
  (☎ 02-233 7250)
  132 Thanon Sathon Neua,
  Bangkok 10500

UK
  (☎ 020-7629 6966, 7499 8841)
  19A Charles St, London W1X 8ER
USA
  (☎ 202-332 9044/5/6)
  2300 'S' St NW, Washington, DC 20008
Vietnam
  (☎ 04-253 369)
  Bldg No A-3, Ground floor,
  Van Phuc Diplomatic Qrtrs, Hanoi

Embassies & Consulates in Myanmar

Yangon can be a good place to get visas for
other countries. If you can manage to pay for
them with free-market kyat they're very
cheap, and because Yangon isn't a big
tourist stopover, visas are usually issued
quickly. However, many embassies for
neighbouring countries are now accepting
only US dollars for payment of visa fees.
Visas for Laos can be obtained directly from
the Lao embassy, for example; in Thailand
you would have to go through a travel
agency for the same visa.

Australia
  (☎ 01-251810, 251797)
  88 Strand Rd
Bangladesh
  (☎ 01-549556, 549557)
  56 Kaba Aye Paya Lan
Canada
  Affairs handled by Australian embassy
China
  (☎ 01-221281)
  1 Pyidaungsu Yeiktha Lan
France
  (☎ 01-282122, 282418)
  102 Pyidaungsu Yeiktha Lan
Germany
  (☎ 01-548951)
  32 Natmauk Lan
India
  (☎ 01-282551)
  545-47 Merchant St
Indonesia
  (☎ 01-254465, 254469)
  100 Pyidaungsu Yeiktha Lan
Israel
  (☎ 01-222290)
  49 Pyay Lan
Italy
  (☎ 01-527100)
  3 Inya Myaing Lan, Golden Valley

Japan
  (☎ 01-549644, 549645)
  100 Natmauk Lan
Laos
  (☎ 01-222482)
  A1 Diplomatic Quarters,
  Taw Win Lan
Malaysia
  (☎ 01-220249)
  82 Pyidaungsu Yeiktha Lan
Nepal
  (☎ 01-545880, 553168)
  16 Natmauk Lan
Netherlands
  Affairs handled by German embassy
New Zealand
  Affairs handled by UK embassy
Pakistan
  (☎ 01-222881)
  A1 Diplomatic Quarters, Pyay Lan
Philippines
  (☎ 01-664010)
  50 Pyay Lan
Singapore
  (☎ 01-525688, 525700)
  286 Pyay Lan
Sri Lanka
  (☎ 01-222812)
  34 Taw Win Lan
Sweden
  Affairs handled by UK embassy
Switzerland
  Affairs handled by German embassy
Thailand
  (☎ 01-533082, 512017)
  45 Pyay Lan
UK
  (☎ 01-281700)
  80 Strand Rd
USA
  (☎ 01-282055)
  581 Merchant St
Vietnam
  (☎ 01-548905)
  6 Wingbar Lan

CUSTOMS

Besides personal effects, visitors are permitted to bring in the following items duty free: 200 cigarettes (or 50 cigars, or 250g of unrolled tobacco), a quart (0.94L) of liquor and 500mL of cologne or perfume. Cameras (including video cameras), radios, cassette players and calculators can be brought into the country, but they're supposed to be declared on arrival and taken out upon departure. In reality no one ever seems to check and if you try to declare your cameras on arrival you're usually waved on through.

Any foreign currency in excess of US$2000 must be declared upon entry. Mobile phones may be confiscated and held by customs personnel on arrival at Yangon international airport and returned upon your departure.

See Export Restrictions in the Shopping section at the end of this chapter for a list of items that cannot be taken out of the country.

MONEY
Currency

Myanmar uses three currencies, two of which are legal tender for everyone, one of which Burmese citizens need a licence to use. All three currencies are strongly linked to the US dollar and the Japanese yen.

Kyat The first is the everyday national currency, called kyat (pronounced chat) and divided into 100 *pyas* with a confusing collection of coins that is rarely seen anymore because the kyat has decreased in value so much over the last few years.

At present the following kyat banknotes were in use: K1, 5, 10, 15, 20, 45, 50, 90, 100, 200 and 500. Towards the end of 1998 the government announced it would soon introduce a much-needed K1000 note. To discourage the black market, K50 and K100 notes were demonetised in the 1960s, and K25, K35 and K75 notes underwent a similar fate in 1987; unscrupulous money-dealers occasionally try to foist these older bills on unsuspecting visitors. Make sure that any K50 or K100 bills you're offered are labelled Central Bank of Myanmar, rather than Union of Burma Bank. In general, any note reading Myanmar rather than Burma should be OK. Exceptions are the K45 and K90 notes, both of which bear Union of Burma Bank but are OK. To make it more confusing, K1 and K5 notes come in both Union of Burma and Central Bank of Myanmar versions, and both are legal tender.

A sum of 100,000 is called *thein* in Burmese, so K100,000 is thein kyat; the Indian term *lakh* (100,000) is also common.

HIGHLIGHTS

ANDERS BLOMQVIST

C urrent visa regulations permit visitors to stay 28 days (up to 56 days with extensions), allowing time to see close to the full range of Myanmar's plentiful attractions. Still, because of the hassles with road travel and flight delays, it usually pays to be under-ambitious with one's travel plans; don't try to see too much in too short an interval, or your travels will quickly become a chore. Old Burma hands have found that more time to travel in Myanmar means more opportunity to become fed up and frustrated if you try to blaze through the country at the same pace as one used to during the one and two-week visa eras of the 1970s and 1980s.

Virtually everyone begins their journey in Yangon (Rangoon). Under the old 'see-everything-in-two-weeks' system, travellers rushed immediately to Mandalay by night express train, leaving perhaps just a day at the end to see the capital. Nowadays there's less reason to rush, and Yangon is a good place to become accustomed to the climate, food and everyday customs before heading upcountry.

Your recreational and aesthetic inclinations will largely determine which direction you take upon leaving Yangon. The basic threads most visitors are interested in following include historic temple architecture, handicrafts, hiking, beaches and culture. These travel aspects are not necessarily mutually exclusive, though it's hard to find one place that has them all!

Glittering Shwedagon at dusk, Yangon.

Historic Temple Architecture

Myanmar's most magnificent temple ruins are of course those at Bagan (Pagan), the country's No 1 tourist attraction and for decades the most popular photo subject for tour brochures and posters. Nearby Salay boasts a little-known set of ruins from the same period, easily visited as a day trip from Bagan.

Nearly as impressive in form and style, if not in number of ruins, are the massive Mrauk U (Myohaung) temples near Sittwe (Akyab) in the Rakhaing (Arakan) State, which so far have seen few tourists. In local colour some people may in fact find Mrauk U superior to Bagan.

Mandalay is surrounded by the ancient cities of Inwa (Ava), Amarapura, Sagaing and Mingun, all easily visited on day trips. Though not as old or impressive in scale as those sites previously described, the atmosphere at the old Mandalay temples is energised by the continued worship of the local population.

The view from Mingalazedi, Old Bagan.

Buddha statue at Mrauk U.

Sun protection provided by a parasol.

A marionette on display, Mandalay.

Myanmar's beaches are yet to be over-run.

Early *stupas* (Buddhist religious monuments) at the former Pyu capital of Thayekhittaya (Sri Ksetra) near Pyay (Prome) rank fourth in architectural interest and are the most accessible of all the ancient capitals from Yangon. Additional Pyu ruins can be seen at the more obscure – and more off-the-beaten-track – sites of Beikthano and Hanlin. See the Architecture section in the Facts about Myanmar chapter for more information on art and archaeological styles.

Handicrafts

Myanmar's incredible ethnic diversity means a wide range of handicrafts are available for study or purchase throughout the country. As the culture and business capital of Upper Myanmar, Mandalay has been the main handicrafts centre for over a hundred years. You'll find virtually every type of craft produced in the immediate region, as well as materials from throughout the north. Mandalay specialities include silverwork, woodcarving, stone sculpture, *kalagas* (embroidered tapestries), Burmese marionettes and jadework.

The Shan State is the country's centre for handrolled *cheroots* (Burmese cigars) and for the ubiquitous embroidered shoulder bags carried by practically every Burmese. Bagan is renowned for its lacquerware and antiques.

Multicoloured cotton *longyis* (a loom-woven length of cloth draped around the lower body and legs and tied at the waist) can be found in municipal markets throughout the country, but the most interesting Burman patterns seem to be those produced in small central Myanmar towns like Inma, Yezin, Pakokku and Lindwin. The various frontier states, ie the Kachin, Kayah, Mon, Kayin and Rakhaing states, produce patterns unique to their regions.

Beaches

Although Myanmar's coastline is the longest in mainland South-East Asia, only the Ayeyarwady Division and Rakhaing State sections stretching from the Ayeyarwady River Delta north-west to Sittwe are so far commonly visited by foreigners. Because of the lengthy travel times involved, stays of at least one night are necessary at most seaside areas. Most suitable for overnight visits are Ngapali, Chaungtha, Kanthaya and Letkhokkon. Between these points you'll find plenty of other beaches, but few facilities and no 'licensed-for-foreigners' accommodation.

Highlights

During the rainy season from June to November, many of the roads in these areas may be washed out and impassable. Only Ngapali is accessible by air. Ngapali is the most attractive beach of the four; the closer you get to the delta, the muddier the beaches become – Letkhokkon being the muddiest.

The beaches and islands south of Mawlamyaing (Moulmein), off peninsular Myanmar, have incredible recreational potential and are just beginning to open up. The drawback so far is that there is virtually no accommodation available at any of the beaches along the Myeik Peninsula or Myeik Archipelago. One of the easiest ways to see these areas is on a liveaboard cruise. Most of the latter are based in Phuket, Thailand, but one foreign company is establishing a base in Myeik (Mergui) itself. See the Activities section later in this chapter for more detail on cruising the Myeik area.

Bamar cuisine – a blend of Asian styles.

Culture

One of the main joys of travelling through Myanmar comes from soaking up the general cultural ambience, which is plentiful throughout the country. You'll obtain less in terms of Burmese culture if you spend most of your time sitting around in foreigner-frequented guesthouses and restaurants in Yangon and Mandalay, both of which are rapidly modernising. Try going to a small to medium-size town well off the main tourist circuit, staying at a local hotel, and eating in Burmese curry shops and teashops. It's not as easy as going with the crowd but you'll learn a lot more about the country.

The balancing boulder, Kyaiktiyo.

Other Highlights

The Mon State's Kyaiktiyo Paya – the famous, stupa-topped gilded boulder perched on a mountain cliff – is fairly accessible these days and is a favourite among visitors interested in Myanmar's syncretic, animistic Buddhism. Mt Popa, the 'home of the *nats*' (spirits) near Bagan, holds a similar lure although the overall atmosphere runs far behind that at Kyaiktiyo.

The old Mon capital of Bago (Pegu) – with the second largest reclining Buddha in the country and a highly revered stupa – makes an easy day trip from Yangon or a stopover on the way to Kyaiktiyo.

Inle, in Shan State, offers a nice variety of old Shan temples, boat tripping and relaxed evenings with nothing much to do except walking to the edge of town for a little stargazing before bed.

Sunset on picturesque Inle Lake, Shan State.

Foreign Exchange Certificates As soon as you exit the immigration checkpoint at Yangon international airport you're supposed to stop at a counter and exchange US$300 for 300 FECs – Myanmar's second legal currency. Printed in China, these Monopoly-like notes issued by the Central Bank of Myanmar 'for the convenience of tourists visiting Myanmar' come in denominations equivalent to US$1, 5, 10 and 20.

Payment for FECs is accepted in US dollars in cash form, British pounds sterling, Australian dollars, Canadian dollars, Swiss francs, French francs, German marks and Japanese yen, or in the form of travellers cheques in US dollars or British pounds only. Credit cards may also be used to purchase FECs in Yangon, but not at the airport. Note that buying FECs with travellers cheques will cost US$2 commission for each cheque exchanged. Only travellers cheques issued by the following banks are accepted in Myanmar: MasterCard, American Express (Amex), Bank of Tokyo, Citicorp, Visa, Bank of America, National Westminster Bank, First National CitiBank, Swiss Bankers and Commonwealth Bank of Australia.

One US dollar always equals one FEC; the rate for other currencies fluctuates according to dollar variance. Along with the FECs you'll also receive a Foreign Exchange Certificate Voucher, which you'll only need to save if you plan to convert more than US$300 at the official rate. Reconversion of FEC to US dollars or British pounds sterling is legal only for conversions in excess of US$300 and only when accompanied by the FEC voucher. At least that's the official story. In everyday practice you can usually exchange surplus FEC back into US dollars at hotels in Mandalay and Yangon, as long as they have enough US dollars on hand. Other currencies? Forget it. From a reader:

Keep the cleanest and crispest FECs for your departure tax. A Thai Airways International employee refused to accept one of our FEC notes because it was slightly soiled.

FECs can be spent anywhere in Myanmar. No special licence or permit is necessary for a citizen of Myanmar to accept FECs; this is not the case for US dollars. Officially approved hotel rooms, airlines, Myanma Railways (some stations) and larger souvenir shops require payment either in US dollars or FECs. So the required US$300 purchase of FECs is not something necessarily to avoid, since they can be used to pay your hotel costs.

FECs can also be exchanged for kyat – at the free-market rate – at shops or from moneychangers that accept FEC. If you run out of FECs while on the road MTT is quite happy to sell you more. FECs may also be purchased at the Central Bank of Myanmar and the Foreign Trade Bank in Yangon and at state-owned hotels.

On the other hand, FECs aren't absolutely necessary for Myanmar travel, and if you can get away without having to purchase them you might as well. The staff at the FEC exchange booth at Yangon airport will usually permit couples to exchange US$300 for both persons rather than US$300 each. Some individuals have also got away with buying less than the US$300 minimum – this usually involves the offering of a small 'present' to the staff behind the exchange counter.

This entire complicated system revolves around the desire of virtually every Burmese person – and of course the government – to get their hands on hard currency, commonly referred to as FE (foreign exchange, pronounced like one word, effee).

If, as we've heard may happen soon, the government banishes FECs and goes to a straight exchange rate, none of this will matter anymore.

US Dollars The FE most desired is the US dollar, Myanmar's third currency – and the most basic to the country's overall economy. Cash dollars can legally be used only at establishments possessing a licence to accept US dollars. In reality all merchants are happy to take them. They can also be used to exchange for kyat from licensed moneychangers or on the black market.

Exchange Rates

With the FEC system in place, it's quite rare – and plain stupid – for any foreign visitor to exchange money at the ridiculously low official exchange rate. Since it's legal for Burmese to possess FECs without any special permit (not so for US dollars, which require a licence issued by the government), the visitor no longer needs to consider the official exchange rate and can instead concentrate on getting the best free- or black-market rate.

This means the old whisky-and-cigarette scheme – buying a bottle of Johnny Walker scotch and a carton of 555s at Bangkok airport's duty-free shop to sell for free-market kyat – is no longer necessary. In fact you'll lose money if you do it! These items are usually less expensive in Yangon than in Bangkok.

One can now choose to change either FECs or US dollars for currency at the free-market rate. Shops, hotels and even permanent moneychangers make FEC exchanges quite legally. Since both FECs and kyat are legal tender for Burmese citizens as well as foreigners, it stands to reason that the currencyholder may trade back and forth.

Only foreign investors doing business in Myanmar need worry about the exchange rate – certain types of investment require a portion of the capital to be converted at official currency exchanges, though even for these the government usually compromises at a higher-than-official rate (usually somewhere around K100 to the dollar).

Where the official rate really comes into play is with regard to joint ventures between the government and foreign investors. For example, Myanma Economic Holdings Ltd, an army-owned company, can contribute 'equal' capital to a joint venture and gain 50% voting rights, while in reality investing only US$55,000 for every US$1 million contributed by the foreign investor (ie US$1 million figured at the official K5.5 rate is only worth US$55,000 in real-world, K100-to-US$1 purchasing ratios).

For the record, the official government exchange rate against the US dollar at the time of writing – established by the Myanma Foreign Trade Bank – was K6.25. Again, these rates are basically meaningless, since no visitor with any sense changes foreign currency for 'official' kyat.

The actual free-market rate, however, as posted at licensed moneychangers and bandied about among street changers, ran closer to:

country	unit		kyat
Australia	A$1	=	216
Canada	C$1	=	226
Germany	DM1	=	212
Euro	€1	=	419
France	1FF	=	64
Japan	¥100	=	294
New Zealand	NZ$1	=	183
Singapore	S$1	=	215
Thailand	1B	=	9
UK	UK£1	=	588
USA	US$1	=	340

These rates vary from day to day, sometimes by as much as K50 per dollar, so you need to keep tabs on the rate if you have enough cash on hand to wait for an optimum rate. The rate is usually best in Yangon – typically 5% to 10% higher than upcountry.

Note that it is illegal to bring kyat into the country.

Exchanging Money

FEC vs Cash US Dollars Some people claim US dollars get a slightly better free-market rate than FECs. Our experience has been that they both get similar rates; any fluctuations between the two depended on which moneychanger we dealt with – and on which day we were changing since the rates bounce up and down from week to week. On any given day, if there seemed to be a difference between the two it was only a matter of K10 to K20.

To maximise your return, though, you can always reserve FECs for hotel, train and air payments, and use US dollars to buy kyat. The rate seems to have stabilised due to the relaxation on foreign exchange holdings (caused by the introduction of FECs in early 1993) and the increase in national hard currency reserves, along with the greater influx of US dollars brought by the increasing number of tourists and foreign businesses coming into Myanmar.

When buying kyat on the free market, you'll get better rates for crisp US$100 bills than for any other denomination or currency. The next most coveted are US$50 notes, after which the rate may drop yet again – meaning in effect that there are three different free-market rates, one for bills smaller than US$50, another for US$50 and yet another for US$100.

When to Change If you're newly arrived, always ask around for the going rate before changing large amounts. It's best to ignore moneychanging touts at the airport – just use cash US dollars for the taxi ride into Yangon. Some people bring a small amount of kyat purchased from travellers or moneychangers in Bangkok, and spend a few kyat on a bus into town if they're pinching pennies. There's a slight risk here, since it's illegal to bring kyat into Myanmar, but it's very seldom that anyone is searched on entry. Once in town you can check into any hotel or guesthouse using FECs or US dollars, then ask other travellers what the current rate is.

Where to Change When you're ready to change US dollars or FECs, it's safest to change in hotels or shops rather than on the street. Official moneychanging booths on Theinbyu Lan are also good places to change, although occasionally these are closed down temporarily when the kyat-dollar rate becomes especially volatile. Unscrupulous moneychangers are very good at short-changing new arrivals for several hundred or more kyat. Always count the kyat before releasing your US dollars/FECs. And take your time counting: short-changing is all the easier with K15, K45 and K90 notes in the mix, as these are difficult for first-time visitors to add up quickly. Rumour says these odd-denominated notes may be discontinued in the near future to

make currency calculations easier – and to make the government appear more 'normal' to the outside world.

ATMs So far only one bank in Myanmar, Mayflower, operates automatic teller machines (ATMs), but these work only for cards issued on Mayflower savings or cheque accounts, and are found only in central Yangon. It's unlikely that international ATMs will be established any time soon, since this would make it somewhat easier for foreign residents and visitors to circumvent Myanmar's banking system and exchange controls. On the other hand, if the FEC/minimum exchange system is abandoned, and is accompanied by liberalised banking regulations, international ATM service can't be far behind.

Credit Cards Amex, Diners Club, Visa and JCB are the only international credit cards accepted in Myanmar, albeit at few places so far. Of these, Visa seems to be the most hassle-free. MTT accepts all four cards in payment for services purchased through its office. Air Mandalay and a handful of hotels and travel agencies in Mandalay and Yangon accept credit cards – and that's about it. The Foreign Trade Bank also accepts foreign credit cards for the purchase of FECs. Don't count on getting by with plastic money, unless you plan to spend most of your time at hotels that do accept plastic.

If the current trend towards banking modernisation continues, you can expect an increasing number of places to accept cards with every passing year. All transactions paid for with foreign credit cards in Myanmar are charged in US dollars, then converted to your home currency by the card's bank of origin.

In 1995 Myanmar Oriental Bank and Yoma Bank became the first private, Burmese-owned banks to issue credit cards. These cards charge in kyat only. Customers must deposit K100,000 to open a credit-card account at either bank.

There is an Amex agent (☎ 01-530206) at Room 6, Bldg 6, Mya Kan Thar Housing,

Mya Kan Thar Lane, Pyay Lan, Yangon. It's really only good for reporting lost or stolen Amex cards or travellers cheques. The agency is not authorised to replace lost travellers cheques, to sell you more travellers cheques, or even to change travellers cheques into cash.

Banking Myanmar now has around 20 private, locally owned banks, plus 38 foreign banks with representative offices. So far, none of the latter are permitted to handle foreign currencies.

Of the private Burmese-owned banks, only Cooperative Bank, Mayflower Bank, Myanmar Industrial Development Bank, Myanmar Citizen Bank, Myanmar Livestock & Fisheries Bank, Myawaddy Bank, Yangon City Bank, Yoma Bank and Yadanabon Bank are currently permitted to manage US dollar accounts. Mayflower appears to be the best managed and most service-oriented. There is a 10% 'tax' (actually a conversion to kyat at the piddling official rate) on such accounts.

Security

Give some thought in advance as to how you're going to organise your finances – whether travellers cheques, cash, credit and debit cards, or some combination of these. Many travellers favour hidden pouches that can be worn beneath clothing. Hip-pocket wallets are easy marks for thieves. Pickpockets work markets and crowded buses throughout the country, so it pays to keep your money concealed. See Dangers & Annoyances later in this chapter for more on petty crime.

It's a good idea not to keep all your money in one place; keep an emergency stash well concealed in a piece of luggage separate from other money.

Costs

Travel in Myanmar today is cheaper than it's been at any time since before the 1988-89 disturbances. Costs depend largely on where you decide to go and in which hotels you choose to stay. Generally speaking, the farther off the beaten track you go, the cheaper (and let's face it, the more uncomfortable) travel becomes.

If you take a package tour or stay in any of the few remaining state-owned hotels, costs are certainly high by South-East Asian standards, especially considering the overall low quality of tourist facilities Myanmar has to offer.

Goods and services may be priced either in kyat or in US dollars/FECs. Hotel rooms, some train tickets, air tickets, car rental and guide services are generally priced in US dollars/FECs – for some of these services, US dollars/FECs may be the only currencies accepted. Duty-free items at the airport and at the Yangon Duty Free Store are also priced in US dollars/FECs. Food, taxis, buses and just about everything else in Myanmar are priced in kyat. In keeping with this two currency system, prices in this guidebook are quoted in either US dollars or kyat; any time US dollars are quoted, FECs are equally acceptable.

Daily Expenses Over the last few years inflation in Myanmar has been high. Many costs – especially for state-owned tourist hotels – have shot up since the 1989 reopening. On the other hand, meals are very cheap if paid for with free-market kyat – US$4 or US$5 worth of free-market kyat per day will more than suffice for food.

Now that the hotel industry has been privatised, it's possible to get rooms in well touristed areas of Myanmar for as low as US$5 per person per night. For shoestring travellers, this is high compared with Thailand and Indonesia, but about the same as in Laos and Vietnam. Virtually all hotels licensed to accept foreigners accept only US dollars or FECs for room payments. A few hotels here and there charge mixed rates for which you may pay a certain portion of the rate in US dollars/FECs and the remainder in free-market kyat. And in very out-of-the-way places you can even pay entirely in kyat, which can bring room rates down to as low as K200 per person (less than US$1).

Most hotels and larger tourist restaurants add a 10% hotel and restaurant tax plus a

10% service charge to the bill. See the Accommodation section later in this chapter for details on potential ways to bring room costs down.

Except for those transport services monopolised by MTT (notably tickets for the Yangon-Mandalay express train and Mandalay-Bagan express boat), public ground transport is inexpensive and so slow that you're unlikely to be able to spend more than US$5 a day on long-distance movement. Using domestic air transportation speeds things up considerably but averages US$50 to US$160 per flight.

Although it's difficult to pin down a one figure travel budget due to all the variables in the equation – particularly whether or not your desired itinerary requires hiring a guide – you can expect to spend a rock-bottom minimum of about US$10 a day. This assumes always taking the cheapest room available, using public ground transport (avoiding the Yangon-Mandalay express train and Mandalay-Bagan express boat), never using the services of a guide, staying clear of places that require buying package tours, and eating in local restaurants and teashops rather than hotel restaurants or places geared to foreign tourists.

A comfortable budget for those seeking the extra convenience of a private, rather than shared, bathroom, the occasional use of a freelance guide (but not a package) and a broader range of restaurant choices, would be around US$25 to US$30 a day. Taking express ground transport and flying a couple of domestic air routes might add another US$5 or US$7 per person per day for anyone staying the full 28 day period permitted under the current tourist visa regulations.

Moving farther upmarket you could easily spend US$25 to US$50 per day on the more well appointed hotels and guesthouses – and in Yangon there are an increasing number of US$75 to US$125 a night places. And for ultra-luxury, there's always The Strand, where rooms start at over US$300 a night and restaurant main dishes cost US$8 to US$16.

Locally purchased travel packages that include guide services, accommodation and meals cost a minimum of US$25 per person a day, or as much as US$100 a day for more deluxe tours.

Inflation It's important to remember that Myanmar has an annual inflation rate of about 50%, so any prices quoted in this book will probably need to be adjusted accordingly. One of the easiest and most accurate ways to calculate overall price increases is to check the price of a cup of tea in a typical Burmese teashop – such prices are more or less standard throughout urban Myanmar. In 1994, for example, you could sip a cup of tea for K6; a year later a sip at the same teashop cost K8. At the time of writing, the same cup of tea had increased to K25. If this formula holds, a cup in mid-2000 will cost about K38. A trishaw ride cited in this guidebook as costing K300 would have increased to around K500 – and so on.

Tipping & Bribes

Tipping as known in the west is not customary in Myanmar. However, minor bribes – called presents in Burmese-English (as in 'Do you have a present for me?') – are part of everyday life and can be seen as the moral equivalent of tipping, except that the range of services covered differs completely. Much as tips are expected for a taxi ride or a restaurant meal in the west, extra compensation is expected for the efficient completion of many standard bureaucratic services. A visa extension or customs inspection will move a little more quickly if a present – a little cash, a package of cigarettes, a tube of lipstick, a ballpoint pen – is offered along with whatever is the regular fee. T-shirts and up-to-date western calendars – basically anything that can be resold for cash – will work minor miracles.

If a Myanma Airways (MA) flight is 'sold out', a whole carton of cigarettes or bottle of liquor – or the equivalent in cash (about US$10) – might buy a seat. Want to ride in the front seat of a passenger pickup truck instead of crammed in the back? Add 30% to 50% of the regular passenger fare. In some cases a present may be requested for no special service at all – just to get a government worker to do his or her job. Some visitors refuse to pay in such cases, though from the Burmese perspective you're liable for the unwritten 'leisure class tax' because of your relative wealth. You may have earned your meagre travel budget washing dishes at the dingiest dive in London, but to the Burmese your presence in Myanmar automatically means you're well-off. The same happens to Burmese of obvious means, so it's not always a case of 'foreigners pay more'. The major exception is when it comes to hotels and plane or train transport, where foreigners really get soaked relative to what locals pay.

No matter how this system might bruise your sensibilities, you probably won't get through a Myanmar trip without paying at least a couple of minor bribes – even if you're not aware you've paid.

Taxes & Refunds

Other than the 10% hotel tax, there are no consumer taxes in Myanmar. Companies based in Myanmar are taxed at a flat 30% of adjusted gross income while branches of companies based outside Myanmar are exposed to a sliding scale of 5% to 40% depending on income. Capital gains are taxed at 10% for resident firms, 40% for non-resident firms. Import taxes vary from 0% to 25%. None of these taxes are refundable.

POST & COMMUNICATIONS
Post

Surprisingly perhaps, most mail out of Myanmar seems to get to its destination quite efficiently. Or at least we think so: a number of letter writers either agreed that everything they sent arrived OK (even from upcountry) or totally disagreed, saying that nothing at all arrived.

International postage rates are a bargain K32 per letter to anywhere in the world. For registered mail anywhere in the world add K50. There is a free poste-restante service on the 2nd floor of the main post office in Yangon.

Officially post offices all over Myanmar

are supposed to be open Monday to Friday from 9.30 am to 4 pm, but in reality, the staff open and close when they feel like it. As a general rule of thumb, the smaller the town, the more the post office deviates from the official schedule. Yangon's main post office keeps fairly rigorous hours; elsewhere it's often difficult to get any kind of service after 3.30 pm. In some places it's worse than that; the post office in Kawthoung appears to stay open only an hour or so in the morning, regardless of advertised hours. Most likely the staff are out trying to earn some real money!

Embassies in Yangon recommend that if you are sending any important correspondence in or out of Myanmar you should send it by air freight rather than trust the mail. DHL Worldwide Express (☎ 01-664423) has an office at 7 (A), Kaba Aye Paya Lan, plus an office in Mandalay (☎ 02-39274). ASAP Express Services (☎ 01-228468) is at 82 8 Lan in Yangon. For larger air or sea freight shipments, Express Air & Sea Transportation Co (EAST; ☎ 01-667057, fax 666364) at 14 A-1 Lane, A-1 Compound, Mile 9, Pyay Lan, is recommended.

Telephone

Domestic Calling other places in Myanmar is relatively simple and very inexpensive from the Central Telephone & Telegraph (CTT) office on the corner of Pansodan and Mahabandoola Lans in Yangon. Only larger cities with area codes can be direct-dialled. Smaller towns still use manual switchboards, so you must ask the national operator to connect you to a specific town operator, then request the local number. These numbers are usually listed with the name of the town. The telephone number for the Inle Inn in Nyaungshwe, eg is 'Nyaungshwe 16' – which means you must first be connected with the operator in Nyaungshwe, then ask for the number 16.

Government-regulated mobile cellular phone service is available, but costs – billed in US dollars only – are quite high compared to elsewhere in the world. All cellphone (or hand phone) numbers begin with the code 09.

Area Codes

The country code for Myanmar is ☎ 95; the area code for Yangon is ☎ 01, for Mandalay ☎ 02. You need to dial the zero when calling from within Myanmar. Other cities with area codes include:

Aungban	☎ 081
Bagan	☎ 062
Bago	☎ 052
Chauk	☎ 061
Dawei	☎ 036
Heho	☎ 081
Hinthada	☎ 044
Hpa-an	☎ 035
Kalaw	☎ 081
Kyaukse	☎ 066
Lashio	☎ 082
Loikaw	☎ 083
Magwe	☎ 063
Mawlamyaing	☎ 032
Meiktila	☎ 064
Minbu	☎ 065
Monywa	☎ 071
Myeik	☎ 021
Myingyan	☎ 066
Myitkyina	☎ 074
Nyaungshwe	☎ 081
Pakokku	☎ 062
Pathein	☎ 042
Pyay	☎ 053
Pyinmana	☎ 067
Pyin U Lwin	☎ 085
Sagaing	☎ 072
Sittwe	☎ 043
Taunggyi	☎ 081
Taungoo	☎ 054
Thanlyin	☎ 065

International There are two ways to make an international call. The fast and expensive way is to use an International Direct Dial (IDD) phone, available in certain hotels in Yangon, Mandalay and Bagan. Calls are charged by the minute, usually at about US$12 to anywhere outside of Asia.

The cheaper way to arrange international telephone calls is at the main telephone office described previously. International calls (or trunk calls) are charged by three-minute blocks; if you stay on the line for less than three minutes you still pay the full three minute charge. If you want to talk longer than three minutes, you must start all over again for each additional three minute block.

You may have to wait for up to half an hour for a line. In Mandalay it's often one or two hours. The Yangon phone office is open Monday to Friday from 8 am to 4 pm, weekends and holidays from 9 am to 2 pm. A similar office is found in Mandalay and other larger cities such as Pathein and Mawlamyaing.

Additionally in Yangon, several central shops, as well as many small hotels, are able to book trunk calls for you while you wait – usually from 10 to 30 minutes. Rates average less than US$1 a minute.

The number of hotels that furnish IDD phones is increasing rather quickly, especially in Yangon and Mandalay. Most mid-range hotels and even some budget guest-houses have IDD service available near reception. The larger Yangon hotels – The Strand, Traders and Equatorial, for example – feature in-room IDD phones, as well as small business centres where guests may make international calls. All add steep service charges onto the regular phone company rates. The Strand permits nonguests to use its business centre, which is open 24 hours, but calls are highly surcharged. Waiting is the norm even at the hotels, since not more than one IDD line is usually available.

Fax

You can also make surcharged phone and fax calls at the International Business Centre (☎ 01-667133) at 88 Pyay Lan (Mile 6½). Sponsored by the Ministry of Forestry, the International Business Centre has a range of secretarial and business services in addition to basic telecommunications. Fax machines are also available at the Central Telephone & Telegraph (CTT) office, and many hotels.

Note that if you bring your own fax machine to Myanmar, or purchase one in Yangon or Mandalay to use there, you're supposed to register the machine with the government. Few people do, although a high profile Yangon resident who donated money to Aung San Suu Kyi was jailed for owning an unlicensed fax machine a few years ago; he later died in prison while serving a sentence for this 'crime'. The International Business Centre can help with registration, or contact the CTT office in Yangon. Note that if you arrive from overseas with a fax machine and a tourist visa, you will certainly be questioned about your intentions.

Email & Internet Access
At the moment, logging onto the Internet from Myanmar is illegal, so there are no Internet Service Providers (ISPs) as yet in the country. The government does provide an email service, which costs a very steep US$150 to set up, plus US$150 annual dues, plus US$1 per kilobyte for each message sent or received. No other service provider is permitted to set up email services, so it's unlikely prices will be dropping any time soon. The government has plans to offer Internet access eventually – probably a heavily screened access of the type officially available in China. Check myanmars.net (www.myanmars.net/myanmar/internet.htm) for the latest. Rates for Internet access via the planned government service have been quoted as US$200 for the initial set-up, plus US$80 per month and a 300kb email limit, in and out; for further info, check www.datserco.com.mm.

Some foreign residents with IDD phones and computer modems access the Net via long-distance calls to Bangkok, at a cost of around US$2.67 per minute – rather steep yet obviously less expensive than the official government service, even if all you're doing is email. The most popular and reliable service out of Thailand at the moment is LoxInfo, based in Bangkok but with 16 local access phone numbers around the country. From a private IDD phone in Myanmar, calls to Bangkok aren't terribly expensive especially if compared to the government alternative. For more information on LoxInfo, log onto its Web site, www.loxinfo.co.th. Temporary accounts may be purchased.

Technically all modems (like all fax machines) are supposed to be registered with the government. In everyday practice only those connected to the government email service are so registered.

INTERNET RESOURCES
For a country that receives fewer than 200,000 visitors per year, Myanmar has a surprising number of Internet sites carrying information on the country. A major problem with most of them is that they tend to represent narrow perspectives. Those attached to Nongovernmental Organisations (NGOs) lobbying for human rights, for example, paint an extremely one-sided, mostly negative picture of the country, while those associated with business or tourism go to the other extreme, imbuing everything in Myanmar with a rosy glow.

One of the best Web sites we've seen – simply because it carries so many links to other Myanmar-related sites and most of all because it's a searchable site – is called Gateway to the Myanmar-Burmese Community (www.shweinc.com/). The copious data on geography, travel, business, history, politics, computers (including hard-to-find, in-country info) and current Myanmar news found on this site is also unique in that it presents several different perspectives on the country, from gung-ho investment news to human rights reports.

Naturally the Myanmar government has its own site, called Myanmar Home Page (www.myanmar.com/), which, despite all the expected government propaganda, contains some hard info on travel and country statistics.

For up-to-date visa information, check www.travisa.com/Myanmar/Myaninst.htm or www.travelfinder.com/visareq/Myanmar (Burma).html.

Human Rights Issues
Of the many NGOs featuring Myanmar pages, the most interesting are Free Burma

(sunsite.unc.edu/freeburma/index.html) and The Burma Project (www.soros.org/burma .html). The fact that neither of these sites uses the United Nations (UN)- and Amnesty International (AI)-accepted (and oldest) name for the country, Myanmar, tells you something about their bias. The Burma Project – sponsored by George Soros' Open Society Institute – goes so far as to list the Embassy of Myanmar as 'Embassy of the SLORC' (State Law & Order Restoration Council). These sites will give you an idea of the mountain of information available out there regarding human rights in Myanmar. Both sites are openly dedicated to bringing down the current regime in Myanmar and stopping all foreign investment and tourism, at any cost. Addresses for many known rebel groups are included. Contact information for AI, oddly, is missing.

Although Myanmar may very well be the most well documented country in the world when it comes to human rights issues, few reports carried on these sites contain independently verified information. Many features, facts and interpretations – particularly on the Free Burma site – are in fact sourced from Burmese refugees living abroad. This does not mean that the reports are false or even exaggerated, it just means that for now most of it must be classified as anecdotal – much like socio-political portraits of Cuba painted by Cuban exiles living in Miami. Both sites mix in occasional mainstream news items from Reuters, Associated Press and so on.

Other sites with human rights info include pages managed by AI (www.amnesty .org/) and the US State Department (www .state.gov/www/global/human_rights/1998 _hrp_report/burma.html).

BOOKS & PERIODICALS
Lonely Planet
In addition to this guidebook, Lonely Planet publishes the *Burmese phrasebook* by David Bradley, a pocket-sized primer to the majority language in Myanmar. For more, see the Language chapter at the end of this book.

Caring for Your Elephant

One of my favourite Burmese books is *Burmese Timber Elephant* by U Toke Gale. It could be subtitled 'selection, care and use of your pet elephant', for it tells you everything you need to know and many things you don't need to know about timber elephants. Even what to do with your elephant when he's in *musth*. There's a chart showing the 90 nerve centres to which an *oozi* applies pressure to control his elephant or to get it to do things. But don't press 13, 25, 60, 61 or 63, for 'the animal will be infuriated'!

Tony Wheeler

Description & Travel
Old Burma: As Described by Early Foreign Travellers, published by the University of Rangoon in 1947, collects together the writings of the first Europeans to visit Myanmar, beginning with Marco Polo. Polo may have relied upon second-hand accounts rather than personal experience to describe the country he knew as 'Mien', a Chinese shortening of 'Myan-ma', in the 14th century. *Old Burma* ends with Captain Symes' stay in the court of Ava in 1795. Packed with historical trivia not found in any other single volume, this little book is out of print and difficult to find. Similar is Gerry Abbott's newer *The Traveller's History of Burma* (Orchid Press, Bangkok), which also compiles and condenses the chronicles of early European travellers in Myanmar. In this case Abbot uses the quotations of traders, priests and explorers to build a history of Myanmar from 1364 Bago to independence in 1948.

Originally published in 1954 by the Burma Oil Co, and revised for the fifth and final time in 1962, the hard-to-find *Motor Roads of Burma* contains information on motor routes all over the country, from roads still used today, such as Kyauk Padaung-Meiktila, to roads that are now seldom used (eg, the Stilwell Road to India).

Although conditions have obviously changed since the book's publication, certain details, such as road distances, have not. Many of the so-called 'circuit houses' described in the book still exist as government or private guesthouses.

Tim Slessor's *First Overland* recounts the journey from London to Singapore made by two Oxford and Cambridge University-crewed Land Rovers in 1956, which saw them travelling the Stilwell Road.

Historical guidebook collectors might also keep an eye out for *A Pocket Guide to Burma*, a tiny 56 page booklet distributed to British soldiers at the close of WWII, or the Burmese-produced *A Handbook on Burma* from 1968. The latter is an interesting read if for no other reason than to compare the country then with the country today. A fold-out colour map in the back of the book shows the political divisions of the time; the Kayin State is called Kawthoolei, the name the Kayin (Karen) themselves tend to call their territory. All of the current divisions (Mandalay Division, Bago Division etc) are lumped into one 'Union of Burma' – proving the point made by the frontier ethnicities that their autonomy has eroded since independence. Another rarity is *Travellers' Guide to Burma* by Kanbawza Win, published by the YMCA in Yangon in 1977 and banned by the government shortly thereafter.

Golden Earth by Norman Lewis, originally written in 1952, is a delightful tale of a ramble around Myanmar at a time when it was both more, and less, open than it is today. At that time the varied rebellions were in full swing, but Myanmar had not yet entered its reclusive period. Much of the book sounds remarkably like Myanmar today, and the author's descriptions of Myanmar's often antiquated trucks have the real ring of truth – no photograph could do a better job of summing up these miracles of mechanical endurance.

Paul Theroux's amusing and cynical bestseller, *The Great Railway Bazaar*, includes chapters on the train trip from Yangon to Mandalay, and from Mandalay to Pyin U Lwin – with a perfect description of Candacraig, and his amusing visit to 'forbidden' Gokteik. Another witty account of pre-1988, seven day-visa Myanmar is found in the essay 'The Raj is Dead! Long Live the Raj!' in Pico Iyer's book *Video Night in Kathmandu*.

Rory Maclean's *Under the Dragon* is a semi-fictional and somewhat over-dramatised account of his travels in the Shan State in search of a Palaung basket, set against descriptions of life in 1990s Myanmar.

History & Politics

GE Harvey's *History of Burma* (1925) remains the classic work, although parts are naturally out of date from today's historiographical perspective. Maurice Collis, a former British civil servant stationed in Burma in the early 20th century, wrote several books chronicling particular episodes in Burma's colonial and pre-colonial history. Perhaps Collis' best books were *Siamese White,* an account of Samuel White's pernicious sojourn as harbourmaster of 17th century Mergui (now Myeik), and the harder-to-find *The Land of the Great Image,* which follows the remarkable adventures of Friar Manrique, a Portuguese Franciscan monk in 17th century Arakan (Rakhaing).

Burma by FSV Donnison gives a concise and very readable history of Myanmar from its earliest development through the British period and into the troubled 1960s. There are also chapters on the country's economy and culture. *The Union of Burma* by Hugh Tinker is a scholarly study of the path to independence in Myanmar and the difficult U Nu period. Frank N Trager's *Burma: From Kingdom to Independence* is an equally scholarly account of this same period and its particular ramifications for Asia.

Recommended French-written histories include *La Birmanie* by Guy Lubeigh and *Birmanie* by E Guillon and C Delachet.

There are other more recent accounts of earlier Burmese history, such as *The Pagoda Wars* by ATQ Stewart, which covers the British takeover of Myanmar.

A number of books concern the dramatic events in Myanmar during WWII, particularly the behind-enemy-lines actions of Wingate's 'Chindit' forces. Find a complete description of their activities in *The Chindits* by Michael Calvert, or read Bernard Fergusson's more personal accounts in *The Wild Green Earth* or *Beyond the Chindwin*. Fergusson's more recent *Return to Burma* provides an account of the author's postwar travels in Myanmar.

A French book, *Les Lautu-L'Organisation Sociale d'une Ethnie Chin de Haute-Birmanie* by André Bereigts, contains a contemporary description of Chin society and culture.

Essays on the History and Buddhism of Burma by Than Tun (Kiscadale Publications) covers a range of social, religious, political and economic topics within the Burmese context.

Anyone interested in colonial Myanmar's steamer era should read *Irrawaddy Flotilla* by Alister McCrae and Alan Prentice (James Paton), a history of the river fleet established by the British and still running today under the auspices of state-owned Inland Water Transport (IWT). Although the title is out-of-print outside Myanmar, re-prints are available in Yangon.

Two books by Myanmar expert David I Steinberg provide what is probably the most complete sociopolitical look at Myanmar between 1962 and 1988. *Burma: A Socialist Nation of Southeast Asia* (Westview Press, Boulder, Colorado) contains an overview of Burmese history, geography, ethnicity, politics and economics, while *Burma's Road Toward Development: Growth & Ideology Under Military Rule* (Westview Press) is a history of the country since 1962, when Ne Win took power.

Myanmar-watcher Martin Smith is without peer when it comes to understanding the country's political situation, and his *Burma – Insurgency & the Politics of Ethnicity* (Zed Press, London) contains an extremely well researched history and analysis of insurgent politics in Myanmar from the 1940s through to 1988. *Burma's Golden Triangle: On the Trail of the Opium Warlords* by André & Louis Boucaud (Asia

Books; or in the French, *Birmanie-Sur la Piste des Seigneurs de la Guerre*, L'Harmattan) presents a collection of accounts detailing the Boucaud brothers' travels in insurgent Myanmar in the 1970s and 1980s, along with some more recently updated material. Although it's sometimes difficult to tell which era is being covered, the book is an entertaining read.

Other French literature worth reading in this vein includes two books by Martial Dasse – *La Face Politique Cachée de la Thailande* and *Montagnards, Revoltes et Guerres Revolutionaires en Asie du Sud-Est Continentale*, both published by Duang Kamol, Bangkok. Another good one on insurgent Myanmar is *La Birmanie où la Quête de l'Unité* by Pierre Fistie (Ecole Francaise d'Extrême Orient).

Outrage: Burma's Struggle for Democracy by Bangkok journalist Bertil Lintner (White Lotus, London and Bangkok) chronicles the violent suppression of Myanmar's pro-democracy movement from 1987 to 1990, with particular focus on the events of 1988. It's a somewhat polemic, onesided look at the student uprisings, but basically it's very informative. Lintner's *Land of Jade* by the same publisher describes a fascinating overland journey he and his Shan wife made through insurgent territories in northern Myanmar in 1985. The reporter's third book-length outing, *Burma In Revolt: Opium and Insurgency Since 1948* (Westview Press), discusses the relationship between opium production and insurgency among the Shan, Kayah, Pa-O, Mon, Lahu and Wa.

Edith Mirante's *Burmese Looking Glass* follows similar political terrain in yet another mid-1980s first-person account featuring the ethnic rebel as noble savage. Among her many brief adventures, the author teaches Mon women to kill using ballpoints and flashlights as weapons.

True Love and Bartholomew: Rebels on the Burmese Border was written by Jonathan Falla, a nurse who worked in the KNU-controlled part of Kayin State during the 1980s. His accounts of Kayin society and the culture of insurgency form an important contribution to the literature on these topics.

Freedom from Fear & Other Writings presents a sometimes brilliant collection of essays by and about Nobel Peace Prize winner Aung San Suu Kyi. She has also published an account of her father titled *Aung San of Burma* and the hard-to-find *Let's Visit Burma* (Burke Publishing), a thin children's guide to the country. A chapter in the latter, 'My Country and People', is an excellent encapsulation of Burmese culture.

In *Dancing in Cambodia, At Large in Burma* (Ravi Dayal, New Delhi), postcolonial scholar Amitav Ghosh impresses with the length and breadth of his travels in contemporary Myanmar and his knowledge of opposition politics.

People, Culture & Society

Anyone interested in quickly obtaining a broad understanding of Burmese customs and etiquette should pick up a copy of *Culture Shock! Burma* by Saw Myat Yin (Times Editions, Singapore). One of the few titles in the *Culture Shock* series to have been written by a local, this book simply and accurately explains male and female roles, business protocol, common Burmese ceremonies and festivals, the naming system, how to extend and accept invitations, and even how Burmese perceive westerners.

Mi Mi Khaing's *Burmese Family*, though first published in 1946 by Longman, remains one of the best references on traditional Burmese customs and values. A blend of amateur sociology and personal memoirs, this book is available in reprinted form in Yangon and Bangkok.

The Thirty-Seven Nats by Sir RC Temple, originally published in 1906 by Griggs in London, has been redone in a beautiful colour edition by Kiscadale Publications. Though it costs an astounding US$180, it's still the most venerable description of the Burmese *nat* (spirit) cult available and the colour plates provide artists' renderings of each of the 37 nats. If you read French, an even more informative book on the nat cult

is *Rites et Possesions en Birmanie*, by Benedicte Brac de la Perriere. This contains detailed descriptions of *nat pwes* (ritualised dance-drama performance) and other spirit ceremonies. *Nat-Pwe: Burma's Supernatural Sub-Culture* by Yves Rodrigue sheds further light on this fascinating topic and includes reproductions of the same colour plates that appear in *The Thirty-Seven Nats*.

Other notable books from Kiscadale include a new edition of *The Burman: His Life and Notions*, a fascinating collection of essays by Shway Yoe, the pseudonym of Sir JG Scott, a colonial official and specialist in Burmese botany, linguistics and archaeology. In his many years in Myanmar, Scott acquired an extraordinary knowledge about every aspect of the country. Kiscadale has also republished *The Silken East: A Record of Life and Travel in Burma*, a chronicle of travels along the Chindwin, Ayeyarwady and Thanlwin (Salween) rivers early in the 20th century by VC Scott O'Connor. Kiscadale, incidentally, devotes itself to Myanmar-related topics; for a catalogue write to Kiscadale Publications, Murray House, Gartmore, Stirling FK8 3RJ, UK.

The Soul of a People by H Fielding was an 1898 attempt to understand the Burmese. *Thibaw's Queen*, by the same author in 1899, is a romanticised story of the collapse of the final Burmese kingdom before British imperial might. It has been republished in Myanmar by the Buddha Sasana Council and is easily found.

For those interested in the Shan State or the Shan people, a mandatory read is Inge Sargent's *Twilight Over Burma: My Life as a Shan Princess*. It's about an Austrian woman who marries Sao Kya Seng, the last *sawbwa* (hereditary Shan chieftain) of Hsipaw, who was arrested in 1962 and never heard from again. Like this guidebook, it's banned in Myanmar.

Somewhere in Myanmar, you may come across a mouldy 1922 booklet on elephant lore entitled *A Short Treatise on the Management of Elephants* by AJW Milroy, deputy conservator of forests for the Raj.

Towards the end of WWII Longman published a series of booklets about Myanmar known as *Burma Pamphlets*. You may see some of these long-since out-of-print books on culture and customs in Myanmar; they make interesting reading.

Bamar culture as it relates to religion is well covered in *Folk Elements in Burmese Buddhism* by Maung Htin Aung (Department of Religious Affairs, 1959), reprints of which are easy to find in Yangon since it's a standard exam text for Burmese students. The book most accurately describes what occurs in villages along the Yangon-Mandalay axis and as far north as Monywa and Shwebo only; customs in outer Myanmar – even in the predominantly Buddhist Shan, Rakhaing, and Mon states – differ greatly. *Burmese Supernaturalism* by Melford Spiro contains decent explanations of nat worship as well as certain Burmese Buddhist themes.

The Vanishing Tribes of Burma, by Richard K Diran, is a remarkable photographic documentation of 28 different ethnic minorities in Myanmar, including several never before recorded on film. Although this represents only around a quarter of the ethnicities found in Myanmar today, it's nonetheless an important contribution to the visual literature on the nation's multicultural milieu.

On the Road to Mandalay, edited and translated by Mya Than Tint (White Orchid, Bangkok), is a Studs Terkel-inspired collection of recent interviews with ordinary Burmese – an elephant *oozi* (handler), a miner, a fortune-teller, a waitress etc – in which they describe their lives, loves, hopes and dreams.

For gourmets and cooking enthusiasts, *Cook & Entertain the Burmese Way* (Myawaddy Press) by Mi Mi Khaing makes interesting reading. This volume contains a wealth of information on preparing, serving and eating Burmese food in the correct style, and includes instructions on how to mix Burmese salads by hand, recipes for 'salivators and tongue titillators', and a very useful appendix that lists fruits, vegetables, spices and fish with their Burmese and English names. It's available at bookshops in Yangon and at tourist hotels throughout the country. A slicker tome, *Under the Golden Pagoda: The Best of Burmese Cooking* by Aung Aung Taik (Chronicle Books, San Francisco), covers much the same territory.

Art, Archaeology & Design

Myanmar Style: Art, Architecture & Design of Burma by John Falconer et al pulls together many elements of Burmese art and design never seen in one volume before. Luscious photos by Luca Tettoni archive, for the first time in print, both contemporary and historical architecture, along with ritual objects, traditional crafts and everyday items such as patent medicine containers and children's toys.

The slim *Kalagas: The Wall Hangings of Southeast Asia* (Ainslie's, Menlo Park, California) by Mary Anne Stanislaw contains photographs and descriptions of the Burmese *kalaga* (tapestry) craft. Sylvia Fraser-Lu's *Burmese Crafts, Past and Present* is currently the most comprehensive volume covering handicrafts in Myanmar.

Burmese Art, written by John Lowry and published by the Victoria & Albert Museum, presents a detailed discussion of nonarchitectural art in Central and Upper Myanmar from the early Bagan through Mandalay period. It's illustrated with 50 black & white photos of works in the museum's Burmese collection.

If you'd like to know a lot more about Shwedagon Paya then get a copy of *Shwedagon* by Win Pe (Printing & Publishing Corporation, Yangon). You might find it in street bookstalls or at the Bagan Bookshop in Yangon.

Several books offer histories and descriptions of the temple architecture at Bagan. The older *Pictorial Guide to Pagan* (Ministry of Culture, Yangon) contains illustrated descriptions of many of the important Bagan buildings plus a map inside the back cover. It's a useful book that you'll find fairly easily in Myanmar. The 1986 release, *Glimpses of Glorious Pagan* by the University of Yangon's history department, is basically an update of the earlier book. *Pagodas of Pagan* (Buddha Sasana Council Press) is also quite readily available, but not so detailed or interesting. Another good general guide is *Pagan: Art and Architecture of Old Burma* by Paul Strachan (Kiscadale). This modern art history of Bagan monuments is available at larger hotels in Yangon, and costs around US$50 hardcover or US$25 softcover.

If you're really serious about studying the monuments of Bagan, don't need any accompanying art history and can afford US$130 per volume, look for the six volume *Inventory of Monuments at Pagan* (Weatherhill) by French archaeologist Pierre Pichard. Basically what you get for your investment is a set of monocolour diagrams. Pichard spent several years living in Bagan during the 1980s compiling this series. A softcover version collecting 302 diagrams in the series is available as *Inventory of Monuments at Pagan: Monuments 1137-1439* for a mere US$160. If you're too cheap to afford that trifle, look for the Department of Archaeology's own two volume *Inventory of Ancient Monuments in Bagan* (Ministry of Culture, Yangon), which uses Pichard's diagrams but adds a colour photo to accompany each and every diagram – at a cost of US$30 per volume. The latter two volume set is generally available only in Myanmar.

It is very difficult to find any material on historical places other than the straightforward Yangon-Mandalay-Bagan triangle. *Historical Sites in Burma* by Aung Thaw (Ministry of Union Culture) is an excellent illustrated description of the major buildings at Bagan, Bago, Yangon, Amarapura, Ava, Sagaing, Mingun, Mandalay and a number of other historical spots. It can be found at Yangon's Bagan Bookshop or in Bagan.

Historic Sites & Monuments of Mandalay & Environs by U Lu Pe Win (Buddha Sasana Council Press) is fairly easy to come across and describes the ancient cities around Mandalay: Ava, Sagaing, Amarapura and Mingun.

One of the few books available with any information at all about archaeological sites other than Bagan or Mandalay is *A Guide to Mrauk U* by Tun Shwe Khine (Sittway Degree College). Available only in Yangon and Sittwe, it contains detailed descriptions and floor plans of the impressive Mrauk U monuments.

Theatre & Dance-Drama

Aung San Suu Kyi's former secretary Ma Thanegi has published an informative volume on marionette theatre called *Burmese Puppets* (White Orchid, Bangkok). Around Yangon you may come across reprints of the dryly written *Burmese Drama* by Maung Htin Aung, originally published by Oxford University Press, India, in 1937.

Burmese Dance and Theatre (Oxford University Press, Kuala Lumpur) by Noel F Singer is a small but well illustrated volume covering the history of Burmese theatre right up into the early 1990s. About the only other printed resource to cover this territory is the out of print *Burmese Drama: A Study, with Translation, of Burmese Plays* (Oxford University Press, Calcutta, 1937) by Maung Htin Aung.

Novels, Short Stories & Poetry

Quite a few writers set novels in Myanmar, the most famous, of course, being George Orwell's *Burmese Days* (1934). It makes an engrossing, if slightly depressing, read on upcountry Myanmar in the British days. Orwell served with the British colonial police in Myanmar and his novel exhibits a strong grasp of expat life.

Michio Takeyama's *Harp of Burma*, first published in Japanese in 1949, then in English in 1966, novelises the desertion of a Japanese soldier in Myanmar during WWII.

In 1983 Burmese author Wendy Law-Yone published *The Coffin Tree*, a well written, sensuous novel that follows the young female narrator on a cultural journey back and forth between the USA and Myanmar some time after the 1962 military coup. Law-Yone updated Burmese political themes and turned up the heat for her novel *Irrawaddy*

Tango, in which the fictional country Daya stands in for Myanmar and a dictator's mistress turns rebel assassin. Set in colonial times, *John Dollar* by Marianne Wiggins is a riveting, haunting tale about another journey that a young woman makes to Myanmar. It recounts the English schoolteacher's experiences in the tight-knit British community in Yangon as well as an exciting death-and-survival adventure on the high seas.

For a taste of Burmese verse, try *Modern Burmese Poetry* (Thawda Press, Yangon), translated by Richard Win Pe and readily available in Yangon bookshops.

One chapter in *A Traveller's Literary Companion to South-East Asia* contains excerpted material from a number of works by foreign and Burmese writers on Myanmar, and includes an account of Orwell's sojourn in the country. The chapter editor, Anna Allott, also translated and edited *Inked Over, Ripped Out* (Silkworm Press, Chiang Mai), which highlights the restrictions faced by Burmese writers in the 1990s, and contains a number of censored and uncensored Burmese short stories from the SLORC period.

Magazine Articles

National Geographic has done a number of features about Myanmar. The November 1940 issue featured an article called 'Burma Road, Back Door to China', which chronicled a trip through Hsipaw, Lashio and other places in northern Shan State to China. The February 1963 issue covered Myanmar as a whole; March 1971 was about Bagan; June 1974 had an article on the Inle leg rowers; while in the June 1979 issue there was an article about the long-necked Padaung women – revealing that they're actually not long-necked at all – the heavy coils they wear around their necks actually push their shoulder blades and collar bones down, rather than extend their necks. Myanmar featured once again in July 1984, in a general article where it emerges that even *National Geographic* writers couldn't wangle more than a seven day visa. Myanmar's latest *National Geographic* appearance occurred in the July 1995 issue,

wherein the author excoriated the military regime in one of the most political articles the magazine has ever published.

Probably the best writing on Myanmar ever to appear in a mainstream magazine was a piece by Amitav Ghosh in the 12 August 1996 issue of the *New Yorker*. The long article not only encapsulates Myanmar exceedingly well, it was the first article published in the west in the 1990s to question opposition politics.

Archaeology magazine ran an inspiring article on the archaeological significance of Bagan, 'The Power of Pagan', in its September/October 1992 issue.

Stan Sesser's detailed 22 page assessment of the country appeared in the 9 October 1989 issue of the *New Yorker* and was reprinted in Sesser's book *Lands of Charm & Cruelty* (1994). Joe Cummings, co-author of this guidebook, published an article about black-market moneychanging in Myanmar called 'For a Few Kyats More' in *Outside* magazine, September 1994.

Hong Kong weeklies *Asiaweek* and *Far Eastern Economic Review* feature pieces on Myanmar at an average frequency of two or three times per month. With regard to Myanmar, *Asiaweek*'s reporting seems more factual and unbiased, though *FEER*'s coverage of guerrilla movements is more detailed.

Political Publications

Various groups outside the country produce newsletters and reports focusing on current political affairs and especially human rights in Myanmar. While all are good sources of otherwise hard-to-find information, occasional articles seem designed more to inflame through anecdotal exaggeration, rather than to inform through substantive reporting. Most groups will gladly send sample copies of their publications.

All Burma Students Democratic Front
(☎/fax 02-379 2002)
PO Box 42, Hua Mak PO, Bangkok 10243, Thailand;
(☎ 02-300 0631)
PO Box 151, Khlong Chan PO, Bang Kapi, Bangkok 10240, Thailand

Amnesty International
(☎ 415-291 9233)
500 Sansome St, San Francisco, CA 94111, USA
Burma Action Group
(☎ 020-7359 7679, fax 7354 3987)
Collins Studios, Collins Yard, Islington Green, London N1 2XU, UK
Burma Affairs Monitor
(☎/fax 020-7924 3146)
3A Chatto Rd, London SW11 6LJ, UK
Burma Alert
(☎ 819-647 5405, fax 647 5403)
RR 4, Shawville, Quebec J0X 2Y0, Canada
Burma Bureau Germany
(☎ 2173-907334, fax 907335)
Fahlerweg 08 D-40764 Langenfeld, Germany
Burma Debate
(fax 301-983 5011)
PO Box 19126, Washington, DC 20036, USA
The Burma Project (Open Society Institute)
(☎ 212-887 0632, fax 489 8455)
888 7th Ave, New York, NY 10106, USA;
(☎ 415-381 6905)
10 Robertson Terrace, Mill Valley, CA 94941, USA
Burma Relief Centre
(☎ 053-216894)
PO Box 48, Chiang Mai University, Chiang Mai 50002, Thailand;
BRC-Japan
(☎ 7442-28236, fax 46254)
Ozuku-cho, Kashihara-shi, Nara-ken 634, Japan
Human Rights Watch – Asia
(☎ 212-972 8400, fax 972 0905)
484 5th Ave, New York, NY 10017, USA
National Coalition Government of the Union of Burma
(☎ 202-393 7342, fax 202-393 7343)
Suite 910, 815 15th St SW, Washington, DC 20005, USA

FILMS

Michio Takeyama's 1949 antiwar novel *Harp of Burma* was made into a beautiful black & white Japanese film directed by Kon Ichikawa in 1956. It's now available on video with English subtitles under the title *The Burmese Harp*.

In 1995, American director John Boorman's graphic *Beyond Rangoon*, a film dramatising the brutal suppression of the 1988 pro-democracy uprising, briefly focused international cinematic attention on Myanmar's plight.

NEWSPAPERS & MAGAZINES

Before the 1962 Burmese military takeover, over 30 daily newspapers – including three in English, six in Chinese, five in Indian languages and 18 in Burmese – were published in the country. Today the only English-language daily newspaper readily available in the country is the *New Light of Myanmar*, a thin, state-owned mouthpiece published by the Ministry of Information. Although much toned down from its socialist predecessors, the *Working People's Daily* and the *Daily Guardian*, it still contains startling Orwellian propaganda of the 'War is Peace', 'Freedom is Slavery' nature, mixed in with a fair amount of noncontroversial wire news.

There are now only four Burmese-language dailies, *Myanma Alin*, *Kyemon*, *Myodaw* and *Yadanabon* (Mandalay only). Only *Myanma Alin* – the Burmese version of the *New Light of Myanmar* – is circulated in greater numbers than the *New Light* itself.

Fortunately the *New Light* isn't the only source of printed news in Myanmar. Recent issues of international magazines like *Time, Newsweek* and the *Economist* are often available at newsstands and bookshops in luxury hotels like The Strand, Traders Hotel, Summit Parkview and Sedona Hotel in Yangon. Whenever a feature about Myanmar appears in one of these magazines, however, that issue mysteriously fails to appear. Older issues are sold on the street by pavement vendors. Western newspapers are available at the British and American libraries. You can also get the *International Herald Tribune* at Trader's.

The *Far Eastern Economic Review* and *Asiaweek*, the Hong Kong-based weekly news magazines, regularly report on the latest major events within Myanmar and on the relatively calm acceptance of these events by Myanmar's neighbours. Thailand's *Bangkok Post* and *The Nation* also regularly carry news on Myanmar.

A tourist-oriented publication called *Today* – published by MTT and available at the MTT office and at many hotels – contains short, noncontroversial articles on

Myanmar's culture and the tourism industry, along with useful lists of embassies, current festivals, airlines and long-distance express bus services. Better for train, air, boat and bus schedules is the privately published monthly *Myanmar Travel Handbook*. Both are usually available from hotel desks or occasionally from street book vendors.

See the Bookshops and Libraries entries in the Information section of the Yangon chapter for information on where to find English- and French-language publications.

RADIO & TV

All legal radio and television broadcasts are state-controlled. Radio Myanmar (formerly Voice of Myanmar) broadcasts news in Burmese, English and eight other national languages three times a day at 8.30 am and 1.30 and 9.30 pm. Only music with Burmese-language lyrics goes out on the airwaves.

Educated Burmese generally listen to shortwave BBC and VOA broadcasts for an earful of the outside world. Although these programs appear nightly, the most popular time to listen is each Wednesday evening from 8.15 to 9 pm, when the BBC broadcasts Burmese-language special reports that contain translated Myanmar news stories extracted from the foreign press. Just as popular – perhaps more so – is the Burmese service of Radio Free Asia (RFA).

TV Myanmar operates nightly from 5 pm to midnight via the NTSC system. Regular features include military songs and marching performances, locally produced news and weather reports, and a sports presentation. Every evening a segment of 'national songs' is performed by women dressed in ethnic costumes; when the songs are over, the national flag is always tellingly hoisted by the singer wearing Bamar dress.

National news in English is telecast on TV Myanmar nightly around 9.15 pm. Whenever a televised government speech or meeting is announced (which pre-empts all other programming for the evening), the local video rental shops are emptied of stock as virtually no one watches these long, drawn-out events. A second military-owned station, Myawaddy TV, telecasts government news every morning from 7 am to 8.30 am only.

One of the most dramatic changes to occur in Myanmar's media since the advent of TV is the relatively recent arrival of satellite TV services. Tens of thousands of satellite dishes have appeared in Yangon and Mandalay over the last four years. The main signal received is the 'southern footprint' of AsiaSat 1 & 2, same as for Thailand and Indochina, which beam in Satellite Television Asia Region (STAR) channels such as BBC World Service, STAR Movies, the Chinese Channel and Channel V (Asia's MTV clone). Myanmar also receives Doordarshan India (India Television), India's Hindi/Urdu Zee TV and Yunnan TV via satellite. Many of the newer hotels now provide satellite TV, although for some reason it seems they re never able to provide a choice of more than two or three satellite channels at a time.

VIDEO SYSTEMS

Although the standard TV system in Myanmar is NTSC, many people also own PAL sets, a format compatible with that used in Thailand and most of Europe (France's SECAM format is a notable exception) as well as in Australia. Some video shops rent NTSC as well as PAL and SECAM tapes; virtually all videos offered for sale or rent in Myanmar are pirated or unlicensed tapes. A 'multisystem' VCR has the capacity to play both NTSC and PAL, but not SECAM (except as black & white images).

PHOTOGRAPHY & VIDEO
Film & Equipment

Myanmar is a very photogenic place, so bring lots of film with you. Colour print films – mostly Kodak, Fuji and Konica brands – are readily and inexpensively available in shops in Yangon and Mandalay. Prices are around K700 for a 36 exposure roll of Fujicolor 100; Kodak costs a bit more.

Slide film is harder to find but some shops stock it. Generally the only types available are Kodak Ektachrome Elite 100 (or the newer Elite Chrome) and Fujichrome

Sensia 100, both of which sell for around K2000 per roll. Pro-grade film like Velvia and Provia are not distributed in Myanmar according to Fuji's head office, but they are occasionally available on the black market for K2000 to K2500. Of course if the kyat devalues further these prices will increase exponentially according to the value of the US dollar – you can figure that whatever film costs in Bangkok it will cost about the same or just a bit more here. Black & white print (or slide) film is very hard to come by. If you're shooting in this medium, be sure to bring your own supply. Bangkok is a good place to stock up on film of all types.

Outside Yangon and Mandalay, film is scarce. Most film you might see on sale in the hinterlands will have come from visitors who sold it while in the country – with no guarantee on age or quality.

Photographic processing services are available but quality is erratic. It's best to wait until you've returned home – or have your film processed in Bangkok, where decent colour labs are plentiful.

Technical Tips

The usual tropical rules apply to taking photographs here. Allow for the intensity of the sun after the early morning and before the late evening. Try to keep your film as cool as possible, particularly after it has been exposed. Beware of dust, particularly at the height of the dry season when Central Myanmar becomes very dusty indeed. And don't drop your camera in the Ayeyarwady!

Restrictions

It is forbidden by law to photograph any military facility or any structure considered strategic – this includes bridges and train stations – and any uniformed person.

If you happen to see a public demonstration taking place, be discreet about taking photographs, as journalists are strictly unwelcome in Myanmar.

Aung San Suu Kyi's University Ave home is absolutely off-limits to photographers, whether amateur or pro. We recently received a letter from an Italian photographer who claimed that when he tried to shoot photos of the house, soldiers promptly confiscated all his film, drove him to the airport and had him deported. Although you might not receive this treatment, we do know of people who have been questioned and turned away from the block on which Aung San Suu Kyi lives.

Also off-limits are any homes in Yangon belonging to government ministers or generals. Often these are the biggest, nicest looking homes, so be careful when shooting any grand residential structures.

For more on the issue of restrictions, see Dangers & Annoyances later in this section.

Photographing People

A benefit of Myanmar's low tourist flow is that the Burmese are not over-exposed to camera-clicking visitors and are not at all unhappy about being photographed. Even monks like to be photographed, although, of course, it's rude to ask them to pose for you and it's always polite to ask anybody's permission before taking photographs.

Airport Security

The X-ray baggage inspection machines at Yangon international airport are all deemed film-safe. Nevertheless if you're travelling with high speed film (ISO 400 or above), you may want to have your film hand-inspected rather than X-rayed. Security inspectors are usually happy to comply. Packing your film in see-through plastic bags generally speeds up the hand-inspection process. Some photographers pack their film in lead-lined bags to ward off potentially harmful rays.

At other airports around the country the X-ray machines are considerably more dubious and we suggest you have all film hand-inspected. On occasion the upcountry machines aren't working at all, in which case there will be no anxiety over the film.

TIME & DATES
Hours

Myanmar Standard Time (MST) is 6½ hours ahead of Greenwich Mean Time (GMT/UTC).

Coming from Thailand you turn your watch back half an hour, from India you turn it forward an hour. When it is noon in Yangon, it's 9.30 pm the previous day in San Francisco, 12.30 am in New York, 5.30 am in London and 3.30 pm in Sydney or Melbourne. When these cities are on daylight-saving time, these times are one hour behind.

Days

Most Burmese Buddhists recognise an eight day week in which Thursday to Tuesday conform with the western calendar but Wednesday is divided into two 12-hour days. Midnight to noon is 'Bohdahu' (the day Buddha was born), while noon to midnight is 'Yahu' (Rahu, a Hindu god/planet). It's rare that the week's unique structure causes any communication problems, however, given that the Wednesday division mainly applies to religious rather than secular matters (for example, which planetary post a worshipper attends at a paya).

Months

The traditional Burmese calendar features 12 28-day lunar months that run out of sync with the months of the solar Gregorian calendar. To stay in sync with the solar year, the Burmese calendar inserts a second Waso month every few years – somewhat like the leap year day added to the Gregorian February. The Burmese months are:

Tagu	March/April
Kason	April/May
Nayon	May/June
Waso	June/July
Wagaung	July/August
Tawthalin	August/September
Thadingyut	September/October
Tazaungmon	October/November
Nadaw	November/December
Pyatho	December/January
Tabodwe	January/February
Tabaung	February/March

Most traditional festivals take place according to this scheme, making it difficult to calculate festival dates using a Gregorian calendar.

Each lunar month is divided into two 14-day halves; the two weeks during which the moon waxes (or appears to increase in size) are called *la-zan*, while the two weeks of the waning moon are *la-gweh*. These lunar phases determine the Burmese religious calendar. Four monthly 'holy days' – when it's most propitious to visit a paya or *kyaung* (Buddhist monastery) – occur on the 8th and 15th days of the waxing and waning moons.

Burmese months are cited more commonly than the Gregorian months in everyday speech. Ask most villagers what the date is and they'll respond with something like: 'It's Pyatho, 8th day of the waning moon'. Educated Burmese are familiar with the Gregorian calendar, which is used in most official capacities and in business situations.

Years

Over the centuries Burmese monarchs have established and counter-established several different year counts. The main one in current use, called *thekkayit*, is 638 years behind the Christian era. Since each new year begins in April (at the end of the Thingyan festival), this means the Christian year 2000 is equivalent to thekkayit 1362 until the month of April, after which it's 1363. Burmese archaeology is particularly challenging since historic chronicles and stone inscriptions use different year counts depending on who was king at the time.

Another calendar in use follows the Buddhist era as reckoned in Thailand counting from 543 BC; hence 2000 is 2543 BE. Private businesses typically cite years following the AD Christian calendar. Some official Burmese documents and many Burmese calendars state the year according to all three systems, ie thekkayit, BE and AD.

ELECTRICITY

Myanmar's national grid system covers only certain parts of Central and Eastern Myanmar. Most of the power comes from a single hydroelectric plant at Lawpita in the Kayah State. Off the national grid, towns and cities may have their own diesel plants or small hydroelectric facilities.

Even in the capital, however, there's never enough electric capacity to power the whole city, so Myanma Electric Power Enterprise (MPPE) rotates the supply from quarter to quarter and from day to day. The voltage often drops to levels that are barely enough for anything more than basic lighting. Brownouts and blackouts are common, except, of course, in the neighbourhoods where military officers or ministers live. In many towns and villages electric power is supplied only during the evening hours from around 6 to 11 pm.

Businesses and homes that can afford it maintain their own gas or diesel-powered generators. Often these are unable to supply enough voltage to power major appliances like air-conditioners; this is why many smaller hotels feature in-room air-con units that don't work. Transformers that 'step up' the voltage are becoming increasingly common, but the cheaper models – those within economic reach of the Burmese middle class – don't seem to work very well.

In many villages lighting, heating and cooking sources are restricted to candles, paraffin and firewood.

Voltages & Cycles
When it's working the current is supposed to run at 230V, 50 Hz AC.

Plugs & Sockets
Most electrical wall outlets take British-style plugs with three flat prongs in a triangle; some older outlets accept round prongs and a few outlets feature combined round/flat holes for either type.

WEIGHTS & MEASURES
For a country with such a professed anti-colonial stance, Myanmar is amazingly Anglo in the standard units of measures employed in everyday life.

Weight
The most common units of weight used in Myanmar are viss (peiqtha), pounds (paun)

and ticals (kyat tha). One viss equals 3.6 pounds (1.6kg) or 100 ticals. One tical equals 16g.

Volume
At the retail level, rice and small fruits or nuts are sold in units of volume rather than weight; the most common measure is the standard condensed-milk can or bu. Eight bu equals one small rice basket or pyi, and 16 pyi make a jute sack or tin.

Petrol and most other liquids are sold by the imperial gallon (4.55L). One exception is milk, which is sold by the viss.

Length & Distance
Cloth and other items of moderate length are measured by the yard (91.5cm), called gaiq in Burmese. A half yard is a taung (45.7cm), which is divided into two htwa (22.8cm). Half a htwa is a maiq (11.4cm).

Road distances are measured in miles (1 mile = 1.61km). Shorter distances in town or in the countryside may be quoted in furlongs. There are 8 furlongs in 1 mile; thus 1 furlong equals about 0.2km.

LAUNDRY
Virtually every hotel and guesthouse in Myanmar offers a laundry service. Rates are generally geared to room rates; the cheaper the accommodation, the cheaper you'll find the washing and ironing. Cheapest of all are public laundries, where you pay by the pound (in weight), but our experience has been that these are available only in Yangon and Mandalay. There are no 'laundromats' or self-service laundries anywhere in the country.

Some hotels and guesthouses also provide laundry areas where you can wash your clothes at no charge; sometimes there's even a hanging area for drying. In accommodation where there is no laundry, do-it-yourselfers can wash their clothes in the sink and hang them out to dry in their rooms – see the What to Bring section earlier in this chapter for useful laundry tools. Laundry detergent is readily available in general mercantile shops.

TOILETS

In Myanmar, as in many other Asian countries, the 'squat toilet' is the norm, except in hotels and guesthouses geared towards tourists and international business travellers. Instead of trying to approximate a chair or stool like a modern sit-down toilet, a traditional Asian toilet sits more or less flush with the surface of the floor, with two footpads on either side of the porcelain abyss. For travellers who have never used a squat toilet it takes a bit of getting used to. If you find yourself feeling awkward the first couple of times you use one, you can console yourself with the knowledge that, according to those who study such matters, people who use squat toilets are much less likely to develop haemorrhoids than people who use sit toilets.

Next to the typical squat toilet is a bucket or cement reservoir filled with water. A plastic bowl usually floats on the water's surface or sits nearby. This water supply has a two fold function; toilet-goers scoop water from the reservoir with the plastic bowl and use it to clean their nether regions while still squatting over the toilet. Since there is usually no mechanical flushing device attached to a squat toilet, a few extra scoops must be poured into the toilet basin to flush waste into the septic system. In larger towns, mechanical flushing systems are becoming increasingly common, even with squat toilets. More rustic toilets in rural areas may simply consist of a few planks over a hole in the ground.

Even in places where sit-down toilets are installed, the plumbing may not be designed to take toilet paper. In such cases the usual washing bucket will be standing nearby so you can wash your hands, or there will be a waste basket where you're supposed to place used toilet paper.

Public toilets are rather uncommon in Myanmar, except in train stations, larger hotel lobbies and airports. While on the road between towns and villages, it is perfectly acceptable to go behind a tree or bush or even to use the roadside when nature calls.

BATHING

Smaller hotels and most guesthouses in the country may not have hot water, though places in the larger cities will usually offer small electric shower heaters in their more expensive rooms (though depending on the generator situation these devices may only function for a few hours per day). Very few boiler-style water heaters are available outside larger international-style hotels.

Many rural Burmese bathe in rivers or streams or at public wells. Those living in towns or cities may have washrooms where a large jar or cement trough is filled with water for bathing purposes. A plastic or metal bowl is used to sluice water from the jar or trough over the body. Even in homes where showers are installed, heated water is uncommon. Most Burmese bathe at least twice a day, and never use hot water.

If ever you find yourself having to bathe in a public place you should wear a longyi; nude bathing is shockingly offensive.

HEALTH

Travel health depends on your predeparture preparations, your daily health care while travelling and how you handle any medical problem that does develop. While the potential dangers can seem quite frightening, in reality few travellers experience anything more than upset stomachs.

Predeparture Planning

Health Insurance Be sure to have adequate health insurance. See Travel Insurance under Visas & Documents in this chapter for details.

Travel Health Guides If you are planning to be away or travelling in remote areas for a long period of time, you may like to consider taking a more detailed health guide.

CDC's Complete Guide to Healthy Travel, by Open Road Publishing, 1997. The US Centers for Disease Control & Prevention recommendations for international travel.

Staying Healthy in Asia, Africa & Latin America, by Dirk Schroeder, Moon Publications, 1994. Probably the best all-round guide to carry; it's detailed and well organised.

Burmese Beauty Secrets

Diet
The typical Burmese dietary intake includes plenty of fibre via pulses, vegetables, fruit and grains (rice and noodles). Fish and chicken are preferred to red meat, and vegetable oils (sesamum, sunflower and peanut) are used instead of animal fat. Few dairy products are eaten. Very weak green tea is drunk in large quantities and clear soups are often taken with main meals.

Even in the cities, women rarely touch alcohol or cigarettes, and the huge cheroots puffed by country women are very mild.

Climate
Except for the central 'dry zone', the country's normally high humidity is kind to the skin. There are no frosts or drying winds and little pollution. Constant sweat keeps the pores active and flushed.

Personal Hygiene
All-over washing with cold water two or three times a day – using unrefined, unscented soap – is a routine for all. It is believed that warm water is bad for the skin. Herbal shampoo is made by boiling the bark of a small shrub called *tayaw (Grewia)* with the pods of soap acacia *(Acacia concinna)*. The resultant brown liquid, which is widely sold in the markets, lathers quite well and leaves the hair soft and glossy. Hair is oiled with coconut oil and adorned with combs of woods, ivory and tortoiseshell.

Cosmetics
The soft outer bark of the *thanakha* tree *(Linoria acidissima)*, which grows in central Burma, is ground on a whetstone with a little water and used as a paste on the face. Alternately, it can be bought prepared as a liquid cosmetic or in powder form. The paste is smeared on the face and body; some women cover their whole bodies with it at night. Thanakha is mildly astringent, and used as a combination skin conditioner, sunscreen, perfume and cosmetic. Older women tend to put cold cream and light oil preparations on their faces before applying thanakha.

Traditionally, eyebrows and lashes were blackened with a mixture of oil and soot, but nowadays 'western' cosmetics – some made domestically, some imported – are readily available. Burmese women are generally very brand-conscious, and genuine Revlon lipsticks are a treasured gift.

Physique
Most Burmese have small bones, high cheekbones in an oval face and slim bodies, although plumpness is frequently considered a sign of health and beauty. The expression *'Wa-laiq-ta!'* ('How fat you're looking!') is considered a compliment. Although they are not tall, the *longyi* (sarong-style garment) makes them appear so.

From early childhood, boys and girls carry water pots or trays of food on their heads, which seems to result in fewer back problems and beautiful carriage. The longyi restricts the stride so the people move slowly and gracefully. Burmese women believe that squatting, rather than standing, helps prevent varicose veins.

Vicki Bowman

Travellers' Health, by Dr Richard Dawood, Oxford University Press, 1995. Comprehensive, easy to read, authoritative and highly recommended, although it's rather large to lug around.

Where There Is No Doctor, by David Werner, Macmillan, 1994. A very detailed guide intended for someone, such as a Peace Corps worker, going to work in an underdeveloped country.

Travel with Children, by Maureen Wheeler, Lonely Planet Publications, 1995. Includes advice on travel health for younger children.

There are also a number of excellent travel health sites on the Internet. From the Lonely Planet home page there are links at www. lonelyplanet.com/weblinks/wlprep.htm#heal to WHO and the US Centers for Disease Control & Prevention.

Other Preparations

Make sure you're healthy before you start travelling. If you are going on a long trip make sure your teeth are OK. If you wear glasses take a spare pair and your prescription.

If you require a particular medication take an adequate supply, as it may not be available locally. Take part of the packaging showing the generic name rather than the brand, which will make getting replacements easier. It's a good idea to have a legible prescription or letter from your doctor to show that you legally use the medication to avoid any problems.

Immunisations

Plan ahead for getting your vaccinations: some of them require more than one injection, while a few vaccinations should not be given together. Note that some vaccinations should not be given during pregnancy or to the allergic – discuss with your doctor.

It is recommended you seek medical advice at least six weeks before travel. Be aware that there is often a greater risk of disease with children and during pregnancy.

There are currently no immunisation requirements for entry into Myanmar except for yellow fever if you come from an infected zone. Discuss your requirements with your doctor, but vaccinations you should consider for this trip include the following

(for more details about the diseases themselves, see the individual disease entries later in this section):

Diphtheria & Tetanus Vaccinations for these two diseases are usually combined and are recommended for everyone. After an initial course of three injections (usually given in childhood), boosters are necessary every 10 years.

Polio You should keep up-to-date with this vaccination, which is normally given in childhood. A booster every 10 years maintains immunity.

Hepatitis A Hepatitis A vaccine (eg Avaxim, Havrix 1440 or VAQTA) provides long-term immunity (possibly more than 10 years) after an initial injection and a booster at six to 12 months. Alternatively, an injection of gamma globulin can provide short-term protection against hepatitis A – two to six months, depending on the dose given. It is not a vaccine, but is ready-made antibody collected from blood donations. It is reasonably effective and, unlike the vaccine, is protective immediately, but because it is a blood product, there are current concerns about its long-term safety. Hepatitis A vaccine is also available in a combined form, Twinrix, with hepatitis B vaccine. Three injections over a six-month period are required, the first two providing substantial protection against hepatitis A

Hepatitis B Travellers who should consider vaccination against hepatitis B include those on a long trip, as well as those visiting countries where there are high levels of hepatitis B infection, where blood transfusions may not be adequately screened or where sexual contact or needle sharing is a possibility. Vaccination involves three injections, with a booster at 12 months. More rapid courses are available if necessary.

Typhoid Vaccination against typhoid may be required if you are travelling for more than a couple of weeks in most parts of Asia, Africa, Central and South America, and Central and Eastern Europe. It is now available either as an injection or as capsules to be taken orally.

Rabies Vaccination should be considered by those who will spend a month or longer in a country where rabies is common, especially if they are cycling, handling animals, caving or travelling to remote areas, and for children (who may not report a bite). Pretravel rabies vaccination involves having three injections over 21 to 28 days. If someone who has been vaccinated is bitten or scratched by an animal, they will require two booster injections of vaccine; those not vaccinated require more.

Medical Kit Check List

Following is a list of items you should consider including in your medical kit – consult your pharmacist for brands available in your country.

☐ **Aspirin** or **paracetamol** (acetaminophen in the USA) – for pain or fever
☐ **Antihistamine** – for allergies, eg hay fever; to ease the itch from insect bites or stings; and to prevent motion sickness
☐ **Antibiotics** – consider including these if you're travelling well off the beaten track; see your doctor, as they must be prescribed, and carry the prescription with you
☐ **Loperamide** or **diphenoxylate** –'blockers' for diarrhoea; **prochlorperazine** or **metaclopramide** for nausea and vomiting
☐ **Rehydration mixture** – to prevent dehydration, eg due to severe diarrhoea; particularly important when travelling with children
☐ **Insect repellent**, **sunscreen**, **lip balm** and **eye drops**
☐ **Calamine lotion**, **sting relief spray** or **aloe vera** – to ease irritation from sunburn and insect bites or stings
☐ **Antifungal cream** or **powder** – for fungal skin infections and thrush
☐ **Antiseptic** (such as povidone-iodine) – for cuts and grazes
☐ **Bandages**, **Band-Aids (plasters)** and other wound dressings
☐ **Water purification tablets** or **iodine**
☐ **Scissors**, **tweezers** and a **thermometer** (note that mercury thermometers are prohibited by airlines)
☐ **Syringes** and **needles** – in case you need injections in a country with medical hygiene problems. Ask your doctor for a note explaining why you have them.
☐ **Cold** and **flu tablets**, **throat lozenges** and **nasal decongestant**
☐ **Multivitamins** – consider for long trips, when dietary vitamin intake may be inadequate

Tuberculosis The risk of TB to travellers is usually very low, unless you will be living with or closely associated with local people. Vaccination against TB (BCG) is recommended for children and young adults living in these areas for three months or more.

Malaria Medication

Antimalarial drugs do not prevent you from being infected but do kill the malaria parasites during a stage in their development and significantly reduce the risk of becoming very ill or dying. Expert advice on medication should be sought, as there are many factors to consider, including the area to be visited, the risk of exposure to malaria-carrying mosquitoes, the side effects of medication, your medical history and whether you are a child or an adult or pregnant. Travellers to isolated areas in high risk countries may like to carry a treatment dose of medication for use if symptoms occur. Antimalarial drugs are readily available in Yangon.

Basic Rules

Food There is an old colonial adage that says: 'If you can cook it, boil it or peel it you can eat it ... otherwise forget it.' Vegetables and fruit should be washed with purified water or peeled where possible. Beware of ice cream that is sold in the street or anywhere it might have been melted and refrozen; if there's any doubt (eg a power cut in the last day or two), steer well clear. Shellfish such as mussels, oysters and clams should be avoided as well as undercooked meat, particularly in the form of mince. Steaming does not make shellfish safe for eating.

If a place looks clean and well run and the vendor also looks clean and healthy, then the food is probably safe. In general, places that are packed with travellers or locals will be fine, while empty restaurants are questionable. The food in busy restaurants is cooked and eaten quite quickly with little standing around and is probably not reheated.

Water The No 1 rule is *be careful of the water* and especially ice. If you don't know for certain that the water is safe, assume the worst. Reputable brands of bottled water or

Nutrition

If your diet is poor or limited in variety, if you're travelling hard and fast and therefore missing meals or if you simply lose your appetite, you can soon start to lose weight and place your health at risk.

Make sure your diet is well balanced. Cooked eggs, tofu, beans, lentils (dhal in India) and nuts are all safe ways to get protein. Fruit you can peel (bananas, oranges or mandarins for example) is usually safe (melons can harbour bacteria in their flesh and are best avoided) and a good source of vitamins. Try to eat plenty of grains (including rice) and bread. Remember that although food is generally safer if it is cooked well, overcooked food loses much of its nutritional value. If your diet isn't well balanced or if your food intake is insufficient, it's a good idea to take vitamin and iron pills.

In hot climates make sure you drink enough – don't rely on feeling thirsty to indicate when you should drink. Not needing to urinate or small amounts of very dark yellow urine is a danger sign. Always carry a water bottle with you on long trips. Excessive sweating can lead to loss of salt and therefore muscle cramping. Salt tablets are not a good idea as a preventative, but in places where salt is not used much, adding salt to food can help.

---

soft drinks are generally fine, although in some places bottles may be refilled with tap water. Only use water from containers with a serrated seal – not tops or corks. Take care with fruit juice, particularly if water may have been added. Milk should be treated with suspicion as it is often unpasteurised, though boiled milk is fine if it is kept hygienically. Tea or coffee should also be OK, since the water should have been boiled.

Water Purification The simplest way of purifying water is to boil it thoroughly. Vigorous boiling should be satisfactory, however, at high altitude water boils at a lower temperature, so germs are less likely to be killed. Boil it for a longer period in these environments.

Consider purchasing a water filter for a long trip. There are two main kinds of filter. Total filters take out all parasites, bacteria and viruses and make water safe to drink. They are often expensive, but they can be more cost effective than buying bottled water. Simple filters (which can even be a nylon mesh bag) take out dirt and larger foreign bodies from the water so that chemical solutions work much more effectively; if water is dirty, chemical solutions may not

work at all. It's very important when buying a filter to read the specifications, so that you know exactly what it removes from the water and what it doesn't. Simple filtering will not remove all dangerous organisms, so if you cannot boil water it should be treated chemically. Chlorine tablets (Puritabs, Steritabs or other brand names) will kill many pathogens, but not some parasites like giardia and amoebic cysts. Iodine is more effective in purifying water and is available in tablet form (such as Potable Aqua). Follow the directions carefully and remember that too much iodine can be harmful.

Medical Problems & Treatment
Self-diagnosis and treatment can be risky, so you should always seek medical help. Although we do give drug dosages in this section, they are for emergency use only. Correct diagnosis is vital.

An embassy, consulate or five star hotel can usually recommend a local doctor or clinic. Antibiotics should ideally be administered only under medical supervision. Take only the recommended dose at the prescribed intervals and use the whole course, even if the illness seems to be cured earlier. Stop immediately if there are any serious

Everyday Health

Normal body temperature is up to 37°C (98.6°F); more than 2°C (4°F) higher indicates a high fever. The normal adult pulse rate is 60 to 100 per minute (children 80 to 100, babies 100 to 140). As a general rule the pulse increases about 20 beats per minute for each 1°C (2°F) rise in fever.

Respiration (breathing) rate is also an indicator of illness. Count the number of breaths per minute: between 12 and 20 is normal for adults and older children (up to 30 for younger children, 40 for babies). People with a high fever or serious respiratory illness breathe more quickly than normal. More than 40 shallow breaths a minute may indicate pneumonia.

reactions and don't use the antibiotic at all if you are unsure that you have the correct one. Some people are allergic to commonly prescribed antibiotics such as penicillin or sulpha drugs; carry this information (eg on a bracelet) when travelling.

Environmental Hazards

Fungal Infections Fungal infections occur more commonly in hot weather and are usually found on the scalp, between the toes (athlete's foot) or fingers, in the groin and on the body (ringworm). You get ringworm (which is a fungal infection, not a worm) from infected animals or other people. Moisture encourages these infections.

To prevent fungal infections wear loose, comfortable clothes, avoid artificial fibres, wash frequently and dry yourself carefully. If you do get an infection, wash the infected area at least daily with a disinfectant or medicated soap and water, and rinse and dry well. Apply an antifungal cream or powder like tolnaftate (Tinaderm). Try to expose the infected area to air or sunlight as much as possible and wash all towels and underwear in hot water, change them often and let them dry in the sun.

Heat Exhaustion Dehydration and salt deficiency can cause heat exhaustion. Take time to acclimatise to high temperatures, drink sufficient liquids and do not do anything too physically demanding.

Salt deficiency is characterised by fatigue, lethargy, headaches, giddiness and muscle cramps; salt tablets may help, but adding extra salt to your food is better.

Heatstroke This serious, occasionally fatal, condition can occur if the body's heat-regulating mechanism breaks down and the body temperature rises to dangerous levels. Long, continuous periods of exposure to high temperatures and insufficient fluids can leave you vulnerable to heatstroke.

The symptoms are feeling unwell, not sweating very much (or at all) and a high body temperature (39°C to 41°C or 102°F to 106°F). Where sweating has ceased, the skin becomes flushed and red. Severe, throbbing headaches and lack of coordination will also occur, and the sufferer may be confused or aggressive. Eventually the victim will become delirious or convulse. Hospitalisation is essential, but in the interim get victims out of the sun, remove their clothing, cover them with a wet sheet or towel and then fan continually. Give fluids if they are conscious.

Jet Lag Jet lag is experienced when a person travels by air across more than three time zones (each time zone usually represents a one hour time difference). It occurs because many of the functions of the human body (such as temperature, pulse rate and emptying of the bladder and bowels) are regulated by internal 24-hour cycles. When we travel long distances rapidly, our bodies take time to adjust to the 'new time' of our destination, and we may experience fatigue, disorientation, insomnia, anxiety, impaired concentration and loss of appetite. These effects will usually be gone within three days of arrival, but to minimise the impact of jet lag:

• Rest for a couple of days prior to departure.
• Try to select flight schedules that minimise sleep deprivation; arriving late in the day means

you can go to sleep soon after you arrive. For very long flights, try to organise a stopover.

- Avoid excessive eating (which bloats the stomach) and alcohol (which causes dehydration) during the flight. Instead, drink plenty of non-carbonated, nonalcoholic drinks such as fruit juice or water.
- Avoid smoking.
- Make yourself comfortable by wearing loose-fitting clothes and perhaps bringing an eye mask and ear plugs to help you sleep.
- Try to sleep at the appropriate time for the time zone you are travelling to.

Motion Sickness Eating lightly before and during a trip will reduce the chances of motion sickness. If you are prone to motion sickness try to find a place that minimises movement – near the wing on aircraft, close to midships on boats, near the centre on buses. Fresh air usually helps: reading and cigarette smoke don't. Commercial motion sickness preparations, which can cause drowsiness, have to be taken before the trip commences. Ginger (available in capsule form) and peppermint (including mint-flavoured sweets) are natural preventatives.

Prickly Heat Prickly heat is an itchy rash caused by excessive perspiration trapped under the skin. It usually strikes people who have just arrived in a hot climate. Keeping cool, bathing often, drying the skin and using a mild talcum or prickly heat powder or resorting to air-conditioning may help.

Sunburn You can get sunburnt surprisingly quickly, even through cloud. Use a sunscreen, a hat, and a barrier cream for your nose and lips. Calamine lotion or Stingose are good for mild sunburn. Protect your eyes with good quality sunglasses, particularly if you will be near water, sand or snow.

Infectious Diseases
Diarrhoea Simple things like a change of water, food or climate can all cause a mild bout of diarrhoea, but a few rushed toilet trips with no other symptoms is not indicative of a major problem.

Dehydration is the main danger with any diarrhoea, particularly in children or the elderly as dehydration can occur quite quickly. Under all circumstances *fluid replacement* (at least equal to the volume being lost) is the most important thing to remember. Weak black tea with a little sugar; soda water; or soft drinks allowed to go flat and diluted 50% with clean water are all good. With severe diarrhoea a rehydrating solution is preferable to replace minerals and salts lost. Commercially available oral rehydration salts (ORS) are very useful; add them to boiled or bottled water. In an emergency you can make up a solution of six teaspoons of sugar and half a teaspoon of salt to a litre of boiled or bottled water. You need to drink at least the same volume of fluid that you are losing in bowel movements and vomiting. Urine is the best guide to the adequacy of replacement – if you have small amounts of concentrated urine, you need to drink more. Keep drinking small amounts often. Stick to a bland diet as you recover.

Gut-paralysing drugs such as Lomotil or Imodium can be used to bring relief from the symptoms, although they do not actually cure the problem. Only use these drugs if you do not have access to toilets, eg if you *must* travel. For children under 12 years Lomotil and Imodium are not recommended. Do not use these drugs if the person has a high fever or is severely dehydrated.

In certain situations antibiotics may be required: diarrhoea with blood or mucus (dysentery), any diarrhoea with fever, profuse watery diarrhoea, persistent diarrhoea not improving after 48 hours and severe diarrhoea. These suggest a more serious cause of diarrhoea and in these situations gut-paralysing drugs should be avoided.

In these situations, a stool test may be necessary to diagnose what bug is causing your diarrhoea, so you should seek medical help urgently. Where this is not possible the recommended drugs for bacterial diarrhoea (the most likely cause of severe diarrhoea in travellers) are norfloxacin 400mg twice daily for three days or ciprofloxacin 500mg twice daily for five days. These are not recommended for children or pregnant women.

The drug of choice for children would be co-trimoxazole (Bactrim, Septrin or Resprim) with dosage dependent on weight. A five day course is given. Ampicillin or amoxycillin may be given in pregnancy, but medical care is necessary.

Two other causes of persistent diarrhoea in travellers are giardiasis and amoebic dysentery.

Giardiasis is caused by a common parasite, *Giardia lamblia*. Symptoms include stomach cramps, nausea, a bloated stomach, watery, foul-smelling diarrhoea and frequent gas. Giardiasis can appear several weeks after you have been exposed to the parasite. The symptoms may disappear for a few days and then return; this can go on for several weeks.

Amoebic dysentery, caused by the protozoan *Entamoeba histolytica*, is characterised by a gradual onset of low-grade diarrhoea, often with blood and mucus. Cramping abdominal pain and vomiting are less likely than in other types of diarrhoea, and fever may not be present. It will persist until treated and can recur and cause other health problems.

You should seek medical advice if you think you have giardiasis or amoebic dysentery, but where this is not possible, tinidazole (Fasigyn) or metronidazole (Flagyl) are the recommended drugs. Treatment is a 2g single dose of Fasigyn or 250mg of Flagyl three times daily for five to 10 days.

Hepatitis Hepatitis is a general term for inflammation of the liver. It is a common disease worldwide. There are several different viruses that cause hepatitis, and they differ in the way that they are transmitted. The symptoms are similar in all forms of the illness, and include fever, chills, headache, fatigue, feelings of weakness and aches and pains, followed by loss of appetite, nausea, vomiting, abdominal pain, dark urine, light-coloured faeces, jaundiced (yellow) skin and yellowing of the whites of the eyes. People who have had hepatitis should avoid alcohol for some time after the illness, as the liver needs time to recover.

Hepatitis A is transmitted by contaminated food and drinking water. You should seek medical advice, but there is not much you can do apart from resting, drinking lots of fluids, eating lightly and avoiding fatty foods. Hepatitis E is transmitted in the same way as hepatitis A; it can be particularly serious in pregnant women.

There are almost 300 million chronic carriers of **hepatitis B** in the world. It is spread through contact with infected blood, blood products or body fluids, for example through sexual contact, unsterilised needles and blood transfusions, or contact with blood via small breaks in the skin. Other risk situations include having a shave, tattoo or body piercing with contaminated equipment. The symptoms of hepatitis B may be more severe than type A and the disease can lead to long-term problems such as chronic liver damage, liver cancer or a long-term carrier state. Hepatitis C and D are spread in the same way as hepatitis B and can also lead to long-term complications.

There are vaccines against hepatitis A and B, but there are currently no vaccines against the other types of hepatitis. Following the basic rules about food and water (hepatitis A and E) and avoiding risk situations (hepatitis B, C and D) are important preventative measures.

HIV & AIDS Infection with the Human Immunodeficiency Virus (HIV) may lead to Acquired Immune Deficiency Syndrome (AIDS), which is a fatal disease. Any exposure to blood, blood products or body fluids may put the individual at risk. The disease is often transmitted through sexual contact or dirty needles – vaccinations, acupuncture, tattooing and body piercing can be potentially as dangerous as intravenous drug use. HIV/AIDS can also be spread through infected blood transfusions; some developing countries cannot afford to screen blood used for transfusions. In Myanmar it is uncertain whether proper screening procedures are being followed.

If you do need an injection, ask to see the syringe unwrapped in front of you, or take a needle and syringe pack with you.

Fear of HIV infection should not preclude treatment for serious medical conditions.

Myanmar has one of the highest HIV infection rates (the rate at which new infections are contracted) in the world, and possibly the highest in South-East Asia. The closer you get to the Chinese border – where neighbouring districts record the highest HIV infection rates in Asia – the more prevalent the virus becomes. Rates among intravenous drug users here are reportedly the highest in the world.

HIV is also making the rounds in Myanmar's thriving prostitution underground. Prostitution exists in two parallel streams: the nearly invisible but larger Burmese trade in which Bamar, Kayin, Shan, Yunnanese and Kachin women service Burmese men on the 'guesthouse' circuit, and the more transparent but rather recent trade developed to service visiting Chinese businessmen from Hong Kong, Taiwan and Singapore through luxury hotels and karaoke lounges. So far no figures concerning the infection rates among Burmese prostitutes are available but it is likely to be quite high – probably much higher than in Thailand or India where condom use is substantially more prevalent. Interviews with sex workers in Myanmar suggest that condom use is comparatively uncommon.

Because of HIV's looming spectre over Myanmar, do not under any circumstances share needles or engage in unprotected sexual intercourse with Burmese nationals while in the country.

Intestinal Worms These parasites are most common in rural, tropical areas. The different worms have different ways of infecting people. Some may be ingested on food such as undercooked meat (eg tapeworms) and some enter through your skin (eg hookworms). Infestations may not show up for some time, and although they are generally not serious, if left untreated some can cause severe health problems later. Consider having a stool test when you return home to check for these and determine the appropriate treatment.

Sexually Transmitted Diseases Gonorrhoea, herpes and syphilis are among these diseases; sores, blisters or rashes around the genitals and discharges or pain when urinating are common symptoms. In some STDs, such as wart virus or chlamydia, symptoms may be less marked or not observed at all, especially in women. Syphilis symptoms eventually disappear completely but the disease continues and can cause severe problems in later years. While abstinence from sexual contact is the only 100% effective prevention, using condoms is also effective. The treatment of gonorrhoea and syphilis is with antibiotics. The different sexually transmitted diseases each require specific antibiotics. There is no cure for herpes or AIDS.

Typhoid Typhoid fever is a dangerous gut infection caused by contaminated water and food. Medical help must be sought.

In its early stages sufferers may feel they have a bad cold or flu on the way, as symptoms are a headache, body aches and a fever that rises a little each day until it is around 40°C (104°F) or more. The victim's pulse is often slow relative to the degree of fever present – unlike a normal fever where the pulse increases. There may also be vomiting, abdominal pain, diarrhoea or constipation.

In the second week the high fever and slow pulse continue and a few pink spots may appear on the body; trembling, delirium, weakness, weight loss and dehydration may occur. Complications such as pneumonia, perforated bowel or meningitis may occur.

Insect-Borne Diseases

Malaria This serious and potentially fatal disease is spread by mosquito bites. If you are travelling in endemic areas it is extremely important to avoid mosquito bites and to take tablets to prevent this disease. Symptoms range from fever, chills and sweating, headache, diarrhoea and abdominal pains to a vague feeling of ill-health. Seek medical help immediately if malaria is suspected. Without treatment malaria can rapidly become more serious and can be fatal.

If medical care is not available, malaria tablets can be used for treatment. You need to use a malaria tablet that is different from the one you were taking when you contracted malaria. The standard treatment dose of mefloquine is two 250mg tablets and another two six hours later. For Fansidar, it's a single dose of three tablets. If you were previously taking mefloquine and cannot obtain Fansidar, then other alternatives are Malarone (atovaquone-proguanil; four tablets once daily for three days), halofantrine (three doses of two 250mg tablets every six hours) or quinine sulphate (600mg every six hours). There is a greater risk of side effects with these dosages than in normal use if used with mefloquine, so medical advice is preferable. Be aware also that halofantrine is no longer recommended by the WHO as emergency standby treatment, because of side effects, and should only be used if no other drugs are available.

Travellers are advised to prevent mosquito bites at all times. The main messages are:

- Wear light-coloured clothing.
- Wear long trousers and long-sleeved shirts.
- Use mosquito repellents containing the compound DEET on exposed areas (prolonged overuse of DEET may be harmful, especially to children, but its use is considered preferable to being bitten by disease-transmitting mosquitoes).
- Avoid perfumes or aftershave.
- Use a mosquito net impregnated with mosquito repellent (permethrin) – it may be worth taking your own.
- Impregnating clothes with permethrin effectively deters mosquitoes and other insects.

Dengue Fever Several travelers have told us recently of getting dengue fever while visiting more remote parts of Myanmar. This viral disease is transmitted by mosquitoes and occurs mainly in tropical and subtropical areas of the world. Generally, there is only a small risk to travellers except during epidemics, which are usually seasonal (during and just after the rainy season). With unstable weather patterns thought to be responsible for large outbreaks in the Pacific, South-East Asia and Brazil, travellers

to these areas may be especially at risk of infection.

The *Aedes aegypti* mosquito, which transmits the dengue virus, is most active during the day, unlike the malaria mosquito, and is found mainly in urban areas, in and around human dwellings.

Signs and symptoms of dengue fever include a sudden onset of high fever, headache, joint and muscle pains (hence its old name, 'breakbone fever') and nausea and vomiting. A rash of small red spots appears three to four days after the onset of fever. Dengue is commonly mistaken for other infectious diseases, including influenza.

You should seek medical attention if you think you may be infected. Infection can be diagnosed by a blood test. There is no specific treatment for dengue. Aspirin should be avoided, as it increases the risk of haemorrhaging. Recovery may be prolonged, with tiredness lasting for several weeks. Severe complications are rare in travellers but include dengue haemorrhagic fever (DHF), which can be fatal without prompt medical treatment. DHF is thought to be a result of second infection due to a different strain (there are four major strains) and usually affects residents of the country rather than travellers.

There is no vaccine against dengue fever. The best prevention is to avoid mosquito bites at all times – see the malaria section earlier for more details.

Japanese B Encephalitis This viral infection of the brain is transmitted by mosquitoes. Most cases occur in rural areas as the virus exists in pigs and wading birds. Symptoms include fever, headache and alteration in consciousness. Hospitalisation is needed for correct diagnosis and treatment. There is a high mortality rate among those who have symptoms; of those who survive, many are intellectually disabled.

Cuts, Bites & Stings
Bedbugs & Lice Bedbugs live in various places, but particularly in dirty mattresses and bedding, evidenced by spots of blood

on bedclothes or on the wall. Bedbugs leave itchy bites in neat rows. Calamine lotion or Stingose spray may help.

All lice cause itching and discomfort. They make themselves at home in your hair (head lice), your clothing (body lice) or in your pubic hair (crabs). You catch lice through direct contact with infected people or by sharing combs, clothing and the like. Powder or shampoo treatment will kill the lice and infected clothing should then be washed in very hot, soapy water and left in the sun to dry.

Bites & Stings Bee and wasp stings are usually painful rather than dangerous. However, in people who are allergic to them, severe breathing difficulties may occur and require urgent medical care. Calamine lotion or Stingose spray will give relief and ice packs will reduce the pain and swelling.

Cuts & Scratches Wash well and treat any cut with an antiseptic such as povidone-iodine. Where possible, avoid bandages and Band-Aids, which can keep wounds wet.

Leeches & Ticks Leeches may be present in damp rainforest conditions; they attach themselves to your skin to suck your blood. Trekkers often get them on their legs or in their boots. Salt or a lighted cigarette end will make them fall off. Do not pull them off, as the bite is then more likely to become infected. Clean and apply pressure if the point of attachment is bleeding. An insect repellent may keep them away.

You should always check all over your body if you have been walking through a potentially tick-infested area as ticks can cause skin infections and other more serious diseases. If a tick is found attached, press down around the tick's head with tweezers, grab the head and gently pull upwards. Avoid pulling the rear of the body as this may squeeze the tick's gut contents through the attached mouth parts into the skin, increasing the risk of infection and disease. Smearing chemicals on the tick will not make it let go and is not recommended.

Snakes To minimise your chances of being bitten always wear boots, socks and long trousers when walking through undergrowth where snakes may be present. Don't put your hands into holes and crevices, and be careful when collecting firewood.

Snake bites do not cause instantaneous death and antivenins are usually available. Immediately wrap the bitten limb tightly, as you would for a sprained ankle, and then attach a splint to immobilise it. Keep the victim still and seek medical help, if possible with the dead snake for identification. Don't attempt to catch the snake if there is a possibility of being bitten again. Tourniquets and sucking out the poison are now comprehensively discredited.

Women's Health
Gynaecological Problems Antibiotic use, synthetic underwear, sweating and contraceptive pills can lead to fungal vaginal infections, especially when travelling in hot climates. Fungal infections are characterised by a rash, itch and discharge and can be treated with a vinegar or lemon-juice douche, or with yoghurt. Nystatin, miconazole or clotrimazole pessaries or vaginal cream are the usual treatment. Maintaining good personal hygiene and wearing loose-fitting clothes and cotton underwear may help prevent these infections.

STDs are a major cause of vaginal problems. Symptoms include a smelly discharge, painful intercourse and sometimes a burning sensation when urinating. Medical attention should be sought and male sexual partners must also be treated. Remember that in addition to these diseases HIV or hepatitis B may also be acquired during exposure. Besides abstinence, the best thing is to practise safe sex using condoms.

Pregnancy Most miscarriages occur during the first three months of pregnancy. Miscarriage is not uncommon and can occasionally lead to severe bleeding. The last three months should also be spent within reasonable distance of good medical care. A baby born as early as 24 weeks stands a chance of survival, but only in a good modern hospital. Pregnant women should avoid all unnecessary medication and vaccinations, and malarial prophylactics should still be taken where needed. Additional care should be taken to prevent illness and particular attention should be paid to diet and nutrition. Alcohol and nicotine, for example, should be avoided.

Less Common Diseases
The following diseases pose a small risk to travellers, and so are only mentioned in passing. Seek medical advice if you think you may have any of these diseases.

Cholera This is the worst of the watery diarrhoeas and medical help should be sought. Outbreaks of cholera are generally widely reported, so you can avoid such problem areas. *Fluid replacement is the most vital treatment* – the risk of dehydration is severe as you may lose up to 20L a day. If there is a delay in getting to hospital, then begin taking tetracycline. The adult dose is 250mg four times daily. It is not recommended for children under nine years nor for pregnant women. Tetracycline may help shorten the illness, but adequate fluids are required to save life.

Rabies This fatal viral infection is found in many countries. Many animals can be infected (such as dogs, cats, bats and monkeys) and it is their saliva that is infectious. Any bite, scratch or even lick from an animal should be cleaned immediately and thoroughly. Scrub with soap and running water, and then apply alcohol or iodine solution. Medical help should be sought promptly to receive a course of injections to prevent the onset of symptoms and death.

Tetanus This disease is caused by a germ that lives in soil and in the faeces of horses and other animals. It enters the body via breaks in the skin. The first symptom may be discomfort in swallowing, or stiffening of the jaw and neck; this is followed by painful convulsions of the jaw and whole body. The disease can be fatal. It can be prevented by vaccination.

Tuberculosis (TB) TB is a bacterial infection usually transmitted from person to person by coughing but which may be transmitted through consumption of unpasteurised milk. Milk that has been boiled is safe to drink, and the souring of milk to make yoghurt or cheese also kills the bacilli. Travellers are usually not at great risk as close household contact with the infected person is usually required before the disease is passed on. You may need to have a TB test before you travel as this can help diagnose the disease later if you become ill.

Typhus This disease is spread by ticks, mites or lice. It begins with fever, chills, headache and muscle pains followed a few days later by a body rash. There is often a large painful sore at the site of the bite and nearby lymph nodes are swollen and painful. Typhus can be treated under medical supervision. Seek local advice on areas where ticks pose a danger and always check your skin carefully for ticks after walking in a danger area such as a tropical forest. An insect repellent can help, and walkers in tick-infested areas should consider having their boots and trousers impregnated with benzyl benzoate and dibutylphthalate.

WOMEN TRAVELLERS
Attitudes Towards Women
Despite the perceived status of women within Myanmar, the 1998 UN Gender Development Index (GDI) ranks Myanmar a low 134th on a list of 174 nations with regard to a matrix of factors, which include education, health care, employment rate and share of earned income relative to male citizens of Myanmar. By contrast, neighbouring countries Thailand and India are ranked 40th and 128th respectively. The adult literacy rate for Myanmar women is 77.6% versus 88.7% for Myanmar men. Average share of earned income, however, totals 46.4%, which beats the US (40%), France (39.1%), Canada (37.9%) and Switzerland (32.4%).

In most respects Burmese women enjoy legal rights equal to those of Burmese men; for example, they own property and aren't barred from any profession. Unlike in the west, females do not traditionally change any portion of their names upon marriage; in the event of divorce, they are legally due half of all property accumulated during the marriage. Inheritance rights are also equally shared. Female children are educated alongside male children and, by university age, women tend to outnumber men in university and college enrolment. Most professions grant women a maternity leave of six weeks before birth and one or two months afterwards.

Religion is one arena in which women perpetually take a back seat. A small number of Buddhist shrines, for example Mandalay's Mahamuni Paya, have small areas around the main holy image that are off-limits to women. Many Burmese – women as well as men – believe a female birth indicates less religious merit than a male birth, and that it is easier for males to attain *nibbana* (nirvana). A small but devoted minority of men and women refute this view, pointing out that the actual *suttas*, or sayings of the Buddha, do not support this assumption.

Just as boys between the ages of five and 15 usually undergo a pre-puberty initiation as temporary novice monks, girls around the same age participate in an initiatory ear-piercing ceremony (often called 'ear-boring' in Burmese English). Some also become temporary nuns at this age. For details on clerical differences between Buddhist monks and nuns, see the Monks & Nuns entry under Burmese Buddhism in the Religion section of the Facts about Myanmar chapter.

Saw Myat Yin, insightful author of *Culture Shock! Burma*, expresses a viewpoint common among the majority of Burmese women, who see their role as equal but 'supportive and complementary ... rather than in competition' and that 'if they accept a role a step behind their menfolk they do so freely and willingly'. Though some westerners may find this difficult to believe, this represents the most commonly expressed perception in Myanmar. Even Aung San Suu Kyi, Myanmar's torchbearer of democracy, has written:

Although theoretically men are considered nobler because only a man can become a Buddha, Burmese women have never really had an inferior status. They have always had equal rights of inheritance and led active, independent lives. Secure in the knowledge of her own worth, the Burmese woman does not mind giving men the kind of respectful treatment that makes them so happy!

Safety Precautions

In Myanmar no Burmese woman would even consider travelling without at least one female companion, so women travelling alone are regarded as slightly peculiar by the locals. Women travelling alone and being seen off on boats and trains by Burmese friends may find the latter trying to find a suitably responsible older woman to keep them company on the trip.

As in most Buddhist countries, foreign women travelling in Myanmar are rarely hassled on the road as they might be in, for example, India, Malaysia or Indonesia. Save for one robbery incident in Bagan a few years ago, we have heard of no reports of foreign women being attacked or otherwise harassed while travelling in Myanmar.

GAY & LESBIAN TRAVELLERS

Most of the cultures of Myanmar are very tolerant of homosexuality, both male and female. Muslim and Christian Burmese communities are exceptions, but as they form relatively small minorities they rarely foist their world perspectives on people of other faiths.

Although it's difficult to tell given the opaqueness of the current military-directed government – which contains no true judiciary branch – there appear to be no laws that discriminate against homosexuals. Certainly we have never heard of anyone facing prosecution or arrest for homosexual behaviour.

The gay/lesbian scene around the country

is relatively low-key – certainly nowhere near as prominent as in neighbouring Thailand. There is no 'gay movement' in Myanmar as such, since there's no antigay establishment to move against. Whether speaking of dress or mannerism, lesbians and gays are generally accepted without comment.

Since homosexuals are free to meet wherever they wish without encountering social prejudice, furtive secrecy is much less common than in western countries and other less liberated parts of the world. Public displays of affection – whether heterosexual or homosexual – are frowned upon.

DISABLED TRAVELLERS

With its lack of paved roads or footpaths – even when present the latter are often uneven – Myanmar presents many physical obstacles for the mobility-impaired. Rarely do public buildings feature ramps or other access points for wheelchairs, nor do any hotels consistently make efforts to provide handicapped access (the single exception is Traders Hotel in Yangon, which has some ramping). Hence you're pretty much left to your own resources. Public transport is particularly crowded and difficult, even for the fully ambulatory.

For wheelchair travellers, any trip to Myanmar will require a good deal of advance planning. Fortunately a growing network of information sources can put you in touch with those who may have wheeled through Myanmar before. There is no better source of information than someone who's done it.

Organisations

Three international organisations that act as clearing houses for information on world travel for the mobility-impaired are: Mobility International USA (☎ 503-343 1284, fax 541-343 6812), PO Box 10767, Eugene, OR 97440, USA; Access Foundation (☎ 516-887 5798), PO Box 356, Malverne, NY 11565, USA; and Society for the Advancement of Travel for the Handicapped (SATH) (☎ 212-447 0027, fax 725 8253), Suite 610,

347 Fifth Avenue, New York, NY 10016, USA. SATH publishes a very good magazine called *Open World*.

Abilities magazine (☎ 416-923 1885, fax 923 9829), Suite 501, 489 College St, Toronto, ON M6G 1A5, Canada, carries a column called 'Accessible Planet', which offers tips on foreign travel for people with disabilities. The magazine is also available online at indie.ca/abilities/magazine/magazine.html. The book *Exotic Destinations for Wheelchair Travelers* by Ed Hansen & Bruce Gordon (Full Data Ltd, San Francisco) contains useful information on South-East Asia (including Thailand), though nothing specific to Myanmar.

If you're passing through Bangkok – as many people who visit Myanmar do – try contacting Disabled Peoples International, Council of Disabled People of Thailand (☎ 02-255 1718, fax 252 3676), 78/2 Thanon Tivanon, Pak Kret, Nonthaburi 11120, and Handicapped International, 87/2 Soi 15 Thanon Sukhumvit, Bangkok 10110.

SENIOR TRAVELLERS

Senior discounts aren't available in Myanmar, but the Burmese more than make up for this in the respect they typically show for the elderly. In all the cultures of Myanmar, status comes with age; there isn't nearly as heavy an emphasis on youth as in the western world. Deference for age manifests itself in the way the Burmese will go out of their way to help older persons in and out of vehicles or with luggage, and – usually but not always – in waiting on them first in shops and post offices.

Cross-generational entertainment is more common than in China, Vietnam or Thailand. Although there is some age stratification in karaoke clubs or discos, all ages are welcome. At more traditional events such as rural paya fairs and other temple-centred events, young and old dance and eat together.

TRAVEL WITH CHILDREN

Like many places in South-East Asia, travelling with children in Myanmar can be very rewarding as long as you come well prepared with the right attitudes, physical requirements and the usual parental patience. Lonely Planet's *Travel with Children* by Maureen Wheeler et al contains useful advice on how to cope with kids on the road and what to bring along to make things go more smoothly, with special attention paid to travel in developing countries.

The Burmese love children and in many instances will shower attention on your offspring, who will find ready playmates among their local counterparts and impromptu nanny service at practically every stop.

Due to Myanmar's overall low level of public sanitation, parents ought to lay down a few ground rules with regard to health maintenance – such as regular hand-washing – to head off potential medical problems. All the usual health precautions apply (see the Health section in this chapter for details); children should especially be warned not to play with animals encountered along the way since rabies is very common in Myanmar.

DANGERS & ANNOYANCES

Tales of insurgents, terrorists, forbidden areas and so on make Myanmar sound as if it is a rather unsafe country to visit, and for certain parts of the country this holds true. Myanmar's insurgency problem is a tricky one; the insurgents and guerrillas do not have enough support, equipment or energy to be more than a major irritation. They certainly have little hope of unseating the government. On the other hand, the government is also sadly short of popular support and enthusiasm, so they have little hope of totally overcoming their armed opponents. The result is a long-running stalemate.

Sporadic fighting continues along the border with Thailand, but unless you're a Kayin refugee this is unlikely to affect you. An Australian and a Thai national were abducted by Kayin rebels at the border in early 1998, but were released unharmed after a few days.

So long as you do not venture into those 'brown' or 'black' no-go areas (a possibility that the Burmese government is firmly determined not to let happen), you're very un-

likely to run into any difficulty. Apart from sometimes blowing up the Yangon-Mandalay railway line, the insurgents seem happy enough to stick to their own territory and leave the government's territory to the government. See the boxed text titled 'Insurgency' in the Facts about Myanmar chapter.

Of course, in the government-controlled areas (the places where you are permitted to go), the possibility of being mugged, robbed, held up or otherwise enjoying any of those other unpleasant, everyday western events is similarly remote. Basically Myanmar is a very friendly and safe country, though we do recommend that you keep a close eye on your valuables, particularly during overnight train trips. The shortage of luxury goods can make some of your possessions just a little bit too tempting at times.

Night-time road travel is not recommended due to the frightful condition of most roads and public vehicles. In some areas there are *dacoits* (highwaymen) who hold up vehicles at night; this is most common in the Kayin State and Mon and Tanintharyi divisions. Since the last edition of this book was published the economic downturn in South-East Asia has begun to bite, and road robberies in the latter three states appear to be on the increase. In some cases the bandits claim to be politically motivated, but their methods and targets leave this seriously in doubt. A group of eight bandits operating in southern Tanintharyi Division, between Myeik and Kawthoung, claim to belong to the All Burma Students Democratic Front (ABSDF), but their activities appear to be confined solely to ripping off passengers in civilian vehicles that ply this road – hardly a revolutionary stance. So far no foreigner has been affected in robberies in any of these areas.

You must also be cautious about talking Burmese politics with the locals, not for your safety but for theirs. The people who have the best chance of filling you in on the latest events are those Burmese who deal with foreign tourists on a regular basis – trishaw drivers, vendors, even the occasional candid MTT guide. Because of their occupations, these people can talk at length with foreigners without arousing suspicion; when not in the presence of other Burmese they can be surprisingly forthcoming with their views. The average Burmese on the street, however, would be very circumspect about conversing openly with a foreigner, especially about politics.

Forget about making bold gestures of political protest, as these, too, may get your Burmese contacts in trouble and yourself deported or jailed immediately. One traveller wrote to tell us that during her trip in Myanmar, two foreign bus travellers refused to show their passports at a military checkpoint as a form of protest. As a result, the bus driver was ordered by the army to stand in the sun for three hours while the travellers waited on the bus, completely unaware of the situation they had caused. The government is unlikely to harass tourists, but may well take it out on the locals behind closed doors. It is one thing to show a form of protest against the junta, but make sure your protest does not affect others. See Western Responses in the History section of the Facts about Myanmar chapter for details on a 1998 incident in which 18 foreigners were arrested in Yangon for handing out political leaflets.

See the earlier Health section for cautions on personal health and conditioning.

Air Travel

Government-operated MA has one of the worst safety records in the world. The year 1998 alone saw two MA crashes that involved fatalities. We recommend that you avoid travel on this airline if at all possible.

LEGAL MATTERS

The Myanmar government contains no judiciary branch as separate from the executive powers vested – by force of totalitarian rule – in the Tatmadaw. Thus you have absolutely zero legal recourse in case of arrest or detainment by the authorities, regardless of the charge. In actual everyday practice, foreigners are not hassled by the police or by the military except when involved in political activities. Certainly if you were ar-

rested, you would most likely be permitted to contact your consular agent in Myanmar for possible assistance.

If you purchase gems or jewellery from persons or shops that are not licensed by the government, you run the risk of having them all confiscated if customs officials find such items in your baggage when you're exiting the country.

Drugs are another area where you must be very careful. We know of a French traveller arrested for possession of opium or heroin in Kengtung and held for several weeks before he was able to bribe his way out.

Many foreigners have entered Myanmar illegally from Northern Thailand, but not all have succeeded in avoiding arrest. We know a Chinese Malaysian reporter, stationed in Bangkok, who was arrested near Kengtung for travelling in Myanmar without a valid visa. He spent an uncomfortable year in prison in Kengtung before being released. In late 1998 three western motorcyclists crossed from Thailand's Mae Hong Son Province into the Shan State illegally; they were held for three months before being released and deported.

See the 'What's My Line?' boxed text in this chapter on the hazards peculiar to journalistic professions.

BUSINESS HOURS

Most government offices are open Monday to Friday from 9.30 am to 4.30 pm (usually posted as 1630, according to the 24 hour system). Don't arrive at a government office at 4 pm expecting to get anything done; most government workers start drifting away to the local teashops after 3.30 pm.

Banks are open from 10 am to 2 pm on weekdays only. Private shops are generally open from around 9.30 or 10 am till 6 pm.

PUBLIC HOLIDAYS & SPECIAL EVENTS

Traditionally Myanmar follows a 12 month lunar calendar, so the old holidays and festivals will vary in date, by the Gregorian calendar, from year to year (see Months under Time & Dates earlier in this chapter for a list of these months). Myanmar also has a number of more recently originated holidays whose dates are fixed by the Gregorian calendar.

Festivals are drawn-out, enjoyable affairs in Myanmar. They generally take place or culminate on full-moon days, but the build-up can continue for days. There's often a country-fair atmosphere about these festivals – at some convenient grounds there will be innumerable stalls and activities that go on all night. Pwes, music and Burmese boxing bouts will all be part of the colourful scene. The normally calm Burmese can get really worked up during these festivals – at a full-moon festival on one of our visits to Yangon the supporters of the defeated favourite in a boxing bout were so enraged they wrecked the arena, and subsequent bouts had to be cancelled.

January/February
Independence Day
Independence Day on 4 January is a major public holiday marked by a seven day fair at Kandawgyi (Royal) Lake in Yangon. There are fairs all over the country at this time.

Union Day
Union Day on 12 February celebrates Bogyoke Aung San's short-lived achievement of unifying Myanmar's disparate racial groups. For two weeks preceding Union Day, the national flag is paraded from town to town, and wherever the flag rests there must be a festival. The month of Tabodwe culminates in a rice-harvesting festival on the new-moon day. *Htamin* (literally, rice), a special food-offering made and eaten at this time, consists of glutinous rice mixed with sesame, peanuts, shredded ginger and coconut. In villages large batches of htamin are cooked over open fires and stirred with big wooden paddles until they become a thick mass, after which the rice is wrapped in small banana-leaf parcels and distributed among all the members of the community.

February/March
Shwedagon Festival
The lunar month of Tabaung brings the annual Shwedagon Festival, the largest *paya pwe* (pagoda festival) in Myanmar. The full-moon day in Tabaung is also an auspicious occasion for the construction of new payas, and local paya festivals are held.

Peasants' Day/Armed Forces Day
Two holidays fall during our month of March: 2 March is Peasants' Day, while 27 March is Resistance or Armed Forces Day, celebrated with parades and fireworks. Since 1989, the Tatmadaw has made it a tradition to pardon a number of prisoners on Armed Forces Day.

April/May
Buddha's Birthday
The full-moon day of Kason s celebrated as the Buddha's birthday, the day of his enlightenment and the day he entered nibbana. Thus it is known as the 'thrice blessed day'. The holiday is celebrated by the ceremonial watering of *bo* trees, the sacred banyan tree under which Buddha attained enlightenment. One of the best places to observe this ceremony is at Yangon's Shwedagon Paya, where a procession of girls carry earthen jars to water the three banyan trees on the western side of the compound.

Workers' Day
Although the government renounced socialism in 1989, the country still celebrates May Day – 1 May – as Workers' Day.

June/July
Buddhist Lent
The full moon of Waso is the beginning of the three month Buddhist 'Lent'. Laypeople present monasteries with stacks of new robes for resident monks, since during the Lent period monks are restricted to their monasteries for a prolonged period of spiritual retreat. Ordinary people are also expected to be rather more religious during this time – marriages do not take place and it is inauspicious to move house. The most devout Burmese Buddhist will observe eight precepts – rather than the usual five – for the duration of the season. This is a good time for young men to temporarily enter the monasteries.

Martyrs' Day
The 19th of July is Martyrs' Day, commemorating the assassination of Bogyoke Aung San and his comrades on that day in 1947. Wreaths are laid at his mausoleum north of the Shwedagon Paya in Yangon. Government officials probably pray the Burmese people don't attempt to reinstall the planned civilian government aborted by Aung San's assassination.

July/August
Wagaung Festival
At the festival in Wagaung, lots are drawn to see who will have to provide monks with their alms. If you're in Mandalay, try to get to Taungbyone, about 30km north, where there is a noisy, seven day festival to keep the nats happy.

The Water Festival

Around the middle of April, the three day Thingyan (Water festival) starts the Burmese New Year. Thingyan, from the Sanskrit *samkranta* (fully passed over), celebrates the passage of the sun from the sign of Pisces into the sign of Aries in the zodiac. This is the height of the dry and hot season and, as in Thailand's Songkran, it is celebrated in a most raucous manner – by throwing buckets of cold water at anyone who dares to venture into the streets. Foreigners are not exempt!

In cities, temporary stages called *pandal* (from the Tamil *pendel*) are erected along main thoroughfares. Each pandal is sponsored by civic groups, neighbourhood associations, student societies or government departments, the members of whom stand next to rows of water barrels and douse every person or vehicle that passes by.

On a spiritual level, the Burmese believe that during this three day period the king of the *nats* (spirits), Thagyamin, visits the human world to tally his annual record of the good deeds and misdeeds humans have performed. Villagers place flowers and sacred leaves in front of their homes to welcome the nat. Thagyamin's departure on the morning of the third day marks the beginning of the new year, when properly brought-up young people wash the hair of their elder kin, Buddha images are ceremonially washed and *pongyis* (monks) are offered particularly appetising almsfood.

Although the true meaning of the festival is still kept alive by ceremonies such as these, nowadays it's mainly a festival of fun. In between getting soaked, there will be dancing, singing and theatre. In the latter, the emphasis is on satire – particularly making fun of the government, the latest female fashions and any other items of everyday interest. Cultural taboos against women acting in a boisterous manner are temporarily lifted, so women can 'kidnap' young men, blacken their faces with soot or oil, bind their hands and dunk their heads in buckets of water until the boys surrender and perform a hilarious monkey dance for the girls.

Joe Cummings

September/October

Boat Races

This is the height of the wet season, so what better time to hold boat races? They're held in rivers, lakes and even ponds all over Myanmar, but the best place to be is Inle where the Buddha images at the Phaung Daw U Kyaung are ceremonially toured around the lake in the huge royal barge, the Karaweik. The latter comes just before the festival of Thadingyut and usually overlaps late September and early October.

Thadingyut

In Thadingyut, the Buddhist Lent comes to an end and all those couples who had been putting off marriage now rush into each other's arms. Monks are free to travel from kyaung to kyaung or to go on pilgrimage to holy spots such as Kyaiktiyo or Mt Popa. The Festival of Lights takes place during Thadingyut to celebrate Buddha's return from a period of preaching

dhamma (Buddhist philosophy) in Tavatimsa (the highest *deva* realm), his way lit by devas who lined the route of his descent. For the three days of the festival all of Myanmar is lit by oil lamps, fire balloons, candles and even mundane electric lamps. Every house has a paper lantern hanging outside and it's a happy, joyful time all over Myanmar – particularly after the solemnity of the previous three months. Pwes may be performed on *pandals* (stage platforms) erected along city streets, particularly in Mandalay.

October/November

Tazaungmon

The full-moon night of Tazaungmon is an occasion for another 'festival of lights', known properly as Tazaungdaing. It's particularly celebrated in the Shan State – in Taunggyi there are fire balloon competitions. In some areas there are also speed-weaving competitions during the night – young Burmese women show their prowess at weaving by attempting to produce robes for Buddha images between dusk and dawn. The results, finished or not, are donated to the monks. The biggest weaving competitions take place at Shwedagon Paya in Yangon.

Kahtein

Tazaungmon also brings *kahtein* (Pali: *kathina*), a one month period at the end of Buddhist Lent during which new monastic robes and requisites are offered to the monastic community. Many people simply donate cash; kyat notes are folded and stapled into floral patterns on wooden 'trees' called *padetha* and offered to the monasteries. This symbolises a much older tradition in which laypeople would leave kathina robes hanging from tree branches in the forest for monks to find.

National Day

Myanmar's national day falls in late November or early December.

November/December

Nadaw

During Nadaw, many nat pwes are held; Nadaw is actually spelt with the characters for nat and *taw* (respectful honorific).

Christmas

Despite Myanmar's predominantly Buddhist background, Christmas Day is a public holiday in deference to the many Christian Kayin.

December/January

Kayin New Year

Held on the first waxing moon of Pyatho, the Kayin new year is considered a national holiday. Kayin communities throughout Myanmar celebrate by wearing their traditional dress of woven tunics over red longyis and by hosting folk dancing and singing performances. The largest celebrations are held in the Kayin suburb of Insein, just north of Yangon, and in Hpaan, the capital of the Kayin State.

Ananda Festival

The Ananda Festival, held at the Ananda Paya in Bagan, also takes place during Pyatho.

Paya Pwes

In addition to these main pan-Myanmar festivals, nearly every active paya or kyaung community hosts occasional celebrations of its own, often called pagoda festivals in Burmese English. The typical paya pwe features the same kinds of activities as a major festival – craft and food vendors, music and dance – on a smaller scale. The biggest proliferation of paya fairs occur on full-moon days and nights during the January to March period, following the main rice harvest, providing local paddy farmers and their families a good excuse to party. The festivals also offer added market venues for local basketweavers, potters, woodcarvers, blacksmiths, longyi-weavers and other artisans.

To the professional *hse-hna pwe thi* (twelve-festival traders) who travel from festival to festival following the lunar calendar, the smaller paya fairs serve as convenient fillers between major gigs. Other assorted camp followers include fortunetellers, movable teashops, tent barbers, homespun beauty consultants, pickpockets and professional beggars.

Particular paya festivals are described in the appropriate destination sections throughout this guidebook.

ACTIVITIES
Cycling

Although one highly publicised package tour group cycling south from Bagan had problems with permits a couple of years ago, many individuals have brought their bikes into Myanmar and cycled around the unrestricted areas of the country with no problems. Cycling is the ideal form of local transport because bikes are cheap, nonpolluting and keep you moving slowly enough to see everything. The terrain – varying from rutted, unsealed dirt or gravel roads to potholed, semi-paved ones – is definitely not for the average touring bike. Instead you'll need a sturdy mountain bike equipped with thick tyres. Shoulders may be nonexistent, but for the most part drivers are courteous and move over for bicycles. Plain black Indian or Chinese bicycles can be hired in Mandalay, but so far nowhere else we've seen. Carefully note the condition of the bike before hiring; if it breaks down you are responsible and parts can be expensive.

There is plenty of opportunity for dirt-road and off-road pedalling in all areas of the country, but be sure to stay well within the boundaries of what's allowed for foreign tourists. Don't even think about going north of Lashio, east of Taungoo, east of Taunggyi or south of Kalaw, as these areas are particularly sensitive. Good touring routes include the two-lane roads along the Ayeyarwady between Mandalay and Yangon via Bagan, Pyay and many other less well known towns. The terrain along the Ayeyarwady is mostly flat and the river scenery is inspiring.

One note of caution: before you leave home, go over your bike with a fine-toothed comb and fill your repair kit with every imaginable spare part. You're highly unlikely to be able to buy that crucial gismo for your machine when it breaks down somewhere in the back of beyond as the sun sets.

No special permits are needed for bringing a bicycle into the country, although bikes may be registered by customs – which means if you don't leave the country with your bike you'll have to pay a customs duty. Most larger cities have bike shops but they usually stock only a few Indian, Chinese, Thai or locally made parts. Japanese bike parts are rare. All the usual bike trip precautions apply – bring a repair kit with plenty of spare parts, a helmet, reflective clothing and plenty of insurance.

You can take bicycles on the trains for a relatively small cargo fee. Buses often don't charge (if they do it will be something nominal); on the ordinary buses they'll place your bike on the roof, and on express aircon buses it will go in the cargo hold.

Hiking

Northern Myanmar's potential as a serious hiking venue remains virtually untapped due to the sensitive political nature of the mountainous frontier states. Out-of-town hikes are now permitted in the 'secure' area of the Shan State stretching from Kalaw east to Inle. So far about the only place you'll find hiking guides are in the small towns of Kalaw and Nyaungshwe (Yaunghwe).

The area around Kalaw and Pindaya offers a variety of possible mountain hikes to minority villages. At present overnight hikes don't seem to be officially permitted, though that hasn't stopped some visitors

from spending the night in the occasional village. Guides in Nyaungshwe can lead hikes into the hills east of Inle, but not too far east, as Shan and Red Pa-O insurgent territory crops up quickly in this direction.

Similar areas east of Taungoo are an interesting possibility, though again this takes one into insurgent areas (Kayin and Kayah).

Kengtung, in the far eastern section of the Shan State, would make an excellent base for treks to nearby Wa, Shan, Kheun and Akha villages. There are guides in Kengtung gearing up for the day when the government OKs such activities. Currently there are a few 'underground' treks in the area – ask around.

Jungle hiking on Lampi Kyun, a long, narrow island off the coast of Tanintharyi Division, can be arranged through Phuket-based adventure tour companies or as an add-on to Myeik Archipelago dive itineraries. The closest mainland jumping-off point for Lampi is the town of Kawthoung at Myanmar's southernmost tip.

Mt Kyaikto, site of Kyaiktiyo Paya (see the Highlights section at the beginning of this book), offers an easily navigated but physically challenging uphill climb if you start from the bottom – about a four hour hike. Branch trails around the mountain provide at least a couple of days worth of side hikes that few foreign visitors have so far experienced.

Mountaineers everywhere are awaiting the day when the highest mountain in South-East Asia, snow-clad Hkakabo Razi (5889m), on the border between Myanmar and Tibet, and nearby Gamlang Razi (5835m) are open to climbers. So far there's been lots of talk about opening this area up but little action. Those few foreigners who have made it as far as Putao – a valley town in the same general region – have been disappointed; until the area north of Putao opens there's little point in going to the trouble of obtaining one of the rare permits issued for Putao.

Motorcycling Tours

In many ways, the combination of Myanmar's hilly terrain and generally bad roads is an off-roader's dream. Quite recently, a well organised off-road motorcycle touring company has started up a 1700km-long road and trail tour. Other companies are planning to follow. Starting in Yangon, a dry-season tour heads up the coast along the Bay of Bengal and takes in Bagan, Mt Popa and Inle Lake. A monsoon-season tour avoids the drenched coastline, but takes in Mandalay and other inland sites.

Each tour has a maximum of five riders, plus a guide on motorcycle and a 4WD back-up vehicle with mechanic, luggage etc. The cost for a 13 day, 12 night tour is about US$1400, which includes everything but entrance fees. For more information contact CSL Travels & Tours Co (☎/fax 01-514047, email tradpra@datserco.com.mm) at 24 Inya Myaing Lan, GPO Box 1062, Yangon.

Diving & Snorkelling

Coastal, insular and marine Myanmar are nearly untouched in terms of their potential for underwater exploration. The only area that has been dived so far – and only since January 1997 – is a small portion of the Myeik Archipelago, a string of some 804 islands running more or less parallel to the coast of the 480km-long Myeik Peninsula.

Myeik Archipelago diving has so far been organised only as liveaboard dive cruises out of Phuket or Kawthoung. Reports say diving conditions are excellent. Many islands feature lofty limestone sea cliffs pockmarked with caves, some of which form extensive submarine networks or lead to enclosed tidal lagoons. The larger islands also contain mountainous, forested interiors with a considerable hiking potential to supplement diving activities. Around a dozen big-league dive sites have so far been identified, from the so-called Burma Banks in the south (claimed by Myanmar but actually in international waters according to international maritime law) all the way to Tanintharyi Kyun (known to the British as Tenasserim Island) west of the port town of Myeik itself.

For the time being the only way to dive in the Myeik Archipelago is to join one of

the liveaboard cruises operated by companies based in Thailand. A typical six day/five night trip costs around US$1000 per person, plus US$90 for a Myanmar customs entry permit. Among the more experienced outfitters offering Myeik diving are:

Asian Adventures
(☎/fax 076-342798,
email info@asian-adventures.com)
231 Thanon Rat Uthit, Hat Patong, Phuket 83150, Thailand
Dive Asia Pacific
(☎ 076-263732, fax 263733,
email info@dive-asiapacific.com)
PO Box 244, Phuket, Thailand
Divemaster
(☎ 02-938 4216, fax 938 4218,
email divemstr@ksc9.th.com)
110/63 Thanon Lat Phrao, Soi 18, Bangkok, Thailand
Fantasea Divers
(☎ 076-340088, 295511, fax 340309,
email info@fantasea.net)
PO Box 20, Hat Patong, Phuket, Thailand
Faraway Sail & Dive
(☎/fax 076-283129,
email info@far-away.net)
45/10 Muu 9, Soi Suki, Thanon Chao Fa, Phuket, Thailand
South East Asia Liveaboards Co
(☎ 076-340406, fax 340586,
email info@sealiveaboards.com)
225 Thanon Rat Uthit, Hat Patong, Phuket, Thailand

Most programs start from Ranong, Thailand, and offer four to six days of diving in the islands for around US$800 to US$1000 per person, all inclusive.

Asian Adventures is currently renovating the colonial Hotel Mergui in Myeik with the intention of turning it into an inn oriented towards divers and others interested in marine tourism. When completed this will become the first land-based diving operation in Myanmar.

Paddling

Myanmar's many great rivers, most of which are relatively clean by international standards, bear incredible potential as venues for long-distance canoeing and kayaking. We don't know anyone who has tried it yet, but one might assume that most rivers in the country would be off-limits to foreign paddlers. One exception might be the Ayeyarwady River between Mandalay and Yangon, which is heavily travelled by IWT boats, as well as the occasional tourist boat. River traffic towards Yangon tends to be heavy, so if you were to attempt this stretch, you might best put in no farther north than Mandalay and no farther south than Pyay.

As with bicycles, we know of no customs regulations forbidding the temporary import of a canoe or kayak. Of course the reality of showing up at Mingaladon airport in Yangon with a 4m kayak might be different.

Sea kayaking is another extraordinary possibility. One outfitter based in Thailand, South East Asia Liveaboards Co (see the Diving & Snorkelling section for contact info), offers a five night 'guided sea kayak safari' in the Myeik Archipelago, which features a kayaking component along with sailing, hiking, snorkelling and diving. Asian Adventures' planned dive centre in Myeik may also offer kayak trips to nearby islands.

MEDITATION STUDY

Several monasteries and meditation centres in Yangon provide opportunities for the study and practice of *satipatthana vipassana,* or insight-awareness meditation, based on instructions in the Maha Satipatthana Sutta of the Theravada Buddhist canon. This type of meditation is also commonly practised in Sri Lanka and Thailand, though the tradition of lay practice is probably stronger in Myanmar. Many westerners have come to Myanmar to practise at the various centres for periods of time ranging from 10 days to more than a year. Visitors typically attach themselves to a respected *sayadaw* (chief abbot) in the Buddhist tradition for the duration.

The most famous centre in Yangon is the Mahasi Meditation Centre (Mahasi Thathana Yeiktha in Burmese), founded in 1947 by the late Mahasi Sayadaw, perhaps Myanmar's greatest meditation teacher. The Mahasi Sayadaw technique strives for intensive,

moment-to-moment awareness of every physical movement, every mental and physical sensation, and ultimately, every thought. This technique has spread well beyond Myanmar's borders and is now commonly taught in Buddhist centres all over the world. The Mahasi Meditation Centre is on Thathana Yeiktha Lan (formerly Hermitage Rd) off Kaba Aye Paya Lan, north of Kandawgyi, about 10 minutes from the city centre or 20 minutes from the airport.

Two of the Mahasi centre's chief meditation teachers, Sayadaw U Pandita and Sayadaw U Janaka, have established their own centres – Panditarama and Chanmyay Yeiktha – which are also highly regarded. Although each presents its own slight twist on the Mahasi Sayadaw technique, the basic meditation instructions are similar.

Another famous centre is the International Meditation Centre, founded by the late U Ba Khin, a well known lay teacher. The U Ba Khin technique focuses on a deep appreciation of impermanence and on consciously moving or 'sweeping' one's mental awareness throughout the body. In India this practice has been perpetuated by SN Goenka. Instruction at all of the above centres is given to foreigners in English.

For practice sessions of less than a month, a tourist visa will suffice. To obtain the necessary 'special-entry visa' for a long-term stay of more than a month, applicants must receive a letter of invitation from the centre where they would like to study, which may in turn require a letter of introduction from an affiliated meditation centre abroad. This invitation is then presented to a Myanmar consulate or embassy that will issue a visa for an initial stay of six to 12 weeks, as recommended by the centre. This may be extended in Yangon at the discretion of the centre and Burmese immigration.

Important points to remember: the special-entry visa takes eight to 10 weeks to be issued and cannot be applied for while a person is in Myanmar on a tourist visa. Food and lodging are provided at no charge at the centres but meditators must follow eight precepts, which include abstaining from food after noon and foregoing music, dancing, jewellery, perfume and high or luxurious beds. Daily schedules are rigorous and may involve nearly continuous practice from 3 am till 11 pm. Students may be given permission to travel in Myanmar at the end of a long period of study but this is not automatic. Finally, westerners who have undergone the training say it is not recommended for people with no previous meditation experience.

For further information, contact:

Chanmyay Yeiktha Meditation Centre
(☎ 01-661479, fax 667050)
655-A Kaba Aye Paya Lan, Yangon; a second branch (☎ 01-620321) is set among 10 acres of gardens in Hmawbi, a 50 minute drive north of Yangon.
Dhamma Joti Vipassana Centre
(☎ 01-549290)
Nga Htat Gyi Paya Lan, Bahan Township, Yangon
International Meditation Centre
(☎ 01-551549)
31-A Inyamyaing Lan, Yangon
Mahasi Meditation Centre
(☎ 01-541971, fax 289960)
16 Thathana Yeiktha Lan, Yangon
Panditarama Meditation Centre (Shwe Taung Gon Sasana Yeiktha)
(☎ 01-531448, fax 527171)
80/A Shwetaunggyaw Lan (Thanlwin Lan), Yangon; Panditarama Forest Meditation Centre, 3km north-east off the highway to Bago, is a second branch.
Saddhamma Ransi Meditation Centre
7 Zeyar Khema Lan, Mayangone Township, Yangon

For further information on the teachings of Mahasi Sayadaw and U Ba Khin, read *Living Dharma: Teachings of Twelve Buddhist Masters* by Jack Kornfield (see the Recommended Reading section under Religion in the Facts about Myanmar chapter for more titles).

Other meditation centres can be found outside Yangon, particularly in Sagaing, which is Myanmar's principal monastic centre in terms of numbers of monks, nuns, monasteries and nunneries. In Sagaing, Kyaswa Kyaung hosts occasional Mahasi

Sayadaw-style retreats oriented towards foreigners, under the direction of Sayadaw U Lakkhana and a couple of foreign lay teachers. For further information contact MettaDana@aol.com by email, or call ☎ 510-290 6148 in the USA.

In Mawlamyaing, Venerable Pak Auk Sayadaw teaches satipatthana vipassana using a penetrative and highly technical approach at Pak Auk Forest Monastery (☎ 032-22132) c/o Major U Khan Sain, 653 Lower Main Rd.

WORK

Although Myanmar is one of the 20 poorest countries in the world, there are, surprisingly, a few employment opportunities around for foreigners. As one might guess, the development game flourishes in Yangon, with plenty of NGO and UN operations in place. Getting information on these can be rather difficult; your best bet is simply to turn up in Yangon and ask around at places where expats hang out, such as the 50th Street Bar & Grill. Or contact known NGOs/UN offices overseas and ask whether they have any programs in Myanmar. To be considered for an NGO or UN position you'll need an educational and experiential background to match, and will most likely have to arrange your visa and work permit outside Myanmar.

English teaching is another possibility. Despite the high demand for English language instruction, the opportunities are much slimmer than in most other Asian countries, simply due to the lack of disposable income. Still there are a few private language schools in Yangon and Mandalay – check the yellow pages of the Yangon phone directory. As might be expected, rates of pay are quite low – basically no more than a subsistence allowance by most standards. Work permits aren't necessarily needed if you're just looking for temporary work.

Foreigners have also obtained temporary work as extras in Yangon's burgeoning film industry. As in India, pay rates are very low – this really isn't a moneymaking proposition as much as it is a sometimes fun experience.

ACCOMMODATION

Following the privatisation of hotels in 1992 after 30 years of state control, the accommodation scene in Myanmar has been turned upside down. In terms of new hotels under construction and on the drawing boards, Myanmar was in fact considered the hottest hotel market in the world in the mid-1990s, as dozens of large and small developers tried to meet the pent-up demand created by years of mismanagement by MHT. The Ministry unloaded its own properties as fast as it could sell them so that at present there are very few government-owned places left in the country.

Between 1988 and 1992 no town or city in the entire country could claim more than four legal places to stay. Now that anyone can open a hotel or guesthouse licensed for foreigners, new hotels and guesthouses in Yangon alone have been opening at an average rate of 40 per year, with a total of over 150 at the end of 1999. In Mandalay the number of new hotels and guesthouses established during a similar interval reached 70, while in Bagan/Nyaung U the total came to 65. Current figures for other cities include around 20 places to stay in Taunggyi, 25 in Inle, 20 in Bago, 10 in Kalaw and seven in Kyaingtong. Many places in Yangon and Mandalay are foreign-owned. Such growth is all the more amazing given the overall political situation and the fact that foreign companies cannot buy land but must lease it instead.

Although there are now around 450 licensed places to stay throughout the country, occupancy rates for hotels in Myanmar average a low 20%. If that rate doesn't improve, it is likely there will be an eventual shakeout of the hotel industry in which many properties may close. Already we are beginning to see some closures in Yangon.

Technically any hotel or guesthouse that accepts foreign guests must have a special lodging licence – this is usually displayed somewhere on the wall behind the reception desk. Such a licence requires these hotels and guesthouses to charge US dollars or FECs, and to have a minimum of five rooms and certain room standards that are substantially beyond the usual local inn. This seems partially designed to justify higher rates so that the government can collect more tax, partially to keep foreigners separate from Burmese and partially out of a concern that Myanmar will develop a poor image if foreigners see the inside of a typical Burmese guesthouse.

Traditionally, the Burmese don't stay in hotels or guesthouses when they travel but rather in the homes of family, friends or business associates, or at monasteries if none of the former are available. As in other countries in South-East Asia, until recently the hotel/guesthouse mainly functioned as a place where men gambled, drank and enjoyed the company of prostitutes – activities strongly discouraged by Burmese Buddhism – away from the disapproving eyes of their families.

While shopping for places to stay, keep in mind that the newer private hotels tend to represent better value than government-owned hotels or hotels that were previously government-owned. Many of the latter are now owned or managed by former MHT hotel managers who have long been accustomed to charging high rates for indifferent service and mediocre room quality. Of the countless new places to stay, among the best are the small, family-run places with fewer than 10 rooms.

Although the upcoming discussion of two tiered rates, nonfunctioning amenities and tiresome breakfasts may sound discouraging, most people will find it's well worth putting up with these frustrations to be able to travel in Myanmar. The situation has actually improved a great deal over previous years when your only choice of places to stay were low-standard, high-priced MHT-owned hotels – of which there were relatively few. Rates and overall variety have improved tremendously over the last four years.

Rates, Services & Taxes

Much of the whirlwind hotel development has arrived in over-anticipation of future tourism growth, so a lot of rooms will probably stay empty for the next few years. This means competition for your accommodation dollar will be keen and rates should continue to settle out on the low side. In 1998 alone, rates fell by at least 30%.

For the time being, many of Myanmar's hotels can be a bit overpriced by most South-East Asian standards. In the first place almost all hotels follow a two tiered pricing system – charging one rate for locals in kyat and another for foreigners in US dollars/FECs. A typical middle-of-the-road, Burmese-owned hotel might charge K3000 for Burmese and US$30 for foreigners – nearly four times the local price figured at the real exchange rate. We stayed at a guesthouse in Dawei that took K400 from Burmese and US$10 from foreigners – close to a ten-fold increase at then-current exchange rates! If you complain, the usual excuse is that hotels that accept payment in US dollars must pay tax to the government in US dollars – an irrational argument considering 10% of one currency's true value for any given amount is exactly the same as 10% of another.

Bargaining is the answer – for budget and mid-range places you should expect to be able to talk the asking rate down. At the top end, rates aren't really much different from elsewhere in South-East Asia and you're not likely to get much of a discount – but it doesn't hurt to try.

Most places offer a 'free breakfast' as part of the room rate. This is where you should begin bargaining, as the breakfasts at most places (there are exceptions) are a uniformly boring plate of white toast and fried eggs with tea or instant coffee. Asking for a room without breakfast can net a savings of as much as US$2 to US$4 per night. You can usually buy a better and more filling breakfast at a local teashop for less than K150. If the hotel won't give you a discount for dropping breakfast, ask if you can at least get a changing variety of breakfasts, such as *mohinga* (pronounced moun-hinga, rice noodles served with a thick, yellow fish soup), *hsi htamin* (turmeric-coloured sticky rice topped with sesame seeds and shredded coconut) or other Burmese specialities, from time to time to break the monotony.

Except for international-class hotels like The Strand, Traders Hotel and the Summit Parkview – where a uniform dollar pricing structure is used – and a few hotels way off the beaten track where everyone pays in kyat, virtually all hotels use the two tiered pricing system. If you're travelling with a hired vehicle and driver, your driver can get a free room at most hotels – or at least he should get the much lower kyat rate reserved for Burmese.

Fortunately for travellers on a tight budget, there are now a smattering of places in the US$5 to US$10 per person range. Typically this gets a bare cubicle with two beds and a cold-water bathroom down the hall. Rooms with a private cold-water bath cost a few dollars more. A toast-and-egg breakfast is usually included. In some places you can now stay in rooms for as low as US$3 a night.

Moving up from this category, room rates seem to make a big leap as hot water, aircon and TV suddenly become part of the picture. In fact, compared with the hotel scene in neighbouring countries, Myanmar seems to have way too many small hotels with air-con, hot water and TV in every room; somehow the Burmese are getting the message that all foreigners need every one of these amenities. Because of problems with inconsistent electric power supplies, the hot water and air-con units in these hotels frequently don't work properly, if at all – an especially frustrating situation when you're paying extra for these. For this type of room the minimum rate ranges around US$12 to US$24 for a single and US$24 to US$36 for a double. Toast-and-egg breakfasts, of course, are included.

The next level of hotels offers larger rooms, usually a bit more atmosphere, and perhaps a sitting garden, for US$40 to US$55. Toast and eggs again! Many of the places in this price range are older hotels that once belonged to the MHT but are now privately owned. The service in these hotels can be terrible at one place, great at another.

Profit margins on foreigner rates are probably among the highest in the world since upkeep is obviously very low. Some hotels in this range are modern but characterless Chinese-owned buildings with tidy rooms and all the amenities. The same problems with nonfunctioning air-con and hot water tend to occur. In this category are a few rare exceptions where the hotel breakfasts include a variety of fresh fruits, eggs cooked in your choice of styles, or where Burmese breakfasts can be taken as an alternative.

Once you're in the US$60 and up range most of the amenities you pay for actually seem to function. At this level many of the hotels are owned by Singaporean, Taiwanese or Hong Kong companies, which usually don't insult you with 'free breakfasts'.

Depending on your luck and the current state of hotel development, you can usually find a few kyat-priced hotels to stay at in out-of-the-way areas, and even in fairly accessible but relatively untouristed towns such as Shwebo, Magwe, Myingyan and Pakkoku. We found other towns where guesthouses cost no more than K1000 a night, sometimes as low as K400. The rooms in such places are very basic – perhaps two hard beds in a room surrounded by wood partitions that stop 30cm short of the ceiling. Once the local government begins enforcing the foreigner licence law this kind of place will become more difficult to find.

Most hotels and guesthouses charge a 10% tax on top of room rates. Larger, more expensive hotels also add a 10% service charge.

FOOD

You can eat very well and very inexpensively in Myanmar. Before 1995 it was often difficult to find decent Burmese food in local restaurants, but the economic development in urban areas has brought substantial improvements in the availability and quality of Burmese cuisine. Chinese and Indian foods are also quite popular in the larger towns and cities. Street and market stalls tend to provide the regional dishes, but with these you must be a little wary of cleanliness. Like most South-East

Asians, the Burmese are great snackers, and in the evening many street stalls sell tasty little snacks.

Myanmar has a wide variety of tropical fruits, and in season you can get delicious strawberries in Pyin U Lwin, Mandalay and even Yangon. Don't miss the huge avocados if you're in the Inle area. In Yangon and Mandalay snack bars have excellent, and seemingly healthy, ice cream but you should avoid the ice cream street vendors unless you have a very strong stomach.

Food can be incredibly cheap in Myanmar if you pay in free-market kyat – and this never seems to be a problem except at the Yangon international airport snack bar and the biggest Yangon hotels.

Bamar & Regional Cuisines

Mainstream Burmese cuisine represents an intriguing blend of Bamar, Mon, Indian and Chinese influences. *Htamin* (rice) is the core of any Burmese meal, to be eaten with a choice of *hin* (curry dishes), most commonly fish, chicken, prawns or mutton. Very little beef or pork are eaten by the Burmese – beef because it's considered offensive to most Hindus and Buddhists, pork because the nats disapprove. Many Buddhists in fact abstain from eating the flesh of any four legged animal, and, during the Buddhist Waso or rains retreat, may take up a 'fire-free' diet that includes only uncooked vegetables and fruit. Virtually all butchers in Myanmar are either Muslim or Chinese.

Bamar curries are the mildest in Asia in terms of chilli power – in fact most cooks don't use chillies at all in their recipes, just a simple *masala* of turmeric, ginger, garlic, salt and onions, plus plenty of peanut oil and shrimp paste. Heat can be added in the form of *balachaung*, a table condiment made from chillies, tamarind and dried shrimp pounded together, or from the very pungent, very hot *ngapi jaw* (shrimp paste fried in peanut oil with chilli, garlic and onions). Curries are generally cooked until the oil separates from all other ingredients and floats on top. Some restaurants will add oil to maintain the correct top layer, as the oil preserves the underlying food from contamination by insects and airborne bacteria while the curries sit in open, unheated pots for hours at a time. When you're served a bowl of hin, you're not expected to consume all the oil; just spoon the ingredients from underneath.

Almost everything is flavoured with *ngapi*, which is a salty paste concocted from dried and fermented shrimp or fish, and can be very much an acquired taste. A thin sauce of pressed fish or shrimp called *ngan-pya-ye* may also be used to salt Bamar dishes. Mi Mi Khaing, author of one of the seminal works on Burmese cuisine, *Cook and Entertain the Burmese Way*, explains:

> It is sometimes observed that cheeses, and the esoteric pleasures therefrom, are strangely absent in East Asian cuisines. Cheese needs milk, and so too herds lovingly bred; whereas our rivers, spreading into immense deltas and other waters, already abound with fish of kind upon kind there for the netting. Adjoining great fisheries are saltbeds of the long Burmese coastline. Deliciously odoriferous foods result from this conjoining.

One of the culinary highlights of Bamar cuisine is undoubtedly *thouq* (also *lethouq*) – light, spicy salads made with raw vegetables or fruit tossed with lime juice, onions, peanuts, chillies and other spices. Among the most exquisite are *maji-yveq thouq*, made with tender young tamarind leaves, and *shauk-thi thouq*, mixed with pomelo, a large citrus similar to grapefruit. *Htamin let-thouq* are savoury salads made with cooked rice.

Another common side dish is Indian-influenced *peh-hin-ye* (lentil soup, or dahl); the better restaurants may serve dahl fortified with chunks of boiled turnips, potatoes and okra. A *hin-jo* (mild soup) of green squash may also be available. At an authentic *htamin zain* (rice shop), once you've ordered one or more curries, then rice, dahl, soup, side dishes and Chinese tea come automatically at no charge. Soft drinks, beer or Indian tea cost extra. Hotel restaurants usually have a few Bamar dishes on their

Table Etiquette

At home, most families take their meals sitting on reed mats around a low, round table about 30cm in height. In restaurants, chairs and tables are more common. The entire meal is served at once, rather than in courses. In ordinary Bamar restaurants, each individual diner in a group eating together typically orders a small plate of curry for himself or herself, while side dishes are shared among the whole party. This contrasts with China and Thailand, for example, where every dish is usually shared.

Traditionally, Bamar food is eaten with the fingers, much like Indian food, but nowadays, it's also common for urban Burmese to eat with a *hkayin* (fork) and *zun* (tablespoon), in the Thai fashion. Such utensils are always available at Bamar restaurants and almost always given automatically to foreign diners. The fork is held in the left hand and used as a probe to push food onto the spoon; you eat from the spoon.

Except for *mohinga* (rice noodles and fish soup), which is eaten with fork and spoon, noodle soups are eaten with a spoon and *tu* (chopsticks).

Joe Cummings

menus but these will be toned-down versions of the real thing, with less chilli and seasonings, and they'll usually come with fewer accompanying dishes.

Noodle dishes are most often eaten for breakfast or as light meals between the main meals of the day. By far the most popular is mohinga. Another popular noodle dish, especially at festivals, is *oun-no hkauq-sweh*, rice noodles with pieces of chicken in a spicy sauce made with coconut milk.

Shan hkauq-sweh (Shan-style noodle soup) – thin wheat noodles in a light broth with chunks of chilli-marinated chicken – is a favourite all over Myanmar but is most common in Mandalay and the Shan State. A variation popular in Mandalay is made with rice noodles and called *myi shay*. Another Shan dish worth seeking out is *htamin chin* ('sour rice', a turmeric-coloured rice salad).

A popular finish to Bamar meals is *lahpeq thouq* (a salad-like concoction of pressed, moistened green tea leaves mixed with a combination of sesame seeds, fried peas, dried shrimp, fried garlic, peanuts, toasted coconut and ginger, and other crunchy flavourings). The 'slimy-looking' mass of leaves puts some foreigners off, but it's actually quite tasty once you get beyond the dish's exotic appearance.

In Mandalay and around Inle (Kalaw, Pindaya, Nyaungshwe and Taunggyi) it is also fairly easy to find Shan food, which is very similar to northern Thai cuisine. Popular dishes are *hkauq sen* (Shan-style wide rice noodles with curry) and various fish and meat salads. Large *maung jeut* (rice crisps), usually translated as rice cracker (which in typical Burmese pronunciation comes out sounding like rice cricket), are common throughout the Shan State.

Mon food, most readily available in towns stretching from Bago to Mawlamyaing, is very similar to Bamar with a greater emphasis on curry selections. Where a Bamar restaurant might offer a choice of four or five curries, a Mon restaurant will have as many as a dozen, all lined up in curry pots for the prospective diner to see. Mon curries are also more likely to contain chillies. Otherwise the two cuisines are quite similar.

Rakhaing cuisine most resembles those of Bangladesh and India's Bengal, featuring lots of bean and pulse dishes, very spicy curries and flatbreads. Because of the Rakhaing State's long coastline, seafood is commonly eaten in the larger towns. Seafood is also available and quite popular in the Tanintharyi Division, which has a similarly lengthy sea coast.

Chinese & Indian Cuisines

Throughout Myanmar in towns large and small you'll find plenty of Chinese restaurants, including quite a few of the regional specialities that are a world (well, half of

---

Betel

Kunya (betel chews) are often passed round at the end of a meal as a 'digestive'. These take a variety of forms, the most basic being small chunks of dried areca nut (betel nut) wrapped in a betel leaf with lime paste. More elaborate kunya may contain flavoured tobacco (usually Indian snuff), peppermint and other spices. In villages in areas where areca palms are cultivated, people chew fresh areca nut as well as dried. Experienced chewers can hold betel cud in their mouths for hours without spitting.

The nut and leaf come from two separate plants, the areca or betel palm (*Areca catechu*) and the betel vine (*Piper betel*). An alkaloid in the nut produces mild stimulation and a sense of well being. It also kills certain worms that may take up residence in the digestive tract; modern veterinarians use an areca extract to deworm pets. Though not habit-forming, the chewed nut stains the teeth dark red and is thought to be carcinogenic.

Vicki Bowman

China anyway) away from Chinese food found in western countries. In a run-of-the-mill Chinese restaurant a meal will cost around K550, often less. In true Chinese fashion you almost invariably get soup with your meal and free Chinese tea.

Indian restaurants are also common, although much more so in Yangon than in other towns. Most are run by Muslim Indians, a few by Hindus. Excellent chicken *dan bauk* (biryani) as well as all-you-can-eat, *thali* (banana-leaf) vegetarian food is easy to find in the capital. The Burmese call Indian restaurants that serve all-you-can-eat thalis 'Chitty' or 'Chetty' restaurants. You can recognise Muslim Indian restaurants by the numeral 786 over the door, sometimes flanked by the star and crescent symbol. This number represents the Arabic phrase 'In the name of Allah the most beneficent and merciful'.

DRINKS
Nonalcoholic Drinks

Only drink water when you know it has been purified – which in most restaurants it should be. One should be suspicious of ice although we've had lots of ice drinks in Myanmar without suffering any ill-effects. Many brands of mineral water are sold in bottles and are quite safe.

Burmese tea, brewed in the Indian style with lots of milk and sugar, is cheap. Many restaurants, the Chinese ones in particular, will provide as much weak Chinese tea as you can handle – for free. It's a good, safe thirst quencher and some people prefer it to regular Burmese tea. You can always buy some little snack if you'd like a drink but not a meal. Teashops are a good place to drink safely boiled tea and munch on inexpensive snacks like *nam-bya*, *palata* or Chinese pastries. See the boxed text on Teashops in the Yangon chapter.

Soft drinks are more costly but reasonable by Asian standards. Since the privatisation of industry there has been a boom in new made-in-Myanmar soft drink brands, including Max, Star, Fruito, Crusher and Fantasy. All are more or less equivalent to international brands like Pepsi, Coca-Cola, Fanta, Bireley's and so on. One of oldest native brands is the formerly government-produced Lemon Sparkling (somewhat similar to Sprite or 7-Up), which since its takeover by private enterprise has improved considerably.

Alcoholic Drinks

The Burmese are not big drinkers; according to the Food and Agriculture Organisation, Myanmar ranks around 90th worldwide in the consumption of alcohol, consuming only about a quarter of a litre per annum. This is partially due to the general lack of disposable income and a socioeconomic context that classifies most alcoholic beverages as luxury items. Alcohol-drinking is also looked down upon by the many Burmese Buddhists who interpret the fifth lay precept against intoxication very strictly.

Beer Since foreign trade was freed up in the early 1990s, the beer brands most commonly seen in Myanmar are international: Tiger, ABC Stout, Singha, San Miguel, Beck and other beers brewed in Thailand, Singapore and Indonesia. At one time these brands were available only on the black market; they are now sold freely in shops and restaurants throughout the country, and typically cost K150 to K200 per 375mL can or bottle.

Myanmar brews a couple of its own brands, including long-running Mandalay Beer, which is very similar to Indian or Sri Lankan beer – rather watery but not bad on those hot and dusty occasions when only a beer will do. Most bottles contain a layer of sediment on the bottom resulting from inadequate filtration. Unfortunately, considering its low quality, Mandalay Beer also happens to be the most expensive beer in Myanmar at K275 per bottle. Hence few Burmese or foreigners drink the national brew. Founded in 1886, Mandalay Brewery (129 Warden Lan, Yangon) also produces the New Mandalay Export label, which is better-tasting and doesn't contain sediment. Newer, better brands brewed in Myanmar include 'Myanmar' and Skol, both of which cost about the same as Mandalay Beer but taste a lot better.

'Bucket beer' is also available here and there, served warm in a bowl and quite cheap.

Toddy Throughout Central Myanmar and the delta, *htan ye* (palm juice) is the farmer's choice of alcoholic beverage. Htan ye is tapped from the top of a toddy palm, the same tree – and the same sap – that produces jaggery, or palm sugar. The juice is sweet and nonalcoholic in the morning, but by mid-afternoon naturally ferments to a weak beer-like strength. By the next day it will have turned. The milky, viscous liquid has a nutty aroma and a slightly sour flavour that fades quickly.

Villages in some areas have their own thatched-roof toddy bars where the locals meet and drink pots of fermented toddy. The toddy is sold in the same roughly engraved terracotta pots the juice is collected in for about K100 per pot (or K25 in a bottle to go), and drunk from coconut half-shells set on small bamboo pedestals. Favourite toddy accompaniments include prawn crackers and fried peas. Some toddy bars also sell *htan-ayeq* (toddy liquor, also called jaggery liquor), a much stronger, distilled form of toddy sap, for around K60 per bottle.

Other Liquors & Wines Very popular in the Shan State is an orange brandy called *shwe leinmaw*, which varies in price from K75 to K150 per bottle, depending on how close to the source you buy it – much of it is distilled in the mountains between Kalaw and Taunggyi. It's a pleasant-tasting liqueur, sort of a poor man's Grand Marnier, and packs quite a punch.

There is also a variety of stronger liquors, including *ayeq hpyu* (white liquor), which varies in strength from brandy-like to almost pure ethyl; and *taw ayeq* (jungle liquor), a cruder form of ayeq hpyu.

Foreign wines – especially those from Australia – are occasionally found in shops and restaurants frequented by foreigners.

ENTERTAINMENT

For most of nonurban Myanmar, local entertainment involves sitting around with friends at home or in a local teashop, telling jokes and recounting the events of the day. Religious and seasonal festivals are an important venue for Burmese folk drama and pop music performances – see Public Holidays & Special Events in this chapter, and Music under the Arts section in the Facts about Myanmar chapter for details.

Most larger towns or cities have a couple of rustic clubs or restaurants where live music can be heard. Many of these are nowadays called 'karaoke', which has become an all-purpose term meaning any sort of nightspot where you can sit, drink alcohol and listen to music. By government decree, the music is mostly Burmese, though in the cities you'll also hear a few Chinese songs mixed into the night's repertoire.

Yangon and Mandalay feature a handful

of discos or dance clubs each, often with live music. Most are associated with hotels but a few operate independently. Western pop songs are expressly forbidden but bands will slip them in every so often or improvise Burmese lyrics to make them more acceptable to the music police. Sometimes discos and 'karaokes' are closed down by the government, either for playing the wrong type of music or, more commonly, because of prostitution. Prostitution has a long history in Myanmar but it is only recently that it has become associated with places that foreign visitors might enter.

More highbrow entertainment, such as classical musical performances, are occasionally sponsored by foreign embassies in Yangon.

SPECTATOR SPORTS
Burmese Martial Arts

Myanmar has a tradition of kickboxing that's said to date back to the Bagan era, although the oldest written references are found in chronicles of warfare between Burma and Thailand during the 15th and 16th centuries. *Myanma let-hwei* (Burmese kickboxing) is very similar in style to *muay thai* (Siamese kickboxing), although not nearly as well developed as a national sport. In fact Burmese boxing matches are never seen or heard on TV or radio, and only occasionally reported in the newspaper.

The most common and traditional kickboxing venues are temporary rings set up at paya pwe rather than sports arenas. Within the last eight years, the martial art's status has raised perceptibly and nowadays occasional championship matches are also held at Aung San Stadium in Yangon. Finding out in advance about such public events can be difficult. If you're interested it's best to drop in on one of the kickboxing classes at Yangon's YMCA and ask whether there are any upcoming matches in the area.

As with Thai boxing, almost anything goes in the ring. All surfaces of the body are considered fair targets and any part of the body except the head may be used to strike an opponent. Common blows include high kicks to the neck, elbow thrusts to the face and head, knee hooks to the ribs and low crescent kicks to the calf. A contestant may even grasp an opponent's head between his hands and pull it down to meet an upward knee thrust. Punching is considered the weakest of all blows and kicking merely a way to 'soften up' one's opponent; knee and elbow strikes are decisive in most matches.

Competition isn't nearly as formalised in Myanmar as in Thailand; in fact you probably won't find two people anywhere in the country who agree on the rules! What's obvious is that the structure and limitations of each match varies with its context and with the calibre of the participants. Unlike Thai boxing, which has borrowed a great deal from the Queensbury rules in international or western boxing, Burmese boxing represents a more traditional form once shared by the two countries. Rules tend to follow situational norms; fighters, managers and judges get together before each match and work out time limits and scoring criteria.

In the simplest rural matches, fought in a dirt circle, there's no time limit and a fighter loses once he has wiped blood from his face or body three times. In more organised amateur matches, boxers fight in square rings (5.8m by 5.5m), for three to five rounds of three minutes each, usually with two minutes rest between. Professional matches in larger towns and cities begin with five rounds but may increase round by round to 12 rounds when the scoring is tight – even longer if no clear winner emerges earlier in the match. When such extensions occur, boxers can request a five minute rest period for every seven rounds fought. Such marathons – gruelling in the extreme by most international standards – are somewhat rare. At both amateur and pro matches, two referees officiate in the ring – this contrasts with Thailand, where there's only one. At ringside are three judges who score the match by pooling their impressions of stamina, skill and bravery.

Fighters bandage their hands but do not wear gloves; they fight barefoot except for nylon anklets worn to absorb perspiration. Simple, dark-coloured shorts rather than baggy boxing trunks are usually worn; if the shorts worn by the contestants appear too similar in colour, the fighters may sew coloured bandanas over the front to make it easier for spectators to differentiate the opponents. In championship matches Burmese fighters are beginning to imitate the Thai boxers they see on TV by wearing big, gaudy trunks.

Before the match begins, each boxer performs a dance-like ritual in the ring to pay homage to Buddha and to Khun Cho and Khun Tha, the nats whose domain includes Burmese kickboxing. The winner repeats the ritual at the end of the match. A small musical ensemble consisting of drums, *hneh* (double-reed wind instrument), cymbals and bamboo clappers performs during the rituals and throughout the match; the volume and tempo of the music rise and fall along with events in the ring.

There are no weight divisions in Burmese boxing – perhaps because the pool of professional fighters is relatively small. Instead boxers are ranked by skill into 1st, 2nd and 3rd class. The best boxers are said to hail from the Ayeyarwady Division, Mandalay Division, Kayin State and Mon State, and these regions are where you'll see the best matches. A pro boxer earns around K20,000 for winning in a big match. Many of the more accomplished Burmese professionals end up migrating to the better paying boxing stadiums of provincial Thailand; some go back and forth.

Myanmar's most famous myanma lethwei teacher is 40-year-old Saya Pan Thu, founder of the Institute of Myanmar Traditional Advanced Boxing and one of three trainers at Yangon University. Pan Thu comes from a teaching lineage that emphasises Myanmar's most traditional style of kickboxing, but also incorporates a few grappling and wrestling techniques from the judo-like Burmese art of *bando*. Due largely to Pan Thu's steady promotion of Burmese martial arts, the country may soon establish the Myanma Traditional Boxing Federation, an organisation that will regulate boxing rules, introduce new safety measures to the ring and develop overall professionalism.

Another thread follows the YMCA school developed by Nilar Win, who now teaches in Paris. The YMCA/Nilar Win tradition appeals to both the amateur and the aspiring professional with its relative emphasis on physical fitness and on precision of movement. It also borrows more from modern martial techniques outside Myanmar, particularly from Thailand.

Chinlon

The Burmese term *chinlon* refers to games in which a woven rattan ball about 12cm in diameter is kicked around. It also refers to the ball itself, which resembles the *takraw* of Thailand and Malaysia. Informally any number of players can form a circle and keep the chinlon airborne by kicking it soccer-style from player to player; a lack of scoring makes it a favourite pastime with Burmese of all ages.

In formal play six players stand in a circle of 22 foot circumference. Each player must keep the ball aloft using a succession of 30 techniques and six surfaces on the foot and leg, allotting five minutes for each part. Each successful kick scores a point, while points are subtracted for using the wrong body part or dropping the ball.

A popular variation – and the one used in intramural or international competitions – is played with a volleyball net, using all the same rules as in volleyball except that only the feet and head are permitted to touch the ball. It's amazing to see the players perform aerial pirouettes, spiking the ball over the net with their feet.

Football (Soccer)

Attending local football matches between different *yaq-kweq* (residential quarters) is good entertainment and a great way to meet locals.

SHOPPING

Shopping in Myanmar is better than ever now that free-market kyat may be used openly for purchases. Bartering is also quite acceptable and many merchants would love to trade their wares for designer watches,

handheld calculators, jeans, T-shirts with English writing on them, and so on.

In larger towns and cities bargains are usually found in the public markets, called *zei*, or *zay*, in Burmese. The main central market is often called *zeigyo* (also spelt *zei-gyo* or *zay-cho*); other markets will be named for the district or township where they're found.

The Bogyoke Aung San Market in Yangon and the Zeigyo Market in Mandalay are good places to look for handicrafts; just about everything that can be bought around the country can be purchased just as cheaply right in these two markets. The big hotel shops, large air-con handicrafts emporiums and the shops in the departure lounge at Yangon airport are very expensive.

Note the following warning on precious stone rip-offs, but beware of other more mundane rip-offs. A couple of travellers wrote of being persuaded to buy betel nut to resell in Bangladesh, which is something like taking coals to Newcastle!

Precious Stones & Jewellery

Myanmar generates a considerable income from the mining of precious stones, mostly in the North. Be very wary of people who come to you with stories of large profits from taking Burmese gemstones to sell in western countries. There are a lot of red glass rubies waiting for the unwary.

Precious stones are supposed to be a government monopoly and they are very unhappy about visitors buying stones from anywhere but licensed retail shops. If *any* stones are found when your baggage is checked on departure, they may be confiscated unless you can present a receipt showing they were purchased from a government-licensed dealer.

The finer imperial jade or pigeon-blood rubies can only be purchased at special dealer sessions during the government-sponsored Myanmar Gems, Jade & Pearl Emporium held each year in October, December and February at a special building next to Kaba Aye Paya in Yangon. Each is typically attended by only around 400 'key' international buyers.

Still, many visitors manage to buy stones from unlicensed dealers, who far outnumber the licensed kind. The government turns a blind eye to most domestic trade; entire districts of southern Mandalay, for example, are engaged in the unlicensed buying, selling, cutting and polishing of jade.

Black-market prices are considerably lower than prices found in licensed retail shops, but of course the risk is far greater as well. The best place to buy unlicensed stones is at the source, where fakes are much less common; the reason being that anyone discovered selling fakes in a well known gem town would be severely punished by dealers of legitimate minerals.

Dug from pit, strip and tunnel mines, Myanmar's finest rubies and sapphires hail from Mogok (Sagaing Division), Pyinlon (Shan State) and Maingshu (or Mong Shu, Shan State). The Kachin State is the sole domain of jadeite, or Burmese jade, which forms inside football-sized boulders in mountain streams. Emeralds are mined at Myadaung in the Kayah State. At the moment only Mogok is open to the average foreign visitor, but all of these precious minerals are traded heavily in Mandalay and Yangon.

Lacquerware

Probably the most popular purchase in Myanmar is lacquerware – you'll find it on sale in the main markets of Yangon and Mandalay, in the Mahamuni Paya entrance walks in Mandalay, and most particularly in Bagan, where most of the lacquerware is made. Burmese lacquerware is fairly similar to that made in the north of Thailand and, although connoisseurs of Japanese lacquerware say that in comparison the Burmese items are inferior, many people find it highly collectable.

Although the earliest lacquerware found in Myanmar today can be dated to the 11th century and was created in the Chinese style, the incised polychrome techniques, known as *yun*, in use today were imported from northern Thailand. Yun is an old Bamar word for the inhabitants of Chiang

Mai; in 1558 King Bayinnaung captured a number of Chiang Mai lacquer artisans and brought them to Bago to establish the Burmese incised lacquerware tradition.

At one time Mandalay artisans made relief lacquerware, a tradition that appears to have all but died out. The oldest bichromatic style applies gold or silver to a black background, a technique dating perhaps to the Pyay era and kept alive by artisans in Kyaukka near Monywa, Mandalay Division. Lacquerware is also made in Kengtung.

Lacquer as used in Myanmar comes from the *Melanorrhea usitata* or *kusum* tree (not to be confused with 'lac', which comes from an insect), and in its most basic form is mixed with paddy-husk ash to form a light, flexible, waterproof coating over bamboo frames.

To make a lacquerware object, the craftsperson first weaves a frame. If the item is top quality, only the frame is bamboo; horse or donkey hairs will be wound round the frame. In lower-quality lacquerware the whole object is made from bamboo. The lacquer is then coated over the framework and allowed to dry. After several days it is sanded down with ash from rice husks, and another coating of lacquer is applied. A high quality item may have seven layers of lacquer altogether.

The lacquerware is engraved and painted, then polished to remove the paint from everywhere except in the engravings. Multicoloured lacquerware is produced by repeated engraving, painting and polishing. From start to finish it can take five or six months to produce a high quality piece of lacquerware, which may have as many as five colours. Flexibility is one characteristic of good lacquerware. A top quality bowl can have its rim squeezed together until the sides meet without suffering damage. The quality and precision of the engraving is another thing to look for.

Lacquerware is made into bowls, trays, plates, boxes, containers, cups, vases and many other everyday items. Octagonal-topped folding tables are another popular lacquerware item.

Tapestries

Along with lacquerware, tapestries are one of the better bargains in Myanmar. They consist of pieces of coloured cloth of various sizes heavily embroidered with silver or gold-coloured thread, metal sequins and glass beads, and feature mythological Burmese figures in padded relief. The greatest variety is found in Mandalay, where most tapestries are produced, but mark-up can be high there because of a tout system (trishaw drivers or guides who hook customers typically receive high commissions). However, if you locate the shops on your own and bargain well, you can get very good prices. You can also purchase tapestries in Yangon at craft shops in the Bogyoke Aung San Market – prices are similar to those in Northern Myanmar but the selection is not as great.

Good quality kalagas are tightly woven and don't skimp on sequins, which may be sewn in overlapping lines, rather than spaced side by side, as a sign of embroidery skill. Metals used should shine, even in older pieces; tarnishing means lower quality materials. Age is not necessarily a factor in value except when related to better quality work. Prices vary according to size and quality, from smaller squares (say 30cm by 30cm) for US$5 to US$10, to the larger (say 1.5m by 1.2m) for US$65. You can usually get better deals by paying in cash US dollars rather than the free-market kyat equivalent.

Clothes & Textiles

Myanmar is the only country in South-East Asia where the majority of the population wear nonwestern clothes as part of their everyday dress. Native fabrics are for the most part limited to the longyi.

Men wear ankle-length patterns of checks, plaids or stripes. To tie them they gather the front of the longyi to create two short lengths of material, then twist them into a half-knot, tucking one end in at the waist while allowing the other to protrude from the knot; this protrusion of cloth can be allowed to hang freely or can be formed into a decorative bunch. It can even be used as a small pouch to hold money or keys. Any kind of shirt, from a T-shirt to the formal mandarin-collar *eingyi*, may be worn with a man's longyi. On very formal occasions such as weddings, the *gaung-baung* (Bamar turban) is added to the outfit.

Burmese women favour calf-length longyis in solid colours, partial stripes or flower prints, topped off by a form-fitting, waist-length blouse. A black waistband is stitched along the waist end, which is folded in front to form a wide pleat, then tucked behind the waistband to one side. The most expensive designs feature wavy or zigzag *acheiq* patterns, the most rare of which are woven using a hundred or more spools of thread and called *lun-taya* (hundred spool) *acheiq*. These are so thick and long-wearing they may be handed down from generation to generation like Persian rugs.

Simple rubber or velvet thong slippers are the most common footwear for both men and women.

Tailoring in Myanmar is very inexpensive compared with just about anywhere else in the world. Many of the textiles seen in tailor shops are imported synthetics. If you want, say, a shirt made from pure cotton, consider buying a longyi in a market or longyi shop and having the tailor cut and sew from that.

Antiques

They're not all as ancient as made out, but many people like to collect *a-le* ('opium' weights); the little animal shapes in descending sizes that are traditionally used for weighing out opium, gems and other precious goods (see Export Restrictions later in this section, however).

The older scale system used a series of nine weights; the newer system uses six weights. Production of the traditional zoomorphic weights came to a halt once the British colonial administration standardised the system of weights and measures in 1885. The pre-1885 weights were made of bronze; reproductions made for the tourist trade are usually brass. The most common animal figures are *to-aung* (a creature that

Do Real Men Wear Longyis?

Men throughout South and South-East Asia commonly wore skirt-like waistclothes until the beginning of this century. European trouser-wearing gradually won over the rest of South-East Asia, and even in India the wearing of the *lungi* (the Indian equivalent to Myanmar's *longyi*, a sarong-style garment) no longer predominates.

Myanmar's isolation since independence and general lack of income have thus far preserved the longyi-wearing tradition. Nowadays only around 10% of males in urban areas wear trousers; in rural parts of the country virtually no male (except for uniformed soldiers) is seen wearing anything other than a longyi. Jokes about what's found beneath a man's longyi parallel similar jokes about Scottish kilts.

The longyi is a very practical clothing choice for Myanmar. In the tropical heat, the billowing cotton keeps one's legs substantially cooler than even the thinnest trousers. The lower length can be pulled between the legs and tucked in at the back of the waist to create 'shorts' for swimming or running. In a country where people often bathe outdoors at riverbanks and streams, the longyi preserves the bather's modesty while he scoops water over his body, and dries quickly afterwards.

And one size fits all. They can easily be loosened at the end of a large meal, and as one's weight moves up or down, there's no need to buy a new set of longyis. More than just an article of clothing, a spare longyi can be used: as a shoulder sling to carry items while travelling; as a bedsheet, picnic blanket or towel; as a baby cradle; tied ankle-to-ankle for safely climbing coconut or toddy palms; and as an impromptu curtain when the hot sun pierces a train or bus window.

Different patterns hail from different parts of the country. In most of central Myanmar, small checks and plaids in relatively bright colours predominate. Solid reds bordered with horizontal stripes at the middle or bottom indicate a Karen-style longyi. Highly favoured – and somewhat expensive – Rakhaing patterns feature a thick, high-relief weave in light, reflective greys and blues. Around Inle Lake, weavers produce red, green and yellow *Zin-me* (Chiang Mai) and blue, brown and green *Ban-gauk* (Bangkok) longyis, modelled after Thai weaving styles introduced to the region in the early 20th century. You can also find *ikat* (tie-dyed) longyis, reminiscent of patterns used in north-eastern Thailand and Laos. Deep indigo, green and purple plaids are the hallmark of the Kachin style, which, during the 1988-90 uprisings, became a symbol of the pro-democracy movement – especially when worn with a white Mandarin-collar shirt and terracotta-coloured waistcoat. For a Burmese to wear the latter outfit today is to risk being branded as an undesirable dissenter by the authorities.

Joe Cummings

looks like a cross between a bull and a lion), *hintha* (a swan-like bird) and *karaweik* (the Burmese crane). Folding scales in carved wooden boxes go with the weights. Check prices in shops in Bangkok before blithely looking for bargains in Myanmar.

Kammawa & Parabaik *Kammawa* (from the Pali *kammavacha* or 'karma-words') are narrow, rectangular slats painted with extracts from the Pali Vinaya – the *pitaka*, concerned with monastic discipline, specifically extracts having to do with clerical affairs. The core of a kammawa page may be a thin slat of wood, lacquered cloth, thatched cane or thin brass, which is then layered with red, black and gold lacquer to form the script and decorations. The resulting 'pages' aren't bound but are tied in stacks with similarly decorated wooden covers.

Traditionally, a new monk may receive a kammawa from his sponsors (usually his family) upon ordination. They have become less common since the advent of the press-printed page in Myanmar and are now mostly seen in museums and antique stores.

The *parabaik* is a similarly horizontal 'book', this time folded accordion-style, like a road map. The pages are made of heavy paper covered with black ink on which the letters are engraved; some parabaiks may feature gouache illustrations, and some can be erased and written over again. Typical parabaiks contain *jatakas* (Buddha biographies) or royal chronicles and, less frequently, Buddhist scriptures. Both kammawas and parabaiks are among the items prohibited for export. So unless you're setting up house in Myanmar, you'd best leave them to the Burmese.

Woodcarving
You can still find some pleasantly carved new Buddha figures and other items from workshops in Mandalay or in the corridors leading to Shwedagon Paya in Yangon, but in general you will not see too much woodcarving on sale.

Older items from the Amarapura, Yadanapon and Mandalay periods are plentiful but you can't be sure Burmese customs will allow them out of the country.

Umbrellas
The graceful and beautifully painted little parasols you see around Myanmar are a product of the port of Pathein – in fact they're known in Myanmar as *Pathein hti* (Pathein umbrellas). Everyday umbrellas have wooden handles, the more ceremonial ones have handles of silver. You can pick up a nice small umbrella for about US$1. The Bogyoke Aung San Market in Yangon is a good place to look. See the Pathein section of the Around Yangon chapter for details on where to observe them being made.

Shan Shoulder Bags
Brightly coloured, embroidered shoulder bags from the Shan State can be found all over Myanmar, but most particularly at Inle. Fancy models have a zip pocket in the front. They are also now made by Chinese and Kachin weavers.

Bookshops
Finding books in Myanmar is not that easy, although there are a number of used-book vendors in Yangon. The best selection of English-language books, including many out-of-print editions, can be found at the Bagan (also called Pagan) Bookshop at 100 37th St, Yangon. Owner U Ba Kyi is a veritable national treasure for rebinding and reprinting rare, out-of-print literature on Myanmar. He has quite a large selection, although you may have to bargain a bit; the most expensive books are not, curiously, necessarily the rarest. Often the high prices are simply due to the books being currently out of favour – such as all books on Mahayana Buddhism! Joe found a 1st edition of Henry Miller's *City of Paris* here.

Along Pansodan Lan near Merchant St, not far from Bagan Bookshop, are a number of outdoor book vendors who stock English-language books on Buddhism, Burmese history, archaeology and other noncensored topics, including such oddities as the Raj-era *Civil List* (read *Burmese Days* to understand its all-consuming importance in the colonial era). Be sure to bargain – the street vendors tend to ask prices 100% or higher than bookshop prices for the same titles.

Inwa Book Store (☎ 01-271076) at 232 Sule Paya Lan, and Sarpay Beikman Book Centre on Merchant St, between 37th and 38th Sts, are both government-owned bookstores with fair selections of new books as well as postcards.

Along Bogyoke Aung San Lan, across from the Bogyoke Aung San Market, are a number of other bookstalls, and there are some in the streets that run back from the main road. Several of these have quite a selection of Burmese books if you ask for them. You can also buy old issues of *Time*, *Newsweek* and other foreign magazines here (and elsewhere in the street markets) for just K50 to K60 per copy.

Outside Yangon you may well come across similar book vendors displaying their wares along the streets.

Export Restrictions

The following items cannot legally be taken out of the country: prehistoric implements and artefacts; fossils; old coins; bronze or brass weights (including opium weights); bronze or clay pipes; kammawas or parabaiks; inscribed stones; inscribed gold or silver; historical documents; religious images; sculptures or carvings in bronze, stone, stucco or wood; frescoes or fragments thereof; pottery; and national regalia and paraphernalia.

Getting There & Away

AIR

Apart from day trips to Three Pagodas Pass from Thailand, five-day trips from Thailand's Mae Sai to the Burmese towns of Tachileik and Kengtung (Kyaingtong), and group travel from China, people who arrive at Myanmar by land or sea are few and far between. That only leaves arriving by air. The good news is that as the military government has gradually extended the allowable visa stay to the current 28 days, more and more airlines have put Yangon (Rangoon) on their schedules.

KLM-Royal Dutch Airlines began flying into Yangon in the 1930s and by the 1950s, Yangon (Rangoon) was an important air hub for a number of European airlines. However, after the 1962 military takeover, increased restrictions and lack of traffic led most carriers to delete Yangon from their schedules – not without a sigh of relief, one suspects. In the late 1980s, in fact, there were so few flights in or out of Myanmar that boarding passes were stamped with the warning 'Don't Miss Your Flight' – the implication being that there wasn't another flight for some time.

These days, Yangon international airport (located in the township of Mingaladon) is still unable to take anything bigger than an Airbus 300 or a Boeing 767, so aircraft such as 747s and DC-10s can't fly there. A new, larger airport (50km north-east of the capital, on the highway to Bago) has been in the planning and rumour stage for several years, but so far it's a no-show.

There are several major air route options. The first and most common is to travel out and back from Bangkok in Thailand. A second possibility is to slot Myanmar in between Thailand and Bangladesh, India or Nepal – many people travelling from South-East Asia to the subcontinent manage a few weeks in Myanmar in between. Other alternatives include travelling out and back from Calcutta, Karachi, Dhaka, Hong Kong, Taipei, Osaka, Kuala Lumpur, Singapore and Kunming.

Bangkok is a good place to look for tickets to Myanmar. Some travel agents will not only sell you tickets at knock-down prices, but will organise your visa too. It's usually cheaper to arrange your visa and ticket separately, however. One discount ticket agency within walking distance of the Myanmar embassy in Bangkok is Sun Far Travel (☎ 02-223 8179) at 48/5 Thanon Pan. Typical costs for Bangkok-Yangon-Bangkok tickets are around US$230 on Thai Airways International (THAI), US$220 on Myanmar Airways International (MAI) and as low as US$140 on Biman Bangladesh Airlines. The latter flies Bangkok-Yangon-Calcutta for a similar figure and Bangkok-Yangon-Kathmandu for around US$200. Return flights to/from Kuala Lumpur, Singapore or

---

Warning

The information in this chapter is particularly vulnerable to change: prices for international travel are volatile, routes are introduced and cancelled, schedules change, special deals come and go, and rules and visa requirements are amended. Airlines and governments seem to take a perverse pleasure in making price structures and regulations as complicated as possible. You should check directly with the airline or a travel agent to make sure you understand how a fare (and ticket you may buy) works. In addition, the travel industry is highly competitive and there are many lurks and perks.

The upshot of this is that you should get opinions, quotes and advice from as many airlines and travel agents as possible before you part with your hard-earned cash. The details given in this chapter should be regarded as pointers and are not a substitute for your own careful, up-to-date research.

Kunming cost US$430 to US$640. Remember that published fares outside South-East Asia are often higher than you'll find in Bangkok, or other regional capitals.

Airlines

The following airlines currently fly into Yangon.

Thai Airways International THAI currently flies Bangkok-Yangon-Bangkok twice daily. THAI use Airbuses and the flight takes about 50 minutes. Although slightly more expensive than the equivalent MAI flight, THAI's departure times are more convenient and the service more reliable.

Myanmar Airways International MAI flies from Bangkok to Yangon and vice versa daily; from Hong Kong twice weekly; from Singapore daily; from Kuala Lumpur twice weekly; and from Kunming and Dhaka once a week. They use Boeing 737s leased from Royal Brunei Airlines, as well as a Boeing 767 leased from EVA Airways. From 1993 to 1998, MAI was a joint venture between Myanma Airways (MA, the government-owned domestic carrier) and a Singaporean company. In 1998 it was purchased by EVA Airways of Taiwan.

Air Mandalay Air Mandalay (AM), one of Myanmar's new, privately owned domestic carriers, has recently started up regular service between Chiang Mai in Thailand and Yangon twice weekly during the high season (November to February); and once a week the rest of the year.

Biman Bangladesh Airlines Biman flies Bangkok-Yangon-Dhaka (via Chittagong) once a week. It is usually the cheapest operator, although it has been known to occasionally cancel flights; a reputation that has actually earned them a small following of folks hoping for a few extra days in Yangon.

If you're flying through to Calcutta with Biman, you (sometimes) get a free night's stopover in Dhaka. Note that if you plan to stop in Bangladesh, it's still worth getting a ticket to Calcutta, as the price is the same and you may, therefore, start your Bangladesh travels with free airport transport and a free night's accommodation.

If you plan on an overnight stay in Dhaka, be sure to get a hotel voucher from Biman before leaving Yangon; in fact it might be best to get it in Bangkok (or wherever you buy the ticket) first, just to be safe. A number of travellers have said they landed in Bangladesh and ended up sleeping in the airport because Biman wouldn't take them to a hotel without a hotel voucher.

Air China China's national carrier flies 737s between Kunming (Yunnan Province, China) and Yangon once a week. In the reverse direction, this flight continues on to Beijing from Kunming. If you are travelling around China and then continuing to South-East Asia this can be an economical choice, since from Western China you would not have to backtrack all the way east to Hong Kong, then fly all the way west to Bangkok. Visas are obtainable from the Myanmar consulate in Kunming.

Silk Air This subsidiary of Singapore Airlines flies daily between Yangon and Singapore using Boeing 737s.

All Nippon Airways All Nippon Airways flies once a week to Yangon from Osaka in Japan but returns via Bangkok on 767s.

Malaysia Airlines Malaysia Airlines flies twice-weekly from Kuala Lumpur to Yangon on 737s.

Pakistan International Airlines Pakistan International Airlines flies once a week to/from Karachi on Airbus A-300s.

Indian Airlines Indian Airlines flies between Calcutta and Yangon twice weekly on Airbus A-300s.

Other Airlines Both China Airlines and EVA Airways fly from Taipei to Yangon thrice weekly on Airbus 300s.

Air Travel Glossary

Baggage Allowance This will be written on your ticket and usually includes one 20kg item to go in the hold, plus one item of hand luggage.

Bucket Shops These are unbonded travel agencies specialising in discounted airline tickets.

Bumped Just because you have a confirmed seat doesn't mean you're going to get on the plane (see Overbooking).

Cancellation Penalties If you have to cancel or change a discounted ticket, there are often heavy penalties involved; insurance can sometimes be taken out against these penalties. Some airlines impose penalties on regular tickets as well, particularly against 'no-show' passengers.

Check-In Airlines ask you to check in a certain time ahead of the flight departure (usually one to two hours on international flights). If you fail to check in on time and the flight is overbooked, the airline can cancel your booking and give your seat to somebody else.

Confirmation Having a ticket written out with the flight and date you want doesn't mean you have a seat until the agent has checked with the airline that your status is 'OK' or confirmed. Meanwhile you could just be 'on request'.

Courier Fares Businesses often need to send urgent documents or freight securely and quickly. Courier companies hire people to accompany the package through customs and, in return, offer a discount ticket which is sometimes a phenomenal bargain. In effect, what the companies do is ship their freight as your luggage on regular commercial flights. This is a legitimate operation, but there are two shortcomings – the short turnaround time of the ticket (usually not longer than a month) and the limitation on your luggage allowance. You may have to surrender all your allowance and take only carry-on luggage.

Full Fares Airlines traditionally offer 1st class (coded F), business class (coded J) and economy class (coded Y) tickets. These days there are so many promotional and discounted fares available that few passengers pay full economy fare.

ITX An ITX, or 'independent inclusive tour excursion', is often available on tickets to popular holiday destinations. Officially it's a package deal combined with hotel accommodation, but many agents will sell you one of these for the flight only and give you phoney hotel vouchers in the unlikely event that you're challenged at the airport.

Lost Tickets If you lose your airline ticket an airline will usually treat it like a travellers cheque and, after inquiries, issue you with another one. Legally, however, an airline is entitled to treat it like cash and if you lose it then it's gone forever. Take good care of your tickets.

MCO An MCO, or 'miscellaneous charge order', is a voucher that looks like an airline ticket but carries no destination or date. It can be exchanged through any International Association of Travel Agents (IATA) airline for a ticket on a specific flight. It's a useful alternative to an onward ticket in those countries that demand one, and is more flexible than an ordinary ticket if you're unsure of your route.

No-Shows No-shows are passengers who fail to show up for their flight. Full-fare passengers who fail to turn up are sometimes entitled to travel on a later flight. The rest are penalised (see Cancellation Penalties).

Air Travel Glossary

On Request This is an unconfirmed booking for a flight.

Onward Tickets An entry requirement for many countries is that you have a ticket out of the country. If you're unsure of your next move, the easiest solution is to buy the cheapest onward ticket to a neighbouring country or a ticket from a reliable airline which can later be refunded if you do not use it.

Open Jaw Tickets These are return tickets where you fly out to one place but return from another. If available, this can save you backtracking to your arrival point.

Overbooking Airlines hate to fly empty seats and since every flight has some passengers who fail to show up, airlines often book more passengers than they have seats. Usually excess passengers make up for the no-shows, but occasionally somebody gets 'bumped' onto the next available flight. Guess who it is most likely to be? The passengers who check in late.

Point-to-Point Tickets These are discount tickets that can be bought on some routes in return for passengers waiving their rights to a stopover.

Promotional Fares These are officially discounted fares, available from travel agencies or direct from the airline.

Reconfirmation If you don't reconfirm your flight at least 72 hours prior to departure, the airline may delete your name from the passenger list. Ring to find out if your airline requires reconfirmation.

Restrictions Discounted tickets often have various restrictions on them – such as needing to be paid for in advance and incurring a penalty to be altered. Others are restrictions on the minimum and maximum period you must be away, such as a minimum of 14 days or a maximum of one year.

Round-the-World Tickets RTW tickets give you a limited period (usually a year) in which to circumnavigate the globe. You can go anywhere the carrying airlines go, as long as you don't backtrack. The number of stopovers or total number of separate flights is decided before you set off and they usually cost a bit more than a basic return flight.

Stand-by This is a discounted ticket where you only fly if there is a seat free at the last moment. Stand-by fares are usually available only on domestic routes.

Transferred Tickets Airline tickets cannot be transferred from one person to another. Travellers sometimes try to sell the return half of their ticket, but officials can ask you to prove that you are the person named on the ticket. This is less likely to happen on domestic flights, but on an international flight tickets are compared with passports.

Travel Agencies Travel agencies vary widely and you should choose one that suits your needs. Some simply handle tours, while full-service agencies handle everything from tours and tickets to car rental and hotel bookings. If all you want is a ticket at the lowest possible price, then go to an agency specialising in discounted fares.

Travel Periods Ticket prices vary with the time of year. There is a low (off-peak) season and a high (peak) season, and often a low-shoulder season and a high-shoulder season as well. Usually the fare depends on your outward flight – if you depart in the high season and return in the low season, you pay the high-season fare.

A few European and Asian airlines that used to fly into Yangon still maintain offices there for ticketing flights out of Bangkok/Singapore. Aeroflot, the Russian airline, stopped flying into Yangon from Moscow and Vientiane in 1992, but may start operating again soon.

KLM has an office in Yangon to service its flights out of Bangkok and Singapore, as do Air France, Asiana Airways (Korea) and Royal Brunei Airlines.

See the Getting There & Away section in the Yangon chapter for a listing of airline offices in Yangon.

Arrival in Yangon

On arrival, you will probably find there is a bit of a race to get into the terminal building. Your first taste of Burmese bureaucracy is likely to be a lengthy one, and the early arrivals will save quite a bit of time. The process is first to squeeze past the immigration counter, where your visa and immigration form are inspected.

Then it's on to the customs counter, where you will have to fill in a form if you have a camera, calculator, computer or any other marvel of western technology. Airport officials are very serious about three items: video cameras, computers with modems and mobile phones. Video cameras or video tapes are not prohibited, but apparently they remind them of reporters; with computers they are even more paranoid. If you bring any of these items, be prepared to do some explaining. The form asks for the number of items, brand names and values – undervalue the items because if they are stolen or lost, it's better to have a lower cost to argue about when departing from Myanmar.

Arriving on a packed-full THAI flight, you may find that the immigration/customs procedures take up to an hour to complete, which is exasperating as it will be the only incoming flight at the time.

Once you've picked up your bags, you must pass the Foreign Exchange Certificate (FEC) counter where you will be asked to change US dollars or British pounds into FECs. In the past, some clever folks managed to bypass the FEC counter but it's nearly impossible to avoid these days. (See the Money section in Facts for the Visitor for details on this latest twist to the government's currency control system.)

Then it's through the arrival area exit, where you can book an official taxi into town for US$2 to US$3, or continue out the door to the street entrance, where you can find an even cheaper taxi to central Yangon. Most taxis, official or otherwise, will offer to stop about halfway to town to change money, but you can get a slightly better rate in town rather than anywhere near the airport.

See the Getting Around chapter for information on getting to/from the airport.

Flight Reconfirmation

If you are counting on flying out of Yangon on your scheduled date of departure, you must reconfirm your outbound flight either at the appropriate airport ticket counter or at the relevant airline office in town. This applies regardless of whether or not your flight is officially confirmed (OK status) on the ticket. You may notice a sign in the airport waiting lounge that reminds you of this requirement.

For most flights, we have found the airline offices in town to be more reliable than the airport ticket counters – mainly because you can't always find someone at the airport to fill out the proper forms. More airline offices in Yangon are now online with computer reservation systems, but a confirmation may still require calling back the next day to see if you have OK status. If you are trying to connect with an airline that does not fly into Yangon, you may need to call its Bangkok office. However, check first with the airline that flew you into Myanmar; it may be able to help reconfirm your connecting flight (eg THAI will reconfirm all United Airlines reservations).

If you do not reconfirm, the airlines (this goes for any airlines flying in and out of Yangon) can't guarantee your outbound seat, especially during the height of the tourist season (November to February), when most flights out of Yangon seem to be intentionally overbooked. On the other hand, if you're looking for a few extra days in Myanmar, just give it a miss and you're quite likely to get bumped – particularly if you neglect to arrive for check-in until an hour or less before departure.

If you do get bumped, make sure you visit immigration to extend your visa sometime before your rescheduled departure (this usually amounts to paying the routine US$3 per extra day fee). Otherwise the airlines may refuse to give you a seat when you arrive for check-in and you will have to deal with the airport immigration office. This process has been known to delay check-in until the very last minute, in which case you may find yourself bumped a second time.

Departure Tax

Leaving Myanmar is much easier than in the recent past, when you had to turn in a currency control form to prove you'd changed foreign currency for *kyat*. With the FEC system in place, no one checks to see what kind of currency you've spent or are leaving the country with.

A US$10 departure tax payable in dollars or FECs is collected at the airport from all ticketholders before check-in.

In the departure lounge, you can buy any handicrafts you missed on your way around the country, or purchase whisky and cigarettes at the duty-free counter – they're cheaper than at Bangkok international airport.

If you have time on your hands between check-in and boarding, there is a restaurant/bar/lounge on the 2nd floor of the departure lounge, where the food's not bad, but rather expensive. Every item on the menu costs US$2, whether it's a sandwich, beer, soft drink or bag of potato chips.

LAND

'Overlanding' through Asia is nowhere near as popular as it was some years back. Nevertheless, the idea of a route through Myanmar has long been a dream for overlanders. If you could only drive through Myanmar (not to mention Afghanistan) it would then be possible to travel by car all the way from

London to Singapore, and Asia overland would be much more of a reality than it has been in the past.

Prior to WWII that route would not even have been a dream – there were simply no roads through Myanmar. After the war three new roads and a railway were built across the Burmese borders, but these fascinating routes had a short civilian life. The railway was built by the Japanese, using the infamous Bridge on the River Kwai. It went up to the Burmese border at the Three Pagodas Pass, from where it ran to Mawlamyaing (Moulmein). After the war most of the railway was torn up, leaving only a stretch from Kanchanaburi in Thailand, which runs into the jungle less than halfway to the border. Forget that one.

China

Originally built to supply the forces of Chiang Kai-shek in his struggle against the Japanese, the famous Burma Road runs from Kunming, in China's Yunnan Province, to the city of Lashio. Nowadays the road is open to travellers carrying permits for the region north of Lashio, although you can only legally cross the border in one direction – from the Chinese side (Ruili) into Myanmar via Mu-se in the Northern Shan State. This appears to be possible only if you book a visa-and-transport package from Chinese travel agencies in Kunming. Once across the border at Mu-se, you can continue on to Lashio and farther south to Mandalay, Yangon and so on.

A second route a little farther north-west from Lwaigyai to Bhamo is also open in the same direction. You cannot legally leave Myanmar by either route, however. There is a military checkpoint just north of Lashio to ensure the smooth flow of black-market goods from China.

India

During WWII the Indians and the British built a road from Imphal in India to Tamu on the Burmese border. Farther north the Americans, under General 'Vinegar Joe' Stilwell, built a 430km-long road running from Ledo in the remote Indian North-East Frontier Province to Myitkyina in the north-east of Myanmar. At a cost (in 1944) of US$137 million it would certainly rank as one of the most expensive roads in the world, because after a few months of use in 1944 it has hardly been used since. Both these roads have now probably returned to the jungle.

You can read a quite fascinating description of driving through Myanmar, using the Stilwell Road, in *First Overland* by Tim Slessor. It tells of a 1956 trip from London to Singapore by two Oxford and Cambridge University-crewed Land Rovers. They may well have been not only the first, but also the last, to go overland, for a 1962 edition of *The Motor Roads of Burma* (published by the Burma Oil Company) states that only the first 190km from Myitkyina to Tanai was 'motorable during all weathers'. The rest of the way to Ledo required a 4WD plus 'preparation, patience, perseverance and luck'. The road from Mandalay to Myitkyina via Pyin U Lwin (Maymyo), Lashio and Bhamo was 780km long and generally motorable according to the same road guide. Turn-offs led to the Chinese border from just beyond Mongyu and Bhamo.

The British-Indian road sounds equally forbidding. Mandalay-Tamu was 490km via Amarapura, Sagaing, Shwebo, Ye-U and Kalewa. After Shwebo, 93km out, the road rapidly deteriorated (according to this 1962 report), with many unbridged *chaungs* (canals) to cross. In wet weather, this would have been an impossible proposition, although the booklet also noted that it was sometimes possible to ship vehicles from Monywa to Kalewa by riverboat – thus avoiding the worst part of the route. Once at Tamu, the road on the Indian side of the border was quite good.

The latest word, at the time of writing, is that the Chin State is about to open to limited group tours. If this happens, travel for individuals may follow, in which case it will be possible to traverse the state via the Chindwin River, all the way to the Indian border at Tamu. Whether foreigners will be permitted

to cross into India (or vice versa) is a matter yet to be decided between the Indian and Burmese governments. Indian traders are already allowed crossing privileges, as is apparent in the bustling town of Monywa.

Thailand

Several border crossings between Thailand and Myanmar are open to day-trippers or for short excursions in the vicinity. As yet, none of these link up with routes to Yangon or Mandalay or any other cities of size.

Mae Sai-Tachileik The infamous bridge, Lo Hsing-han's former 'Golden Triangle' passageway for opium and heroin, spans the Sai River between Thailand's northernmost town and the border boomtown of Tachileik. Nowadays, border permits (for up to 14 days) can be obtained from Burmese immigration officials at the border for excursions to Tachileik and beyond (as far north as Kengtung), at a cost of US$18 and the exchange of US$100 into FECs. However, if you only want to cross the border to Tachileik, the cost is US$5 and there is no FEC requirement. On occasion, the border shuts down for security reasons – usually involving skirmishes between the Yangon military and the Shan State's splintered Mong Tai Army (MTA) over the opium poppy harvest.

For similar reasons, travel west from Kengtung to Taunggyi is still off-limits to non-Burmese, even though the road is in useable condition. It is 163km farther from Tachileik to Kengtung, and another 450km from Kengtung to Taunggyi.

Farther to the south, in Thailand's Mae Chan district, it is possible to cross the border almost everywhere – with a local and reliable guide. This too is opium country, and Sunday strollers are not welcome.

Rumour has it that an overland route all the way to China via Kengtung will eventually open here, but so far Kengtung is the end of the line, and you must leave the way you came, via Tachileik.

Three Pagodas Pass A gateway for invading armies and a major smuggling route for many centuries, this is one of the most interesting and accessible of the border crossing points.

Now that the Burmese have wrested control from Mon and Kayin (Karen) armies, there is much legal trade going on at Three Pagodas Pass. The settlement on the Burmese side, called Payathonzu (Three Pagodas), is open on-and-off to foreign tourists for day trips. Travellers have been allowed to go as far as a dozen kilometres or so inside Myanmar from this point, but the roads are so bad that almost no one makes it even that far. However, at the time of writing, this crossing was closed.

From Kanchanaburi (the site of the Bridge on the River Kwai) you can get a minibus or rent a motorcycle, and drive 150km along dusty, winding mountain roads to Sangkhlaburi. The trip takes about half a day. The road is OK as far as Thong Pha Phum, but deteriorates somewhat after that little town.

Pickup trucks make regular trips to Three Pagodas Pass from Sangkhlaburi. Along the way, you must stop at a Thai military checkpoint, and at the Burmese border you're required to sign your name and present your passport at this checkpoint. The pass itself is unreal – three little pagodas standing on a crest.

Payathonzu itself is not that interesting, just a collection of wooden teashops, a cinema, a couple of markets and several souvenir shops. The nearby Kloeng Thaw Falls take a couple of hours by motorcycle from Payathonzu. The road to the falls is only open in the dry season – reportedly the Kayin control the waterfall area during the rainy season. No one actually stops you from going to the falls at that time, though many people will try to wave you back. Even in good weather, the two-rut track is very rugged; not recommended for motorcycle novices.

Mae Sot-Myawaddy This crossing begins a route from Myawaddy to Mawlamyaing via Kawkareik, along a rough road that has long been off-limits to foreigners

due to Mon and Kayin insurgent activity in the area. There are regular buses from Tak to Mae Sot on the Thai side. In 1994 the Myanmar government signed an agreement with Thailand to build a bridge across the Moei River between Myawaddy and Mae Sot, and it opened in 1997 – briefly. After much bickering over reclamation of the river banks, it was finally opened again in 1998, only to close again. This pattern seems to be continuing. Even when the bridge is open, travel has only been permitted between Myawaddy and Mae Sot, about 6km east of the border. The military government in Yangon claims the road will eventually open all the way through to Hpa-an in the Kayin State.

On the Myawaddy side, there's nothing very interesting, just a Buddhist temple, a village school and thatched-roof compounds. Here the government has kept the Myawaddy-Mawlamyaing route open to black-marketeers – in order to avoid civil unrest in Yangon, due to shortages of consumer goods and rising prices.

Just north of Myawaddy is Wangkha, and just to the south is Phalu (Waley on the Thai side), former Kaayin and Mon smuggling posts now controlled by Yangon. Between Mae Sot and Tha Song Yang, south of Mae Sariang on the Thai side, are several Kayin refugee camps (at last report there are 12 camps totalling about 100,000 refugees). These camps are populated by civilians who have fled Burmese-Kayin armed conflicts, and by political dissidents from Yangon. The fighting was particularly bad in 1995, when dissident Kayin Buddhists – backed by Burmese troops – routed the leading Christian faction; this area continues to be a military hotspot.

Chiang Dao A dirt track turns left 10km north of Chiang Dao and leads through the small town of Muang Ngai to Na Ok at the border. This was the most popular opium route from Myanmar in the mid-1970s, but the main trading items now are water buffalo and lacquer. It's still wise to be very careful in this area.

Prachuap Khiri Khan Not only is there a road over the Mawdaung Pass between Ban Huay Yang and Tanintharyi (Tenasserim), but there is a major business smuggling timber from Myanmar. The 'toll gate', formerly controlled by Kayin guerrillas from the Karen National Union (KNU)/Karen National Liberation Army (KNLA), is now once again controlled by Yangon forces. If you can find a local who knows the area well, it's possible to visit near the border crossing point of Dan Singkon.

Getting Around

AIR

Myanmar has 66 airstrips around the country, 20 of which are served by regularly scheduled domestic flights. Most are short, one strip fields that can land only one plane at a time. None have instrument landing capability, a situation that can be especially tricky during the monsoon season (May to November), even though all 23 are considered 'all-weather aerodromes'.

Planned construction seems to have stalled indefinitely on a new international airport between Yangon (Rangoon) and Bago, on a site used by B-29 bombers during WWII. Airports at Mandalay and Heho are soon to add sorely needed runways and expanded passenger facilities.

To/From the Airport

Since 1994, Burmese citizens without special permission or guide licences have been barred from the airport, hence nowadays you usually aren't approached by taxi drivers until you leave the airport. A transportation desk with helpful staff just outside the arrival area can arrange taxis into Yangon for US$2 to US$3 per person; if several people are going to one hotel you might get a taxi for US$5 (up to four passengers). Some hotels will provide free transport if you book a room at their airport hotel desk. You can also book your own taxi (to the destination of your choice) from the assorted collection of vehicles parked outside the airport gate, for around US$2, but be prepared to bargain and give directions to small hotels or guesthouses.

Coming to the airport from Yangon you can pay in free-market *kyat*, though the fare works out to be about the same as the journey to Yangon from the airport – about US$2 or kyat equivalent.

Departing from Myanmar (Burma) is much easier than arriving, unless you have an early-morning Myanmar Airways International (MAI) flight out and have to crawl out of bed. If you happen to be flying out of Yangon on Union Day, 12 February, you need to get out to the airport before noon because the road to the airport is closed to nonparade traffic after that time.

Luggage In Myanmar it's wise to travel as lightly as possible and carry your own baggage out to the aircraft, rather than trust that it will find its own way there. At many airstrips everyone (except package-tour groups) carries their own luggage anyway, regardless of quantity. You will save time if you also carry it at the other end.

Myanma Airways

Until 1989, Myanma Airways (MA) was known as Burma Airways Corporation and, before that, Union of Burma Airways. MA's airline code remains UB.

MA's small fleet consists of two Fokker F-28 jets and four F-27 turboprops. Legroom and carry-on luggage space is minimal, as the airlines have opted for the maximum number of seats the aircraft are designed to carry. All craft are in decidedly tatty condition and the whole operation seems to be a little haphazard, which does not do wonders for one's nerves. The airline employs safety procedures that haven't been updated since the 1950s, and since 1989 MA has logged eight fatal crashes, including two in 1998 – one at Ngapali and another near Tachileik.

Of course – safety aside – there are reasons to use MA, even though there are now two very reliable private domestic carriers, Air Mandalay (AM) and Yangon Airways (YA). Both YA and AM have much smaller route nets, flying only to the more popular tourist destinations. MA flies to virtually every airport in the country and is cheaper than either AM or YA – though if you care about comfort, service, safety and punctuality, the extra fare is definitely a worthwhile investment.

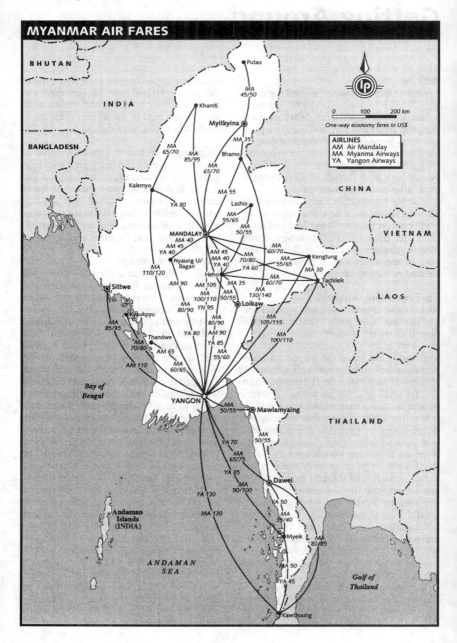

MYANMAR AIR FARES

BHUTAN

INDIA

BANGLADESH

CHINA

VIETNAM

LAOS

THAILAND

Bay of
Bengal

Andaman
Islands
(INDIA)

ANDAMAN
SEA

Gulf of
Thailand

0   100   200 km

One-way economy fares in US$

AIRLINES
AM Air Mandalay
MA Myanma Airways
YA Yangon Airways

Putao

MA
45/50

Khamti

Myitkyina

MA 35

Bhamo

MA
65/70

MA
85/95

MA
65/70

Kalemyo

YA 80

MA 55

Lashio

MA
55/65

MA
50/55

MANDALAY
MA 40
AM 45
YA 40

MA
60/70

Kengtung

Nyaung U/
Bagan

AM 45
MA 40
YA 40

MA
70/80

MA
55/65

MA 30

Heho

YA 60

MA
60/70

Tachileik

Sittwe

AM 90

AM 105

MA 35

Kyaukpyu

MA
100/110

MA
50/55

Loikaw

MA
130/140

MA
85/95

Thandwe

MA
80/90

YN 95

MA
105/115

MA
70/80

AM 65

YA 80

MA
80/90

AM 110

MA
60/65

AM 90

YA 85

MA
55/60

MA
100/110

YANGON

MA
50/55

Mawlamyaing

YA 70

MA
50/55

MA
65/75

YA 85

YA 130

MA
90/100

Dawei

YA 50

MA 130

MA
35/40

Myeik

MA
80/85

MA 50

YA 45

Kawthoung

Schedules On MA, even with ticket in hand, things may not go strictly to plan. Schedules don't mean much – if the passengers turn up early the flight may go early. If insufficient passengers show up the flight may not go at all.

Even having a confirmed reservation and being first in line may not get you there, because Burmese VIPs can jump the line with ease and package-tour people also get preference over independent travellers. Dates and departure times are rarely written on MA tickets, so they don't have to honour these on the day and hour for which reservations were originally made.

Fares & Payment Foreigners must purchase all MA tickets using Foreign Exchange Certificates (FECs) or US dollars. Burmese citizens pay much lower fares in kyat. If you cancel your booking within 24 hours of departure, MA collects a 25% cancellation charge; within six hours it jumps to 50%. Also note that you're not able to purchase tickets for MA outside the country – you can, however, with AM.

Another wrinkle in booking procedures is that you can't take an MA flight that involves an intermediate connection straight through the connecting stop. For example, on Mondays, MA flight UB 787 goes from Mandalay to Bhamo, arriving at 11 am. Twenty minutes after arrival in Bhamo, the same plane continues northward to Myitkyina. But you can't book this flight straight through from Mandalay to Myitkyina; this is because the MA office in Mandalay apparently can't figure out how many people hold reservations on the Bhamo-Myitkyina leg. So you must stop over in Bhamo, and make a new reservation for a seat to Myitkyina. The same goes for flights to Mawlamyaing via Dawei (Tavoy), flights from Kengtung to Yangon via Heho and other such routings.

Though MA uses both F-27 turboprops and F-28 jets, in everyday practice the more expensive F-28s are used only for long hauls (Yangon-Sittwe (Akyab), or Yangon-Myeik (Mergui)), so you'll usually end up paying the lower fare. By the way, all the

Air Safety in Myanmar

At the time of writing, the majority of foreign embassies in Yangon (including the US, UK, Australian and French, among others) had issued travel advisories warning their citizens to avoid flying Myanma Air (MA). One of the largest travel agencies requires a signed waiver from clients who insist on flying MA. Until there's a turnaround in MA's safety record, we see no reason to risk it. Travellers on MA have reported broken seats, lousy toilets, cancelled flights etc. To make matters worse, recent crashes have been met by a combination of government denials and misinformation, with confusion and fear the final results. In 1998 EVA Airways, based in Taiwan, purchased Myanmar Airways International (MAI), the international division of the government airline. Rumours have since circulated that EVA might also buy MA. If true, it's very good news, since EVA would no doubt invest a great deal in safety, maintenance and service.

Michael Clark

MA crashes in the last ten years have been on the F-27 turboprops.

Air Mandalay & Yangon Airways

AM, the first private carrier in the country, appears to have been created so that foreigners won't compete with Burmese citizens for perpetually tight seating space on MA aircraft. In other words, the government would just as soon see you fly with upscale AM (or YA) rather than with government-subsidised MA.

Flying with either AM or YA saves visitors a whole list of headaches. In the first place, they fly to places for which permits aren't necessary, so that's one layer of bureaucracy eliminated in their ticket lines. Secondly, both AM and YA are usually punctual in arrivals and departures. Finally, both AM and YA planes – recent French-built ATR-72s – are substantially more comfortable, and the attentive, professional service contrasts strongly with the cattle-car ambience at MA. The ATR-72s are comfortably configured to seat 66 passengers, allowing for ample legroom.

AM's Toulouse-trained pilots hail from Australia, France, Singapore and Myanmar; all flight attendants are trained in Singapore. The company has updated safety procedures for flying to each of the airports it serves in Myanmar – the first airline in Myanmar to undertake this task since the 1950s. YA seems to have closely followed AM in terms of safety procedures and customer service.

For the moment, AM flies only to Yangon, Mandalay, Bagan/Nyaung U, Thandwe, Sittwe and Heho. Plans are under way to add more domestic routes to the shedule. AM also operates the only arriving international flight into Mandalay. Of course, it's from Chiang Mai in Thailand, and it stops in Yangon first.

YA currently flies to Yangon, Mandalay, Bagan/Nyaung U, Heho, Kalemyo, Kengtung, Tachileik, Dawei and Kawthoung.

Ticketing & Reservations Unlike MA, AM has ticketing services overseas – Bangkok and Chiang Mai in Thailand, and Singapore: Mekong Land (☎ 66-2-712 5842, 381 0881, fax 391 7212), 399/6 Soi Thonglor 21, Bangkok, Thailand; AM (☎ 053-279992), Chiang Mai, Thailand; and MAS Travel Centre (☎ 65-235 4411, 737 8877, fax 235 3033), 19 Tanglin Rd, Tanglin shopping centre, Singapore.

Fares Both AM and YA flights cost a bit more than MA flights to the same destinations. Also, AM requires all passengers – foreign or Burmese – to pay in US dollars; YA allows Burmese citizens to pay in kyat, at about a third of the dollar amount. Both AM and YA fares are slightly higher during the busier November-March period. Ticket prices are cheaper from travel agents than from the airlines. (See the Travel Agencies entry under Information in the Yangon chapter later, for a list of travel agents.)

BUS & TRUCK

Within the last few years, a fleet of new private, air-con express buses have caught on for services from Yangon to Meiktila, Pyay (Prome), Mandalay, Taunggyi, Mawlamyaing and Pathein (Bassein) – with more sure to come with the ongoing privatisation of the transport industry. This new class of private service has essentially eliminated the need to consider buses operated by the state-owned Road Transport Enterprise, which tend to be very crowded, ancient and unreliable.

These new express buses also beat Myanma Railway's express trains in both speed and ticket price; they also stop for meals along the way. Another major difference between bus and train is that all bus tickets may be purchased using kyat; if there's a dollar/FEC fare posted it's usually close to the kyat fare, figured at the free-market rate.

There are also many modern Japanese pickup trucks installed with bench seats known as *lain-ka* (for line car, rather like an Indonesian *bemo* or Thai *songthaew*) coming into use in the country. In fact, nowadays, most intercity travel off the main routes is accomplished by Toyota pickups carrying 20 or more passengers plus cargo.

These days, foreigners are permitted to buy bus tickets of any class, using kyat, to any destination within or near the main Yangon-Mandalay-Bagan-Taunggyi quadrangle. We also found that buses were easily boarded in most other places in the country too, except for 'brown' areas towards the Thai border.

Trip durations for public road transport are very elastic. Burmese superstition says when you're on a journey, you shouldn't ask 'How much longer?', or 'When will it arrive?', as this is only tempting fate. Upcountry roads in Central Myanmar are generally in reasonable condition on the main routes, but they're always narrow. When oncoming vehicles meet, or when one has to overtake another, both vehicles have to pull partly off the road. Breakdowns and tyre punctures are common.

TRAIN
Myanma Railways

Myanmar maintains 4684km of metre-gauge railway line – much of which is now open to foreign tourists – and 550 train stations. As of 1995, rolling stock consisted of 318 locomotives – 48 steam and the remainder diesel – plus 1130 passenger coaches.

The 647km-long trip from Yangon to Mandalay is the only train trip most visitors consider – there are daily and nightly reserved cars on express trains on this route, where you can be sure of getting a seat. One way to tell whether an approaching train is express or local is to check the engine colour; express engines are painted yellow, local ones blue. Another train journey worth considering is the Mandalay (or Pyin U Lwin) train to Lashio (or Hsipaw), which is a scenic and relatively comfortable ride.

Express trains hold the edge over buses for comfort, atmosphere and scenery. But if speed, punctuality or cost are important criteria, then the new private express buses are usually a better choice. The express trains are far superior to the general run of Burmese trains. In fact we'd recommend avoiding most other trains for any long trip – one 12 hour train trip that ends up running 15 hours late is enough for most people The Mandalay to Myitkyina route, though scheduled to take around 24 hours, often takes 40 hours; in 1995 this train derailed, killing 120 people. Even on the more travelled Yangon-Mandalay route, delays are common.

Apart from the straightforward Yangon-Bago-Thazi-Mandalay line, you can also take the branch line from Pyinmana to Kyauk Padaung (about 50km south of Bagan) or the branch from Thazi to Shwenyaung (about 11km from Inle Lake). Another express line now runs between Bagan/Nyaung U and Mandalay. At Mandalay there are three branches: one running slightly northwest across the Ava Bridge (Inwa) and up to Yeu, one directly north to Myitkyina in the Kachin State and one north-east through Pyin U Lwin (Maymyo) to Lashio in the northern part of the Shan State. From Yangon, lines also run north-west to Pyay, with

a branch-off to Pathein, while from Bago there is a branch off south-east to Kyaikto (jumping-off point for Mt Kyaiktiyo) and Mawlamyaing (Mottama train station).

Note also that Burmese trains are classified by a number and either the suffix Up for northbound trains, or Down for southbound trains.

Private Railways

Although most trains are operated by state-owned Myanma Railways, a few private enterprises have come into existence as well. Between Yangon and Mandalay, the private Dagon Mann (DM) line runs express trains that are more pleasant than the state-run express trains. However, the steep US dollar fares are clearly designed to dissuade foreigners from taking the train, which caters to upper crust Burmese rather than tourists. In fact, the only reason the DM accepts foreigners is that the government requires the company to set aside a few seats to help fill the demand for space during the tourist season. For more detail, see the Train entry in the Getting There & Away section of the Yangon chapter.

Two private companies, Malihka and Santhawta, operate trains along the Mandalay-Myitkyina line. In this case the only alternative is the very slow and uncomfortable government train. Ticket prices for foreigners are, as usual, in US dollars – and of course, are much higher than those for locals.

Classes

Express trains offer two classes of passage: upper class and ordinary class. The main differences between ordinary and upper are that the seats recline in the latter and can be reserved in advance, while ordinary class features hard upright seats that can't be reserved. Some trains also offer a 3rd class of service called 1st class, which is a step down from upper in comfort

The No 15 Up/No 16 Down train between Yangon and Mandalay is a 'special express' that uses relatively new Chinese equipment. The upper-class Chinese cars contain 30 wide seats in rows of three; other express

Train Schedules & Fares

train	departure	arrival	fare
Yangon to Mandalay			
11 Up	6.00 am	9.10 pm	US$30
17 Up	3.15 pm	5.20 am	US$18 to US$50 (special express)
5 Up	5.00 pm	7.00 am	US$30
15 Up	6.30 pm	8.20 am	US$38 (special express)
3 Up	7.30 pm	10.35 am	US$30
7 Up	9.00 pm	11.30 am	US$30
Yangon to Thazi			
11 Up	6.00 am	5.52 pm	US$27
5 Up	5.00 pm	4.14 am	US$27
17 Up	3.15 pm	2.35 am	US$33 (special express)
15 Up	6.30 pm	5.36 am	US$33 (special express)
3 Up	7.30 pm	7.17 am	US$27
Mandalay to Yangon			
6 Down	3.15 pm	5.20 am	US$30
18 Down	4.15 pm	6.20 am	US$38 (special express)
16 Down	5.30 pm	7.30 am	US$38 (special express)
4 Down	6.30 pm	10.00 am	US$30
8 Down	8.30 pm	12.30 pm	US$30
Thazi to Yangon			
18 Down	4.15 pm	6.20 am	US$33 (special express)
6 Down	6.00 pm	5.20 am	US$27
16 Down	8.16 pm	7.30 am	US$33 (special express)

trains may use older, South Korean cars that also seat three across but contain a total of 40 seats (so there's less room).

Myanma Railways and Myanmar Travels & Tours (MTT) no longer deny the existence of sleeping cars, but the one or two pulled by the No 15 Up/No 16 Down are usually occupied by Burmese VIPs or foreign tour groups. These sleeping cars contain five cabins, each with four berths, a fan, light and a small table with washbasin underneath. If demand is high enough, the No 17 Up/No 18 Down may also pull a sleeper.

Private Railcars

Myanma Railways keeps a couple of private railcars at the Yangon train station,

which are available for hire when not being used by government VIPs. Each comes with a kitchen, dining area, sitting area, double-berth cabin and six fold-down beds (in the dining and sitting cabins). The cars can be hooked on to any train along the Yangon-Mandalay and Thazi-Nyaungshwe (Yaunghwe) lines – and possibly other lines by special permit. The price is negotiable depending on how long the car is needed; a typical arrangement would be US$500 for up to nine days, including the services of an on-board cook. At night, these private cars are usually parked on sidings within train station limits along the way. For more information, see the stationmaster at Yangon's main train station.

Reservations

For tickets along the Yangon-Mandalay trunk line, all foreigners are supposed to purchase train tickets from MTT or from the windows labelled Foreigner Ticket Centre at the Yangon and Mandalay train stations, open daily from 8 am to 6 pm. Only Mandalay, Yangon and Thazi tickets are available from these sources. For Bago you must go to the Advance Booking Office (no English sign) on Bogyoke Aung San Lan adjacent to the station; the latter is only open from 6 to 10 am and 1 to 4 pm.

There are two advantages to booking your express train tickets through MTT in Yangon: this office accepts Visa and American Express (Amex) – MasterCard withdrew in 1998 – and a seat quota set aside for foreigners means you might be able to get a seat even when the station window says the train is full. Contrary to rumour, we found the fares to be exactly the same at both places, though fares differ according to which express train you take, even along the same line. A day's notice is usually enough for booking a seat. (Also, whenever you try to use a credit card in Myanmar, be prepared to pay a surcharge – 10% or more – and to wait for the extra paperwork to be completed; despite being accepted by some big hotels, credit cards are not a convenient method of payment in Myanmar.)

If you want to try your luck at getting a coveted sleeper, you'll need at least a couple of weeks notice. During the November-March tourist season berths are booked months in advance; assuming you hold a seat on a train pulling a sleeper car (No 15 Up/No 16 Down or No 3 Up/No 4 Down), your best bet is to try to upgrade to a berth after boarding. If any are available due to last-minute cancellations, you should be able to move from seat to berth for a US$3 to US$5 additional fare, paid directly to the conductor.

To buy tickets at other train stations you can use the same ticket windows as the Burmese. For common tourist destinations – Bago, Pyin U Lwin, Kyaikto – an inflated US dollar/FEC fare is usually collected. To other points via nonexpress trains, you may

be able to pay in kyat. Some foreigners riding the scenic (but slow) train between Shwenyaung and Thazi have been charged US dollars/FECs while others have paid in kyat – even on the same day! US dollar/FEC fares run roughly ten times the local fare in real kyat; an upper-class seat on an express train from Yangon to Mandalay costs foreigners US$30 to US$38 (depending on the train), while locals pay K1050 for upper class, K350 for ordinary. Foreigners aren't permitted to ride ordinary class on this line; on most other branch lines where foreigners are allowed to pay in kyat rather than US dollars/FECs, there's usually no problem buying an ordinary ticket if that's what you want – at least, not at the time of writing.

If you're having trouble buying a ticket or making yourself understood at a train station, try seeking out the stationmaster – the person at the station most likely to speak English, and most inclined to help you get a seat.

CAR

Hiring a car and driver is an increasingly popular way to get around the country. Prohibitions on car hire in Myanmar have lifted over the last few years and it's now very easy to hire a reasonably new, air-conditioned car with driver for around US$35 to US$40 a day, less for older, non-air-con cars. The usual per-day asking price will be around US$50, including driver and all fuel. If you hire for five days or more and pay for fuel yourself, the cost can drop to as low as US$30 a day. The cost will usually go up a few US dollars per extra person in the car or van. And the price should go down slightly if you plan on having a car for more than a week; the longer you intend to hire the car, the better your bargaining position.

There are no car rental agencies per se, but most travel agencies in Yangon, Mandalay or Bagan – and some guesthouses and hotels elsewhere – can arrange cars and drivers. In most cases, you will be asked to sign a simple contract and pay a good-faith deposit.

Foreigners with business or residence visas are permitted to drive themselves, although most still hire drivers. Driving conditions are

Car Rental Precautions

As a rule, it's a good idea to see your car and meet your driver before you agree to anything, or put down a deposit for car rental. You may want to look for a couple of essentials: a spare tyre and working seat belts. I was once offered a seat belt that looked fine at first glance, but had no buckle, or receiving end, to snap into. When the driver noticed the dilemma, he helpfully motioned for me to loop the belt around my neck!

Michael Clark

poor and a driver adds little to the hire cost. Of the 24,000km of roads in Myanmar, slightly less than half are bituminous or metalled; the remainder are graded gravel, unimproved dirt or simple vehicle tracks. To compound the difficulty, Myanmar traffic law requires vehicles be driven on the right-hand side of the road, even though the vast majority of cars and trucks – because they are low-cost, basic Japanese models – have right-hand drive. Supposedly Ne Win changed driving customs from the left side of the road to the right in 1970 on the advice of a fortune teller who vaguely suggested he move the country from left to right to improve his karma. This contradictory arrangement is brilliant for keeping an eye on pedestrians and oxcarts alongside the road, but terrible for observing oncoming traffic.

Among the most popular and reliable rental cars in the country are second-hand, reconditioned Toyota hatchbacks imported from Japan and called Super-roofs. Also called vans, one fresh off the boat costs US$5000. Myanmar assembles its own Mazda jeeps – or MJs – using 85% local parts. Though mostly a monopoly of the government, these jeeps make decent off-road vehicles. The old US-made, WWII-era Willys jeeps that once characterised outback Myanmar travel are becoming few and far between. You'll see a few of them in Mrauk U, usually without windows.

Myanmar is no longer quite self-sufficient in oil, and petrol can usually only be purchased in the area where the vehicle is registered. Officially, petrol from a Myanma Electric Power Enterprise (MPPE) station costs just K25 a gallon, but is rationed at four gallons a week (an increase from two gallons per week a year ago). At makeshift black-market pumps – often located just around the corner from an MPPE station – petrol costs up to K350 a gallon, over K400 in remote areas and small towns. When Burmese vehicle owners make an upcountry 'road trip' (the Burmese English term for any ex-Yangon driving), they either have to buy fuel on the black market, or carry along numerous jerry cans of petrol.

Another small cost to consider when travelling by car is the customary K5 to K20 'toll' collected upon entering many towns and villages throughout Myanmar – a legacy of the tributes paid to warlord states in centuries past. More a curiosity than a true financial burden, the road toll means you or the driver should carry lots of small kyat bills – Burmese drivers are adept at handing these to the toll collectors while barely slowing down.

MOTORCYCLE

Apparently there's no longer any restriction on hiring motorcycles in Myanmar – you may even drive them yourself if you possess a valid International Driving Permit. Almost any large motorcycle dealer will entertain a hire offer. In Yangon, the latest to offer motorcycles is CSL Travel & Tours (☎ 01-514047) at 24 Inya Myaing Lan. Also try Super Star Motorcycle Sale Centre (☎ 01-272290) at 222 Pansodan Lan, or Mandalay Central Enterprise (☎ 01-273652) at 146 Pansodan Lan. Rates are high compared to Thailand, up to US$30 per day for nothing larger than a Japanese 125cc, and about US$35 for a 200cc bike. A substantial deposit may be required. You might also consider buying a used bike and selling it back to the dealer at a slightly reduced price after a few weeks on the road.

Always check a machine over thoroughly

before you take it out. Look at the tyres to see if they still have tread, look for oil leaks, test the brakes. You may be held liable for any problems that weren't duly noted before your departure. Newer bikes cost more than clunkers, but are generally safer and more reliable.

If you get a flat tyre you can't deal with or just need air, you'll find plenty of tyre repair places along the road – look for oil drum tops painted with two Burmese characters spelling *lei* (air), or a suspended inner tube.

Precautions

Wear protective clothing and a helmet (the dealer should be able to provide a helmet with the bike, if asked). Without a helmet, a minor slide on gravel can leave you with concussion, cuts or bruises. Shoes, long pants and long-sleeved shirts are highly recommended as protection against sunburn and as a second skin if you fall. If your helmet doesn't have a visor, then wear goggles, glasses or sunglasses to keep bugs, dust and other debris out of your eyes. It is almost suicidal to ride on Myanmar's highways without taking these minimum precautions for protecting your body. Gloves are also a good idea, to prevent blisters from holding on to the twist-grips for long periods of time.

Distribute whatever weight you're carrying on the bike as evenly as possible across the frame. Too much weight at the back of the bike makes the front end less easy to control and prone to rising up suddenly on bumps and inclines.

For distances of over 100km or so, take along an extra supply of motor oil and, if riding a two stroke machine, carry two stroke engine oil. On long trips, oil burns fast.

BICYCLE

Bikes can easily be hired in Mandalay, Bagan, Pyin U Lwin and around Inle Lake. Guesthouses often have a few for rent at only K300 to K400 per day. Just about anywhere outside Yangon, bikes are the ideal form of local transport since they're cheap, nonpolluting and keep you moving slowly enough to see everything. Outside Yangon

and Mandalay vehicular traffic is generally very light. Carefully note the condition of the bike before hiring; it's not unusual to get one that needs a brake job or new pedal. And if it breaks down you are generally responsible and parts can be expensive.

If renting doesn't appeal, you can buy a sturdy new made-in-India Hero for US$40, a slightly better Five Rams from China for US$50 or a top of the line Crocodile from Thailand for US$150. All are plain, utilitarian, all-black city bikes with moderately heavy frames.

A few visitors bring their own touring bikes into Myanmar; nowadays there doesn't seem to be any problem with customs as long as you make the proper declarations upon entering the country. Grades in most parts of Myanmar open to tourism are moderate. Frontier regions, on the other hand – particularly the Shan, Kayin, Kayah and Chin states – tend to be mountainous. You'll find plenty of opportunity everywhere for dirt-road and off-road pedalling – in fact you must come prepared for it! Especially in the north, where main roads can resemble off-roads elsewhere, a sturdy mountain bike would make a good alternative to a touring rig.

One of the most scenic routes starts in Thazi (accessible by train) and runs east through hilly Kalaw and Pindaya to Inle Lake. Another starts in Mandalay and down the flat Ayeyarwady (Irrawaddy) River plains to Bagan. Shorter trips out of Mandalay to Monywa, Pyin U Lwin, Sagaing, Inwa (Ava) and Amarapura also make satisfying rides.

Anyone with previous Third World cycling experience will find Myanmar a fairly straightforward pedal, though an extra measure of resourcefulness and cycling savvy is called for, due to the overall lack of accommodation and transport infrastructure. November to February are the best cycling months in terms of weather. Larger towns have bike shops – there are several in Mandalay and Yangon – but they often stock only a few Indian, Chinese or locally made parts. All the usual bike trip precautions apply – bring a small repair kit with plenty of spare parts, a helmet, reflective clothing and plenty of insurance.

BOAT
River Ferry

A huge fleet of riverboats, heir to the old Irrawaddy Flotilla Company (IFC), still ply Myanmar's major rivers. In the last few years, several newer boats have been put into service – mostly for visitors. But many of the boats date back 80 or 100 years to the British era. In Burmese-English they're still called steamers, even though the original stern-wheelers have all been converted to diesel. River ferry is, without doubt, one of the most enjoyable ways to cover long distances in Myanmar. The main drawback is speed; where both modes of transport are available, a boat typically takes three to four times as long as road travel along the same route.

Inland Water Transport (IWT) has over 500 boats totalling nearly 1.5 million tonnes and carrying at least 14 million passengers annually. Another thousand or so private cargo and passenger boats travel the waterways. That is just a pale shadow of the former glory of the original Glasgow-owned IFC, which ceased operations in 1948 – only to be revived in 1995. Its old Siam Class steamers carried 4200 deck passengers each plus 40 more in staterooms; they were 100m long and travelled faster upriver than the present-day government boats can manage downriver! The captains of these mighty riverboats were so important that a Mandalay shop once had a sign announcing they were 'Silk Mercers to the Kings and Queens of Burma and the Captains of the Steamers'. IFC was struck a disastrous blow by WWII, and many wrecks of their boats are still at Mandalay, scuttled in the river in 1942.

There are 8000km of navigable river in Myanmar, with the most important river being the Ayeyarwady. Even in the dry season, boats can travel from the delta all the way north to Bhamo, and in the wet they can reach Myitkyina. Other important rivers include the Twante Chaung, which links the Ayeyarwady to Yangon, and the Chindwin River, which joins the Ayeyarwady a little above Bagan. The Thanlwin (Salween) River in the east is only navigable for about 200km from its mouth at Mawlamyaing.

Today most of the red-and-black boats of the nationalised water transport corporation are rather rundown and ramshackle, but it still takes great expertise to navigate Myanmar's waterways. Rapidly changing sandbanks and shallow water during the dry season mean the captains and pilots have to keep in constant touch with the changing pattern of the river flows. For example, seven pilots are used on the stretch from Mandalay to Pyay. Each is an expert on his own particular segment of the river. Many of the passengers on the long-distance ferries are traders who make stops along the way to pick up or deliver goods. Along the heavily travelled 423km-long Yangon-Pyay-Mandalay route, there are 28 ferry landings, where merchants can ply their trade.

Only a few riverboat routes are regularly used by visitors. These new 'tourist boats' carry foreigners on the upper deck, locals on the lower. Best known is the Mandalay-Bagan service. Others routes include Sittwe-Mrauk U, and Mawlamyaing-Hpa-an. On the Ayeyarwady, there is a quite amazing amount of transport shuttling up and down this riverine 'road to Mandalay' and it's a trip that most people seem to enjoy. Other boats can extend the trip south to Pyay, or all the way to Yangon; it's two days travel downriver from Bagan to Pyay, where you change boats and have another couple of days travel before reaching Yangon.

Mandalay-Bagan Express Ferry There is now a better alternative to the government's (MTT) Mandalay-Bagan ferry, which still departs from Mandalay every Wednesday and Sunday. The new Mandalay-Bagan Express ferry departs every Monday, Tuesday, Thursday, Friday and Saturday, and the trip takes about nine hours, as opposed to MTT's 13 hours. (See the Boats entry in the Getting There & Away section of the Bagan Region chapter for more information.)

A slower, much cheaper ferry does the

same Mandalay-Bagan route daily, taking roughly 26 to 29 hours and costing just K200 for deck class. The slower boat stops overnight at Pakokku.

Ayeyarwady River Luxury Cruises There are several luxury ferries now travelling the upper and lower reaches of the Ayeyarwady River. The most conspicuous, and by far the most expensive, is the *Road to Mandalay*, an E&O luxury liner (Orient-Express Cruises, London). Five-night package tours between Mandalay and Bagan cost about US$2000 per person.

Since 1996 the revived IFC has been operating old-fashioned 'expedition cruises' along several sections of the upper and lower Ayeyarwady River. If you've got the money, these boats are by far the most interesting vessels in Myanmar, relying on shallow-draft technology pioneered in Scotland over 100 years ago by naval architects; the RV *Pandaw* has a draft of just three feet – helpful on a river that bulges with sand bars during the dry season. Although the original stern-paddle design has been replaced by modern engines, the boats have the feel of a classic river steamer, with breezy promenades and teak and brass fittings throughout. Prices range from US$150/250 for one/two-night cruises between Bagan and Mandalay; up to US$3000 for a 12 day cruise that reaches Bhamo on the upper Ayeyarwady.

Thanlwin River Ferry Double-decker ferries from the Hpa-an jetty, on the river's eastern bank in Mawlamyaing, depart twice daily to Hpa-an. This four hour cruise (three hours downriver) is one of the most scenic river trips in the country. The fare for foreigners is US$2 for upper deck class, and US$12 for a stuffy cabin. See Getting There & Away in the Hpa-an section of the South-Eastern Myanmar chapter for more details.

There are other, lesser known, river trips that the adventurous traveller can also consider. For example, Twante is only a few hours from Yangon via the Twante Chaung, and you can continue all the way to Pathein.

The overnight river journey between Bhamo and Mandalay on the upper Ayeyarwady has only recently opened up to river travel. The shorter four hour ferry running between Mawlamyaing and Hpa-an is probably the most scenic short trip you'll find in the country.

Another shorter trip you can make quite easily is the trip upriver from Mandalay to Mingun. You can also make short day-excursions by rented boat from Yangon, Mandalay and Bagan.

Reservations

The government's IWT fares, calculated by mileage, used to be quite inexpensive when you could pay in kyat. As with train travel, the collection of US dollars/FECs versus kyat seems to be somewhat arbitrary. However, we've noticed more and more that foreigners are asked to pay the US dollar amounts. That goes for the privately owned ferries as well. Of course, with small boats that you might charter for part of a day, you can pay in kyat.

The main IWT ticket office in Yangon is one street back from Lan Thit jetty, in Bldg No 63. This is where all the locals purchase tickets. Foreigners are always referred to a small white building next to Transit Shed No 1, opposite nearby Kaingdan Lan jetty. Here you can reserve tickets directly from IWT deputy division manager U Win Shwe (☎ 01-284055), who has held the position for over a decade. To be safe, try to book a week in advance of travel, although a day's advance purchase may sometimes be sufficient.

The IWT office (☎ 02-86035) in Mandalay is on 68th St near the Mandalay Swan Hotel. For information on ferries to Bagan or Pyay, see the appropriate Getting There & Away sections in the Bagan Region chapter, the Pyay section in the Around Yangon chapter, and the Bhamo section in the North-Eastern Myanmar chapter.

Boats & Classes

The standard long-distance ferry features two large decks, a lower deck consisting of the bare steel hull and an upper deck finished in wood. These ferries typically hold 286 passengers, 123 on the more costly upper deck and the remainder below. Only upper deck passage can be reserved in advance; assigned numbers painted on the deck indicate the reserved spots. Some boats feature a dozen or so sling chairs toward the bow of the upper deck; these cost a bit more than regular upper deck class. Boats running day routes usually feature a saloon compartment in the upper deck of the bow, with a few wooden chairs and an attached toilet. Monks usually ride in a separate, wired-off section of the upper foredeck.

Those craft running overnight routes may contain a few beds in the saloon compartment. A few boats even have cabins with sleeping berths in the bow, usually no more than six cabins sleeping two people each. On most routes, saloon and cabin-class space is very difficult to come by, though foreigners have a better chance than the Burmese. Military officers, of course, always have first choice.

The Mandalay-Bagan express boats have forward-facing row seating, though you're free to roam the decks for the price of a ticket. All the express boats have a snack bar serving noodles, beer, soft drinks etc.

Three new Chinese-built ferries featuring a triple-deck design have recently gone into service along the Yangon-Pathein route and along the Ayeyarwady River from Mandalay to Pyay via Bagan/Nyaung U. These vessels feature 18 double cabins in 1st class, 10 double cabins in 2nd class, three 16-berth cabins in 3rd class and deck space for 270 passengers. First class cabins on the tripledeckers have attached toilets and showers.

Ship
Myanma Five Star Line Although the obstacles standing in your way are daunting, it's possible to travel along Myanmar's coastline via Myanma Five Star Line (MFSL), the country's state-owned ocean transport enterprise. MFSL maintains just 21 craft, which sail north and south from Yangon about twice a month. Only eight vessels offer passenger service: MV *Taung-*

gyi, MV *Hakha*, MV *Myitkyina*, MV *Loikaw*, MV *Lashio*, MV *Bagan*, MV *Hpa-an* and MV *Htonywa*. Shipping dates vary from month to month and are announced via a public chalkboard at the main MFSL office in Yangon. There's another office and chalkboard in Sittwe.

Southbound MFSL ships sail regularly to Kawthoung, a two-day and two-night voyage from Yangon, to pick up goods shipped through Thailand's Ranong Province, with calls at Dawei and Myeik. During the rainy season, the journey can take a week.

Northbound ships call at Thandwe (a full day from Yangon), Taunggup and Kyaukpyu (one night ashore) before docking in Sittwe (five more hours) for cargo from India and Bangladesh.

Schedules can be irregular and you may have to wait several days for a ship going your way. If you're bent on trying for a ticket, it would be best to have a Burmese citizen make inquiries on your behalf, as the bureaucracy can be staggering. Tickets can only be purchased two days ahead; at times they are in such demand that locals are only able to buy them via a lottery system.

Foreigners who have persevered will usually be issued one of the 20 coveted berths in saloon (upper) class. All Yangon ships leave from the MFSL jetty (also known as the Chanmaye Seikkan jetty), just west of Pansodan Lan jetty. Saloon fares are: Kawthoung K4423; Dawei K2474; Myeik K2696; Thandwe K1538; Kyaukpyu K2179; and Sittwe K2592.

Cargo Ships If you don't mind sleeping on potato and onion sacks, cargo ships are a cheap alternative to the government-MFSL ships that sail up and down the Bay of Bengal. See the Getting There & Away section for Sittwe in the Western Myanmar chapter for more information.

LOCAL TRANSPORT
Larger towns in Myanmar offer a variety of city buses *(ka)*, bicycle rickshaws or trishaws *(saiq-ka,* for side-car*)*, horsecarts *(myint hlei)*, vintage taxis *(taxi)*, more modern

little three-wheelers somewhat akin to auto-rickshaws *(thoun bein,* or three wheels), tiny four-wheeled Mazdas *(lei bein,* or four wheels) and modern Japanese pickup trucks (also *lain ka).*

Small towns rely heavily on horsecarts and trishaws as the main mode of local transport. In the five largest cities (Yangon, Mandalay, Pathein, Mawlamyaing and Taung-gyi), public buses take regular routes along the main avenues for a fixed per-person rate, usually no more than K5. Standard rates for taxis, trishaws and horsecarts are sometimes 'boosted' for foreigners. A little bargaining may be in order; ask around locally to find out what the going fares are. The supply of drivers and vehicles often exceeds demand, so it's usually not hard to move the fare down towards normal levels.

You can rent bicycles in Mandalay, Bagan, Pyin U Lwin and Nyaungshwe at most hotels and guesthouses.

ORGANISED TOURS

Itineraries for Myanmar tours booked anywhere in the world look much the same. The cheapest (around US$400) is a four day-three night Yangon package that includes a visa, airport transfers in Yangon,

guide service and accommodation only, booked through travel agencies in Bangkok. With a package of this sort, you must book your own round-trip flight to Yangon, arrange your own local transport outside Yangon and buy your own meals.

More expensive trips costing US$2000 or more run for 14 or 15 days in Yangon, Mandalay, Pyin U Lwin, Bagan, Kalaw, Pindaya, Inle Lake, Taunggyi and Bago, including visa, return air fare from Bangkok, local transport, accommodation, all meals and guide service. Such tours can be booked easily in the USA, Europe, Japan, New Zealand and Australia, or from agencies in Bangkok.

Deluxe river cruises on the upper and lower reaches of the Ayeyarwady River are available for periods of two to 14 days. See the River Ferry section in this chapter for more information.

It's also possible to arrange tours locally, out of Yangon and Mandalay. There are well over 100 travel agencies in Yangon, so it pays to shop around (see the Travel Agencies entry under Information in the Yangon chapter later). Many will custom-design a tour according to your requests, for about the same price as a package tour booked abroad.

Yangon

Yangon (formerly Rangoon) lies in the fertile delta country of Southern Myanmar, on the wide Yangon River, about 30km from the Andaman Sea. Although the population hovers around four million, the city gives a very different impression from other Asian capitals of similar size. It seems full of trees and shade – even old growth teak here and there – and some outlying neighbourhoods are refreshingly overgrown. Shimmering stupas float above the treetops. If you can close your eyes to the neglected colonial architecture in the city centre, you'll probably agree that this could be one of the most charming cities in South-East Asia. In the city centre, the streets are wide and carefully laid out on a typical British colonial grid system.

The city has changed dramatically following the 1989 banishment of socialism. Since 1992, when the relatively moderate, pro-capitalist General Than Shwe (often referred to as 'No 1') took power, many new cars and trucks have taken to city roads, mobile phones are commonly seen in the city centre and satellite dishes dot the horizon. The capital is still easygoing and there's little of the frenetic, neon-lit clamour of Bangkok. Nevertheless, the word rushhour can now be applied in relation to the city centre. Of course, the Yangon rush hour is a combination of weaving cars, buses, trucks, trishaws, taxis, bicycles and pedestrians. Somehow, people and vehicles coexist in the middle of large intersections. The sound of horns seems constant at times, and there are even posted signs here and there on city centre alleyways forbidding their use. Of course, no one seems to pay attention to either the signs or the honking.

History

As Myanmar's capital city, Yangon is comparatively young – it only became capital in 1885 when the British completed the conquest of Upper Myanmar and Mandalay's

HIGHLIGHTS

- Glittering Shwedagon Paya with its dazzling mix of pavilions, stupas, images and bells.
- Colonial architecture of old 'Rangoon' including the legendary Strand Hotel.
- Serene Sule Paya in the heart of the busy city centre.
- Pro-democracy landmarks such as Aung San's house museum and the Martyrs' Mausoleum.
- Sprawling Bogyoke Aung San Market and Theingyi Zei.
- Peaceful Kandawgyi and Inya Lake.

brief period as the centre of the last Burmese kingdom ended.

Despite its short history as the seat of national government, Yangon has been in existence for a long time – although very much as a small town, in comparison to places like Bago (Pegu), Pyay (Prome) or Thaton. In 1755 King Alaungpaya conquered Lower

Myanmar and built a new city on the site of Yangon, which at that time was known as Dagon. Yangon means 'end of strife': the king rather vainly hoped that with the conquest of Lower Myanmar, his struggles would be over.

In 1756 with the destruction of Thanlyin (Syriam) across the river, Yangon also became an important seaport. In 1841 the city was virtually destroyed by fire; the rebuilt town again suffered extensive damage during the Second Anglo-Burmese War in 1852. The British, the new masters, rebuilt the capital to its present plan and corrupted the city's name to Rangoon.

Yangon's early history as Dagon is tied very closely to its grand Buddhist stupa, the Shwedagon Paya. It doesn't stand in the city centre, rather about 3km to the north – yet it totally dominates the Yangon skyline.

In 1988 around 15% of Yangon's city centre population – all squatters – were moved to seven *myo thit* (new towns) northeast of the city centre. Many of the old colonial buildings once occupied by the squatters have now been refurbished for use as offices, businesses and apartments.

Starting in the early 1990s, the government began sprucing up the city's appearance by cleaning the streets and painting many public buildings. To try and keep blood-red spittle off the streets, the selling of betel nut was banned in 1995. As with many such decrees, the streets are no better or worse.

Orientation

The city is bounded to the south and west by the Yangon River (also known as the Hlaing River) and to the east by Pazundaung Chaung, which flows into the Yangon River. The whole city is divided into townships, and street addresses are often suffixed with these (eg 126 52nd St, Botataung Township – or Botataung t/s). North of the centre, the city opens up like the top of a funnel and spreads along a network of long, curving avenues.

At the northern end of the city, most businesses and hotels are found along Pyay Lan,

Kaba Aye Paya Lan or Insein Lan – long avenues running south from the airport area to the city centre. Addresses in this northern area often quote the number of miles from Sule Paya – the landmark *paya* (pagoda) in the city's centre. For example, 'Pyay Lan, Mile 8' means the place is 8 miles north of Sule Paya on Pyay Lan.

Two of the most important townships outside the central area are Dagon – where you'll find Shwedagon Paya, People's Park and several embassies – and Bahan, site of many of the city's mid-range and top end hotels and inns.

Central Yangon is a relatively simple area to find your way around, and pleasant enough to explore on foot. The main central streets are laid out in a grid system, with the minor north-south streets numbered in the North American fashion. Many of the major roads were renamed after independence, but some of the old names persist, and this can be confusing. Anawrahta Lan, for example, is often referred to by locals as Fraser St, and has both new and old street signs.

Most of the other old names are fading from memory, however, and are of interest perhaps only to those in search of a bygone era. Mention of Sparks St (Bo Aung Gyaw Lan), China St (Shwedagon Paya Lan), Godwin Rd (Madaw Lan) or Montgomery St (Bogyoke Aung San Lan) will probably elicit little more than a shrug. One exception: locals may indicate their political opinions by their choice of pre-junta terms such as Burma and Rangoon.

The English terms street and road are used interchangeably in Yangon for the single Burmese word *lan*. Hence, some maps may read Shwegondaing St, while others will say Shwegondaing Rd; in Burmese, it's simply Shwegondaing Lan.

Maps The *Yangon Tourist Map,* printed by Design Printing Services (DPS) and distributed by Myanmar Travels & Tours (MTT), is usually free and useful enough for most people. If you anticipate spending a lot of time in the capital, look for a new bilingual atlas, *The Map of Yangon,* a detailed street

YANGON

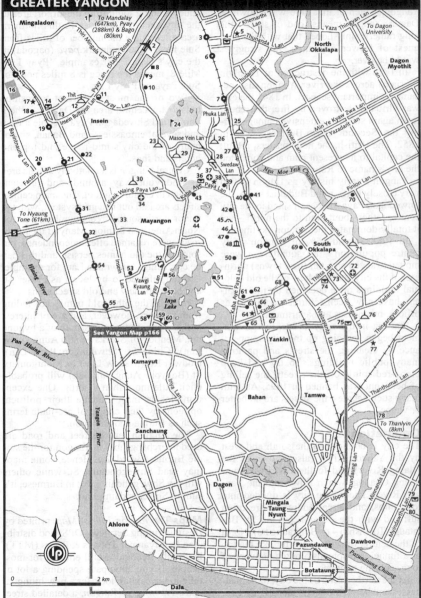

GREATER YANGON

Mingaladon

15
16
17 ★
18 ●
19

Lan Thit
Insein Butteyon Lan
Pyay Lan
Thin Mingala Lan (Station Road)

To Mandalay
(647km), Pyay
(288km) & Bago
(80km)

1
2
3
4 ★ 5
6
Khemarthi
Lan
Thunanda Lan
Yaza Thingyan Lan
To Dagon
University

North
Okkalapa

Dagon
Myothit

8
9
10

11
12
13
14

Insein

Thudamar Lan

Phuka Lan
7
25
U Wisara Lan
Min Ye Kyaw Zwa Lan
Yazadarit Lan
Pyidaungsu Lan

Bayinnaung Lan

20
21 22

24
Masoe Yein Lan
23
26
29
27
28
35 36 37
38
39
Swedaw
Lan
Nga Moe Yeik Chaung

Sawa Factory Lan

30
34
31
33
32
54
Kyaik Waing Paya Lan
43
Kaba Aye Paya Lan
40 ● 41
42 ●
45
46
47 ●
48
49
50 ●
Param Lan
Pinlon Lan
70
Thanthumar Lan
South
Okkalapa
71
69
72
73
74
Tnitsa Lan

Mayangon

44

To Nyaung
Tone (61km)

Hlaing River

Inya
Lake

Yawgi
Kyaung
Lan
52
53
56
57
55
58
59 60
51
61 62
63 66
64 ★ 65 67
68
Kanbe Lan
Kaba Aye Paya Lan
Insein Lan
Pyay Lan
Waizayanta Lan
Thumingala Lan
Thuminzalar Lan
Yadana Lan
76
75
Thingangyun Lan
77 ★
78
To Thanlyin
(8km)

Pan Hlaing River

See Yangon Map p166

Kamayut
Yankin

Inya Lan

Bahan
Tamwe

Sanchaung

Yangon River

Dagon

Mingala
Taung
Nyunt

Upper Pazundaung Lan
Thanthumar Lan
79
80
Minnanda Lan
Myindawtha Lan

Ahlone

81
Dawbon

Pazundaung

Pazundaung Chaung

Botataung

Dala

0   1   2 km

PLACES TO STAY	20	Department of Health	48	Myanma Gems Museum
8 Ramada Airport Hotel		(Malaria Control)		& Gems Mart
51 Inya Lake Hotel	21	Gyogone Train Station	49	Parami Train Station
56 Best Executive Suites	22	Yangon Institute of	50	Chanmyay Yeiktha
		Technology		Meditation Centre
PLACES TO EAT	23	Shan Kyaung Paya	52	Philippines Embassy
9 Airport Oasis Restaurant	24	Myanmar Golf Association	53	Na-Gar Glass Factory
33 Nawarat Hotel Restaurant	25	Me La Mu Paya	54	Thirimyaing Train Station
58 Silom Village Restaurant	26	Naga Cave Paya	55	Kamayut Train Station
59 Malai Thai Restaurant	27	Tadagale Train Station	57	International Business Centre
65 L'Opera Restaurant	28	Swedawmyat Paya (Buddha	60	Yangon Boat Club
		Tooth Relic Pagoda)	61	Ministry of Forestry
OTHER	29	Nagayon Paya	62	Ministry of Agriculture
1 City Golf Club	30	Kyaikwaing Paya	63	Survey Department
2 Yangon International	31	Thamaing Train Station	64	Police Station
Airport	32	Okkyin Train Station	66	Teacher Training College
3 Okkalapa Train Station	34	Hospital of the Disabled	67	Post Office
4 Post Office	35	Myaing Haywun Park	68	Kanbe Train Station
5 Police Station	36	Post Office	69	Nandawun Market
6 Pweseikkon Train Station	37	Yangon Psychiatric Hospital	70	Pinlon Market
7 Kyaukyedwin Train Station	38	Police Station	71	South Okkalapa Paya
10 Department of Civil	39	Nawaday Cinema	72	Women and Children
Aviation	40	Yegu Train Station		Hospital
11 Highway Bus Station	41	Radio Transmitting Station	73	Police Station
12 Ah Lain Nga Sint Paya	42	Department of Religious	74	Post Office
13 Insein Park		Affairs	75	Post Office
14 Post Office	43	DHL Express Mail	76	Kyaikkasan Paya
15 Ywama Train Station	44	Sangha Hospital	77	Police Station
16 Insein Prison	45	Maha Pasana Guha	78	Thuwunna Bridge
17 Police Station	46	Kaba Aye Paya	79	Post Office
18 Insein Market	47	State Pariyatti Sasana	80	Police Station
19 Insein Train Station		University	81	Thaketa Bridge

directory with both a street and place index, first published in 1998, and easily found in most bookshops or large hotels for about US$3 or the *kyat* equivalent.

Harder to find, but still useful, is the older *Yangon City Map* (Printing & Publishing Enterprise), or the more detailed *Yangon Guide Map* (Ministry of Forestry, Survey Department). Both of these maps were first published in 1993. You might find used versions of these and other maps at the rambling sidewalk bookstalls on Pansodan Lan, just north of Merchant St.

Information

Tourist Office The MTT office (☎ 01-275328), at 77-91 Sule Paya Lan, on the corner of Mahabandoola Lan and across the street from Sule Paya, is the main centre for

tourist inquiries. Basically nothing more than a government-run travel agency, its main purpose seems to be to discourage visitors from venturing away from the main tourist quadrangle, while encouraging the use of government-sponsored transportation like Myanma Airways (MA) and the Yangon-Mandalay express train. Decent city maps of Bagan (Pagan), Mandalay and Yangon are sold for K20 to K30 each; postcards are also cheap here. Though seemingly helpful, information here is inconsistent at best, and should be double-checked; this means destinations, prices – everything.

The office is open daily from 8.30 am to 5 pm.

Money With the Foreign Exchange Certificate (FEC) system in place, no one bothers to change money at the so-called official rate any more. If you're foolish enough to want to, you'll have to convince someone you're serious. Even the MTT cashier will take foreign currency at close to the going rate.

Yangon is usually the best place in the country for changing money at the free-market rate. On the other hand, we've found that news of a drop in rates sometimes takes longer to reach the provinces. Ask around to establish what the current rate is. If you've bought FECs at the airport, the best place to change them is at a hotel or shop licensed to accept FECs. In general, Bogyoke Aung San Market is a good place to shop for moneychangers; several here are licensed to exchange kyat for FECs. If you don't have FECs, US dollars are the only alternative; free-market moneychangers usually aren't interested in other foreign currencies.

Post The main post office is a short stroll east of The Strand Hotel on Strand Rd. It's open Monday to Friday from 9.30 am to 4.30 pm, though it's best to arrive by 4.15 pm.

Telephone & Fax The Central Telephone & Telegraph (CTT) office, on the corner of Pansodan and Mahabandoola Lans, was recently the only public place in the country where international telephone calls could be conveniently arranged. There are now two more methods: International Direct Dial (IDD) and trunk calls. IDD calls are very expensive, and can be made from many hotels; trunk calls are quite cheap, and can be made from many shops in the city centre area. The CTT office also has fax machines and is open Monday to Friday from 8 am to 4 pm, weekends and holidays from 9 am to 2 pm. Some hotels also have fax machines.

The area code for Yangon is 01.

Travel Agencies Most visitors to Myanmar only use domestic travel agencies to book a tour, hire a car or book a domestic flight (air ticket prices are usually cheaper through a private travel agency). However, of the more than 100 enterprises in Yangon calling themselves travel agencies, only a handful can be considered full-service, experienced tour agencies.

Among the more reliable agencies are:

Columbus Travels & Tours
   (☎ 01-221881, fax 229246,
   email columbus@mtpt400.stems.com)
   586 Strand Rd (corner of Strand Rd and 7th St)
Diethelm Travel
   (☎ 01-527110, fax 527136,
   email leisure@diethelm.com.mm)
   1 Inya Lan
Free Bird Tours
   (☎ 01-245489, fax 275638,
   email freebird@myanmars.net)
   357 Bo Aung Gyaw Lan
Golden Express Limited
   (☎ 01-225569,
   email getour@datserco.com.mm)
   97-B Wadan Lan
Insight Myanmar Tourism
   (☎ 01-297798, fax 295599,
   email insight@mtpt400.stems.com)
   85-87 Theinbyu Lan, Botataung Township
Santa Maria Travel & Tours
   (☎ 01-254625, fax 297946,
   email maria99@ksc.th.com)
   195-B 32nd St, Pabedan Township
Tour Mandalay
   (☎ 01-294729, fax 297917,
   email KZN.TMC@mtpt400.stems.com)
   2nd floor, 194/196 Mahabandoola Lan
Woodland Travels
   (☎ 01-246636, fax 240377,
   email woodland@datserco.com.mm)
   24 Yawmingyi Lan

Bookshops Inwa Book Store, at 232 Sule Paya Lan between Anawrahta and Bogyoke Aung San Lans, has a fair collection of new books in English. Sarpay Beikman Book Centre, on Merchant St between 37th and 38th Sts, carries most of the government-published books and maps on Myanmar.

Bagan Bookshop (also called Pagan), at 100 37th St, has the country's most complete selection of English-language books on Myanmar and South-East Asia. The owner often has the front gate pulled across the entrance, but this doesn't necessarily mean the place is closed unless the door inside the gate is closed, too. Also check out the many bookstalls around Bogyoke Aung San Market (sometimes known as Scott

Market) or along 37th St. See the Books & Periodicals section in the Facts for the Visitor chapter for more details.

Myanmar Book Centre (MBC) (☎ 01-531732; fax 524580), at 477 Pyay Lan, Kamayut Township, is located inside the Nandawun building (Myanmar Gems & Handicrafts). MBC also has smaller branches in the National Museum and the Sedona Hotel. It carries a good variety of books and periodicals dealing with Burmese history and culture, including some rare and out-of-print books. MBC is open daily from 9 am to 6 pm.

Libraries The British Council Library (☎ 01-295300), in the UK embassy, has a small library of English-language magazines and books; it's open to the public Monday to Saturday from 8.30 am to 3.30 pm. The American Center (☎ 01-223140), at 14 Taw Win Lan, behind the Ministry of Foreign Affairs also has a collection of books and magazines, which can be perused Monday to Friday from 9 am to 4 pm.

For French-language material, check the Alliance Française (☎ 01-282122), attached to the French embassy; it's open Tuesday and Friday only.

If visiting Shwedagon Paya, you can visit the Library & Archives of Buddhism, located in the Western Arch.

Religious Services For those seeking houses of worship:

Anglican/Episcopal/Protestant
Holy Trinity Cathedral
(☎ 01-272326) 446 Bogyoke Aung San Lan
English Methodist Church
(☎ 01-284165) 65 Alaungpaya Lan
Immanuel Baptist Church
(☎ 01-250079) Mahabandoola Garden St
Kuo Yu Chinese Methodist Church
(☎ 01-225141) 47 Min Ye Kyaw Swar Lan, Ahlone Township

Catholic
St Mary's Cathedral
(☎ 01-294896) 372 Bo Aung Gyaw Lan
St Augustine's Church
(☎ 01-530620) 64 Inya Lan

Armenian Orthodox
St John the Baptist Armenian Orthodox Church
113 Bo Aung Gyaw Lan

Jewish
Moseah Yeshua Synagogue
(☎ 01-275062) 85 26th St (services on special occasions only)

Muslim
Cholia Jama Mosque
Bo Sun Pet Lan
Narsapuri (Moja) Mosque
227 Shwebontha Lan
Surti Suni Jama Mosque
Shwebontha Lan

Sikh
256 Theibyu Lan

Meditation Centres
Chanmyay Yeiktha Meditation Centre
(☎ 01-661 479)
55A Kaba Aye Paya Lan
Mahasi Meditation Centre
(☎ 01-541 971, 552 501, fax 289 960/1)
16 Sasana Yeiktha Lan
Panditarama Golden Hill Meditation Centre
(☎ 01-531 448)
80A Shwetaunggyaw Lan
The International Meditation Centre
(☎ 01-531 549)
31A Inya Myaing Lan

Laundry Professional laundry services usually do a better job of washing and ironing than Yangon's guesthouses and small hotels. Ava Laundry and Anglo Myanmar Laundry Service, two places on the southern side of Mahabandoola Lan, between 41st and 42nd Sts, are fast, reliable and cheap. Both shops are open daily from 7.30 am to 9.30 pm.

Medical Services If you want medical attention in Yangon, your best bet is the Asia Emergency Assistance (AEA) International Clinic, on the ground floor of the New World Inya Lake Hotel, Kaba Aye Paya Lan (☎ 01-667879; alarm centre ☎ 667877); you can also call the hotel (☎ 01-662866), and ask for AEA International.

There are several private and public hospitals in Yangon, but the fees, service and

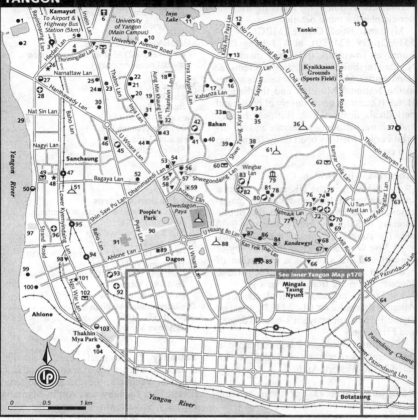

YANGON

quality may vary. Two that have been recommended to us are the Kandawgyi Hospital, on Natmauk Lan, at the north-eastern edge of Kandawgyi (Royal Lake) (☎ 01-542486) and the Pacific Medical Centre & Dental Surgery, at 81 Kaba Aye Paya Lan (☎ 01-548022).

Pharmacies There are two pharmacies just north of Sule Paya and opposite one another – the AA Pharmacy, at 142/146 Sule Paya Lan; and Global Network Co, at 155/161 Sule Paya Lan. May Pharmacy is nearby, at 542 Merchant St (on the north-west corner of Pansodan Lan). All three shops have 24-hour counters.

Emergency An ambulance can be summoned by dialling ☎ 192 or ☎ 01-295133. For police, call ☎ 199 or ☎ 01-284764. At neither of these numbers can we guarantee an English-speaking operator; you may have to enlist the aid of a Burmese friend or acquaintance to make these calls.

PLACES TO STAY
4 Aurora Inn
12 Sedona Hotel
18 Motherland Inn
19 Windermere Inn
21 Yoma Hotel 2
24 Summer Palace Hotel
33 Mya Yeik Nyo Royal Hotel
43 Winner Inn
44 Comfort Inn
46 Liberty Hotel
53 Savoy Hotel
73 Hotel Nikko Royal Lake Yangon
74 Green Hill Inn
75 Bagan Inn
81 Beauty Land Hotel
84 Kandawgyi Palace Hotel
89 Summit Parkview Hotel

PLACES TO EAT
7 Danubyu Daw Sawyi Restaurant
13 Royal Taj Restaurant
20 Green Elephant Restaurant
32 Malai Thai Restaurant
34 Mr Guitar Café
38 Vietnam House Restaurant
54 Top Choice Food Centre
55 Sabai Sabai Thai Restaurant
57 Aung Thuka Restaurant
58 Hla Myanma Htamin Zai (Shwe Ba)
66 Sei Taing Kya Teashop
67 Royal Garden Restaurant
68 Karaweik Restaurant
76 Le Planteur Restaurant & Bar
77 Lone Ma Lay Restaurant
87 Dolphin Seafood Restaurant
98 Jack of Clubs

OTHER
1 Institute of Marine Technology
2 Myanma Dockyards Enterprise
3 Hledan Train Station
5 Hledan Zei (Market)
6 Judson Baptist Church
8 Post Office
9 University of Foreign Languages
10 UNICEF
11 Tatmadaw Boat Club
14 Sanpya Zei (Market)
15 Bauktaw Train Station
16 Pacific Medical Centre & Dental Surgery
17 Golden Valley Art Centre
22 Inya Gallery of Art
23 Institute of Medicine 1
25 MBC Bookshop
26 Police Station
27 Hsimmalaik Bus Station
28 Orthopaedic Hospital
29 San Pya Fish Market
30 Myanma TV and Radio Department
31 Diethelm Travel
35 Mahasi Meditation Centre
36 Chaukhtatgyi Paya
37 Tamwe Train Station
39 Home for the Aged Poor
40 Yangon International School
41 Traditions Gallery
42 Italy Embassy
45 Singapore Embassy
47 Kyemyindaing Train Station
48 Police Station
49 Post Office
50 Htee Dan Jetty (Passenger Ferry to Dalah)

51 Kohtatgyi Paya
52 Yuzana Supermarket
56 Air Mandalay
59 Martyrs' Mausoleum
60 Post Office
61 Ngahtatgy Paya
62 Post Office
63 Manlwagon Train Station
64 Thaketa Bridge
69 UNDP & FAO
70 Kandawgyi Hospital
71 Eye, Ear, Nose & Throat Hospital
72 Germany; Nepal Embassy
78 Mogok Meditation Centre
79 Bogyoke Aung San Museum
80 Japan Embassy
82 Jivitdana Hospital
83 Vietnam Embassy
85 Yangon Zoological Gardens
86 National Aquarium
88 Maha Wizaya Paya
90 People's Square
91 Pyithu Hluttaw (National Assembly)
92 Children's Hospital
93 Chinese Embassy
94 Ahlone Lan Train Station
95 Panhlaing Train Station
96 People's Hospital
97 Thirimingala Zei (Market)
99 Myanma Fisheries Enterprise
100 Myanmar Timber Enterprise
101 Police Station
102 Post Office
103 Buses to Thanlyin
104 Myanma Electric Power Enterprise

Your embassy (see the list of foreign embassies in the Embassies & Consulates section in the Facts for the Visitor chapter) may also be able to assist with emergencies or serious problems. Many embassies and consulates maintain after-hours phone numbers, which they'll disclose to passport holders from the appropriate country. It's a good idea to register with your embassy upon arrival, so that the embassy staff will know where to reach you in case of an emergency at home.

Shwedagon Paya

The highlight of any visit to Yangon, and indeed Myanmar itself, Shwedagon Paya is located to the north of central Yangon, between People's Park and Kandawgyi. See the special section starting opposite page 176 for full details about Shwedagon, its design and historical significance.

In the compound's north-western corner is a huge bell that the butter-fingered British dropped into the Yangon River while trying to take it. Unable to recover it, they gave the bell back to the Burmese, who refloated it by tying a vast number of bamboo lengths to it.

The official admission fee for Shwedagon is US$5, which includes an elevator ride to the raised platform of the stupa. Of course, like most Burmese, you may walk up one of the long graceful entrances. If you come before 7 am, you may be able to get in for free. On the other hand, if you're taking photos rather than praying, a roving foreigner-ticket-checker may ask you to the pay US$5 on the spot.

Maha Wizaya (Vijaya) Paya

Almost opposite the southern gate to Shwedagon Paya, a pedestrian bridge links the Shwedagon complex with a well proportioned *zedi* (Buddhist stupa) built in 1980 to commemorate the unification of Theravada Buddhism in Myanmar. The king of Nepal contributed sacred relics for the zedi's relic chamber and Burmese strongman Ne Win had it topped with an 11-level *hti* (decorated top) – two more levels than the hti at Shwedagon.

Foreign media and some locals often refer to the monument as 'Ne Win's paya', due to Ne Win's involvement in the project (a common practice among top military figures). However, many Burmese citizens resent this phrase, pointing out that since the zedi was built by donations from the people, it should rightfully be called the 'people's paya'. They emphasize that any *kutho* (Buddhist merit) created by its construction should accrue not to Ne Win, but to the Burmese people, who have enriched the man and his regime since 1962. Politics and religion aside, the Maha Wizaya is one of the most attractive to have been built in Myanmar in decades. Admission is free.

Sule Paya

Situated in the centre of Yangon, across from the MTT office, the tall zedi at Sule Paya makes an excellent landmark; in fact it's used as a milestone from which all addresses to the north are measured. Legend says it's over 2000 years old but, as with

many other ancient Burmese shrines, it has been rebuilt and repaired many times over the centuries, so no one really knows when it was built. The central stupa is said to enshrine a hair of the Buddha; its Mon name, Kyaik Athok, translates as 'the stupa where a Sacred Hair Relic is enshrined'. Most likely, as with the zedi at Shwedagon, it was originally built by the Mon in the middle of this century.

The golden zedi is unusual in that its octagonal shape continues right up to the bell and inverted bowl. It stands 46m high and is surrounded by small shops and all the familiar nonreligious activities that seem to be a part of every Burmese zedi. In fact, unlike the more pristine Shwedagon Paya, Sule's busy location seems to enhance its soulful place in daily Yangon life, and it's a popular meeting place for many Burmese. Admission is free.

Botataung Paya

Bo means leader (usually in a military sense) and *tataung* means 1000 – the Botataung Paya was named after the 1000 military leaders who escorted relics of the Buddha, brought from India over 2000 years ago. This ancient monument was completely destroyed during WWII. It stood close to the Yangon wharves, and during an Allied air raid on 8 November 1943, a bomb scored a direct hit on the unfortunate paya.

After the war, the Botataung was rebuilt in a very similar style to its predecessor, but with one important and unusual difference: unlike most zedis, which are solid, the Botataung is hollow, and you can walk through it. There's a sort of mirrored maze inside the stupa, with glass showcases containing many of the ancient relics and artefacts, including small silver and gold Buddha images, which were sealed inside the earlier stupa. Above this interesting interior, the golden stupa spire rises to 40m.

To the western side of the stupa is a hall containing a large gilded bronze Buddha, cast during the reign of King Mindon Min. At the time of the British annexation, it was kept in King Thibaw Min's glass palace, but after King Thibaw was exiled to India, the British shipped the image to London. In 1951 the image was returned to Myanmar and placed in the Botataung Paya.

Also on the grounds is a *nat* (spirit) pavilion containing images of Thurathadi (the Hindu deity Saraswati, goddess of learning and music) and Thagyamin (Indra, king of the nats) flanking the thoroughly Burmese nat Bobogyi.

A short walk from Botataung Paya at Botataung jetty, you can watch ferryboats and oared water taxis cross the Yangon River.

Kaba Aye Paya

The 'world peace' zedi was built in 1952 for the 1954-56 Sixth Buddhist Synod. The 34m-high stupa also measures 34m around its base. It stands about 11km north of the city centre, a little beyond the Inya Lake Hotel. This attempt to construct a modern paya was not terribly successful – it does not have the same visual appeal of Myanmar's older, more graceful stupas. The interior of the monument, however, is hollow and inside are some nice Buddhist sculptures, including a *lei-myet-hna* (four-sided Buddha sculpture).

Maha Pasana Guha

The 'great cave' is a totally artificial one, built close to the Kaba Aye Paya. It was here that the Sixth Buddhist Synod was held to coincide with the 2500th anniversary of the Buddha's enlightenment. The participants at the Synod were attempting to define a definitive text for the *Tripitaka* (Buddhist canon). The cavern measures 139m by 113m.

Chaukhtatgyi Paya

The reclining Buddha at Chaukhtatgyi is almost as large as the enormous figure in Bago. It's housed in a large metal-roofed shed on Shwegondaing Lan, only a short distance north-east beyond the Shwedagon Paya. Surprisingly, this huge figure is little known and hardly publicised at all – if you can't get to Bago to see the Shwethalyaung, then don't miss this colossal image. Fortune-tellers on the surrounding platform offer astrological and palm readings.

Other Payas, Temples & Shrines

South of the Chaukhtatgyi Paya, there's a huge seated Buddha image at the **Ngahtatgyi Paya**. It's appropriately known as the five storey Buddha and is located in the Ashay Tawya monastery. In Kyemyindaing (also called Kyimyindine and Kemmedine), in the west of the city, there's another huge seated Buddha in the **Kohtatgyi Paya** on Bagaya Lan; it stands (or sits) 20m high. There are many monasteries in the vicinity. Kyemyindaing also has a busy night market.

Near the airport, the **Me La Mu Paya** has a series of images of the Buddha in his previous incarnations, and a reclining Buddha image. The paya is named after the mother of King Ukkalapa, the founder of the city of Dagon. In Insein, west of the airport, the **Ah Lain Nga Sint Paya** has a five storey tower and a particular connection with the nats and other spirit entities of Burmese Buddhism.

Near the International Buddhist University is **Swedawmyat Paya** (Buddha Tooth Relic Pagoda), on Swedaw Lan, between Kaba Aye Paya Lan and Thudhamar Lan, architecturally one of the best new payas in Yangon. However, it contains not just another tooth relic from the Buddha, but a replica of a relic brought from China in 1997 by pilgrims.

The **Yau Kyaw Paya** is a 30 minute drive from the city, past the Kyaikkasan Paya. It's an interesting complex of buildings with tableaux depicting Buddhist legends, pet monkeys, deer and peacocks and an interesting museum crammed full of Burmese antiques. The paya is beside the Pazundaung Chaung in a rural setting.

Kheng Hock Keong, on Strand Rd, is the largest Chinese temple in Yangon. Supported by a Hokkien association, the 100-year-old temple is most lively from around 6 to 9 am, when it's thronged with worshippers offering candles, flowers and incense to the Buddhist and Taoist altars within. Old men play Chinese checkers in the temple compound throughout the day. If you hang around long enough you may meet Mr Chan, an octogenarian *tai chi* and chi gong teacher, who visits every morning after exercising at Mahabandoola Gardens.

YANGON

INNER YANGON

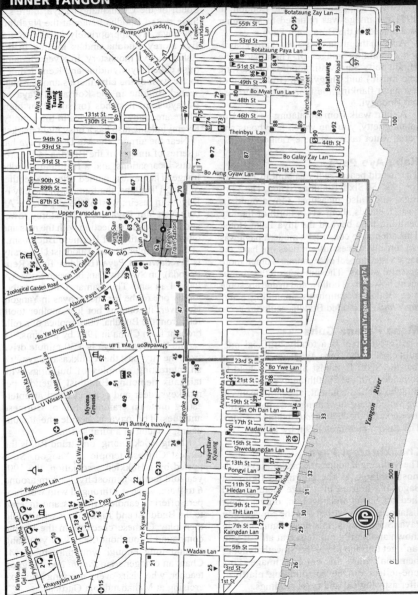

55th St
53rd St
Botataung Zay Lan
Botataung Paya Lan
51st St
49th St
Bo Myat Tun Lan
48th St
46th St
Theinbyu Lan
Bo Galay Zay Lan
41st St
Bo Aung Gyaw Lan
Upper Pazundaung Lan
Lower Pazundaung Lan
Yay Kyaw Lan
Min Nandar Lan
Merchant Street
Botataung
Strand Road
131st St
130th St
94th St
93rd St
91st St
90th St
89th St
87th St
Upper Pansodan Lan
Daw Thein Tin Lan
Myama Gonyi Lan
Mya Yar Gon Lan
Mingala Taung Nyunt
Aung San Stadium
Gyo Byu
Kun Chan Lan
Yangon Train Station
Bo Min Gaung Lan
Kan Taw Galay Lan
Zoological Garden Road
Alaung Paya Lan
Pantra
Nawaday Lan
Yawmingyi Lan
Shwedagon Paya Lan
Bo Yar Nyunt Lan
Bogyoke Aung San Lan
Bo Ywe Lan
23rd St
21st St
Anawahta Lan
19th St
Latha Lan
Mahabandoola Lan
Sin Oh Dan Lan
17th St
Madaw Lan
15th St
Shwedaungdan Lan
13th St
Pongyi Lan
11th St
Hledan Lan
9th St
Thit Lan
7th St
Kaingdan Lan
5th St
Thayettaw Kyaung
Myoma Kyaung Lan
Samon Lan
Za Ga War Lan
U Wisara Lan
Maw Kon Teik Lan
Zi Wa Ka Lan
Myoma Ground
Padonma Lan
Pyay Lan
Min Ye Kyaw Swar Lan
Wadan Lan
Thantaman Lan
Za Ga War Lan
Kin Won Min Gyi Lan
Pyidaungsu Yeikha Lan
Khayaybin Lan
3rd St
1st St
Strand Road
Yangon River

See Central Yangon Map pg174

500 m
250
0

INNER YANGON

PLACES TO STAY

11 Pansea Yangon;
    Pansea Restaurant
21 Panda Hotel
37 Lai Lai Hotel
59 Hotel Equatorial
60 Thamada Hotel
67 Sunflower Inn
76 Yoma Hotel
78 Motherland Inn 2
79 Queen's Park Hotel
80 Haven Inn
82 Cozy Guest House
83 Three Seasons Hotel
88 YMCA

PLACES TO EAT

1 Ashoka Indian Restaurant
14 Sei Taing Kya Teashop
17 Sei Taing Kya Teashop
25 Maw Shwe Li Restaurant
36 Singapore's Kitchen
38 Indian Street Stalls
39 Chinese Street Stalls
40 Shwe Pu Zun Bakery
56 Café D
58 Yuzana Garden Hotel
    Snack Bar
62 Sakhantha Hotel
    Restaurant
81 Sei Taing Kya Teashop
84 Home Sweet Home
86 Mya Sabe Food Centre
91 Palai Kywe Restaurant
94 50th Street Bar & Grill

OTHER

2 Sri Lanka Embassy
3 Malaysia Embassy
4 Pakistan Embassy
5 Indonesia Embassy

6 France Embassy
7 National Archives
8 Ein Daw Yar Paya
9 National Museum
10 Laos Embassy
12 American Center & USIS
13 Ministry of Foreign
   Affairs
15 Central Women's
   Hospital
16 Israel Embassy
18 No 2 Military Hospital
19 School
20 Mary Chapman Deaf &
   Dumb School
22 Than Zei (Market)
23 New Yangon General
   Hospital
24 Institute of Medicine No 1
26 Wadan St Jetty
27 Columbus Travels & Tours
28 Inland Water Transport
   Office (Tickets to Pathein)
29 Kaingdan St Jetty
30 Lan Thit St Jetty
31 Hledan St Jetty
32 Pongyi St Jetty
33 Sin Oh Dan St Jetty
   (Vehicle Ferry to Dalah)
34 Kheng Hock Keong
   (Chinese Temple)
35 Myanma Agricultural Bank
41 Pickups to Bago
42 Yangon General Hospital
43 Institute of Dental
   Medicine
44 School
45 School
46 Holy Trinity Cathedral
47 Bogyoke Aung San
   Market

48 FMI Centre
49 National Theatre
50 National Swimming Pool
51 Tatmadaw Military Hall
52 Defence Services
   Museum
53 Yuzana Pickle Tea
54 School
55 Amusement Park
57 Nature History Museum
61 Thamada Cinema
63 City Bus Ticket Offices
   (Long Distance Buses)
64 School
65 School
66 Infectious Diseases
   Hospital
68 Muslim Cemetery
69 Theinbyu Zei (Market)
70 Morning Market
71 St Mary's Cathedral
72 School
73 Salvation Army Church
74 Sikh Temple
75 Ivy Gallery
77 Shwe Pon Pwint Paya
85 Tour Mandalay Travel
87 Ministers' Offices
89 Myanma Five Star Line
90 FEC Money Exchange
92 Insight Myanmar Travel
93 Myanma Railways Office
95 East Yangon General
   Hospital
96 University of Yangon
   (Botataung Campus)
97 Botataung Paya
98 Saw Mill
99 Botataung Jetty
100 Myanma Five Star Line
    Cargo Jetty

The **Moseah Yeshua Synagogue**, at 85 26th St, near Mahabandoola Lan, was founded over a hundred years ago by Sephardic Jews. In the classic Sephardic style, it contains a *bimah* (platform holding the reading table) in the centre of the main sanctuary and a women's balcony upstairs. The wooden ceiling features the original blue-and-white Star of David motif. Myanmar had around 2500 Jews – a combination of B'nai Israel, Cochin (Indian) and Iraqi heritages –

until nationalisation in the 1960s and 1970s, when many began leaving the country. Today there are no more than 50 or so Burmese Jews left in Myanmar, but surviving trustees maintain the synagogue for the occasional special service given by visiting rabbis from India. Caretaker Moses Samuels is happy to talk with visitors and show them the nearby Jewish cemetery, with over 700 graves dating back to 1856.

Several Hindu temples can be found in

the centre of the city, including **Sri Sri Siva Krishna**, 141 Pansodan Lan, **Sri Kali**, on Anawrahta Lan, between 26th and 27th Sts, and **Sri Devi**, on the corner of Anawrahta Lan and 51st St. These are the centres for the city's annual Murugu Festival, famous for colourful street processions featuring acts of ritual self-mutilation.

National Museum

In 1996 the national museum (☎ 01-282563) was moved to a larger site on Pyay Lan, about 1km north of Bogyoke Aung San Lan, and just south of the Indonesian embassy. The collection remains unspectacular and cavernous; most explanations are in Burmese.

Nevertheless, you can find several interesting exhibits, especially the 8m-high Sihasana Lion Throne, used by King Thibaw Min, the last Burmese king, and returned to Burma in 1908 by Lord Mountbatten. The British took the throne from the Mandalay Supreme Court, outside the Mandalay Palace complex, and placed it in the Indian Museum in Calcutta, following the annexation of Burma to the British Raj. Thus, it survived the destruction of the palace during WWII, and after independence was returned to Yangon. The carving on the throne depicts the *Lokanat* (World Preserver legend) from Hindu-Burmese mythology, in which a battling lion and elephant cease fighting when a singing and dancing *deva* (Pali: spirit-being) arrives on the scene.

The main floor contains jewellery, old black & white photos of Mandalay Palace and Yangon, royal relics, Hintha opium weights and inscribed tablets.

Note that the museum has three other floors that are very easy to miss. Upstairs you'll find Burmese archaeological finds as well as traditional musical instruments. The fourth floor features about 40 mannequins dressed in the traditional dress of various ethnic groups in the country. Other exhibits include the Mandalay Regalia, a collection of gem-studded arms, swords, jewellery, bowls and other items. This too was taken by the British after the Third Anglo-Burmese War, and was returned to Myanmar in 1964 from the Victoria & Albert Museum in London. The museum also contains the royal couch that belonged to King Mindon's queen, excellent old maps and modern Burmese paintings by the talented U Ba Nyan and others.

The museum is open daily from 10 am to 4 pm. Admission is US$5 for foreigners (compared to 10 kyat for monks, nuns, children and students). Camera use is discouraged by a sign near the entrance announcing a US$100 fee for using still cameras, and US$200 for video.

Bogyoke Aung San Museum

Located on Bogyoke Aung San Museum St in Bahan Township, this quiet and secluded house-museum (☎ 01-550600) is the former home of General Aung San and his wife Daw Kin Kyi, and contains remnants of another era. The house itself dates from the 1920s and the rooms, stairway, railings and furniture are fairly intact. There are several old family photos, which of course include daughter Suu Kyi as a little girl. A glass-encased English-language library reveals the general's broad interests; titles range from *Cavalry Training, Armoured Cars, Children's Play Centre* and *The Mahatma Letters* to *Schemes of Constitutional Reform in Burma – if Separated, Left-wing Democracy in the English Civil War* and Adam Smith's *The Wealth of Nations*.

The museum is open Tuesday to Sunday from 10 am to 3.30 pm. Admission is US$2.

Martyrs' Mausoleum

Close to Shwedagon, on a hill offering a good view over the city, stands this memorial to Bogyoke Aung San and his fellow cabinet officers who were assassinated with him. It was also here that a bomb set off by North Koreans killed a number of South Korea's top government officials in late 1983.

Mahabandoola Garden

Just south-east of Sule Paya, this square urban park offers pleasant strolling in the city centre's heart, especially in the early morning, when the Chinese come to practice tai chi, and the air hasn't yet filled with traffic fumes. Occupying the centre of the park's northern half, an **Independence Monument** is surrounded by two concentric circles of *chinthe* (half-lion/half-griffin sculptures). A large fountain in the north-west corner sometimes functions; geese live in the somewhat stagnant pond at the park's southern end, where there is also a children's playground with a couple of mechanical rides.

For a year or two following the 1988-90 uprisings, the park was occupied by Burmese soldiers; many of the more violent events of the time took place nearby.

Entry to the park costs K5 for both locals and foreigners.

Yangon Zoological Gardens

These 70-acre gardens (☎ 01-285871, 284252) on Alaung Paya Lan (formerly King Edward Ave) are a nice place for a stroll and encompass a fairly decent zoo as well. Originally developed in 1906 by the British, the nicely landscaped grounds include a couple of artificial lakes, a playground and a miniature train circuit for kids, English and Latin labels (even on many of the trees) and maps of distribution. On weekends, it's a favourite family picnic spot.

Tigers and lions pace about in the stately **King Edward VII Carnivora House**, built in 1915. Other open-air exhibits display an elephant house and a fair selection of both common and scarce Asian animals (including sambar, leopard, serow, Eld's deer, Malayan sun bear, goral, Indian muntjac, great hornbill, python, cobra and the huge marsh crocodile).

A two storey school-like building on the grounds contains a **Natural History Museum** (☎ 01-272156), free with zoo admission, with labelled static exhibits on rocks and minerals, mammals, birds, fish, reptiles and amphibians – most of the specimens are stuffed or bottled. A separate room in the museum displays samples of tropical hardwood and bamboo native to the forests of Myanmar.

Zoo admission costs US$5 for foreigners,

but US$2 for residents. The zoo is open daily from 6 am to 4 pm. A restaurant on one of the lakes offers cafeteria-style service.

Across the street from the northern end of the zoo, on Kandawgyi, stands the **National Aquarium** (☎ 01-283304). When we visited the aquarium, few of the tanks were labelled. All in all, a disappointing contrast with the zoo, but very popular with Burmese families on weekends. Admission to the aquarium is K5.

Kandawgyi

Also known by its literal translation, Royal (Dawgyi) Lake (Kan), this natural body of water, located close to the city centre, is another good place for strolling or picnicking. The lake seems its most attractive at sunset, when the glittering Shwedagon is reflected in calm waters; you'll find the best sunset view from the lake's south-west edge.

Several of the city's embassies, clinics and smaller hotels are found in the lake's vicinity. Just east of the Kandawgyi Palace Hotel (formerly the Baiyoke Kandawgyi Hotel, and before that, the British Boating Club), on the southern side of the lake, floats a **Shin Upagot shrine**. Upagot is a bodhisattva or Buddhist saint who is said to protect human beings in moments of mortal danger.

The renovated **Karaweik**, a reinforced concrete reproduction of a royal barge, sits (it certainly doesn't float) at the eastern edge of the lake. Apart from being something of a local attraction in its own right, the Karaweik (Sanskrit: Garuda), the legendary bird-mount of the Hindu god Vishnu, is also a restaurant – see the later Places to Eat section. Traditional dance performances are held here in the evenings.

Inya Lake

Further north of the city, stretching between Pyay Lan to the west and Kaba Aye Paya Lan to the east, Inya Lake is roughly five times larger than Kandawgyi. Like the latter, it's a popular weekend relaxation spot for locals, although certain areas along the lake-shore – occupied by state guesthouses

YANGON

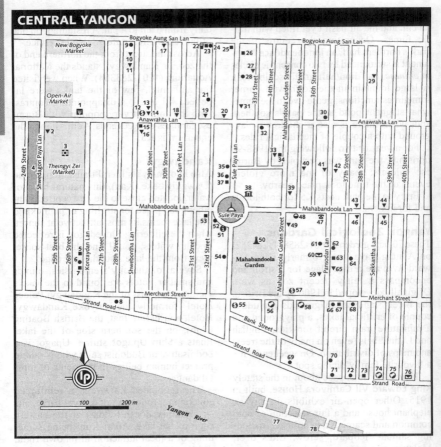

CENTRAL YANGON

and ministerial mansions – are off-limits to the general public.

Two important figures in contemporary Burmese history reside on opposite sides of the lake, like powerful nats locked in a battle of wills. At the southern end, at 54 University Ave, is Aung San Suu Kyi, under involuntary house arrest until 1995, with only her democratic ideals to keep her company; at the other end is willing recluse Ne Win, housed with his wizards and astrologers. Curiosity has a price: there are

roadblocks within a few blocks of Suu Kyi's home, and approaching foreigners will surely be questioned, if not searched. More than one foreigner has recently been escorted to the airport for immediate deportation, after having their film confiscated.

University of Yangon

Like most universities and colleges in Myanmar, the University of Yangon has been closed since student uprisings in 1990, following a national election that was nullified

CENTRAL YANGON

PLACES TO STAY
5 Daddy's Home
7 White House Hotel
15 Sunflower Hotel
23 Central Hotel
25 Traders Hotel
26 Dagon Hotel
34 Pyin Oo Lwin II Guest House
37 Mayshan Guest House
53 Mahabandoola Garden Guest House
63 Best Inn
67 Zar Chi Win Guest House
73 The Strand Hotel

PLACES TO EAT
2 Theingyizei Plaza Rooftop Restaurants
10 Pizza Corner
11 J' Donuts
13 Danubyu Daw Sawyi Restaurant
14 New Delhi Restaurant
16 Thei War Restaurant
17 Hollywood Bakery
18 Shwe Htoo Restaurant
19 Nila Biryane Shop
20 New Nila Biryane Shop
27 Lay Tan Kon Teashop
29 Theingi Shwe Yee Tea House
31 Golden City Chetty Restaurant

33 999 Khauk Swai
39 Tokyo Fried Chicken
40 Cherry Restaurant
41 J' Donuts
42 MacBurger
43 Golden Crown Café
44 Bharat Restaurant
45 Yahta Teashop
46 Nilar Win's Cold Drink Shop
49 Mandarin Restaurant
59 Nan Yu Restaurant
65 Donburiya Japanese Restaurant

OTHER
1 Sri Kali Temple
3 Moseah Yeshua Synagogue
4 Theingyizei Plaza
6 Diamond Luck Ticketing
8 Ministry of Trade
9 Super One Department Store
12 Myanma Oriental Bank
21 Santa Maria Travel & Tours
22 Diamond Ice Bar
24 Malaysia Air
28 Inwa Book Store
30 Ava Tailoring
32 Camera/Film Shops
35 Yangon Duty Free Store

36 Myanmar Airways International
38 City Hall
47 Central Telephone & Telegraph Office
48 Buses to Thanlyin
50 Independence Monument
51 Myanmar Travels & Tours (MTT)
52 THAI Airways International
54 Air France
55 Central Bank of Myanmar
56 US Embassy
57 Myanma Foreign Trade Bank
58 India Embassy
60 Post Office
61 Supreme Court
62 Biman Bangladesh
64 Bagan (Pagan) Bookshop
66 Silk Air
67 Sarpay Beikman Book Centre
69 Customs
70 Yangon Airways Office
71 Myanma Port Authority
72 Myanma Airways
74 Australia Embassy
75 UK Embassy
76 Main Post Office
77 Myanma Five Star Line Passenger Jetty
78 Pansodan St Jetty (Passenger Ferry to Dalah)

by the current military regime. Offices there are still open, and people have visited the library to do research. Ask around, however, before venturing onto the campus and past the security gate.

Other Attractions

Opposite Shwedagon Paya to the west, **People's Park** is a huge expanse of grass and trees bisected by **People's Square**, a wide, socialist-style pedestrian promenade. Near a set of fountains south of People's Square is a children's playground area, and in the south-eastern corner of the park a couple of armoured tanks are on display. The park entrance faces the eastern side, opposite Shwedagon's western gate; admission costs US$4 for foreigners, plus US$2 for still cameras, US$4 for video.

Myanma Gems Museum & Gems Market

Just north of Parami Lan, on Kaba Aye Paya Lan, the museum (☎ 01-531071) is meant to impress – starting with the world's largest sapphire that comes from Mogok and measures 6¾ inches in height, and nearly 12kg in weight; this somehow translates to 63,000 carats. Other exhibits display gemstones from the raw to the polished. In a poor country famous for valuable resources, the museum offers an unintended lesson in beauty, politics and money. Open daily except Monday and government holidays. Admission is US$3.

Na-Gar Glass Factory

The Factory (☎ 01-526053), at 152 Yawgi Kyaung Lan, Hlaing Township, is a very interesting place to visit, with lots of hand-blown glass on display, in a surprisingly pleasant indoor-outdoor setting. Unusual wine glasses, small vases and the like are also for sale at very reasonable prices. It's free, and worth a visit.

Swimming & Golf

Three public pools in Yangon charge small fees for daily use: Kandawgyi Swimming Pool (☎ 01-551327) on Lake Rd by Kandawgyi; Kokkin Swimming Club (☎ 01-550034), at 23 Sayasan Lan; and National Swimming Pool (☎ 01-278550), on U Wisara Lan.

Yangon has three golf courses open to the public. City Golf Club (Ngwe Thaw Tar Club; also know as YCDC; ☎ 01-641324), Thiri Mingala Lan, Mile 10, Insein Township, and near the university; Myanmar Golf Association (☎ 01-661702), Pyay Lan, Mile 9, Mayangon; and Yangon Golf Club (☎ 01-635563), Lower Mingaladon Lan, Insein Township. All three have ties to the Burmese military. Players tend to be a cross-section of Tatmadaw (armed forces) officers and Singaporean and Japanese business executives. Greens fees, on average, range from US$20 to US$30 for foreigners; a caddy is about US$3 for 18 holes. Clubs can be rented for about K2000.

Martial Arts & Weight Training

Burmese kickboxing instruction for beginners is offered on the ground floor of the YMCA (the Y) on Mahabandoola Lan near Theinbyu Lan (☎ 01-294128, 296435), on Tuesday, Thursday and Saturday from 7 to 9 am; experienced students meet Monday, Wednesday and Friday from 3 to 5 pm. The instructor is Ko Chit, a young but accomplished student of the renowned Nilar Win, who founded the Y program and is now teaching Burmese kickboxing in Paris. There's usually someone around who can translate the essentials, though you should mostly expect to learn by example. The techniques taught at the Y incorporate some moves borrowed from Thai and international boxing.

A bodybuilding/weight room, next to the kickboxing room at the Y, features a full range of cast-iron free weights. Visitors are welcome to participate in boxing or weight training upon becoming members; if you're staying at the Y, you're welcome to use the facilities for a small donation. Inquire at the main office on the upper floor for more information.

Saya Pan Thu, founder of the Institute of Myanmar Traditional Advanced Boxing, at 15 Aung Chan Tha Lane, Hledan Lan, Kamayut Township, teaches a more traditional Burmese kickboxing style on most Saturdays at 4 pm at the Yangon University campus. Pan Thu doesn't speak much English, nor apparently do any of his students. If you're interested in learning Burmese kickboxing, watch a few training sessions at both the Y and Pan Thu's to see which style seems more suitable.

The art of Tai Chi is practiced daily at dawn at Mahabandoola Park, near Sule Paya.

Running & Walking

The Yangon Hash Harriers meet at the Sailing Club (☎ 01-531298), at 132 Inya Lan, every Saturday at 4 pm, with a walk/run beginning at 4.30 pm. The walk/run through central Yangon takes about 30 to 45 minutes, at an easy pace that allows even children to keep up. Another informal group does a 3km and 6km run between the Traders Hotel and the Zoological Garden/Kandawgyi area every Sunday. Inquire at the Traders Hotel (☎ 01-242828), located on the corner of Sule Paya and Bogyoke Aung San Lans.

Train Ride

More in the category of sightseeing rather than transportation, the Yangon Circle Line is a three hour trip around Yangon and the neighbouring countryside. It's a great way to get a quick overview of the sprawling capital. The train is least crowded on weekends and the cost is K15. For more information contact the Yangon train station (☎ 01-274027).

continued on page 188

SHWEDAGON
PAYA

Shwedagon Paya

RICHARD I'ANSON

BERNARD NAPTHINE

BERNARD NAPTHINE

Title Page: A serene smile at Shwedagon Paya (Photograph by Bernard Napthine).

Top: Surrounded by some of the many Buddha statues at Shwedagon Paya.

Middle: A skyline dominated by spires.

Bottom: A menacing Shwedagon demon.

Facing Page: Shwedagon Paya reveals a wealth of detail.

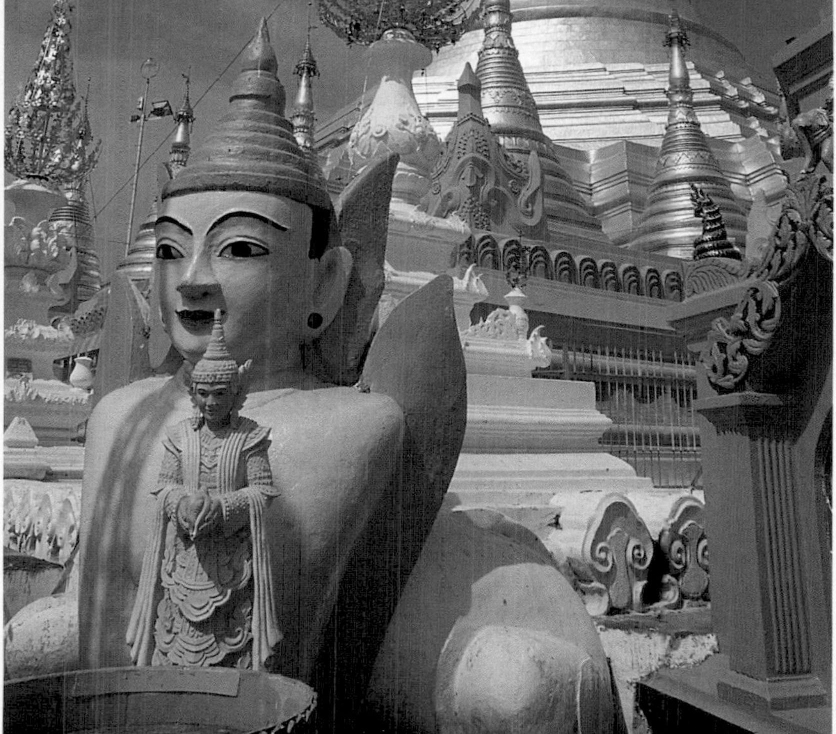

BERNARD NAPTHINE

Shwedagon Paya

THE GOLDEN DAGON

Kipling called it 'a golden mystery ... a beautiful winking wonder'. As the setting sun casts its last rays on the soft orange dome of the great Shwedagon Paya, you can feel the magic in the air. In the heat of the day, the *stupa* (Buddhist religious monument) glitters bright gold. It can be quiet and contemplative; colourful and raucous. The Golden Dagon is the essence of Myanmar, and a place that never fails to enchant.

For Burmese Buddhists, Shwedagon is the most sacred of all Buddhist sites in the country, one which all Burmese hope to visit at least once.

The great golden dome rises 98m above its base. According to legends, this stupa – of the solid *zedi* (bell-shaped monument) type – is 2500 years old, but archaeologists are nearly unanimous in suggesting the original stupa was built by the Mon, sometime between the 6th and 10th centuries. In common with many other ancient zedis in earthquake-prone Myanmar, it has been rebuilt many times and its current form dates back only to 1769.

History

The legend of Shwedagon Paya tells of two merchant brothers meeting the Buddha, who gave them eight of his hairs to take back to be enshrined in Myanmar. With the help of a number of *nats* (spirits), the brothers and the king of this region of Myanmar discovered the hill where relics of the previous Buddhas had been enshrined. When the chamber that would house the hairs was built and the hairs were taken from their golden casket, some quite amazing events took place:

> ... there was a tumult among men and spirits ... rays emitted by the Hairs penetrated up to the heavens above and down to hell ... the blind beheld objects ... the deaf heard sounds ... the dumb spoke distinctly ... the earth quaked ... the winds of the ocean blew ... Mount Meru shook ... lightning flashed ... gems rained down until they were knee deep ... all trees of the Himalayas, though not in season, bore blossoms and fruit.

Fortunately, hairs of the Buddha are not unveiled every day.

Once the relics were safely enshrined, a golden slab was laid on their chamber and a golden stupa built on it. Over this, a silver stupa was built, then a tin stupa, a copper stupa, a lead stupa, a marble stupa and finally, an iron-brick stupa. Or so the legend goes. Later, the legend continues, the stupa at Dagon fell into disuse and it is said the great Indian Buddhist-emperor Asoka came to Myanmar, finding the site only with great difficulty, and subsequently had the encroaching jungle cleared and the stupa repaired.

During the Bagan period, the story of the stupa emerges from the mists of legend and becomes hard fact. Near the top of the eastern

Facing page: The great golden dome of Shwedagon Paya at dusk.

stairway you can see an inscription recording the history of the stupa to 1485. King Anawrahta visited Dagon from his capital at Bagan (Pagan) in the 11th century, while King Binnya U, during his reign at Bago (Pegu) (1353-85), had the stupa rebuilt to a height of 18m. Succeeding kings alternately neglected, then improved, the stupa. During the 15th century, it was rebuilt several times, eventually reaching 90m a little under its present height.

During this period, the tradition of gilding the stupa also began – Queen Shinsawbu, who was responsible for many improvements to the stupa, provided her own weight (40kg) in gold, which was beaten into gold-leaf and used to gild the structure. Her son-in-law, Dhammazedi, went several better, by offering four times his own weight and that of his wife's in gold. He also provided the 1485 historical inscription on the eastern stairway.

The Great or Golden Pagoda, from the S.E. Rangoon.

Below: An etching of Shwedagon Paya from *Rough Pencillings of a Rough Trip to Rangoon in 1846* by Colesworthy Grant.

In 1586 the English visitor Ralph Fitch made probably the best early European description of the great stupa:

... it is called Dogonne, and is of a wonderful bignesse, and all gilded from the foot to the toppe ... it is the fairest place, as I suppose, that is in the world it standeth very high, and there are foure ways to it, which all along are set with trees of fruits, such wise that a man may goe in the shade above two miles in length ...

The zedi suffered from a series of earthquakes that caused great damage during this time. In 1612 De Brito raided the stupa from his base in Thanlyin and carried away Dhammazedi's great bell, with the intention of melting it down for cannons. As the British were to do later, with another bell, he dropped it into the river. During the 17th century, the monument suffered earthquake damage on eight occasions. Worse was to follow in 1768, when a quake brought down the whole top of the zedi. King Hsinbyushin had it rebuilt to virtually its present height, and its current configuration dates from that renovation.

SHWEDAGON PAYA

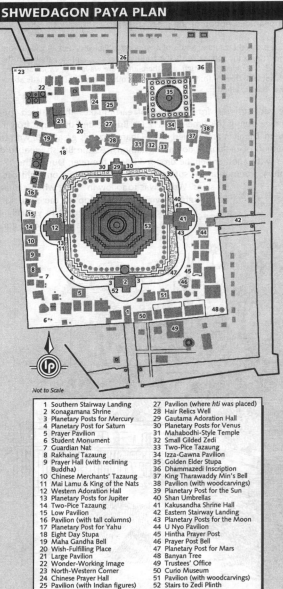

SHWEDAGON PAYA PLAN

Not to Scale

1 Southern Stairway Landing
2 Konagamana Shrine
3 Planetary Posts for Mercury
4 Planetary Post for Saturn
5 Prayer Pavilion
6 Student Monument
7 Guardian Nat
8 Rakhaing Tazaung
9 Prayer Hall (with reclining Buddha)
10 Chinese Merchants' Tazaung
11 Mai Lamu & King of the Nats
12 Western Adoration Hall
13 Planetary Posts for Jupiter
14 Two-Pice Tazaung
15 Low Pavilion
16 Pavilion (with tall columns)
17 Planetary Post for Yahu
18 Eight Day Stupa
19 Maha Gandha Bell
20 Wish-Fulfilling Place
21 Large Pavilion
22 Wonder-Working Image
23 North-Western Corner
24 Chinese Prayer Hall
25 Pavilion (with Indian figures)
26 Northern Stairway Landing

27 Pavilion (where *hti* was placed)
28 Hair Relics Well
29 Gautama Adoration Hall
30 Planetary Posts for Venus
31 Mahabodhi-Style Temple
32 Small Gilded Zedi
33 Two-Pice Tazaung
34 Izza-Gawna Pavilion
35 Golden Elder Stupa
36 Dhammazedi Inscription
37 King Tharawaddy Min's Bell
38 Pavilion (with woodcarvings)
39 Planetary Post for the Sun
40 Shan Umbrellas
41 Kakusandha Shrine Hall
42 Eastern Stairway Landing
43 Planetary Posts for the Moon
44 U Nyo Pavilion
45 Hintha Prayer Post
46 Prayer Post Bell
47 Planetary Post for Mars
48 Banyan Tree
49 Trustees' Office
50 Curio Museum
51 Pavilion (with woodcarvings)
52 Stairs to Zedi Plinth
53 Tawa-gu Image

British troops occupied the compound for two years after the First Anglo-Burmese War in 1824. In 1852 during the Second Anglo-Burmese War, the British again took the paya, the soldiers pillaged it once more and it remained under military control for 77 years, until 1929. In 1871 a new *hti* (the decorative top of a paya), provided by King Mindon Min from Mandalay, caused considerable head-scratching for the British, who were not at all keen for such an association to be made with the still independent part of Myanmar.

During this century, Shwedagon Paya was the scene for much political activity during the Burmese independence movement and also suffered from a serious fire in 1931. It started at the bottom of the western stairway, which had been reopened to the public for less than two years, after the British military occupation had closed that entrance. The fire rushed up the stairway and right round the northern side of the paya, before being halted halfway down the eastern stairway. The huge earthquake of 1930, which totally destroyed the Shwemawdaw in Bago, only caused minor damage to Shwedagon. After another minor earthquake in 1970, the zedi was clad in bamboo scaffolding beyond King Mindon's 100-year-old hti, and was refurbished.

Design
There are four covered walkways up Singuttara Hill to the platform on which Shwedagon stands. The southern entrance, from Shwedagon Paya Lan, is the one which can most properly be called the main entrance. Here, and at the northern entrance, there are lifts available, should you not feel fit enough for the stroll up the stairs. The western entrance features a series of escalators in place of stairs, and is the only entrance without vendors. The eastern stairway has the most traditional ambience, passing adjacent *kyaungs* (monasteries) and vendors selling monastic requisites. Foreigners are required to pay US$5 to enter the complex. A camera permit for Shwedagon costs K5, but this fee is not always enforced.

Two 9m-high *chinthes* (the legendary half-lion, half-griffin leogryphs) guard the southern entrance. You must remove your shoes and socks as soon as you mount the first step. Like the other entrances, the southern steps are lined with a whole series of shops, where devotees buy flowers – both real and beautifully made paper ones – for offerings. Ceremonial paper umbrellas, Buddha images, golden thrones, ivory combs, books, antiques and incense sticks are also on sale. However hot it may be outside, you'll find the walkway cool, shady and calm. It's this quiet, subdued atmosphere on the entrance steps that makes the impact so great as you arrive at the platform.

You emerge from semigloom into a visual cacophony of technicoloured glitter – for Shwedagon is not just one huge glowing zedi. Around the mighty stupa cluster an incredible assortment of smaller zedis, statues, temples, shrines, images and *tazaungs* (small pavilions). Somehow, the bright gold of the main stupa makes everything else seem brighter and larger than life.

SHWEDAGON PAYA

Stupas, indeed all Buddhist structures, should be walked around clockwise, so turn left at the top of the steps, and like the crowds of Burmese, start strolling. During the heat of the day, you'll probably have to confine yourself to the mat pathway laid around the platform – unless your bare feet can take the heat of the uncovered marble paving.

The hill on which the stupa stands is 58m above sea level and the platform covers over 5 hectares. Prior to the British takeover of Lower Myanmar, there had been Burmese defensive earthworks around the paya, but these were considerably extended by the British, and the emplacements for their cannons can still be seen outside the outer wall.

The main stupa, which is completely solid, rises from its platform in a fairly standard pattern. First there is the plinth that stands 6.4m above

Left: Painting of the entrance to Shwedagon Paya, from the 1905 *Burma Painted and Described* by R Talbot Kelly.

the clutter of the main platform and immediately sets Shwedagon above the lesser structures. Smaller stupas sit on this raised platform level – four large ones mark the four cardinal directions, four medium-sized ones mark the four corners of the basically square platform and 60 small ones run around the perimeter.

From this base, the zedi rises first in three terraces, then in the 'octagonal' terraces and then in five circular bands – together these elements add another 30m to the stupa's height. This is a normal solution to a standard architectural problem associated with stupas – how to change from the square base to the circular upper elements? Here, as in many other Burmese zedis, that transition is achieved with the help of the octagonal sections, which make a transition from the horizontal design of these lower elements to the smooth vertical flow of the bell.

Earlier stupas were commonly hemispherical; a good example in Myanmar is the Kaunghmudaw at Sagaing near Mandalay. The more graceful bell design, as seen here, is a comparatively recent development. The shoulder of the bell is decorated with 16 'flowers'. The bell is topped by the 'inverted bowl', another traditional element of stupa architecture, and above this stand the mouldings and then the 'lotus petals'. These consist of a band of down-turned lotus petals, followed by a band of up-turned petals.

The banana bud is the final element of the zedi before the hti tops it. Like the lotus petals below, the banana bud is actually covered with no less than 13,153 plates of gold, measuring 30 sq cm each – unlike the lower elements, which are merely covered with gold-leaf. The seven-tiered hti is made of iron and again plated with gold. Even without the various hanging bells, it weighs well over a tonne. The hti tiers descend in size from bottom to top, and from the uppermost tier projects the shaft which is hung with gold bells, silver bells and various items of jewellery. The topmost vane, with its flag, turns with the wind. It is gold and silver plated and studded with 1100 diamonds totalling 278 carats – not to mention 1383 other stones. Finally, at the very top of the vane rests the diamond orb – a hollow golden sphere studded with no less than 4351 diamonds, weighing 1800 carats in total. The very top of the orb is tipped with a single 76 carat diamond.

This central zedi is regilded every year. By 1995 it had reportedly accumulated 53 metric tonnes of gold leaf.

Around the Stupa

The mighty zedi is only one of many structures on the hilltop platform. Reaching the platform from the southern stairway (1), you encounter the first shrine (2), which is to Konagamana, the second Buddha. Almost beside the shrine stand the planetary posts for Mercury (3). If you were born on a Wednesday morning (as was the Buddha), then this is your post, and the tusked elephant is your animal sign. Continuing around the plinth, you pass a double-bodied lion with a man's face, a laughing necromancer with his hands on his head, and an earth goddess. At the south-west corner of the plinth, you reach the planetary post for Saturn (4). Come here if you were born on a Saturday; your animal sign is the *naga* (dragon serpent). The pavilion (5) directly opposite has 28 images to represent the 28 *avatars* (previous incarnations) of the Buddha.

Back towards the corner of the platform is a monument (6) with inscriptions in four languages, recounting a 1920 student revolt against British rule. Continuing around the platform, you come to a glass case with two figures of nats (7) – one is of the guardian nat of Shwedagon Paya. Close to these figures is a prayer hall (8), bare inside, but with fine woodcarving on the terraced roof. It is known as the Rakhaing Tazaung, since it was donated by brokers from the Rakhaing (Arakan) coast bordering Bangladesh. An 8m-long reclining Buddha can be seen in the next prayer hall (9). Next to this is the Chinese Merchants' Tazaung (10), with a variety of Buddha figures in different poses.

On the plinth opposite this prayer hall are figures of Mai Lamu and the king of the nats (11), the parents of King Ukkalapa who, according to the legend, originally enshrined the Buddha hairs here. The figures stand on top of each other. The western adoration hall (12) was built in 1841, but was destroyed in the fire that swept the zedi platform in 1931. The planetary posts for the Thursday-born (13) stand to the right and left of this pavilion – your planet is Jupiter; your animal sign is the rat. A figure of King Ukkalapa can be seen further to the left, on the zedi plinth.

Directly opposite the west adoration hall is the Two Pice Tazaung (14) at the head of the western stairway. It was built with the proceeds of a daily collection of two *pice* (an extinct unit of Burmese currency) from the stalls in Yangon market. The western stairway, the steepest of the four entrances, was also built from this collection after the 1931 fire. The low pavilion (15) next to the entrance was built by manufacturers of monastery requirements – in contrast to the rather Chinese-looking roof. Next round is a pavilion (16), with tall columns and the *pyatthat* (wooden, multiroofed pavilion) rising from the upper roof. Almost opposite this tazaung, at the north-western corner of the main zedi, is the planetary post (17) for those born on Wednesday afternoon, whose animal symbol is the tuskless elephant, and whose planet is Yahu (Rahu, a mythical planet in Hindu astrology that allegedly causes eclipses).

A small stupa with a golden spire (18) has eight niches around its base, each with a Buddha image. Between the niches are figures of animals and birds – they represent the eight directions of the compass and the associated sign, planet and day of the week. To get over the small complication of having an Eight Day Stupa and a seven day week, Wednesday is divided into Wednesday morning and Wednesday afternoon. The eight days, which can also be found with their corresponding planetary posts around the main stupa are (from the southern entrance):

direction	day	planet	sign
south	Wed am	Mercury	tusked elephant
south-west	Sat	Saturn	naga (dragon serpent)
west	Thu	Jupiter	rat
north-west	Wed pm	Yahu	tuskless elephant
north	Fri	Venus	guinea pig or mole
north-east	Sun	Sun	garuda
east	Mon	Moon	tiger
south-east	Tue	Mars	lion

Close to this small stupa stands the bell pavilion (19) housing the 23 tonne Maha Ganda Bell. Cast between 1775 and 1779, it was carted off by the British after the First Anglo-Burmese War in 1825. They dropped it into the Yangon River while trying to get it to the port for shipping to England; after repeatedly trying to raise it from the river bottom, they gave up and told the Burmese they could have the bell back if they could get it out of the river. The Burmese placed logs and bamboo beneath the bell until it eventually floated to the surface. Venturing back into the open area of the platform, you come to the star-shaped 'wish-fulfilling place' (20), where there will often be devotees, kneeling down and looking towards the great stupa, praying that their wishes come true.

Right: Painting of a view towards Shwedagon Paya, from the 1905 *Burma Painted and Described* by R Talbot Kelly.

The large pavilion (21) across from the bell pavilion houses a 9m-high Buddha image and is often used for public meetings. Behind this pavilion stands a small shrine (22) with a highly revered 'wonder-working' Buddha image covered in gold leaf. From the north-western corner of the platform (23), you can look out over some of the British fortifications and the country to the north of the hill. There are also two banyan trees growing here, one of them grown from a cutting from the actual tree at Bodhgaya in India, under which the Buddha sat and was enlightened.

Among the cluster of buildings on this side of the platform is the Chinese prayer hall (24), with good woodcarvings and Chinese dragon figures on the sides of the zedi in front of it. The adjacent pavilion (25) has life-size figures of Indians guarding the side and front entrance doors. No one quite understands their relevance or that of the very British lions that guard the next pavilion.

In 1824 a force of Burmese 'Invulnerables' fought their way up the northern stairs to the entrance (26) of the platform before being re-pulsed by the better-armed British forces occupying the paya. The crocodile-like stair bannister dates from 1460. The Martyrs' Mau-soleum of Bogyoke Aung San and his compatriots stands on the western side of the hill reached from this stairway; it doesn't open till 9 am and admission costs US$3.

Walking back towards the stupa, you pass the pavilion (27) built on the site where the great zedi's hti, provided by King Mindon Min, was placed before being raised to the zedi summit. The Hair Relics Well was located at the position of the Sandawdwin Tazaung (28) and is said to reach right down to the level of the Ayeyarwady (Irrawaddy) River and to be fed from it; the Buddha hairs were washed in this well before being enshrined in the zedi. In the northern adoration hall (29), the main image is of Gautama, the historical Buddha. On either side of the hall stand planetary posts for Friday (30), domain of the planet Venus, and the guinea pig or mole.

Modelled after the Mahabodhi temple in Bodhgaya, India, the temple (31) a few steps away is distinctively different from the general style of buildings on the platform. A small gilded zedi (32) stands next to this temple, and next again is another 'two-pice' tazaung (33) en-shrining a 200-year-old Buddha image. An opening behind this image is, according to legend, the entrance to a passage that leads to the chamber housing the Buddha hair relics. Although seen from the 'two-pice' tazaung, the image is actually in the adjacent stupa.

Izza-Gawna (the name means goat-bullock) was a legendary monk whose powers enabled him to replace his lost eyes with one from a goat and one from a bullock. In his pavilion (34) the figure off to the left of the main Buddha image has eyes of unequal size as a reminder of this unique feat. The golden Elder Stupa (35) is built on the spot where the hair relics were first placed before being enshrined in the great zedi. A straight line drawn from the centre of this stupa to the centre of Shwedagon would pass through the small stupa reputed to be the entrance to the passage that leads to the relic chamber. Women are not allowed to ascend to the platform around the Elder Stupa, which is also known as the Naungdawgyi Stupa.

Back in the corner of the platform is the Dhammazedi inscription (36), which dates from 1485 and was originally installed on the eastern stairway. It tells in three languages – Pali, Mon and Burmese – the story of Shwedagon.

Cast in 1841, King Tharawaddy Min's bell is housed in an elegant pavilion (37). The Maha Titthadaganda (three-toned bell) weighs 42 tonnes. Note the ceiling made of lacquer inlaid with glass. If you look closely, you can also discern red-billed green parrots nearly hidden in the scrolling among the *devas* (Pali-Sanskrit for spirit-beings). The adjacent small pavilion (38) has some good panels of woodcarvings. Back on the main platform the planetary post (39) for those born on Sunday (the sun) stands at the north-eastern corner of the stupa platform. The bird-like creature beneath the post is the garuda of Hindu-Buddhist mythology, called *galoun* by the Burmese. Further round you will see golden Shan umbrellas (40) among the plinth shrines; there is also one over the Friday planetary post by the north pavilion.

Facing the eastern stairway, the eastern shrine hall (41) is said to be the most beautiful on the platform. It was renovated in 1869, but destroyed by the 1931 fire, and subsequently rebuilt. The main image is that of Kakusandha, the first Buddha. The eastern stairway (42) is the longest and is lined with shops selling everyday articles as well as religious goods and antiques. On either side, the Monday-born worship at the planetary posts (43) ruled over by the moon and the tiger.

The graceful U Nyo pavilion (44), beside the eastern entrance, has a series of interesting woodcarved panels illustrating events in the life of Gautama Buddha. The prayer post (45) close to the south-eastern corner of the zedi is topped by a mythological *hintha* bird. An interesting bell (46) hangs near this prayer post. Opposite these on the zedi plinth is the planetary post for Tuesday (47), presided over by the lion and the planet Mars.

In the corner of the platform stands another sacred banyan tree (48), also said to be grown from a branch of the original tree under which Gautama Buddha gained enlightenment in India. There is a good view from this corner of the platform over Yangon and across the Yangon River towards Thanlyin. On a clear day, you can see the Kyaikkhauk Paya, just beyond Thanlyin. The paya trustees have their office (49) on this side of the platform, and there's also a small curio museum (50). In front of the museum is a pavilion (51) with very fine woodcarvings. There is also a revolving hti and a telescope, possibly for looking at the real hti on top of the zedi.

Beside the southern shrine (2), the first stop on this circular tour, stairs (52) lead up onto the zedi plinth. With permission from the paya trustees, men only are allowed to climb up to the plinth terrace. Men come up here to meditate; the terrace is about 6m wide – a circular walkway between the great zedi and its 68 surrounding zedis. There's a K5 fee for entering the terrace. Behind the eastern shrine is a Buddha image (53) known as the Tawa-gu, which is reputed to work miracles.

Visiting Shwedagon is far more than just wandering around and looking at the shrines, pavilions, images, bells and stupas. It's a place you feel as much as see. There's a quite amazing atmosphere here – sometimes serene, sometimes exciting, but always enjoyable. Sunrise and sunset are the best times for a visit.

continued from page 176

Places to Stay

Since the privatization of the hotel industry in 1993, there has been an explosion of hotel and guesthouse development in Yangon. The number of places licensed to accept foreigners leapt from eight in 1992 – when you still had to book a package deal to receive a tourist visa – to 104 by the beginning of 1995. By the beginning of 1999, the number had climbed to 160. At that time, occupancy at many of the top-end hotels (many of them joint ventures) was running at about 20% on average. The hotel boom has slowed considerably since the time of the failed Visit Myanmar Year 1996, when central planning and overbuilding reigned. Yangon's budget and mid-range hotels and guesthouses, however, have continued to enjoy considerable success.

Places to Stay – Budget

When Yangon's smaller hotels and guesthouses began receiving licences allowing them to accept foreigners as guests in 1993, many proprietors reckoned they'd strike it rich by charging US$15 to US$20 per person per day for very basic rooms with shared bath. By 1996 most budget places had dropped their rates quite a bit – several to as low as US$5 to US$10 per person. There still seems to be a general surplus of rooms, and rates may continue to decline. Price quotes at the following places almost always include tax and service, as well as a rudimentary eggs-and-toast breakfast. Payment is accepted in US dollars or FECs only. Note that some categories overlap; the same guesthouse or hotel may have budget rooms for US$5 per person, but air-con doubles for US$25. Most of the budget spots are in the city centre area.

The conveniently located *Zar Chi Win Guest House* (☎ *01-275407, 59 37th St)* sits on the western side of 37th St, just south of Merchant St and near the book vendors and Bagan (also called Pagan) Bookshop, and comes with a funky red-and-yellow colour scheme. The usual windowless cubicles cost US$5/10 a single/double with shared bath and toilet, or US$8/15 with private bath. Rates include breakfast and a left-luggage service is available. Like many places in this price range, you may be able to bargain for a dollar's reduction, if you can do without the bleak breakfast. The *Tea Camp*, next door, has decent Burmese breakfasts for less than K100.

A few blocks west, *Pyin Oo Lwin II Guest House* (☎ *01-243284, 3rd floor, 184 Mahabandoola Garden St)*, just south of Anawrahta Lan, is much better than it looks from the outside. Windowless but clean rooms with hot water cost US$10/18. It's in a good location and has helpful staff.

Back in the city centre, the friendly and popular *White House Hotel* (☎ *01-240779, 69/71 Konzaydan Lan)*, west of Sule Paya, between Merchant St and Mahabandoola Lan, offers cubicle rooms with fan and shared bath facilities for US$8 per person. Air-con rooms are shared bath too, and cost US$10 per person. The guesthouse occupies two floors over a shophouse, on a crowded street – a design pattern seen repeatedly in this price range. A few doors up from the White House is *Daddy's Home* (☎ *01-252169, 107 Konzaydan Lan)*, with similar prices, facilities and service.

Half a block north of Sule Paya is the *Mayshan Guest House* (☎ *01-283599, 252986, 115/117 Sule Paya Lan)*, which is clean and friendly, well managed and centrally located, with air-con rooms with bath, TV and phone, at US$10/15, and US$15/25 in the high season. It has a very comfortable lobby, and breakfast is included.

Mahabandoola Garden Guest House (☎ *01-248104, 93 32nd St)*, on the southeast corner of Mahabandoola Lan, has 18 rooms – all small, windowless and clean. This is one of the cheapest deals in Yangon, at US$3 per person, with common bath and no breakfast.

Near the train station, on the corner of U Pho Kya and Bo Min Yaung (U Ohn Khine) Lans, are the best of the budget places. From the street it doesn't look like much, but upstairs, the *Sunflower Inn* (☎ *01-252196, 253954, 59 U Pho Kya Lan)* offers clean, if small, air-con rooms with communal bath for US\$10/15, including breakfast. For US\$15/25 you can have one of four superior rooms with private hot-water bath, fridge and TV. There are also two single economy rooms with fan for US\$8 per person. The Indian proprietors are friendly and helpful.

Towards Bogyoke Aung San Lan is another old standby, the *Dagon Hotel* (☎ 01-289354, 256-260 Sule Paya Lan). The tall, narrow hotel has a bit of character; there are city views from the balcony and a couple of good Chinese restaurants downstairs and nearby. However, at the time of writing, the Dagon was closed for repairs, but scheduled to reopen, with rooms for US\$12/18, with air-con, fridge, and shared bath and toilet.

Owned by the same family that runs the Sunflower Inn, the slightly more expensive *Sunflower Hotel* (☎ 01-240014, 259/263 Anawrahta Lan), on the corner of Shwebontha and Anawrahta Lans in the Indian quarter, offers a variety of clean and airy rooms from a single economy with fan for US\$6 to a single/double with air-con, bath, TV and fridge for US\$20/32. Rooms over the street are noisy.

For many years budget travellers have stayed at Yangon's spartan but reliable *YMCA* (☎ 01-294128, 296435, 263 Mahabandoola Lan), near Theinbyu Lan. The 18 rooms are large and in reasonable, if somewhat tatty, condition; and all rooms have windows, a plus in the budget category. The Y offers clean economy rooms (shared bath) with a fan for US\$8/15, and US\$10/16 with air-con. Two air-con rooms with private bath and fridge cost US\$20/30. The Y offers free transport to/from the airport and allows guests to store luggage while travelling upcountry. Both men and women are welcome at this Y, although double rooms are ostensibly for married couples.

Out past the YMCA in Pazundaung township, the family-run *Cozy Guest House* (☎ 01-291623, fax 292239, 126 52nd St) has five small air-con rooms (three with windows), all with a shared hot-water bath down the hall. Rates are US\$10 per person, including breakfast.

Motherland Inn 2 (☎/fax 01-291343, 433 Lower Pazundaung Lan) is one of the nicest guesthouses in Yangon. Though a bit far from the central area, it is exceptionally clean and friendly, and good value, with standard air-con rooms with private bath costing US\$8 per person. An economy room with fan and bath is just US\$6. It also has a huge air-con dorm for US\$3 per person, which is decent. All rates include breakfast.

Motherland Inn (☎ 01-513182, 99(0) Than Lwin Lan) is further out of the city centre, in a quiet neighbourhood. A decent standard air-con room at this location is US\$7; it's US\$5 per person for fan and shared toilet. All rates include breakfast.

Places to Stay – Mid-Range

Yangon's accommodation in this category has expanded rapidly. Many of the newer, mid-range places consist of large converted residences in the Bahan, Dagon and Mingala Taung Nyunt townships, just north of the city centre in the vicinity of Kandawgyi and Shwedagon Paya. Unless otherwise noted, rates do not include the 20% tax and service charges. This tax often appears only at more expensive establishments, many of them joint ventures, or government-backed. Some hotels in this price range will accept credit card payment. Visa is the most commonly accepted card – when cards are accepted. MasterCard withdrew in August 1998. Cash is generally the way to go in Myanmar, as there are very few ATMs in the country, and they're for Burmese only.

City Centre *Best Inn* (☎ 01-272835, fax 240084, 96/98 Pansodan Lan) sits on a busy street, but is surprisingly cool and quiet inside. Clean, comfortable rooms with air-con, carpet, TV and private hot-water baths cost US\$24/36/48 a single/double/triple; rates include breakfast, tax and service.

Not far from the Y, just north of Mahabandoola Lan, the two storey *Three Seasons Hotel* (☎ 01-293304, fax 297946, 83/ 85 52nd St) offers seven large rooms for US\$15/20 a single/double, plus two large four-bed rooms priced at US\$30 to US\$40 per room. All rooms come with hot-water showers, fridge, air-con, high ceilings and wooden floors. This is one of the quieter central neighbourhoods; other pluses include a tastefully decorated lobby, and the very friendly and resourceful staff. Rates include breakfast, served in an airy room overlooking the street; breakfasts of *mohinga* (rice noodles and fish soup) or *htamin bei* (sticky rice) can be arranged with a day's notice.

Lai Lai Hotel (☎ 01-225913, 783 Mahabandoola Lan), on the edge of Chinatown, is a modern, eight storey, thoroughly Chinese-style hotel, with good city views from the upper floors. All rooms come with hot showers, satellite TV, phones, minibars and air-con for US$15/30/45. A Chinese restaurant is downstairs.

The six storey *Thamada Hotel (☎ 01-662866, 37 Alaung Paya Lan)*, just across the railway line from the town centre, at the northern end of Sule Paya Lan, has very helpful staff and nicely furnished rooms. The Thamada is a very popular venue for local wedding receptions. Done in the old socialist style, the hotel's 58 large rooms each cost US$40 single, US$45 to US$50 double, or US$78 triple. All rooms feature high ceilings, air-con, TV and hot water; some have fridges. Roadside rooms offer bathtubs as well as showers but these get the most street noise. Rooms at the rear don't have tubs, but they're quieter.

A popular city centre choice is the new, 11 storey *Queen's Park Hotel (☎ 01-296447, fax 293596, 132 Anawrahta Lan)*, on the corner of Bo Myat Tun Lan. The hotel has a helpful staff, a generator to cover frequent power outages, and the room rates are a steal. A single room with TV, fridge, telephone, private bath and air-con is US$15. The standard double is US$18, while superior rooms are US$25/30. A few larger suites are available for US$35/40.

Haven Inn (☎ 01-295500, fax 297946, 216 Bo Myat Tun Lan) is a small family-run retreat, close to the central area, and quiet. It has only five rooms, so it's often full during the high season. Rooms cost US$15/20. All rooms have air-con, hot-water shower,

telephone and include a good breakfast. Two of the larger rooms have a desk and fridge. It also has a generator, so it can handle the power outages. The place has a very homey feel to it, even though none of the rooms have windows.

The small, 16 room *Yoma Hotel (01-297725, fax 297957, 146 Bogyoke Aung San Lan)*, like its Yoma 2 counterpart (see the North, Inya Lake Area entry later in this section), is a popular mid-range place with business travellers, offering computer use complete with email access. A single superior room is US$24 and a double is US$32. A junior suite is US$28/36/44. All rates include breakfast. Monthly rates are available upon request.

Shwedagon & Kandawgyi Area This area of the city is generally quieter than central Yangon. It's also convenient for walking to Shwedagon Paya, the zoo and Kandawgyi.

A residential compound-style inn, typical of those found in Bahan Township, *Beauty Land Hotel (☎ 01-549772, 9 Bo Cho Lan)* offers a wide variety of rooms from US$10 to US$50, depending on whether you get hot water or cold water, shared bath or attached bath, air-con or fan. All rooms come with breakfast and the proprietors offer free airport transport.

The well managed *Bagan Inn (☎ 01-541539, fax 549660, 26 Natmauk Lan 2 (Po Sein Lan))* sits in its own large, landscaped compound on a quiet street, just north of Kandawgyi. Owned by Hong Kong Chinese, the inn's 25 rooms, in three separate two storey buildings, are large and nicely decorated with Burmese *kalagas* (tapestries). All rooms feature fridge, TV, air-con and phone; IDD phone and fax services are available. Standard singles cost US$40, doubles US$60 to US$70, superior doubles US$70 to US$80; there are also more expensive suites. Rates include full breakfast and laundry service. Next door and under the same ownership, the *Silver Palace Restaurant* offers a European, Thai, Chinese and Burmese menu.

The six storey *Summer Palace Hotel (☎ 01-527211, fax 525424, 437 Pyay Lan)* is a popular business-oriented hotel near the TV and radio broadcast station. They have an efficient business centre and a large pool. There are 56 rooms, at a very reasonable US$20/25 a single/double.

Near Kandawgyi, the **Green Hill Inn** (☎ 01-550330, fax 549388, 12 Po Sein Lan) has clean and simple air-con rooms for US$10 and US$15. A larger superior room is US$20, and a junior suite is US$30. All rooms have attached toilets and hot water. Prices are the same for single or double occupancy, and breakfast is included.

The two storey **Comfort Inn** (☎ 01-533377, fax 524256, 4 Shwe Lin Lan) sits in a large compound between Inya Lan and U Wisara Lan, and north of People's Park. Similar in standard to the Bagan Inn, the Comfort Inn offers two standard rooms with air-con and TV for US$35/45, and 10 superior rooms with air-con, large bathrooms, TV and fridge for US$55/65 per room. There is a putting green on the grounds, and rates include breakfast and free airport transfer.

North of the centre, between Inya Lake and Shwedagon Paya, in a quieter part of Yangon, **Winner Inn** (☎ 01-531205, 42 Thanlwin Lan) is great value with rooms for either one or two guests at US$25, complete with private bath, air-con, fridge and satellite TV, and a dining room overlooking the garden.

At the nearby **Windermere Inn** (☎ 01-524613, fax 533846, 15A Aung Min Khaung Lan), near Thanlwin Lan, rooms cost US$15/25. Roughly located between the University of Yangon and Hledan Lan Market, this is one of the quieter small hotels off the main roads. Rooms have air-con, bath, TV and fridge, and breakfast is included.

Panda Hotel (☎ 01-212850, 205 Wadan Lan), on the corner of Min Ye Kyaw Swar Lan, is another excellent mid-range hotel in a residential area, west of the city centre. All rooms in the 10 storey Panda are air-con, with fridge, telephone, TV and private bath. The standard room costs US$20/30, and a larger junior suite is US$30/40.

North & Inya Lake Area The remainder of the hotels in this category are located well north of the centre; the majority are found along or just off Insein Lan or Pyay Lan, which are both long avenues running north to south.

The small, 17 room **Yoma Hotel 2** (01-531065, fax 526945, 24A Inya Lan), like its Yoma 1 counterpart, is very service-oriented and a popular spot with business travellers in this price range (both Yoma hotels have computers with email access). A superior room with either king or twin beds is US$21/28 a single/double. A junior suite costs US$25/32/40 a single/double/triple. Lower long term rates are available.

A 15 minute bus ride north of Sule Paya is the French-owned **Aurora Inn** (☎ 01-525961, fax 525400, 37 Thirimingalar Lan), hidden between Paya Lan and Hledan Lan. The inn encompasses two older buildings. The one at the back is decorated with antiques and contains a dandy small French restaurant and bar, **Chez Sylvie**. Spacious guest rooms are priced at US$10 to US$16 single, US$20 to US$30 double and US$30 to US$45 triple, depending on whether they come with fan or air-con. All room rates include continental breakfast (with a French accent) and laundry. IDD phone service is available.

Another converted colonial building, the **Shwe Hinthar Inn** (☎ 01-533295, fax 524170, 51 Pyay Lan) offers 18 well appointed rooms on spacious grounds for US$30/40, including continental breakfast. All rooms have air-con, fridge and private bath, and there is a large garden and poolside bar on the grounds.

Liberty Hotel (☎ 01-530050, fax 524144, 343 Pyay Lan), near the Hanthawady roundabout, in an elite residential neighbourhood, is a two storey colonial mansion converted to a hotel. Large, high-ceilinged, standard rooms cost US$20/25, and a much larger family room is US$45, plus tax. Rates include breakfast.

Farther north is **Best Executive Suites** (☎ 01-525795, 69 Pyay Lan, Mile 6), a more expensive branch of the city centre's Best Inn. Its 12 well kept rooms, each with air-con, TV and fridge, cost US$45/55.

Places to Stay – Top End

With the exception of The Strand Hotel, hotels in this category often discount rooms depending on demand.

City Centre 'When in Singapore stay at the Raffles', the saying used to go. (Actually it was 'feed at the Raffles' and stay somewhere else, but never mind.) Similarly, when you are in Yangon, the place to stay, if you can afford it, is *The Strand* (☎ *01-243377, fax 289880, 92 Strand Rd)*, between 38th St and Seikkantha Lan. Originally constructed by the Sarkies brothers of Raffles and Bangkok Oriental fame, in 1896, The Strand was one of those glorious outposts of the British empire early this century. During WWII it was forced to close, only to reopen in 1948, under the auspices of London's Steel Brothers Co.

Ne Win nationalised the property in 1963 and in its latter-day socialist role The Strand became a run-down shadow of its former self – certainly no competition for the well kept likes of Raffles or The Oriental. Yet somehow, the old colonial era lived on at The Strand. Many hardened travellers actually preferred staying here rather than the heavily commercial (and high-priced) Raffles and Oriental, insisting that The Strand had more character than either of those glossy stables.

All of this changed again in 1991, when Dutch-Indonesian resort impresario Adrian Zecha and his company began spending US$36 million to renovate the grande dame. By the beginning of 1995, 32 rooms had been totally redone and opened to the public. A planned renovation of the once-popular annexe was abandoned in 1998.

Our verdict: of the three major Sarkies hotel renovations in South-East Asia, this one seems the most faithful to the original spirit. Though perhaps well beyond the budget of many visitors to Myanmar as a place to spend the night, The Strand is well worth a visit for a drink in the bar, high tea in the lobby lounge or a splurge lunch at the cafe. Unlike the Oriental or Raffles, the hotel isn't appended to touristy shopping malls and souvenir shops. The decor doesn't bowl you over with a surplus of ornamentation either, and the staff seem to be a bit more laid-back and less snobbish to nonguest visitors – as long as you dress decently for your visit.

The renovated guest rooms are divided into eight superior suites for US$425 a single/double a night, 23 deluxe suites at US$450 and one apartment-like Strand Suite for US$900. To all rates, add the mandatory 20% tax and service. Each suite is elegantly finished in the colonial style, with plenty of brass and teak, and has air-con as well as ceiling fans; IDD phone, satellite TV and all the other amenities expected at hotels of this calibre. Among the public facilities are a dinner-only restaurant, an opulently finished bar decorated with local art, a cafe and a small business centre. All guests are met at the airport.

The best of the newer upscale city centre hotels is the 500 room *Traders Hotel* (☎ *01-242828, fax 242800, 223 Sule Paya Lan)*, on the corner of Bogyoke Aung San Lan, owned by the Shangri-La chain. Despite its imposing size, the hotel has a reputation for good service. It has a very decent book/gift shop, business centre, pool and fitness centre and excellent restaurant and bar facilities. As usual in Yangon, rooms generally go for less than the advertised tariff. Most rooms range from US$90 to US$120, plus 20% tax and service. Large suites are available for up to US$800 per room. All rates include breakfast, airport transfer, laundry and local phone calls.

The swanky new 350 room *Hotel Equatorial* (☎ *01-250388, fax 252478, 33 Alan Pya Paya Lan)* is just north of the city centre, complete with wood and rattan furnishings, Japanese and Chinese restaurants, cafe, disco/pub, business centre, fitness centre, tennis court and swimming pool. Room rates are US$120/140. Prices go up to US$220 for a deluxe suite.

The six storey *Central Hotel* (☎ *01-241007, 335-357 Bogyoke Aung San Lan)*, next to the Traders Hotel and across the road from Bogyoke Aung San Market, offers

A young monk, Yangon.

Colonial architecture on Pansodan Lan, Yangon.

Pick a winner! Yangon shopfront lottery tickets.

Street signs in Burmese and English, Yangon.

Yangon bus – a cow may well be faster.

The 55m Shwethalyaung Buddha, Bago

large and clean, if unremarkable, rooms for US$50/70, and larger suites from US$86 to US$125. All rooms are air-con with private bath, fridge and phone. The hotel has a good Chinese restaurant and a very popular bar/cafe, adjacent to the large lobby.

Shwedagon & Kandawgyi Area The *Pansea Yangon (☎ 01-221462, fax 228260, 35 Taw Win Lan)* is a very elegantly restored colonial teak mansion tucked away in the embassy quarter, north-west of the central area. The hotel was recently featured in a coffee-table book on South-East Asian architecture, and it's worth a visit just to see the beautiful grounds. The Pansea has 45 spacious rooms, in addition to four family suites. The Pansea Restaurant serves excellent French and Asian cuisine in a pond-side setting. Rooms for single/double occupancy cost US$125/135, plus tax.

For those visitors who want luxury without the glitz, a number of converted mansions in Bahan Township provide more intimate digs. Among the best is *Mya Yeik Nyo Royal Hotel (☎ 01-548310, fax 548318, 20 Pa-le Lan)*, off Kaba Aye Paya Lan, between Kandawgyi and Inya Lake. This stately, 50-year-old, two storey edifice was built by the British as an office for the legendary Irrawaddy Flotilla Company (IFC) and served later as a bank, kindergarten and state guesthouse. Large, high-ceilinged rooms contain IDD phones, adjustable air-con, and minibars; rates here start at US$50/60. The MYN Royal's 6 acre landscaped perch affords clear views of Shwedagon Paya. A Burmese music ensemble performs nightly in the spacious lobby/dining room, which is decorated with antiques and handicrafts. On the grounds are a pool and tennis court.

Kandawgyi Palace Hotel (☎ 01-249255, fax 280412, Kan Yeik Thar Lan) is a striking 200 room teak building on the lakeside. Before its extensive renovation in the mid-1990s, it was known as the Baiyoke Kandawgyi Hotel, a state-owned enterprise. The original building once housed the British Boating Club. The hotel has several fine

restaurants with Myanmar, Asian and European fare, including a 24 hour coffeeshop. There is also a business centre, fitness centre and large outdoor swimming pool – which is free to nonguests for the price of a drink poolside. Single/double rooms here are US$80/90, plus 10% tax and 10% service charge.

A top choice among business travellers, the *Summit Parkview Hotel (☎ 01-227966, fax 227993, 350 Ahlone Lan)* stands within walking distance of Shwedagon Paya. The voluminous marble lobby is designed to impress; the US$30 million hotel is owned by a three company consortium, which includes Singapore's Tiger Balm Corp (owned by the Ow family, originally from Myanmar). All 252 rooms come with IDD phones, satellite TV, in-house movies and 24 hour room service for US$70/80; suites and junior suites cost more. In addition to a useful hotel clinic and dispensary, the Summit offers a swimming pool, fitness centre, newsstand, bakery/cafe, and restaurant.

Overlooking Kandawgyi, *Hotel Nikko Royal Lake Yangon (☎ 01-544500, fax 544400, 40 Natmauk Lan)* has 303 rooms and suites, a business centre with secretarial service and email access, a fitness centre and large pool (US$5 for nonguests), a grand ballroom, a very good Japanese restaurant and a brasserie serving excellent Bamar, Mediterranean and Thai cuisine. Rooms are priced at US$100/120 for a superior room, and US$120/140 for a larger deluxe room.

Close to Shwedagon Paya, the *Savoy Hotel (☎ 01-526289, fax 524891, 129 Dhammazedi Lan)* seems to be a cozier version of The Strand – without the history. Only open since 1996, the hotel has 30 teak- and antique-adorned rooms in addition to six suites, a small business centre, pool, a fine international restaurant, plus cafe and bar – all are open till late. Rooms are good value for a top-end hotel. A single superior room costs US$120, a double US$135; suites are US$160 and US$180. A full breakfast is included in the tariff. This is a popular place in this price range.

North & Inya Lake Area The *Sedona Hotel (☎ 01-666900, fax 666911, 1 Kaba Aye Paya Lan)* is near Inya Lake and offers well appointed rooms in this price range. Tariff prices range from US$120/140 for single/double superior rooms and US$140/160 for deluxe rooms. Discounts are usually available for stays of three days or more. The hotel boasts a popular fitness centre, sauna, large swimming pool, tennis courts, business centre and good bookshop. *Paddy O'Malley's* is a popular Irish pub with live (non-Irish) music most nights.

One of the nicest renovations in Yangon is the 239 room *Inya Lake Hotel (☎ 01-662857, fax 655537)* on Kaba Aye Paya Lan, about 6km north of the city centre on Inya Lake. Originally built in 1961 with Russian aid and run by Israelis, the hotel was completely renovated in 1995 by the same company that did The Strand. The hotel offers excellent facilities, including outdoor pool, fitness centre, tennis courts, business centre and several restaurants and cafes. Room rates here are quite reasonable for a top-end Yangon hotel. Superior rooms are US$82/92, plus 10% tax and 10% service charge.

Ramada Airport Hotel (☎ 01-666699, fax 663575), on Airport Road, near the Department of Aviation, is adjacent to the international airport and is frequented largely by business travellers. A deluxe room (single or double) costs US$50 and a superior is US$84. The hotel offers facilities such as a swimming pool, fitness centre and business centre.

Places to Eat

Yangon has some interesting culinary possibilities for those willing to do some exploring. At the mid-range and top end of the scale are the ubiquitous Chinese restaurants, while the many Indian and Bamar places are cheap and basic. Eat early in the evening – by 9 pm all but a couple of 24 hour places, a few large hotel cafes and The Strand will be ready to close. There are also a few music clubs/cafes that serve food until 11 pm.

Bamar Two humble-looking restaurants in the Shwedagon Paya area enjoy reputations for serving the best traditional Bamar cuisine in the capital. *ATK: Aung Thuka (17(A) 1st St)*, between Shwegondaing and Dhammazedi Lans near Shwedagon Paya, People's Park and the Royal Hotel, features a clean, simple dining room decorated with Burmese calendars and movie posters, and furnished with linoleum-top tables and wooden chairs. A long table along one side of the room displays dozens of cookpots containing the day's curries and special dishes, so all you need to do is point to what appeals to you. Curries made with prawn or venison are particularly good here, as are such side dishes as *kazun ywet* (stir-fried watercress and mushrooms) and *shauk thouq-thi* (citron salad). If you order one or more curries, you'll automatically receive soup, dahl, rice and side dishes. Prices are very reasonable.

The nearby *Hla Myanma Htamin Zain* (Beautiful Myanmar Rice Shop) *(27 5th St)* is sometimes called Shwe Ba (along with its neighbour, ATK) because a famous Burmese actor of the same name once had his house nearby. Like Aung Thuka it's a very simple, plain restaurant, where the food is served from rows of curry pots. They also have some Chinese and Indian dishes. It's a difficult place to find; it's best to go by taxi with a driver who knows the place. Both Shwe Ba restaurants are open from around 10 am to 7 pm. Figure on spending no more than K400 per person for a full spread, not including beverages.

Danubyu Daw Sawyi Restaurant is a slightly more modern-looking Bamar restaurant, with colourful tiled walls at the five way intersection of Hledan Lan, University Ave, Pyay Lan and Insein Lan, quite near the main University of Yangon campus, a little north of the Aurora Inn. The food is traditional Bamar – a selection of curries, soups and vegetable side dishes. Daw Sawyi is also open for breakfast, when it serves fried vegetable rolls and noodles; like most Burmese rice shops, it closes around 7 pm. A second branch of Daw Sawyi can be found at 194 29th St, five blocks west of Sule Paya.

A recent addition to the Myanmar cuisine scene is *Green Elephant Restaurant* (☎ 01-530263, 12 Inya Lan), which offers upscale and slightly westernised Bamar curries, salads, meat and fish dishes in an attractive covered garden setting. The food and service are excellent. Most dishes are K350 to K500.

Foodstalls serving curries and rice – for experienced stomachs only – can be found along the eastern side of Bo Galay Zay Lan. The *noodle stalls* on 32nd St, near Sule Paya, are very cheap and very good.

Shan *999 Khauk Swai* (Triple 9) (130/B 34th St), behind City Hall, a short walk from Sule Paya, is a small shop serving some of the best Shan-style noodles in Yangon. The menu, printed in English and Burmese, includes delicious and filling *Shan hkauq sweh* (thin rice noodles in a slightly spicy chicken broth), *gyon hkauq sweh* (same with wheat noodles), *Shan htamin chin* ('sour' rice salad), *myi shay* (Mandalay-style noodle soup) and other delights. Most noodle dishes cost K100 and are served with fried tofu triangles and jars of pickled cabbage. It's open from 6.30 am to around 7 pm, though we'd recommend eating no later than 6 pm, since the kitchen may sell out of some items. Another good spot for Shan noodles is the *Cherry Restaurant* (203A 35th St), two blocks over.

Another good Shan eatery is *Maw Shwe Li Restaurant* (316 Anawrahta Lan), Lanmadaw Township, west of the city centre. This small, friendly out-of-the-way place is usually crowded with Burmese people, and the curries are excellent and cheap; Shan specialties include *pei pot kyaw* (sour bean condiment) and *hmo chawk kyaw* (fried mushrooms).

Thai *Sabai Sabai Thai Restaurant* (☎ 01-526526, 126 Dhammazedi Lan), just across from the Savoy Hotel, serves excellent and authentic Thai food, in a cosy Thai-style wooden building. Prices are in US dollars and kyat (K600 to K800 a dish). The *Malai Thai Restaurant* (116B Inya Lan), near the

Yangon Yacht Club, is popular with visiting Thais, and the prices are moderate. Another location is at 75 Than Lwin Lan, near the Windermere Inn.

The *Silom Village Restaurant* (647A Pyay Lan) is just north of Inya Lan. The Thai food is quite good, and the bustling outdoor atmosphere is fun – although the service can be spotty when they're busy.

The *Vietnam House Restaurant* (☎ 01-550957, 287 Shwegondaing Lan), between Kaba Aye Paya Lan and Chaukhtatgyi Paya, has an excellent local reputation, and the prices are moderate, with most dishes in the K450 to K700 range.

Indian Along Anawrahta Lan, west of Sule Paya Lan, towards the Sri Kali temple, are a number of *shops* serving Indian biryani (*kyettha dan bauk* in Burmese), and at night the *roti* and *dosa* (North and South Indian pancakes) makers set up along the pavement on the side streets. Indian food is probably the cheapest way of eating in Yangon, particularly at places that serve *thali* (all-you-can-eat meals of rice and various vegetable curries piled on a fresh banana leaf or stainless steel thali plate), which often cost only K200. Biryani costs a bit more, around K220 to K260.

The most popular biryani place in the city centre is still the *Nila Biryane Shop*, on Anawrahta Lan, between 31st and 32nd Sts. It's always crowded but the service is snappy. Equally tasty is *New Nila Biryane Shop*, a block east on the same side of Anawrahta Lan, owned by the same family. Both offer vegetarian biryani, as well as the usual chicken. If one place is out of your favourite biryani, they may send an order to the other shop.

For more variety, try the *New Delhi Restaurant*, on Anawrahta Lan, between 29th St and Shwebontha Lan. This reasonably clean place serves a wide selection of North and South Indian dishes, including *puris* (puffy breads), *idli* (rice ball in broth) and *dosa* (thin crepe filled with potato and spelt toeshay on the menu) with curry and coconut chutney in the morning, banana-leaf thalis and a variety of curries for lunch and dinner. Most Indian places serve tea; the New Delhi serves only coffee, South Indian-style. Open later than most and good for a quick *palata* (fried flatbread) or biryani plate is the nearby **Shwe Htoo Restaurant** on Anawrahta Lan, between the New Delhi and Nila Biryane.

On Mahabandoola Lan, on the corner of Seikkantha Lan, is the dependable and cheap **Bharat Restaurant**, which is similar to the New Delhi with more of a focus on South Indian flavours. Bharat's a bit smaller – it's generally easier to get served – and the marble-topped tables make a nice change from the long cafeteria-style tables at the Indian places on Anawrahta Lan.

Golden City Chetty Restaurant *(170 Sule Paya Lan)*, just north of Sule Paya, on the eastern side of the street, follows the usual pattern for Yangon's Indian restaurants – white-tile walls and bright fluorescent lights. The dosas, thalis etc are nothing special, but it's one of the few city centre Indian places open after 7 pm.

Thei War Restaurant, on Shwebontha Lan, is two doors south of Anawrahta Lan, and the **Sunflower Hotel** serves tasty dahl as well as chicken, mutton and vegie curries – all on banana leaves, South Indian-style. You're supposed to use your fingers (after washing up), but if you insist on a fork and spoon, be careful not to tear a hole in your banana leaf. Good, cheap and authentic – it's about K400 for two people.

Two more upscale Indian restaurants away from the central area are worth a try. The **Ashoka Indian Restaurant** *(☎ 01-221134, 77 Pyidaungsu Yeiktha Lan)* serves excellent and mostly North Indian cuisine; entrees start at US$5. Another very good North Indian eatery is the **Royal Taj Restaurant** *(☎ 01-542899, 138-C University Ave Extension)* (sometimes called New University Ave), just east of Kaba Aye Paya Lan and Inya Lake. Excellent tandoori dishes and vegie curries. Prices are moderate.

Chinese You can sample the whole range of Chinese cuisine in Yangon – from the familiar Cantonese through to the less well known Shanghai, Sichuan, Beijing or Hokkien dishes.

In the city centre area, between Strand Rd and Merchant St, the **PK: Palai Kywe Restaurant** *(44 Bo Aung Gyaw Lan)*, near the main post office, serves excellent northern Chinese fare at reasonable prices. Roasted duck is a speciality, and the menu has several vegetarian dishes. Open daily from 10 am to 9 pm.

The **Mandarin Restaurant** *(126 Mahabandoola Garden St)*, near the corner of Mahabandoola Lan and Sule Paya, just across from the bus park and next door to the Methodist Church, is owned by the same family that runs the Mayshan Guest House. The Mandarin offers the usual wide assortment of reasonably priced northern Chinese dishes, vegetarian fare and fresh fish, in a clean and friendly setting.

One of the best new restaurants in town, **Singapore's Kitchen** *(☎ 01-226297, 524 Strand Rd)*, between 12th St and Phoone Gyee Lan, offers excellent food and good service in a unique setting, with fresh fish on display, an open kitchen and tables that spill onto the footpath during fair weather. At night it's a bright and busy place, and even better is the 1 am closing time. Besides seafood, they do a good job of crispy-fried duck, as well as lots of vegie, noodle and meat dishes. For a variety of dishes and a couple bottles of beer expect to pay about K3000 for two.

Near the Three Seasons Hotel, **Mya Sabe Food Centre** *(71 51st St)* is a very good open-front Chinese eatery with great fried rice, fresh fish and various noodle dishes. It also features a deli case with excellent Chinese pastries – some sweet and some filled with vegetables or chicken. This eatery is open from 6 am to 9 pm. The air-con **Nan Yu** has been in business at 81 Pansodan Lan since 1968 and has all the usual Cantonese specialities (including crabs' thumbs) – soups are particularly good here.

One of the oldest Chinese restaurants in the city is the **Palace** *(84 37th St)*, once widely considered by locals to be the best Chinese eatery in Yangon. Of course, times have changed, but it's still reliable and the servings are generous. Popular specialities include sour-hot fish, which makes heavy use of garlic.

The *Lakeview Terrace Restaurant* (☎ 01-249255, Kan Yeik Thar Lan), a covered outdoor restaurant overlooking the lake at the Kandawgyi Palace Hotel, has a quiet, unpretentious atmosphere, and the Bamar food is decent and plentiful. Most dishes are K400 to K600, which is quite reasonable, given the lakeside perch.

The *Yadana Garden Restaurant* (☎ 01-543561), on the corner of Palae and Kaba Aye Paya Lans, has an extensive offering of Chinese, Bamar and international entrees. The food is good, and prices are moderate to expensive.

The *Royal Garden Restaurant* (☎ 01-297716), on Kampat Lan, overlooking Kandawgyi, serves excellent Singapore-Chinese cuisine. Prices are moderate to expensive.

Not far from Shwedagon Paya, the *Top Choice Food Centre* (135 Inya Lan), on the corner of Dhammazedi Lan, is a small indoor-outdoor Chinese cafe, across the street from the Savoy Hotel, with a variety of good, quick Chinese, Shan and Thai dishes. It's open daily from 6 am to 10.30 pm.

For noodles, fried rice and other quick Chinese meals, try the *night market* on Madaw Lan in Chinatown, around the corner from the Cantonese temple. The *Chinese street stalls* on 19th St, at Mahabandoola Lan, are particularly tasty and clean; try the *Tin Ohn* stall for good pork and squid satay. Another good *Indian stall* (selling good barbecued fish) is nearby on Latha Lan, just south of Mahabandoola, next to Vilas Beauty Salon.

Good Chinese food is also available at the larger, banquet-style places described as dinner show restaurants in the Entertainment section of this chapter.

French French food at a good price is the emphasis at *Chez Sylvie* (☎ 01-525961, 37(A) Thirimingala Lan), in a small dining room in the Aurora Inn. Patrons may also choose to dine in an outdoor garden area. The fixed price menu changes daily and costs around K1200. Live musical performances are provided on many evenings. It's open daily for lunch and dinner.

The serene *Pansea Restaurant* (☎ 01-22146235), on Taw Win Lan, at the Pansea Yangon serves outstanding French- and Burmese-style cuisine. Prices begin at about US$10, and they have a good assortment of imported wines.

Le Planteur Restaurant & Bar (☎ 01-549389, 16 Sawmaha Lan), near Hotel Nikko Royal Lake, serves fine French-Swiss food, with main meals costing US$10 to US$25. It has a smokehouse and produces its own smoked hams and salamis. The bar offers the speciality of the house, 'Les Planteurs' (planters' punch), plus a variety of delicious fruit punches at US$3 per jug. To find it, look for a small wooden signboard saying Le Planteur, just off Natmauk Lan.

Italian For excellent, though pricey, Italian cuisine, try *L'Opera Restaurant* (☎ 01-566662, 20 Thu Ka Waddy Lan), east of Inya Lake and just south of Kanbe Lan. A full dinner with wine will cost you about US$25 per person.

Fast Food Modest western-style restaurants serving 'short eats', and catering to well heeled Burmese clientele by offering sandwiches, burgers, pizza, spaghetti, donuts and the like, are multiplying quickly in the city. Typical of the genre is *Home Sweet Home* (☎ 01-293001), on the corner of Mahabandoola Lan and 52nd St. When the voltage is running, the place is air-conditioned. White-shirted waiters serve sandwiches and a variety of burgers made with a choice of chicken, beef, fish or pork, for around K140 each. Other menu items include grilled lobster, pizza, omelettes, spaghetti, macaroni and cheese, ice cream, fried cashews, milkshakes and imported beers; set menus are available for K650 to K800. Home Sweet Home is open daily from 9 am to 10 pm. *Tokyo Fried Chicken* (156 Mahabandoola

Garden St), just north of Mahabandoola Lan, is another popular spot; there are tables, but you order and pick up your meal at the counter.

In the central area, try *Pizza Corner* and *J' Donuts*, both on Shwebontha Lan, just south of Bogyoke Aung San Lan; *Mac-Burger* and *J' Donuts* on Pansodan Lan, between Mahabandoola and Anawrahta Lans. There's even a new 24 hour restaurant in town, *Donburiya Japanese Restaurant* (☎ 01-280528, 112 Pansodan Lan), across from the High Court, serving very good Japanese rice and noodle dishes.

At 377 Mahabandoola Lan, four blocks east of Sule Paya (between 37th and 38th Sts), you'll find the long-running *Nilar Win's Cold Drink Shop* (☎ 01-278364). Founded by a famous Burmese boxer who now lives in Paris, it's a clean little cafe where you can get yoghurt, *lassi* (a delicious Indian yoghurt drink, plain or blended with fruit) as well as fruit salad, avocado salad, toast and egg (just K80), French toast and other traveller delicacies. It's open daily from 8 am to 11 pm.

Hotel Restaurants For years, The Strand Hotel been among the very best hotel kitchens in town. *The Strand Grill* (☎ 01-243377, 92 Strand Rd) features a changing continental menu and is open from 6 to 11 pm only; the Grill is also one of Yangon's most expensive restaurants, with dinners starting at about US$25. Less formal (and less expensive) is the hotel's *Strand Café*, off the southern end of the lobby facing Strand Rd. The menu offers well prepared soups, salads and sandwiches, as well as a number of Burmese and Asian-inspired dishes, with entrees starting at US$9. The cafe's open daily from 6.30 am to 11 pm. There is also a proper and filling high tea, daily from 2 to 5 pm. The cost is US$14 per person.

Worth a look for the swank colonial-era interior is the *50th Street Bar & Grill* (☎ 01-298096, 9-13 50th St), near the corner of Merchant St, a hangout popular with expats and Burmese. A pool table, plenty of newspapers and magazines and a bulletin board for locals gives the place a homely touch that goes with the excellent brick-oven pizzas, sandwiches, pastas and meat and seafood dishes. Like most upscale eateries in Yangon, prices are in US dollars, though you may pay in kyat as well. On some weekends, a local house band performs upstairs, and the bar often stays open till midnight or later, especially on the weekend.

The *Traders Hotel Restaurant* (☎ 01-242828, fax 242800, 223 Sule Paya Lan), on the corner of Bogyoke Aung San Lan, serves fine international, Cantonese, Japanese and Burmese cuisine. There is also a good cafe and bakery. The small Gallery Bar on the 2nd floor serves drinks and snacks. For an expensive splurge on a Sunday morning, you'll get your fill at the lavish brunch, which includes well prepared Bamar curries, Chinese steam pot, roast duck, soufflés, deserts – you name it. The tab is US$12. While you're there, check out the pianist in the lobby.

The *Yuzana Garden Hotel Snack Bar* (☎ 01-240993, 44 Alaung Paya Lan) looks like a giant greenhouse; it's all glass and a very popular and busy nightspot in Yangon. It has good food, quick service and moderate prices.

Restaurants at the *Summit Parkview* and *Nawarat* hotels offer somewhat predictable, but reliable, menus featuring a variety of Chinese, European and pseudo-Bamar dishes. Both are open daily for breakfast, lunch and dinner. Food at the *Inya Lake* and *Kandawgyi Palace Hotels* is excellent, and includes both Bamar and international cuisines. The *Thamada Hotel Restaurant* also gets good reviews for Chinese cuisine, and the prices are moderate.

The restaurant at the *Sakhantha Hotel* has Chinese, Bamar and western dishes on its menu. The food is nothing special, but it's part of the train station and it's definitely got atmosphere. There are two dining rooms, one for hotel guests and one for nonresident diners and drinkers (usually people waiting for a train). They're both throwbacks to colonial days, with high ceiling fans and people waiting to go somewhere else.

Bakeries In Myanmar, bakeries where cakes and sweet pastries are produced are usually called confectioneries. Yangon's teashops are where you'll find the Bamar-style pastries and sweet snacks. For more western-style breads and cakes try *Hollywood Bakery*, near the Central Hotel and *A & T Bakery Confectionery (☎ 01-526763, 150 Dhammazedi Lan)*, near the Air Mandalay office.

The better places seem to be those that stick to the tried-and-true Bamar style of baking – itself an interesting blend of local, Chinese, Indian and English styles. One find of this sort is *Shwe Pu Zun Bakery (☎ 01-222305, 248 Anawrahta Lan)*, just west of Lan Madaw. When it comes to the quality and variety of both Bamar and western-style cakes and pastries, the Shwe Pu Zun has no peer.

The restaurant in the *Summit Parkview Hotel* stocks a small selection of European-style pastries in a bakery cabinet at the front for ordering in the dining room or for takeaway. Both the *Traders Hotel* and the *Sedona Hotel* have good bakeries. The Sedona has fresh bread every morning, although if you happen to drop by later in the day, you'll find that whatever's left has been discounted.

Teashops Yangon abounds in teashops, where cups of milk tea or coffee, followed by endless tiny pots of Chinese tea and cheap Burmese, Chinese and Indian snacks are available. For breakfast, in fact, you're often better off spending a few kyat in a teashop, rather than eating the boring toast, egg and instant coffee breakfasts provided by many hotels and guesthouses.

The most famous tea-tippling spot in Yangon, perhaps all Myanmar, is *Sei Taing Kya Teashop*, which has six branches. The most happening branch is the one around the corner from the Russian and Israeli embassies at 53 Za Ga War Lan, on the corner of Padonma Lan. It's open from 7 am to 5 pm and serves first-quality tea, samosa, palata, mohinga and *ei-ky-kwe* (deep-fried pastries). A branch east of the city centre is

at 103 Anawrahta Lan, on the corner of 51st St, near the taxi stand. There's another just south of the Theinbyu Playground and Kandawgyi, on Theinbyu Lan.

Another famous teashop – and conveniently located if you're staying in the city centre – is the smaller, more intimate *Theingi Shwe Yee Tea House (☎ 01-289542, 265 Seikkantha Lan)*. Quality tea is served here, along with sliced *bei moq* (opium cake), a moist, delicious brown cake made with poppyseeds and topped with slivered coconut. Other house specialities include seasoned sticky rice with pigeon peas, flaky coconut puffs, curry puffs and *sanwin makin* (literally, turmeric unavoidable; sweetened sticky rice steamed in banana leaves). The teashop also makes hamburgers, which are popular throughout the day: Theingi Shwe Yee is open daily from 7 am to 8 pm.

Mahabandoola Lan has a couple of more modest establishments that typify the general division between Chinese-influenced and Indian-influenced teashops. *Yatha Teashop*, on the southern side of Mahabandoola Lan, between Seikkantha Lan and 39th St, represents the latter, providing fresh samosas and palatas.

The *Golden Crown Café*, on the other side of the street, offers Chinese pastries, steamed buns and eggrolls. Both places serve tea of average quality – nothing to compete with Sei Taing Kya or Theingi Shwe Yee.

The train station platform teashop attached to the *Sakhantha Hotel* features worn wooden booths under a corrugated metal shelter cooled by huge ceiling fans. Since it's rarely crowded, it's a quite relaxed spot to sip a slow tea or coffee, compared to the average Yangon teashop. Snacks are limited: in addition to the very average tea and coffee there's a small selection of cakes and curry puffs, plus *dan bauk* (chicken biryani).

A certain crowd of Burmese writers often congregate at *Lay Tan Kon Teashop (165 33rd St)*, on the upper block near Sarpe Lawka Bookshop.

Burmese Teashops

At all times of day you'll see Burmese sitting in teashops, where the tea flows freely and the assorted pastries are very inexpensive. Teashops are an important social institution in Myanmar, serving as meeting places for friends, family and business associates, as well as a source of inexpensive nutrition and caffeine.

The shops come in all shapes and sizes, indoor and outdoor, morning-oriented and evening-oriented. The morning teashops are typically open from 5 am to 5 pm, and generally serve the best quality tea; many will also serve Burmese-style coffee. Evening teashops open from 4 or 5 pm and stay open till 11 pm or later – even all night in some places.

The tea quality can vary dramatically from one teashop to the next. The best use only fresh, first-quality Indian-style tea for every brewing cycle, while the worst recycle tea leaves until the flavour and colour are gone – to be replaced by ground tamarind and other natural flavour enhancers. The price differences between the good and the bad differ by only K1 or K2 per cup, so it's usually worth seeking out the top-quality places – ask around, everyone knows the superior ones. For example, in a city of 12 teashops, two will stand out clearly as the best. If Burmese tea has received bad international press in the past, it most likely comes from the low quality brews served in the lower class teashops. At a good place, the tea is very drinkable.

Most teashop servers know the English word 'tea' if nothing else, but if you want to order in Burmese ask for *lahpeq ye* (tea water). Burmese tea is always served with milk and sugar. The shops will lighten up on the sugar if you say *cho bouk* (less sweet), or add more if you say *kyauk padaung* (the name of a famous sugarpalm-growing region near Bagan).

Many tea drinkers pour hot tea from the cup into the saucer and sip from the latter, as it cools faster. Some Burmese add a dash of salt to their tea, perhaps a legacy of their Tibetan origins. A thermos of *ahka ye* (Chinese tea, also known as *lahpeq ye gyan*) sits on every table and is drunk as a chaser after finishing a cup or two of the Burmese-style milk tea. Don't remove the steel wool plug stuffed into the top of the thermos – it's meant to filter the tea leaves while pouring.

Tea Snacks

A good deal more than tea is available in a Burmese teashop. Cigarettes and cigars can be purchased singly, along with an array of snacks. Teashop menus fall into two main types, depending on whether they're mostly Chinese or Indian-influenced. A Chinese-style place typically offers *paug-si* (steamed buns), *kaw pyant sein* (fried eggrolls) and *ei-kya-kwe* (long, deep-fried pastries known as *youtiao* in China).

An Indian-style teashop – slightly more common than the Chinese style – typically serves *samosa* (fried triangular-shaped pastries stuffed with vegetables) and *palata* (Indian *paratha*, or fried flatbread). The latter sounds like bladder in Burmese pronunciation; a tasty variation is palata filled with mashed banana (ask for banana bladder!). Another popular variation, *bei palata* is stuffed with pigeon peas. Some Indian-style teashops also offer *nam-bya* (baked, unleavened bread similar to Indian *nan*, often served with a spicy split-pea dip).

Other more Burmese snacks that may be available at a teashop include *hsi htamin* (turmeric-coloured sticky rice topped with sesame seeds and shredded coconut); *kauk hnyin bauq* (sticky rice with salted and mildly spiced pigeon peas); *kua pyant leiq* (deep-fried Burmese egg rolls stuffed with potatoes and vegetables); and *sanwin makin* (literally, turmeric unavoidable, a packet of sweetened sticky rice and banana hunks steamed in banana leaves). Some urban teashops also sell hamburgers, which are gaining popularity as a breakfast food in Myanmar.

Joe Cummings

Entertainment

Yangon entertainment, never the highlight of any foreigner's Myanmar visit, was dealt a near-deathblow by the 11 pm curfew imposed from 1988 to late 1992. The main form of local recreation is hanging out in the teashops or 'cold drink' shops.

On festival days, local bands occasionally organise live outdoor concerts. During the water festival, sizeable rock-music shows are set up along Inya Lan and University Ave and feature local underground rockers such as Iron Cross, Emperor and Aurora. Foreign observers who have seen the leather-clad performances said they are amazed the events are allowed by the State Peace & Development Council (SPDC), the gang formerly known as the State Law & Order Restoration Council (SLORC).

National Theatre The Yangon government recently revived the performance of Burmese classical dance-drama at the National Theatre, a state-sponsored facility on Myoma Kyaung Lan, north-west of Bogyoke Aung San Market.

Scenes from *Ramayana* – called *Yama thagyin* in Burmese – are only occasionally held. Finding out about them is the trick; check at the theatre itself or try asking staff at the larger hotels.

Dinner Shows In the last couple of years, a number of large, semi-outdoor, banquet-style restaurants with floorshows have opened in Yangon. Heavily used by the visiting business community, these dining spots are typically Chinese-owned and feature extensive Chinese menus plus a few Burmese dishes. Entertainment is provided by Burmese bands that perform a mixture of Burmese, western, Chinese and Japanese pop songs – usually sung by a changing roster of female vocalists. Some places also feature Burmese classical dance and/or marionette theatre. There is no charge for entertainment, and no set charges for dinner – you simply order from a menu. Tax and service charges amounting to 20% of the bill are usually added.

Kandawgyi seems almost ringed by such places, as a lake view is considered a prime asset for an evening out on the expense account. If this sounds like your cup of tea, among the best of the bunch is *Lone Ma Lay Restaurant* (☎ 01-559357), off Natmauk Lan on Kandawgyi. Entertainment focuses on Burmese classical and folk dance early in the evening, and pop later on. The Chinese food here is quite respectable, with huge portions and fresh ingredients at lunch and dinner. The Burmese dishes aren't too shabby, even if they show a little extra Chinese influence. The restaurant is also open in the morning for Burmese teashop snacks and noodles; breakfast is served from 6 to 10 am, lunch and dinner from 10 am to 11 pm.

Also on the lake, near the aquarium, is *Dolphin Seafood Restaurant* (☎ 01-250240), on Kan Yeik Thar Lan (Lake Rd). It's a little less formal and is known for employing the best Burmese pop singers in town. A recent addition to the restaurant is karaoke in English, Burmese and Chinese.

There are four similar *rooftop restaurants* in Theingyizei Plaza, on Shwedagon Paya Lan in Chinatown. Access to all four is provided by a single lift open to the street. Directly opposite the lift exit on the roof is *RSR*, with the usual Chinese food and pop singers. Turn left and you'll soon come to *Seafood*, which specialises in fresh seafood, with no musical distractions. Turn right to reach *Ambassador*, which is similar to RSR, followed by the popular *Smile World*, whose dynamic pop music show packs in lots of Burmese who let their *longyis* (sarong-style garments) fly on the dance floor. The food isn't bad at Smile World either. Be prepared for the occasional tethered and neurotic bear, peacock or lemur in some of these restaurants; it's apparently part of the show.

The first restaurant on the lake to offer musical entertainment was the state-owned *Karaweik* – you can't miss this huge replica of an old Burmese floating palace, which is made out of concrete and is definitely not about to float anywhere. Inside this superbly kitsch Yangon wonder you can get fairly ordinary Bamar, Indian or Chinese food, and its prices are not too outrageous. A traditional Burmese music ensemble sometimes plays the Burmese equivalent of 'music to dine by' in one of the several dining rooms, while a separate theatre-style room features a nightly performance of classical Burmese dance.

If you're waiting for a plane and haven't had enough fun yet, repair to *Airport Oasis Restaurant (☎ 01-665865)*, a karaoke-style restaurant near the airport, with good Chinese and European food.

Cinemas A half-dozen or so cinemas along Bogyoke Aung San Lan, east of Sule Paya, show films for K50 or less per seat. The normal fare is pretty awful; a succession of syrupy Burmese dramas, kung-fu smashups and 'made for Third-World consumption' European or American action thrillers. On the other hand, it's quite a scene.

Easily the best cinema for foreigners is *Thamada Cinema (☎ 01-246962, 5 Signal Paya Lan)*. The theatre is newly renovated, quite popular and bookings can be made in advance for the fairly recent American and international films. There are usually five screenings per day, the first at 10 am, the last at 9.30 pm. Prices range from K50 to K150.

The American Center, behind the Ministry of Foreign Affairs at 14 Taw Win Lan, shows free American movies every Monday at noon. Older music programs such as *Austin City Limits* are also sometimes shown.

Bars, Cafes, Discos & Karaoke *The Strand Bar*, far more sophisticated than its funky predecessor, is open from 11 am to 11 pm. Any foreign liquors you may be craving are bound to be among the huge selection of bottles behind the polished wooden bar. Modern watercolours of Burmese scenes decorate the walls and occasionally there's someone around to play the baby grand. Friday afternoon is a two-for-one happy hour, usually graced by a couple of fine musicians playing near the end of the bar.

Two other popular bars with local Burmese and expats are the *50th Street Bar & Grill*, at 50th and Merchant Sts, which has a pool table and brick-oven pizza, and all-day happy hour on Sunday; and *The Bar* at the Savoy Hotel, on the north-west corner of Dhammazedi and Inya Lan, which is open till midnight.

Diamond Ice is a popular bar and cafe on the ground floor of the Central Hotel, on Bogyoke Aung San Lan, just west of Traders Hotel. It's roomy and well lit, with satellite TV, and prices are in kyat.

Founded by famous Burmese vocalist Nay Myo Say, *Mr Guitar Café (☎ 01-550105, 22 Sayasan Lan)* is a small cafe/bar decorated with old guitars. Live folk music is featured nightly from about 7 pm to midnight. Well known Burmese musicians drop by frequently, especially on weekends, to sit in with the regular house group (during music breaks Mr Bean videos are shown). The clientele is a mix of Burmese and local expats. Along with music, the cafe offers espresso and coffee drinks, plus Asian and European food. Open from 6 pm to midnight, sometimes later.

Café D (☎ 01-700446, Amusement Park, Zoological Garden, Bo Min Gaung Lan) is a very popular nightspot with good food (mostly Chinese) and live acoustic music, all in a spacious and handsome setting. The original name was Café Dangerous, but the uniforms who decide such matters found that too close for authoritarian comfort. Open from about 4 pm to midnight, sometimes later.

Jack of Clubs (☎ 01-220546, 329 Lower Kyimyindaing Lan, Ahlone Township), just north of Ahlone Lan and Harmony Amusement Park, is one of Yangon's cooler spots and features a number of monthly events, including blues music evenings, art exhibitions, and locally produced documentaries about travel in Myanmar (a recent trip about the southern Shan State featured a traditional Shan dinner on the menu). There's also a pizza oven and pool table. Open from 11 am to midnight, sometimes later.

The Pioneer Club at the Yuzana Garden

Hotel (☎ 01-240993) is the place to see Yangon's hip crowd gyrate under disco lights. Nearby is the **London Music Club** (☎ 01-250388, 33 Alan Pya Phaya Lan), at the Hotel Equatorial, a bustling basement scene with a huge U-shaped bar; there is a cover charge of K1500. The London features regular concerts by touring musicians; the price is usually K2000, which also buys you two drinks.

A word of warning: prostitutes are a regular feature at many of Yangon's hot night spots. Though the government keeps them on the move, there is little concern for their health or safety, or that of their clients.

Shopping

Markets Shopping at the various zei (markets, often spelt zay) in central Yangon can be fun and very educational. The sprawling, 70-year-old Bogyoke Aung San Market (sometimes called by its British name, Scott Market), appropriately located on Bogyoke Aung San Lan, has the largest selection of Burmese handicrafts you'll find under one roof (actually several roofs). Along the maze-like aisles you'll find a whole variety of interesting Burmese souvenirs, from lacquerware and Shan shoulder bags to T-shirts and cheroots. Gems and jewellery are also on hand, but be sure to read the Precious Stones & Jewellery entry in the shopping section of the Facts for the Visitor chapter before buying any.

Some of the more interesting shops in Bogyoke Aung San Market include: Depi Store, 39 West Block, for cheroots and cigars; Myanmar Lacquerware, 1/2 East Wing, for lacquerware; Eastern Queen, 1st floor, 18 Face Wing, for rattan furniture; Maung Maw & Brothers, 115 Inner West Wing, for both modern and traditional musical instruments; Myat Sanda, 138 West Wing and Sein Pan 69 West C, for lephet (pickle tea); and Mya Malar Longyi (Myanmar Traditional Nether Garments), West Wing. At least 20 other places in the market also specialise in longyis.

The long south stairway at Shwedagon Paya is lined with small shops catering to pilgrims and tourists alike. Popular items

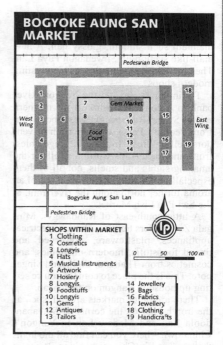

BOGYOKE AUNG SAN MARKET

Pedestrian Bridge

West Wing

East Wing

Gem Market

Food Court

Bogyoke Aung San Lan

Pedestrian Bridge

SHOPS WITHIN MARKET
1 Clothing
2 Cosmetics
3 Longyis
4 Hats
5 Musical Instruments
6 Artwork
7 Hosiery
8 Longyis
9 Foodstuffs
10 Longyis
11 Gems
12 Antiques
13 Tailors
14 Jewellery
15 Bags
16 Fabrics
17 Jewellery
18 Clothing
19 Handicrafts

0   50   100 m

include sandalwood bracelets, small drums, papier maché animals etc. Bargaining is expected here.

Another major market, especially for locals who find Bogyoke Aung San Market a little too pricey, is Theingyi Zei, the biggest market in Yangon. This rambling affair extends four blocks east to west from Konzaydan Lan to 24th St, and north to south from Anawrahta Lan to Mahabandoola Lan. Most of the merchandise for sale represents ordinary housewares and textiles, but the market is renowned for its large section purveying traditional Burmese herbs and medicines. A snake section features the fresh blood and organs of various snakes – including the deadly branded krait – disembowelled on-the-spot for medicinal consumption. Of more general interest is traditional Burmese herbal shampoo, made by boiling the bark of the tayaw shrub with big black kin pun (acacia pods) and sold in small plastic bags; this is the secret of how Burmese women maintain such smooth, glossy hair. A new mall-like section on Shwedagon Paya Lan, Theingyizei Plaza, contains less-interesting modern shops.

Thirimingala Zei, on the Yangon River bank in Ahlone Township off the northern end of Strand Rd (straight west about 1km from People's Park), is a labyrinth of vendors selling fresh foodstuffs, vegetables, fruits and meat – it's worth a stroll for the amazing sights and smells, not all of them especially pleasant. Catch even more of an aroma further north along the riverfront, at the San Pya Fish Market.

A little south-east of Kandawgyi, Mingala Zei proffers textiles, clothes, electrical appliances, plasticware, preserved and tinned foodstuffs, modern medicines, and cosmetics from Thailand, China and Singapore. This is the place to come if you're setting up house in Yangon on the cheap.

There are other markets around, such as the iron bazaar on the corner of Mahabandoola Lan and Madaw Lan in Yangon's Chinatown – here you can find all the items that are used in Chinese cooking. Itinerant vendors set up along Anawrahta Lan east and west of Sule Paya Lan nightly from around 6 to 10 pm, selling everything from Chinese toothbrushes to fresh fruit and shishkebab. Chinatown itself extends east-west between Madaw Lan and Shwedagon Paya Lan, and north-south between Mahabandoola Lan and Strand Rd.

The FMI Centre just east of Bogyoke Aung San Market is a recent and upscale air-con addition to the city centre's shopping scene with music stores, jewellery and clothing shops.

Speciality Shops Myanmar Elephant House (☎ 01-532773), located at 24A Aung Min Khaung Lan, off Thanlyin Lan, produces a variety of high-quality, handmade wood, cane and rattan furniture plus design accessories.

Yuzana Pickle Tea (☎ 01-242526), at 22 Nawaday Lan, Dagon Township, sells the city's best quality lephet in sweet, sour and chilli-laced varieties. You can buy an all-in-one kit containing prepared tea leaves, fried garlic, sesame, peanuts, fried peas etc, or buy each of the ingredients separately. The kit makes a unique souvenir. There is a second branch on the ground floor of Theingyi Zei, Shed D, E-60.

Myanmar Orchid and Flora Centre at 119 Sule Paya Lan offers fresh and artificial flowers, orchid plants and seeds; if you're moving to Yangon they can also provide landscape design. The morning market at 38th St and Bogyoke Aung San Lan has fresh flowers at cheap prices. Also try the back entrance to Bogyoke Market, or early mornings/evenings at Hledan, Myaynigone or Kyimyindaing markets.

J's Irrawaddy Dream (☎ 01-221695), at 59 Taw Win Lan (a block north of the Pansea Hotel), is a handsome shop featuring Burmese textiles, clothes, lacquer and other handicrafts. Open daily from 9 am to 8 pm.

Arts & Crafts There is a small but thriving local gallery scene in Yangon. Traditions Gallery (Claudia Saw Lwin, director) (☎ 01-513709), at 24 Inya Myaing Lan, has quality reproductions of traditional Burmese handicrafts. Ivy Gallery (Myat Min, director) (☎ 01-297654), at 159 45th St, between Bogyoke Aung San and Anawrahta Lans, features a fine collection of modern Burmese art. Ivy also has a shop in Bogyoke Aung San Market at 438 West Row. Yone Yang Antique Shop (☎ 01-240167) at 1B Kabaaye Paya Lan, at Inya Ave, is a good place to browse, even if much of its stock is not for export.

Both Golden Valley Art Centre (☎ 01-533830) at 54(D) Golden Valley, and Inya Gallery of Art (☎ 01-530327) at 50(B) Inya Lan feature exhibits by contemporary Burmese painters.

For recommendations on where to buy books, see the Bookshops section at the beginning of this chapter.

Tailors Yangon isn't a place you would usually think of for tailor-made clothes, but prices for tailoring are among the lowest in South-East Asia. The selection of fabrics at tailor shops, however, is mostly restricted to synthetics. Cotton lengths in prints, plaids, solids and batiks can easily be found in the larger markets, so you may do better to buy cloth at a market and bring it to a tailor shop for cutting and sewing.

If you want a traditional, Mandarin-collar Burmese shirt (for men, try Ava Tailoring (☎ 01-248156), at 124 Pansodan Lan, near the train station at the Anawrahta Lan intersection. If you're measured the day you arrive, they can have it ready by the time you return from upcountry. Sein Shwe Tailors (☎ 01-281979), at 84A 26th St, Mahamed Esoof, at 142 Bo Galay Zay Lan, and Globe Tailoring (☎ 01-273416), at 367 Bogyoke Aung San Lan, are well regarded by local expats for women's and men's tailoring. Globe is especially good for quick alterations.

Photography Supplies Along Anawrahta Lan, between Sule Paya Lan and Mahabandoola Garden St, are at least a dozen shops that sell film and photography supplies. Several stock slide film – usually Kodak Ektachrome 100 and Fujichrome Sensia 100 – for around K1800 per roll. Colour print film is plentiful and cheap, black & white film is very scarce. Slide film isn't common in Myanmar, and it's a good idea to check the date on the packaging. For camera repair, Pacific Camera Repair, on the same block, has been recommended.

Photocopy Service Try Thazin Photocopying Centre (☎ 01-27599), at 207 Pansodan Lan, between Mahabandoola Lan and Merchant St, in the city centre.

Duty-Free Goods Most merchandise at the duty-free shop at Yangon international airport is cheaper than Bangkok, Hong Kong or Singapore. There's also a branch in town at the former location of the Tourist Department Store on Sule Paya Lan just north of Sule Paya. It's now called Yangon Duty Free Store. Both branches carry the usual airport stuff – perfume, cigarettes (US$9 a carton), alcohol (average US$10 per litre) and watches – plus a variety of other imported goods, such as chocolate candy and breakfast cereal.

Getting There & Away

Air See the introductory Getting There & Away chapter for information on air travel to/from Yangon.

Airline Offices Ten airlines have offices or agents in Yangon, though only Biman Bangladesh Airlines, Air China, Myanmar Airways International, Thai Airways International and Silk Air actually have flights to/from Yangon international airport.

Air China
  (☎ 01-665187)
  206 Bagwa Lane, Pyay Lan (Mile 9)
Air France
  (☎ 01-252708, fax 274199)
  69 Sule Paya Lan
Air Mandalay
  (☎ 01-525488, fax 525937)
  146 Dhammazedi Lan
All Nippon Airways
  (☎ 01-248901, fax 248904)
  380 Bogyoke Aung San Lan, FMI Centre
Asiana Airlines
  (☎ 01-524112, fax 531317)
  Wizaya Plaza, 301 Dhammazedi Lan
Biman Bangladesh Airlines
  (☎ 01-275882)
  106-108 Pansodan Lan
China Airlines (Taiwan)
  (☎ 01-245484, fax 246330)
  353 Bo Aung Gyaw Lan
EVA Airways (Taiwan)
  (☎ 01-298001, fax 296272)
  47/49 Bogalay Zay Lan
Indian Airlines
  (☎ 01-253597, fax 248175)
  127 Sule Paya Lan
Japan Airlines
  (☎ 01-243030, fax 246859)
  380 Bogyoke Aung San Lan, FMI Building
KLM Royal Dutch Airlines
  (☎ 01-274466)
  c/o Myanma Airways, 104 Strand Rd
Korean Air
  (☎ 01-282226)
  341 Mahabandoola Lan

Malaysia Airlines
(☎ 01-241007, fax 241124)
335 Bogyoke Aung San Lan
Myanma Airways
(☎ 01-274874)
104 Strand Rd
Myanmar Airways International
(☎ 01-289772, fax 289609)
123 Sule Paya Lan
Pakistan International Airlines
(☎ 01-245069)
184 Bo Aung Gyaw Lan
Silk Air
(☎ 01-284600, fax 283872)
537 Merchant St
Thai Airways International
(☎ 01-285006, fax 289564)
441-445 Mahabandoola Lan
Yangon Airways
(☎ 01-251934, fax 251932)
22-24 Pansodan Lan

Bus The bus scene has improved with the influx of several private lines, many of which have city centre offices and shuttle stations.

To the North Most public and private buses to destinations outside of Yangon leave from the Highway bus station (also known as Sawbwa- gyigon), at the intersection of Pyay Lan and Station Rd, just south-west of Yangon's international airport in Mingaladon. Each bus line has an office at the station; for the most part, these offices are lined up according to general routes, eg one section for Nyaung U/Bagan, another for the Mandalay area, another for Taunggyi/ Inle Lake and one for Mawlamyaing/Dawei. There are snack shops with rice and noodle dishes if you get hungry while waiting for a departure.

Ordinary government buses are the cheapest and slowest: so slow that the Road Transport Enterprise won't even give arrival times. Private bus companies generally run better vehicles on tighter schedules, for up to twice the government fare. You can buy tickets at the station (a day or two in advance is recommended), or at several central locations, mostly opposite the central train station, alongside Aung San Sta-

dium. There are several offices and you can quickly check schedules and compare prices and services.

Most impressive of all are the newer aircon express buses, which run to Pyay, Meiktila, Mandalay, Taunggyi and Mawlamyaing. These buses typically feature large Japanese, Chinese or Korean air-con (more or less) buses with around 45 reclining seats, and even on-board video. Typical fares are K2000 (or US$7/FEC) for Mandalay, Meiktila or Taunggyi; K800 (or US$4/ FEC) to Pyay or Mawlamyaing. These lines also may stop in Bago and Taungoo, where small offices are maintained at roadside restaurants.

The major players on the popular Yangon to Mandalay route are Leo Express, Kyaw Express and Transnational Express, all of whom maintain offices at the Highway bus station as well as in central Yangon, across from the train station near Aung San Stadium. Meals, snacks and water are usually provided. Most companies transfer passengers from several central locations to the Highway bus station in vans or pickups for no extra charge.

Express bus offices opposite the central train station include:

Kyaw Express
(☎ 01-242473) 8-11 Aung San Stadium (South)
Leo Express
(☎ 01-249512) 23-25 Upper Pansodan Lan at Aung San Stadium (East)
Sun Moon Express
(☎ 01-641201) Aung San Stadium (South)
Transnational Express (TNE)
(☎ 01-249671) 22-29 Aung San Stadium (South) at Kunchan Lan

Mawlamyaing Buses for Mawlamyaing depart from the Highway bus station (Mottama is the actual stop; from there you take a ferry or longtail boat across the river).

Bago, Kyaiktiyo, Pathein & Thanlyin Buses for Bago and Pathein leave from the Hsimmalaik Bus Centre near the intersection of Hanthawady and Hledan Lans in the north-western part of Yangon. Hsimmalaik is a bustling, dusty compound, and mostly caters for bus trips within 320km of Yangon. Most signs are in Burmese, but people are very helpful, and patience pays.

There are two private buses to Pathein, with departures at 4.30, 6 and 9 am, and noon and 2 pm. The cost is K400. The best of the Pathein bus companies is Ktet Aung Express (☎ 01-5131730); its office at Hsimmalaik is open daily from 7 am to 6 pm. You can continue to Chaungtha Beach or Gwa for an additional K300 to K350, although you must change buses at the ferry crossing. The bus to Pathein takes approximately 4½ hours; to Chaungtha Beach another three hours. Minibuses to Pathein are also available from the less convenient Highway bus station. For Pathein, you can buy same-day tickets for the noon or 2 pm departure, but for morning departures, you should definitely try to purchase tickets the day before.

Minibuses to Kyaiktiyo (and Kinpun, the basecamp to Kyaiktiyo Paya) leave hourly from 6 to 11 am for the five hour trip. The cost is K400.

Pickups to Bago leave hourly from 6 am to 3 pm for K100 per person. Small pickups to Bago and Kyaiktiyo also leave from the eastern side of Latha Lan, south of Anawrahta Lan. Buses to Thanlyin leave from the southern side of Mahabandoola Lan, east of Sule Paya.

Train In addition to the many trains operated by state-owned Myanma Railways, one private company runs out of Yangon train station along the Yangon to Mandalay line. Dagon Mann (☎ 01-249024) reserves just four berths and six upper class seats for foreigners on its private express train (No 17 Up on the public schedule), which departs from Yangon at 3.15 pm on Wednesday, Friday and Sunday, arriving in Mandalay at 5.40 am the next morning. Obviously this service is no quicker than the Myanma Railways trains, because they use the same engines and tracks. In fact, the train really caters to Burmese residents, who pay a

good deal less – K500 for a wooden seat in 64-seat ordinary class. As usual, foreigners are charged much more. For this privilege, they are rewarded with a meal choice of hamburger, fried noodles or fried rice, plus one soft drink, and video programs. A 1st class seat costs US$30 (no air-con or video); upper class with air-con US$42; upper class reclining US$45; and US$50 for a four person air-con sleeper with attached bath and fridge. A few two person cabins are also available at the same price but it's rare that these become available for foreigners.

Dagon Mann upper class tickets may be reserved up to a month in advance of departure. All tickets must be purchased in advance; the company recommends four days. Reservations and tickets are available at the Dagon Mann ticket office on Bogyoke Aung San Lan, on the platform of the train station. You must pay K1 to get on the platform without a ticket.

See the Getting Around chapter for information on rail travel between Yangon and Mandalay using Myanma Railways.

Boat Along the Yangon River waterfront, which wraps around southern Yangon, are a number of jetties with boats offering long-distance ferry services. Four main passenger jetties service long-distance ferries headed up the delta towards Pathein or north along the Ayeyarwady (Irrawaddy) River to Pyay, Bagan and Mandalay: Pongyi, Lan Thit, Kaingdan and Hledan. Named for the respective streets that extend north from each jetty, all four are clustered in an area just south of Lanmadaw township and south-west of Chinatown. When you come to purchasing a ticket for a particular ferry from the Inland Water Transport (IWT) deputy division manager's office (☎ 01-284055), at the back of Lan Thit jetty, be sure to ask which jetty your boat will be departing from.

Myanma Five Star Line (MFSL) (☎ 01-295279) ships leave from the MSFL jetty – also known as Chanmayeiseikan jetty – next to Pansodan Lan jetty.

Getting Around

To/From the Airport See the Air section in the Getting Around chapter for details on getting to/from the airport.

Bus Over 40 numbered city bus routes connect the townships of Yangon. Many buses date back to the 1940s and carry heavy teak carriages. Often, they're impossibly crowded; a Burmese bus is not full until every available handhold for those hanging off the sides and back has been taken. Other routes use newer air-con Japanese and Korean buses that aren't too bad; some routes also use pickup trucks with benches in the back. If you can find a space you can go anywhere in central Yangon for K5. Longer routes cost from K10 to K20. Prices often double at night – still cheap and still crowded.

Useful bus routes include:

Bogyoke Aung San Market to Mingala Zei (south-east of Kandawgyi) – Japanese pickup No 1 (၁)

Sule Paya to Thamaing Junction (Eight-Mile Junction) along Insein Lan – bus No 44 (၄၄), No 45 (၄၅) and No 53 (၅၃)

Sule Paya to Hledan junction, then Pyay Lan University of Yangon, along the west side of Inya Lake to Yangon City Hotel and the airport – blue bus No 51 (၅၁), No 53 (၅၃) and air-con No 51 (၅၁)

To Kaba Aye Paya and on to Mae La Mu Paya – bus No 43 (၄၃)

Similar route to No 8, starting from Insein, continuing on to Theinbyu Lan in the vicinity of the YMCA, Three Seasons Hotel, Cozy Guest House – green pickup No 48 (၄၈)

Mahabandoola Garden St to the Highway bus station – yellow No 51 (၅၁)

To Shwedagon Paya – bus No 37 (၃၇), No 43 (၄၃) and No 46 (၄၆)

To the Chaukhtatgyi Paya – bus No 42 (၄၂), No 47 (၄၇)

Train A circular train route loops out north from Yangon to Insein, Mingaladon and North Okkalapa townships and then back into the city. There are actually two trains, one clockwise (left-bound) and one counterclockwise (right-bound), and it takes three

hours to complete the loop in either direction. A run around this loop will give you a cheap (K15), but not particularly comfortable, look around; trains depart every 30 minutes between 6 am and 8 pm.

This train isn't any good for getting around central Yangon – there's only one central station, the main one – but it can be useful for moving back and forth between the various townships north of the city centre. If you want to use the train to get around the city, the Ministry of Forestry's *Yangon Guide Map* shows the stations most clearly. The Kyaukyedwin station is not far from the airport, and there are also convenient stations for Hledan, Kamayut and Insein north-west of the city centre. Buses to these same areas are quicker, of course, unless you've just come from upcountry by train and are at Yangon train station anyway. Yangon's main station is off Sule Paya Lan, north of Bogyoke Aung San Lan; to buy tickets for the circular train, look for the ticket window next to an oval track map at the eastern end of the station.

Sunday is the least crowded time to use the circular train to get a quick glimpse of the city and surroundings.

Taxi Licensed taxis carry red licence plates, though there is often little else to distinguish a taxi from any other vehicle in Yangon. The most expensive are the car taxis – usually older, mid-sized Japanese cars. Fares are highly negotiable – most trips around the central area shouldn't cost more than K180 one way, K200 to K300 for longer trips. You can also hire a taxi for about K500 an hour. For the entire day, you should pay about K4000 or US$12 to US$15. Be sure to work out all details before you agree to a price and itinerary.

For all types of taxis the asking fares usually leap by 30% or so after sunset and on weekends, when rationed petrol isn't available. Late-night taxis – after 11 pm or so – often cost double the day rate, mainly because the supply of taxis on hand is considerably lower than in the day, so the drivers are able to charge more.

Trishaw Every Asian country seems to have its own interpretation of the bicycle trishaw. In some countries the passengers sit beside the rider, side by side in a sort of sidecar; in others they sit in front or in the back. In Myanmar, trishaw passengers ride beside the driver, but back to back – one facing forward, one backward. These contraptions are called *saiq-ka* (as in side-car) and to ride one costs roughly K10 per person for every kilometre.

Nowadays trishaws are not permitted on the main streets between midnight and 10 am. They're most useful for side streets and areas of town where traffic is light. So far, trishaws have outlasted the rumours about their imminent banning from the city centre.

Boat Cross-river ferries to Dala on the southern bank of the Yangon River, leave about every 20 minutes from Pansodan Lan jetty (for pedestrians), at the foot of Panso-

dan Lan; the cost is K5. Sin Oh Dan Lan jetty (for vehicles) at the foot of Sin Oh Dan Lan. Dalah is the departure point for excursions to Twante and Letkhokkon; departure times are 9 am, and 1 and 5 pm (from Dalah, it leaves at 8.30 am, and 12.30 and 4.30 pm). See the Getting There & Away in the Twante section of the Around Yangon chapter for further details on cross-river transport.

You can hire *sampans* (flat bottomed skiff) from the Pansodan or Botataung jetties for K200 per hour if you just want to have a look at river life. On a grander scale, for US$1000 you can charter a deluxe double-decker (normally reserved for VIP dinners and the like) from the IWT office near Lan Thit jetty for a four hour cruise between Thanlyin to the north-east and Bayinnaung Bridge to the north-west.

Since the completion of the Thanlyin Bridge, there are no more passenger ferries to Thanlyin across the Bago River from Yangon.

Around Yangon

Several destinations in the Yangon, Bago and Ayeyarwady divisions surrounding the capital make good one to three-day excursions from Yangon (Rangoon). Thanlyin (Syriam) and Twante can be seen in out-and-back day-trips, while relaxing Letkhokkon requires an overnight stay. If your tastes are broad, the varied sights in Bago may well be worth an overnight stay; Pathein and Chaungtha Beach perhaps warrant several nights between them. Pyay (Prome), in the north-western corner of Bago Division on the Ayeyarwady (Irrawaddy) River, is a rewarding two day detour for the modest ruins of Thayekhittaya (Sri Ksetra), a Pyu kingdom that was in existence around 1500 years ago.

Taungoo, a Bago Division town, off the highway between Yangon and Mandalay, once held little interest for the average visitor except as a good resting place between Yangon and Mandalay. These days it's also the starting point for an excursion to nearby Seine Forest Camp, a working elephant teak forest area.

Delta Region

A vast basin stretching from the Bay of Bengal coast across to the Bago Range receives year-round drainage from several major rivers, including the Ayeyarwady, Bago, Yangon (Hlaing) and Pathein (Ngawun). Intercut with canals, streams and tributaries, this riverine network irrigates millions of hectares of farmland, making the delta the central, and essential, 'rice bowl' of Myanmar. Estuarine environments along the coast provide much of the country's saltwater and freshwater fish harvest as well. Because of such natural abundance, the delta has attracted Burmese people from all around the country; hence it's one of Myanmar's most populated – and interesting – regions.

THANLYIN & KYAUKTAN

If you've got a morning or afternoon to spare in Yangon, you can make an excursion across the river to Thanlyin and on to the 'mid-river' *paya* (pagoda) at Kyauktan. Thanlyin was the base during the late 16th century and early 17th century for notorious Portuguese adventurer Philip De Brito. Officially a trade representative for the Rakhaing, he actually ran his own little kingdom from Thanlyin, siding with the Mon (when it suited him) in their struggle against the Bamar. In 1599 his private army sacked Bago, but in 1613 the Bamar besieged Thanlyin and De Brito received the punishment reserved for those who defiled

AROUND YANGON

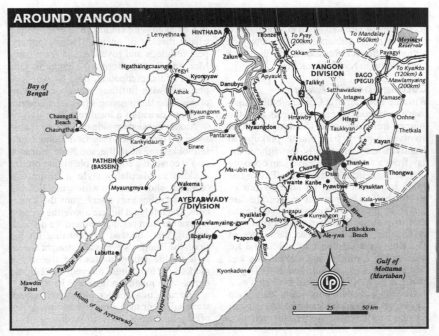

Buddhist shrines – death by impalement. It took him two days to die, due, it is said, to his failure to take the recommended posture where the stake would have penetrated vital organs. Thanlyin continued as a major port and trading centre until it was destroyed by Alaungpaya in 1756, after which Yangon took over this role.

Although there is no longer any of this ancient city to be seen, Thanlyin is a relaxing change of pace, with shaded streets and a busy market to stroll through. A short bus ride out of town will take you to the large, golden **Kyaik-khauk Paya**, rising on a hillock to the north of the road. It's said to contain two Buddha hairs delivered to the site by the great sage himself, although the paya looks to be no more than a couple of hundred years old. Most likely the first stupa on this hillock was erected by the Mon 600 to 800 years ago. Just before this

stupa are the tombs of two famous Burmese writers: Natshingaung and Padethayaza. If it's too hot to climb the stairs, you can always take the lift for K5.

If you continue 12km further, until the road terminates at a wide river, you can visit the **Yele Paya** (Mid-River Pagoda) at Kyauktan. It's appropriately named since the complex is perched on a tiny island in the middle of the river. In the temple there are pictures of other famous payas all over Myanmar and further afield. To reach the islet shrine, catch one of the many launch ferries from the riverbank for a few *kyat*. Near the ferry landing are several food vendors.

Places to Stay & Eat

So far, none of the several guesthouses in Thanlyin is licensed to accept foreigners. Until that changes, check out the friendly *White House Restaurant & Guest House*, about 100m off the main road, which serves good Chinese fare in a small air-conditioned cafe. For more ambience, try the courtyard setting at **Bonsai Restaurant** on the main road leading to Kyaik-khauk Paya.

Getting There & Away

With the opening of a Chinese-built bridge over the Bago River several years ago, the journey from Yangon to Thanlyin no longer involves a ferry trip. Large pickups to Thanlyin leave frequently throughout the day from a spot on Sule Paya Lan opposite City Hall, a little east of Sule Paya. The 25km trip takes about an hour by bus or pickup; half an hour by car or taxi. The fare is K15 by pickup. Minibuses also make the short trip out to Thanlyin from a spot next to Thakhin Mya Park, near the corner of Tha Khin Mya Garden Lan and Strand Rd west of the central Yangon area. The bus fare is K30 to Thanlyin, and K40 if you continue on to Kyauktan and the Yele Paya.

Once in Thanlyin, horse carts are a good way to get around. You can hire one to go to Kyaik-khauk Paya for about K500 each way.

TWANTE

It's an interesting day trip from Yangon to Twante; a small town noted for its pottery and cotton-weaving, and for an old Mon paya complex. One can travel there by public jeep from Dala (on the opposite bank of the Yangon River) or by ferry along the Yangon River and Twante Canal. The latter mode of transport is slower but provides a glimpse of life on and along the famous canal, which was dug during the colonial era as a short cut across the Ayeyarwady Delta.

A large market in the centre of town near the canal banks was destroyed by fire in January 1995 but has since been rebuilt.

Shwesandaw Paya

Standing 76m tall, this Mon-built *zedi* (bell-shaped paya), a kilometre or two south of the canal, is just a few years younger than the one at Yangon's Shwedagon Paya. Though the stupa itself fits the standard central Burmese mould, a walk around the

compound will yield a few minor surprises. In a chicken-wire enclosure to one side is a casual display of ancient Twante pottery, plus religious and royal regalia from early Mon and Bamar (Burman) kingdoms. One corner of the compound, used by worshippers as a 'wish-fulfilling' station, commemorates King Bayinnaung's (also spelt Bayint Nyaung) defeat of a local rebellion.

Along the western side of the stupa stand some old bronze Buddhas. Continuing counterclockwise, near the southern entrance you'll come to a 100-year-old sitting bronze Buddha in Mandalay style with unusual 'capped' shoulders in which the flowing monastic robes curl away from the shoulders. The left hand hovers above the crossed legs rather than resting on them – a difficult casting feat. Instead of focusing on the floor, the Buddha's eyes stare straight ahead. A low blue ledge in front of the image marks off 'footprints' allegedly left by an ogress who made a pilgrimage here.

The ruins of a smaller, older-looking zedi stand adjacent to the main compound, just off the road from the ferry landing.

Oh-Bo Pottery Sheds

Pottery is a major cottage industry in Twante, which supplies much of the delta region with well designed, utilitarian containers of varying shapes and sizes. The pots are made in huge thatched-roof sheds in the Oh-Bo district south of the canal, about 15 minutes walk from the dock.

Near the entrance to the sheds are the potters' wheels. Twante pots are typically half wheel-thrown, half coil-shaped, then air dried on huge racks in the middle of the shed. After drying, the pots are fired in large wood-fired adobe kilns set towards the back of the sheds. To one side of the sheds stand piles of cut wood – assorted jungle hardwoods, but especially rubberwood, are the fuels of choice. The kilns are divided into two chambers, one for drying wood and one for firing the pots with a brown-black glaze. It takes around 15 days for the firing and cooling of one kiln-full. The typical shed turns out 70,000 pots a year, all of them handmade.

Twante pots can be purchased directly from the sheds or, perhaps more conveniently, at the central market near the Twante ferry landing.

Getting There & Away

The quickest way to get to Twante is via a short cross-river ferry and public jeep or pickup ride. Pedestrian ferries from Pansodan Lan jetty (near the foot of Par sodan Lan and opposite The Strand Hotel) take passengers across the Yangon River to Dala on the opposite bank in 20 minutes for K3 per person. In Dala catch one of the dark green jeeps that leave for Twante every 45 minutes or so throughout the day. The jeeps are gradually being replaced by Hi-Lux pickups. The ride takes 30 to 45 minutes and the fare is K30 for a jeep; K35 (K70 for a front seat) for a Hi-Lux. Come prepared for a crush – drivers cram as many people as possible into and onto the vehicle – or charter your own saloon car for about K200 per person. Minibuses round out the possibilities at K50 per person.

The seemingly slower but more scenic trip along the Yangon River and Twante Canal takes two hours – even though it's only 24km from landing to landing. Although there are several boats that pass by Twante on their way across the western delta, including the Yangon-Pathein ferry (which leaves from Lan Thit jetty), the most frequent departures are aboard Hpayapon-bound craft. These leave from the Hledan and Kaingdan Lan jetties in Yangon daily at noon, 1, 2, 3 and 4 pm, returning hourly till 7 pm. The fare is US$1 (or FEC); only K20 for locals.

When you add up the wait times for the cross-river ferry/jeep departure versus the canal ferry, both modes of transport end up taking about the same amount of time from start to finish. A good way to vary the trip would be to do the ferry-jeep combo out to Twante, then catch one of the canal ferries back to Yangon around sunset when the waterways look their best.

Getting Around

Trishaws from the ferry dock to the Oh-Bo pottery sheds cost K30 per person. From the dock to Shwesandaw Paya, the cost is K100 A horsecart from Shwesandaw back to the dock is about K150.

LETKHOKKON BEACH

Letkhokkon, about three to four hours by road from Dala, is the closest beach to the capital. Located in Kunyangon township, near the mouth of the Bago River, Letkhokkon is a delta beach facing the Gulf of Mottama (Martaban), with fine powder-beige sand and a very wide tidal bore that tends towards mudflats at its lowest ebb. Copious coconut palms along the beach help make up for the less than crystalline waters. The lack of clarity is part of the estuarial milieu here and doesn't mean the water isn't clean. At low tide the local kids like to stage mudfights.

A day or overnight excursion to Letkhokkon is more than just a beach trip; it offers a glimpse of relaxed delta life. Along the way, the road passes by rice paddies, betel-leaf gardens and several Karen villages. At Kunyangon a large stupa called **Payagyi** (Big Paya) is a common stop for Burmese day-trippers. West of the road between Kawhmu and Ingapu is a hilly area studded with the porcelain remains of ceramics left behind by hundreds of years of sea trade.

Adjacent to the main beach area, the village of **Letkhokkon** itself is a fairly typical seaside town that prospers from coconuts and fishing. Farther south-east in a neighbouring village is a **monastery** with a bizarre collection of mutant fruits, including a pineapple plant that bears a blossom not seen on other pineapples; coconuts whose outer husks bear likenesses to Kyaiktiyo Paya and the late *sayadaw* (chief abbot); and dead logs that bear fruit. Using a magnifying glass, the abbot likes to show visitors markings in the fingerprint of his left index finger resembling a dancing peacock.

Myaseinthaun, a delta island offshore, is visited by many native and migratory waterfowl. **Daedaye,** on a delta peninsula northwest of Letkhokkon, is a small town that thrives on the production of processed

AROUND YANGON

seafood for export. Though the town itself isn't so interesting, there's a long beach nearby called **Anauntphettokan** (Westward-moving Beach, named for its heavy sand drift). The beach can be approached by boat from Ingapu or other spots along the coastline. You can rent a launch for visiting these areas from the Letkhokkon Beach Hotel. The asking price is K3000 per hour, but you should be able to arrange a better deal for multi-hour hires.

Places to Stay & Eat
As you approach Letkhokkon from the north, you'll see a two lane, palm-flanked avenue leading off to the right to the *Letkhokkon Beach Hotel*, a tidy row of brightly painted wooden beach bungalows. The hotel charges US$38/45 a single/double for spacious rooms with air-con, mosquito nets and attached hot-water showers. However, when we visited the power was not on for more than six hours a day. Rates include a choice of western or Asian breakfasts. Good seafood is sometimes available at the hotel restaurant. The hotel maintains a booking office in Yangon (☎ 01-224346) at 68 11th St, Lanmadaw Township.

There are a couple of other simple *eateries* in the village, as well as a thatched-roof *bar* where various palm distillates are available.

Getting There & Away
Vehicle ferries cross the Yangon River to Dala from Sin Oh Dan Lan jetty between 18th and 19th Sts in Yangon at 9 am, and 1 and 5 pm; from Dala they leave at 8.30 am, and 12.30 and 4.30 pm. The fare is K160 for autos and small trucks, plus a K20 tax to be paid on either side of the river. The crossing takes just 15 minutes.

Pedestrian ferries cross to Dala from Pansodan Lan jetty about every 20 minutes in either direction, starting at 5 am and stopping at 8 pm. The cost is K5.

The road between Dala and Letkhokkon is in very poor condition in places. Count on close to four hours to complete the journey without stops, more by public transport. It's not easy getting to Letkhokkon by the latter.

First you must cross to Dala via the Pansodan Lan jetty pedestrian ferry (K5) or charter a sampan for K100. Near the row of restaurants and teashops on the Dala side you'll see a cluster of pickup trucks and jeeps; ask around to see if anyone's going to Letkhokkon. This isn't too common – usually only a couple of vehicles a day do this route direct. There are more frequent departures to Kunyangon, but there's no guarantee you'll find a vehicle there to continue to Letkhokkon.

Expect to pay about K3500 each way to hire a car or jeep from Dala to make the trip. Of course you could always hire a car and driver in Yangon; however, some drivers refuse to do the trip because the road is so hard on their vehicles.

Once in Letkhokkon it's usually not difficult to find a vehicle heading back to Dala.

PATHEIN
Situated on the eastern bank of the Pathein River (also known as the Ngawan River) in the Ayeyarwady Delta, about 190km west of Yangon, Pathein is the most important delta port outside the capital, despite its distance from the sea. It is surrounded by a major rice-growing area that produces the best rice available in Myanmar, including a high quality variety called *pawsanmwe htamin* (fragrant rice).

Noted for its colourful hand-painted umbrellas, the town is of some historic interest and was the scene for major clashes during the struggle for supremacy between the Mon and the Bamar. Later it became an important trade relay point for goods moving between India and South-East Asia. The city's name may derive from the Burmese word for Muslim – *pathi* – due to the heavy presence of Arab and Indian Muslim traders here centuries ago. The colonial Brits – or more likely their imported Indian civil servants – corrupted the name to Bassein.

Today, Pathein's population of 200,000 includes large contingents of Kayin (Karen) and Rakhaing. Although one part of a Mon kingdom, Pathein is home to only a few Mon today. During the 1970s and 1980s, the Kayin villages surrounding Pathein generated insurgent activity that has quelled to the point that Pathein is now open to foreign tourists. The recent growth of delta trade, particularly rice exports, has contributed to a general air of prosperity in Myanmar's fourth largest city.

The scenic waterfront area, markets, umbrella workshops and colourful payas make the city worth a stay of at least a night or two. It also serves as a jumping-off point for excursions to the small beach resort of Chaungtha and further north to Gwa and Thandwe in the Rakhaing State.

Post & Communications

The main post office is located towards the western end of Mahabandoola Lan near the clock tower. Since there's no air service between Pathein and Yangon, mail is slow, but the Pathein postal service is supposed to be reasonably reliable.

You can make domestic trunk calls and international calls from the telephone office next door. However, the wait can be up to an hour for either.

Shwemokhtaw Paya

In the centre of Pathein, near the riverfront, looms the golden, bell-shaped stupa at Shwemokhtaw Paya. One legend says it was originally built by India's Buddhist king Asoka in 305 BC as a small stupa called Shwe Arna. Standing 2.3m tall, this original stupa supposedly enshrined Buddha relics and a 6 inch gold bar. Another legend says a Muslim princess named Onmadandi requested each of her three Buddhist lovers to build a stupa in her honour. One of the lovers erected Shwemokhtaw, the others the less distinguished Tazaung and Thayaunggyaung payas.

Whichever story you believe, Bagan's King Alaungsithu is thought to have erected an 11m stupa called Htupayon over this site in 1115 AD. Then, in 1263, King Samodagossa took power, raised the stupa to 40m and changed the name to Shwemokhtaw Paya, which means Stupa of the Half-Foot Gold Bar. The stupa's main shape has re-

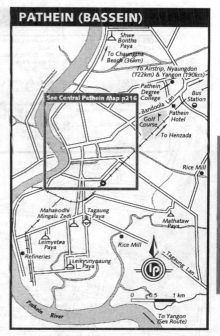

mained the same since then, although the changing of the decorative *hti* (umbrella-like decorated top) has increased the height to its present 46.6m. The current hti consists of a topmost layer made from 6.3kg of solid gold, a middle tier of pure silver and a bottom tier of bronze; all three tiers are gilded and reportedly embedded with a total of 829 diamond fragments, 843 rubies and 1588 semiprecious stones.

The southern shrine of the compound houses the **Thiho-shin Phondaw-pyi** sitting Buddha image, which supposedly floated to the delta coast on a raft from Sri Lanka in ancient times. According to legend, an unknown Sinhalese sculptor fashioned four different Buddha images using pieces from the original bodhi tree mixed with a cement composite. He then placed them on four wooden rafts and set the rafts adrift on the ocean. One landed in Dawei (Tavoy), and is

AROUND YANGON

CENTRAL PATHEIN

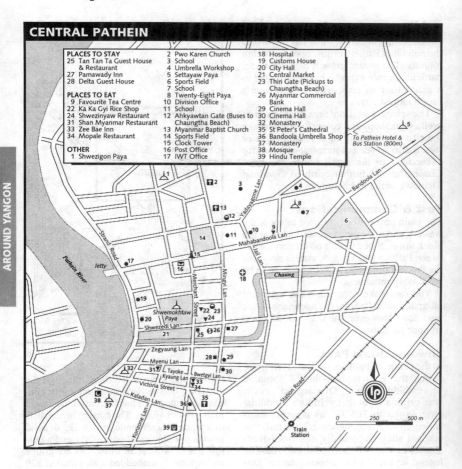

PLACES TO STAY
25 Tan Tan Ta Guest House
   & Restaurant
27 Pamawady Inn
28 Delta Guest House

PLACES TO EAT
9 Favourite Tea Centre
22 Ka Ka Gyi Rice Shop
24 Shwezinyaw Restaurant
31 Shan Myanmar Restaurant
33 Zee Bae Inn
34 Mopale Restaurant

OTHER
1 Shwezigon Paya

2 Pwo Karen Church
3 School
4 Umbrella Workshop
5 Settayaw Paya
6 Sports Field
7 School
8 Twenty-Eight Paya
10 Division Office
11 School
12 Ahkyawtan Gate (Buses to
   Chaungtha Beach)
13 Myanmar Baptist Church
14 Sports Field
15 Clock Tower
16 Post Office
17 IWT Office

18 Hospital
19 Customs House
20 City Hall
21 Central Market
23 Thiri Gate (Pickups to
   Chaungtha Beach)
26 Myanmar Commercial
   Bank
29 Cinema Hall
30 Cinema Hall
32 Monastery
35 St Peter's Cathedral
36 Bandoola Umbrella Shop
37 Monastery
38 Mosque
39 Hindu Temple

now housed at the Shin-Mokhti Paya; another landed at Kyaikkami (Amherst), and is now at Yele Paya; the third landed at Kyaikto and is now at Kyaikpawlaw; and the fourth landed near Phondawpyi, a fishing village about 97km south of Pathein. In 1445 the Mon queen Shinsawpu purportedly brought the latter image to Pathein, then known as Kuthima.

A marble standing Buddha positioned in a niche in the fence running along the western side of the stupa marks a spot where Mon warriors once prayed before battle. In the north-western corner of the compound is a shrine to Shin Upagot, the bodhisattva who floats on the ocean and appears to those in trouble. At this shrine his lotus raft is flanked by blue dragons representing the sea; live turtles swim in the water surrounding the small pavilion.

The people of Pathein celebrate Vesakha (Thrice-Blessed Day) with a huge *paya pwe* (pagoda festival) during the full moon of Kason (April/May).

Settayaw Paya

Of the several lesser-known payas in Pathein, perhaps the most charming is this one dedicated to a mythical Buddha footprint left by the Enlightened One during his legendary perambulations through mainland South-East Asia.

The paya compound wraps over a couple of green hillocks dotted with well constructed *tazaungs* (shrine buildings) – altogether a nice setting and a change from the flat paya compounds near the river. The footprint symbol itself is the usual oblong, 1m-long impression and not very interesting. In the same pavilion, however, a well done Mandalay-style bronze Buddha stands over the footprint. All too visible in the compound is a garishly painted 11m standing Buddha. The group of whitewashed stupas on the slight rise below were built by the famous Burmese musician Po Sein.

Other Religious Monuments

One of the standard sights in town is the so-called **Twenty-Eight Paya**, a rectangular shrine building containing 28 sitting and 28 standing images – none of them is particularly distinguished except that the latter appear in the open-robe Mandalay style rather than the closed-robe pose typical of Mandalay standing images. At one end of the hall stands a group of crude sculptures depicting a *jataka* (scene from the Buddha's life), in which Buddha teaches a disciple the relativity of physical beauty by comparing a monkey, the disciple's wife and a *deva* (spirit-being) Although it's not that interesting a sight, the shrine is a short walk from Pathein's main umbrella workshops. You may have to ask the caretaker to unlock the building.

More interesting from an artistic perspective is **Tagaung Mingala Zeditaw** (Tagaung Paya), centred around a graceful stupa that swoops inward from a wide, whitewashed base to a gleaming silver superstructure. Look for the small squirrel sculpture extending from the western side of the upper stupa and representing a previous incarnation of Buddha as a squirrel. One of the pavilions at the base of the stupa contains a very large sitting Buddha image. Local legend says the stupa is the same age as Shwemokhtaw, but like most famous stupas in Myanmar, the truth is buried beneath several layers of royal renovations. The latest refurbishing was carried out in 1979. Tagaung Paya is about 3km south of Kaladan Lan, past the railway line.

West of Tagaung Paya, a little way towards the river, stands **Mahabodhi Mingala Zedi**, patterned after the world-famous Mahabodhi stupa in Bodhgaya, India. **Leikyunynaung Paya**, a couple of kilometres directly south of Mahabodhi, was renovated by the State Law and Order Restoration Council (SLORC), now the State Peace and Development Council (SPDC), using conscript labour in the early 1990s to create a facsimile of Ananda Paya in Bagan. Its main distinguishing characteristic is that it can easily be seen at a distance from boats passing along the river. Since the renovation few people outside the government worship here.

A kilometre or so north-east of Leikyunynaung is **Leimyetna Paya**, which features a large, but particularly ugly, sitting Buddha. Even worse is the gaudily painted sitting Buddha at **Shwezigon Paya**, at the northern end of town.

Parasol Workshops

Most of the 'umbrellas' made in Pathein are actually parasols; ie they aren't waterproof, but are used as a defence against the hot delta sun. Around 25 parasol workshops are scattered throughout the northern part of the city, particularly in the vicinity of the Twenty-Eight Paya shrine, off Mahabandoola Lan. The parasols come in a variety of colours; some are brightly painted with flowers, birds and other nature motifs. One type that can be used in the rain is the saffron-coloured monks' umbrella, which is waterproofed by applying various coats of tree resin; a single umbrella may take five days to complete, including the drying process. Parasols and umbrellas can be ordered in any size directly from the workshops. Bargaining usually isn't too fierce as the parasols are reasonably priced, even cheap, for basic ones.

Most workshops welcome visitors who

want to observe this craft. One of the easiest to find – and one with high-quality work – is the workshop opposite the entrance to the Twenty-Eight Paya.

Other Attractions

At the **night bazaar** that is set up each evening in front of Customs House along Strand Rd, vendors purvey food, clothing, textiles, tools, housewares and just about every other requisite for daily life at low prices. Just south of Shwemokhtaw Paya is the central market, and just south of that is a newer market, with all manner of goods. Both markets are closed on Sunday.

The **golf course** next to the Pathein Hotel has 18 holes that can be played for a reasonable K1500 greens fee.

Places to Stay

The centrally located **Tan Tan Ta Guest House & Restaurant** (long known as the Golden Dove Hotel) on Merchant St on the corner of Shwezedi Lan offers simple, clean rooms with air-con, TV and attached bath for US$7/15 a single/double. Three similar economy rooms are available without TV or aircon for US$5 per person. There are also nine single economy rooms with fan and common bath for US$3 per person. The restaurant serves decent Chinese and Bamar food.

The **Pamawady Inn** (☎ 042-21165, 14-A Mingyi Lan) is a 10 minute walk from the harbour and is the best of the bunch. Set back in a garden compound, the little hotel offers nine very clean air-con rooms for US$15/20. There are also a couple of economy rooms with fan and shared bath for US$5/10.

The **Delta Guest House** (☎ 042-22131, 44 Mingyi Lan) is a good central choice. Small, simple and well kept rooms cost US$3 per person with common bath downstairs; US$8 a room (one or two people) upstairs with air-con and private bath.

The only other place to stay is at the **Pathein Hotel** (☎ 042-22599), an L-shaped, two storey building on spacious grounds near the bus station off Bandoola Lan. Large rooms on the upper floor come with air-con, fridge, TV and hot-water shower

for US$20/40. Not bad overall, but a bit pricey considering the distance from town.

Places to Eat

Pathein has several decent restaurants, most of them central. Thanks to the Bamar restaurant revival that started in Yangon and Mandalay, there's now a choice in Pathein, to go with the usual assortment of Chinese or Indian dishes. **Shan Myanmar Restaurant** on the corner of Konzone and Bwetgyi Sts and **Ka Ka Gyi Rice Shop**, across Merchant St from Shwemokhtaw Paya, both offer good curries and hot-sour soups for lunch or dinner.

Shwezinyaw Restaurant (24/25 Shwezedi Lan), near Merchant St is a Bamar/Indian-Muslim hybrid with good curries and biryani. It's open daily from 8 am to 9 pm. The biryani (dan bauk) at nearby **Mopale Restaurant**, on Merchant St is even better, though the place closes by 7 pm.

Among the more well known and longest-running Chinese places is the **Zee Bae Inn** on Merchant St. This narrow, two storey spot has been serving large bowls of noodles and other Chinese dishes since the 1950s. The downstairs area opens onto the street, while upstairs there's an air-con dining room. The restaurant usually opens around 9 or 10 am and closes around 7 or 8 pm.

Favorite Tea Centre, on Mahabandoola Lan near Jail Rd, serves good quality tea and snacks. Opposite the golf course on Bandoola Lan, near the Pathein Hotel, is the **Shuginthat Tea Shop** (the English sign reads Golf Restaurant). This tranquil, indoor/outdoor spot is a good place to enjoy tea and Bamar snacks at a leisurely pace.

Several **noodle shops** occupy 1940s-vintage buildings along Konzone Lan, near the central market.

Yegyi If you're coming by car from Pyay, the town of Yegyi makes the best mid-point stop. **U Ba Gyi Rice Shop** (no sign), behind the train station in the central market, is a dirty-looking place with decent Bamar food. A very good hot-sour vegetable soup comes as a side dish with all meals.

Getting There & Away

Air Pathein has an airstrip out at the northeast edge of the city, but at the time of writing it didn't field any regularly scheduled flights. If it's ever expanded to handle Myanma Airways' (MA) Fokkers, it will only be a half-hour flight from Yangon.

Bus Buses are available from Yangon's Hsimmalaik bus centre for K400. Departures are at 4.30, 6 and 9 am, noon and 2 pm. The trip averages five hours. Tickets should be purchased at least a day in advance for morning departures; you can usually get a ticket the same day for the noon or 2 pm departure. All buses and minibuses are air-con, more or less. There are several bus companies operating between Yangon and Pathein. The best of the group seems to be Htet Aung Express (☎ 01-513173); its Hsimmalaik office is open daily from 7 am to 6 pm. Be prepared to ask around; most of the signs are in Burmese. Also be prepared to follow your fellow passengers when you transfer to another bus at the first ferry crossing on the way to Pathein. Buses will generally drop you anywhere you request in Pathein.

Buses depart from Pathein for Yangon from 5 am until about noon from Yinsuntan bus station. Most buses will also pick up passengers from Pathein hotels.

Train Pathein is accessible by train, but since you have to travel some distance north towards Pyay and then turn south, making a ferry crossing along the way, the train trip takes a lengthy 14 hours minimum.

Car Pathein can be reached by car from Yangon in about five hours. The usual route is to drive 1½ hours (68km) north-west to Nyaungdon (Yandoon or Yangdon on some maps) on the eastern bank of the Ayeyarwady River. Experienced drivers will know when it's best to leave to meet the vehicle ferry across the Ayeyarwady – it leaves every two hours between 6 am and 6 pm. From Nyaungdon to Pathein is another 122km; about 2½ to three hours under normal driving conditions. Along the way you

must cross several rivers and streams by bridge. There are a few military checkpoints along this route – including one where Aung San Suu Kyi was detained while on her way to a National League for Democracy (NLD) political rally in Pathein, after slipping unnoticed out of Yangon. This 1998 stand-off between the country's most outspoken dissident and the embarrassed military lasted six days. Ma Suu stayed with the car and her companions the entire time, before returning to Yangon.

To reach Pathein from Pyay, you must first drive a little north to meet the ferry across the Ayeyarwady. Once across the river you continue west towards Taungup, turning south at the first major junction. From here, a new road south to Myanaung runs smooth and wide for 60km or so, then deteriorates considerably for the rest of the journey to Pathein. There are many checkpoints along this route. Yegyi is the most well equipped stop-off point for trucks, buses and cars along the Pyay-Pathein road.

Boat New Chinese triple-deckers (Bala series) have recently started making the Yangon-Pathein trip, and foreigners have had to pay in dollars; ordinary class costs US$9 per person, and puts you on the middle deck. For US$33 per person you can get an air-con cabin on the top deck. Two of these express boats leave Yangon's Lan Thit jetty daily at 3 and 5 pm, each arriving the next morning in Pathein. Foreigners must buy tickets from the deputy division manager's office next to Building 63 on Lan Thit jetty. Older boats with much cheaper ticket prices are available for Burmese, but so far foreigners have been encouraged to use the new class of service.

AROUND PATHEIN

Horseshoe-shaped **Inye Lake**, 70km northeast of the city near the village of Kyonpyaw, is a favourite weekend picnic spot. Local fishermen sell fresh fish from the lake.

If you follow the Pathein River till it empties into the Andaman Sea you'll reach **Mawdin Point** (Mawdinsoun), the site of a famous festival during the lunar month of Tabodwe (February/March). On the sea side of the cape, at its point, is a sandy beach and the revered stupa of **Mawdin Paya**. Once a week or so, a boat to Mawdin leaves the main Pathein jetty around 6 am and arrives at 2 pm, but since there's no lodging licensed for foreigners at Mawdin, this is strictly a trip for risk-takers.

During the Mawdin Point festival there are special boats running daily – this would probably be the best time of year to attempt a trip since more guesthouses open especially for the festival.

Huge **Diamond Island** lies in the midst of the mouth of the Pathein River and is an important sea-turtle hatchery.

Other interesting delta towns include **Labooda** and **Hpayapon**, both of which can be reached by long-distance ferry from Yangon.

Chaungtha Beach

West of Pathein, on the Bay of Bengal coast, Chaungtha Beach has recently opened to foreign tourists. As western coast beaches go, this one fits somewhere between Letkhokkon, farther south, and Ngapali, to the north, in terms of quality. At low tide the very wide beach has a touch of the 'muddy delta' look, but overall at medium and high tide it's attractive enough, with fine, beige sand, backed by coconut palms and casuarina trees. **Kyaukpahto**, at one end of the beach near a cluster of boulders, is a large rock that's been carved into a *gu* (cave shrine). Offshore lies a modest coral reef with decent snorkelling except during the rainy season, when water clarity is poor.

At the opposite end of the beach is the mouth of the U Do Chaung, which wraps around the back of Chaungtha village to create a small peninsula. Because there's a military post at the southern end of the peninsula, it seems to be a restricted zone – the Burmese don't usually walk in the area. Two islands can be seen offshore, **Theinbyu** and **Hpokkala**; although mainly inhabited by Burmese fisherfolk, the latter island is off-limits to foreign visitors, also due to some kind of military presence.

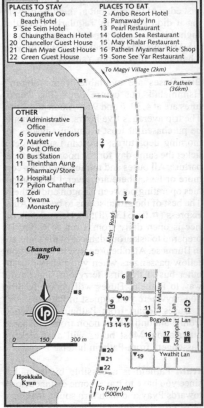

The village has a network of sand roads lined with simple wood or thatch houses. Most Chaungtha residents fish, or farm coconuts for a living; a couple of families also make furniture using rattan collected in nearby jungles. Many villagers speak the Rakhaing dialect. The village market is most active from 6 to 9 am. Towards the beach is a string of restaurants and handicraft vendors.

If you follow a path east, past a solar-powered hospital, you'll pass through a mangrove swamp and end up at a canal beach with a wooden jetty. On the canal side of the peninsula are rickety stilted structures used by the villagers for drying fish. Ferry services to nearby villages along the canal are still available from the jetty. You can also rent canoes for about K700 a half-day, or bicycles for about K500 a day.

Places to Stay Chaungtha receives heavy rainfall and high waves during the southwest monsoon season. Few people from the interior visit then, and traditionally all but a few hotels close down from 15 May to 15 September. In the past few years over 20 hotels and guesthouses have opened for business at Chaungtha. For reservations, some of the hotels list Yangon (01) or Pathein (042) telephone numbers.

The *Chaungtha Beach Hotel (☎ 042-22587)* used to be the only place to stay for foreigners, aside from a few army-owned bungalows. It's still there and has improved a bit since the competition arrived. Standard rooms with fan and attached bath cost US$8 per person. Superior rooms with a r-con, fridge and TV cost US$20/36 a single/couble. You'll get more for your money, though, at other beach chalets, including *See Seim Hotel (☎ 042-22509)*, on the beach, with clean rooms for US$15/20, all with fan and attached bath. There is also a five bed 'family room' that costs US$7 per person. The restaurant here is also quite good. The *Chaungtha Oo Beach Hotel (☎ 01-254708)* is at the far end of the beach north of the village, with bright blue and white chalet-type rooms for US$20/30.

Several good budget-level guesthouses are clustered around the village. Among the cleanest and friendliest are *Green Guest House*, *Chan Myae Guest House* and *Chancellor Guest House*, with fan and attached bath for US$4 to US$5 per person.

Places to Eat The main street into the village from the beach is lined with rustic seafood restaurants. The better ones include *Pearl Restaurant*, *Sone See Yar Restaurant*, *Golden Sea Restaurant*, *Pathein Myanmar*

Rice Shop and *May Khalar Restaurant*, all of which serve fresh lobster, clam, scallop and fish. There are also a few *teashops* along this strip, one of which opens early in the morning and serves decent *hsi htamin* (turmeric-coloured sticky rice topped with sesame seeds and shredded coconut) and other Bamar tea snacks.

The *restaurants* at the See Seim Hotel, Ambo Resort Hotel and Chaungtha Beach Hotel are quite good, and offer the advantage of a beach view.

Getting There & Away The rough 36km road to Chaungtha from Pathein can be traversed in two hours by private car; public minibuses and pickups usually take about three hours. Two buses leave the Pathein bus station daily at 7 and 11 am for Chaungtha for K300 per person. Pickups are also available from a roadstop near the Shwemokhtaw Paya at 1 pm for half the bus fare. Buses and trucks from Chaungtha Beach to Pathein leave at the same times, 7 and 11 am, and 1 pm from the bus station in the village. Several of the Yangon to Pathein buses continue to Chaungtha Beach. Unless you're in a hurry to get to the coast, stop in Pathein for a night before continuing on the rugged delta roads.

Whether by public or private vehicle, from Pathein you first cross the Pathein River by ferry; the ferry runs daily, roughly every hour from 6 am to 6 pm. In the reverse direction, if you get stuck waiting for a ferry back from Pathein, there are five thatched-roof restaurants where you can hang out.

Parts of the road to Chaungtha are sealed, some are unsealed. The road passes through nearly barren scrubland before crossing the U Do Chaung by bridge, and after that climbs forested hills to an elevation of around 300m. This area is said to be inhabited by elephants, monkeys and leopards; at one point you'll pass through a lush forest reserve with an upper canopy of tall dipterocarps. From there, the road descends into an area of coconut groves and rice paddies. Over half the villages passed along the way are Kayin.

Until the road was cut from Pathein, the only way to reach Chaungtha was by ferry along the U Do Chaung. From the Chaung jetty in Chaungtha, you may be able to book a passage on a boat to Mawdin Point, 12 hours south by schooner.

North of Yangon

HTAUKKYANT

On the road to Bago, beyond Yangon's airport at Mingaladon, you reach Htaukkyant, where the road to Pyay forks off to the north-west, while the Bago and Mandalay road continues on to the north-east. Shortly beyond the junction is the huge Htaukkyant War Cemetery with the graves of 27,000 Allied soldiers who died in the Burma and Assam campaigns of WWII. Maintained by the Commonwealth War Graves Commission, the cemetery is beautifully landscaped.

You can get to Htaukkyant on a No 9 bus from Yangon or aboard any Bago-bound bus from either the Highway bus centre or Hsimmalaik bus centre.

BAGO (PEGU)

Situated only about 80km from Yangon, Bago is easily reached from the capital yet is just far enough off the beaten track to avoid tourists. There are now several hotels and guesthouses where you can spend the night, and if you're on your way to Mt Kyaiktiyo or Mawlamyaing (Moulmein), an overnight stay here will break up the journey nicely.

Bago was reputedly founded in 573 AD by two Mon princes from Thaton, who saw a female goose standing on the back of a male goose on an island in a huge lake. Taking this to be an auspicious omen of some kind, they founded a royal capital called Hanthawady (from the Pali-Sanskrit Hamsavati, Kingdom of the Goose) at the edge of the lake. During the later Mon dynastic periods (1287 to 1539), Hanthawady became the centre of the Mon kingdom of Ramanadesa, which consisted of all Lower Myanmar.

The Bamar took over in 1539 when King Tabinshwehti annexed Bago to his Taungoo

kingdom. The city was frequently mentioned by early European visitors – who knew it as Pegu – as an important seaport. In 1740 the Mon, after a period of submission to Taungoo, re-established Bago as their capital, but in 1757 King Alaungpaya sacked and utterly destroyed the city. King Bodawpaya, who ruled from 1782 to 1819, rebuilt it to some extent, but when the river changed its course the city was cut off from the sea and lost its importance as a seaport. It never again reached its previous grandeur.

In deference to legend, the symbol for Bago is a female *hamsa* (*hintha* or *hantha* in Burmese; a mythological bird) standing on the back of a male hamsa. At a deeper level, the symbol honours the compassion of the male hamsa in providing a place for the female to stand in the middle of a lake with only one island. Hence, the men of Bago are said to be more chivalrous than men from other Burmese areas. In popular Burmese culture, however, men joke that they dare not marry a woman from Bago for fear of being henpecked!

Kanbawzathadi Palace & Museum

Recently, the original Hanthawady site surrounding a former Mon palace was excavated just south of the huge Shwemawdaw Paya. Walled in the Mon style, the square city measured 1.8km along each side and featured 20 gates in total. The palace compound in the centre, known as Kanbawzathadi, housed King Bayinnaung from 1553 (or 1566 according to some sources) to 1599 and covered 204 acres. About 64 acres of this area have been excavated. Bayinnaung, the brother-in-law of a Taungoo king, moved to Bago after conquering an older Mon principality called Oktha-myo, east of the Hanthawady site.

Only the palace's brick foundations are visible today. Everything else is being built anew, as at the Mandalay Palace (see the Mandalay Fort section in the Mandalay chapter), including the king's apartment and audience hall. Among other copied marvels, the original audience hall featured a seven level roof, two levels higher than Mandalay Palace, and was topped with solid gold tiles. The entire palace compound was originally surrounded by a teak stockade, a few stumps of which can be seen in the new museum. The government is keen to make the site into a showpiece of sorts, since King Bayinnaung ruled during an era when Burmese domains reached their farthest in South-East Asia. The nearby Mon site of Okthamyo, meanwhile, is all but ignored.

The small but well stocked, octagonal-shaped museum displays Mon, Siamese, and Bagan-style Buddhas; clay tobacco pipes; glazed tiles and pots; 'Martaban' jars (huge water jars from the delta area); bronze weights and scales; pieces of the original teak stockade; and weaponry. The museum is open Wednesday to Sunday from 9 am to 4 pm. Admission is US$4 (plus a K50 camera fee).

Shwemawdaw Paya

Shwemawdaw (Great Golden God) Paya stands north-east of the train station. You can't miss it, since its height of 114m dominates the town. The Shwemawdaw is said to be over 1000 years old and was originally built by the Mon to a height of 23m to enshrine two hairs of the Buddha. In 825 AD it was raised to 25m and then to 27m in 840. In 982 a sacred tooth was added to the collection; in 1385 another tooth was added and the stupa was rebuilt to a towering 34m. In 1492, the year Columbus sailed the Atlantic, a wind blew down the hti and a new one was raised.

King Bodawpaya, in the reconstruction of Bago after the ravages of Alaungpaya, rebuilt the stupa to 91m in 1796, but from that point it has had a rather chequered career. A new hti was added in 1882, but a major earthquake in 1912 brought it down. The stupa was repaired, but in 1917 another major quake again brought the hti down and caused serious damage. Again it was repaired, but in 1930 the biggest quake of them all completely levelled the stupa and for the next 20 years only the huge earth mound of the base remained.

Reconstruction of the Shwemawdaw commenced in 1952 and was completed in 1954, when it reached its present height. The glittering golden top of the stupa reaches 14m higher than the Shwedagon in Yangon. Shady trees around the base make it a pleasant place to stroll or simply sit and watch the Burmese. At the north-eastern corner of the stupa a huge section of the hti toppled by the 1917 earthquake has been mounted into the structure of the stupa. It is a sobering reminder of the power of such geological disturbances.

Like the Shwedagon, the stupa is reached by a covered walkway lined with stalls – a number with interesting collections of antique bits and pieces. Along the sides of the walkway a collection of rather faded and dusty paintings illustrates the terrible effects of the 1930 earthquake and shows the subsequent rebuilding of this mighty stupa.

The mouths of the two *chinthe* (a half-griffin/half-lion guardian beast) at the western entrance contain two Mahayana bodhisattvas, Shin Upagot (Upagupta, on the left) and Shin Thiwali (Sivali, on the right).

On the full moon of the Burmese lunar month of Tagu (March/April) the Shwemawdaw Paya festival attracts huge crowds of worshippers and merrymakers.

Admission costs US$2 (plus K25 camera fee; K200 video fee).

Hintha Gon Paya

Located behind the Shwemawdaw, this shrine has good views over Bago from the roofed platform on the hilltop. According to legend, this was the one point rising from the sea when the mythological bird (the hintha) landed here. A statue of the bird, looking rather like the figures on opium weights, tops the hill. The stupa was built by U Khanti, the hermit monk who was also the architect of Mandalay Hill. You can walk to it by taking the steps down the other side of the Shwemawdaw from the main entranceway. Admission is free.

Shwethalyaung Buddha

To the west of the Yangon-Bago road, only a little over a kilometre on the Yangon side of

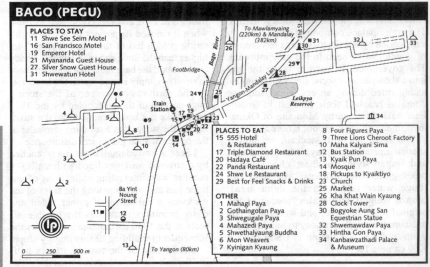

BAGO (PEGU)

PLACES TO STAY
11 Shwe See Seim Motel
16 San Francisco Motel
19 Emperor Hotel
21 Myananda Guest House
27 Silver Snow Guest House
31 Shwewatun Hotel

To Mawlamyaing
(220km) & Mandalay
(382km)

Footbridge

Train
Station

Leikpya
Reservoir

Ba Yint
Noung
Street

0   250   500 m

To Yangon (80km)

PLACES TO EAT
15 555 Hotel
     & Restaurant
17 Triple Diamond Restaurant
20 Hadaya Café
22 Panda Restaurant
24 Shwe Le Restaurant
29 Best for Feel Snacks & Drinks

OTHER
1 Mahagi Paya
2 Gothaingotan Paya
3 Shwegugale Paya
4 Mahazedi Paya
5 Shwethalyaung Buddha
6 Mon Weavers
7 Kyinigan Kyaung

8 Four Figures Paya
9 Three Lions Cheroot Factory
10 Maha Kalyani Sima
12 Bus Station
13 Kyaik Pun Paya
14 Mosque
18 Pickups to Kyaiktiyo
23 Church
25 Market
26 Kha Khat Wain Kyaung
28 Clock Tower
30 Bogyoke Aung San
     Equestrian Statue
32 Shwemawdaw Paya
33 Hintha Gon Paya
34 Kanbawzathadi Palace
     & Museum

the train station, the Shwethalyaung is a huge reclining Buddha. Measuring 55m long and 16m high, it is a good 9m longer than the reclining Buddha at Wat Pho in Bangkok, but still 19m short of the Buddha in Dawei. A sign on the platform in front of the image gives the measurements of each body part; the little finger alone extends 3.05m.

The Shwethalyaung is reputed to be one of the most lifelike of all reclining Buddhas. The Burmese say the image represents Buddha in a 'relaxing' mode – instead of *parinibbana* (death) – since the eyes are wide open and the feet lie slightly splayed rather than parallel.

The sturdy iron shed that houses the image may look rough and ready, but it's spacious and airy and gives you a far better view than offered by the cramped cells of most reclining Buddhas. The walkway up to the platform is crowded with souvenir and handicraft stalls.

Originally built of brick and stucco in 994 AD by the Mon King Migadepa II, the Shwethalyaung was allowed to deteriorate and was then restored several times during

its existence before the destruction of Bago in 1757. The town was so completely ravaged that the huge Buddha was totally lost and overgrown by jungle. It was not found until the 1880s British era, when an Indian contractor, digging in a large earth mound for fill to be used in the construction of the railway line, rediscovered the image. Restoration began in 1881 and the present iron and steel tazaung, a product of a Calcutta engineering company, was completed in 1903. The 1930s saw another flurry of renovative activity, as mosaic was added to the great pillow on which the Buddha's head rests, and Italian marble was laid along the platform.

Near the huge head of the image stands a **statue of Lokanat** (Lokanatha or Avalokitesvara), a Mahayana Buddhist deity borrowed by Burmese Buddhism. Behind the reclining Buddha image is a set of huge painted reliefs depicting the legend of the founding of the image. Foreigner admission is US$2 and is worth it.

A Japanese war cemetery, **Kyinigan Kyaung**, can be seen on the grounds of a monastery just north of Shwethalyaung.

North-west of this monastery, a settlement of **Mon weavers** use handlooms to produce cotton *longyis* (sarong-style garments) and other textiles.

Maha Kalyani Sima (Maha Kalyani Thein)

This 'Sacred Hall of Ordination' was originally constructed in 1476 by Dhammazedi, the famous alchemist king and son of Queen Shinsawpu. It stands beside the road en route from the train station to the Shwethalyaung. It was the first of 397 similar *simas* (ordination halls) he built around the country, copying plans brought back from Ceylon. De Brito, the Portuguese adventurer, burnt it down in 1599 during his period of plunder, and during the sack of Bago, it was destroyed once again.

Subsequently it suffered from fires or quakes on a number of occasions before being levelled by the disastrous 1930 quake. As with the Shwemawdaw, reconstruction was completed in 1954. Next to the hall are 10 large tablets with inscriptions in Pali and Mon. The hall itself features rows of vented arches around the outside, with an impressive separate cloister and marble floors inside. Niches along the inside upper walls contain 28 standing Buddha images.

Across the road from the Maha Kalyani Sima, by the corner, is a curious monument with four Buddha figures standing back to back, in somewhat similar fashion to the four seated Buddhas at the Kyaik Pun (see later Kyaik Pun Paya entry later in this section) on the outskirts of town. An adjacent open hallway has a small reclining Buddha image, thronged by followers, and some macabre paintings of wrongdoers being tortured in the afterlife.

Mahazedi Paya

Continuing beyond the Shwethalyaung brings you to the Mahazedi (Great Stupa) Paya. Originally constructed in 1560 AD by King Bayinnaung, it was destroyed during the 1757 sack of Bago. An attempt to rebuild it in 1860 was unsuccessful and the great earthquake of 1930 comprehensively levelled it, after which it remained a ruin. This current reconstruction was only completed in 1982. Stairways lead up the outside of the stupa, and from the top there are fine views over the surrounding area. Note the model stupa by the entrance.

The Mahazedi originally had a Buddha tooth, at one time thought to be the actual Buddha tooth of Kandy, Sri Lanka. After Bago was conquered in 1539, the tooth was later moved to Taungoo and then to Sagaing near Mandalay. Together with a begging bowl supposed to have been used by the Buddha, it remains in the Kaunghmudaw Paya, near Sagaing, to this day. Admission here is US$2.

Shwegugale Paya

A little beyond the Mahazedi, this zedi has a dark *gu* (tunnel) around the circumference of the cylindrical superstructure. The monument dates to 1494 and the reign of King Byinnya Yan. Inside are 64 seated Buddha figures. From here you can take a short cut back to the corner in the road, just before the Shwethalyaung. Admission is free.

Kyaik Pun Paya

About 1.5km out of Bago on the Yangon road, and then a couple of hundred metres to the west of the road, stands Kyaik Pun Paya. Built in 1476 by King Dhammazedi, it consists of four 30m-high sitting Buddhas placed back-to-back around a huge, square pillar. According to legend, four Mon sisters were connected with the construction of the Buddhas; it was said that if any of them should marry, one of the Buddhas would collapse. One of the four disintegrated in the 1930 earthquake, leaving only a brick outline. It has since been fully restored.

En route to the Kyaik Pun Paya, you can detour to the picturesque **Gaung-Say-Kyan Paya**, reached by crossing a wooden bridge over a small lake. Admission is free.

Other Attractions

North of the main town centre, near the eastern bank of the river, is one of the three largest monasteries in the country, **Kha Khat**

Wain Kyaung. Watching the long line of monks and novices file out of the monastery in the early morning for their daily alms round is quite a sight.

Many Bago women work in local cheroot factories – there are around 15 large ones, many smaller ones. The **Three Lions factory** lies a little north of the road to Shwethalyaung, from the main avenue through town; the proprietors don't mind receiving visitors. Farther west, towards Mahazedi Paya, you can visit a **woodcarving workshop**.

Bago has a very interesting **market** just across the river from the train station. Take some time to wander around the various market buildings. The market serves as a distribution point for cloth, household items, and other imports from Thailand and beyond.

On the highway to Yangon, south of town, is **Hanthawady Golf & Country Club**, a military-built 18 hole golf course, now operated by a Japanese company. Greens fees are US$15; a caddy is US$2, and you can rent clubs.

Places to Stay

The best budget places are on the busy main road. Rooms towards the back of these hotels will be quieter. The six storey, modern-looking *Emperor Hotel (☎ 052-21349)*, on the main avenue through town between the railway and the river, has a friendly, English-speaking manager. Small but clean rooms cost US$6/10 a single/double with fan and attached Asian-style toilet and bath; US$8/16 with air-con and hot water. A much larger family room goes for US$40.

The small and friendly *Myananda Guest House (☎ 052-22275)* is on the main road a few doors towards the river from the Hadaya Café, and is a good budget choice. Economy rooms with fan, shared bath and toilet are US$4 per person. One triple room has air-con, fridge, TV and attached cold-water bath for US$12.

Farther south-west near the railway crossing, the *San Francisco Motel (☎ 052-22265)* has rooms with shared toilet and bath for US$4 to US$6 per person, or US$8/12 with attached bath. Double rooms in the

new wing (west) are cleaner and brighter looking, and cost US$10.

Across the Bago River, near the reservoir and opposite the clock tower, is the *Silver Snow Guest House*, with clean economy rooms at US$5 per person, and rooms with attached bath for US$15/20. There is no air-con, but all rooms have fan and a mosquito net upon request.

Slightly fancier is the nine room *Shwe See Seim Motel (☎ 052-22118, 354 Ba Yint Noung Lan)*, near the bus station. Bungalow units and regular rooms both cost US$24/30. There is a small and fairly dirty pool.

Out towards the Shwemawdaw Paya, on the road east to Mawlamyaing, the sprawling government-owned *Shwewatun Hotel (☎ 052-21263)* offers clean rooms for US$24/30, with ceiling fans and cold-water bath; US$42/60 with air-con, hot water and fridge. This is clearly overpriced in comparison with the rates for central hotels. The hotel restaurant has decent food.

Places to Eat

The friendly but shabby *555 Hotel & Restaurant*, a few doors west of the Emperor Hotel, is a popular eatery and not a hotel. The menu is a combination of Bamar, Chinese, Indian and European; the food is cheap and good, and the menu includes 'goat fighting balls' (goat testicles) prepared in a number of ways. Next door is *Triple Diamond Restaurant*, popular with locals and a bit cheaper than 555. The standard rice or noodle dish is K200. The medium-priced *Panda Restaurant*, just west of river, offers a good, standard Chinese menu.

Half a block north of the main road is a clean and quiet gem, *Shwe Le Restaurant (194 Strand St)*, just west of river. The menu features Shan, Indian and Malaysian curries from K200 to K400.

The *Hadaya Café*, opposite the Emperor Hotel, is a very popular teashop with a nice selection of pastries, ice cream and good-quality tea. *Best for Feel Snacks & Drinks (248 31st St)* features both western-style snacks and good Bamar curries in a quiet and comfortable setting.

In the centre of town on the small street facing the market are a number of *food stalls*, including some good Indian biryani stalls.

Getting There & Away

You can get to Bago by either rail or road; in either case the trip takes about two hours. It's very easy to day trip to Bago from Yangon, but put aside the whole day. An early start is probably the best idea, as Bago can get very hot around noon.

By road, the route to Bago follows the Mandalay road to Taukkyan, about 30km from the capital, where the Pyay road branches off. From here to Bago the country is much more open and the traffic somewhat lighter.

Air A new international airport south-west of town, towards Yangon, has been talked about for several years, but at the time of writing, the plan seemed to be on semi-permanent hold.

Bus The buses from Yangon operate approximately hourly from 5 or 6 am and depart from the Highway bus centre near the airport. The fare is K150. GEC Bus Company and Taung Hta Ban Company both make the two hour trip in relative comfort. Pickups depart from Hsimmalaik bus centre; the fare is K100 (K150 for a front seat). Avoid Sunday, however, when Bago is a very popular excursion from Yangon and the buses get very crowded. It can also be difficult to get back to Yangon because the buses will be booked out until late in the evening; you may want to catch a train back.

Mandalay Most of the private bus companies running air-con express buses between Yangon and Mandalay stop in Bago. While they usually won't sell tickets for the short distance between Yangon and Bago, you can book tickets from Bago onward to Mandalay – for the full Yangon-Mandalay fare (around K2000); the Mandalay buses usually arrive in Bago by 7 pm; inquire at the Bago bus station, or the travel desk in the lobby of the Emperor Hotel.

Train It is possible to visit Bago by breaking the Yangon-Mandalay train journey here. During the high season (November to February), it is wiser to do this coming down from Mandalay rather than going up from Yangon, because of the difficulties of getting a seat from Bago to Mandalay; from Bago to Yangon you could easily stand, so wait for another train or change to the bus.

From Yangon, there are about six trains a day from around 6 am to 8 pm. The foreigner fare from Yangon is US$2/5 for ordinary/upper class on the express train.

Another train runs between Bago, Kyaikto and Mawlamyaing three times a day. The cost between Bago and Kyaikto is US$3/6; between Bago and Mawlamyaing the fare is US$6/15. These are not express trains and, as usual, the buses are faster.

Taxi A more expensive but more convenient alternative is to hire a taxi from Yangon. A taxi between Yangon and Bago will cost about US$12 to US$15 each way, with a bit of bargaining – and has the additional advantage of giving you transport from place to place once you get to Bago. Inquire at any Bago hotel. Some drivers may feel that getting you to Bago and back, and to the two big attractions – the Shwemawdaw and the Shwethalyaung – is quite enough for one day. Don't accept excuses that other sites are 'too far off the road', are down tracks 'only fit for bullock carts' or are simply 'closed'. A good place to hire taxis for a Bago trip is near The Strand Hotel. Choose a driver with reasonable English-language skills.

If you hire a taxi in Bago, be sure that your driver agrees to drop you in Yangon at your hotel. Some drivers who lack the proper licence may get close to central Yangon, only to announce they risk a fine by continuing farther.

Kyaiktiyo A guide and driver to Mt Kyaiktiyo can be hired through any of the central Bago hotels for around US$40. The same tour booked in Yangon costs US$80. See the Kyaiktiyo section in the South-Eastern

Myanmar chapter for more information. Pickups to Kyaikityo depart from in front of Hadaya Café. The five hour trip costs K500.

Getting Around

Trishaw is the main form of local transport in Bago. A one way trip in the central area should cost no more that K30 to K35. If you're going further afield – say from Shwethalyaung Paya, at one end of town, to Shwemawdaw Paya, at the other – you might as well hire a trishaw for the day, which should cost no more than K300.

TAUNGOO

Although Taungoo (often spelt Toungoo) was once the centre of one of the most powerful post-Bagan kingdoms, virtually nothing visibly historic remains to indicate its former 15th to 16th century glory. Today it's simply a typical central Myanmar town supported by the timber trade. It's situated towards the northern end of the Bago Division, within sight of mountain ranges to both the east and west, the source of teak and other hardwoods.

Among Burmese the town is most known for its bounteous areca palms, which yield the nut used in betel chews. In Myanmar, when someone receives unexpected good fortune they are likened to a betel-lover receiving a paid trip to Taungoo.

Kayin State is less than 35km east, and another 65km or so further east is Kayah State. Karen and Kayah insurgents have been known to operate within these distances, and until very recently, Taungoo was considered off-limits for foreigners. A dry-weather road continues east all the way to Loikaw, but any travel beyond the Sittoung (Sittang) River a few kilometres to the east of Taungoo still requires special permission. Such permission is nearly impossible to obtain unless you're a teak buyer or mineral engineer.

Shwesandaw Paya

Situated in the centre of town west of the main road, this is Taungoo's grandest pilgrimage spot. The central stupa, a standard-issue bell shape, is gilded and dates to 1597; local legend says an earlier stupa on the site was built centuries before and contains sacred hair relics. A pavilion on the western side of the stupa contains a large bronze Mandalay-style sitting Buddha, given to the paya in 1912 by a retired civil servant who donated his body weight in bronze and silver for the casting of the image. He died three years after the casting, at age 72; his ashes are interred behind the image, which stands 3.6m high.

Another pavilion in the north-western corner of the compound houses a garish reclining Buddha surrounded by devas and monastic disciples. Glass cabinets along the wall display small religious objects and Buddhas donated by the faithful; only a few are old. Among the other tazaungs is one that displays sculptures of the seven Taungoo kings, a small Kuan Yin pavilion to placate the Chinese, a *nat* (spirit) shrine with images of Saraswati and her attendants, and a Shin Upagot shrine.

Myasigon Paya

Though not as well known as Shwesandaw, this is the most interesting of the three famous zedis in towns. A brick pahto beneath the stupa features glass mosaic arches, paintings of Taungoo kings and a huge, bronze-and-silver-faced sitting Buddha in royal attire. The image is surrounded by planet Buddhas, an arrangement usually reserved for stupas. Smaller Buddhas, some of them old, are displayed in glass cases in the same building. Opposite the large sitting image, against a couple of pillars, are two Chinese bronze goddess statues, one sitting on an elephant, the other on a Fu dog. An inscription says the figures were donated to the paya in 1901 by a German Buddhist.

A small museum on the grounds contains bronze images of Erawan (the three headed elephant who serves as Indra's mount), a standing Buddha captured from Thailand by King Bayinnaung and two British cannons dated 1897. Other items of lesser artistic or historic import include modern sculptures of famous disciples of the Buddha, such as

Mogalla and Sariputta, 100-year-old *hsun ok* (food-offering pedestals), terracotta votive tablets, old coins and stamps.

Other Attractions

In spite of the fact that seven kings reigned over Taungoo for a total of 155 years, all that's left of the secular kingdom known then as Kaytumadi are a few earthen ramparts and a moat on the western side of town. Nearby **Lay Kyaung Kandawgyi**, the town's 'royal lake', features a few small islands topped with pavilions.

Follow the road west of the lake to reach **Kawmudaw Paya**, said to be the oldest religious site in Taungoo. The central pink-and-white, bell-shaped stupa is not that impressive. A mirrored pillar marks the 'earth-conquering' spot from which Taungoo kings set off to conquer other armies. Worshippers walk clockwise around the pillar in the hope of conquering their personal problems.

Elephant Camp Over the past few years, Taungoo has become the starting point for trips to nearby **Sein Ye Forest Camp**, a working elephant camp in a mountainous area of Karen villages and teakwood plantations. Visitors who reach the camp can proceed into the forest either on foot or by riding an elephant. How far you get and how much you see simply depends on whether you're on a day-return trip, or on spending the night at a camp 'resort', or even in one of the villages.

There are two ways to do the trip, either by making your own arrangements, or by arranging a one or two-day tour out of Taungoo. In either case, inquire at the Sawasdee Restaurant & Guest House, or at the Myanmar Beauty Guesthouse (see the following Places to Stay entry for contact details). The manager at Sawasdee can arrange a day-return trip for US$40 per person, which includes the necessary permits, transportation there and back, a walk into the forest area and a chance to ride on an elephant. The price includes a Chinese lunch and plenty of bottled water. Tours can also be arranged in Yangon. Contact Woodland Travel (☎ 01-246636) for 'eco-tour' information; expect to pay about US$100 a day.

The more adventurous alternative is to hire your own jeep or pickup with driver for about US$25 to US$30 (or kyat equivalent), obtain the necessary permits (US$20 per person total) and go. If you visit overnight, you can make arrangements to stay in one of two Karen villages (Shwe Daung or Mgwe Taung), or splurge at the Sein Yee camp 'resort' that costs US$60 for a double room; it's not fancy, but it has hot water and everything you'll need for a comfortable night's sleep.

Places to Stay

From the main road through Taungoo, turn west before the Taungoo Baptist Church onto Bo Hmu Pho Kun Lan to reach *Myanmar Beauty Guest House* (also known as Myanma A-Hla) (☎ *054-21270, 21527, 7/134 Bo Hmu Pho Kun Lan*). It's just a couple blocks north of the main market. This is easily the best value in town, with sparkling clean rooms with bath and air-con for US$6 per person. Similar rooms with fan and common bath are just US$3 per person. All rooms have mosquito netting upon request, and an excellent Bamar-western breakfast is included – complete with fresh fruit and local coffee and tea. The guesthouse is owned by two doctors (husband and wife), Dr Tin and Dr Yee, who seem to delight in conversing with international travellers. They also maintain a clinic at the front of the compound.

Other places to stay in Taungoo include the government-leased *Myanma Thiri Hotel* (☎ *054-21764*). It's well off the eastern side of the main road towards the southern end of town and is a two storey, thick-walled, colonial-style building with colonnaded front. Large, well maintained rooms with good beds, satellite TV, fridge, air-con, ceiling fans and private hot-water showers cost US$24/36/48 a single/double/triple including breakfast. Though usually on the empty side, the hotel is off the main road in a quiet compound, with a decent Chinese/Bamar restaurant within.

Min Kyee Nyo Guest House (652 Nanda Kyaw Hti Lan) is a small place off the main road, offering clean and comfortable rooms for US$10/15, and a couple of economy rooms for US$3 with fan and common bath facilities.

The *Sawasdee Restaurant & Guest House* (☎ 054-21614), on the main road, has three decent economy rooms with fan and common cold-water bath for US$5 per person, and two air-con rooms with bath for US$7 per person.

Places to Eat

For tasty, Chinese-Bamar fare, try either *Happy Restaurant*, opposite the Myanmar department store, or the similar *Golden Myanmar Restaurant*, across the road. Both of these indoor-outdoor eateries are on the main road through town, near the corner of Bo Hmu Pho Kun Lan.

South of the Myanma Thiri Hotel, the *Sawasdee Restaurant* is owned by a local man who worked in Thailand for a couple of years. In addition to an indoor dining room, there are a handful of little thatched-roof dining areas outdoors. The menu features a long list of Chinese dishes, and a few Bamar and Thai dishes as well. Prices are reasonable. Fresh prawns from the Sittoung River are a house speciality. It's open daily from 7 am to 10 or 11 pm. The *Khayanpya Restaurant*, next door, is similar.

Mandalay Htamin Zain (Mandalay Rice Shop) has been serving Bamar food since 1914 (at its current location since 1964), and thus claims the honour of being the oldest restaurant in Myanmar. It's on a side street, off the western side of the main road, near the main market – look for two peacock reliefs over the door.

At the night market that convenes next to the central market, *vendors* specialise in *chapatis* and meat-stuffed *palata* (fried flatbread). *Win Sanda* and *Sein Taik*, around the corner from Nansanda Guest House at the corner of the market, are two popular side-by-side teashops. One focuses on samosas, the other on *paug-si* (Chinese buns); they're open from 5.30 am to around 9 pm.

Getting There & Away

Bus Taungoo is considered a midway point for road trips between Yangon, Mandalay and Taunggyi. Kyaw Express and Leo Express stop at the Golden Myanmar Restaurant on the main road just after midnight. Fares to either Yangon or Mandalay should be about K1000, but in reality you may have to pay closer to K1500 to either destination, especially during the high season (November to February). The trip in either direction takes seven to eight hours. One bus, the air-con Yangyi Aung Express, collects passengers near the central market in Taungoo, and makes the overnight trip to Yangon for K450.

Cheaper public buses are available to Yangon and Mandalay around 6 pm daily for just K250. These can be flagged down anywhere along the main road or at the central market. Count on around 10 hours to either city. See the Getting There & Away section in the Yangon chapter for bus departure times from Yangon.

Train The express train No 18 Down leaves Taungoo for Yangon around midnight, and No 16 Down leaves at about 1.30 am. Both trains reach Yangon in about six hours, and the fare (upper class only) is US$18. Two other ordinary class trains leave for Yangon at 6 and 8 am and reach Yangon in about seven hours. The fare is US$4 to Bago, and US$6 to Yangon.

In the northerly direction, the No 17 Up to Mandalay leaves around 2 am and arrives at 10 am; the No 15 Up departs at 11 pm and arrives at 5 am; and the No 7 Up leaves at 3 am and gets to Mandalay around 11 am. Step lively, as the train only stops in Taungoo for 10 minutes. The fares are US$18 for upper class, and US18 for upper class. Two other ordinary class trains leave for Mandalay at 3 pm and 10 pm and reach Mandalay in about seven hours. The fare is US$7 for ordinary class.

See the Getting There & Away section in the Yangon chapter for information on the Mandalay-bound express trains, which stop briefly in Taungoo. The same applies for

Mandalay (see the Getting There & Away section in the Mandalay chapter for more information). If you're coming from Yangon or Mandalay, express bus would be a considerably cheaper option.

Car Taungoo makes an especially good stopover if you've hired a car. If you have your own vehicle and are feeling adventurous, the 100km unpaved logging road from Oktwin (15km south of Taungoo) to Pakkaung provides a unique shortcut to Pyay. From Pakkaung the road is sealed the remaining 39km to Pyay. This is a lengthy and tiring all day trip; start early and bring at least one spare tyre, plus food and plenty of water.

Forget about travelling east to Loikaw. Not only is the road beyond the Sittoung River in miserable condition, you may have to deal both with military checkpoints (at the river) and bandits (in the mountains).

PYAY (PROME)

Seven hours north of Yangon by road or an overnight riverboat trip south of Bagan, the town of Pyay lies on a sharp benc in the Ayeyarwady. Nearby are the ruins of the ancient Pyu capital of Thayekhittaya (Sri Ksetra) and, although few visitors get there, it has been the centre of the most intensive archaeological work in Myanmar almost all of this century.

The current town site was established as a trade centre during the Bagan era, but Pyay didn't really hit its stride until the British developed the Irrawaddy Flotilla Company in the late 1890s. Today the town serves as an important transshipment point for cargo moving between Upper and Lower Myanmar along the Ayeyarwady River, and between the Rakhaing coast and the interior along the road from Taungup to Sinte (just across the river from Pyay). Sometimes the name of the city is spelt Pyi, although the everyday pronunciation is always Pyay. The British called it Prome.

Shwesandaw Paya

In the centre of the small town of Pyay it-

self, the Shwesandaw Paya is the main point of interest. A lift (K2) takes visitors from street level to the elevated main stupa platform, which, like the Shwedagon in Yangon, is perched on top of a hill.

As the name Golden Hair Relic suggests, the zedi Shwesandaw purportedly contains a couple of Buddha hairs. Just over 1m taller than the main zedi at Shwedagon, the Shwesandaw stupa follows classic Bamar Bagan lines similar to those seen at Bagan's oldest paya, Shwezigon. Along with Kyaiktiyo, Shwemawdaw, Mahamuni (see the Mandalay chapter) and Shwedagon, this is one of the most sacred Buddhist pilgrimage spots in Myanmar.

It's also one of the country's more impressive zedis, especially on its hillside setting. Looking east from the stupa you'll see an enormous seated Buddha figure rising up from the treeline. From the Shwesandaw terrace you look across to the image eye-to-eye; it's known as **Sehtatgyi Paya** (Big Ten-Storey) for its height. Shwesandaw is at its most atmospheric at night, when the zedi is illuminated and the cityscape sparkles below.

Places to Stay

Since Pyay opened to tourists several years ago, it has become a convenient stopover on the road between Bagan and Yangon – with new places to stay continuing to open.

Near the Bogyoke Aung San statue (known as Bogyoke Cheyo) in the middle of town, not far from the train station, is *Aung Gabar Guest House* (☎ 053-22743, 1436 Bogyoke Lan). Although its rooms are a bit small and dark, they're clean and the management is helpful. Bath and toilet are down the hall. Rates are US$3 (or kyat equivalent) per person, or US$4 with aircon. One room is available with attached bath for a flat rate of US$10. A simple breakfast is provided.

The well managed *Yoma Royal Hotel* (☎ 053-21824, 43 Pyay-Yangon Lan) has small but decent economy rooms at US$4/7 a single/double, and larger rooms with bath at US$24/36, including a nice breakfast on the 2nd floor with a view of the river.

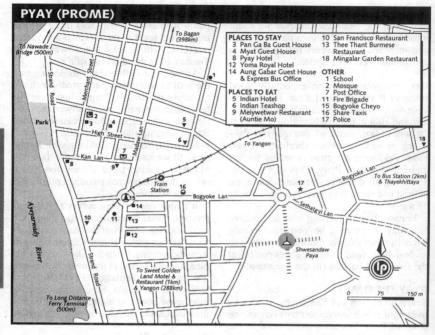

PYAY (PROME)

To Nawade /
Bridge (500m)

To Bagan
(398km)

Strand Street

Merchant Street

Strand Road

Park

High Street

Madaw Lan

Kan Lan

Ayeyarwady River

Train Station

Strand Road

To Long Distance
Ferry Terminal
(500m)

Bogyoke Lan

To Yangon

Sethatgyi Lan

Shwesandaw
Paya

To Sweet Golden
Land Motel &
Restaurant (1km)
& Yangon (288km)

To Bus Station (2km)
& Thayekhittaya

0   75   150 m

PLACES TO STAY
3   Pan Ga Ba Guest House
4   Myat Guest House
8   Pyay Hotel
12 Yoma Royal Hotel
14 Aung Gabar Guest House
    & Express Bus Office

PLACES TO EAT
5   Indian Hotel
6   Indian Teashop
9   Meiywetwar Restaurant
    (Auntie Mo)

10 San Francisco Restaurant
13 Thee Thant Burmese
    Restaurant
18 Mingalar Garden Restaurant

OTHER
1   School
2   Mosque
7   Post Office
11 Fire Brigade
15 Bogyoke Cheyo
16 Share Taxis
17 Police

The *Pyay Hotel* (☎ *053-21890*), on the corner of Strand Rd and Kan Lan, is comfortable, if a bit overpriced. It's just off the main road, not far from the river. Economy rooms (common bath) cost US$6/9, or pay up to US$24/30/36 for a double room with bath, fan and air-con (when the electricity is working). All rates include a bleak breakfast of eggs and toast.

The turn-off for the *Sweet Golden Land Motel & Restaurant* (☎ *053-22526, 12 Nawaday Lan*) is just south of the town gate and, unless you have a car, it's a good 20 minute walk from the main road. You can also hire a three wheeled taxi from town for about K50. This collection of clean and spacious bungalows is picturesque and peaceful, if a bit isolated. Rooms with private bath and satellite TV cost $20/30, possibly cheaper in the low season. The owners can also arrange boat tours of nearby weaving

villages and Shwe Bone Daw Paya along the river.

Pan Ga Ba Guest House (☎ *053-21277, 342 Merchant St*) features basic rooms, with two beds and a mosquito net, in a big house-like building for just US$2 to $3 per person. The manager speaks decent English, and offers area maps and rental bikes. We continue to receive raves about this place from travellers. In front of the guesthouse the proprietors run a restaurant that is popular with locals.

Myat Hotel (☎ *053-21361*) is a converted bungalow with a homey feel, even though the rooms are small. Rooms with shared bath cost US$8/12; and US$10/16 with bath and air-con.

Places to Eat

The clean, friendly and inexpensive *Meiy-wetwar Restaurant* (English sign states

Auntie Mo), opposite the post office and near the Pyay Hotel, serves excellent traditional Bamar food. It offers curries made with chicken, prawn, venison or steamed fish, plus fried chicken, roast duck, fried mackerel eggs and delicious Bamar salads made with your choice of tomato, fishtail, pickled tea, horseshoe leaf or pomelo. Staff speak some English here, but it's easier to point. It's open from 11 am until around 7 pm.

Similar to the Meiywetwar s another very tasty and reasonably priced restaurant, *Thee Thant Burmese Restaurant* on Mawdaw Lan, between the Yoma Royal Hotel and Aung Gabar Guest House.

A block south of the Pyay Hotel, on the same side of Strand Rd, the *San Francisco Restaurant* offers decent Chinese fare.

Further from the town centre, try the restaurant at *Sweet Golden Land Motel & Restaurant*, and the *Mingalar Garden Restaurant* for good Chinese-style food.

The *Indian Hotel*, two streets north of the train station, serves all-you-can-eat *thalis* (set meals) in a long, narrow, somewhat grubby, dining room with tables along each wall; despite its name the Indian Hotel is a restaurant only. The *Indian teashop* (no name) half a block south offers decent potato curry and stuffed palatas for breakfast. There are also a number of *teashops* located along Bogyoke St, east of the Bogyoke Cheyo.

If your tastes run to palm toddy, there's a *toddy bar* behind the Ministry of Forestry's 'Static Workshop', just a bit west of Payagyi, on the road to Hmawzaw. Take the narrow dirt road alongside the workshop till it ends next to a field of toddy palms. The rustic, thatched-roof bar is on the left; in addition to toddy sold by the pot or by the bottle, the bar sells prawn crackers and other snacks.

Getting There & Away
Bus Pyay lies 288km north-west of Yangon via a decent, sealed two-lane road (considered the best road in the country). From Yangon there are several choices from the Highway bus station at the northern end of Yangon, starting with Rainbow Express's

air-con, 45 seat bus for US$3 (or kyat equivalent). Two other companies run good buses between Yangon and Pyay: Sun Moon Express and Rubyland Express, for US$3. Departures begin at 7 am and continue hourly until about 5 pm. All three companies have shuttle offices opposite the Yangon train station and you can usually catch a free shuttle from this central location out to the Highway bus centre; from there it's about a six hour trip to Pyay.

From Yangon, ask to be dropped off at the centrally located Bogyoke Cheyo, rather than the bus centre, which is 2km east of town. In fact, any help you can get in Pyay regarding buses will usually save you a lot of hassle at the bus station where information is hard to come by.

Other companies at Yangon's Highway bus station operate passenger transport to/from Pyay in the K300 to K400 range for ordinary pickups (seven to eight hours).

To reach Bagan/Nyaung U from Pyay, try the Ye Thu Aung Express Bus. The cost is K1000, departing at 6 am. Another popular bus to Bagan is the New Bagan Express – same cost and same time. Given a day's notice, both bus companies will pick you up at your hotel.

From the main bus station in Mandalay you can get an overnight express bus (three a day) for K900; these take a grinding 12 to 15 hours to reach Pyay, however. If you're coming from the north it would be better to break your journey in Nyaung U, Kyauk Padaung or Magwe. The road between Magwe and Pyay is decent, but it's still a five hour stretch.

Other bus routes to/from Pyay include: Kyauk Padaung (K500, three times daily, 10 hours), Taungup (K650, once daily, 13 hours), Taundwingyi (K200, three daily, four hours), Magwe (K100, three daily, five hours), Meiktila (K500, three daily, 12 hours) and Pathein (K400, once daily, 10 hours). The eight hour bus trip from Pyay to Thandwe costs K600.

The Pyay bus station is about 2km east of Shwesandaw Paya off the road to Paukkaung.

Train A branch railway line north of Yangon terminates at Pyay. There is only one express train per day, the No 71 Up, which leaves Yangon train station at 1 pm sharp and is scheduled to arrive in Pyay at 8 pm. This train may arrive up to two hours late. From Pyay, the No 72 Down is scheduled to depart at 10 pm for a 5 am Yangon arrival. This is an ordinary train with 1st, not upper, class seats available to foreigners for US$9.

Car A car and driver from Yangon to Pyay will cost less per day than hire to most other places outside the capital, since the road is decent and it's no more than a day's drive one way. Figure on paying around US$40 for an older, non-air-con car and up to US$50 for a newer model with air-con.

If you're coming to Pyay by private vehicle, you may wish to break your journey in Paungde, a small town with a very trim, old colonial-style market building. It's only about 64km short of Pyay, but is well endowed as far as small Burmese towns go, as it was Ne Win's birthplace (another reason why the Yangon-Pyay road is so good).

The **Nawade Bridge** that crosses the Ayeyarwady between Pyay and Sinte opened in January 1998, and allows for easier road access to Ngapali Beach and Thandwe on the Rakhaing coast, 218km to the west over a good but hilly road. A car can be hired, but you may have to pay the return trip price, about US$50 or kyat equivalent. This same road crosses the road south to Pathein.

Boat A new Chinese-built triple-decker ferry is scheduled to begin service by 2000 along the Ayeyarwady River between Pyay, Bagan/Nyaung U and Mandalay. The vessel features 18 double cabins in 1st class and deck space for 270 passengers. First class cabins have attached toilets and showers. Prices are usually in dollars for foreigners; from Pyay to Bagan expect to pay about US$9 for ordinary deck class to about US$27 for a 1st class cabin for the overnight journey.

You can continue to Yangon on a government boat for US$2 lower deck, or US$7 upper deck cabin, though most people find the cabins very stuffy; this stretch takes 2½ days, with overnight stops in Myaungmya and Wakema. From Yangon, you could take the ferry upriver from Kaingdan Lan jetty, but it's a slow four day journey.

The ferry pier in Pyay is about 500m south of the San Francisco Restaurant. As the river level lowers during the dry season, the pier usually migrates downriver. You can book tickets at the Inland Water Transport (IWT) office on the opposite side of Strand Rd from the high-water pier or, for deck class only, on the boat itself.

From Pyay, other ferry trip possibilities include Pakokku and Mandalay.

Getting Around

Shared taxis are the main way to get around Pyay. There are still a few three wheeled taxis and horsecarts, either of which should cost no more than K50 per trip anywhere in town, including the bus station. You can hire a horsecart for most of the day for about K500. Most of the taxis gather in a dirt site about 200m west of the Bogyoke Cheyo.

AROUND PYAY
Hmawza & Thayekhittaya

The ancient site of Thayekhittaya – known to Pali-Sanskrit scholars as Sri Ksetra – lies 8km north-east of Pyay in the village of Hmawza, along a good road that leads to Paukkaung. Taking this road, you'll first come to the towering **Payagyi**, an early, almost cylindrical roadside stupa about 2km from the edge of the city.

Legend says Payagyi was erected by mythical King Duttabaung in 443 BC, but most likely it dates to the early Pyu kingdom that ruled the surrounding area from the 5th to 9th centuries AD – or from the 3rd to 10th centuries according to some sources. Nearby stand a couple of lofty teak trees, safe from the woodcutter's axe since they occupy sacred ground. Payagyi is thought to mark one of four corners that delineated Thayekhittaya. Only two others are visible today; Bawbawgyi and Payama.

Very little is known about this kingdom or about the Pyus themselves. The earliest Pali inscriptions found here date to the 5th or 6th centuries and indicate the coexistence of Mahayana and Theravada Buddhism. A Chinese chronicle based on a Tang dynasty (618-905) survey of the Pyu kingdom reads:

> When the Pyu king goes out in his palanquin, he lies on a couch of golden cord. For long distances he rides on an elephant. He has several hundred women to wait on him ... (The Pyus) are Buddhists and have a hundred monasteries, with bricks of glassware embellished with gold and silver ...

A few kilometres further brings you to the junction where you turn off the Bagan road towards Paukkaung. The road runs alongside the extensive city walls of Thayekhittaya, and ahead on the left to the north of the road you can see the decaying **Payama**, similar in form to the Payagyi, to the north of the road. Surrounded by rice fields, Payama is at its most picturesque in the rainy season but well worth a look anytime. To reach it you must walk 500m or so from the highway along a trail that winds through these fields. On the grounds stands a stone plinth that once supported a *thein* (monastic ordination hall). A large brick-and-plaster pedestal near the stupa was a gift from the British to hold a large Buddha image (now in the Hmawza museum) excavated at the site. Some stucco relief still adheres to the pedestal. Two venerable banyan trees flank the stupa.

Just before crossing a stream, there's a turn-off south that leads into the village of Hmawza. This road terminates at a small train station on the Yangon-Pyay line, which was built straight through the middle of Thayekhittaya. About 1.5km from the highway turn-off (6km total from Payagyi), by the old palace site, stands a small **museum** and a map of the area. Inside the museum is a collection of artefacts collected from Thayekhittaya excavations, including royal funerary urns, stone reliefs; a couple of bodhisattvas; a *dvarapala* (gate guardian); statues of the Hindu deities Tara Devi, Vishnu and Lakshmi; several 6th century

Buddha images; tile fragments; terracotta votive tablets; and silver coins minted in the kingdom. There are no regular hours but the museum is usually unlocked for visitors. Entry is US$4, although the most interesting stuff can be seen by just walking around the grounds.

Inquire at the museum for a guide to the outer ruins to the south, as these ruins can be hard to find. There's no charge for the service if someone's available, but a K100 tip is appreciated. At one time this area was considered dangerous due to the presence of 'insurgents' but it now appears secure. Archaeological enthusiasts could easily spend some time here investigating these rarely visited ancient sites. The village itself holds some interest as an example of a typical farming settlement where rice, vegetables and flowers are brought to market, or for shipment by train. Handmade basketry and pots are also for sale in the village.

South of the museum, outside the city walls, are the cylindrical **Bawbawgyi Paya** and cube-shaped **Bebe Paya**. Standing over 45m high, the brick-and-plaster Bawbawgyi is the oldest stupa in the area. Bebe looks like a prototype pahto for some of the temples at Bagan; some sources say it was constructed in the 9th century, but it actually may have evolved during the Bagan era. The *sikhara* (a mound-like superstructure atop the cubic base) has been partially restored. Other cube-shaped pahtos in the area include one thought to have been used by a hermit, featuring eight Buddha reliefs along the lower half of the interior wall and a vaulted ceiling of brick. **East Zegu Paya** exhibits a similar vaulted brick ceiling, while **West Zegu Paya** lies in total ruins.

Leimyethna Paya is wider and squatter than the others; its doorways have been blocked off to prevent destruction by looters seeking valuable relics. The vaulted ceiling, no longer accessible for viewing, is reportedly supported by a pillar faced with original Buddha reliefs. The blocking of the doorways may be temporary until these precious reliefs can be restored and moved to a museum.

The best English-language reference available on the Thayekhittaya/Sri Ksetra monuments is an article entitled 'Excavations at Hmawzaw, Prome', which appeared in the 1911-12 annual report of the *Archaeological Survey of India*. The article contains detailed descriptions of objects and inscriptions found at each site, but almost no architectural information on the Pyu stupas.

Getting There & Away The most convenient way to reach Hmawza from Pyay is by pickup, which should cost around K100 one way and take no more than 15 or 20 minutes.

To hire a taxi for a half-day to visit Payama, Payagyi and Hmawza plus the ruins, expect to pay about K3000.

There are three local trains per day between Pyay and Hmawza at 7 and 10 am and 5 pm. The fare is K5 and the journey takes about 15 minutes. Hitching might also be possible as far as the turn-off to Hmawza, as the road to Paukkaung is fairly well travelled.

Shwedaung

This small town about 14km south of Pyay, via the road to Yangon, contains two famous payas. The more well known is **Shwemyetman Paya** (Paya of the Golden Spectacles), a reference to a large, white-faced sitting Buddha inside the main shrine. The Buddha wears a gargantuan set of eyeglasses with gold-plated rims. Coming south from Pyay, the turn-off for Shwemyetman is located on the right-hand side of the road, opposite a small whitewashed mosque bearing a 1962 imprimatur. At the roadside, there's also a small green and white sign in English that reads 'Shwemyethman Buddha Image – 1 furlong'.

Spectacles were first added to the image during the Konbaung era, when a local nobleman offered them to the temple in an attempt to stimulate local faith through curiosity. Word soon spread that the bespectacled Buddha had the power to cure all kinds of ills, especially afflictions linked to the eyes. The first pair of spectacles was stolen at an early stage, and a second pair was made and enshrined inside the image to protect it from thieves.

An English officer stationed in Pyay during the colonial era had a third pair fitted over the Buddha's eyes after his wife suffered from eye trouble and the abbot suggested such a donation. Naturally, as the story goes, she was cured. It requires nine monks to remove the glasses for their fortnightly cleaning. The attendant who watches over this charming paya seems to have the duty of clapping his hands loudly whenever a few birds try to alight on the huge pair of classic gold wire-rims.

The second major paya in Shwedaung, located to the north of the first, is **Shwenattaung Paya** (Golden Spirit Mountain). As a stupa site, Shwenattaung reportedly dates back to the Thayekhittaya (Sri Ksetra) era, though the current 37m stupa features the post-Bagan style. Legend takes it back all the way to 283 BC, from which point it was supposedly reconstructed by a long line of Bamar kings – hardly likely since there were no Bamar in the area before the 9th century AD – with the aid of local nats. Although there is a nat shrine in the paya compound, there is little to suggest that nats play a more important role here than at any other central Burmese paya. A large paya pwe is held here each year on the full moon of Tabaung (February/March), the same time as Yangon's Shwedagon festival.

The town of Shwedaung is also famous for *hkauq sweh* (rice noodles). Several *noodle shops* along the main road through town sell them from early morning till early evening.

Getting There & Away Large and small pickups leave for Shwedaung frequently throughout the day, from the bus station east of Pyay, for around K50 per person for the 20 minute ride. The last pickup back to Pyay passes the turn-off for Shwemyetman Paya around 5 pm.

Mandalay

Mandalay was the last capital of Myanmar (Burma) before the British took over and for this reason it still has great importance as a cultural centre. Historically, it's the most Burmese of the country's large cities, a place where you'll come close to the 'heart' of Myanmar despite China-style modernisation. Mandalay still has considerable cultural and religious significance and its Buddhist monasteries are among the most important in the country – about 60% of all the monks in Myanmar reside in the Mandalay area. It's also said that Mandalay residents speak better Burmese than anyone in the country.

The city takes its name from Mandalay Hill, the 236m-high bluff that rises just to the north-east of Mandalay Fort and its royal palace. Today the population ranges somewhere between 600,000 and 800,000 people; the largest in the country after that of the capital, Yangon (Rangoon), located 695km to the south. It lies in the centre of Myanmar's 'dry zone' and is a surprisingly sprawling place – you'll find wandering around the city in the hot season to be a dry and dusty experience.

New townships are springing up along the edges of the city, many inhabited by former squatters who are being pushed out of the central area in the city's rush to modernise. The Chinese presence has become very large since the easing of foreign trade restrictions. Government truces with northern insurgents and trade with China have brought a boomtown atmosphere to Mandalay, with an assortment of new hotels, office buildings and department stores, not to mention a flourishing vice scene – especially in Kywezun and Ma Yan Chan, two districts on the river in the north-western part of the city, long considered 'black' by the authorities, due to the presence of gambling, prostitution and heroin.

Although it suffered considerable damage in the fierce fighting at the end of WWII –

HIGHLIGHTS

- Traditional dance and drama from cultural centre of Myanmar.
- Mandalay Hill, with spiralling stairways, temples and sweeping views.
- Ancient Rakhaing Buddha image at Mahamuni Paya.
- Kuthodaw Paya, the world's 'biggest book'.
- Bustling markets with produce and handicrafts from Upper Myanmar.

Mandalay Fort was completely burnt out – there is still much to be seen both in Mandalay and in the surrounding deserted cities of the old capitals.

History

Despite erroneous references to the contrary, Mandalay is a comparatively young city, and its period as the capital of the last Burmese kingdom was a short one. Most of the monuments and buildings are therefore fairly recent, although some temples long pre-date the city. For centuries this area of

MANDALAY

Ayeyarwady River

0   0.5   1 km

Golf Course

Mandalay Hill

Old Racecourse

● 4

● 3

■ 2

5 ⚑

⚑ 6

North Moat Street (12th Street)

⚑ 8

⚑ 9

10th Street

11th Street

14th Street

16th Street

Canal

Shweta

Fort Moat

Mandalay Fort

Nandawun Park

Mandalay Palace

🏛

Myinghaywun Park

12th Street

14th Street

16th Street

To Yankin Hill (2.5km)

19th Street

21st Street

East Moat Street

Inwa Lan

18th Street

20th Street

Pinya Lan

To Mingun Ferry (500m)

Bayintnaung Lan

32 ▼

31 ●

See Central Mandalay Map p248

23rd Street

24th Street

25th Street

● 10

85th Street
84th Street
83rd Street
82nd Street
81st Street
80th Street

26th Street

26 ●

▼ 25

27th Street
28th Street

▼ 24

23 ● ▼ 22

14 ■

15 ● 13 ■
11 ■
12 ■

● 16

29 ●
30 ●

28 ●

30th Street

▼ 27

31st Street

74th Street
73rd Street
71st Street

18 ▼

21 ■ 19 ■

70th Street
68th Street
66th Street
65th Street

63rd Street
62nd Street

17 ■

32nd Street

20 ■

Kankaw Lan

To Gawain Jetty for Bagan Ferry & Pyay Ferry (500m)

37 ●

42 ■ 43 ■

41 ■

44 ■

33rd Street

34th Street

Yangyiaung Lan

34 ●
35 ⚑
36 ⚑

Thinsa

38 ⚑

40 ▼

47 ●
45 ●

48 ●

35th Street

46 ●
36th Street

37th Street

55 ✚

To Pyin U Lwin (68km)

Yarzar Chaung

39 ●

79th Street
78th Street

49 ●

38th Street

39th Street

Salgaing-Mandalay Road

50 ●
51 ●

40th Street

41st Street

Patheingyi Creek

54 ●

52 ●

To Amarapura, Inwa & Sagaing (10km)

⚑ 53

To Airport (2km), Highway Bus Station (4km) & Yangon (695km)

MANDALAY

MANDALAY

PLACES TO STAY
1 Emerald Land Inn
3 Novotel Mandalay
11 Mandalay View Inn
13 Sedona Hotel Mandalay
15 Mandalay Swan Hotel & MTT
17 Si Thu Tourist Hotel
19 Mandalay Royal Hotel
20 Golden Land Inn
21 Taim Byu (Silver Cloud) Hotel
30 Pacific Hotel
43 Myit Phyar Ayer Hotel
48 Tiger Hotel
49 Great Guest House
51 Power Hotel

PLACES TO EAT
14 Pyigyimon Restaurant
18 Honey Garden Restaurant
22 Sakhantha Restaurant
24 Tu Tu Restaurant

25 Marie-Min Vegetarian Restaurant
26 BBB (Barman Beer Bar)
27 Daw Lay May Restaurant
32 Thai Yai Restaurant
33 Emerald Green Restaurant
40 Minn Thi Ha Teashop
47 Aya Myit Tas (Tar) Myanmar Restaurant

OTHER
2 Yadanapon Zoo
4 Military Cemetery
5 Kyauktawgyi Paya
6 Kuthodaw Paya
7 Sandamani Paya
8 Shwenandaw Kyaung
9 Atumashi Kyaung
10 School of Fine Arts, Music & Drama
12 Mandalay Marionettes & Culture Show
16 Police Academy

23 Mann Swe Gon Handicrafts
28 Kachin Clothing 2
29 Yangon Airways
31 Main Post Office
34 Inland Water Transport Office (IWT)
35 Shwe In Bin Kyaung
36 Thakawun Kyaung
37 Kachin Clothing 1
38 Kin Wun Kyaung
39 Jade Market
41 Myawady Travel & Tours (Permits to Mogok)
42 Judson Baptist Church
44 Father Lafon's Catholic Church
45 Bamboo Fan Factory
46 Goldleaf Workshop
50 Moustache Brothers Troupe
52 Buddha Image Makers
53 Mahamuni Paya
54 Mandalay Arts & Sciences University
55 Drug Addicts Hospital

Myanmar was the site of the capitals of the Burmese kingdoms; while in Mandalay you can easily visit three former royal cities – all now deserted.

King Mindon Min, penultimate ruler in the Konbaung dynasty, founded the city in 1857 and began construction of his new capital. The actual shift from nearby Amarapura to the new royal palace took place in 1861. In true Burmese tradition, the new palace was mainly constructed from the dismantled wooden buildings of the previous palace at Amarapura. Mandalay's period of glory was short – Mindon was succeeded by the disastrous Thibaw Min and in 1885, Mandalay was taken by the British. Thibaw and his notorious queen were exiled and 'the centre of the universe' or 'the golden city' (as it was known) became just another outpost of the British empire.

Fifteen years after independence, Mandalay slumbered, like the rest of the country, through the socialist mismanagement of Ne Win and company. With the reopening of the Burma Road through Lashio to China however, the city is now undergoing an economic boom. The money fuelling this boom is generated by three trades, known locally as the red, green and white lines – rubies, jade and heroin – and controlled by Kachin, Wa, Shan, Kokang and Chinese syndicates.

Orientation

The hill with the huge grounds of old Mandalay Fort at its base is the natural focus of Mandalay. The city sprawls away to the south and east of the fort, bounded on the west by the busy Ayeyarwady (Irrawaddy) River.

The city streets are laid out on a grid system with numbered streets running north-south and east-west. Some people may make a distinction between east-west roads and north-south streets, but in everyday practice the Burmese use these terms interchangeably, and also the word lan. The east-west streets run into the 40s only, while the north-south streets start in the 60s and run through the 80s. For moving across the city quickly, 35th St serves as the main east-west thoroughfare, while 80th St is the main north-south street. The two major business thoroughfares are 26th and 84th Sts.

MANDALAY

Ambitious plans to build a circular road around the city, which would speed travel to Sagaing and other outlying areas, has been postponed indefinitely. The plan eventually calls for all households now living along the river to move to a new town in Anisakan District, halfway between Mandalay and Pyin U Lwin (Maymyo). Needless to say, the idea has not been well received. (No one we talked to expects the government to do more than simply give the order and maybe provide a couple of trucks; the rest would be up to the displaced families.)

If you're thinking of making day trips to the ancient cities outside Mandalay, it's best to do Sagaing one day and save Inwa (Ava) and Amarapura for another day,

Addresses In Mandalay a street address that reads 66th (26/27) means the place is located on 66th St between 26th and 27th Sts. Some of the longer east-west streets take names once they cross the Shweta Chaung (canal) heading west. Hence 18th St becomes Inwa Lan, 22nd St becomes Pinya Lan, 26th St changes to Bayintnaung Lan and 35th St is Yangyiaung Lan.

Information

Tourist Offices Myanmar Travels & Tours (MTT) has an office (☎ 02-27193) in the Mandalay Swan Hotel on the corner of 68th and 26th Sts. It's open daily from 8.30 am to 6.30 pm.

MTT also have a desk at the airport to meet flights, and at the train station to meet tourist trains – in order to steer you towards their favourite hotels.

The Ministry of Information's *Map of Mandalay* is useful for getting to the main tourist sites, and has a fairly extensive restaurant and hotel key.

Admission Fees Fees in historical Mandalay can add up quickly – US$3 per person for Mandalay Hill, US$5 for Kuthodaw (Biggest Book) Paya and Sandamani Paya together, US$5 for both Shwenandaw (or Shwe Dangi) and Atamushi Kyaung (Incomparable Monastery), US$2 for Kyauk-

tawgyi Paya, US$5 for Mandalay Palace and US$4 for Mahamuni Paya. If you continue to the ancient cities, add US$3 to see Mingun, US$4 to visit Sagaing Hill and US$6 to visit Inwa. On the other hand, the five minute ferry ride to Inwa is only K10.

If you visit all these sights, the fees will total a steep US$30. Admission fees can be paid at each site; some people manage to avoid paying by visiting before 7 am or after 5 pm, or by claiming to be on a Buddhist pilgrimage. The MTT office will also collect fees for the various tourist attractions around the city, but most people pay as they go.

The Ministry of Hotels & Tourism (MHT) receives a steady trickle of complaints about these relatively high entrance fees. They typically respond by either raising the fees, or creating new ones.

Guides Although most places in and around Mandalay can easily be visited on your own, if you want someone to take care of all the travel details and provide a running commentary, there are several good guides in town. The going rate for a licensed guide is around US$20 a day, not including extras like car or driver.

Soft-spoken Richard at the Marie-Min Vegetarian Restaurant, located on 27th St between 74th and 75th Sts, can arrange individual or small group tours in and around Mandalay and to Pyin U Lwin, Bagan (Pagan), Monywa and Inle Lake. An Indian Catholic, Richard is one of the few licensed non-MTT guides in Mandalay.

Another guide is friendly English instructor U Nyunt, who specialises in tours to Bagan and Mogok. Experienced, French-speaking Than Tun (Dominique) covers all of Upper Myanmar. Both guides can usually be contacted through the Royal Guest House, Sabai Phyu Hotel or the Classic Hotel. You'll find several tour agencies in town as well.

Some trishaw drivers act as guides for just a few US dollars a day. Generally, their foreign language skills aren't great and neither is their knowledge of Burmese history and architecture, but at least they know where everything is.

Also, since the military government's closing of the universities, many former students have taken to the streets with trishaws. Trishaw drivers accustomed to transporting foreigners through town usually park near the popular guesthouses. But you don't have to worry about finding them – they'll find you. Bear in mind that the typical trishaw driver will try to steer you to at least one or two handicraft shops, where he'll earn commissions from anything you buy. Figure on paying K800 per day for all-day trishaw sightseeing in the central part of city, or K1000 with jaunts to Mahamuni Faya to the south, or Mandalay Hill to the north. A better idea might be to hire your trishaws one-way only, so you don't feel pressured to hurry to the next spot. A one-way ride from the clock tower to Mahamuni should cost between K100 and K150.

Post & Communications The Central Telephone & Telegraph (CTT) office is on the corner of 80th and 25th Sts, where both domestic and international calls can be made at low government rates. Many of the top-end hotels now offer expensive international Direct Dial (IDD) phone service, and most of the budget and mid-range hotels and guesthouses offer some sort of booking call service, in which you place the call and wait for a call back from the local operator. As at the CTT office, expect to wait an hour on average.

The main post office is on the corner of 22nd and 81st Sts. A new DHL Worldwide Express office is next door. It opens at 9.30 am and is supposed to close at 4 pm. In typical Burmese government fashion, the staff wander off for tea at around 3 pm, and by 3.30 pm there's usually no one at the windows.

Mandalay Fort

King Mindon Min ordered the construction of his imposing walled palace compound in 1857. The immense walls measure 8m high and 3m thick at the bottom, tapering to 1.5m thick at the crenellated top, and are made of fired brick backed by earth ramparts. Each of the four sides extends 2km; the surround-

ing moat is 70m wide and over 3m deep. A channel from the Mandalay irrigation canal fills the moat. After the British occupied the city in 1885, the compound was named Fort Dufferin and became the seat of the colony's government house and British Club.

On 20 March 1945, in fierce fighting between advancing British and Indian troops and the Japanese forces, who had held Mandalay since 1942, the royal palace within the fort caught fire and was completely burnt out. The traditional wooden construction of Burmese palaces had often in the past led to severe damage by fire, and this – the last and most magnificent palace complex – was no exception. All that remains of the original palace today are the huge walls and moat, the base on which the wooden palace buildings and apartments stood, and a few masonry buildings or tombs. The Burmese army has reoccupied the fort; soldiers grow their own fruit and vegetables in the middle of the base to supplement meagre wages.

There were originally three gates to the fort on each of the walls. There were also five bridges leading into the fort, four running to the main gates. Each of the gates was topped by a *pyatthat* (wooden pavilion). Smaller pyatthats stood at each corner and between the large ones – making 32 in all. Apart from some damage repaired after the war and changes made when the railway was directed through the palace grounds, the wall and its pavilions are original.

Mandalay Palace was far more than just royal living quarters – it was really a walled city within Mandalay. A massive reconstruction project and a new palace is nearly completed – all for the benefit of tourists. Some visitors like the reconstruction, while others abhor it. Instead of flammable wood, the new version sports concrete construction topped by aluminium roofs. Only the renovated moat surrounding the fort seems to have improved.

A 33m-high watchtower, *Nan Myint Saung*, reached via a spiral staircase, commands a view of the entire compound and cityscape. Nearby is the partly original 'tooth relic tower' and the tomb of King Mindon. The

An early print of Mandalay Palace

MANDALAY

latter was once gilded and decorated with glass mosaics, but an 1898 restoration obliterated all traces of the earlier craftsmanship. The large open sheds here contain over 600 inscribed stone slabs that were collected by King Bodawpaya (1782-1819) and were later moved to the palace from Amarapura just before WWII. Other reminders of the former glory of the old palace are the Royal Mint and the Sabbath Hall, which are also close by.

Much of the restoration of the palace and moat has been carried out using prison labour. For a while, the municipal government required all young males in the city to contribute one day's worth of 'volunteer' labour per month to the project, but this practice was discontinued, due to the negative publicity generated in the foreign press. Many locals as well as visitors still refuse to enter the new palace for this reason. Apparently, an old term for the west gate, *Ah Luwe* (Gate of Ill Omen), still applies. This entrance was once used for condemned prisoners and funeral processions.

The palace Cultural Museum has not yet reopened. Plans are to eventually combine this museum with the equally drab Mandalay Museum & Library on 80th St, outside the fort walls.

Admission for foreigners to the palace compound costs US$5. The main entrance is the gate on the eastern wall. The admission also entitles you to visit the still-drab palace Cultural Museum. You can get a K10 glimpse of the compound by taking one of the public Mann Sit Thi buses, which run from Zeigyo (Central Market) through the fort from east to west.

Mandalay Museum & Library
Opposite the south-western corner of Mandalay Fort's wall, on the corner of 24th and 80th Sts, this mildly interesting museum and library contains a collection of Mandalay regalia, royally commissioned art and palm-leaf manuscripts that were formerly housed in the palace. Most of the articles date from the reigns of the last two Mandalay kings – Mindon and Thibaw. It's open Wednesday to Sunday from 10 am to 4 pm and admission is US$2 for foreigners. There

are plans to eventually combine the holdings at this museum with those from the palace museum.

Mandalay Hill

An easy half-hour barefoot climb up the sheltered steps brings you to a wide view over the palace, Mandalay and the *paya* (pagoda)-studded countryside.

A US$3 fee is collected at the bottom of the hill, though you could take a minitaxi the back way to the top of the hill and enter freely, then walk down. Two immense carved lions guard the south-west entrance to the hill and the south-east entrance is watched over by the *Bobokyi Nat* (Boboki spirit). If you're certain to leave the way you came, it's perfectly safe to leave your shoes

---

A Stroll Up Mandalay Hill

Since it's such a natural focus for the city, and the only place with a good view over the pancake-flat central plain, Mandalay Hill is where many people start their visit to Mandalay. The famous hermit monk, U Khanti, is credited with inspiring the construction of many of the buildings on and around the hill in the years after the founding of the city.

From the south, two covered stairways wind their way up the hill, meeting about half-way up. Another path ascends more steeply from the west. It's a pleasant stroll, with plenty of places to stop for a rest. Shoes must be removed as you enter the walkways. For those who don't want to make the climb, a minibus to the top can be boarded for K3 to K5 per person. For the majority of the year, it makes most sense to climb before 10 am or after 4 pm, to avoid the midday heat.

Close to the top of the hill, you come to a huge standing Buddha image, looking out towards the royal palace with an outstretched hand pointing in that direction. This image, known as the **Shweyattaw**, represents a rather interesting legend. The Buddha, accompanied by his disciple Ananda, was said to have climbed Mandalay Hill while on one of his visits to Myanmar. In the 2400th year of his faith, he prophesied, a great city would be founded below the hill. By our calendar that 2400th year was 1857 – the year King Mindon Min decreed the move from Amarapura to Mandalay. The statue represents the Buddha pointing to where the city would be built.

The first shrine you come to, half-way up the hill, contains the so-called **Peshawar Relics**, three bones of the Buddha. The relics were originally sent to Peshawar, now in Pakistan, by the great Indian king Asoka. The stupa into which they were built was destroyed in the 11th century, but in 1908, the curator of the Peshawar Museum discovered the actual relic casket during excavations. Although Peshawar had once been a great Buddhist centre, it had by that time been Muslim for many centuries; so the British government presented these important relics to the Burmese Buddhist Society, and this relatively neglected temple was built to house them.

From the summit, 230m above the surrounding plain, there's a fine view back over the battlements of the palace to the city of Mandalay, while to the east you can see the hazy blue outline of the Shan hills. Those interested in military history can also find, in a small building attached to one of the shrines at the top of a wide, steep flight of steps, a monument to the British regiment which retook the hill from the Japanese in fierce fighting in 1945. The Mandalay Hill monasteries were renovated and enlarged in the early 1990s to accommodate Burmese army sentries.

Admission to the hill is US$3; there's an additional US$3 for the use of video cameras. Mandalay Hill can be reached via bus No 4 or 6, or via the red Mann Sit Thi bus.

Joe Cummings

with one of the attendants. If you keep them with you, it's considered respectful to keep them in a bag and out of view.

Kyauktawgyi Paya

Close to the southern entrance to Mandalay Hill stands the Kyauktawgyi Paya, the construction of which commenced in 1853 and was completed in 1878. It was originally intended that this paya, like its namesake a few kilometres south in Amarapura, would be modelled after the Ananda Pahto (temple) of Bagan, but due to a palace rebellion this grand plan was not carried through.

It is chiefly interesting for the huge seated image of the Buddha carved from a single block of marble. The marble block from the mines of nearby Sagyin was so colossal that it required 10,000 men labouring for 13 days to transport it from a canal to the current site. Ornamented with royal attire, the image was completed and dedicated in 1865. Around the shrine are figures of the Buddha's 80 *arahats* (disciples), arranged in groups of 20 on each of the four sides. Admission for foreigners is US$2.

Mandalay's biggest festival is held here for seven days in early to mid-October to commemorate Thadingyut.

Sandamani Paya

To the south-east of Mandalay Hill, close to the bus stop, is the Sandamani Paya, a cluster of slender whitewashed *stupas* (Buddhist religious monuments) built on the site of King Mindon's temporary palace – used while the new Mandalay Palace was under construction. King Mindon had come to power after the successful overthrow of King Pagan Min, an operation in which he had been assisted by his younger brother Prince Kanaung.

Mindon tended to concentrate on religious matters and leave the niceties of secular rule to his brother, but in 1866 Prince Kanaung was assassinated in an unsuccessful revolt inspired by Prince Myingun. The Sandamani Paya was built as a memorial to Prince Kanaung on the spot where he was killed.

The Sandamani Paya enshrines an iron image of the Buddha cast in 1802 by Bodawpaya and transported here from Amarapura in 1874. Around the stupa lies a large collection of marble slabs inscribed with commentaries on the *Tripitaka* (Buddhist canon). They were another project of the venerable U Khanti. Do not confuse them with the 729 inscribed marble slabs of the Kuthodaw Paya, which stands to the east of the Sandamani Paya.

Admission to Sandamani is combined with admission to nearby Kuthodaw, and costs US$5.

Kuthodaw Paya

Also known as the Maha Lawka Marazein Paya, the central stupa here was modelled after Shwezigon Paya at Nyaung U near Bagan. Building commenced in 1857, at the same time as the royal palace. The paya complex has been dubbed 'the world's biggest book', for standing around the central stupa are 729 marble slabs on which are inscribed the entire Tripitaka. Each slab is housed in its own individual small stupa.

It took an editorial committee numbering over 200 to produce the original slabs. It has been estimated that, reading for eight hours a day, one person would take 450 days to read the complete 'book'. King Mindon convened the Fifth Buddhist Synod and used a team of 2400 monks to read the whole book in a nonstop relay lasting nearly six months! In 1900 a paper edition of the stone original was printed in 38 volumes, each with about 400 pages. A 730th slab in the corner of the inner enclosure tells of the construction of this amazing book.

Foreigner admission is US$5, which includes admission to nearby Sandamani Paya.

Atumashi Kyaung

The ruins of Atumashi Kyaung (Incomparable Monastery), built by King Mindon in 1857, stand a little to the south of Kuthodaw Paya. Built at the same time as the Kuthodaw Paya, this *kyaung* (monastery) was of traditional Burmese monastic construction – a masonry base topped by a wooden building – but instead of the usual multiroofed design it consisted of graduated rectangular terraces. By all accounts, it was one of the most magnificent temples in all South-East Asia. Inside was a famous Buddha image, clothed in the king's silk clothing and with a huge diamond set on the forehead. The image was stolen in 1885, during the British takeover of the city.

In 1890 the monastery caught fire and, together with its contents, which included four complete sets of the Tripitaka in teak boxes, was completely gutted. Today a huge quadrangle of colonnaded and arched walls, the main stairway and a few fine stucco reliefs survive. Although only a pale shadow of its original form, the ruined building is still impressive. Inside you can see the stumps of teak pillars that once supported the roof. Using convict labour, the government is currently renovating the site – one hopes the atmosphere won't be ost completely, as at Mandalay Fort. In the nearby Shwenandaw Kyaung you can see an early photograph of the Atumashi Kyaung prior to its destruction.

Admission for foreigners to Atumashi Kyaung is another government two-for-one deal – the US$5 fee includes nearby Shwenandaw Kyaung.

Shwenandaw Kyaung

Close to the Atumashi Kyaung stands the Shwenandaw Kyaung (Golden Palace Monastery). This monastery is of great interest, not only as a fine example of a traditional Burmese wooden monastery, but as a fragile reminder of the old Mandalay Fort. At one time, this building was part of the palace complex and was used as an apartment by King Mindon and his chief queen, and it was in this building that he died. After Mindon's death, King Thibaw Min had the building dismantled and reassembled on its present site in 1880 as a monastery. It is said that Thibaw used the building for meditation, and the couch on which he sat can still be seen.

The building is covered inside and out with carved panels; though unfortunately, many of the exterior panels have weathered badly and some have been removed. At one time the building was gilded and decorated with glass mosaics. The carved panels inside are still in excellent condition, particularly the 10 *jataka* (scenes taken from the Buddha's life).

A couple of years ago an admission of US$3 was collected but this practice was recently discontinued. One rumour says the old *sayadaw* (chief abbot) in charge of the attached monastery thought it was disgraceful to charge admission to a religious building. Not even the State Peace & Development Council (SPDC) goes against the most highly ranked sayadaws in matters of this kind.

Mahamuni Paya

South-west of the town, or about 1.5km north-west of Mandalay airport, stands the Mahamuni Paya (Great Sage Pagoda). It is also sometimes called Payagyi (Big Paya), or the Rakhaing Paya. It was originally built by King Bodawpaya in 1784, when a road paved with bricks was constructed from his palace to the paya's eastern gate. You can still find traces of this royal highway. In 1884 the shrine was destroyed by fire; the current one is comparatively recent.

The centrepiece of the shrine is the highly venerated Mahamuni image that was transported to Myanmar from Mrauk U (Myohaung) in Rakhaing (Arakan) in 1784. It was believed to be of great age even at that time – it may have been cast during the 1st century AD – and the surrounding complex was specially built for it. The 4m-high seated image is cast in bronze, but over the years countless thousands of devout Buddhists have completely covered the figure in a 15cm-thick layer of gold leaf. Only men are permitted to walk up to the Mahamuni image and apply gold leaf. In the rainy season it is cloaked in monastic robes.

During festivals, the image is thronged by so many worshippers that caretakers have installed video monitors in other parts of the complex so that the Burmese can pay their respects to the Mahamuni's video image; you'll actually see people bowing down before the TV screens. Each morning at 4 am, a team of monks washes the Mahamuni's face and even brushes its teeth – an event well worth getting up early to see. Photography of the image is forbidden.

In the courtyard a small building houses six bronze Khmer figures brought back from Rakhaing along with the Mahamuni Buddha. Three are lions, two are male warriors and one is Erawan (the three-headed elephant). Originally, these figures stood sentry at Angkor Wat in Cambodia, then were taken from Angkor by the Thais in 1431. King Bayinnaung subsequently looted them from Ayuthaya in 1564 and brought the figures to Bago (Pegu), where in 1663 they were nabbed by King Razagyi of Rakhaing. According to legend, rubbing a part of the image will cure any affliction on the corresponding part of your own body – knee and stomach ailments seem to be the main preoccupation of the Burmese, who have polished these parts to a high gloss. Bars now protect the sculptures from further rubbing.

The temple courtyard contains more inscription stones collected by King Bodawpaya, who appears to have had quite a thing about this pursuit. Another small building, next to the one containing the bronze figures, has two large statues shouldering a pole between them, from which is slung a traditional Burmese gong said to weigh five tonnes. There are many interesting shop stalls at the entrance to the shrine; this was one of the few places in the country where photographs of Aung San Suu Kyi were openly sold during the long period of her house arrest.

During the Mahamuni Paya *pwe* (festival) in early February, thousands of people from nearby districts make pilgrimages to Mahamuni. The temple is always a centre of activity and during this festival it explodes with energy.

Admission to the Mahamuni Paya is US$4 for foreigners. The blue No 1 bus goes to Mahamuni from Zeigyo and from Kuthodaw Paya.

Shwekyimyint Paya
Located on 24th St between 82nd and 83rd Sts, a little north-east of Zeigyo or the clock tower, this quiet paya's original construction considerably predates Mandalay itself. It was founded in 1167 by Prince Minshinzaw during the Bagan period. He was the exiled son of King Alaungsithu and settled near the present site of Mandalay.

The shrine is notable because it contains the original Buddha image consecrated by the prince. It also contains many other images, made of gold, silver or crystal that were collected by later Burmese kings and removed from Mandalay Fort after it was occupied by the British. These images are generally kept under lock and key and only shown to the general public on very important religious occasions. Here, and at the Setkyathiha Paya, you can find the ridiculous in close proximity to the sublime – glass cases with figures of the Buddha and disciples which, when you put a coin in the slot, parade around to noisy music.

Shwekyimyint is often a good place to meet Burmese people who wish to serve as unofficial tour guides to other religious sites, for nothing more than a chance to practise their tourist-English skills. Of course, a tip or small gift is always appreciated. Admission to the paya is free.

Setkyathiha Paya
A short distance south-west of the Zeigyo on 85th St, this stupa rises from an elevated masonry platform. It was badly damaged during WWII, but was subsequently repaired. Its main point of interest is the impressive 5m-high seated Buddha image cast in bronze by King Bagyidaw in Inwa in 1823 just before the First Anglo-Burmese War broke out.

In 1849 King Pagan Min moved the image to Amarapura, just as the second war was about to begin. When the third and final conflict was about to commence, the image was brought to Mandalay in 1884. Reclining Buddha images can be seen in the paya courtyard, along with a sacred bodhi tree planted by U Nu, a former prime minister of Myanmar.

Admission is free.

Eindawya Paya

The beautifully proportioned stupa at Eindawya Paya stands west of Zeigyo. It is covered in gold leaf and makes a fine, shimmering sight on a sunny day. The stupa was built by King Pagan Min in 1847, on the site of the palace where he lived before he ascended the throne – which at that time was still at Amarapura.

The shrine houses a Buddha image made of chalcedony – a quartz mineral with an admixture of opal – which was said to have come to Myanmar from Bodhgaya, India in 1839. Because the Eindawya Paya is a little more remote and less visited by the usual stream of tourists, you're likely to get an unusually open reception here.

Admission is free.

Shwe In Bin Kyaung

This large and elegant wooden monastery was commissioned in 1895 by a pair of wealthy Chinese jade merchants. The woodcarved ornamentation along the balustrades and roof cornices is of exquisite quality. You'll find it west of Shweta Chaung and south of 35th St. It is seldom crowded and is well worth a visit. Admission is free.

Other Attractions

Something is always happening on the streets of Mandalay, whether bustling street markets or neighbourhood pwes. Mandalay's centre is a short walk west from the south-western corner of the fort. Here you will find the clock tower, and nearby, the relocated Zeigyo. The sprawling old market, designed in 1903 by Count Caldari (the Italian first secretary of the Mandalay Municipality) was dismantled – much to the dismay of the local folk – around 1990 and moved to two new three storey buildings done in the People's Republic of China-style on 84th St between 26th and 27th Sts. In spite of the less atmospheric location, the market still represents a fascinating collection of stalls selling every sort of Burmese ware you could imagine – and a fair assortment of smuggled goods from outside Myanmar. In the usual Asian manner, here

are sections for everything from jewellery or textiles to books or hardware. When a lift and escalators were added several years ago, it proved to be quite a marvel. Nowadays however, people in power-erratic Mandalay often ignore the high-tech facilities and take the stairs.

In the evening, busy **night markets** spring up around the intersections of 84th and 27th Sts, and 79th and 29th Sts. A picturesque **open-air market** west of Zeigyo specialises in onions, potatoes, and jaggery (the old English term for sugar produced by the sugar palm).

If you continue west along 26th St beyond the market you will eventually come to the **riverfront**, a scene of constant activity and interest; something is always happening down here. The boat landing at the end of 26th St (called Bayintnaung Lan at this point) is where you must come for the riverboats heading upriver to Mingun. You can see working water buffaloes at the western end of Pinya Lan (22nd St), the next landing north. A short distance north of the Mingun jetty is an area where people come to do their laundry; it can be a very colourful place. This may change if the government pursues its plan to move everyone out of the riverfront districts.

Yankin Paya, perched on Yankin Hill about 2.5 to 3km east of Mandalay Fort, is a good spot for watching sunsets. If you go by rented bicycle you can park at the bottom and climb the hill on foot. Or you can take a white No 5 bus for K8 to the foot of the hill, then board one of the local pickups that climb the hill for K10 per person (K20 in a pickup). Unlike at Mandalay Hill, there's no charge for climbing Yankin Hill.

Yadanapon Zoo, opposite the northern side of the fort moat, has a small collection of animals, but is a quiet place to wander around for a K10 entry fee.

Churches

Mandalay has some churches among the many temples. On the western side of 80th St between 34th and 35th Sts, **Father Lafon's Catholic Church** was built by the French in

MANDALAY

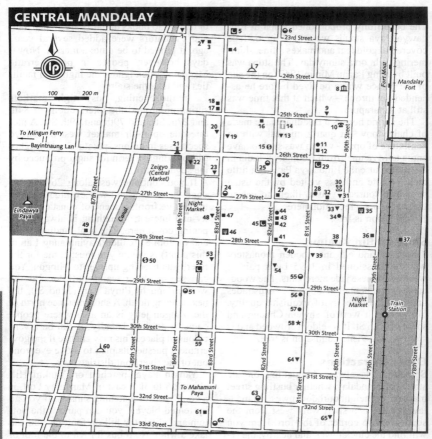

CENTRAL MANDALAY

the gothic style in 1894, then rebuilt in 1919. Its gothic facade remains intact. **Sacred Heart Cathedral**, on the eastern side of 82nd St between 25th and 26th Sts, was constructed in 1873, bombed in WWII and rebuilt in 1951. Masses are held daily at both churches, twice on Sunday. The congregations are predominantly Indian and Chinese.

The **Judson Baptist Church**, named for the American missionary who has virtually become a saint in Myanmar, stands on 82nd St between 33rd and 34th Sts. A sign posted

on the church claims the church fathers oppose 'liberalism, modernism, ecumenism, formalism and worldliness'.

Places to Stay – Budget

Room rates at the budget end have dropped considerably, as more hotels and guesthouses obtain licences to accept foreigners. Rates now average US$4 to US$8 per person – high by Burmese standards but the lowest they've been in years. Many budget hotels also have a few larger and slightly

CENTRAL MANDALAY

PLACES TO STAY
3 Classic Hotel
4 ET Hotel
12 Sabai Phyu Guest House
16 Royal Guest House
17 Nylon Hotel
18 Garden Hotel
27 Unity Hotel
32 Dream Hotel
36 Mother's World Hotel
37 Popa II Hotel
41 Bonanza Hotel
42 New Star Hotel
43 New York Hotel
47 Universe Hotel
49 AD-1 Hotel
61 Silver Swan Hotel

PLACES TO EAT
1 Mingalar Confectionery
2 Lashio Lay Restaurant
9 Shwe Pyi Moe Teashop
13 Devi Indian Restaurant
19 Mann Restaurant
20 Nylon Ice Cream Bar
22 Ambassador Restaurant & Grand Restaurant
23 Min Min Restaurant

31 Punjab Food House
33 Everest Restaurant
38 Laksmi Restaurant
39 Chan Myae South Indian Restaurant
40 Thinn Biryani
48 Shwe Let Yar Myanmar Fast Food
53 May Myo Biryani
54 Chin Shin Restaurant
64 Htaw Yin Restaurant
65 Golden Land Cold Drink

OTHER
5 Mosque
6 Buses to Taunggyi
7 Shwekyimyint Paya
8 Mandalay Museum & Library
10 Central Telephone & Telegraph Office
11 Myanma Airways Office
14 Sacred Heart Cathedral
15 MEB (Myanmar Economic Bank) No 1
21 Clock Tower
24 Pickups to Monywa

25 Main/Central Bus Centre (Buses/Pickups to Pyin U Lwin, Hsipaw & Lashio)
26 Air Mandalay Office
28 Shining Star Tours
29 Central Mosque
30 Sikh Temple
34 Bamboo Fan Factory
35 Hindu Temple
44 Seven Star Travel Agency; Penta Money Exchange
45 Am Yauk Tan Mosque
46 Hindu Temple
50 Myanmar Economic Bank (MEB) No 2
51 Pickups to Amarapura, Ava & Sagaing
52 Mosque
55 Bus to Hsipaw
56 Fire Lookout Tower
57 Mayflower Money Exchange
58 Police
59 Small Paya
60 Setkyathiha Paya
62 Leo Express; Kyaw Express (Buses to Yangon)
63 Shwe La Min (Golden Moon) (Bus to Bagan)

more expensive rooms – just as several mid-range places have a few economy rooms. Discounts are often available, especially during off-peak times.

At all of these places, you can expect electric power and water pressure to be intermittent. The importance of a fan can become apparent during a low-electricity episode. Quite often, the power required for the air-conditioning units is cut off, but enough power is provided to keep the lights on and the fans turning. In Mandalay, it's a good idea to ask upon check-in about the power schedule in general, and your room in particular.

Prostitution is no longer as common at most of the budget places as it was just a few years ago, although a few continue as part-time brothels. Some guesthouses are reputed to employ young Shan prostitutes.

At the moment, several hotels and guesthouses in the central district stand out in terms of quality and variety of accommoda-

tion. One very popular place is the well managed, 32 room *Royal Guest House* (☎ 02-22905, 41 25th St). Clean, if small, rooms cost US$4/8 for singles/doubles with shared toilet and cold-shower facilities; the corridors adjacent to these rooms are air-conditioned, and open transoms allow some of the cool air to reach the room, though on a hot night it's a stretch. For US$10/12 you can get a room with attached toilet and hot-water shower. There are two triple rooms with bath, air-con and small fridge for US$15.

Another popular place in the same vicinity is the tidy *Sabai Phyu Guest House* (☎ 02-25377, 58 81st St), a modern, multistorey building, which offers economy fan rooms with common bath for US$4 to US$8 a single, US$8 to US$12 a double. Breakfasts are served on the rooftop, which affords views of Mandalay Hill.

The convenient *ET Hotel* (☎ 02-25491, 129A 83rd St), between 23rd and 24th Sts,

MANDALAY

has 22 fan- and air-con rooms and another five with fan only. All rooms come with hot-water shower and a decent breakfast. The ET is a good spot to get information on travelling out of Mandalay. Rooms cost US$8/12, and a few larger family-style rooms go for US$15/20.

The *AD-1 Hotel* (☎ 02-34505), just east of Eindawya Paya, near the corner of 87th and 28th Sts, is for the moment one of the best bargains in Mandalay. Clean and basic rooms with fan and hot-water shower cost US$4/6, with breakfast. Another dollar gets you a room with air-con.

Moving north to the Shan district, the quiet *Classic Hotel* (☎ 02-25635, 59 23rd St) between 83rd and 84th Sts offers comfortable air-con rooms with TV, fridge and attached bath for US$10/16, breakfast included. Some rooms have hot water; others only cold water – though it doesn't seem to affect the price. The Lashio Lay Restaurant is next door.

The ever-popular *Nylon Hotel* (☎ 02-33460) is on the corner of 25th and 83rd Sts, a block west of the Royal Guest House, and has clean economy single rooms with fan and common bath for US$4. Larger rooms with air-con, fan, TV and bath range from US$8/10 a single to US$12/15 a double. As usual, quieter rooms are towards the back. Next door is the *Garden Hotel* (☎ 02-25184, 174 83rd St), a typical Burmese-style hotel with decent economy rooms with common bath for US$8/12, and rooms with private bath for US$10 to US$20. All rooms come with air-con, TV, fridge and breakfast.

Moving east of the city centre, the friendly *Taim Byu (Silver Cloud) Hotel* (☎ 02-27059), on the corner of 73rd and 29th Sts, is very good value with economy rooms with fan and attached bath for US$10 per person, and larger superior rooms with air-con, fridge, and TV for US$20/30. All rates include breakfast. In the same vicinity, the quiet and cheap *Si Thu Tourist Hotel* (☎ 02-26201, 29 65th St) between 30th and 31st Sts offers the usual cubicles-along-a-corridor setup with shared bath and toilet facilities for US$3 per person.

The *Great Guest House* on the northern side of 39th St, between 80th St and the railway, sees few foreigners. This location is close to where the Moustache Brothers and other pwe troupes often perform. Rooms cost US$5 per person.

Places to Stay – Mid-Range
Mandalay has added a number of hotels with rooms in the US$25 to US$45 per night range. South of the train station, the *Silver Swan Hotel* (☎ 02-32178, fax 36567, 568 83rd St), between 32nd and 33rd Sts, has very helpful staff, clean and airy rooms with teakwood floors, air-con, tub and shower, fridge and TV. A great-value hotel in this price range, with most rooms costing US$20/25 a single/double, plus a few economy rooms available at US$15/18. All rates include breakfast, tax and service.

The new 42 room *Myit Phyar Ayer Hotel* (☎ 02-27242, fax 35646, 568 80th St) between 33rd and 34th Sts has an inviting lobby decorated with marionettes and classical musical instruments. This well managed new addition to the upper end of the mid-range hotels is very good value for the money. A variety of smart-looking rooms with teak furnishings start at US$25 for a single, US$35/45 a single/double for standard rooms, US$45/60 for slightly larger rooms with the addition of a tub, and four suites at US$75 (single or double).

The *Power Hotel* (☎ 02-52406, 686 80th St) between 39th and 40th Sts is fairly typical of the Chinese-style multistorey box hotels. Rooms feature air-con, fridge, TV and attached hot-water bath, and cost US$25/35, including breakfast. Similar in features and price is the nearby *Tiger Hotel* (☎ 02-23234, 628 80th St) between 37th and 38th Sts.

Moving east of the train station you'll find one of the nicer and quieter places to stay outside the central district – the Indian-operated *Mandalay View Inn* (☎ 02-22347), a two storey residential compound on 66th St between 26th and 27th Sts, just north of the Mandalay Marionettes' theatre. Well maintained standard rooms cost US$30/40;

slightly larger rooms US$40/50. These rates include breakfast but not tax and service. Discounts are available for multiday stays. All rooms come with air-con, TV, phone and hot-water showers; IDD phone service is available.

The attractive **Mandalay Royal Hotel** (☎ 02-23702, 5 71st St) between 29th and 30th Sts offers comfortable rooms with air-con, TV and fridge. Most rooms have a balcony. Rates are a reasonable US$15/20 for a standard room, and US$25/30 for a larger room with a small desk. Similar in price, but with sometimes unhelpful staff, is the quiet **Golden Land Inn** (☎ 02-33560, 47 Kankaw Lane) near the corner of 32nd and 71st Sts.

When the new train station is completed, a more upscale place is expected to replace the rather funky Popa I Hotel, currently adjacent to the station. However, just a block north of the train station, the **Popa II Hotel** (☎ 02-22555) has clean and quiet air-con rooms at US$30/36. Although this is still a government hotel, it is far better than either the state-owned Innwa Inn or Mya Mandalar Hotel – both near the south-east corner of Mandalay Palace and both run-down and overpriced.

The four storey **Pacific Hotel** (☎ 02-32507), on the corner of 30th and 78th Sts, is a new Chinese hotel opposite the train station, with clean and airy rooms at US$30/45, breakfast included. All rooms are air-con, with TV, fridge and attached bath.

A cluster of hotels west of the train station includes the nine storey **Universe Hotel** (☎ 02-33246, fax 33245, 215 83rd St), between 27th and 28th Sts, which has clean, air-con rooms and private bath for US$30/36. Breakfast is included and the hotel will pick up guests from the airport or train station. Slightly larger rooms with fridge go for US$36/42. The spacious lobby has satellite TV and IDD phone service.

The **Dream Hotel** (☎ 02-26054, fax 35656, 152 27th St) between 80th and 81st Sts presents a strong contrast between the busy outside world and a quiet interior. Run by an Indian family, the hotel offers a variety of lodgings, beginning with a couple of econ-omy rooms with shared bath for US$10 per person. Superior rooms with attached bath cost US$25/30, and the hotel has a few larger suites for US$35 to US$45. All rooms come with TV, hot water, air-con and fridge.

The **Unity Hotel** (☎ 02-28860) on the corner of 27th and 82nd Sts is another centrally located Chinese-style place with clean, though dark, rooms that go for US$20/30, breakfast included. The Unity's lobby is a popular hangout for travellers who need to make IDD calls, or who want to catch a bit of satellite TV. Free airport transportation is also provided.

On the north-east corner of 82nd and 28th Sts, the Chinese-style **Bonanza Hotel** (☎ 02-31032) offers good-sized rooms with air-con, TV, fridge and private hot-water showers for a reasonable US$15/25. The lobby is up one flight of stairs.

South of the Air Mandalay office in two connected five-storey buildings on 82nd St, between 27th and 28th Sts, are the **New York Hotel** (☎ 02-28917) and the **New Star Hotel** (☎ 02-27210). Air-con rooms with cold-water shower and fridge cost US$15/25 at both places.

Mother's World Hotel (☎ 02-33627, fax 36599, 58 79th St) between 27th and 28th Sts offers large, carpeted rooms with TV, fridge, air-con, hot water and a small writing desk for US$20/35.

North and west of the city centre is the new and out-of-the-way **Emerald Land Inn** (☎ 02-26990, fax 35645) on the southern side of 14th St, between 87th and 88th Sts. The hotel features 32 rooms including six chalet-type bungalows, plus a restaurant and swimming pool. All rooms come with air-con, satellite TV, minibar fridge and phone. Room rates are a reasonable US$30/40, with a few larger suites for US$50/60, plus tax and service. Free airport transport is provided.

Places to Stay – Top End

Mandalay's recent hotel boom has produced three new top end hotels. Like similar establishments in Yangon, occupancy is running well below expectations. The rates mentioned here reflect the going rates – which are usually 30% to 40% below published rates. The three hotels in this category are also the only ones in Mandalay where you can reliably use a credit card (Visa or American Express (Amex)). Add another 10% service and 10% tax to the listed rates.

The *Mandalay Swan Hotel* (☎ 02-31625, 31587, fax 35677, 44(B) 26th St) between 66th and 68th Sts is a joint venture between the Burmese government and a Singaporean company. The centrally located Mandalay Swan is also home to the government's MTT travel agency. The 106 room low-rise hotel is spread out among landscaped gardens and features a pool and tennis court. It has the usual upscale cafe and restaurant offerings, plus Kipling's Bar and karaoke lounge. Rooms (single or double) range from a reasonable US$45 to US$70 for a junior suite. The more expensive rooms get you a complimentary lunch or dinner as well. All room rates include a full breakfast and free airport transportation.

The *Novatel Mandalay* (☎ 02-35638, 02-35680, fax 35639, 9 10th St), at the foot of Mandalay Hill, is an impressive affair complete with a large pool and fitness centre, business centre, several shops, cafe, Chinese restaurant and yet another Burmese bar called Kipling's. A variety of smart rooms is available starting at US$75 (all rates for single or double) and ranging from US$125 to US$200 for larger suites. All room rates include full breakfast, air-con, minibar, satellite TV and airport transport.

The 247 room *Sedona Hotel Mandalay* (☎ 02-36488, fax 36499), just opposite Mandalay Palace, on the corner of 26th and 66th Sts, easily meets all the large resort hotel expectations, from pool bar and gymnasium to business centre and banquet facilities. Well appointed single/double rooms begin at US$90/100. For US$130/140 you get a balcony with a view of Mandalay Hill. Larger suites are available for US$150 to US$300. All rates include a full western-style breakfast, satellite TV, and free airport transportation.

Places to Eat

As in Yangon, the variety and quality of restaurants in Mandalay have multiplied with the recent economic development. Bamar, Shan and Chinese restaurants are particularly good, but Indian food in Mandalay isn't quite up to Yangon's standards.

Bamar The long-running *Tu Tu Restaurant*, on the southern side of 27th St between 74th and 75th Sts, serves traditional Bamar food from pots lined up on a table, in typical Burmese fashion. It's a little more expensive than other restaurants of this type but the place is clean and the food is very good.

The similarly clean and reasonably priced *Shwe Let Yar Myanmar Fast Food* on 83rd St between 27th and 28th Sts opposite the Modern Hotel serves traditional Bamar dishes and Burmese-style *biryani* (dan bauk).

Aya Myit Tas (Tar) Myanmar Restaurant on the west side of 81st St, between 36th and 37th Sts, serves excellent Bamar curries. The owners are friendly and the food is plentiful and cheap. Similar is quality and price is *Daw Lay May Restaurant* (no English sign) on 76th St between 30th and 31st Sts. There's no English menu, but the owners are helpful and it's easy to point to what you'd like.

A very pleasant upscale Bamar restaurant in a patio setting is *Sakhantha* (☎ 02-21066, 24 72nd St), between 27th and 28th Sts, which offers consistently good Bamar food. The long list of traditional Bamar *thouq* (salad), including the hard-to-find tamarind leaf salad, is particularly appetising. It's open daily from 10 am to 9 pm. A popular tourist venue is the *Pyigyimon Restaurant*, a replica of Yangon's Karaweik floating restaurant at the south-eastern corner of the moat. There are as many Chinese dishes as Bamar dishes on the menu. In the evening, dinner is accompanied by a Burmese puppet show put on by Mandalay Marionettes.

Along the eastern side of 80th St between 28th and 30th Sts, many food stalls open up at night, selling everything from *mohinga* (rice noodles and fish soup) and chicken biryani to *ayeq hpyu* (moonshine) and tea.

Food is generally quite tasty here and you'll meet interesting people – it's less insular than most indoor restaurants in town.

Shan The best Shan restaurants are found in the vicinity of 23rd St, west of the moat. The popular *Lashio Lay Restaurant*, next to the Classic Hotel on 23rd St between 83rd and 84th Sts, offers a large array of spicy and mild Shan dishes which changes on a daily basis and usually includes four or five vegetarian dishes. The food is very good and it's easy enough to point out the dishes that look most appetising; virtually no English is spoken.

Thai Yai Restaurant, on the southern side of 22nd St between 83rd and 84th Sts, serves both Shan and Thai dishes. Among the house specialities are Thai-style roast chicken, papaya salad, noodles and chicken rice. It's open from 6 am to 10 pm, later than most of the other Shan places. Lashio Lay and Thai Yai each serve delicious *Shan hkauq sweh* (spicy rice noodles) in the morning; this makes a nice change from teashop fare or the standard toast-and-egg breakfasts served at most guesthouses and hotels.

Indian & Vegetarian Strictly vegetarian – though not strictly Indian – *Marie-Min Vegetarian Restaurant* on 27th St between 74th and 75th Sts, is a godsend to many travellers, and has one of the cleanest kitchens we've seen. Owned and operated by an Indian Catholic family, Marie-Min serves delicious *chapatis* (flatbread), *pappadums* (thin cracker), curries, pumpkin soup and eggplant dip, plus such delights as strawberry *lassis* (yoghurt shakes), muesli, guacamole, hash-brown potatoes, pancakes and various western-style breakfasts (served all day). The menu, written in 12 languages, is quite reasonably priced, with most dishes costing less than K160. This traveller-friendly oasis has an information bulletin board and also offers a breakfast box for early morning riverboat or train trips. It's open daily from 8 am to 10 pm. On Christmas Eve the devout owners arrange special candlelit dinners accompanied by live Burmese music. (Of course, like many Mandalay eateries, you may have a candlelit dinner anytime the power suddenly goes out.)

Other traditional Indian places can be found near the Hindu and Sikh temples and the Central Mosque around the intersection of 81st and 26th Sts. A good find among these is the cozy *Punjab Food House* on 80th St near 27th St. This friendly, Sikh-run curry shop serves tasty chapatis, rice and vegetarian curries. In the morning they usually have *aloo puri* (fried flatbread with potato curry). It's open from 8.30 am to 7.30 pm.

Across the street from Punjab Food House, next to the Nepali temple, is the slightly larger *Everest Restaurant*, with a tasty 'morning *nasta*' of chapati with vegetables, *dosai* (crepe and vegetables) and *aloo puri* (potato curry) on occasion. Rice and vegetable curry is served for lunch and dinner. It's open from 7 am to 7 pm. The roomy *Chan Myae South Indian Restaurant* (English sign: India restaurant) is on 81st St near the corner of 28th St. The food is good, and there's lots of it for the price – and they serve beer.

In the same general vicinity, *Laksmi Restaurant* opposite the Hotel Venus on 28th St between 80th and 81st Sts isn't bad for curries and rice. The very basic *Devi Indian Restaurant* (English sign: restaurant), opposite the Arya Samaj temple on the eastern side of 82nd St between 25th and 26th Sts, does puri and dosa from 6 to 8 am, rice and curries from 10 am to 9 pm. Though it's basically a grubby hole-in-the-wall place, it's one of the few Indian eateries in town that serves beer (also tea and soft drinks).

Several nearby shops also serve biryani. *Thinn Biryani* on the southern side of 28th St between 81st and 82nd Sts serves both vegetarian and chicken biryani, plus rich *ohn htamin* (coconut rice). Look for the sign that says: 'Taste of Thinn will make you win; try Thinn's speciality, delicious Persian biryani in the heart of Mandalay City.' It's open from 5 am to 10 pm. Another reliable biryani shop, *May Myo Biryani*, opposite the Hotel Sapphire on 83rd St between 28th and 29th Sts, is open from 10 am to 10 pm.

Chinese There's quite a selection of Chinese eating places on 83rd St, between 26th and 25th Sts, not far from Zeigyo. You'll find the popular *Mann Restaurant* – one of the city's better Chinese eateries. The nearby *Min Min Restaurant*, on 83rd St between 26th and 27th Sts, has Chinese Muslim food (indicated by the number 786 throughout Myanmar) – it's reasonably cheap, and the food is quite OK. A similar Chinese Muslim place, *Chin Shin Restaurant*, on the eastern side of 82nd St between 28th and 29th Sts, serves curries, noodles, duck and Yunnan noodles.

Moving upmarket, the posh *Honey Garden Restaurant (☎ 02-24098)*, on the corner of 70th and 29th Sts, offers superb service and a long list of well prepared Chinese dishes (and a few Bamar ones) in outdoor dining areas. It's open from 9 am to 10 pm. *Emerald Green Restaurant (☎ 02-24725)* on Yangyiaung Lan (35th St) between 88th and 89th Sts is another upscale Chinese place with white tablecloths, air-con and a full bar. The food is very good, and it's an easy dinner stop-off if you're returning from Mingun at the end of the day.

On the east rooftop of Zeigyo, the *Ambassador Restaurant* features an extensive Chinese banquet-style menu with Burmese singing and dancing. The *Grand Restaurant* on the west rooftop is similar.

There are many small *Chinese restaurants* along 80th and 81st Sts in the central district, most open till 9 or 10 pm – late for Mandalay. The hygienic-looking Chinese eatery *Htaw Yin Restaurant (396 81st St)*, near 31st St, is quite good. Another string of basic *Chinese eateries* is found along 29th St, between 83rd and 84th Sts, and along 30th St, between 70th and 76th Sts.

Teashops & Cafes Although Mandalay is absolutely jammed with teashops, two stand out from the pack. *Shwe Pyi Moe Teashop* on 25th St between 80th and 81st (look for the thick phalanx of bicycles parked out front) serves probably the best tea in town and is open from 5 am to 5 pm. The selection of snacks leans towards Chinese, with

ei-kya-kwe (long, deep-fried pastries, known as *you tiao* in Chinese) a house speciality. *Minn Thi Ha Teashop*, on the south side of 38th St between 83rd and 84th Sts near the entertainment district, is of similar high quality and is also very popular; it's open from 5 am to 4 pm.

Near the south-east corner of Mandalay Palace and the Sedona Hotel, *Shudaunk Teashop* (no English sign) is a comfortable teashop serving cold drinks and mostly Indian snacks.

Western Food, Snacks, Ice Cream & Beer The *BBB (Barman Beer Bar) (☎ 02-25623)*, on the western side of 76th St between 26th and 27th Sts, offers an extensive menu of well prepared western, Bamar, Indian and Chinese dishes served in an air-con dining room furnished in rattan. Indian and European breakfasts cost K200, meat dishes K600, grilled lobster K1000; plentiful set dinners cost K1100. Other menu items include sandwiches, milkshakes and fresh fruit juices. BBB is open from 7 am to 11 pm daily.

Across the road from Mann Restaurant at 176 83rd St there's the very popular *Nylon Ice Cream Bar* – it's a strange name (actually Nai Lon), but the ice cream is excellent and seems to be safe. In the evening you can sit out at the pavement tables and try large servings of strawberry, pineapple or orange ice cream for just a few kyat. *Golden Land Cold Drink*, on 80th St between 32nd and 33rd Sts, is owned by the same family as Nylon, and they do delicious lassis. Friendly *Man Thu Yein (314 81st St)*, between 26th and 27th Sts, is also quite popular.

At Myainghaywun Park, inside Mandalay Fort, an informal outdoor *cafe* serves cheap draught beer from the Mandalay Brewery.

Towards the end of the dry season Mandalay becomes a very dusty, thirsty place. All over town there are sugar-cane vendors with their big, heavy crushing wheels ready to fix you a glass of iced sugar-cane juice (with a dash of lime). It's very refreshing and appears to be fairly safe. In season there are strawberry vendors around town; take a basket (after rinsing) to one of the ice-cream bars and try strawberries and ice cream!

For good Bamar sweets, try **Mingalar Confectionery** on the north-west corner of 23rd and 84th Sts, near the Classic Hotel and Lashio Lay restaurant.

Entertainment

Marionette Theatre *Mandalay Marionettes and Culture Show* (☎ 02-38718), on 65th St between 26th and 27th Sts, is a small theatre where marionette shows, music and dancing are performed nightly at 8.30 pm. The same company puts on similar performances at the *Pyigyimon Restaurant* earlier in the evening at 7 pm. The show lasts around an hour and features selections from the *zat pwe* (recreation of an ancient legend or Buddhist jataka) and *Yamazat* (Tales from the Indian epic *Ramayana*) traditions. This includes colourful marionette dances that represent the *zawgyi* (immortal alchemist), *naga* (dragon serpent), *galoun* (Sanskrit: *garuda*, the royal birdmount of Vishnu) and ogre figures from Burmese mythology. The puppetmasters are former students of the famous master Shewi-bo U Tin, who passed away some time ago. Preceding the marionette theatre are short performances of traditional music played on the *saung gauq* (Burmese harp) and *pattala* (xylophone). The admission fee is K500. Trishaw drivers often badmouth the show or say it's closed because the theatre owners refuse to pay commissions. Handmade marionettes are available for sale.

Folk & Classical Pwe Mandalay is the cultural heart of Myanmar, and there is an active entertainment scene, most notably dozens of *pwe troupes* that combine music, drama and improvisation to the delight of Burmese audiences. Pwe troupes often perform at important Burmese social functions including paya festivals, novitiations, weddings and monastic ceremonies.

If you'd like to delve a little deeper into the art of the Burmese pwe, pay a visit to the *Moustache Brothers troupe* on 39th St between 80th and 81st Sts. One of several pwe troupes headquartered in this district, brother Lu Maw and family have opened their house to visitors interested in learning more about Burmese dance, comedy, music and puppetry. The Moustache Brothers' ensemble is somewhat unusual, in that they use nothing but traditional instruments in their performances. Comedian Lu Maw speaks fair English and is very knowledgeable about the history of Burmese dance-drama and comedy.

Performances at the small theatre on 39th St are narrated in English by Lu Maw, a master of improvisation. The family of dancers, musicians and storytellers are as talented as they are dedicated to the fine line between art and politics. In true pwe fashion, performances always include improvised material about news of the day – from the recruiting of Shan girls into prostitution to the increasing price of cooking oil.

The Moustache Brothers gained unwanted notoriety on 7 January 1996 when the oldest brother, U Par Par Lay, and cousin U Lu Zaw were arrested following an independence day performance at the invitation of Aung San Suu Kyi, at a gathering of 2000 members of the opposition NLD (National League for Democracy) outside her Yangon home. Their crime was to tell a joke on the government: 'In the past, thieves were called thieves. Now they are known as cooperative workers'. Both performers are currently serving seven-year prison terms near Myitkyina, north of Mandalay. We learned that when Par Par Lay's wife travels to the prison to bring food every couple of months, she is not allowed to actually visit or even see her husband. Instead, guards only show her the prisoner's signature for the 'receipt of goods'.

Although blacklisted from tour group itineraries by the government, the talented family performs nightly at 8 pm in a small theatre-room facing the street. The price for a group of up to seven people is about K500 per guest. If you go alone, a donation may be acceptable. The family will also perform during the day by appointment. The brothers also make and sell Burmese marionettes

A-Nyeint Pwe – From Slapstick to Satire

Call it folk opera, call it vaudeville or even guerrilla street theatre – the *a-nyeint pwe* is one of the most fluid and adaptable, yet traditional, of contemporary Burmese entertainment forms. In a-nyeint pwe, the emphasis shifts among comedy, dancing, melodrama and instrumental music – in the typically lengthy performance there is plenty of time for all. Accessible and enjoyable even to non-Burmese-speaking visitors, a-nyeint pwe is the everyday, all-purpose Burmese entertainment genre: a religious festival, wedding, funeral, celebration, monastic ordination, fair, sporting event – almost anything can be a good reason to host one. Once under way a performance traditionally goes on all night in rural areas (or from around 8 pm till midnight in the cities), which is no strain – if the audience gets bored at some point during the performance they simply fall asleep and wake up when something more to their taste is on.

These old-time variety shows appeal to all generations, from young children to grannies. During the comedy segments in particular, it is very easy to understand what is happening – slapstick comedy hardly needs to be translated. In one pwe we saw in Yangon, a prolonged skit involved an obviously henpecked and accident-prone husband who, at every opportunity, showed his nervousness by untying, hitching up and then retying his longyi. An equivalent gesture in western culture might be compulsively straightening a necktie or fiddling with a ballpoint pen. It soon had the audience, and us, falling around with laughter.

Pwe comedians often work subtle political commentary into their routines. U Par Par Lay, a famous comedian with a Mandalay a-nyeint pwe troupe called the Moustache Brothers, was arrested for comparing farmers' hats with his cohort on stage. The cohort said 'My hat

is so large it protects my head from sun and rain all day long', to which the comedian replied, 'My hat is so large it protects all Myanmar', a reference to the star-topped hat that served as a symbol for the NLD before Aung San Suu Kyi was arrested in 1989. Par Pay Lay spent six months in jail for that innocuous-sounding reference. He and 13 other performers were arrested again following an Independence Day performance at Aung San Suu Kyi's compound in January 1996 in which more pointed satire poked fun at the generals running the country. This time the pwe comedian was sentenced to seven years hard labour in a Myitkyina prison camp; even his family has not been permitted to visit him since September 1996. While the Moustache Brothers have been blacklisted from taking their performing troupe on the road, a video of their 1996 performance has since become one of the hottest selling underground videos in the country.

Joe Cummings

Par Par Lay

which are reasonably priced. If you give them advance notice, the families will prepare a Bamar meal and perform for small groups.

All of the pwe troupes in this area practice their craft during the months of June and July daily from 10 am to 4 pm. Visitors are welcome to wander from house to house and watch for free. During other times of year the troupes perform locally as well as intermittently travelling to festivals and religious ceremonies.

Abbreviated examples of Burmese classical music and dance are performed at the *Grand* and *Ambassador restaurants* on the west and east rooftops of Zeigyo.

Burmese Kickboxing You can watch Burmese kickboxing at a small *training facility* on 76th St between 27th and 28th Sts. If you're interested in attending a full-fledged match, this is the place to find out where and when the next one will be held in the Mandalay area. As with most places in Myanmar, matches commonly take place at paya festivals.

Shopping

Markets Zeigyo Market – an obsolete term, as *zeigyo* (*zei-gyo*, or *zei-cho*) means central market – encompasses two large buildings on 84th St; one between 26th and 27th Sts, the other between 27th and 28th Sts. You can find just about anything made in Myanmar here, from everyday consumer goods to jewellery and fine fabrics. Several markets have sprung up in the surrounding area, including the large open-air Kaingdan Market a couple of streets west of Zeigyo, which specialises in fresh produce and jaggery. A night market that extends southwards from the intersection of 84th and 27th Sts offers all kinds foods, audio tapes and clothing.

In Mandalay's unofficial and expanding Chinatown, there's a daily market that sets up along each street between 29th and 33rd Sts, running east of 80th St and west of the railway. General produce and household goods are cheaper to buy here than anywhere else in Mandalay.

Arts & Crafts Mandalay is a major crafts centre and you can get some really good bargains if you know what you're looking for. There are many little shops in the eastern part of the city near the Mya Mandalar and Mandalay Swan hotels selling a mixture of gems, carvings, silk, *kalaga* (tapestries) and other crafts. If you enter without a tout (most of the younger trishaw or horsecart drivers are into this), you'll get better deals, as they are usually paid high commissions.

Among the better shops is Mann Swe Gon Handicrafts on 27th St between 72nd and 73rd Sts. The proprietors maintain a particularly good selection of kalagas as well as other handicrafts. Nearby Sunflower Arts & Crafts (adjacent to Marie Min restaurant) has a good number of decent puppets, lacquerware and kalagas at moderate prices.

Sein Myint Artist (☎ 02-26553) at 42 Sanga University Lan in Nan Shei Quarter makes excellent kalagas. You're also free to wander the indoor-outdoor workshop which is adorned with antique looms, as well as a small gallery of very fine antique paintings and carvings, which are not for sale.

Try the east entrance of Mahamuni Paya for religious crafts. Thein Hteik Shin Myanmar Handicrafts is a reliable shop with reasonable prices.

A quality shop for *longyis* (sarong-style garments), ready-made silk and cotton clothing (also in big sizes) and colourful shoulder bags is Manaw Myay Kachin (MMK) Traditional Store with two locations: on 84th St between 33rd and 34th Sts (☎ 02-25226); and on 30th St between 77th and 78th Sts (☎ 02-32737).

Handicrafts are also available at a few vendor stalls in Zeigyo. Keep in mind that some of the items sold at these shops aren't legally supposed to be taken out of the country – older kalagas, *parabaiks* (folding manuscripts), *kamawas* (lacquered scriptures), gems, jade and any authentic antiques.

The very plush Yadanapura Art Centre, a government-run enterprise on 78th St towards the airport, purveys a high-quality selection of handicrafts and jewellery. As long as you keep the receipt, you'll be able

MANDALAY

to take any purchase from this shop out of the country.

If you have a dilapidated stupa in need of refurbishing, then head for the western exit of the Mahamuni – here you will find workshops manufacturing all sorts of temple paraphernalia. If the *hti* (umbrella-like decorated top of stupa) has toppled then this is the place to come for a new one.

Mandalay's gold-leaf makers are concentrated in the south-east of the city, near the intersection of 36th and 78th Sts. Sheets of gold are beaten into gossamer-thin pieces which are cut into squares and sold in packets to devotees to use for gilding images or even complete stupas. The typical gold-leaf square measures just .000127cm, thinner than ink on the printed page. Gilding a Buddha image or a stupa with gold leaf brings great credit to the gilder, so there is a steady growth of gold leaf on many images in Myanmar. Gold-leaf stickers cost a few kyat. Other crafts you may be able to see around Mandalay include silk weaving and silversmithing.

You can visit a bamboo fan factory on 80th St between 36th and 37th Sts, where the artisans make fans of paper and bamboo for weddings and banquets.

Precious Stones & Sculpture Kyawzu and Minthazu, two villages attached to the urban sprawl of Southern Mandalay, specialise in the cutting, polishing and carving of jade. Just north of the villages, outdoor jade markets meet daily in several spots along 86th St. The best quality jade is generally purveyed during the late morning (from 10 am to 1 pm) at the intersection of 38th and 86th Sts, where you'll see throngs of Burmese standing and squatting on the roadside or sitting in teashops, poring over red, white and green chunks laid out on empty rice sacks. Both rough and polished pieces, some carved, can be purchased here. None of the trade, of course, is 'government approved'. While most of the jade seen here is genuine, not all is of high quality. Beware of vendors selling jade 'boulders' smuggled in from Kachin State. Some are fakes with

thin sheets of jade peering through the brown outer 'skin'; the inside may contain cement or worthless stone.

A street close to Mahamuni Paya has a whole series of stone-carvers' workshops. Buddha images of all sizes are hewn from solid stone slabs. The best stone and marble cutters are found on the corner of 45th and 84th Sts. Bronze foundries and woodcarving workshops are clustered off Aung San Lan in the Tampawadi Quarter, south of Mahamuni. Bells and gongs are hand-beaten at workshops near the Myohaung train station (take bus No 7).

Photographic Supplies Eastern Photo Studio, on 28th St and the north-east corner of 81st St, usually has colour slide film. Around the corner and across the street from the Air Mandalay office is Konica Half Hour Colour Lab, which does a decent job on colour prints. Sein Photo Studio on the south-east corner of 28th and 84th Sts has good prices on film and processing.

Getting There & Away

For information on travel between Mandalay and Bagan or Mandalay and Taunggyi, see the Bagan or Inle Lake sections in the relevant chapters.

From Yangon you can fly, bus or rail upcountry. Mandalay is the starting point for travel to most of upper Myanmar – by riverboat, bus, train or air.

Air As elsewhere in much of the country, there are now two alternatives to flying on the government's risky Myanma Airways (MA). Both Air Mandalay (AM) and Yangon Airways (YA) have daily flights between Mandalay from Yangon; between Mandalay and Bagan (Nyaung U); and between Mandalay and Heho.

The AM (☎ 02-27439) office is on 82nd St between 26th and 27th Sts; the YA (☎ 02-36012) office on 78th St between 29th and 30th Sts; and the MA (☎ 02-22590) office on 81st St between 25th and 26th Sts.

The Yangon-Mandalay fare averages US$95 each way for all three airlines. The only significant difference between AM and YA seems to be that the latter allows Burmese citizens to pay in kyat. Both AM and YA utilise French-built ATR-72s, which are better equipped, safer and all-round more pleasant than MA's small and over-worked fleet of F-27 turboprops or F-28 jets.

A taxi from the airport to the city centre costs about K500, or US$2 at the most. Bus Nos 10 and 12 also head downtown from the airport for K15 per person.

As elsewhere in Myanmar, tickets are cheaper purchased from an agent. Even the airlines will usually send you to a nearby agent to purchase your ticket. In the city centre, try Seven Stars Travel Agency (☎ 02-28909) at 269 82nd St between 27th and 28th Sts, or nearby Shining Star Tours (☎ 02-36335) at 279 81st St between 26th and 27th Sts. The government's MTT office (☎ 02-27193) is located in the lobby of the Mandalay Swan Hotel.

Bus Kipling never actually took the 'road to Mandalay', but you can. Private air-con buses from Yangon's Highway bus station cost less than US$10 (K1800 to K2000), payable in kyat. Both Leo Express (☎ 02-31885) and Kyaw Express (☎ 02-27611) depart for Yangon at 5 pm from the corner of 83rd and 33rd Sts. Shuttle vans take you out to the Highway bus station that's near the airport. Another good long-distance bus company, Aung Kyaw Moe (AKM) (☎ 02-38346), operates from the Highway bus station, with similar prices and departure times. The Mandalay-Yangon fare is K2000. For most other destinations outside Mandalay, the usual mode of transport is Japanese pickup truck (Hi-Lux) or minibus.

For fares, departure times and trip durations, see the Getting There & Away section in the Yangon chapter.

Bagan Minibuses make the trip from Mandalay to Bagan in about 7 hours, roads permitting, and leave thrice daily from the Highway bus station (☎ 02-21807). The fare is K650. Buy tickets at least a day in advance from Nyaung U Mann Bus Co. inside

the second building under the circular stairway, or from New Bagan Express in the same area. Closer to the city centre, Shwe La Min (Golden Moon) buses depart for Bagan from the corner of 82nd and 32nd Sts. Pickups to Bagan are available from the Highway bus station for same-day departures and for about half the bus fare.

Taunggyi Buses bound for Taunggyi leave from the Highway bus station. Golden minibuses (25 seats) depart at 5.30 am. The cost is K1000. Slightly larger and more expensive, both Tiger Head (Kya Khaung) (☎ 02-28814) and Lion King (Chinthay Min) (☎ 02-21280) express buses depart for Taunggyi at 5 am. The cost is K1500. All three companies also do central district pickups near the north-east corner of 82nd and 23rd Sts.

Pyin U Lwin, Hsipaw, Lashio Pickups and buses leave for Pyin U Lwin, Hsipaw and Lashio from the Central bus station (also called Main bus station) in a bustling lot near the corner of 26th and 82nd Sts in the city centre. Pickups to Pyin U Lwin cost about K75 (K150 in the front) or K200 for a minibus. Buses to Hsipaw cost K400; to Lashio K650.

With most pickups, if you want to ride at the front of the cab, figure on paying at least 50% more of the regular fare.

For departures to the following towns, inquire at the Highway bus station: Monywa (3½ hours, K200), Nyaungshwe (Yaunghwe, near Inle Lake) (eight hours, K1500), Kyauk Padaung (five hours, K400), Shwebo (three hours, K150), Pyinmana (six hours, K350), Taungoo (11 hours, K800) and Bago (14 hours, K1000).

Pickups and minibuses to Meiktila (four hours, K200) leave from both the Highway bus station and the Central/Main bus station, on the corner of 82nd and 26th Sts.

Train The old British-designed Mandalay train station is being replaced with a new seven storey complex, including two floors devoted to a hotel. Service continues at the

MANDALAY

station, but until construction is completed (around 2000) it's advisable to arrive early to allow time to find your track and platform.

Although there are a number of trains each day between Yangon and Mandalay, you should only consider the day or night expresses, as the other trains represent everything that can be wrong with Burmese rail travel – slow, crowded and uncomfortable. Additionally, it's possible to reserve a seat on the express services, and on these special 'impress the tourists services' you really do get a seat – not a half or a third of a seat. Upper class even has reclining seats and is quite comfortable. Sleepers are available but hard to reserve.

Trains leave from both ends at the same time and in theory should arrive at the same time – but in fact they are frequently a few hours late. However, your chances of boarding an on-time train are better if you take one of the 'special express' trains between Mandalay and Yangon, which depart at 5.30 pm and are scheduled to arrive at 7 am the next morning. The cost is US$38 per person, one-way. Get an excellent chicken biryani wrapped in a banana leaf at one of the stations on the way or, if you take the night train, on the platform. Meals in the dining car, which is often packed, aren't bad; Myanmar Beer is available.

Upon arrival in Mandalay you may be given a ticket for 'free transport' to your hotel, endorsed by Myanma Railways. Although this does entitle you to a free ride to the hotel or guesthouse of your choice, it means Myanma Railways takes a small commission from the place you stay. As with any kind of tout/commission system, this means they may try to steer you away from places that don't pay commissions.

Myanma Railways also operates daily trains from Mandalay to Hsipaw, Lashio, Monywa, Myitkyina and Pyin U Lwin; see the Getting There & Away sections in the appropriate chapters for details.

For schedule and fare information for the trains to and from Yangon, see the Getting Around chapter towards the beginning of this book.

Car & Taxi Cars (with licensed driver) can be rented through a number of sources, including most hotels and guesthouses. Expect to pay about US$25 to US$35 a day for trips outside Mandalay. Prices will vary according the number of passengers and the price of petrol. One of the most common cars in use is the reliable Toyota 'Super-roof' van/station wagon. As always, check out the vehicle before you sign an agreement. Your hotel or guesthouse should be of help. Drivers can usually be found at the ET Hotel, the Royal Guest House and the Mandalay Royal Hotel, among others.

The MTT office quotes the following rates for saloon car taxis, but you can usually beat these prices by about 20% with a privately owned taxi:

destination	cost (US$)
Mandalay city tour	$25 to $30
Mandalay, Amarapura and Sagaing	$30 to $35
Mandalay to Pyin U Lwin	$35 to $40
Mandalay to Bagan (one-way)	$75 to $80
Mandalay to Taunggyi (one-way)	$80 to $85

Motorcycle Although motorcycle rental hasn't really caught on yet in Mandalay, you may be able to rent a motorcycle at one of the following places: Honda Motorcycles (☎ 02-22620) at Building 5, Room 2, 35th St, between 81st and 82nd Sts; Suzuki Mandalay (☎ 02-28144) on 28th St between 83rd and 84th Sts; or Yamaha (☎ 02-24243) at 216 27th St between 82nd and 83rd Sts.

Boat The Inland Water Transport (IWT) office (☎ 02-86035) is located near the Gawwein jetty, at the western end of Yangyiaung Lan (35th St). They sell tickets here to Bagan, Pyay, and Bhamo. The office is open daily from 10 am to 2 pm, but they do not sell tickets to Bagan on Tuesday or Saturday. Boat tickets can also be purchased from the MTT office at the Mandalay Swan Hotel, but you'll have to pay an additional US$2.

Mandalay-Bagan Ferry There is now a private ferry service from Mandalay to Bagan, in addition to the old government ferry. The private ferry *Shwe Kein Nayi* is faster, making the trip in about nine hours. Departures are every Monday, Tuesday, Thursday, Friday and Saturday. Food is available on board but it's pricey. You can buy tickets the day before at the jetty at the end of 35th St, or most guesthouses and hotels will get tickets for you for an extra charge of about K200.

MTT's government boat departs twice weekly, on Wednesday and Sunday, at a cost of US$11 deck class or US$33 for a stuffy cabin. MTT also sells ferry tickets, but adds an extra US$2 for the service.

For more information on ferries to Bagan, Bhamo or Pyay, see the appropriate Getting There & Away sections in the relevant chapters.

Getting Around

Bus Mandalay's buses are virtually always crowded, particularly during the 7 to 9 am and 4 to 5 pm rush hours. The atmosphere on the buses is also surprisingly friendly – so if that's more important to you than smooth comfort, you'll probably quite enjoy bussing around Mandalay. Some of the useful services include:

From Mahamuni Paya to Zeigyo and Kuthodaw Paya – blue bus No 1 (၁)
To Gawwein jetty, train station and airport – blue bus No 2 (၂)
To Mandalay Hill from the clock tower and Zeigyo – bus No 4 (၄)
Between Yankin Hill, Zeigyo and the boat jetty to Mingun – white bus No 5 (၅)
To the other side of Mandalay Hill, to the Institute of Indigenous Medicine – bus No 7 (၇)
Via Setkyathiha Paya, Mahamuni Paya and Amarapura to Inwa; starts from the corner of 27th and 84th Sts – red or black bus No 8 (၈)
To U Bein's Bridge – yellow bus No 8 (၈)
Mandalay Hill to south of the city and airport – red bus No 12 (၁၂)
Mahamuni Paya to Mandalay Hill through Mandalay Fort – red and yellow Mann Sit Th bus

Pickup Pickups to Amarapura, Inwa and Sagaing leave throughout the day from Zeigyo at 26th and 84th Sts for around K20 each. You can also hop on at any point along the way.

Taxi There are now many taxis in Mandalay, and fares average about K150 for trips within the central district. Around Zeigyo you'll find a few three-wheelers and more four-wheelers – tiny Mazda pickups that hold four passengers. They operate within the city for around K75 to K100 per trip. The level of English among most drivers is virtually nil; our experience is that it's easier for non-Burmese speakers to take a little time to make sense of the city bus system than it is to try and work out your destination with a taxi driver. It helps if you have the address of the place you're going to written in Burmese.

There is usually a group of taxis waiting at the airport; these cost a standard K500 for the whole vehicle into town. Jeeps are also occasionally available, although there are fewer than in previous years.

Car Cars (with licensed driver) can be rented through a number of sources, including most hotels and guesthouses. Expect to pay around US$10 for a half day in Mandalay and about US$15 for the whole day. MTT also arranges car hire, but as usual it's more expensive. To visit nearby Amarapura and Sagaing, expect to pay around US$20 for the day.

It's also possible to hire pickups by the day for tours around Mandalay. Count on around K2500 to K3000 for a day trip to Amarapura and Sagaing that includes an English-speaking guide; the trucks take up to eight people, so it needn't be expensive.

Trishaw The familiar back-to-back trishaws are the usual round-the-town transport. Count on K50 for a short ride in a trishaw, K100 for a longer one – say, from Mandalay Hill to Zeigyo. Figure on K500 to K800 per day per trishaw for all-day sightseeing in the central part of the city.

You must bargain for your fare, whether by the trip, by the hour or by the day. In the evening, expect to pay a bit more.

Trishaws can easily be flagged down just about anywhere. Many drivers tend to hang out near the popular guesthouses, like the Royal Guest House or the Nylon Hotel. Some of the trishaw drivers (especially former university students) in these areas speak English or French. However, unless you know the driver, it is best not to shop in a trishaw, as drivers often have 50% deals with shop owners. Shops that refuse to go along with this may still be hassled by the driver later on, or the driver might tell you that a particular shop is now closed.

Bicycle There are several places in the city centre to rent bicycles, including near the Royal Guest House on 25th St and opposite the Mann Restaurant on 83rd St. The average cost is K50 to K60 per hour or K300 to K400 per day, depending on the bike's condition. If you're looking for bicycle parts and accessories, try Ye Yint in Zeigyo (No 1 Myout Bet Tait Tan).

Horsecart Once a charming Mandalay staple, horsecarts are seldom seen nowadays in central Mandalay. The few we've seen recently were usually laden with goods. You will find them on the city's outer edges and also in the nearby ancient cities – Inwa in particular.

Walking Mandalay is a surprisingly sprawling place. Think three times before setting out on a little stroll around the fort walls or out to Mandalay Hill. The central district area is easily traversed on foot, however.

Around Mandalay

The area around Mandalay has a number of attractions well worth visiting. The four ancient cities (Amarapura, Inwa (Ava), Sagaing and Mingun) are all within easy day-tripping distance, as is the atmospheric old 'hill station' of Pyin U Lwin (Maymyo). To the north-west, bustling Monywa is not as historic, but it is one of Myanmar's most typically Burmese cities.

Ancient Cities

After the fall of Bagan (Pagan), right up to when the third and last Anglo-Burmese War reached its final (and for the Burmese, disastrous) conclusion in 1885, the capital of one of Myanmar's kingdoms stood in, or close to, Mandalay. Perhaps it's part of the Buddhist belief in the temporary nature of life, but many kings developed an overpowering urge to commence their reign with a new capital and a new palace. Thus, the capital seemed to play musical chairs around the countryside.

Additionally, masonry or brick construction was reserved almost solely for religious buildings. The palaces, though magnificent and extensive, were made of wood. When the shift was made to a new capital, the wooden palace buildings were often dismantled and taken along. When the royal entourage departed, the mighty cities soon reverted to farming villages – with neglected *stupas* (Buddhist religious monuments) picturesquely dotting the fields.

In the chaos after the fall of Bagan, it was Sagaing that first rose to prominence in the early 14th century, but in 1364 Inwa succeeded it. Not until 1760 was the capital shifted back across the river to Sagaing, where it remained for just four years. Inwa regained its pre-eminent position only from 1764 to 1783, after which time Amarapura became the capital. In 1823 Inwa was again the capital, but following the terrible earthquake of 1838, which caused great damage to

HIGHLIGHTS

- Day trips to the 'deserted' royal capitals of Inwa, Amarapura and Sagaing.
- Rickety and picturesque U Bein's Bridge at Amarapura.
- Ferry rides along the Ayeyarwady River to the massive Mingun Paya.
- The scenic colonial hill station of Pyin U Lwin.
- Bustling Monywa and nearby Borobodur-like Thanboddhay Paya.

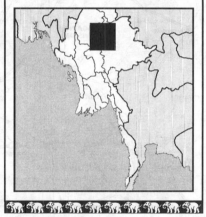

all these cities, the capital was moved back to Amarapura in 1841. Amarapura was capital again for only a short period, and in 1860 the seat of power was transferred to Mandalay, where it remained until the end of the British conquest of Myanmar 25 years later. This seemingly constant moving or abandoning of capitals around Mandalay gives the area its second nickname: Deserted Cities.

Three of the ancient cities are south of Mandalay. Amarapura and Inwa are on the eastern (Mandalay) side of the Ayeyarwady

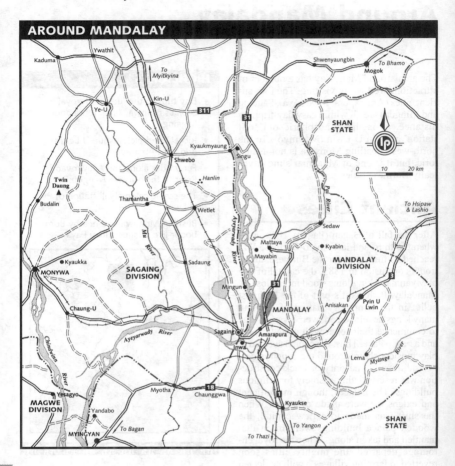

AROUND MANDALAY

(Irrawaddy) River, while Sagaing lies to the west of the river, but is easily reached by the long Inwa Tada (more commonly known as Ava Bridge). Mingun, which was never a capital, is on the western bank of the Ayeyarwady to the north of Mandalay. It's easily reached by frequent riverboats running from Mandalay.

Don't try to do all the cities in one day. It's best to devote a half day each to Sagaing and Mingun; Amarapura and Inwa can be seen together on a separate day.

The Last Kings

Alaungpaya founded the last dynasty (the Konbaung dynasty) of Burmese kings in 1752. It ended 133 years later, when King Thibaw was deposed by the British and exiled to India. Two of the kings, Hsinbyushin and Bodawpaya, were Alaungpaya's sons.

The kings were:

Alaungpaya	1752-1760
Naungdawgyi	1760-1763
Hsinbyushin	1763-1776

Singu Min	1776-1782
Bodawpaya	1782-1819
Bagyidaw	1819-1837
Tharawaddy Min	1837-1846
Pagan Min	1846-1853
Mindon Min	1853-1378
Thibaw Min	1878-1385

AMARAPURA

Situated 11km south of Mandalay, the modern town of Amarapura is often referred to as Taungmyo (The Southern City) to distinguish it from Mandalay, the northern city. The name Amarapura means City of Immortality, but its period as capital was brief. Amarapura was founded by Bodawpaya as his new capital in 1783, not long after he ascended the throne, but in 1822 Bagyidaw moved his court back to Inwa. In 1841 Amarapura again became the capital, but in 1857 Mindon Min decided to make Mandalay the capital, and the changeover was completed in 1860. Amarapura was also the site for the first British embassy in Myanmar in 1795.

Today, little remains of the old Amarapura palace area, although there are several interesting sites to be seen. They are widely scattered, so if you don't have transport, allow enough time and energy for walking. The city walls were torn down to make quarry material for railway lines and roads, while most of the wooden palace buildings were dismantled and taken to the new palace in Mandalay.

Pahtodawgyi

Built by King Bagyidaw in 1820, this well preserved *paya* (pagoda) stood outside the old city walls. The lower terraces have marble slabs illustrating *jatakas* (scenes from the Buddha's life). There's a fine view over the surrounding countryside from the upper terrace. An inscription stone within the temple precincts details the history of the monument's construction.

Bagaya Kyaung

The Bagaya Kyaung in Amarapura was built when Bodawpaya moved the capital to

Amarapura, but was destroyed by fire in 1821. Its Inwa predecessor of the same name is still standing (Ba is Mon for monastery, Kaya – or Gaya – means starflower tree). A second Amarapura version, built in 1847, was again burnt down in 1866, leaving only eight brick stairways. These were gradually overgrown until the Myatheindan *sayadaw* (chief abbot) built a two storey brick building in 1951, in which he deposited 500 Buddha images and 5000 sets of *pe-sa* (palm leaf manuscripts) from throughout Burma. Between 1993 and 1996, the State Law & Order Restoration Council (SLORC), now known as the State Peace & Development Council (SPDC) reconstructed the monastery, based on drawings and ground plans in frescoes in the Kyauktawgyi Paya, near U Bein's Bridge. It's no longer a monastery, but houses a museum and library, of interest for its collection of palm-leaf manuscripts. The museum is kept locked, but the caretaker will open it on request.

Palace Ruins

Little remains of the old Amarapura palace, but you can find two masonry buildings – the treasury building and the old watch tower – in its old grounds. King Bagyidaw and King Bodawpaya were both burnt here on the site of their 'tombs' and their ashes placed in velvet bags and thrown into the Ayeyarwady. The corner stupas still stand at the four corners of the once square city.

U Bein's Bridge

South of Pahtodawgyi, the shallow Taungthaman Lake is crossed by a long and rickety teak bridge, curved to withstand the wind and waves. During the dry season, the bridge crosses mostly dry land. U Bein was the 'mayor' of Amarapura at the time of the shift from Inwa, and he wisely salvaged material from the deserted Inwa Palace to build this 1.2km-long footbridge. Although some of the original 984 teak posts have now been replaced by concrete blocks, most remain. It has stood the test of time for two centuries and remains the longest teak span in the world.

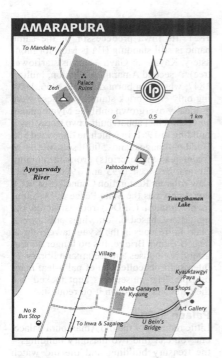

AMARAPURA

To Mandalay

Palace Ruins

Zedi

0   0.5   1 km

Ayeyarwady River

Pahtodawgyi

Taungthaman Lake

Village

Kyauktawgyi Paya

Maha Ganayon Kyaung   Tea Shops

No 8 Bus Stop

To Inwa & Sagaing   U Bein's Bridge

Art Gallery

At the start of the bridge is the **Maha-gandhayon Kyaung**, home to several thousand young monks. It was founded around 1914 and is renowned as a centre for monastic study and strict religious discipline. If you visit at about 11 am, you can watch the whole monastery eating silently. There is also a new and garish-looking temple with a gigantic seated Buddha. Near the bridge is a cluster of shaded tables where you can take tea, beer and snacks under an arcade of *meh-zeh* trees planted in 1875. The best times to visit the bridge are just after sunrise or just before sunset, when hundreds of villagers commute by foot or bicycle back and forth across it. You can also hire a small boat to take you in either direction for about K200 if you only want to cross the bridge once.

During the dry season, look for a cement stairway leading down to a little island with a single *teashop* (no sign) serving cold drinks and a few snacks. It's situated about half-way across the bridge and makes a nice break on a hot day.

Kyauktawgyi Paya

If you stroll across the bridge (there are fine views across the lake to Pahtodawgyi, and rest places where you can shelter from the sun and sample fresh palm toddy), you'll come to Taungthaman village and Kyauktawgyi Paya. Constructed in 1847 by Pagan Min, it is said to have been modelled on the larger Ananda Pahto at Bagan, but it has the look of a Tibetan or Nepali temple, with its five tiered roof.

While the paya does not have the perfectly vaulted roofs or the finer decorations of the original, it does have an excellent seated Buddha image and interesting and well preserved frescoes in the four entrance porches. Religious buildings, zodiac charts and scenes from everyday life are all illustrated in the frescoes. You can even find some suspiciously English-looking figures in the crowds – they were beginning to make their presence felt at the time of the temple's construction. The *paya pwe* (pagoda festival), known as the Festival of Lights, takes place during Thadingyut (October).

The atmosphere around Kyauktawgyi is very peaceful and shady, and this is a good place to be at sunset, when people, bicycles and bullock carts pass on their way back from a day's work in the fields surrounding the shrine. There are several smaller overgrown stupas in the vicinity, including a unique honeycomb-shaped stupa covered with Buddha niches. Lay people come here to practise meditation, away from the worldly distractions of Mandalay. There are a couple of traditional outdoor *teashops* where those with time on their hands sit on woven mats or small stools around low tables, drinking small pots of Chinese tea and eating snacks such as fried gourd, soy cake and fried lentil balls dipped in a tasty tamarind sauce.

Look for a small and friendly **art gallery** near the teashops.

Other Attractions

On the bank of the Ayeyarwady, just north of the bridge, stand two 12th-century payas – the **Shwe-kyet-kya** and the **Shwe-kyet-yet**, or Golden Fowl's Run, a string of *zedis* (stupas) cascading down from a high bluff. If the river level is not too high, you can pay a boatman about K200 to take you out in a local *hgnet* (swallow-tailed boat) for a fabulous view of the two payas, the Sagaing hills, and the sun setting behind the Ava Bridge. Amarapura also has a **Chinese joss house**; when the decision was made to shift to Mandalay, the Chinese traders preferred to remain.

Amarapura is noted for silk-and-cotton weaving, and there are reportedly around 40,000 Siamese-style, four-heddle looms in the area. As you wander through the modern town you'll hear the looms' steady clackety-clack. Bronze casting is also done in Amarapura.

In August, a week after the end of the Taungbyone *nat pwe* (spirit festival) and the full moon of Wagaung, Myanmar's nat worshippers move to the Irinaku Yadanagu) Festival, just south of Amarapura, and to the east of the road. The festival celebrates Popa Medaw, the mother of the Taungbyone brothers. The authorities have clamped down on some of the wilder activities in recent years, but this festival and Taungbyone are still the main nat festivals of the year, and important dates in Myanmar's gay scene.

Getting There & Away

A No 8 bus from 83rd St, near the corner of 29th St in Mandalay, will take you to Amarapura for K20 and on to Inwa for another K20. Get off the bus when you come to the palace wall on the left of the road, and a temple guarded by elephants on the right, with the Ayeyarwady visible behind it. From here you can walk to Pahtodawgyi and through the village of Taungthaman to U Bein's Bridge.

Touring by bicycle is another alternative. Bikes can be rented in Mandalay for around K350 a day. Pedalling to Amarapura should take 45 minutes or so.

INWA (AVA)

The ancient city of Inwa (Mouth of the Lake), for a long time a capital of Upper Burma after the fall of Bagan, is on the Mandalay side of the Ayeyarwady River close to the Ava Bridge, a few kilometres south of Amarapura. Just south of the bridge, the Myitnge River flows into the Ayeyarwady, and south of this river stands Inwa. A channel, known as the Myittha Chaung, was cut across from the Myitnge to the Ayeyarwady to make Inwa an island.

From 1364 Inwa was the capital of a Burmese kingdom for nearly 400 years (apart from brief interludes), until the shift was made to Amarapura in 1841. No other capital has lasted as long. Although Inwa was known to the outside world as Ava until comparatively recently, the classical Pali name of the city was Ratnapura (City of Gems), pronounced Yadanabon in Burmese.

Prior to 1364, Sagaing had been the capital of the central Bamar kingdom, but after Sagaing fell to the Shan, the capital was moved across the river to Inwa. The kings of Inwa set about re-establishing Bamar supremacy, which had been in decline since the fall of Bagan. Although the power of Inwa soon extended as far as Pyay (Prome), the Mon rulers of Bago (Pegu) proved to be a strong match for the Bamar.

In 1555 Inwa fell to another Bamar kingdom, that of Taungoo, but in 1636 the capital of Taungoo was returned to Inwa. This period as capital lasted only a century. The Mon again rose up and destroyed Inwa in 1752. A few years later Alaungpaya vanquished the Mon forever, and after a period with Shwebo in the north as capital, Inwa once again became the centre of the kingdom.

When the British occupied Lower Myanmar following the Second Anglo-Burmese War, much of Upper Myanmar was known as the Kingdom of Ava. An embassy report of a visit to Inwa in 1795 enthused:

The Burmans are certainly rising fast in the scale of Oriental nations. They have an undeniable claim to the character of a civilised and well instructed people. Their laws are wise and pregnant with sound morality; their police is better regulated than in most European countries; their natural disposition is hospitable to strangers.

During his reign, Bodawpaya moved the capital to Amarapura, but his successor Bagyidaw shifted it back to Inwa. When the disastrous earthquake of 1838 caused serious damage, the city was finally abandoned as a capital, in favour of Amarapura, in 1841.

A number of small villages have sprung up inside the city walls, and peasants till the soil where once the palace used to stand – the massive old city walls are still easily traced. To the south, an ancient brick causeway leads from the city gate towards the town of Tada-u, where an Italian-Thai company has recently completed a $150 million international airport for Mandalay, capable of receiving jumbo jets.

Nanmyin

The 27m-high masonry watch tower, the Nanmyin, is all that remains of the palace built by Bagyidaw. The upper portion was shattered by the 1838 earthquake and the rest has taken on a precarious tilt – it's known as the 'leaning tower of Inwa'.

Maha Aungmye Bonzan

Also known as the Ok Kyaung, this is a brick-and-stucco monastery built by Meh Nu, the chief queen of Bagyidaw, for her royal abbot U Po (Nyaunggan Sayadaw) in 1818. Monasteries were generally built of wood and were prone to deterioration from the elements or destruction by fire. Although this monastery was built in imitation of the traditional wooden style, its masonry construction has ensured its survival. The 1838 earthquake badly damaged it, but it was restored in 1873.

Bagaya Kyaung

Fire and earthquake aren't the only threats to Myanmar's architectural heritage, and one of Inwa's finest attractions is the happily unrenovated Bagaya Kyaung, which dates from 1834. The entire monastery is built of teakwood and supported by 267 teak posts (the largest measures 18m in height and 2.7m in circumference). The cool and dark interior feels old and inviting. On the outside, look for the Keinayi peacock – half-bird and half-female. How long this pristine wooden structure will escape the heavy hand of renovation is not certain, but visit it while you can. A small sign in Burmese at the entrance warns: 'No footwear; if you are afraid of the heat on the floor, stay in your own house.'

Ava Bridge

This British-engineered, 16-span bridge dates to 1934 and was the only structure that crossed the Ayeyarwady River, until 1998 when a new Chinese-engineered bridge was completed at Pyay, followed shortly afterwards by one at Myitkyina. The Ava Bridge (also called Inwa Tada) was put out of action by the British in 1942, when they demolished two spans in order to deny passage to the advancing Japanese. Not until 1954 was the bridge repaired and put back into operation. It carries two lanes of traffic, plus a railway line.

Tolls are collected for every moving vehicle that crosses, from bullock carts and trishaws to cargo trucks. Due to the route's strategic importance, photography of – or from – the bridge is strictly forbidden.

Other Attractions

Farms, villages, *kyaungs* (monasteries) and ruined zedis are scattered around the area within the old city walls. The walls are in particularly good condition near the northern gate, facing the Ayeyarwady. This was known as the **Gaung Say Daga** (Hair-Washing Gate), since kings had their hair ceremonially washed at this gate. In places the moat outside the walls is also visible.

Located nearby, **Htilaingshin Paya** dates back to the Bagan period; in a shed in the compound an inscription records the construction of the wooden palace during the first Inwa dynasty.

To the southern side of the city stand the remains of the huge four-storey **Le-htat-gyi**

Paya. There is also the **Lawkatharaphu Paya**, while to the south of the city stands the **Inwa Fort** and nearby **elephant stockade**.

The Inwa Nat Pwe celebrates the nat Thon Ban Hla from the 10th day of the waxing moon through to the full moon of Tabaung (February/March).

Getting There & Away

Bus No 8 to Amarapura, Inwa and Sagaing leaves from the clock tower, near the *zeigyo* (central market) in Mandalay. Bus numbers are in Burmese script. The cost is about K20 for each segment along the way. Pickups bound for Sagaing leave from the corner of 83rd and 29th Sts and will drop you off at the Ava Bridge. You can then follow the extremely dusty (in the dry season) track down to the ferry landing on the Myitnge River. You'll be ferried across for K5. During the wet season, you have to take a ferry from the Thabyedan Fort near the Ava Bridge. Ferries also shuttle across the Ayeyarwady between Inwa and Sagaing for K5.

A taxi can be hired from Mandalay for US$15 to US$20 to take you to Amarapura, Inwa and Sagaing, and back again.

A few miles south-east of Inwa, but best accessed by car from the Mandalay-Meiktila road, is Paleik and the Yadana Labamuni Hsu-taung-pye Paya, said to have been founded in 1093 by Alaungsithu. It is better known as **Hmwe Paya** (Snake Pagoda) after the two pythons that sleep curled around a Buddha image and are lovingly washed and fed every morning at 11 am. Although it receives very few foreign visitors, there is an entrance fee of 3 Foreign Exchange Certificates (FECs). A festival including *a-nyeint* (similar to vaudeville/slapstick) and *zat* (recreation of an ancient legend or Buddhist jataka) performances takes place in the two weeks following the full moon of Waso (June/July).

Paleik is a well kept village surrounded by an estimated 325 stupas and payas in varying states of repair, many from the Konbaung period. It is like a mini-Bagan, but with much more greenery, and worth a visit if you are travelling between Mandalay

and Meiktila by car. The turn-off to the right for Paleik is about 20km south of Mandalay, after the river and beyond Myitnge, or 30km north of Kyaukse.

Getting Around

Inwa makes an interesting break in the ancient city circuit because so few travellers seem to make it there – due, in part, to the high admission fee of US$5, collected at the ferry crossing. However, to get around you'll either need a bicycle (which may be available at the small ferry landing), or you must hire a horse cart; several await the arrival of each small ferry, and the cost is about K400 for a three hour tour.

SAGAING

If you're unable to get to Bagan to poke around the ruins, Sagaing may also provide an interesting substitute. There are certainly plenty of stupas here, and those scattered over the Sagaing hills – which rise on the western bank of the Ayeyarwady, just north of the modern town – provide a very picturesque spectacle from across the river. Flying in or out of Mandalay provides you with an even better view, but make sure you're sitting on the correct side of the plane – on the right when flying Mandalay-Bagan, on the left when flying Bagan-Mandalay.

Sagaing became capital of an independent Shan kingdom around 1315, after the fall of Bagan had thrown central Myanmar into chaos. Its period of importance was short, for in 1364 the founder's grandson, Thado Minbya, moved his capital across the river to Inwa. For four brief years, from 1760 to 1764, Sagaing was once again the capital, but its historic importance is comparatively minor.

Today, it's mostly known as a religious centre that supports dozens of Buddhist monasteries and nunneries as well as a major monastic hospital. During the full moon of Tazaungmon (October/November), devotees from Mandalay and beyond flock to Sagaing to offer robes. Kyaswa Kyaung offers an annual 'foreign yogis retreat' (in the Mahasi Sayadaw tradition) each January.

AROUND MANDALAY

Thabyedan Fort

Just to the left of the Ava Bridge, on the Mandalay and Inwa side, is the fort of Thabyedan, which was built as a last-ditch defence by the Burmese before the Third Anglo-Burmese War. It was taken by the British with little effort.

Kaunghmudaw Paya

The best known of the Sagaing stupas, this huge whitewashed edifice is actually situated 10km beyond the town of Sagaing. The enormous dome, whose name means work of great merit, rises 46m in the shape of a perfect hemisphere and was modelled after the Mahaceti (Great Stupa) in Sri Lanka – although legend also says that it represents the perfectly shaped breast of a well endowed Burmese queen. Also known by its Pali name Rajamanicula, the zedi was built in 1636 to commemorate Inwa's establishment as the royal capital of Myanmar.

Around the base of the zedi are 812 stone pillars, each one to 1.5m high and with a small hollow for an oil lamp. Images of nats can be seen in the 120 niches that also circle the base. A nearly 3m-high polished marble slab stands in a corner of the paya grounds – the 86 lines of Burmese inscriptions on the slab record details of the monument's construction.

Tupayon Paya

Constructed by King Narapati of Inwa in 1444, Tupayon is of an unusual style for Myanmar: it consists of three circular storeys each encircled with arched niches. A temporary wooden bridge was constructed across the Ayeyarwady when the *hti* (the umbrella-like decorated top) was raised, and a huge festival was held. The 1838 earthquake toppled the superstructure, and although it was partially repaired in 1849, the reconstruction was never completed.

Aungmyelawka Paya

Situated on the riverfront, near Tupayon Paya, this zedi was built in 1783 by Bodawpaya on the site of the residence he owned before he became king. It is built entirely of sandstone, in imitation of the Shwe- zigon Paya at Nyaung U, Bagan. It is also known as the Eindawya Paya.

Other Payas

The **Datpaungzu Paya** is comparatively recent, but houses many relics from other, older temples that were demolished when the railway was built through Sagaing. **Ngadatkyi** to the west of Sagaing was built in 1657 and houses a fine and very large seated Buddha image.

Hsinmyashin Paya is on the way to the Kaunghmudaw Paya and is known as the Pagoda of Many Elephants, because of the elephant statues stationed at each entranceway – a departure from the usual half-lion, half-dragon *chinthes* (guardian statues). Built in 1429, it was badly damaged in an earthquake in 1485. Although subsequently repaired, it suffered even worse damage in a 1955 earthquake.

Sagaing Hill

The hill itself has a number of zedis and kyaungs, some of which are comparatively recent. **Padamya Zedi** dates from 1300, while **Umin Thounzeh** (30-Caves), contains 45 Buddha images in a crescent-shaped colonnade. The impressive **Soon U Ponya Shin Paya** nearby was constructed in 1312 and reaches 29.3m high with a 7.8m hti above that; in front of the principal altar, large bronze frogs on wheels serve as collection boxes. The view of Sagaing from Soon U Ponya Shin and its approach are outstanding. Mural paintings can be seen in the **Tilawkaguru** cave temple, which was built around 1672. The **Pa Ba Kyaung** is typical of the many monasteries on the hillside. Sagaing also has the remains of a fort by the riverbank. The nearby village of **Ywataung** is renowned for its silversmiths.

The village of Sagaing, at the foot of Sagaing Hill, makes an interesting visit – it's chock-a-block with markets, shops and restaurants. Foreigners are charged an entry fee of US$3 to climb Sagaing Hill.

If you don't want to pay, you can still soak up Sagaing's atmosphere by roaming along the pathways that cover the hills des and link up the hundreds of *tazaungs* (retreats). Covered walkways lead down to Thayetpin jetty where you can hire a row boat down the river and pick up other pathways.

Places to Stay & Eat

Although a day trip to Sagaing seems sufficient to many visitors, an overnight stay allows you to take in the sights at a leisurely pace while absorbing the local ambience.

Near the central market in Sagaing, on a side street of the main road through town, the quiet *Happy Hotel (☎ 072-21420)* offers 21 basic but clean rooms for US$5 per person, including breakfast. Shower and toilet facilities are down the hall. Downstairs, you'll find a very decent *restaurant* serving Chinese and Bamar food. Coming from Mandalay, turn right, just past the cinema on the right side of the road, then make the first left and you'll see it on your left.

Some travellers have managed to stay at *unlicensed guesthouses* in Sagaing for as little as K2000 a night. There are plenty of *teashops* and *restaurants* in the vicinity of the Happy Hotel and central market, including *Kant Kaw Thu Zar Ywataung*, on the main road.

Getting There & Away

Sagaing is about 20km south-west of Mandalay and is easily reached by road. The Ayeyarwady flows south by Sagaing, then turns west and north, encircling the town in a loop. The road to Sagaing crosses the river on the 16-span Ava Bridge, which is well over a kilometre long and also carries the railway line.

A Sagaing-bound pickup (from the intersection of 83rd and 29th Sts in Mandalay, and from Amarapura and other stops along the way) will take you right to the middle of town for about K20. To continue to the Kaunghmudaw Paya, it costs another K5.

MINGUN

If we had to choose just one of the four ancient cities around Mandalay to visit, it would be Mingun. Not only are there some

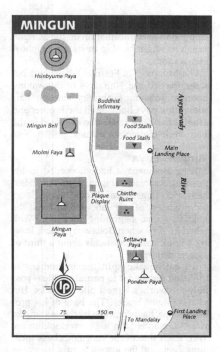

very interesting things to see within a comparatively compact area, but just getting there is half the fun. Count on a half-day to go there and return.

Mingun, located about 11km upriver from Mandalay, on the opposite bank of the Ayeyarwady, is accessible only by river. It's just long enough a trip to give you a pleasant feel for the river and a glimpse of river life.

The village itself is a very friendly place and worth exploring. Several *teashops* and *curry stalls* in the vicinity of the huge Mingun Bell offer snacks, noodles and beverages. A footpath parallel to the river runs the length of the ruins area and beyond and makes an interesting walk, plus it's less dusty than the main road in dry weather.

The Mingun Sanitarium (also called the Buddhist Infirmary), a nursing home for the elderly, is worth checking out. Visitors are welcome. The head nurse here is Than Than

Sue – she speaks excellent English and is happy to impart information on the Mingun area. You might be able to stay the night if there's room.

The Mingun Nat Festival takes place between the 5th and 10th days of the waxing moon of Tabaung (February/March). This celebration pays homage to the brother and sister of the Teak Tree, who drowned in the river while clinging to a trunk.

Mingun Paya

If King Bodawpaya had succeeded in his grandiose scheme, Mingun might now boast the world's largest zedi. Thousands of slaves and prisoners of war laboured to build the massive stupa, beginning in 1790. Work halted in 1819 when Bodawpaya died, leaving a brick base that stands about a third of its intended height.

An earthquake split the monument in 1838 and reduced it to partial rubble – possibly the world's largest pile of bricks. But what a pile of bricks! The base of his projected stupa, badly cracked by the earthquake of 1838, stands 50m high overlooking the river. Each side of the enormous base measures 72m, and the lowest terrace measures 140m. There are projecting four-layer lintels over the porticoes on each of the four sides. Beautiful glazed tiles in brown, pale brown, cream and green were intended to be set in panels around the terrace; some of these tiles can be seen in the small building in front of the enormous ruin. Had the stupa been completed, it would have stood 150m high.

Despite its dilapidated state, you must still go barefoot if you intend to climb the base. You can climb the zedi on the crumbled corner, and from the top you have a fine view of the Hsinbyume Paya, Mingun village and the river.

A pair of commensurately large chinthes are crumbling away at their guard posts closer to the river. They, too, were badly damaged by the 1838 quake.

Pondaw Paya

Closer to the riverbank, a little downstream from the Mingun Paya, is this 5m-high

working model for the gigantic structure. It gives a clear picture of just what Bodawpaya intended to achieve with Mingun Paya. During the 15 years it took to build the base of his stupa, he frequently set up residence on an island in the Ayeyarwady to supervise the construction.

Mingun Bell

In 1808 Bodawpaya had a gigantic bell cast to go with his gigantic zedi. Weighing 55,555 viss (90 tonnes), it is claimed to be the largest hung, uncracked bell in the world. There is said to be a larger bell in Moscow, but it is cracked.

The same earthquake that shook the zedi base also destroyed the bell's supports, so it was hung in a new tazaung, close to the riverboat landing. The bell is about 4m high and over 5m in diameter at the lip. You can scramble right inside it and some helpful bystander will give it a good thump so that you can hear the ring from the interior.

Between Mingun Paya and the bell stands a new pavilion sheltering a life-size standing bronze statue of Molmi Sayadaw, a famous Buddhist abbot from the nearby village of Molmi.

Hsinbyume Paya

Also known as Myatheindan, and built by King Bagyidaw in 1816, three years before he succeeded Bodawpaya as king, this stupa was constructed in memory of his senior wife, the Hsinbyume princess. It is built as a representation of the Sulamani Paya, which, according to the Buddhist plan of the cosmos, stands atop Mt Meru. The seven wavy terraces around the stupa represent the seven mountain ranges around Mt Meru, while the five kinds of mythical monsters can be found in niches on each terrace level. This zedi was also badly damaged in the 1838 quake, but King Mindon had it restored in 1874.

Settawya Paya

Close to the riverbank, upstream from the Pondaw Paya, this hollow, vaulted shrine has a footprint of the Buddha that was brought to Mingun by King Bodawpaya

1838 earthquake damage visible at Mingun Paya.

Mingun women sporting *thanakha* paste, which acts as a sunscreen.

BERNARD NAPTHINE

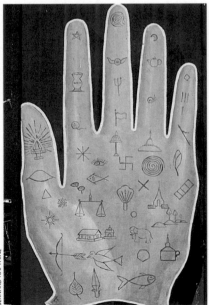

BERNARD NAPTHINE

Poster for a palm reader, Mandalay.

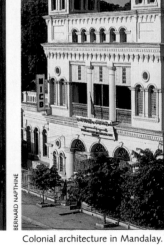

BERNARD NAPTHINE

Colonial architecture in Mandalay.

U-Bein's Bridge on Taungthaman Lake, Amarapura.

Enjoying a *cheroot* (Burmese cigar), Mandalay.

BERNARD NAPTHINE

Mt Popa – home of the *nats* (spirits), Bagan Region.

when the relic chamber in the base of his huge *pahto* (temple) was sealed up. The temple was built in 1811.

Getting There & Away

Riverboats to Mingun depart from Mandalay from the Foreigners River Transport jetty, at the western end of 35th St, with reasonable frequency. The upriver journey usually takes about 45 minutes, though sometimes it can take as long as two hours. Depending on the currents, coming back may be rather quicker. It's best to get a boat out of Mandalay between 7 and 8 am; arrange transport to the jetty the night before. Boats leave every half-hour, or when full. The last boat back to Mandalay from Mingun usually leaves around 4 pm, so don't start this trip too late in the day. The cost is K200 For around K2000, you can hire an entire boat seating 20 or more people. Some travellers have reported being told at the jetty that, as foreigners, they must hire the entire boat. However, we were only told that it was possible to hire a boat. It's best to buy tickets at the nearby Inland Water Transport (IWT) office on 35th St the day before you travel, although you can usually buy a ticket at the jetty.

It's a pleasant, interesting trip with plenty to see along the way – fishing villages, bullock carts, corn fields, market boats, laundering. The boat stops at a sandbank at the southern end of the Mingun area, then continues to the main landing place, beyond the Mingun Paya base.

Pyin U Lwin (Maymyo)

In 1887, during the British annexation of Myanmar, Lwin was renamed Maymyo (May-town) after a British Colonel May, of the 5th Bengal Infantry, which was stationed in the military headquarters there, and among many locals (and tourist touts) the town is still known by its colonial name. From 1896, Pyin U Lwin was a British hill station where, during the hot season, the

servants of the Raj went to escape the heat and dust of the plains. It is 67km east of Mandalay and, at 1070m, is considerably higher. The altitude makes all the difference. Even at the height of the hot season, Pyin U Lwin is pleasantly cool and at certain times of the year it can get quite chilly. Best of all, the air is fresh.

Originally a Shan Danu village, as a legacy of the influx of South Asians during the British colonial era, Pyin U Lwin is home to around 5000 Nepalis and 10,000 Indians. Sweater-knitting is a prominent occupation in town; most of this work is done by women, while the men roam the streets and hang out in teashops. The town has a heavy khaki hue, thanks to the much expanded Defence Services Academy, Myanmar's elite military training school. The cadets can often be found in the teashops.

Getting to Pyin U Lwin is part of its attraction. From Mandalay, you take a pickup or bus that chugs its way across the plains, then up the twisting road into the hills. There's no hurry about the trip, which is interspersed with stops to top up the vehicle's radiator. At the halfway mark you pass View Point, which has spectacular views. Along the way, villagers sell wooden blocks that are supposed to keep truck tyres from slipping while parked on the steep grades.

Getting around Pyin U Lwin can be equally enjoyable; the standard transport around town is a miniature, enclosed wagon pulled by a pony. You're never sure if it's a half-scale replica from the Wells Fargo days of the American West or something from the British 'stand and deliver' era. The lodgings can be the most fun of all – see Candacraig, later in the Places to Stay section, or read Paul Theroux's delightful account of Pyin U Lwin in his book *The Great Railway Bazaar*.

Many of the colonial-era buildings along the town's main streets are being replaced by modern ones built by Chinese developers. You'll find the most intact colonial mansions along the circular road west and east of the centre. Chinese immigrants from Yunnan Province are buying up many of

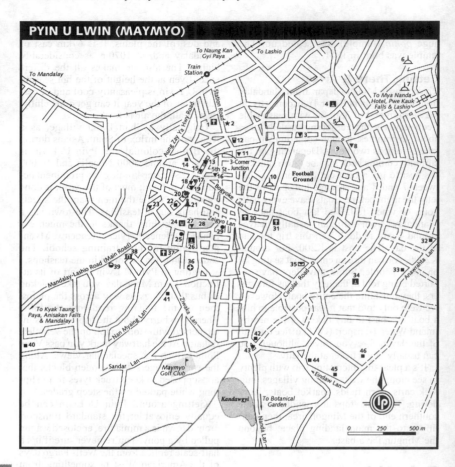

PYIN U LWIN (MAYMYO)

these old mansions, using profits earned in the border trade.

Pyin U Lwin is a centre for growing many English vegetables and flowers that do not flourish in the hotter conditions of the plains. Strawberries are one of the products of this higher altitude – in season (February/March) they're cheap and delicious. There is a flower market on the main road to Mandalay just south of town that sells gladioli, roses, dahlias and other flowers typical of an English country garden. Mulberry trees,

used to raise silk cocoons, are another important township product, and coffee is grown nearby.

The town itself is easygoing and full of interest – a good place for an evening stroll, or an interesting morning at the markets. There are still many English signs around.

Botanical Garden

Colonel May used Turkish prisoners of war to develop this 237-acre botanical garden during WWI. The garden features wide

PYIN U LWIN (MAYMYO)

PLACES TO STAY
14 Da Shanghai Hotel & Restaurant
22 Golden Dream Hotel
32 Thiri Myanmar Hotel
33 Thiri Myaing Hotel (Candacraig)
40 Nann Myaing Hotel
41 Grace Hotel
42 Gandamar Myaing Hotel
44 Royal Parkview Hotel
45 Dahlia Motel
46 April Inn

PLACES TO EAT
3 Win Yatana Restaurant
8 Aung Padamya Restaurant
11 Lay Ngoon Restaurant
12 Tawthagyi Cold Bar

13 Summer Feeling Café; Daw Khin Than Restaurant; Diamond Confectionery
15 Shanghai Restaurant
16 Rainbow Bar & Restaurant
17 Maymyo Restaurant
18 Family Restaurant
19 Myitta Thit Tea Shop
23 Yoe Yar Restaurant
27 Win Shwezin Café
43 Tea Line Milkshake Shop

OTHER
1 Methodist Church
2 Police Station
4 Cantonese Temple
5 Aung Chantha Paya
6 Shwe Myan Tin Paya
7 U Chanti Paya

9 Shan Market
10 Shwezigone Paya
20 Mosque
21 Purcell Tower
24 Hindu Temple
25 Cinema
26 Monastery
28 Zeigyo (Central Market)
29 Fire Brigade
30 St Matthew's Kachin Baptist Church
31 Church of the Immaculate Conception
34 Chinese Temple
35 Post Office
36 Hospital
37 Church
38 Town Hall
39 Pickups & Jeeps to Mandalay & Lashio

expanses of manicured grass, large flower beds, 49 acres of natural forest with walking trails, a rose garden, an orchid house, a small stupa on an islet in a pond and several other ponds. It's very popular with picnicking families on weekends and holidays.

An open-air snack shop sits on a slope overlooking the park. It's open daily from 7 am to 5.30 pm; admission is K10 per person.

Other Attractions
Purcell Tower, the clock tower near the town entrance coming from Mandalay, was a present from Queen Victoria who offered an identical tower to Capetown in South Africa. Another version of the story has it that the clock was made in 1934 by Gillette & Johnson of England, in commemoration of George V's Silver Jubilee. Part of the cost was paid by Mr Purcell, a resident of Mandalay, descended from Armenian traders who were favourites of Kings Mindon and Thibaw. Naturally, its chime copies Big Ben's.

There's a good view from **Naung Kan Gyi Paya** on a hilltop overlooking town, just north of the train station. You can leave your bicycle at the shops at the bottom of the hill.

The 100-year-old **Church of the Immaculate Conception**, south of the central area,

features a large brick sanctuary with a bell-tower and cruciform floor plan. The vaulted wooden ceilings and well appointed interior are more impressive than the outside. According to the Mother Superior here, Pyin U Lwin has around 5000 Catholics; there are two other Catholic churches in town and a Lisu Baptist Theological Seminary.

A few minutes walk from Candacraig is a colourful **Chinese temple** built by Yunnanese immigrants. There is an orphanage and nursing home within the temple compound.

On the north-eastern outskirts of town is a small **Japanese war cemetery** containing around 50 graves. Each year, during the months of December and January, friends and families of the deceased come from Japan to pay their respects. For five days after the full moon of Tabaung (February/March), Pyin U Lwin holds a nat festival for Ko Myo Shin, the main nat of northern Shan State.

Maymyo Golf Club
This fairly well tended 18 hole golf course near the Botanical Garden is one of the best in Myanmar. Greens fees are K1000 per player; clubs (K500), shoes (K150) and caddies (K500 each) can be hired at the pro shop. With club rental you are provided 10

balls; you'll be fined K200 for each ball you lose. Men may be refused play if they're not wearing collared shirts (polo or tennis-style shirts are OK).

Places to Stay – Budget

There are several decent places in the vicinity of Purcell Tower that are licensed to accept foreigners. *Golden Dream Hotel (☎ 085-22142, 42/43 Lashio-Mandalay Rd)*, close to the tower and HMV pickup stop, is a rambling four storey place, where rooms with cold-water shower and toilet down the hall cost US$4 per person. Larger rooms with hot-water shower are US$8/15 a single/double, including Indian or western breakfast. Rooms towards the back are quieter than those facing the street.

The *Grace Hotel (☎ 085-21230, 114 Nan Myaing Lan)* is a one storey inn, with 11 rooms priced at US$8 to US$10 per person. Bicycles can rented for the short ride to town. The main advantages to the Grace are its quiet location away from the main streets and its garden sitting area out front.

The new *Dahlia Motel (☎ 085-22255, 105 Eindaw Lan)* is a bit far from the town centre, but is easily the best value. Tidy economy rooms cost US$5 per person, and the larger standard rooms with bath, TV and fan go for US$10/20 a single/double. A few larger superior rooms are available at US$15 per person. All rooms have hot water, and breakfast and free transport to town. *April Inn (☎ 085-21001, 51(F) Eindaw Lan)* is further from town than the Dahlia, but easy to get to on a bike and worth the effort. It's clean and quiet, and they'll pick you up from either the train station or bus stop. Bungalow rooms cost US$5 a person. A good Bamar- or western-style breakfast is available for K200. Bikes can be rented here for K150 for a half-day, and K250 for the whole day.

Da Shanghai Hotel & Restaurant (☎ 085-22397, 55 How Go Lan), off the main road, is a sprawling Chinese place on a quiet side street, with lots of clean economy rooms for US$5/8, and standard rooms with bath for US$10/15.

At the turn of the century, old Maymyo was considered a 'hornet's nest of *dacoits* (highwaymen)'. Today, a local mafia still tries to keep tabs on all foreigners coming into town from Mandalay. As the number of visitors arriving here by private vehicle increases, their operation seems less secure. But it works like this: Upon arrival in Pyin U Lwin you may be approached by a friendly chap asking where you plan to stay. Whatever your answer is – and regardless of whether you take the tout's recommendation or not – he will later make a trip to collect a 'commission' from the hotel or guesthouse owner of the place you stay. There are two main gangs running this operation, both centred at Indian-owned crafts shops in Pyin U Lwin.

Places to Stay – Mid-Range & Top End

The 15 room *Royal Parkview Hotel (☎ 085-21210)* on Eindaw Lan, near the corner of Thaya Lan, is the town's best hotel, and is easily the best value in this price range. A standard room costs US$30/36 a single/double, and a superior costs US$42/48, with breakfast included. All rooms have hot water, fridge, satellite TV and teak furnishings. A small restaurant serves good Bamar and European dishes.

Two recently built hotels offer decent facilities on the outskirts of town. The 23 room *Thiri Myanmar Hotel (☎ 085-22483, 38B Forest Rd)*, east of town, is a Chinese-style two storey place with a restaurant and small swimming pool (unheated). Decent, if functional, rooms with hot water cost US$24/36. The 24 room *Mya Nanda Hotel (☎ 085-21015)*, just out of town, on the road to Lashio, has clean and comfortable rooms for US$24/30, including breakfast.

For many visitors, half the reason for coming to Pyin U Lwin is to visit or stay at *Candacraig* – even if it is now officially known as the *Thiri Myaing Hotel (☎ 085-22047)*, on Anawrahta Lan. In the colonial era, this was the 'chummery', or bachelor quarters, for employees of the Bombay Burmah Trading Company. This trading firm was engaged in extracting teak from

Upper Myanmar, and the chummery was built in 1906 in the form of an English country mansion – constructed, naturally, of the finest teak.

Today you can sweep up the imposing staircase to the upper landing, where you will find huge, old-fashioned rooms with high ceilings and wooden balconies overlooking the grounds. Although fires are no longer permitted in the rooms, the hotel staff will light a fire in the large sitting room fireplace downstairs – guests must often chip in to pay for firewood.

There are only seven rooms in all, including one smaller economy room for US$18/24. Three larger standard rooms cost US$24/30; and the three largest rooms cost US$30/36. Despite recent renovation work, some travellers have lamented the somewhat dingy conditions and spotty service. To others, it's part of the appeal.

Much of Candacraig's appeal was that Mr Bernard, the chummery cook during the British era, ran the place exactly as if the British had never left. Unhappily, Mr Bernard has now departed this world, but roast beef and roast chicken still appear on the set menu every night, and most travellers find it a great place to stay. You can sip a beer in front of the roaring log fire in the lounge, and at breakfast or lunch staff may put a table on the lawn so you can dine in open-air splendour. The hotel tends to be booked out in the December-January and July-August tourist seasons; at other times of the year you're liable to have the place to yourself. The hotel is still government-owned, although continuous rumours have it up for sale.

The Ministry of Hotels & Tourism (MHT) maintains two other large hotels in Pyin U Lwin. *Gandamar Myaing* (☎ 085-22007), at the corner of Thaya Lan and Myopaq Lan (Circular Rd), is a brick, two storey Tudor-and-Victorian mansion – similar in design to Candacraig – on the way to the Botanical Garden. Large rooms with attached bathrooms will cost you US$24/36. Two economy rooms with cold-water shower cost US$6 per person.

Off the Mandalay-Lashio road, coming from Mandalay, is the *Nann Myaing* (☎ 085-22112), a large cluster of buildings vaguely designed in the Tudor style. The separate reception building is the grandest; the guest rooms are rather more simple and modern. All rooms have wooden floors, high ceilings and blocked fireplaces. Standard rooms with hot-water shower and toilet cost US$36/48, larger superior rooms are US$44/56 and junior suites with sitting rooms and slightly nicer furnishings (fridge, TV, hot shower, portable radiators) cost US$65/90, breakfast included.

All three MHT hotels accept Visa and American Express (Amex) for room payments – sort of. If you want to use a Visa card, it must be franked at either the Candacraig or the Nann Myaing. If you want to use an Amex card, it must be franked at the Nann Myaing, regardless of where you stay. The Gandamar Myaing will accept credit-card payment, but you'll have to visit one of the other hotels to use it. In other words, you can stay at one hotel but may have to cross town to pay your bill with a credit card.

Under construction at the time of writing, and near the golf course on Sandar Lan, is the *Golf Rest House*, a group of bungalows. Whether it will accept foreigners is still unknown. Another new top-end place under construction at the time of writing is the *Aden Motel* on Cherry Lan, east of town.

Places to Eat

Apart from the hotels, there are a number of assorted places to eat in the town centre, including several inexpensive Chinese and Indian restaurants.

Close to the clock tower on the northern side of the street, the large *Myitta Thit Tea Shop* serves good quality tea, crispy biscuit-like *nam-bya* (flat bread cooked in a clay over, similar to Indian *nan*) with dahl dip and fresh butter from local Gurkha-run dairies, *samosas* (stuffed pastries; morning only) and *mohinga* (noodles, fish and egg dish; evening only). The *Maymyo Restaurant* next door serves decent and cheap Chinese food.

AROUND MANDALAY

A couple of blocks south-west of the Hindu Temple is the roomy *Yoe Yar Restaurant* on Ashe Pyithu Panjan Lan. It serves very good Bamar, Thai and Chinese dishes.

Nearby, on a side street off the main road, is the clean and popular *Family Restaurant* at 13 Block 4, 3rd St. The menu mixes Bamar and Indian dishes; order a chicken, vegetable or mutton curry and you'll also receive three or four side dishes, including vegetables and a delicious dahl, plus rice.

Further east near the Shan Market, the family-run *Aung Padamya Restaurant*, at Site 44, 28 Thumingala Quarter, Zaythit Lan, serves excellent and reasonably priced home-cooked Indian food daily from 11 am to 6 pm. The restaurant is owned by the golf pro from Maymyo Golf Club and his Indian Catholic family. The same family operates *Win Yatana Restaurant* on the main road, opposite the football ground.

Near the central market, *Hlaing Tea Shop* is a Nepali-style place serving good egg fried rice, chapatis, *aloo puri* (potato curry) samosas for breakfast, plus other snacks during the day. Away from the town centre is the delightful *Tea Line Milkshake Shop*, which sits in the middle of a strawberry field, opposite the Gandamar Myaing Hotel.

A cluster of good eateries along the main Mandalay-Lashio road begins with *Shanghai Restaurant*, a few blocks north-east of Purcell Tower, which specialises in Shanghai and Szechuan-style food. Several blocks further east, the Cantonese *Lay Ngoon Restaurant* is equally popular.

Indulge your sweet tooth at nearby *Diamond Confectionery*, founded by an Italian who left Myanmar following nationalisation. Although it may not look like much from the street, the shop produces a nice variety of baked goods and Indian snacks, including shortbread, butter cookies, chocolate-cashew muffins, coconut puffs, vegetable puffs and various cakes. Next door is *Daw Khin Than Restaurant*, which serves good Bamar and Chinese food, and the *Summer Feeling Café*, a popular teashop. Opposite these eateries is the *Rainbow Bar & Restaurant*, a small popular Chinese place at 16, Block 7, 5th St.

The open-air *Tawthagyi Cold Bar*, on Station Rd leading to the train station, serves delicious *lassis* (yoghurt-based drinks) made with strawberries, papaya, banana, avocado or coconut. Beer and soft drinks are also available.

Shopping

The main shed of the central market near the clock tower contains vendor stalls selling textiles and household goods from India, China, Thailand and Myanmar. Behind this main shed is a large area where fresh produce and other goods from the countryside are sold. Don't believe any touts in town who say there's nothing local for sale at this market; they're just trying to steer you away from the rival commission mafia and towards their own mafia at the smaller Shan market in the eastern part of town. Both markets are visited by tribespeople; the only real difference between the two markets is size, though it's true there are more Shan people at the Shan market. The Shan market is only open in the morning.

Several handicraft shops on the main street vie for your dollars and kyat: Pacific World Curio (near the Myoma Cinema) at 75 Main Rd (the Mandalay-Lashio road) and Zaw Crafts (a few doors north towards the clock tower, next to the Golden Dream Hotel). Both carry similar collections of marionettes, *kalagas* (tapestries), Shan bags, wood carvings, old British clocks, lacquerware, brass and other materials from Upper Myanmar. Most of this stuff comes from Mandalay. Some Shan textiles and jewellery may be available but that's about it. Beware of shipping things back to your home country from these shops. We've had reports of less than successful results. Also beware of offers of precious stones at these or any other shops; Pyin U Lwin has a very low reputation when it comes to dealing in gems. Many travellers have ended up with handfuls of worthless sapphires that they thought represented a big score.

La Vie Art Gallery (☎ 085-21266) at 7-8 Duwan Lan, AM Block, in the central market, displays paintings and other art by local artists, some of it very good. The owner, Muu Muu, speaks English and is knowledgeable about the artwork.

Getting There & Away

Bus & Pickup The famous WWII-era jeeps that once plied the route between Mandalay and Pyin U Lwin have been almost entirely replaced by buses and Japanese Hi-Lux pickups. From Mandalay, you can take a bus or pickup to Pyin U Lwin for about K150 or K250 (front seat) per person. These now depart from one central location in an alley lot near the north-east corner of 82nd St and 26th Sts, from 5 am until about 3 pm. As soon as a full load of passengers is on board, your truck will depart; for comfort and view, you are better off grabbing the front seats and letting the hardier Burmese people cram themselves into the back. The cost is K40 in the back, K100 up front, and the trip takes three to 3½ hours up, two to 2½ hours down – barring breakdowns of course, which are always possible.

On the way up, the trucks stop mid-way to allow passengers to grab a snack, to give the driver a chance to sort out the radiator and touts time to try and steer you towards specific hotels and restaurants in Pyin U Lwin.

From Pyin U Lwin, pickups depart in the opposite direction from the Shan market, train station, Chinese temple, clock tower and central market. They're all pretty much the same – you might make your selection based on which staging point is most convenient for you. The trip takes about two to three hours up, and about two down. A private taxi to Mandalay costs about K3000, or US$15.

Pickups and buses to Hsipaw and Lashio leave from the same area near 26th and 82nd Sts. The buses from Pyin U Lwin to Hsipaw and Lashio are very cold. Comfortable Toyota 'Super-roof' share-taxis take up to four passengers for around K1000 per person to Hsipaw, and another K500 to Lashio. It takes about six hours to cover the 209km to Lashio, about four hours to Hsipaw. (See the entries on Hsipaw and Lashio in the North-East Myanmar chapter for more information.)

Train There is a daily train to Pyin U Lwin from Mandalay, but this is more for train enthusiasts than a sensible means of transport. The train (No 131 Up) departs Mandalay at 4.35 am and climbs the hills by a switchback system; the schedule says it takes 3½ hours to reach Pyin U Lwin, but this is optimistic – count on four to five hours. The same train continues to Hsipaw and Lashio. This trip across the spectacular Gokteik viaduct is well worth taking, and the armed guards standing about 2m away from the track seem friendly enough. The mandatory-for-foreigners 1st class fare from Mandalay to Pyin U Lwin is US$6; to Hsipaw another US$7; to Lashio another US$4. Purchase tickets the day before travel.

Getting Around

Most of the town's colourful horsecarts are stationed near the mosque on the main road. Fares are steep by Myanmar standards: roughly K70 to K80 to travel from the mosque to the Shan market, K500 for the return trip to Candacraig or the Botanical Garden, K1000 for half-day sightseeing. You can hire bicycles to explore the town at the Grace Hotel, the Dahlia Motel, April Inn and Golden Dream Hotel, or at either of the two crafts shops on the Mandalay-Lashio road. The going rate is K50 per hour or K300 per day.

AROUND PYIN U LWIN
Waterfalls & Caves

There are several natural attractions around Pyin U Lwin, including a number of caves, waterfalls and tribal villages. Most can be reached by a combination of public transport and hiking, though Pacific World Curio or Zaw Crafts in Pyin U Lwin can arrange a guided trip to any, or all, of them. Rates are negotiable depending on where you want to go.

Pwe Kauk Falls Called Hampshire Falls in British times, Pwe Kauk is about 8km from town, off the Lashio road. Although the falls themselves aren't that spectacular, it's a very pleasant picnic spot – popular on weekends and holidays with the locals. During, or just after, the rainy season, you can swim in the upper reaches, but not at the bottom, where the undertow can be quite dangerous.

Three **Shan villages** – Mogyopyit, Yechando and Ye Ngeye – can be visited on the way to Pwe Kauk Falls. Or from Pwe Kauk, you can take a one hour hike to **U Naung Gu**, a natural cave containing several Buddhas and used by local meditators. You can ask around at Pwe Kauk for a local guide to the cave.

You can charter a pickup out to the falls from any of the truck stops in Pyin U Lwin for K150 each way. To visit the Shan villages, you can sometimes hire a bullock cart at Pwe Kauk.

Anisakan Falls Although a fairly long and steep walk is required to get to these falls, the hike is worth it. At the village of Anisakan, about 8km towards Mandalay, turn right at the train station, continue about 600m to the railway crossing, then turn left on a dirt road for about 800m to a fork, where you again take a left turn. After about 500m, you reach a parking place from where you continue on foot. It's a 45 minute descent through a river gorge to reach the falls, which consist of five sections; the third is particularly impressive.

Pickups go to Anisakan village from Pyin U Lwin for K30 per person – catch them in front of the cinema opposite the central market. You should allow at least a half-day for the whole trip. It's possible to ride a bicycle there, but the ride back is more up than down.

Peik Chin Myaing

This large Hindu-Buddhist shrine cave, 27km towards Lashio and another 3.5km off the main road, was developed by local Nepalis and later coopted by the government as a tourist attraction in 1990. (They also managed to rename it Maha Nan Damu Sacred Cave, though everyone seems happy with the old name.) A 600m path leads through the cave, which is decorated with

quite new Buddha images and models of Myanmar's most famous stupas, eg the Shwedagon Paya and Kyaiktiyo. Pickups make the one hour trip direct to Peik Chin Myaing for K400 per person. You can also charter a pickup and driver for around K3000; ask around at the handicraft shops near the Golden Dream Hotel, or at the Lashio truck stop.

On the way, a few kilometres outside Pyin U Lwin, you will pass a new shrine. On 17 April 1997, four stone Buddhas were being transported by truck to China, when one fell off the truck and could not be hauled back on. The driver of the vehicle claims that the night before he had dreamt that one of them did not want to leave Myanmar. A shrine and souvenir stall has now grown up around the Buddha. Four months after the event, pilgrims in this desperately poor country had already donated about 19 million kyat to the Buddha.

Shwesayan Paya

The paya was built in 1054 by Shan princess Saw Mon Hla, daughter of the *sawbwa* (hereditary chieftain of the Shan) of Maingmaw. The wife of Anawrahta, she was on her way home to the Shan State from Bagan, having been expelled from court for alleged witchcraft. A festival takes place in the two weeks following the full moon of Tabaung (February/March). A bamboo platform and teashop is built out into the river, and there is plenty of water splashed around for those who can't wait for Thingyan. Shan traders descend to sell products such as sesame brittle, dried tofu and medicinal herbs and roots. The trademarks of the festival are the colourful locally made *htan-yweq ba-di* (necklaces) and fish, all made out of dyed toddy palm leaves. By car, turn off to the south at Tonbo, the limestone quarry and prison labour camp town at the foot of the Shan plateau on the Mandalay-Pyin U Lwin road. After a few kilometres, you reach the paya on the Myitnge (Dohtawadi) River. During the festival, you can catch a Mandalay-Pyin U Lwin pickup as far as Tonbo, and then a ponytrap to the paya.

Monywa, Shwebo & Mogok

These cities in Sagaing Division, to the north-west and north of Mandalay, are known as three of the most typically 'Burmese' towns in all Myanmar. Although thriving Monywa has been open to foreigners for some time, Shwebo only opened in 1994; neither place has so far received many tourists at all. Visiting Mogok requires a government permit and package tour.

MONYWA

Monywa is a worthwhile trip for temple enthusiasts or others who just want to go where there are few travellers. It lies 136km north-west of Mandalay along the Mandalay-Budalin branch railway line, but is best reached by bus or car.

Situated on the eastern bank of the Chindwin River, with a population of 300,000, Monywa is now the second biggest town in Upper Myanmar and serves as a major trade centre for agricultural produce from the surrounding Chindwin Valley, especially beans, pulses and jaggery (palm sugar). In addition to some 600 warehouses, Monywa supports mills for the production of cotton, flour, noodles and edible oils. Rough cotton blankets from Monywa are famous in Myanmar; some even end up sewn into knapsacks sold to tourists in Bangkok. Other regional crafts include mats and baskets made of bamboo and reed, bullock carts and agricultural implements such as hoes and machetes.

Goods coming from India pass through Monywa on their way to other parts of Myanmar. A forest reserve, west of the Chindwin River, produces teak and various other hardwoods. The Monywa area – particularly the region west of the river – was for many years a centre for the Burmese Communist Party (BCP).

The old market near the river is still active, despite the large new market sheds built by the government near the Monywa Hotel and Great Hotel. This is probably because the government ordered the relocation of a Muslim cemetery to make way for the new market; people fear the nats that may have been left behind.

The first bridge across the Chindwin is being built south of Monywa as part of the so-called Western Highway that may some day link Pathein (Bassein) in the south-west delta with Ye-U in the north-west. One and a half kilometres long, it will join Tawkyaunggyi on the east bank with Monywa on the west. With the northern reaches of Sagaing Division opening up to foreigners, Monywa can serve as a stepping stone for Chindwin River trips north-west to Kalewa. From Kalewa, it's just a short road trip to the Chin State.

Monywa is one of the hottest places in Myanmar in April and May, when temperatures approaching, or exceeding, 40°C are not uncommon.

Festivals

Monywa sits at the north-western edge of what might be termed the nat belt, a region of Upper Myanmar where the nat cult is particularly strong. Nat pwe followers will find the Zeedaw Nat Festival at Zeedaw and Maungdon (cross the Chindwin River at Monywa and travel 22km west along the Yinmabin road) in the fortnight around the new moon of Tabaung (February/March).

Coinciding with the festival at Zeedaw, the Ma Ngwe Daung Nat Festival is celebrated at Ahlone (12km north of Monywa on the Shwebo road). Ma Ngwe Daung was unlucky in love, and the festival is frequented by those who have suffered similar misfortune.

Places to Stay & Eat

The best value in town is *Central Guest House* (☎ 071-21548) on Bogyoke Lan, facing the roundabout. All the rooms are spacious and clean, and the helpful staff speak a bit of English. Small single rooms with fan and attached bath cost US$5 and US$8, depending on size, and much larger rooms with air-con, fridge and local TV at US$10/15 a single/double. Mosquito nets are provided, along with a good breakfast.

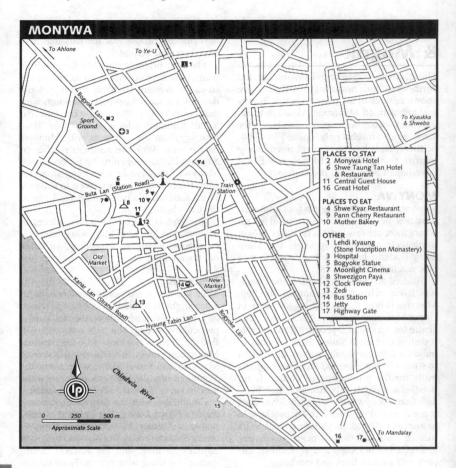

MONYWA

To Ahlone

To Ye-U

To Kyaukka
& Shwebo

Sport
Ground

Bogyoke Lan

Buta Lan (Station Road)

Train
Station

Old
Market

Kanar Lan (Strand Road)

New
Market

Bogyoke Lan

Nyaung Tabin Lan

Chindwin River

0   250   500 m
Approximate Scale

To Mandalay

PLACES TO STAY
2 Monywa Hotel
6 Shwe Taung Tan Hotel
   & Restaurant
11 Central Guest House
16 Great Hotel

PLACES TO EAT
4 Shwe Kyar Restaurant
9 Pann Cherry Restaurant
10 Mother Bakery

OTHER
1 Lehdi Kyaung
   (Stone Inscription Monastery)
3 Hospital
5 Bogyoke Statue
7 Moonlight Cinema
8 Shwezigon Paya
12 Clock Tower
13 Zedi
14 Bus Station
15 Jetty
17 Highway Gate

The *Shwe Taung Tan Hotel & Restaurant*
(☎ 071-21478), near the Moonlight Cinema,
is good value for the money. Small rooms
with air-con (when the power is working)
and cold-water bath cost US$5 per person,
basic breakfast included.

On the north-eastern side of the main road
into town, the so-so *Great Hotel* (☎ 071-
22431) on Bogyoke Lan, has fairly dirty
rooms with attached cold-water shower and
toilet for US$7/10. Although the rooms
aren't air-conditioned, the corridors are.

A bit farther, past the town centre and on
the same side of Bogyoke Lan as the accommodation listed before, is the recently
privatised *Monywa Hotel* (☎ 071-21581).
Wooden bungalows with corrugated metal
roofs are divided into four rooms, each with
fridge, air-con and attached hot-water bath
for US$18/24, or US$30/36 for slightly better furnished rooms with TV. The rooms are
clean, and rates include breakfast. One of
the Monywa Hotel's main advantages is its
pleasant outdoor bar and rambling grounds.

The *Shwe Kyar Restaurant*, a block north-east of the Bogyoke roundabout on Thazi Lan, serves quite good Bamar and Chinese dishes. The *Pann Cherry Restaurant*, in the centre of town near the old market, serves good Chinese food in both the open-sided dining room downstairs and the air-con room upstairs.

Getting There & Away

Bus From Mandalay, you can catch a pickup to Monywa from 27th St, near the corner of 83rd St, or from the Central/Main bus station in the lot near the north-east corner of 26th and 82nd Sts. Pickups leave about every 45 minutes between 4 am and 3 pm for K150 (K300 front) in either direction and take about three hours. Private minibuses leave hourly between 5 am and 3 pm in either direction. The fare is K200.

The Aung Kyaw Moe Express Co runs a large air-con bus between Monywa and Mandalay for K400. In Mandalay, it leaves from the Highway bus station; in Monywa from the bus stop near the new market. The same company runs a bus from Monywa to Yangon for K2000, which leaves town at 12 noon, arriving the next morning at 7.30 am.

Train Myanma Railways operates twice-daily trains from Mandalay to Monywa at 5.35 am (No 123 Up) and 1.45 pm (No 125 Up), but the journey is a slow six hours, compared to the 3½ hours by bus. The return journeys are scheduled for 1.20 pm (No 124 Down) and 6.50 am (No 126 Down). The fare is just K80.

Car By car it's only a 2½ hour drive from Mandalay via a decent two lane road. The going rate for car and driver between the two cities – as a long day trip only – is US$35, although it can vary according to the price of petrol. You may be able to find a driver willing to stay overnight in Monywa.

Boat Ferries upriver to Kalewa take around four days and cost K250 per person in funky two-bed cabins, about half that price for deck class. If more foreigners take this ferry,

expect the price to be in US dollars soon. Food can be arranged through the crew, or at ferry stops along the way.

Getting Around

Horsecart and trishaw are the main forms of local transport. A trip between the Chindwin River and the Monywa Hotel will cost around K50 by trishaw, K100 by horsecart.

AROUND MONYWA
Thanboddhay Paya

The big attraction in Monywa is this magnificent, Mt Meru-type structure. From the outside, the central stupa is vaguely reminiscent of Borobudur in Indonesia, though considerably smaller. There are 845 small stupas that surround and rise up to the richly decorated central stupa.

Thanboddhay was built between 1939 and 1952 by Moehnyin Sayadaw. The solid section of the monument is said to enclose 7350 relics and other holy materials. Inside the attached pahto, votive Buddhas of bone and other materials decorate every wall and archway halfway to the ceiling, and there are larger sitting and standing Buddhas in niches. Altogether, these images reportedly number 582,357.

Ancillary buildings in the compound resemble palace architecture from the Konbaung era (18th and 19th centuries) and feature three-dimensional jataka reliefs on their exteriors.

The paya complex is open daily from 6.30 am to 5 pm; admission is free. The annual festival takes place in the month of Tazaungmon (October/November). Thanboddhay is located 19km south-east of Monywa on the north-eastern side of the main road from Mandalay, just past a small bridge.

Four kilometres past Thanboddhay Paya is a 90m-long reclining Buddha, with a very small (and free) museum on the inside containing 9000 Buddha images. Nearby is **Boddhi-tataung** (1000 Buddhas), a grove of banyan trees, each with a Buddha at its foot, and **Aung Setkya Paya**, standing 130m high on the Po Khaung hills, surrounded by 1060 smaller zedis.

AROUND MANDALAY

Twin Daung

About 3km east of the river in Budalin township, Twin Daung (Well Hill) stands only 200m above the surrounding plain, but features a 50m-deep round lake known as Myitta Kan (The Lake of Love), whose water level reportedly rises and falls with the Chindwin. According to some sources the depression holding the lake was left behind by a volcanic eruption; others say a meteorite bounced off the earth's crust here and went on to land in a similar depression in Kani, further north. Whatever the source, there is now an algae processing plant there. To reach the lake by car, take the road west from Budalin for about 12km.

Ledi Kyaung

This monastery, at the north-eastern edge of the town, 21km north-east of town on the road to Ye-U, was constructed in 1886 by order of renowned Pali scholar Ledi Sayadaw. Similar in concept to Kuthodaw Paya in Mandalay, the kyaung features 806 stone slabs inscribed with Buddhist scriptures.

Shwe Gu Ni Paya

About 20km east of town, via a scenic two lane road, is one of the most important pilgrimage spots in Upper Myanmar. Dating to the 14th century, the main zedi of Shwe Gu Ni Paya rises to 33m (an auspicious height, made even more so when measured in feet – 108) and is famous for its 'wish-fulfilling' powers. The main antechamber to the shrine hall contains exemplary jataka paintings and is well decorated with mosaics.

Kyaukka

This village just beyond Shwe Gu Ni Paya has been a centre for the crafting of lacquerware since the Konbaung era. The pieces produced are for the most part more basic and utilitarian than those made in Bagan. Consisting of simple bamboo frames finished in black, silver or gold (or some combination thereof), the lacquerware shows more links to the pre-Chiang Mai styles that existed before the Bagan artisans began using a wider palette, finer materials, more

layers of lacquer and incising techniques, which allowed different colours to show through the outer layers. Because Kyaukka is less frequented by tourists, prices are particularly low, though you won't find any pieces quite as striking as in Bagan. In output, however, the village is second only to Bagan and the pieces made here are very strong.

Just east of the village, look for the small **Paw Daw Mu Paya**, which commands a good view of the countryside.

The road to Kyaukka is lined with picturesque tamarind trees and rice paddies. Pickups to Kyaukka leave a couple of times in the morning from Monywa's central market; the last one back leaves around 4 pm.

Hpo Win Daung Caves

It's a short ferry ride across the Chindwin River to Nyaungbingyi, followed by a 25km drive to this system of quite impressive sandstone caves situated in a cleft in the Hpo Win Daung (Hpo Win Hills). The hills have probably been occupied since the dawn of human habitation in Myanmar; to the south-west lies the Pondaung-pon-nya mountain range, where the fossilised remains of 'Pondaung Man' – who may have lived 30 million years ago – were found.

The caves and surrounding hills are named after U Hpo Win, a famous *zawgyi* (alchemist) who once lived among them. The caves themselves contain Buddhist statues, wood carvings and murals dating to the 17th and 18th centuries. Most exhibit the Inwa style, though some may date as far back as the 14th to 16th centuries. A covered stairway climbs a hill to the main cave shrine, but there are dozens of large and small caves in the area filled with old Buddhas. There are said to be over 400,000 images in these and other nearby caves. The main festival takes place in the week leading up to the full moon of Tazaungmon (October/November). There is a US$2 admission to the cave area. Some travellers have been able to stay overnight at the nearby monastery.

Shwebataung Paya, just beyond Hpo Win Daung, features unique pavilions cut from the surrounding sandstone and filled with plain Buddha images. The hill is reached via a series of steps beginning in the village of Minzu.

The last ferry in either direction across the Chindwin River departs at 6 pm.

SHWEBO

The flat plain that lies between the Mu and Ayeyarwady rivers around Shwebo has been continuously inhabited since at least the 3rd century AD, when the Pyus founded a city-state at nearby Hanlin. With the coming of the Bamar from the north, Hanlin crumbled and the area became an agricultural supply satellite for the rotating Bamar kingdoms of Upper Myanmar.

During the early 17th century, when the Portuguese adventurer Philip De Brito was defeated at Thanlyin (Syriam), all the Portuguese and Eurasians living at De Brito's 13-year-old colony were exiled to the villages of **Monhla** and **Chantha** near Shwebo. Called *bayingyis*, the rare fair-haired resident may occasionally be seen in these villages, although no linguistic or cultural legacies remain.

Shwebo served as a royal capital from 1760 to 1764 under King Alaungpaya. A Shwebo native, Alaungpaya used the city as a base for the reconquest of Inwa and Lower Myanmar, establishing what is known as the Third Burmese Empire. It was previously called Yangyiaung, Yadanatheinga, Konbaung (Embankment) and Moke-so-po (The Hunter Po), but Alaungpaya changed the name to the more royal Shwebo – Golden Banyan Tree. After defeating the Shan and the Mon, Alaungpaya destroyed several British trading posts, one of the first aggravated assaults against the Raj. His successor Hsinbyushin, moved the capital to Amarapura in the 1780s.

Shwebo today has a Bamar majority with sizeable Muslim and Christian communities. The town has little of Monywa's energy or appeal but like Monywa, the local economy depends on the trading of nuts, pulses, rice and sesame cultivated on the surrounding plains. A signboard in Burmese and English is posted at either end of town

proclaiming this a 'Hi-Tech Model Township'. During the months of April and May, Shwebo is extremely hot and dry.

Things to See & Do

You can get a good view of the city from **Maw Daw Myin Tha Paya**, on Eindathaya Hill at the north-eastern corner of town. The paya was built in 1755 by Alaungpaya and is said to enshrine an emerald alms bowl belonging to Gautama Buddha. Other famous religious monuments include the typical Burmese-style **Myo Daung Zedi** nearby and **Shwe Daza Paya** in the southern part of town (said to have been built by King Narapatisithu over 500 years ago).

Nay Rapan Paya, which is distinguished by the fact that the complex boasts five entrances instead of the usual four, is located south-west of the town centre. Aung Mye Hsu Taung (the town's wishing-ground) is said to be the spot used by King Alaungpaya as a staging point before going into battle. You'll find it just outside the city entrance towards Mandalay, within a larger paya compound.

The water-filled eastern moat, the most visible legacy of Alaungpaya's original city plan, stretches a couple of kilometres and is about 10m deep. The British built a jail on the **Alaungpaya palace grounds**, next to the central market north of the centre. Burmese residents recently moved the jail to the outskirts of town to excavate the site. Alaungpaya's remains, entombed nearby, are marked with a headstone inscribed in English. To enter the gated compound, you must first find the market administrator whose office is about 50m east.

Places to Stay & Eat

Only three guesthouses are licensed to accommodate foreigners in Shwebo. Of those, only one is particularly worth recommending. The relatively new *Zin Wai Lar Guest House* (sign in Burmese) (☎ 075-21263) is located in the eastern part of town on Yangyiaung Lan towards Kyaukmyaung. It's a somewhat modern, three storey affair with 14 ordinary doubles with common bath and

AROUND MANDALAY

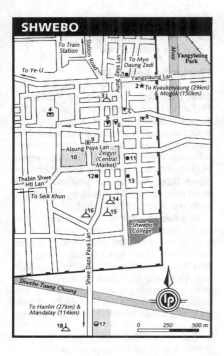

SHWEBO

To Train Station
Station Road
To Ye-U
Aung Zeya Lan
To Myo Daung Zedi
Moat
Yangylaung Park
Yangyiaung Lan
To Kyaukmyaung (29km) & Mogok (150km)
Alaung Paya Lan
Zeigyo (Central Market)
Thabin Shwe Hti Lan
To Seik Khun
Shwebo College
Shwebo Taung Chaung
To Hanlin (27km) & Mandalay (114km)

0   250   500 m

SHWEBO

PLACES TO STAY
1   Zin Wai Lar Guest House
12 Myoma Guest House
13 Tun Tauk Guest House

PLACES TO EAT
5   Khine Thazin Restaurant
6   Shwe Taung Chinese Restaurant
7   Eden Culinary Garden
8   Win Myint Gyi Muslim Restaurant

OTHER
2   Police Station
3   Shwekyettho Paya
4   Post Office
9   Alaungpaya's Tomb
10 Alaungpaya Palace Grounds
11 Aung Mitha Pharmacy
14 Chanthaya Paya
15 Chanthaya-gyi Paya
16 Shwe Daza Paya
17 Highway Bus Station
18 Aung Mye Hsu

squat toilet for K400 each a night. Two double rooms with attached bath and western toilet each go for K1300, and one triple costs K1800 with attached bath, fridge and local TV. Rates include service and tax.

The *Tun Tauk Guest House* (sign in English), a converted private residence, stands opposite the central market on Aung Zeya Lan (Madaw Lan). It costs K300 per person and is sometimes full with local clients. It's fairly clean and well run; shower and toilet facilities are shared throughout. The very basic and friendly *Myoma Guest House* (sign in English), just south of the market on Shwe Daza Paya Lan, has small cubicle-style rooms with common cold-water shower and squat toilets for K200 per person.

The *Eden Culinary Garden*, located on Aung Zeya Lan, offers a mixed menu of European, Chinese and Bamar dishes in a

relatively clean setting. *Shwe Taung Chinese Restaurant*, north of the market and opposite the petrol station on the same road, is Shwebo's most popular Chinese restaurant. The quiet, well decorated *Khine Thazin Restaurant* serves Bamar and Chinese food on Min Nyo San Lan, near the cinema north of the town centre. There are several small no-name *Bamar restaurants* north of the central market along Aung Zeya Lan. For good biryani and other Indian Muslim dishes, head for *Win Myint Gyi Muslim Restaurant*, near the central market.

Getting There & Away

Bus & Pickup Several transport companies operate along the 113km route between Shwebo and Mandalay. The busiest line, ie the one with the most departures, is the Yangyiaung Mahn 35 seat minibus, which costs K350 for the three hour trip. All lines leave hourly from the Central/Main bus station in Mandalay between 6 am and 3 pm. Shwebo's Highway bus station stands opposite Alaungpaya's wishing-ground paya, just outside the city entrance towards Mandalay.

Dyna Transport Co runs several small and medium-sized pickups throughout the day between Shwebo and Mandalay for K100 (K150 front seat).

Even if you have a permit, it's unlikely you'll be able to board a pickup to Mogok, since the permit usually entails signing on for an expensive government-sponsored Myanmar Travels & Tours (MTT) package tour out of Mandalay. Nevertheless, Shwebo is a popular starting point for Burmese people travelling to Mogok. Pickups make the six hour trip for about K500 (K600 front seat). The Padamya Bus Co leaves Shwebo at 7 am for Mogok for K500. Should the Mogok permit situation change, Shwebo might see more foreigners. Meanwhile, all vehicles must pass a military checkpoint before reaching Mogok.

Train Shwebo is linked to Katha and Myitkyina in the north, and to Mandalay in the south by rail. From Mandalay the No 55 Up leaves at 3 pm and normally arrives in Shwebo at 6 pm.

Getting Around
Trishaws and horsecarts are the main modes of public transport. Pickups can be chartered for K2000 a day for around town excursions, K5000 for half-day out-of-town excursions.

AROUND SHWEBO
Hanlin
The architectural remains of the Pyu kingdom (3rd to 9th centuries) at Hanlin (also called Halin and Halingyi) consist of a few crumbling city walls, gates, pillars and melting zedis, but little else. Pots and other artefacts excavated at the site are displayed in a small museum in the local monastery.

Hanlin is 26km south-east from Shwebo. There are no buses to Hanlin, but it's possible to hire a jeep for around US$20 return the same day.

Kyaukmyaung
This small town, 29km east of Shwebo on a good road, is known for its glazed pottery, including the large Martaban jars used to

hold water throughout rural Myanmar. During the dry season, local residents pan for gold along the riverbanks.

Although nothing in Kyaukmyaung justifies a special trip, if you're travelling by road between Shwebo and Mogok, you'll have to stop there to wait for the ferry across the Ayeyarwady River to Singu.

Should you need to spend the night, ask permission first at the police station in Shwebo. A small *guesthouse* here offers basic but clean rooms.

MOGOK
Famed for its surrounding natural beauty, and for the brilliant rubies and sapphires pulled from its red earth, Mogok was, until recently, completely off-limits to foreigners. Even now you're supposed to obtain a travel permit endorsed for Mogok before being permitted to enter Mogok or to stay overnight.

The municipality of Mogok, roughly 200km north of Mandalay and 150km northeast of Shwebo, belongs to Pyin U Lwin District of Mandalay Division. From what we've gathered, the permit requirement is strictly enforced. Should you even attempt to reach Mogok in the company of a Burmese person, the chief risk is to your companion. Mogok used to be reachable by helicopter from Mandalay. These days, permits are only granted for road travel.

At 1170m above sea level, the mountain basin surrounding 'Rubyland' enjoys a fairly temperate climate. Unlike much of Lower Myanmar, the rainy season runs from January to May. Bamar people are a majority in the township of 150,000, but there are also substantial numbers of Shan, Lisu, Palaung, Kachin, Nepali, Indians and Chinese, all vying for a piece of the gem action, or its attendant industries.

Royalty throughout the world has sought Mogok rubies and sapphires for centuries. Alluvial limestone gravels are the source, and deposits are exploited by means of tunnelling, pit-digging or panning – all by hand. Other precious and semiprecious stones found in Mogok District include peridot, lapis lazuli, moonstone, garnet and chrysoberyl.

AROUND MANDALAY

MOGOK

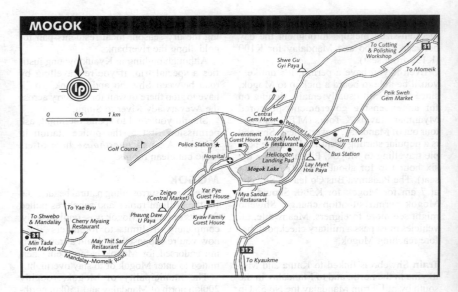

To Cutting
& Polishing
Workshop

To Momeik

Shwe Gu
Gyi Paya

Peik Sweh
Gem Market

Central
Gem Market

Padamyar Lan

Gem EMT

Government
Guest House

Mogok Motel
& Restaurant

Police Station

Golf Course

Hospital

Helicopter
Landing Pad

Bus Station

Lay Myet
Hna Paya

Mogok Lake

Zeigyo
(Central Market)

Yar Pye
Guest House

Mya Sandar
Restaurant

To Yae Byu

Phaung Daw
U Paya

Kyaw Family
Guest House

To Shwebo
& Mandalay

Cherry Myaing
Restaurant

Min Tada
Gem Market

May Thit Sar
Restaurant

Mandalay-Momeik Road

To Kyaukme

0   0.5   1 km

Information
At the time of writing, the Mogok Motel
was the best source for local information.
Operator-assisted trunk calls to Yangon can
be made from the Mogok Motel and from
private houses and businesses with tele-
phones. The post office is generally considered to be unreliable.

Religious Monuments
The hilltops surrounding town are dotted
with stupas and kyaungs. On a hillside north
of the centre, **Min Paya Taun Chantha-gyi
Paya**, said to have been built by King Min
Gaun of the Inwa Dynasty (1364-1555), offers the best panoramic view of Mogok.

Phaung Daw U Paya, on another hill
south-west of Mogok Lake, was built by
King Alaungsithu. A shrine in the complex
contains two very old gilded Buddha images,
one mounted on a ruby-studded pedestal, the
other on a silver pedestal.

Lay Myet Hna Paya, on Bidaung Hill to
the south, and **Shwe Gu Gyi Paya**, on a hill
to the north, are also highly revered, though
of less visual interest.

Gem Markets
Rubies and sapphires are Mogok's life-
blood, and several markets dispense the red
and blue stones on a rotating basis, depending on the time of day. Best for the casual
visitor is the Peiq Sweh Gem Market towards
the eastern end of the Mandalay-Momeik
(Mong Mit) road, where moderately priced
gems are displayed on small metal trays
daily from 9 am to noon.

An unnamed central gem market, near the
cinema on Padamya Lan, west of the Mogok
Motel, purveys high-priced stones to a nearly
all-male crowd daily from noon to 2 pm.

Finally, the Min Tada Gem Market, on the
westernmost edge of town on the Mandalay-
Momeik road, near Min Tada (Min Bridge),
does business daily from 3 pm to 6 pm.

Photography in the gem markets is
frowned upon by both sellers and buyers.

Buying Gems In Mogok, the main thing
you must be concerned about isn't whether
the stones are real or fake, but whether
they're of good quality and the price is fair.
Fake stones are rarely seen in town; simply

because the supply of genuine rubies and sapphires is too great. One of the reasons Mogok has been a prohibited area for foreigners is that it's much harder for the government to control gem sales here, at the source, than in Mandalay or Yangon. In Mogok, no one seems to care who's government-licensed and who's not. On the other hand, customs officials at Yangon international airport will have something to say if they catch you with 'non-government' stones. Be warned.

Other Markets
Every fifth day the Zei Thit (New Market) or Zeigyo (Central Market) is held at a site on the west side of Mogok Lake. It's most active in the morning, when it attracts several groups of tribespeople.

The Aung Chantha Zei, in the centre, is open daily and is busier overall than Zeigyo.

Places to Stay
The only officially licensed lodging in town is the three storey, 42 room *Mogok Motel*, south of the centre on Myopaq Lan (Circular Rd). Still government-owned, the hotel has a complicated tariff schedule that theoretically allows payment with a combination of kyat and US dollars or FECs. In reality, accommodation is included in the package price set by Myawaddy Travel & Tours in Mandalay (or Yangon). The tariff schedule is as follows for a one night/two day visit: US$220 for one person, US$280 for two, and US$420 for three. For a two night/three day package, the rates are US$330 for one person, US$420 for two, and US$630 for three. All rooms come with TV, fridge, attached toilet and hot-water shower. Joined to the hotel are a restaurant and karaoke lounge. There is no electric power from midnight till 6 am.

If the Mogok Motel is full, you're permitted to stay at the *Yar Pye Guest House* or *Kyaw Family Guest House*, which share a four storey building near the central market, in the southern part of town and are owned by the same family. The *Golden Butterfly Park Bungalow*, in the western end of town off the main road, is a very nice guesthouse that, unfortunately, cannot accept foreigners.

Places to Eat
In addition to the *Mogok Motel Restaurant*, there are plenty of *Chinese, Shan and Bamar restaurants* around town, though none of them is outstanding. The *Cherry Myaing Restaurant*, on the west side of town on Yae Byu Lan, near the town entrance from Mandalay, is good for both Chinese and Bamar cuisine. *May Thit Sar*, on the Mandalay-Momeik road, towards the same end of town, and *Mya Sandar* near the lake, east of Zeigyo on the same road as the Yar Pye and Kyaw Family guesthouses, are two of the better spots for Chinese food. We understand that the *Sein Lay Nadi teashop* in Bidaung Quarter holds a literary discussion group every Sunday.

Getting There & Away
As long as the permit requirement is in force, you must apply for one of the package tours (one night/two days; or two nights/three days) from Myawaddy Travel & Tours in Mandalay (☎ 02-27618) on 35th St between 81st and 82nd Sts, or in Yangon (☎ 01-72324) at 189 Sule Paya Lan.

Should the permit situation change, several bus lines operate transport services to Mogok from Shwebo and Mandalay; it's mostly pickups, with a few full-size buses and minibuses mixed in.

From the Highway bus station in Mandalay, there are departures every half-hour from 6 to 9.30 am, all of which arrive between 3.30 and 4.30 pm. In the reverse direction buses leave Mogok every half-hour from 5.30 am to 8 am. The fare is K700.

Pickups leave Shwebo between 5 am and 7 am and arrive in Mogok approximately six hours later. The fare is K500 (K600 in the front seat).

Getting Around
Mogok has no trishaws, taxis or horsecarts; local transport is limited to walking, renting a bicycle or hitching a ride on a private vehicle. Because of the lack of local transport in Mogok, out-of-town buses and pickups generally drop passengers anywhere they like in central Mogok.

Bagan Region

Bagan (Pagan) is the most wondrous sight in Myanmar, if not South-East Asia. Across 40 sq km of country, stretching back from the Ayeyarwady (Irrawaddy) River, stand thousands of *stupas* (Buddhist religious monuments) and *pahtos* (temples). In every direction you'll see ruins of all sizes – huge and glorious temples like the Ananda Pahto soar towards the sky; small, graceful *zedis* (stupas) stand alone in fields. Some come with all manner of historical tales, while others are identified only by a number. Still others, like 900-year-old Gubyaukgyi in Myinkaba, contain elegant mural paintings that require a light to see.

One could easily spend a week or more exploring the Bagan region. In addition to the more well known monuments found in the main archaeological zone of Old Bagan, there are sites worth visiting in several other nearby towns and villages.

What you will be able to see is very much limited by the amount of time at your disposal and how you intend to use it. If you can afford to hire a car (or horsecart) and a guide, you'll be able to visit more temples, particularly those off the beaten track. The availability of bicycles for rent also makes the sites much more accessible than on foot.

If your time is very limited – just an afternoon or a day, for example – we suggest that you restrict yourself to the temples and stupas in the central Bagan Archaeological Zone, which is where most of them are concentrated.

Detailed descriptions about the history and archaeological styles of Bagan's ancient temples and stupas have been combined in a special section titled 'Temples of Bagan' in this chapter.

HISTORY

The extraordinary religious fervour that resulted in this unique collection of buildings lasted two and a half centuries. Although human habitation at Bagan dates back almost

HIGHLIGHTS

- Spectacular plain of Bagan dotted with thousands of 800-year-old temple ruins.

- Sunset over the Ayeyarwady River, viewed from the top of Mingalazedi or Bupaya.

- Mystical Mt Popa, home to Myanmar's nats.

- Little-known Bagan Era ruins and monastery museum of Salay.

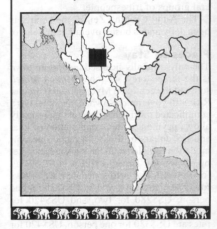

to the beginning of the Christian era, Bagan only entered its golden period with the conquest of Thaton in 1057 AD. Just over 200 years later, Bagan declined and in 1287 was over-run by the Mongols of Kublai Khan. But what fantastic effort went into those two and a half centuries! It's as if all the mediaeval cathedrals of Europe had been built in one small area, and then deserted, barely touched over the centuries.

Originally, this bend in the Ayeyarwady River was occupied by a stable and thriving Pyu city-state, perhaps allied with Beikthano and Thayekhittaya (Sri Ksetra) to the south as well as Hanlin to the north-east. Excavations along the ruined city walls indicate that by 850 the city had reached complex proportions. The name Bagan may in fact derive from Pyugan, a name first written down by the Annamese of present-day Vietnam in the mid-11th century as Pukam. In post-18th century Burmese parlance the name became Bagan, which was corrupted as Pagan by the British.

Bagan's prime began with the Bamar King Anawrahta's ascent to the throne in 1044. At this time, Myanmar was in a period of transition from Hindu and Mahayana Buddhist beliefs to the Theravada Buddhist beliefs that have since been characteristic of Myanmar. Manuha, the Mon king of Thaton, sent a monk to convert Anawrahta; the latter met with such success that Anawrahta asked Manuha to give him a number of sacred texts and important relics. Manuha, uncertain of the depths of Anawrahta's beliefs, refused the request. Anawrahta's reply to this snub was straightforward – he marched his army south, conquered Thaton and carted everything worth carrying to Bagan – including 32 sets of the *Tripitaka* (the classic Buddhist scriptures), the city's monks and scholars and, for good measure, King Manuha himself. All in all, some 30,000 Mon prisoners of war were brought to Bagan from Thaton.

Immediately Anawrahta set about a great program of building, and some of the greatest Bagan edifices date from his reign. Among the better known monuments he constructed are the beautiful Shwezigon Paya, considered a prototype for all later Burmese stupas; the Pitaka Taik (Pitaka Library), built to house the scriptures carried back from Thaton by 30 elephants; and the elegant and distinctive Shwesandaw Paya, built immediately after the conquest of Thaton. Thus began what the Burmese call the First Burmese Empire, which became a major centre for Theravada Buddhism and a pilgrimage point for Buddhists throughout South-East Asia.

King Anawrahta's successors, particularly

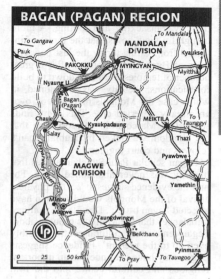

Kyanzittha, Alaungsithu and Narapatisithu, continued this phenomenal building program, although the construction work must have been nonstop throughout the period of Bagan's glory. Pali inscriptions of the time called the city Arimaddanapura (City of the Enemy Crusher) and Tambadipa (Copper Land). Marco Polo described the city-state in his famous 1298 chronicle:

> The towers are built of fine stone; and then one of them has been covered with gold a good finger in thickness, so that the tower looks as if it were all of solid gold; and the other is covered with silver in like manner so that it seems to be all of solid silver ... The King caused these towers to be erected to commemorate his magnificence and for the good of his soul; and really they do form one of the finest sights in the world, so exquisitely finished are they, so splendid and costly. And when they are lighted up by the sun they shine most brilliantly and are visible from a vast distance.

Historians disagree on what exactly happened to cause Bagan's apparently rapid decline at the end of the 13th century. The popular Burmese view is that millions of

Mongols sent by Kublai Khan swept over the city, ransacking and looting. A more thoughtful view holds that the threat of invasion from China threw the last powerful ruler of Bagan into a panic; after a great number of temples were torn down to build fortifications, the city was abandoned, in which case the Mongols merely took over an already deserted city. This view finds support in Marco Polo's observation that the kingdom was taken by Kublai Khan's 'clowns and court jugglers'.

Bagan scholar Paul Strachan argues that the city was never abandoned at all. For him the evidence suggests: '… the physical arrival of the Mongols would seem to have affected Pagan little … Despite the political imbalances that the Mongols brought about Pagan remained a cultural centre, possibly even up to the present'. Evidence suggests Bagan may have continued as an important religious and cultural centre into the 14th century, after which its decay can be blamed on the three way struggle between the Shan, Mon and Bamar for supremacy over Upper Myanmar. Whatever happened, although some minor rebuilding and maintenance continued through the centuries, the state's growth was effectively halted by 1300. Many of the religious monuments were later damaged by looters seeking precious metals and stones hidden in Buddha images and shrine walls.

From the 14th to 18th centuries, Bagan was considered a spooky region, riddled with bandits and *nats* (guardian spirits). The Burmese only began moving back to Nyaung U and Bagan in some numbers after the British established a presence in the area to provide protection from robbers and marauders.

It's hard to imagine Bagan as it once was because, like other Burmese royal cities, only the major religious buildings were made of permanent materials. The kings' palaces were all constructed of wood, and even most *kyaungs* (monasteries) were partly or wholly wooden. So what remains is just a frail shadow of Bagan at its peak. Today, a few small farming villages are the only occupants of the great city. Grain fields stand where there were palace grounds.

The kings who reigned over Bagan during its golden period were:

Anawrahta	1044-1077
Sawlu	1077-1084
Kyanzittha	1084-1113
Alaungsithu	1113-1167
Narathu	1167-1170
Naratheinkha	1170-1173
Narapatisithu	1174-1211
Nantaungmya	1211-1234
Kyaswa	1234-1250
Uzana	1250-1255
Narathihapati	1255-1287

1975 Earthquake & Restoration

In 1975 Bagan was shaken by a powerful earthquake, registering 6.5 on the Richter scale in magnitude. Contrary to initial fears, this 1000-year-old site was not totally ruined. Many of the more important temples were badly damaged, but major reconstruction started almost immediately.

Since renovation of these important religious monuments has been an ongoing project for many centuries, the old skills have not been lost and many monuments were rebuilt using traditional means. The United Nations Educational, Scientific, and Cultural Organization's (UNESCO) recent restoration projects now support dozens of local artisans and, although you certainly won't see any modern construction equipment in Bagan, modern techniques are being employed as well. For example, UNESCO engineers are reinforcing some of the monuments by inserting iron beams in the masonry to preserve the structural integrity in case of earthquake.

As for the hundreds of lesser monuments, anything that was likely to fall off in an earthquake would have fallen off centuries ago. While it was quite evident which of the major temples were repaired, Bagan has never looked like a huge building site. Some of the restoration, such as the repairs to the Gadawpalin Pahto, took until the early 1980s to complete. Others continue.

Bagan Archaeological Zone

Although Old Bagan is no longer inhabited (except by hotel and government employees), it represents the core of the Bagan Archaeological Zone and contains several of the main temple sites, city walls and museum. It's right on a bend of the Ayeyarwady River – sometime during your stay, wander down to the waterfront and watch the coming and going of the river trade. Boats will be passing by or pausing to unload goods, and villagers will come down to the river with oxen carts to collect water. You can even take a boat across the river to the village on the other side. Note how Bagan's water supply is pumped up from a point just below the Aye Yar Hotel.

Orientation

Old Bagan sits on the eastern bank of a deep bend of the Ayeyarwady. A paved road follows the river bend from Nyaung U, the largest town in the area, and through the Bagan Archaeological Zone to the village of Myinkaba, and finally to Thiripyitsaya and Bagan Myothit (New Bagan). Branching off this road is a vast network of tracks and trails between the various monuments.

Although the whole area is known to tourists as Bagan, only the Archaeological Zone is properly called Bagan nowadays. The village that grew up in the middle of the zone during the 1970s was moved to the middle of a peanut field several kilometres away just before the May 1990 elections – much to the disgruntlement of Old Bagan residents who were given about a week's notice by the government to move and rebuild in the new location – known as Bagan Myothit. Now it's hard to tell that a village ever existed here, so thorough were the authorities in erasing all traces. The resilient residents of Bagan Myothit have put together a respectable existence, and many continue to depend on tourist services – lodging, food, souvenirs and moneychanging – for their livelihood.

Clearing Old Bagan of guesthouses has had at least one beneficial effect – it has dispersed visitors around the area and eliminated the tourist ghetto that had developed in Old Bagan. Accommodation is now scattered around Nyaung U, Wetkyi-in, Myinkaba, Bagan Myothit, Tetthe and Old Bagan.

The main town in the area, Nyaung U, is about 5km upriver from Bagan. Nyaung U is also the terminus for buses and riverboats from Mandalay or further afield, and the airport is a couple of kilometres south-east near the village of Tetthe. The train station is another 2km beyond the airport.

Photography & Sunset-Viewing For a panoramic view of as many temple ruins and stupas as possible, Mingalazedi is the best choice, now that the upper terraces of the tallest monuments (Thatbyinnyu, Gawdawpalin, Dhammayangyi, Sulamani) are closed to visitors. The light for the eastward view from Mingalazedi is at its best in the late afternoon.

The westward view from Mingalazedi is, of course, also good at sunset, though some people prefer the sunset view from Shwesandaw Paya, as it encompasses silhouettes of the monuments within Old Bagan to the north-west.

For Ayeyarwady River views at sunset, the best choices are Bupaya in Old Bagan or Lawkananda Paya in Bagan Myothit; both stupas stand on the eastern bank of the river. Upali Thein in Wetkyi-in and Nanpaya in Myinkaba are also good spots for catching a sunset, especially if another favourite is crowded.

Information

Old Bagan itself contains just four hotels, the offices of Myanma Airways (MA), Air Mandalay (AM) and Yangon Airways (YA), as well as Myanmar Travels & Tours (MTT). The latter is open daily from 9 am to 6 pm; its main function seems to be to administer the US$10 admission fee system for the Bagan Archaeological Zone and to post timetables on the wall.

You can also purchase two useful maps

BAGAN REGION

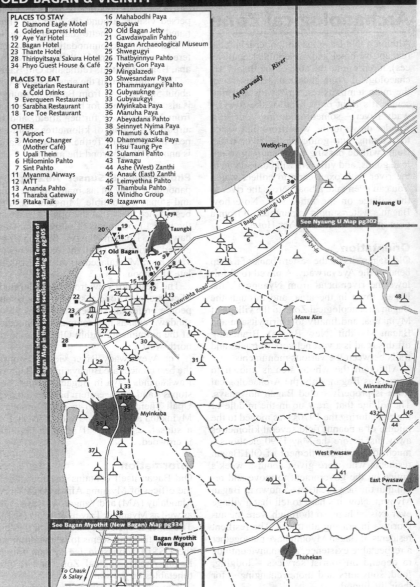

OLD BAGAN & VICINITY

PLACES TO STAY
2   Diamond Eagle Motel
4   Golden Express Hotel
19 Aye Yar Hotel
22 Bagan Hotel
23 Thante Hotel
28 Thiripyitsaya Sakura Hotel
34 Phyo Guest House & Café

PLACES TO EAT
8   Vegetarian Restaurant
    & Cold Drinks
9   Everqueen Restaurant
10 Sarabha Restaurant
18 Toe Toe Restaurant

OTHER
1   Airport
3   Money Changer
    (Mother Café)
5   Upali Thein
6   Htilominlo Pahto
7   Sint Pahto
11 Myanma Airways
12 MTT
13 Ananda Pahto
14 Tharaba Gateway
15 Pitaka Taik

16 Mahabodhi Paya
17 Bupaya
20 Old Bagan Jetty
21 Gawdawpalin Pahto
24 Bagan Archaeological Museum
25 Shwegugyi
26 Thatbyinnyu Pahto
27 Nyein Gon Paya
29 Mingalazedi
30 Shwesandaw Paya
31 Dhammayangyi Pahto
32 Gubyaukne
33 Gubyaukgyi
35 Myinkaba Paya
36 Manuha Paya
37 Abeyadana Pahto
38 Seinnyet Nyima Paya
39 Thamuti & Kutha
40 Dhammayazika Paya
41 Hsu Taung Pye
42 Sulamani Pahto
43 Tawagu
44 Ashe (West) Zanthi
45 Anauk (East) Zanthi
46 Leimyethna Pahto
47 Thambula Pahto
48 Winidho Group
49 Izagawna

For more information on temples see the Temples of Bagan Map in the special section starting on pg305

Ayeyarwady River

Wetkyi-in

Nyaung U

See Nyaung U Map pg302

Leya

Taungbi

Old Bagan

Bagan-Nyaung U Road

Wetkyi-in Chaung

Anawrahta Road

Manu Kan

Minnanthu

Myinkaba

West Pwasaw

East Pwasaw

See Bagan Myothit (New Bagan) Map pg334

Bagan Myothit
(New Bagan)

To Chauk
& Salay

Thuhekan

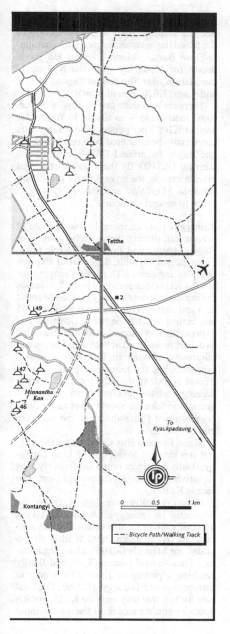

Tetthe

Minnanthu
Kan

To
Kyaukpadaung

0   0.5   1 km

--- Bicycle Path/Walking Track

Kontangyi

here: MTT's own *Bagan Tourist Map* and the independently produced, and much more detailed, *The Map of Bagan*.

Post & Communications There is a post office in Nyaung U; airmail letters are carried aboard daily flights to Yangon (Rangoon), so it's fairly reliable.

Most of the hotels in the area have International Direct Dial (IDD) phones, but they cost a steep US$12 a minute, and the service can be erratic. Fax machines are sometimes available, but they are slow and therefore expensive. When telephoning to/from anywhere in the Bagan area you must go through an operator.

You can make much cheaper 'booking' calls, but from only three locations in the vicinity. A new telephone office in Nyaung U near the Thante Hotel charges K3000 for a three minute overseas call. As usual, you first book the call, then wait at least half an hour for the switchboard to contact the Yangon operator, who then calls back to Nyaung U. A smaller branch telephone office is on the main road between Old Bagan and Nyaung U. Another one is on the main east-west road in Bagan Myothit and is open 24 hours.

Admission MTT charges a US$10 entry fee for the first two nights spent in the archaeological zone. In theory, an additional US$2 is levied per night thereafter, although no one bothers to collect it. For those arriving by air, boat or train, the US$10 fee is collected upon arrival on behalf of MTT. Hotels collect the fee from those arriving overland. Hotels are also required to ask to see your entry receipt, so it's difficult to get around the entry fee. Even if you manage to avoid it, you risk getting a Burmese person in trouble with the authorities.

Getting There & Away
Air All three airlines (MA, AM and YA) fly to Nyaung U-Bagan airport from Yangon, Mandalay and Heho.

From Yangon, AM flies daily; the flight takes an hour and 15 minutes and costs

US$90. From Mandalay, the AM or YA flight costs US$45 each way and takes about half an hour. MA flies the same routes daily for US$80 and US$35, respectively. On any flight, if you sit on the right-hand side of the aircraft flying Mandalay-Bagan or the left-hand side flying Bagan-Mandalay, you can keep the Ayeyarwady in sight for most of the way and obtain a good view of Amarapura, Inwa (Ava), the Ava Bridge (Inwa Tada) and Sagaing while climbing out of, or descending into, Mandalay. You also get an excellent view of Bagan on the Bagan-Yangon flights.

From Heho, all the airlines fly daily to Bagan with a stopover in Mandalay. Aboard AM or YA, a ticket for this route costs US$80; on MA it's US$65.

AM flights can be booked or confirmed at the AM office in Bagan Myothit. AM plans to open another office in Nyaung U as well. The YA office is in Nyaung U near the *zeigyo* (central market). Ostensibly, MA flights can also be booked at the MA office on the opposite side of the road in Old Bagan, but repeated visits indicate that the staff are less than helpful. It's very difficult to find out whether you have a confirmed seat on the plane until it's too late to book the bus-train connection. Our recommendation – especially in light of MA's abysmal efficiency and horrible safety record – is to forget about trying to fly in/out of Bagan on MA. Stick to AM or YA on this route – even though it costs a little more – or come via land or river.

Bus, Pickup & Share Taxi There are a number of options for travelling to the Bagan region by bus:

Mandalay After flying, the fastest way to get to Bagan is on the bus from Mandalay to Nyaung U. Buses operate daily from Mandalay's Highway bus station, also known as the Central/Main bus station, at 26th and 82nd Sts, for around K650 per person for the seven hour trip. Pickups also go from Mandalay to Bagan for a bit less. Along the way you make a couple of tea

stops – breakfast at Kumeh, lunch at Yewei. See the Getting There & Away section in the Mandalay chapter for more information.

From Bagan, Mann Express Co buses depart for Mandalay from the Nyaung U bus station near Shwezigon Pagoda at 4, 7 and 9 am (K650, non air-con).

There are also share taxis – Toyota 'Super-roof' hatchbacks – available to Bagan for around K2000 per person. These same cars can usually be chartered between Mandalay and Bagan for around US$60; new air-con vans for US$100. By share taxi or chartered private vehicle, the drive time for the 305km between Mandalay and Bagan/Nyaung U drops to around six hours.

Taunggyi You can travel by bus, pickup or private car, directly between Nyaung U or Bagan Myothit and Taunggyi, to Inle Lake. From Bagan Myothit, Tiger Head Express operates Japanese pickups to Taunggyi for around K1000 per person. The pickup leaves the main north-south road in Bagan Myothit at 4 am and arrives in Thazi around 8.45 am, in time to catch the No 12 Down special express train to Yangon, which is scheduled to depart from Thazi at 9.28 am. The pickup continues, arriving in Taunggyi around 2 pm, stopping for lunch along the way in Yemabay. Most travellers get off before Taunggyi at the junction town of Shwenyaung and take the short bus or taxi ride to Nyaungshwe (Yaunghwe) at the northern end of Inle Lake.

Mann Express Bus Co operates the only bus (no air-con) from Nyaung U to Taunggyi. Daily departure is at 5 am from Nyaung U, arriving in Taunggyi at around 1 pm. The fare is K1100.

If you're really counting kyat you can hopscotch to Taunggyi/Inle Lake by taking a public pickup from Nyaung U to Kyaukpadaung (K75), changing to another pickup bound for Meiktila (K100), changing again to a Thazi-bound pickup (K30) and finally catching a pickup in Thazi all the way to Shwenyaung or Taunggyi (K200). The total fare for this trip may only be K125, but it's doubtful you'd make it all the way without having to spend the night somewhere. If you decide to stay overnight along the way, Thazi is your least expensive choice.

Those with a less limited budget can charter a car all the way from the Bagan region to Taunggyi or Inle Lake for around US$45, or a new air-con van for up to US$90. Up over the hills east of Thazi, the road is winding – beware if you suffer from motion sickness. Whether by public pickup or chartered van, this is a long and trying trip. You can usually arrange to stop at Mt Popa on the way for the same price, to make it approximately a 10 hour trip. If you want to break the journey with an overnight stop in Kalaw, expect to pay another K3000.

Meiktila & Thazi If seats are available, Tiger Head Express will drop passengers off in Meiktila or Thazi on the way to Taunggyi for K500. If there's competition for the seats, Tiger Head sometimes charges the full Taunggyi fare, which is K1000.

Yangon Several buses leave daily from Nyaung U for Yangon, via Pyay (Prome). Two companies stand out from the rest. The best is the air-con Ye Thu Aung Express bus, departing at 4 pm and arriving early the next morning at Yangon's Highway bus station. The fare is K1500. In the same price range is the New Bagan Express bus, which will also pick you up in the Bagan/Nyaung U area. A slower and less comfortable government bus makes the same trip for K600.

There's also the two hour trip from Nyaung U to Kyaukpadaung, about 50km south-east and costing K75. The Dagon-Popa bus line in Kyaukpadaung departs for Yangon twice daily at 4 and 8 am. It should get to Yangon 12 to 14 hours later, for about K800. Book tickets the day before in Kyaukpadaung.

You could also take a bus to Meiktila and catch one of several Yangon-bound air-con express buses from Mandalay – see the Getting There & Away section in the Mandalay chapter for details.

Pyay The air-con New Bagan Express bus departs from Nyaung U at 8.30 pm for Yangon and will drop you in Pyay for K1000. Arrival time is around 6 am.

From Pyay you can continue to Yangon by public bus (three departures daily) for just K400 and a ride of around seven hours. Air-con Sun-Moon Express or Rainbow Express buses from Pyay to Yangon are also available once a day at around 5 pm for K400 – see the Pyay section in the Around Yangon chapter for more details.

By private vehicle you can drive between Bagan and Pyay in as little as six or seven hours, now that the road has been improved.

Train There are a few train options to/from Bagan:

Mandalay There is a daily 10 pm departure from Mandalay to Bagan that should arrive at 6 am. Upper-class fare is US$9, US$4 for ordinary class. Tickets must be purchased the day before at the Mandalay train station. The same train departs from Bagan for Mandalay at 9 am, arriving in Mandalay at 5 pm.

Yangon There are two routes between Bagan and Yangon, each departing on different days. A train departs for Yangon via Pyay on even-numbered days of the month at 10 pm, arriving the following day at 5.30 pm. Another train departs for Yangon via Pyinmana and Bago (Pegu) on odd-numbered days at 8 pm, arriving the following day at about 3 pm. Although these trains are officially called express trains, they are slower than the more established Mandalay-Yangon express trains. The fare from Bagan to Yangon is US$31 for upper class, US$11 for ordinary class.

The Bagan train station is about 5km south-east of Nyaung U. The taxi fare from Nyaung U to the train station is about K700, more from the big hotels.

Bus/Train via Thazi This is an interesting way to break up the Bagan-Yangon trip. You first have to get to Thazi, which is about half-way from Bagan to Inle Lake. A very efficient Tiger Head Express pickup goes straight to Thazi from Bagan Myothit in plenty of time for the Mandalay-Yangon express. Departure time from Bagan Myothit is around 4 am. A Mann Express minibus also makes the run from Nyaung U to Thazi on its way to Taunggyi – also in time to catch the morning Mandalay (No 12 Down) express train to Yangon.

The Bagan-Thazi road is very scenic, with a view of the Mt Popa volcanic dome in the distance at the beginning of the trip, as well as glimpses of villages, farms, bullock carts, pedestrians bearing cargo on their heads etc. The ride is rather cramped, with 18 official passengers in the back, two with the driver in front and three or four hangers-on. There are rest stops in Kyaukpadaung and Meiktila – the first a short intermission for fuel and the second a longer stop, where you can refuel yourself with tea and *nam-bya* (Bamar roti). The fare is K500 per passenger.

If you want to spend the day in Thazi, you can wait for the 6.30 pm evening express from Mandalay that arrives around 9.30 pm and leaves a few minutes later. You can book your Thazi-Yangon tickets in Mandalay or Thazi, but if you wait till Thazi to buy your ticket there's no guarantee of a seat. An MTT official is sometimes at the station to meet foreigners coming from Bagan. See the Thazi section in the North-Eastern Myanmar chapter for things to do while you're waiting for the train. See the boxed text labelled 'Train Schedules & Fares' in the Getting Around chapter at the start of this book for the Thazi-Yangon train schedule.

Boat It's possible to travel along the Ayeyarwady in both directions from Bagan, although the trip from Mandalay to Bagan is the one most commonly taken by travellers.

Mandalay There is now a better alternative to the MTT *Mandalay-Bagan* ferry (which departs from Mandalay at 5.30 am every Wednesday and Sunday at a cost of US$11 deck class or US$33 for a stuffy cabin). The new *Mandalay-Bagan Express* ferry departs every Monday, Tuesday, Thursday, Friday and Saturday. The trip takes about nine hours and costs US$16. Food is available on board, but it's pricey.

Travelling upriver from Bagan to Mandalay involves another night stop on the way, so unless you can spare at least two full days, the upriver trip (on either ferry) is not worth considering unless you really have formed an attachment to Burmese river travel. In Mandalay, you must purchase tickets for the ferry at either the Mandalay MTT office or the Irrawaddy Water Transport (IWT) office. Most guesthouses or hotels will also help you get boat tickets. The IWT office in Nyaung U is near the jetty.

A slower, much cheaper ferry does the same route daily, except Thursday and Sunday, taking approximately 26 to 29 hours and costing just K100. The slower boat stops one night on the western bank of the river at the busy riverport of Pakokku, where there are several places to stay, including the ***Myayatanar Inn*** at 75 Madaw Lan (Main Rd). It's about 250m down the main street from where you turn left out of the dock road. Rooms are K500 per person per night and staff will pick you up from the boat. You can also sleep on the boat if you wish.

The next morning it's a further two hours downriver to Nyaung U, but don't worry if you oversleep in Pakokku and miss the boat, as other boats pass by later in the morning. If you find yourself stranded in Pakokku, you can usually charter a long-tail boat to make the three hour trip for about K2000.

Only the faster express ferries go all the way to Old Bagan; all other boats land at the Nyaung U jetty, about 6km north-east of Old Bagan. Pickups, taxis and horsecarts from the Nyaung U jetty to Old Bagan are always plentiful.

Although it's quite an experience to travel by boat on the mighty Ayeyarwady, the river is wide and the banks flat, with most of the villages set well back due to the risk of seasonal flooding, so you won't see too much from the river. There are plenty of stops, however, and people are always on hand to sell food and drink.

Towards the end of the dry season (March to early May), inquire about river conditions before leaping on a Mandalay-Bagan ferry. Getting stuck on sand bars can happen at any time of the year, but as the river level falls, you're more likely to get stuck and it's likely to take longer to get unstuck. People have wasted days while at a standstill on the Ayeyarwady.

Pyay & Yangon From Nyaung U, the slow ferries continue daily, except Thursday and Sunday, downriver to Pyay, where you could change boats and continue all the way to Yangon. The first day takes you from Bagan to Magwe, the second day from there to Pyay. From Pyay it's another two and a half-day boat trip to Yangon. You'd use up a quarter of your four week visa on this trip, but it would be quite a ride. At the time of writing, a new Chinese-built triple-deck ferry was scheduled to begin service along the Ayeyarwady River between Pyay, Bagan/ Nyaung U and Mandalay. See the Pyay section in the Around Yangon chapter for more details about the boat.

Getting Around

To/From the Airport The Nyaung U-Bagan airstrip is about 5km south-east of Nyaung U, which is 5km north-east of Old Bagan. A taxi from the airport to Nyaung U or Wetkyi-in costs K700; to Old Bagan or Myinkaba it's around K800; and to Bagan Myothit it's around K900.

Bus There is a bus service (pickup trucks once again) between Nyaung U and Bagan for K5; it departs about 200m from the bus station in Nyaung U.

Horsecart & Trishaw You can hire horsecarts from place to place or by the hour; count on an hourly rate of around K200, K800 for a half-day, K1500 for the whole day. A horsecart from the Old Bagan jetty to Bagan Myothit costs around K300 (with bargaining). Some of the horsecart drivers are pretty knowledgeable too, and some visitors prefer carts to bikes. Technically speaking, drivers are not supposed to act as guides – guides are required to have MTT licences and charge a separate guide fee – but with an informed driver, who needs a guide?

Trishaws are mostly confined to Nyaung U and Bagan Myothit, though they're occasionally seen elsewhere and always show up to meet the boats coming from Mandalay. A trishaw ride costs approximately K50 per kilometre.

Bicycle Although you can comfortably walk around the more central Bagan sites, if you want to travel further afield you'll need transport. Bicycles – available for hire at most hotels and guesthouses – are a great way to get around. Traffic around Bagan is so light that bike riding is a joy, although you should steer well clear when the occasional motor vehicle does chance by. The usual cost is K70 per hour, or K300 to K500 for the day. Riding can be hard-going down the dustier tracks and punctures are inevitable, but they're fixed, or the bike is replaced with alacrity. An early morning or late afternoon ride along the sealed road between Wetkyi-in and Myinkaba is particularly pleasant.

When renting a bike, check it thoroughly before accepting it – make sure it steers properly, the brakes work and the tyres hold air. One traveller told of seeing a rider discover his machine's total lack of braking just at the bottom of the long slope. People picked him up and carried him inside to a bar, where a few beers restored his equilibrium. The same traveller was offered a bike with the suggestion that he pedal back every hour or so, 'to refill the tyres'.

Riding out to some of the more remote temples (eg Minnanthu) can be hard-going through the deep and dusty sand; for these destinations a horsecart is preferable.

Boat From the jetty near Bupaya in Old Bagan you can charter small boats for scenic trips along the river and to visit riverside shrines such as Lawkananda (near Bagan Myothit) and Kyauk Gu Ohnmin (east of Nyaung U). Hire rates are around K1000 an hour. To Salay and back, expect to pay about K10,000 for a charter.

Any of the riverside hotels in Old Bagan can arrange hourly charters.

OLD BAGAN
Bagan Archaeological Museum
The present museum, near the Gadawpalin Pahto, was completely rebuilt in 1998 and now competes in size with the surrounding temples. But it still makes an interesting introduction before you start exploring the actual sites. The central gallery contains a large number of religious images and other fine works found in temples around Bagan, including a bronze Buddha from Bago, dating to the 16th century, and many terracotta votive tablets from the 11th and 12th centuries. The stone images at the museum are crudely restored; the bronzes are better and many show Pallava influence. An 11th century bronze lotus with Buddhas inside is particularly interesting.

Other museum pieces of note include fragments of painted cloth that were kept in the hollow forearms of large Buddha images, plus gems from the chests and heads of some images (many of the images in Bagan temple ruins have holes in the chest area where temple thieves made off with the gems). A lacquer Buddha in the museum's outside pavilion dates from the 13th century. Bagan-style Buddhas vary greatly in the proportion of head to body – some have huge heads and small bodies, some huge bodies and small heads – but all exhibit arched, connected eyebrows and a knife-edged nose on a squarish face.

There is also a small exhibit on the 1975 earthquake. The museum is open Monday to Saturday from 9 am to 4.30 pm; admission is US$4.

Tharaba Gateway
The ruins of Tharaba Gateway (also known as Sarabha Gateway), on the eastern side, are all that remain of the old 9th century city wall. Traces of old stucco can still be seen on the gateway. The gate is guarded by highly revered brother and sister nats, the male (Lord Handsome) on the right, the female (Lady Golden Face) on the left. In their human histories, the siblings died in a fire, so worshippers offer the images flowers and water, rather than candles or incense.

Anawrahta's original palace is thought to have been located near Tharaba.

Places to Stay
The accommodation situation in Old Bagan has changed often since the 1990 elections, when the entire village (guesthouses included) was forced to move to a new settlement called Bagan Myothit in 15 days. For several years afterwards, the only places open to foreigners were government-owned hotels in Old Bagan. However, with the continuing privatisation of hotels and guesthouses, a variety of accommodation can now be found in Old Bagan, Nyaung U, Wetkyi-in, Myinkaba, Bagan Myothit and Tetthe (near the airport). There are close to 125 guesthouses and hotels in the area. Competition for customers is keen and it's not unusual to meet touts whose job is to persuade tourists to jump from one guesthouse to another.

In, or just outside, Old Bagan proper there are four hotels, three of them now privately owned. The best value in Old Bagan is the private *Thante Hotel* (☎ 062-70144, fax 70143), just west of the Bagan Archaeological Museum. Small economy rooms with bath and air-con cost US$10/15 a single/double. Larger rooms in the two storey 'guesthouse' building cost US$16/20. The upstairs corner rooms are best, as these get cross-ventilation. There are also eight attractive bungalow units with small verandahs that cost US$30/35. A patio breakfast buffet overlooking the Ayeyarwady is included. According to the manager, the hotel's main building dates from 1922 and its first guest was the visiting Prince of Wales.

The 108 room *Bagan Hotel* (☎ 062-70146, fax 70313) is one of the newest upscale hotels in the Bagan area, and it's very good value for money. Brick pathways connect several one-storey buildings on landscaped grounds with Gawdawpalin Pahto looming to one side and the Ayeyarwady just beyond. Superior rooms cost US$40/50, and several larger suites are available from US$60 to US$80. A full breakfast is included, and all rooms have shower and bath, air-con, satellite TV and IDD telephone. There is a good cafe on the grounds and a large lounge in the lobby decorated with teak furnishings and local artwork.

Just north of the city wall, near Bupaya, is the government-owned *Aye Yar Hotel* (☎ *062-70027, fax 70055)*, with 83 rooms, many overlooking the Ayeyarwady. Standard rooms with air-con, hot-water shower, fridge and TV cost US$36/42. Slightly larger superior rooms with balcony views of the river, wood floors and a few more teakwood touches cost US$42/48. Two much larger suites and a separate chalet are available for US$60/ 68. During off-peak times (April to November) rooms may be discounted by about 20%. All rates include breakfast and free airport transfers but do not include the 20% service charge and tax. The hotel verandah is a good spot for a cold beer as you watch the sun set over the Ayeyarwady River.

About 500m south of the Old Bagan city walls – about a 20 minute walk from the centre – is the privately owned 60 room *Thiripyitsaya Sakura Hotel* (☎ *062-70285, fax 70286)*, which does manage to take advantage of its location and looks like it belongs to an exotic place like Bagan – something which certainly cannot be said of most Bagan hotels. There is a new wing of well appointed rooms, but a group of swanky garden bungalows with private verandahs is its attraction. The nightly cost is US$120 for one or two persons. All rooms are teak-furnished, with satellite TV, fridge and air-con. The hotel also has a swimming pool, comfortable lounge area, and an excellent (if pricey) restaurant featuring both international and Bamar cuisine. An outdoor verandah bar overlooks the river. If, after a hard day's temple-seeing, you haven't the energy to drag yourself to a temple top to catch the sunset, this is a very acceptable substitute.

Located between Old Bagan and Nyaung U, the *Golden Express Hotel* (☎ *062-70101)* has 20 spiffy bungalows with air-con, fridge and attached bath for US$20/30, breakfast included.

Finally, if you want to spend the night in Old Bagan, but not the money, you can usually sleep on a platform at the old Bupaya stupa overlooking the river.

See the Nyaung U & Wetkyi-in, Myinkaba and Bagan Myothit sections later in the chapter for details on other places to stay in the area.

Places to Eat

Of the four hotel restaurants in and around Old Bagan, the food at the *Thiripyitsaya* and the *Bagan* hotels is particularly good.

Just outside Tharaba Gateway, the friendly *Sarabha Restaurant* serves well-seasoned and reasonably priced Bamar, Chinese and Thai food in a simple, quiet, indoor-outdoor setting. Just a bit further up the road toward Wetkyi-in, about 200m outside the city gate and north along a dirt road, is the inexpensive *Everqueen Restaurant*, which has a similar menu and garden setting. The Bamar-style tomato and cucumber salad is particularly good.

The simple and decent *Vegetarian Restaurant & Cold Drinks* is just outside the old wall near Tharaba Gate. It serves a few snacks and curry dishes. It's a nice place to rest from the heat if you're bicycling around. A sign in the small dining room says 'Be kind to animals by not eating them'.

Convenient to the Aye Yar Hotel and next to the boat landing below the hotel is a cluster of local *cafes* and *teashops*. Although they're very rustic, the relaxed atmosphere makes for a pleasant evening. *Toe Toe Restaurant*, on the left on a bluff as you walk towards the jetty, serves teashop snacks in the morning and quite decent curries in the afternoon.

Shopping

With most of the businesses in Old Bagan banished to either nearby Nyaung U or Bagan Myothit, the hotels are the only choice for shopping. The Bagan and Thiripyitsaya Sakura hotels have the largest selection of Burmese artefacts, cards, jewellery and books.

For a wider shopping selection, spend an afternoon wandering around Nyaung U or Bagan Myothit.

Getting There & Around

Nyaung U and Bagan Myothit are the main transportation centres for the area. See the Getting There & Away and Getting Around sections earlier in this chapter for details.

NYAUNG U & WETKYI-IN

Nyaung U, about 5km north-east of Old Bagan, is the major population centre in the Bagan area; you'll pass through Nyaung U if you arrive in Bagan by road or air, and by river if you take the slow boat from Pyay or Mandalay. It's an interesting little place for a wander – it has lots of shops (look out for the cigar dealers), an excellent and colourful market, and even a Burmese billiard hall. Recently several inexpensive guesthouses have opened their doors to foreigners. Several small restaurants offer Indian, Chinese and Bamar food.

The small village of Wetkyi-in, roughly

halfway between Nyaung U and Old Bagan, flanks the mouth of Wetkyi-in Chaung (canal). Along the 2km stretch between Wetkyi-in and Nyaung U are several guesthouses and restaurants for travellers.

Although some of the monuments listed in this section are close to Wetkyi-in and Bagan, or conveniently situated between both, others are located far east of Nyaung U. You'll probably see some of them from the river, or if you fly in/out of Bagan.

Aung Myi Bodhi Dhamma Yeiktha

Directly opposite Shwezigon Paya near Gubyaukgyi, this *kammathan kyaung* (meditation monastery) is home to the well regarded 'Pakistan Sayadaw'. Also known by his Pali name U Ariyawananda, the *sayadaw* (chief abbot) teaches a simple technique of breath- and-body awareness that attracts monks and lay practitioners from as far

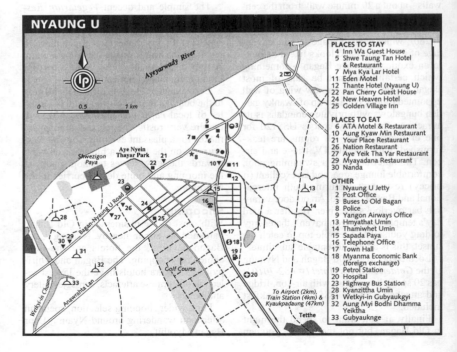

away as Yangon, and even overseas. There's very little to see among the simple collection of huts and buildings – no glittering stupas, just *dhamma* (Pali: Buddhist teachings) practice.

Places to Stay

Places to stay in Nyaung U and Wetkyi-in are increasing in number, turning this side of the Bagan area into a budget accommodation centre. A number of guesthouses and hotels are located near Shwezigon Paya, between Nyaung U and Wetkyi-in. The main advantage to these places is their proximity to the Nyaung U market and Highway bus station. Due to the general activity in the area, these places can be a little noisy during the day, though nights are usually quiet.

In Nyaung U, just west of the roundabout and central market, there's a cluster of guesthouses, including the well managed and friendly *Inn Wa Guest House* (☎ 062-70125), with small clean rooms with fan and hot shower for US$6/10 a single/double. Larger rooms with air-con and a fridge cost US$10/20. Across the street, the *Shwe Taung Tan Hotel & Restaurant* is another good deal with clean, air-con rooms with bath for US$4 per person, including breakfast.

Friendly and bright, the nearby *Mya Kya Lar Guest House* (☎ 062-70065) has a variety of rooms and prices. Small clean air-con economy rooms with separate bath cost US$4 per person, and larger attractive rooms with attached shower, air-con and fan cost US$8/15/20 a single/double/triple. All rooms have wooden floors, and a western or Bamar-style breakfast is included.

On the road going due south from the roundabout and market, the popular *Eden Motel* (☎ 062-70078) has small rooms with fan and hot shower for US$4/7, and larger air-con rooms with TV off an upstairs terrace for US$8/10. One triple room is available for US$15. Breakfast is included; for a good Bamar breakfast, notify the manager the day before.

The central *Thante Hotel (Nyaung U)* (☎ 062-70317), just north of the market, is managed by the same owners as the Thante

Hotel in Old Bagan. Rooms in the main building facing the street feature air-con, satellite TV and attached bath, as do several quieter bungalows by a small pool. Rooms cost US$24/30, including breakfast.

In Wetkyi-in, the comfortable *Pan Cherry Guest House* (☎ 062-70147), just north-east of Shwezigon, has 11 fan-cooled singles/doubles with shared bath for US$4 per person, and three rooms with air-con and attached cold-water shower for US$10/15. The well constructed, residential-style building stays fairly cool, even in hot weather.

The small and friendly *New Heaven Hotel* (☎ 062-70061), at Thiripyitsaya (Block 5), is a few blocks south-east of Shwezigon Paya in a quiet courtyard setting. Rooms come with fan, air-con, bath and breakfast and cost US$4/8. In the same residential area is the *Golden Village Inn* (☎ 062-70088), with prices and accommodation similar to the New Heaven.

About a kilometre south-west of this area, toward Old Bagan, is the *Golden Express Hotel* (☎ 062-70101), which offers 15 cottage-style doubles on landscaped grounds for US$20/35/70 a single/double/triple, including breakfast, plus 24 economy rooms for US$10/15/20, not including breakfast. All rates are subject to 20% tax and service. The hotel is a 10 minute walk to Shwezigon Paya, five minutes to Htilominlo and 20 minutes to Nyaung U.

If you need to stay closer to the airport, try the *Diamond Eagle Motel* near the village of Tetthe. Economy rooms with fan and attached bathroom cost US$10/15, while more comfortable air-con rooms cost US$20/35/45.

Places to Eat

Staying near Shwezigon Paya puts you in the vicinity of several decent places to eat. The *Nation Restaurant* and nearby *Aye Yeik Tha Yar Restaurant* offer the usual fried rice, curries and noodles, and the English-language menus include several brands of beer, yoghurt, *lassi* (yoghurt drinks) and fruit juice. The thatched-roof Nation is popular, but service and quality can vary.

The cafe at nearby *Shwe Taung Tan* is similar in price and variety, and it often has fresh fish on the menu. Across the road is *ATA Motel & Restaurant*, which serves good Pakistani, Indian and Chinese Muslim (halal) food.

South of the central market and opposite the Bagan Golf course is *Peace Restaurant*, serving mostly Chinese dishes, curry snacks, cold drinks and beer. Up the road, and next to the Thante Hotel, is *Thante Bakery & Café*, with a good assortment of snacks and sweets ranging from tasty curry puffs to gooey cakes. It serves tea, coffee and cold drinks, and there are a few tables inside.

In the village of Wetkyi-in, about 1km toward Old Bagan, is the excellent *Myayadana Restaurant*, which serves a variety of Bamar and Chinese dishes in an indoor-outdoor setting. Prices are reasonable, and menus are in English and French as well as Burmese; if you're serious about sampling the Bamar food at Myayadana, ask staff in the morning so they can show off their stuff. Almost as good is the nearby *Nanda Restaurant*, with a similar menu. Both places put on a low-key marionette show most evenings when enough tourists are in town.

In Nyaung U you'll find several less-than-clean *rice and noodle shops*, plus a couple of *biryani* (spiced rice with chicken) *places*. The basic *Aung Kyaw Min Restaurant* (Burmese sign), across the street from the Eden Motel, is a popular spot for its excellent *chin hin* (sour tamarind soup) and *pi hin* (prawn curry).

Shopping

Aside from the all-day central market, several small shops in town sell earthy, utilitarian ceramics, lacquerware and other crafts; what might be called 'folk utensils' elsewhere in Asia are regarded as everyday requisites here.

Getting There & Around

See the Getting There & Away and Getting Around sections earlier in this chapter for transport information to Nyaung U and Wetkyi-in.

MYINKABA

Only a kilometre or two south of Bagan, Myinkaba has a number of interesting pahtos and stupas from the Early Bagan period, including **Gubyaukgyi**, which contains the oldest mural paintings in all of Bagan. Nearby is **Manuha Paya**, built by King Manuha, the 'captive king'. The four Buddhas squeezed within are reputedly representations of the king's own physical discomfort with captivity. Note the north-facing Buddha: north and east positions represent death (with hands flat and feet parallel); south and west represent the relaxed or sleeping position (hands at head, feet crossed).

Excellent lacquerware workshops can be visited in Myinkaba. Some of these accomplish the complete process of producing lacquerware in the one centre, while others specialise in a single phase of the production – such as making the bamboo frames on which the lacquer is coated.

Places to Stay & Eat

Next to Gubyaukgyi, at the northern end of the village, is the quiet and well managed *Phyo Guest House & Café* (☎ 062-70086). Eight rooms along an air-con corridor share three bathrooms; the rates are US$8/15 a single/double including breakfast.

Down the street, opposite Manuha Paya, are a couple of decent teashops. One of them, the *Aung Mya Thi*, makes very tasty samosas.

Shopping

A large lacquerware facility on the western side of the road is a good place to observe craft techniques or purchase a wide variety of well priced lacquer items.

Getting There & Around

Old Bagan is an approximately 2km walk north of Myinkaba. Bicycles can be rented at Phyo Guest House & Café for touring the ruins. Horsecarts are plentiful in Myinkaba. Bagan Myothit is located a few kilometres south – a K40 to K50 horse-cart ride.

TEMPLES
OF BAGAN

Temples of Bagan

BERNARD NAPTHINE

GLENN BEANLAND

Title Page: Ananda Pahto, Old Bagan (Photograph by Bernard Napthine).

Top: A view through the dawn mist at Old Bagan.

Bottom: Looking towards Thatbyinnyu Pahto from Mingalazedi.

GLENN BEANLAND

GLENN BEANLAND

GLENN BEANLAND

Top: September greenery at Old Bagan.

Middle: Temple art, Sulamani Pahto, Old Bagan.

Bottom: The early 14th century Shweguyi Pahto, Old Bagan.

Temples of Bagan

ARCHAEOLOGY OF BAGAN

Classification

Classifying the ancient monuments of Bagan by style and age is made difficult by the vast number of archaeological sites. The official count by the end of the 13th century is said to have been 4446. By 1901 surveys found 2157 monuments still standing and identifiable. According to resident Burmese archaeologist U Aung Kyaing, the last count was taken in 1978, when archaeologists found 2230 identifiable sites, however, most contemporary references on the subject quote a figure of 2217. These figures do not include brick mounds, which would give a total of nearly 4000 separate visible sites.

The sheer variety of motifs and measurements to be studied also presents a challenge, though certain unifying factors can be found throughout. For the most part, the proliferation of temples, *stupas* (Buddhist religious monuments) and *kyaungs* (monasteries) are constructed of fired brick covered with plaster and decorated with stucco relief, polychromatic murals and glazed tiles. Sculpture materials included bronze, teak, brick and stucco, sandstone and lacquer. The most delicate of these media, the mural paintings, are endangered by the peeling of the plaster behind them, droppings left by bats and soot from cooking fires lit during WWII, when the Burmese sought shelter inside the monuments.

Temple paintings of such figures as Avalokitesvara, Manjusri and Shiva show an unmistakable Mahayana, and possibly Tantric, influence. Much of the mural work at Bagan is thought to be similar to how the interiors of Buddhist temples in North-Eastern India may have appeared during the late Pala period, before their destruction at the hands of Muslim invaders.

Looting & Restoration

Looters have made away with many of the sculptures and other religious objects once contained in the monuments. In the 1890s, a German oilman removed glazed plaques from Mingalazedi, Dhammayazika and Somingyi, as well as Vishnu figures from Natlaung Kyaung, all of which ended up at the Berlin Völkerkunde Museum. Around the same time, another German, Th H Thomann took some of the finest mural paintings known in Bagan from Wetkyi-in's Gubyaukgyi and Theinmazi Pahto. The latter were sold to the Hamburg Ethnographical Museum; the exquisite Wetkyi-in paintings never resurfaced (fortunately Thomann left some murals behind, and they're still visible today).

Another complication comes in deciding what's original and what's been added or reformed since the Bagan period. Restorations of several monuments, for example, were under way when British diplomat Michael Symes visited Bagan in 1795. Although, for the most part, writings from the colonial era show a great appreciation for Bagan art and architecture, the British did very little to further Bagan archaeology in terms of excavation or exploration.

Facing page:
Gawdawpalin Pahto, with earlier ruins in the foreground, Old Bagan.

Surveys

An example of the early carelessness with which research was carried out can be found in the early 1900s' *Archaeological Survey of India*. During the survey, a representative from Yangon was accompanied by a local village headman who identified the monuments. When the headman didn't know a monument's name, he simply made one up to please the representative! Many of these names are still in use today.

It wasn't until a couple of decades later that inscriptions were seriously examined to learn Bagan's historical context. The eminent Cambridge scholar GH Luce published a pre-WWII three volume study of the Early Bagan period monuments entitled *Old Burma-Early Pagan* that stands as the classic work. A well researched art history of Bagan was finally carried out by Scotland's Paul Strachan in 1986 and 1987. Strachan published the results in his book *Pagan: Art and Architecture of Old Burma*, in which he divides everything from artefacts to buildings into three stylistic periods: Early (circa 850 to 1120), Middle (circa 1100 to 1170) and Late (circa 1170 to 1300).

The book has its flaws: for example, the author questions why the reclining Buddha next to Shwesandaw Paya couldn't have been lying on its left side instead of its right – an alternative that would have been a violation of classical Buddhist iconography never dared in Myanmar. Nonetheless, it is a very welcome addition to the literature on Bagan.

Strachan's book notwithstanding, no thorough archaeological study has been published since Myanmar's 1948 independence. UNESCO's work focuses on restoration rather than excavation or archaeology; this was perhaps mandated by government fears of any deep historical studies.

Pierre Pichard, an archaeologist from the École Française d'Extrême Orient (EFEO), the same faculty responsible for most of the authoritative work on Angkor and Champa in Indochina, has been working on a new treatise on the archaeology of Bagan for the last 20 years or so. The initial results of his study have appeared in the six volume *Inventory*

Left: Painting of Shwezigon Paya, from the 1905 *Burma Painted and Described* by R Talbot Kelly.

Principal Bagan-era Monuments

monument	estimated date	location
Ananda Pahto	early 12th C	Old Bagan
Ananda Ok Kyaung	11th C	Old Bagan
Shwegugyi	early 14th C	Old Bagan
Thatbyinnyu Pahto	mid-12th C	Old Bagan
Pitaka Taik	mid-11th C	Old Bagan
Nathlaung Kyaung	10th C	Old Bagan
Gawdawpalin Pahto	late 12th or early 13th C	Old Bagan
Pahtothamya	late 11th or early 12th C	Old Bagan
Bupaya	mid-9th C	Old Bagan
Mahabodhi Paya	early 13th C	Old Bagan
Shwesandaw Paya	late 11th C	Old Bagan
Dhammayangyi Pahto	late 12th C	Old Bagan
Sulamani Pahto	late 12th C	Old Bagan
Mingalazedi	late 13th C	Old Bagan
Mimalaung Kyaung	late 12th C	Old Bagan
Shwezigon Paya	late 11th C	Wetkyi-in
Kyanzittha Umin	mid-11th C	Myinkaba
Somingyi Kyaung	early 13th C	Myinkaba
Lawkananda Kyaung	mid-11th C	Thiripyitsaya & Bagan Myothit (New Bagan)
Leimyethna Pahto	early 13th C	Minnanthu
Payathonzu	late 13th C	Minnanthu
Thambula Pahto	mid-13th C	Minnanthu
Nandamannya Pahto	mid-13th C	Minnanthu
Dhammayazika Paya	late 12th C	Pwasaw

of *Monuments at Bagan*, which provides schematic diagrams of many of the Bagan religious ruins. If and when Pichard takes his work any further, it may very well bring with it a whole new set of intriguing theories about the origins and demise of the kingdom of Bagan.

ARCHITECTURAL STYLES

Though there are a number of distinct architectural styles at Bagan, it is easy even for amateurs to trace the developments of temple design over the 240 years of construction. Buildings are primarily either solid *zedis* (stupas) or hollow *pahtos* (temples or shrines). The latter large, square buildings, containing arched passageways, are sometimes referred to as temples in their English names. A zedi customarily houses some relic from the Buddha (hair, tooth or bone), while the focal point of a pahto will be a number of Buddha images. The zedis can be seen in an earlier, more bulbous style and in a clearly Sinhalese design before they evolved into the more distinctively Burmese pattern.

Early pahtos were heavily influenced by late Pyu architecture, as characterised by the monuments of Bebe and Leimyethna at Thayekhittaya

TEMPLES OF BAGAN

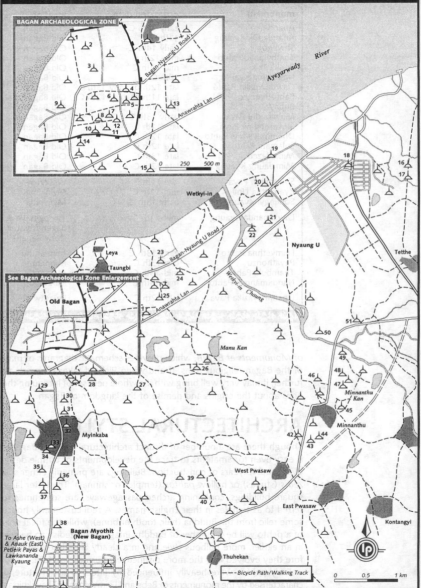

BAGAN ARCHAEOLOGICAL ZONE

Ayeyarwady River

Wetkyi-in

Leya (Taungbi)

See Bagan Archaeological Zone Enlargement

Old Bagan

Nyaung U

Tetthe

Manu Kan

Minnanthu Kan

Minnanthu

Myinkaba

West Pwasaw

East Pwasaw

Kontangyi

Bagan Myothit (New Bagan)

To Ashe (West) & Anauk (East) Petleik Payas & Lawkananda Kyaung

Thuhekan

--- Bicycle Path/Walking Track

0   0.5   1 km

TEMPLES OF BAGAN

1	Bupaya	19	Shwezigon Paya	37	Somingyi Kyaung
2	Pebinkyaung Paya	20	Kyanzittha Umin	38	Seinnyet Nyima
3	Mahabodhi Paya	21	Wetkyi-in		Paya
4	Pitaka Taik		Gubyaukgyi	39	Thamuti & Kutha
5	Thandawgya	22	Gubyauknge		Dhammayazika
6	Shwegugyi	23	Upali Thein		Paya
7	Ngakywenadaung	24	Htilominlo Pahto	40	Dhammayazika
	Paya	25	Sint Pahto		Paya
8	Pahtothamya	26	Sulamani Pahto	41	Hsu Taung Pye
9	Gawdawpalin	27	Dhammayangyi	42	Tawagu
	Pahto		Pahto	43	Ashe (West)
10	Mimalaung Kyaung	28	Shinbinthalyaung		Zanthi
11	Nathlaung Kyaung	29	Mingalazedi	44	Anauk (East)
12	Thatbyinnyu Pahto	30	Gubyauknge		Zanthi
13	Ananda Pahto	31	Gubyaukgyi	45	Leimyethna Pahto
14	Nyein Gon Paya	32	Myinkaba Paya	46	Tayok Pye Paya
15	Shwesandaw Paya	33	Manuha Paya	47	Payathonzu
16	Hmyathat Umin	34	Nanpaya	48	Thambula Pahto
17	Thamiwhet Umin	35	Abeyadana Pahto	49	Nandamannya
18	Sapada Paya	36	Nagayon		Pahto
				50	Winidho Group
				51	Izagawna

(Sri Ksetra) near Pyay (Prome). These early square temples are characterised by their perforated windows and dimly lit interiors. The common Burmese view holds that these early Bagan styles are Mon-style buildings, created by Mon architects imported from Thaton after its conquest, although no such architecture exists in the Mon lowlands. The latest theories suggest the Mon influence at Bagan was primarily confined to the religious and literary spheres, rather than the artistic or architectural. Bagan's kings looked instead to the Pyu kingdoms, and to India, for architectural inspiration.

The pahtos can be primarily divided into two types: those having one entrance to a vaulted inner area, and few windows, and those having four entrances with images around a central cube. The smaller pahto, characteristic of early Bagan, is often called a *gu* or *ku* (Pali-Burmese for cave temple); these monuments are particularly common around the town of Nyaung U. Seventeen pentagonal monuments – considered the earliest known five-sided buildings in the world – have also been found at Bagan.

Later pahtos added Indian design elements to the mix, to produce a truly Burmese design in bright and well lit pahtos like Gawdawpalin, Htilominlo and Thatbyinnyu. Ananda and Dhammayangyi are examples of an earlier transitional phase; indeed, the Ananda is thought by some to have been built by imported Indian labour.

Other unique structures include the *pitaka taik* (Buddhist scripture library), *thein* (ordination hall) and kyaung. These are buildings that would normally have been constructed of wood, and therefore would have disappeared; fortunately, a few were constructed of brick and stone. Monastery buildings served as living quarters and meditation cells for resident monks. At one time, much of the ground space between all the monuments visible today was filled with wooden monastery buildings, said to rival or even exceed the royal palace in design.

Old Bagan
Ananda Pahto

One of the finest, largest, best preserved and most revered of the Bagan temples, Ananda suffered considerable damage in the 1975 earthquake but has been totally restored. Thought to have been built around 1105 by King Kyanzittha, this perfectly proportioned temple heralds the stylistic end of the Early Bagan period and the beginning of the Middle period. In 1990 on the 900th anniversary of the temple's construction, the temple spires were gilded. The remainder of the temple exterior is whitewashed from time to time.

The central square measures 53m along each side, while the superstructure rises in terraces to a decorative *hti* (umbrella-like decorated top) 51m above the ground. The entranceways make the structure a perfect Greek cross; each entrance is crowned with a stupa finial. The base and the terraces are decorated with 554 glazed tiles showing *jataka* scenes (life stories of the Buddha), thought to be derived from Mon texts. Huge carved teak doors separate interior halls from cross passages on all four sides.

Facing outward from the centre of the cube, four 9.5m standing Buddhas represent the four Buddhas who have attained *nibbana* (nirvana). Only the Bagan-style images facing north and south are original; both display the *dhammachakka mudra* (a hand position symbolising the Buddha's first sermon). The other two images are replacements for figures destroyed by fire. All four have bodies of solid teak, though guides may claim the southern image is made of a bronze alloy. Guides like to point out that if you stand by the donation box in front of the original southern Buddha, his face looks sad, while from a distance he tends to look mirthful. The eastern and western standing Buddha images are done in the later Konbaung, or Mandalay, style.

Below: The magnificent Ananda Pahto built in 1105 – representative of the Early Bagan style of architecture.

A small nut-like sphere held between thumb and middle finger of the east-facing image is said to resemble a herbal pill, and may represent the Buddha offering *dhamma* (Buddhist philosophy) as a cure for suffering. Both arms hang at the image's sides with hands outstretched, a mudra unknown to traditional Buddhist sculpture outside this temple. The west-facing Buddha features the *abhaya mudra* (the hands outstretched, in the gesture of no fear).

At the feet of the standing Buddha, in the western sanctum, sit two life-size lacquer statues, said to represent King Kyanzittha and Shin Arahan, the Mon monk who initiated the king into Theravada Buddhism. Inside the western portico are two Buddha footprint symbols on pedestals.

The British built a brick museum next to Ananda Pahto in 1904 in the provincial colonial style. It's now used as a storage facility and is closed to the public. Around the old museum stand a few ordination markers, inscribed stelae and Buddha images.

On the full moon of Pyatho (December/January), a huge *paya pwe* (paya festival) attracts thousands to Ananda. Up to 1000 monks chant day and night during the three days of the festival.

Ananda Ok Kyaung

The name of the smaller *vihara* (Pali-Sanskrit word for sanctuary or chapel for Buddha images), next door to Ananda Pahto, means Ananda brick monastery. It's one of the few surviving brick monastery buildings from the Early Bagan era. The interior of the building is lined with well preserved murals, whose colour palette stretches beyond the traditional brown, black and dull red to include a brighter red, plus a little green here and there. The paintings depict everyday scenes from the Bagan period, including Arab traders, market vignettes, bathing and cooking, and musicians playing *saing waing* (Burmese drums) and *saung gauq* (Burmese harp).

Although the building is often locked, someone around the temple should have the keys to let you in.

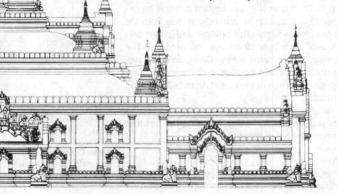

Shwegugyi

Built by Alaungsithu in 1311, this smaller but elegant pahto is an example of the Middle period, a transition in architectural style from the dark and cloistered to the airy and light. This brighter design was carried out through the use of more open doorways and windows. The basic profile of the temple, whose name means Great Golden Cave, presages the magnificent Gawdawpalin Pahto with its corncob *sikhara* (temple finial), a scaled-down version of the one at Ananda Pahto, and the move towards verticality.

Shwegugyi is also notable for its fine stucco carvings and for the stone slabs in the inner wall that tell its history, including the fact that its construction took seven and a half months.

Thatbyinnyu Pahto

This 'Omniscient' temple, one of the highest in Bagan, rises to 61m and was built by Alaungsithu around the mid-12th century. The structure

Left: The elegant Shwegugyi Pahto, with its distinctive corncob finial.

Right: Detail of the elaborate front entrance of Alaungsithu's Thatbyinnyu Pahto.

consists of two huge cubes; the lower one merges into the upper with three diminishing terraces, from which a sikhara rises. Its monumental size and verticality make it a classic example of Bagan's Middle period. Indentations for 539 jataka plaques encircle the terraces; the plaques were never added, leading some scholars to surmise the monument was never consecrated.

In order to better preserve one of Bagan's greatest architectural achievements, since 1994 visitors have been barred from climbing through Thatbyinnyu's amazing inner passages to the top terrace. It was quite a maze climbing to the top – from the main eastern entrance you ascended a stairway flanked by two guardian figures. You then reached a corridor and climbed a narrow, steep flight of steps in the outer wall, and then some external steps to the huge Buddha image on the upper floor. Another claustrophobic stairway within the wall took you to the upper terraces. Of course, military officers and other VIPs are permitted to climb to the top.

In a monastery compound slightly to the south-west of the Thatbyinnyu, you can see the stone supports that once held the temple's huge bronze bell. North-east of the temple stands a small 'tally zedi', which was built of one brick for every 10,000 bricks used in constructing the main temple.

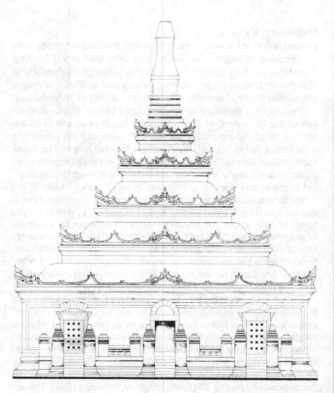

Ngakywenadaung Paya

Close to Thatbyinnyu Pahto, this ruined 9th century stupa features the bulbous shape favoured by the Pyu. Many of the green glazed tiles that covered it can still be seen.

Pitaka Taik

Following the sacking of Thaton, King Anawrahta carted off some 30 elephant-loads of Buddhist scriptures and built this library to house them in 1058. The design follows the basic Early Bagan gu plan, perfect for the preservation of light-sensitive, palm-leaf scriptures. It was repaired in 1738. The architecture of the square building is notable for the perforated stone windows – each carved from single stone slabs and the plaster carvings on the roof – in imitation of Burmese woodcarvings.

Left: Cross-section of Thatbyinnyu Pahto, a classic Middle period temple, constructed around 1150.

Right: King Anawrahta's Pitaka Taik, an Early Bagan period Buddhist scripture library.

Thandawgya

Slightly north of the Thatbyinnyu, this 6m-high stone image of the Buddha was built in 1284, just before the Mongol invasion. It was in poor condition even before the earthquake.

Nathlaung Kyaung

Situated slightly to the west of the Thatbyinnyu, this is the only Hindu temple remaining in Bagan. It is said to have been built in 931 by King Taunghthugyi; if true, this was about a century before the southern school of Buddhism came to Bagan, following the conquest of Thaton. In design, it resembles the Pyu Leimyethna, or four-sided shrines of Thayekhittaya.

The temple is dedicated to the Hindu god Vishnu. Gupta-style reliefs of the 10 Avatars, of whom Gautama Buddha was said to be the ninth, were placed around the outside wall; seven of these survive. As a Vaishnava shrine, it's main function was to serve as a site for Brahmanic rituals deemed necessary adjuncts for royal ceremonies – an aspect of the Burmese monarchy that continued through the country's last kingship, and one that still survives in neighbouring Thailand.

The central square of brick supports the dome and crumbled sikhara, and once contained free-standing figures of Vishnu, as well as Vishnu reliefs on each of the four sides. The statues were stolen by a German oil engineer in the 1890s, but the badly damaged brick-and-stucco reliefs can still be seen. The temple may have been built by Indian settlers in Bagan, possibly the skilled workers brought to construct other temples. The Bagan scholar Paul Strachan, however, vigorously maintains the work was carried out by indigenous artisans.

This temple's name means Shrine Confining Nats, a reference to a purported time when King Anawrahta tried to banish *nat* (spirit) worship in Bagan. He is said to have confiscated all non-Buddhist religious images – both indigenous Burmese nats and Hindu *devas* (Pali-Sanskrit word for spirit-beings) – and placed them in this shrine as part of an effort to establish 'pure' Theravada Buddhism. The king eventually gave in to the cult and standardised the current roster of principal Burmese nats by placing 37 chosen images at Shwezigon Paya. The veracity of this account has never been confirmed, but most Bagan residents – in fact virtually all Burmese – accept it as fact.

Right: Mural from the interior passages of Pahtothamya.

Below: Pahtothamya, a Pyu-style temple with lotus-bud sikhara.

Gawdawpalin Pahto

One of the largest and most imposing of the Bagan temples, Gaw-dawpalin was begun during the reign of Narapatisithu and finished under Nadaungmya (1211-34) but was very badly damaged in the 1975 earthquake. Reconstruction of the Gawdawpalin probably represents the largest operation undertaken after the earthquake; it was not until the early 1980s that it was completed. The name literally means Platform to which Homage is Paid.

In plan, the temple is somewhat similar to the Thatbyinnyu cube shape, with Buddha images on the four sides of the ground floor, with several refinements. It features the use of full pediments over the windows, and stairways that ascend through the walls, rather than from within the central cubes. The top of the restored sikhara, which toppled off in the earthquake, reaches 55m in height. Gawdawpalin is considered the crowning achievement of the Late Bagan period.

Although the top terrace was once a popular place to catch the sunset over the Ayeyarwady River, the passageways are now closed to visitors.

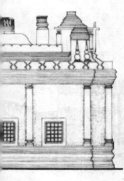

Pahtothamya

In the same temple-crowded central area, the Pahtothamya (or Thamya Pahto) was probably built during the reign of Kyanzittha (1084-1113), although it is popularly held to be one of five temples built by the nonhistorical king Taunghthugyi (931-964). The interior of this single storey building is dimly lit, typical of the early type of Pyu-influenced temples, with their small, perforated stone windows. In its vertical superstructure and lotus-bud sikhara, however, the monument is clearly beginning to move forward from the Early period.

Painting remnants along the interior passages may rate as the earliest surviving murals in Bagan.

Bupaya

Right on the bank of the Ayeyarwady, this cylindrical Pyu-style stupa is said to be the oldest in Bagan. Local residents claim it dates to the 3rd century, although there is little proof to support this belief. More likely it was erected about the same time as the city walls, that is around 850, a dating that still distinguishes it as one of Bagan's earliest stupas.

Bupaya was destroyed when it tumbled into the river in the 1975 earthquake, but has since been totally rebuilt. The distinctively shaped bulbous stupa stands above rows of crenellated terraces.

Pebinkyaung Paya

If you have been to Sri Lanka, you'll recognise the distinctly Sinhalese character of this small stupa. It was probably built in the 12th century and stands towards the river, near the Bupaya.

Below: The Late Bagan period Mahabodhi Paya features an unusual pyramidal spire.

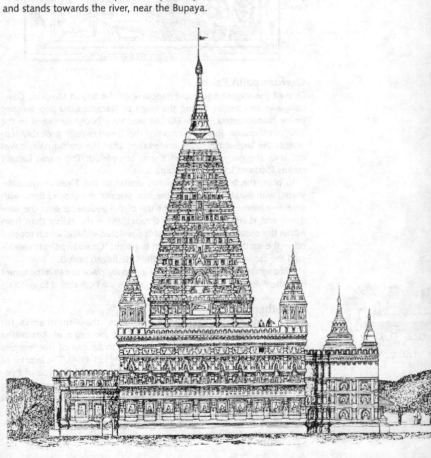

Mahabodhi Paya

Modelled after the famous Mahabodhi temple in Bodhgaya, India, which commemorates the spot where the Buddha attained enlightenment, this monument was built during the reign of Nantaungmya (1211-34). The pyramidal spire, covered in niches that enclose seated Buddha figures, rises from a square block. Stupas of this nature only appeared during the Late Bagan period; they were most common in the city of Salay, further south.

Shwesandaw Paya

Following his conquest of Thaton in 1057, King Anawrahta built this graceful circular stupa at the centre of his newly empowered kingdom. The five terraces once bore terracotta plaques showing scenes from the jatakas, but traces of these, and of other sculptures, were covered by rather heavy-handed renovations. The zedi bell rises from two octagonal bases, which top the five square terraces. This was the first monument at Bagan to feature stairways leading from the square bottom terraces to the round base of the stupa itself. This stupa supposedly enshrines a Buddha hair relic, brought back from Thaton.

The hti, which was toppled by the earthquake, can still be seen lying on the far side of the paya compound. A new one was fitted soon after the quake.

Since the closing of the stairways to the upper terraces of Bagan's tallest monuments, the upper terrace of Shwesandaw Paya has become a very popular sunset-viewing spot. This monument, and Mingalazedi, now offer the highest accessible points within the archaeological zone.

Close to Shwesandaw Paya stands **Lawkahteikpan Pahto** – a small but interesting Middle period gu containing excellent frescoes and inscriptions in both Burmese and Mon.

Shinbinthalyaung

Alongside a south-eastern portion of the wall around Shwesandaw, this long, vaulted-brick structure houses an 18m-long reclining Buddha from the 11th century.

Within the context of Burmese art history, the iconography of the image is a bit confusing. Although the head is oriented towards the south, which would indicate that the Buddha depicted is in a resting, rather than *parinibbana* (dying) state, the flat position of the right arm, and the toes-together position of the feet, suggests the opposite. A resting Buddha is usually propped up on a crooked right arm, with his feet slightly splayed.

One view holds that the orientation and iconography clash because the architects didn't want the Buddha's back to face Shwesandaw. Naive critics might question why the builders couldn't simply have placed the figure on its left side, so as to point the head north while still facing Shwesandaw. In Buddhist iconography throughout Asia, however, reclining Buddha figures always lie on their right side, a preferred

sleeping and dying posture with antecedents in Indian yoga (to keep the left nostril clear, thus stimulating the *ida* nerve channel along the spine, to induce a clear, restful state). The historical Buddha was thought to have passed into parinibbana while lying on his right side; even today, Theravada Buddhist monks are often exhorted to sleep on the right, rather than left, side.

One explanation might be that, as the Cambridge scholar GH Luce suggested, this is an Early period image. Perhaps it shows relatively more Indian influence than later reclining images; in Tantric India, the direction of the *dakshina* (south) is associated with death. At any rate, other parinibbana images, with heads pointing south, exist elsewhere in Myanmar. An appropriate conclusion may be that iconography overrides directional orientation.

Dhammayangyi Pahto

Similar in plan to Ananda Pahto, this later temple seems massive in comparison. It is usually ascribed to Narathu (1167-70), who was also known as Kalagya Min (the king killed by Indians), although other sources state that it was the invaders from Sri Lanka who slew him. Other sources believe it was constructed a little earlier, during the reign of Alaungsithu.

As at Ananda, the interior floor plan of the temple includes two ambulatories. Almost all the entire innermost passage, however, was intentionally filled with brick rubble centuries ago. No one knows for sure why the passage was blocked off; small open places near the top of the passage show intact stucco reliefs and paintings, suggesting that work on the structure had been completed. Local legend says that the work was so demanding – the king mandated the mortarless brickwork fit together so tightly that even a pin couldn't pass between any two bricks – that when the king died, the slave-workers filled the inner ambulatory with rubble in revenge.

Three out of the four Buddha sanctums were also filled with bricks. The remaining western shrine features two original side-by-side images of Gautama and Maitreya, the historical and future Buddhas. Perhaps someday, when Myanmar's archaeological department, or UNESCO, or some other party, clears out all the brick rubble, one of the great architectural mysteries of Bagan will be solved.

The interlocking, mortarless brickwork at Dhammayangyi, best appreciated on the upper terraces, is said to rank as the finest in Bagan. Unfortunately, the highest terraces and hidden stairways leading to them are now off-limits to visitors.

Sulamani Pahto

Like Htilominlo and Gawdawpalin, this is a prime example of later, more sophisticated temple styles, with better internal lighting. This temple, known as the Crowning Jewel, stands beyond Dhammayangyi Pahto and was constructed circa 1181 by Narapatisithu (1174-1211). Combining the horizontal planes of the Early period with the vertical

Facing page: Local villagers following a well worn path, Old Bagan.

Temples of Bagan

ANDERS BLOMQVIST

BERNARD NAPTHINE

Top: View across to Ananda and Thatbyinnyu pahtos, Old Bagan.

Bottom: Tending to the huge reclining Buddha in Manuha Paya, Myinkaba.

GLENN BEANLAND

ANDERS BLOMQVIST

MARK KIRBY

Top: *Jataka* (scenes from the Buddha's life) tiles on Mingalazedi, Old Bagan.

Middle: Monks at Ananda Pahto during the full moon of Pyatho, Old Bagan.

Bottom: Sulamani Pahto, Old Bagan.

lines of the Middle, the temple features two storeys standing on broad terraces assembled to create a pyramid effect. The brickwork throughout is considered some of the best in Bagan. The sikhara, badly damaged by the 1975 earthquake, remains unrestored. Stupas stand at the corners of each terrace, and a high wall, fitted with elaborate gateways at each cardinal point, encloses the entire complex. The interior face of the wall was once lined with 100 monastic cells, a feature unique among Bagan's ancient monasteries.

Carved stucco on mouldings, pediments and pilasters represents some of Bagan's finest ornamental work and is in fairly good condition. Glazed plaques around the base and terraces are also still visible.

Buddha images face the four directions from the ground floor; the image at the main eastern entrance sits in a recess built into the wall. The interior passage around the base is painted with fine frescoes from the Konbaung period, and there are traces of earlier frescoes. Stairways lead very close to the top of this temple, from where the views are superb. As at Thatbyinnyu and Gawdawpalin, however, ascents are now prohibited.

A walled enclosure in the north of the compound contains the remains of **Sulamani Kyaung**, a monastery building that housed Sulamani's senior monk and the *Tripitaka* (Buddhist scriptures); it may also have served as an ordination hall. A water tank in the compound is thought to be the only original Bagan reservoir still in use by local residents.

Mingalazedi
Close to the riverbank, a little south of the Thiripyitsaya Hotel, Mingalazedi (Blessing Stupa) was built in 1277 by Narathihapati. It was the very last of the large Late period monuments to be built before the kingdom's decline, thus representing the final flowering of Bagan's architectural skills.

Mingalazedi is noted for its fine proportions and for the many beautiful glazed jataka tiles around its three square terraces. Although many have been damaged or stolen, there are still a considerable number left. The smaller square building in the zedi grounds is one of the few Tripitaka libraries made of brick; most were constructed of wood, like monasteries, and were destroyed by fire long ago.

Mingalazedi's uppermost terrace is one of the highest points now accessible to visitors. Being the westernmost monument at Bagan, it's a particularly good spot for a panoramic afternoon view of all the monuments lying to the east.

Mimalaung Kyaung
A nice set of *chinthes* (half lion/half dragon mythical beasts) guard the stairway leading up this small, square monastery platform, constructed in 1174 by King Narapatisithu. On top of the platform, a tiered-roof shrine contains a large Bagan-style sitting Buddha. Archaeologists discovered a remarkable 6cm dolomite votive tablet here that was so intricately carved it depicted 78 fully sculpted figures.

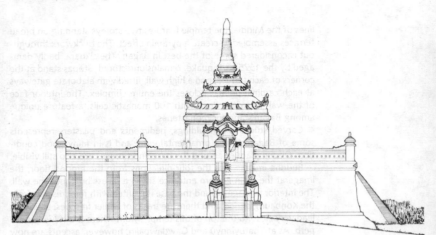

In front of the monastery stands a brick-and-stucco pitaka library next to a large acacia tree. The juxtaposition of venerable tree, library and shrine makes for a special atmosphere, yet few tourists ever visit this easily accessible monument.

Nyuang U & Wetkyi-in
Shwezigon Paya

Actually standing between the village of Wetkyi-in and Nyaung U, this beautiful zedi was started by Anawrahta but not completed until the reign of Kyanzittha (1084-1113). The latter is thought to have built his palace nearby. Supposedly, the Shwezigon was built to enshrine one of the four replicas of the Buddha tooth in Kandy, Sri Lanka, and to mark the northern edge of the city; the other three tooth replicas went to Lawkananda, a smaller stupa to the south; to Tan Kyi, a stupa on the western bank of the Ayeyarwady; and to Tuyan Taung, a stupa on the summit of a hill 32km to the east.

The stupa's graceful bell shape became a prototype for virtually all later stupas over Myanmar. The gilded zedi sits on three rising terraces. Enamelled plaques in panels around the base of the zedi illustrate scenes from the previous lives of the Buddha. At the cardinal points, facing the terrace stairways, are four shrines, each of which houses a 4m-high bronze standing Buddha. Gupta-inspired and cast in 1102, these figures are Bagan's largest surviving bronze Buddhas. Their left hands exhibit the *vitarka* (exposition) mudra while the right hands are held palms outwards, fingers straight up, portraying the gesture of abhaya (no fear).

A 10cm circular indentation in a stone slab, near the eastern side of the stupa, was filled with water to allow former Burmese monarchs to look at the reflection of the hti without tipping their heads backwards (which might have caused them to lose their crowns). For a few

Left: The delightful Mimalaung Kyaung, with its guardian chinthes and pitaka library.

Top right: Aerial-view plan of Shwezigon Paya.

Bottom right: The beautiful bell-shaped Shwezigon Paya – its design became a virtual prototype for all stupas in Myanmar.

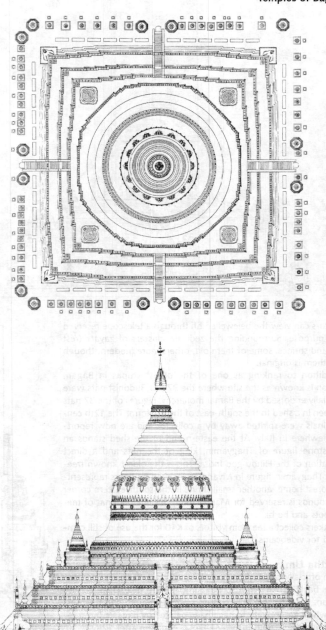

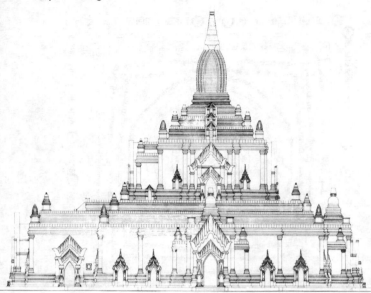

kyat visitors can view the bejewelled hti through a telescope reserved
for that purpose. Surrounding the zedi are clusters of *zayats* (rest
houses) and shrines, some of them old, others more modern, though
none of them is original.

In addition to ranking as one of the oldest stupas in Bagan,
Shwezigon is known as the site where the 37 pre-Buddhist nats were
first officially endorsed by the Bamar monarchy. Figures of the 37 nats
can be seen in a shed to the south-east of the platform. The 12th century originals were spirited away by a collector and are now reportedly somewhere in Italy. At the eastern end of the shed stands an
original stone figure of Thagyamin, king of the nats and a direct
appropriation of the Hindu god Indra. This is the oldest known free-
standing Thagyamin figure in Myanmar. Flanked by tigers representing her forest home, another small shrine in the south-eastern corner
of the grounds is reserved for Mae Wanna, the guardian nat of medicinal roots and herbs.

Caretakers collect a fee from visitors of K10 for the use of still cameras, K25 for videocams.

Kyanzittha Umin

Although officially credited to Kyanzittha, this cave temple may actually date back to Anawrahta. Built into a cliff face close to the
Shwezigon, the long, dimly lit corridors are decorated with frescoes,
some of which are thought to have been painted by Bagan's Tartar invaders during the period of the Mongol occupation after 1287.

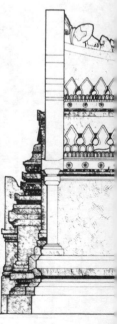

Htilominlo Pahto

Situated close to the road between Nyaung U and Bagan, this large temple was built by King Nantaungmya in 1218. The name is a misreading of the Pali word for Blessings of the Three Worlds. Nantaungmya erected the temple on this spot because it was here that he was chosen, from among five brothers, to be the crown prince.

Inside the 46m-high temple, which is similar in design to Sulamani Pahto, there are four Buddhas on the lower and upper floors. Traces of old murals are also still visible. Fragments of the original fine plaster carvings and glazed sandstone decorations have survived on the outside. The doorways feature nice carved reliefs.

Upali Thein

Named after Upali, a well known monk, this ordination hall was built in the mid-13th century and stands across the road from the Htilominlo Pahto. The rectangular building has roof battlements imitative of Burmese wooden architecture, and a small central spire rising from the

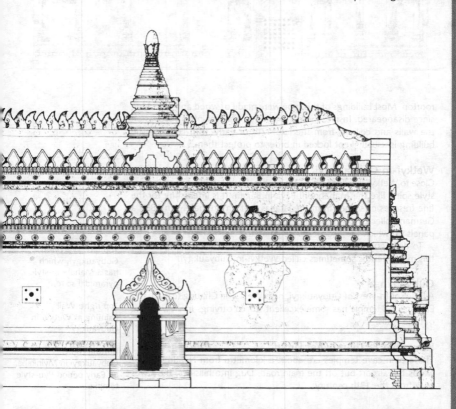

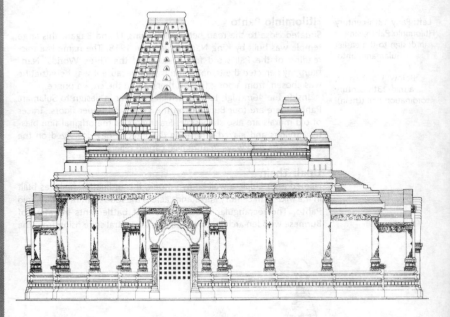

rooftop. Most buildings of this type were made of wood and have long since disappeared. Inside, there are some brightly painted frescoes on the walls and ceilings from the late 17th or early 18th century. The building is usually kept locked in order to protect them.

Wetkyi-in Gubyaukgyi
Close to Wetkyi-in village, this 13th century 'cave temple' has an Indian-style spire, like the Mahabodhi Paya in Bagan. It is interesting for the fine frescoes of scenes from the jatakas, but unfortunately, in 1899 a German collector came by and surreptitiously removed many of the panels on which the frescoes were painted.

To distinguish it from the temple of the same name in Myinkaba, this monument is sometimes called Wetkyi-in Gubyaukgyi.

Gubyaukgne
A little south-west of Gubyaukgyi, near Wetkyi-in Chaung (canal), this Early period temple has some excellent stucco carvings to view on the outside walls.

Hmyathat & Thamiwhet Umin
These twin cave temples are about a kilometre from Nyaung U, to-wards the airport but off the main road. Dug into hillsides, the caves date from the 13th century.

Top left: Wetkyi-in Gubyaukgyi, which has a Mahabodi-style pyramidal spire.

Top right: Wall painting at Wetkyi-in Gubyaukgyi

Bottom right: Gubyaukgyi in Myinkaba, an Early period Pyu-style temple.

Sapada Paya

Sited close to the road as you approach Nyaung U from Kyauk Padaung or the airport, this Late period zedi from the 12th century was built by Sapada, who originally came from Pathein (Bassein), but became a monk in Sri Lanka. His stupa is Sinhalese in style, with a square relic chamber above the bell.

Other Monuments

Closer to the river, about 3km east of Nyaung U, you can find the 13th century **Thetkyamuni** and **Kondawgyi** pahtos. The 11th and 12th century **Kyauk Gu Ohnmin** cave temple, further from the river and built into the side of a ravine, is of the same period of Myinkaba's Nanpaya and contains some very impressive sandstone reliefs. It's best visited by boat.

Myinkaba
Gubyaukgyi

Situated just to the left of the road as you enter Myinkaba, this temple was built in 1113 by Kyanzittha's son Rajakumar, on his father's death. In Indian style, the monument consists of a large shrine room attached to a smaller antechamber. The fine stuccowork on its exterior walls is in particularly good condition.

This Early period temple is also of particular interest for the well preserved paintings inside, which are thought to date from the original construction of the temple and to be the oldest remaining in Bagan. The temple is typical of the Pyu, or Early Bagan, style in that the interior is dimly lit by perforated, rather than open, windows; you need a powerful light to see the ceiling paintings clearly. It is generally kept locked – ask in the village for someone to open it. However, in high tourist season (December to February) it's open most of the day.

Next to the monument stands the gilded **Myazedi** (Emerald Stupa). A four sided pillar in a cage between the two monuments bears an inscription consecrating Gubyaukgyi and written in four languages – Pyu, Mon, Old Burmese and Pali. Its linguistic and historical significance is great, since it establishes the Pyu as an important cultural influence in early Bagan and relates the chronology of the Bagan kings.

Myinkaba Paya

Situated in the village of Myinkaba, this 11th century paya was built by Anawrahta to expiate the killing of his half-brother, the preceding king, Sokkade, in man-to-man combat. It stands at the Myinkaba stream, into which Sokkade's body and saddle were allegedly disposed. Since it was built before Anawrahta's conquest of Thaton, it is also an interesting example of the religious architecture existing before the influence of the southern school of Buddhism had made itself felt.

Manuha Paya

Manuha was named after the Mon king from Thaton, who was held captive in Bagan by Anawrahta. Legend says that Manuha was allowed to build this temple in 1059, and that he constructed it to represent his displeasure at captivity. Stylistically, the dating isn't consistent with the story, though intervening renovations may be responsible for any discrepancies.

The exterior and overall floor plan resemble the more remote Kyauk Gu Ohnmin, a rectangular box topped by a smaller rectangle. Inside, three seated Buddhas face the front of the building, and in the back there's a huge reclining parinibbana Buddha. All seem too large for their enclosures, and their cramped, uncomfortable positions are said to represent the stress and lack of comfort the captive king had to endure. However, these features are not unique in Bagan.

It is said that only the reclining Buddha, in the act of entering nibbana, has a smile on its face, showing that for Manuha, only death was a release from his suffering. You can climb to the top of this paya via the stairs at the entrance to the reclining Buddha chamber at the back

Top right: The mid-11th century Manuha Paya, supposedly built by the captured Manuha.

Bottom right: The unusual interior plan of Manuha Paya, allegedly illustrating King Manuha's discomfort in captivity.

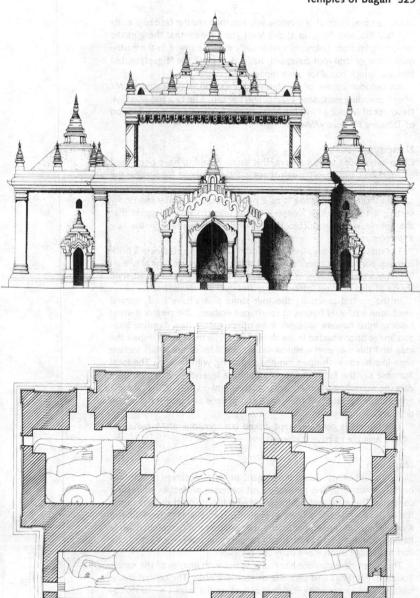

of the temple. Through a window you can then see the face of the sit-ting Buddha, and from up at this level you'll realise that the gigantic face, so grim from below, has an equally gigantic smile! In the earth-quake, the central roof collapsed, badly damaging the largest, seated Buddha, which has since been repaired.

An outdoor corner of the temple compound is dedicated to Mt Popa's presiding nats, Mae Wanna and her sons Min Lay and Min Gyi. Devotees of Manuha Paya celebrate a large paya pwe on the full moon of Tabaung (February/March).

Nanpaya

Close behind the Manuha Paya, this shrine is said to have been used as Manuha's prison, although there is little evidence supporting the legend. In this story the shrine was originally Hindu. Supposedly his captors thought that using it as a prison would be easier than con-verting it to a Buddhist temple. Recent research now suggests that the temple was constructed by Manuha's grandnephew in the late 11th century.

The masonry work – sandstone block facings integrated over a brick core – is particularly fine. Perforated stone windows are typical of ear-lier Bagan architecture – in fact it was probably Bagan's first gu-style shrine. It also features interesting arches over the windows.

In the central sanctuary the four stone pillars have finely carved sandstone bas-relief figures of four-faced Brahma. The creator deity is holding lotus flowers, thought to be offerings to a free-standing Bud-dha image once situated in the shrine's centre, a theory that dispels the idea that this was ever a Hindu shrine. The sides of the pillars feature ogre-like heads with open mouths streaming with flowers. The local Burmese say the face represents a Burmese legend, in which an ogre eats (or, according to others, regurgitates) flowers. In fact the face is a typical representation of the Indian god of time and death, Kala, who devours all in his path.

This temple is generally kept locked but someone at Manuha can usually arrange to have it opened.

Nagayon

Slightly south of Myinkaba, this elegant and well preserved temple was built by Kyanzittha. It is generally kept locked to protect its interesting contents. The main Buddha image is twice life-size and shelters under the hood of a huge *naga* (dragon serpent). This reflects the legend that Kyanzittha built the temple on the spot where he was sheltered while fleeing from his angry brother and predecessor Sawlu – an activity he had to indulge in on more than one occasion.

The outer, dark corridor has many niches with images of the earlier Buddhas. Paintings also decorate the corridor walls. The central shrine has two smaller standing Buddhas as well as the large one. Unfortu-nately the walls have been whitewashed, obscuring any traces of pos-sible murals.

The small ruined stupa of **Pawdawmu Paya** is located nearby.

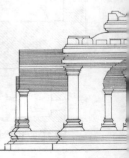

Below: King Kyanzittha's Abeyadana Pahto, built in honour of his wife.

Abeyadana Pahto

While Kyanzittha sheltered at Nagayon during his flight from Sawlu, his wife Abeyadana waited for him a short distance away. At that site he subsequently constructed this temple, which is quite similar in plan to Nagayon.

The inner shrine contains a large, brick seated Buddha (partly original, partly restored), but the fine frescoes are the main interest here. These paintings are now in the process of being cleaned by UNESCO staff. Of the many Buddha niches lining the walls, most are now empty. Some contain Bodhisattvas and Hindu deities – Avalokitesvara, Brahma, Vishnu, Shiva, Indra – showing a Mahayana influence accredited to the tastes of Kyanzittha's Bengali bride, who was said to have been a Mahayanist.

This temple is usually kept locked, though you can ask around in Myinkaba to find someone to open it.

Seinnyet Nyima Paya & Seinnyet Ama Pahto

This stupa and shrine stand side by side and are traditionally assigned to Queen Seinnyet in the 11th century, although the architecture clearly points to a period two centuries later. The zedi rests on three terraces and is topped by a beautiful stylised umbrella.

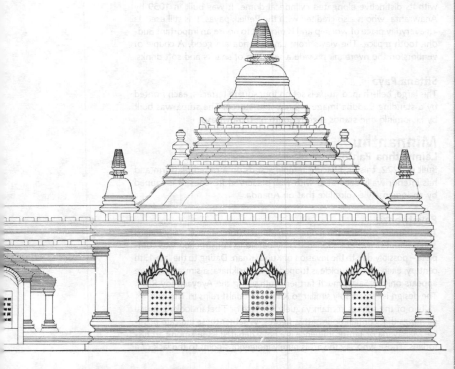

Somingyi Kyaung

Named after the lady who supposedly sponsored its construction, this typical Late Bagan brick monastery is thought to have been built in 1204. A zedi to the north and gu to the south are also ascribed to Somingyi. Many brick monasteries in Bagan were single block structures; Somingyi is unique in that it has monastic cells clustered around a courtyard.

Thiripyitsaya & Bagan Myothit

Ashe (West) & Anauk (East) Petleik Payas

When the lower parts of these twin 11th century payas were excavated in 1905, they revealed quite a surprise. The payas were built not on a solid base as expected, but on vaulted corridors, the walls of which were lined with hundreds of unglazed terracotta tiles illustrating scenes from the jatakas. New roofs were built over these twin tiers of tiles, many of which are still in excellent condition – particularly in the better preserved Anauk Petleik Paya. The buildings themselves are unimpressive.

Lawkananda Kyaung

At the height of Bagan's power, boats from the Mon region, Rakhaing (Arakan) and even Sri Lanka would anchor by this riverside monastery with its distinctive elongated cylindrical dome. It was built in 1059 by Anawrahta, who is also credited with the Petleik payas. It is still used as an everyday place of worship and is thought to house an important Buddha tooth replica. The views from Lawkananda are good. A couple of vendors on the riverbank provide a selection of snacks and soft drinks.

Sittana Paya

This large, bell-shaped stupa is set on four square terraces, each fronted by a standing Buddha image in brick-and-stucco. The stupa was built by Htilominlo and stands slightly south of Thiripyitsaya.

Minnanthu

Leimyethna Pahto

Built in 1222, this east-facing temple stands on a raised platform and has interior walls decorated with well preserved frescoes. It is topped by an Indian-style spire like that on Ananda.

Payathonzu

This complex of three interconnected shrines (the name literally means Three Shrines) was abandoned shortly before its construction was complete – possibly due to the invasion of Kublai Khan. Dating to the late 13th century, each square cubicle is topped by a fat sikhara; a similar structure appears only at Salay, much farther south along the Ayeyarwady River. The design is remarkably similar to Khmer Buddhist ruins in Thailand.

Two of the shrines contain vaguely Chinese or Tibetan-looking mural paintings that contain Bodhisattva figures. Whether these indicate possible Mahayana or Tantric influence is a hotly debated issue among art historians. Those who say the art is purely indigenous point to the lack of a scriptural context for the paintings; others argue from a purely aesthetic view that the overall iconography suggests Mahayana or Tantric content. The three-shrine design hints at links with the Hindu *trimurti* (triple form) of Vishnu, Shiva and Brahma, a triumvirate also associated with Tantric Buddhism. Although one might just as easily say it represents the Triple Gems of Buddhism (dhamma, Buddha, sangha), such a design is uncommon in Asian Buddhist archaeology although it does appear in the Hindu shrines of India and Nepal. At any rate Mahayana/Tantric versus indigenous was never a mutually exclusive polarity, despite Anawrahta's efforts to the contrary. The complex is usually locked. It's best to inquire at the museum in Old Bagan to make an appointment for an inspection; in high season, it will probably be open most of the day for group tours.

Thambula Pahto

This square temple is decorated with faded jataka frescoes and was built in 1255 by Thambula, the wife of King Uzana. On the eastern wall of the southern transept is an apparently secular painting of a boat race.

Nandamannya Pahto

Dating from the mid-13th century, this small, single-chambered temple has very fine frescoes and a ruined, seated Buddha image. The murals' similarity with those at Payathonzu has led some art historians to suggest they were painted by the same hand.

One of the murals represents the 'temptation of Mara' episode in which nubile young females attempt to distract the Buddha from the meditation session that led to his enlightenment. The undressed nature of the depicted females, actually quite tame by all but the most straight-laced standards, shocked French epigraphist Charles Duroiselle, who wrote in 1916 that they were '... so vulgarly erotic and revolting that they can neither be reproduced or described'.

Pwasaw

Dhammayazika Paya

This circular zedi is similar to the Shwezigon or the Mingalazedi, but has an unusual and complex design. Built in 1196 by Narapatisithu, the stupa rises from three five-sided terraces. Five small temples, each containing a Buddha image, encircle the terraces; some of them bear interior murals added during the Konbaung era. An outer wall also has five gateways. Departing from the usual Leimyethna, or four faced type, the plan adds a fifth aspect in tribute to Mettaya or Maitreya, the Buddha to come. This Buddha plays a major role in historical Mahayana Buddhism. In the context of all the other Mahanayist art seen in Late Bagan temples, one cannot help but wonder if, during the Late period, the kings weren't drifting towards Mahayana Buddhism.

The source of the temple illustrations appearing in this section is the publication Architectural Drawings of Temples in Pagan *(Department of Higher Education, Ministry of Education, Yangon, 1989).*

BAGAN MYOTHIT (NEW BAGAN)

For the first couple of years after residents of Old Bagan were forced by the government to move to the new town site, Bagan Myothit was a depressing and treeless place with little spirit. Since then, however, the residents have made the best of their unchosen new home, and there are a number of new hotels and guesthouses, restaurants, souvenir shops and homes. Nyaung U remains the main population centre in the region, but this growing little town is beginning to show signs of life.

The growth of Bagan Myothit, for the most part, has swallowed the small village of Thiripyitsaya that stands at the former site of a Bagan royal palace about 2km south of Myinkaba, and the whole area is now more commonly known as New Bagan. Lots of smaller ruins dot the area, including three very interesting monuments.

A telephone office for making domestic and international calls is on the main road across from Mya Kan Tha Motel.

Places to Stay

Bagan Myothit currently offers a greater choice of mid-range accommodation than any other town or village in the Bagan region. For several years there was a government monopoly on hotels; now that private hotels are again permitted to accept foreigners, many of the Burmese who had experience running guesthouses in Old Bagan are participating in the development.

The main east-west road in town is Khaye Lan, but most of the businesses there still refer to it as Main Rd, and many new small streets and dirt tracks branch out from it. A string of rather new hotels and guesthouses line both sides of the street.

Bagan Central Hotel (☎ 062-70141), on

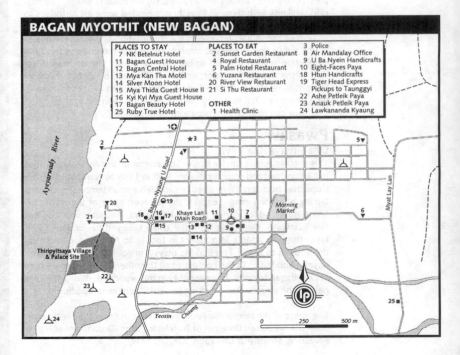

BAGAN MYOTHIT (NEW BAGAN)

PLACES TO STAY	PLACES TO EAT	
7 NK Betelnut Hotel	2 Sunset Garden Restaurant	3 Police
11 Bagan Guest House	4 Royal Restaurant	8 Air Mandalay Office
12 Bagan Central Hotel	5 Palm Hotel Restaurant	9 U Ba Nyein Handicrafts
13 Mya Kan Tha Motel	6 Yuzana Restaurant	10 Eight-Faces Paya
14 Silver Moon Hotel	20 River View Restaurant	18 Htun Handicrafts
15 Mya Thida Guest House II	21 Si Thu Restaurant	19 Tiger Head Express
16 Kyi Kyi Mya Guest House		Pickups to Taunggyi
17 Bagan Beauty Hotel	**OTHER**	22 Ashe Petleik Paya
25 Ruby True Hotel	1 Health Clinic	23 Anauk Petleik Paya
		24 Lawkananda Kyaung

Ayeyarwady River

Bagan-Nyaung U Road

Khaye Lan (Main Road)

Morning Market

Myat Lay Lan

Thiripyitsaya Village & Palace Site

Yeosin Chaung

0   250   500 m

the south side of the main road. is one of the most attractive of the mid-range places to stay. The rooms are large and a ry. The hotel lobby opens out to a courtyard of flowers and bungalows, all with air-con, fridge and hot-water bath. At US$15/25 a single/double, this is great value.

Quiet and friendly, the *Bagan Beauty Hotel* (☎ 062-70238) is on the main road near the Bagan-Nyaung U roac. This thick-walled, two storey house has three single rooms with common bath ard toilet for US$5, and nine double rooms with air-con and hot-water bath for US$10/15. Breakfast is included, and *mohinga* (noodle, fish and egg dish, pronounced *mou1-hinga*) is served on request. Further east on the same side of the street, the new *NK Betelnut Hotel* (☎ 062-70110) features 10 small, but clean and airy, bungalows with air-con, hot water, fan and fridge for US$18/24, including breakfast.

The *Silver Moon Hotel* (☎ 062-70161) is typical of many moderately priced places in Bagan Myothit. Clean and cuiet rooms come with air-con, fridge, sate lite TV and a small desk. Rates are US$20/30, including breakfast. Opposite the telephcne office is the friendly *Mya Kan Tha Motel* (☎ 062-70191), with air-con, hot water, fridge and minibar for US$15/25, including a good complimentary breakfast.

Three more places to stay along the main road offer good value. The small and clean *Mya Thida Guest House II* (☎ 062-70036) has six air-con, hot-water rooms for US$5/8/12 a single/double/triple, including break-fast. Across the road, *Bagan Guest House* (☎ 062-70021) has clean, large rooms with air-con, fridge and hot water for US$5 per person, including a simple breakfast. The 10 room *Kyi Kyi Mya Guest House* (☎ 062-70037), across from Htun Hardicrafts, is one of the cleaner budget places in town. Air-con rooms with fan and hot-water shower cost US$6/10/15.

Typical of Bagan Myothit's upscale look is the 30 room *Ruby True Hotel* (☎ 062-70262), on Myat Lay Lan in the town's south-east corner. Large air-con rooms with

private bath, satellite TV, fridge, minibar and telephone cost US$42/54, including a full breakfast in the hotel restaurant.

Places to Eat
On the western end of Khaye Lan, near the Thiripyitsaya Palace site, three restaurants handle most of the upscale visitor dining trade. The *Si Thu Restaurant* is near the river and prices on the Bamar/Chinese menu are moderate to high; a full course is about K600 to K1000. Check out the large lacquer mural. The nearby *River View* and *Sunset Garden* restaurants stand on high ground above the river, off the western side of the road. The menu, prices and setting at both are similar to the Si Thu. All three restaurants usually feature a marionette show in the evening.

The nearby *Royal Restaurant* is clean and dependable, and the largely Chinese menu is reasonably priced. *Yuzana Restaurant* is a decent Chinese/Bamar eatery at the eastern end of Khaye Lan.

In a quiet north-eastern corner of Bagan Myothit, surrounded by an unnamed temple and stupa ruins, is the friendly *Palm Hotel Restaurant*, serving some of the best Bamar food in the Bagan region.

Shopping
One of the largest lacquerware shops in the area, U Ba Nyein, is on Khaye Lan, opposite Eight-Faces Paya on the roundabout next the AM office. Htun Handicrafts features an interesting factory-workshop where you can see the various stages of lacquerware production. It's on the main road, opposite Kyi Kyi Mya Guest House.

Getting There & Away
Tiger Head Express has its office on the eastern side of the Bagan-Nyaung U road, just north of Kyi Kyi Mya Guest House. See Getting There & Away at the start of this section for details on Tiger Head's pickups to Meiktila and Taunggyi.

Getting Around
Pickups to/from Nyaung U run roughly four times daily from the market for K20 per

person. A horsecart between Old Bagan or the ferry jetty near Old Bagan costs around K150 to K200 each way.

Htun Handicrafts or the Bagan Central Hotel can arrange a car and driver for half-day or full day use. Expect to pay US$25 to US$30 per day for two or three passengers.

Bicycles are a good way to get around, and they can be rented through any of the hotels or guesthouses for K250 to K350 per day.

MINNANTHU

Situated more or less directly south of Nyaung U, Minnanthu's monuments are of a later period than those in the central Bagan area. Temples are quite a way off the beaten path, and the track to the village can be very sandy, making bicycle riding difficult. Nevertheless, the temples are well worth the effort required to see their faded fresco interiors. Some of the horsecart drivers in Old Bagan make good (if unofficial) guides to Minnanthu and can often find someone to unlock the most frequently locked temples.

PWASAW

Between Myinkaba and Minnanthu, Pwasaw was the site of the royal palace after it was transferred from Thiripyitsaya, and before it was moved to Bagan in 874 AD. There are now two small villages, Anauk (West) Pwasaw and Ashe (East) Pwasaw.

Around Bagan

SALAY

During the Late Bagan Era, specifically the late 12th and 13th centuries, Salay (also known as Sale) developed as the expanding spiral of Bagan's influence moved southward along the Ayeyarwady River.

Today, Salay is much more of a religious centre than Bagan, with many more working monasteries than found in Bagan today. Among the Burmese, it's most famous as the historic home of Salay U Ponya, a Bagan Era writer/poet whose works are read by students all over the country.

The British established a presence here, as testified by several old two-storey colonial buildings in town, including one that still bears royal crown reliefs (generally removed in other parts of the country) on the facade. Following independence, the city was virtually abandoned until a Japanese firm built a huge fertiliser plant north of town around 25 years ago. The Japanese eventually turned the plant over to the Burmese, leaving behind the Salay Golf Club – a golf course built to serve the Japanese executives in charge of the project – near the town entrance.

Today the town, with its Bamar majority, is bubbling with activity again. Aside from the atmospheric old colonial buildings and the ruins north of town, the primary attraction is the small museum at Youqson (Yoe San) Kyaung. A trip to Salay is warranted for anyone who develops a passion for Bagan-style architecture. For other visitors less consumed with Bagan, it's simply more of the same, although its laidback atmosphere may be of interest for those who find Bagan and Nyaung U a little too crowded with tourists.

Bagan Era Monuments

Little of Salay's history is known outside a small circle of Burmese archaeologists working with limited funds. Archaeologists from other countries have yet to carry out a thorough study either, so details on the 103 ruins – most of them known only by number rather than name – are sketchy. It is said that most of the monuments in Salay weren't royally sponsored but were built by the lower nobility or commoners. Thus, there are no structures on the grand scale of Bagan's Ananda, Thatbyinnyu or Dhammayangyi.

Salay architects favoured designs similar to those found in the 'outer circle' Bagan monuments of Minnanthu and Pwasaw, particularly mid-sized *gu*-style sanctuaries (small, hollow temples) with prominent *sikharas* (corncob-like temple finials). The latter feature was often inspired by the Bagan namesake copy of the Mahabodhi stupa in Bodhgaya, India.

Among the named sites worth a look is **Payathonzu**, an interconnected complex of three brick shrines with sikharas. All three shrines contain some form of mural painting, but the most extensive painting graces the third one in the series, located to the south-west. This one also has a set of stairs that lead through a very narrow passage to reach the upper terrace. Legend has it that it was constructed by three sisters, but tripartite pahtos exist elsewhere in Salay and Bagan. If Payathonzu is locked, you may have to ask a caretaker for keys, or ask at Youqson Kyaung (see the following entry).

In the same area, near the functioning monastery of **Thadanayaunggyi Kyaung** and the meditation centre of **Mogok Vipassana Yeiktha**, a 19th century shrine shelters a large lacquer Buddha known as **Nan Paya** (also known as Mann Paya). This image, said to date back to the 13th century, may be the largest lacquer image in Myanmar; the fingertips alone measure about 2m high.

A short walk from Payathonzu stands what the locals call **Hkinkyiza Kyaung**, actually an old brick-and-stucco *pitaka taik* (Buddhist scripture library). Unlike similar libraries in Bagan, this one bears an intact superstructure. There is also some original stucco relief remaining on the lintels and pediments. Of the four entranceways, three are blocked off. The remaining unobstructed passage is bare except for an antique pitaka chest sitting at the back. The interior walls have, unfortunately, been whitewashed, probably covering the murals underneath.

Youqson Kyaung

On the other side of the main road from Kyaukpadaung is the oldest surviving wooden monastery hall in the Bagan area, south of Pakokku. The hall sports a new corrugated metal roof to protect the carved wooden structures below from rain or stray sparks from cooking fires. Despite the metal roof, the interior is surprisingly cool. Only two sides of the 23m-long hall actually bear the original 120-year-old sculptures, which include nearly three dimensional carvings of 19th century court life, *jatakas* (stories

from the Buddha's life) and *Ramayana* (one of India's best known legends) tales. Some panels are missing and there are some newer wood carvings mixed in with the old, but those that remain are lovingly cared for by the monks and caretakers, who apply oil regularly to prevent cracking. The monks have also provided detailed English translations identifying the most interesting religious works.

Brick-and-stucco stairs featuring a *naga* (dragon serpent) design lead up to the hall, which is supported by 170 teak pillars 2m off the ground. The structure measures 23m long. Inside the hall is a collection of antique religious objects from the area, including small wooden Buddha figures, heads, old pottery and votive tablets that may date from the 11th to 13th centuries, plus many wooden Konbaung or Mandalay-style images. A wooden Bagan-style naga Buddha is particularly distinctive. A lacquer Konbaung-era Buddha image about 1m high sits in a separate section of the hall, which features a painted, carved-wood ceiling. In the same section is a graceful bronze-and-silver Mandalay-style sitting Buddha in the earth-touching pose; whether by design or not, the head is intriguingly tilted very slightly to the left.

Admission to the monastery's museum is US$3.

Places to Stay & Eat

Salay has no hotels or guesthouses – for foreigners or Burmese – but determined overnighters might be able to stay in one of the many *monasteries*. The *central market* has the usual noodle and sticky rice vendors, and there are also a few *teashops* around town.

Getting There & Away

Salay is 36km south of Bagan along a new sealed road. You pass through the town of Chauk on the way. From Chauk, another road goes east to Kyaukpadaung.

Nyaung U/Bagan By public transport you can catch an early morning pickup from Nyaung U to Salay for about K100. If you hire a car and driver in Bagan, expect to pay about US$15 (or kyat equivalent) for a half-day trip. The drive takes about 40 minutes each way.

You could also take a Pyay-bound ferry from Nyaung U, arriving in Salay around noon. The ferry leaves at 5 am daily, except Thursday and Sunday, and arrives in Pyay in the late afternoon; the deck-class fare is around K50.

From Pyay The 380km drive between Pyay and Salay takes six to seven hours by private vehicle along a paved road. By public transport you'll have to change buses or pickups in Magwe and Kyaukpadaung, making it a very long trip – plan to spend the night in Magwe or Kyaukpadaung and get an early start the next day for onward travel to Salay.

MT POPA

If you look towards the range of hills that rise, shimmering in the heat, behind Bagan, you'll see a solitary peak behind them. Rising to 737m from the flat, surrounding Myingyan Plain, Mt Popa (Popa Daung Kalat in Burmese) is said to be the core of an extinct volcano last active 250,000 years ago. The ground either side of the road is strewn with the remains of a petrified forest.

Volcanic ash makes the surrounding plains fertile and the heights capture the moisture of passing clouds, causing rain to drop on the plateau and produce a profusion of trees, flowering plants and herbs. In fact, the word Popa is derived from the Sanskrit word for flower. One of Mt Popa's presiding nats, Mae Wunna, is considered the patron nat of medicinal and magicoreligious herbs, many of which still grow in the area today. At one time, the surrounding forests were home to elephants, rhinos, sambar and tigers; all had disappeared by the time a 1908 mammal survey was undertaken by the British Raj.

Mt Popa has been described as the Mt Olympus of Myanmar, and it's considered the abode of Myanmar's most powerful nats and, as such, is the most important nat worship centre. The Mahagiri shrine, at the base of the rock outcropping at the summit, contains a display of mannequin-like figures representing the 37 nats and is a major pilgrimage destination. Burmese superstition says you shouldn't wear red or black on the mountain, nor should you curse, say bad things about other people or bring along any meat (especially pork) – any of these actions could offend the residing nats who might then retaliate with a spate of ill fortune.

Atop the impressive rocky crag clings a picturesque complex of monasteries, stupas and shrines that you can climb to, via a winding, covered walkway, complete with curious monkeys. The 25 minute climb is steep and stiff, but it gets cooler as you get higher. When you reach the top the views are fantastic. You'll meet many other pilgrims along the way, including a class of nonordained hermit monks called *yeti* (from the Pali-Sanskrit *rishi)* who wear tall peaked hats; part of their meditation involves walking very slowly and mindfully while in the vicinity of Mt Popa.

Special Events

Mt Popa hosts two huge *nat pwes* (spirit festivals) yearly, one beginning on the full moon of Nayon (May/June) and another on the full moon of Nadaw (November/December). Before King Anawrahta's time, thousands of animals were sacrificed to the nats during these festivals, but this practice has been prohibited since the Bagan era. Spirit possession and overall drunken ecstasy are still part of the celebration, however.

There are several other minor festivals, including ones on the full moons of Wagaung (July/August) and Tagu (March/April), which celebrate the departure and return of the famous Taungbyone nats – Min Gyi and Min Lay – each year. The latter nats are brothers who were born to a marriage between Mae Wunna and an Indian Muslim in Anawrahta's employ. The two sons were murdered at Taungbyone, where Anawrahta built a shrine in their honour. Once a year, the Taungbyone nats are believed to travel a spirit circuit that includes Mt Popa, Taungbyone (22km north of Mandalay) and China.

Places to Stay & Eat

On the 1518m mountain (Popa Yoma) to the north of Mt Popa, there are two new places to stay. The moderately priced *Zay Yar Thein Gi Restaurant & Guest House* (☎ *Popa 28*) offers clean and spacious rooms for US$12 per person. A tasty Bamar or western breakfast is included. There are great views here, but not of Mt Popa.

Opened in 1999, the deluxe *Popa Mountain Resort* (☎/fax 062-70141) commands spectacular views of Mt Popa and the Bagan plain below. There are 24 chalet-style rooms set in a sandalwood grove, each with all the amenities of an international class resort, including local textiles and teak furnishings. In addition to a pool, terrace restaurant and bar overlooking Mt Popa, the resort offers a number of activities on the mountain, including trekking, birdwatching and horseback riding in the forest. Published rates are US$180/200 for a single/double, but 50% discounts are common. For reservations, contact the Popa Mountain Resort office (☎ 01-246636, fax 240377) in Yangon.

Most travellers visit Mt Popa as a day trip from Bagan or on their way east of Meiktila or Inle Lake. There's a rather utilitarian *Forestry Guest House* at the base of the mountain that may take visitors; or you could ask at the nearby monastery.

Near the Mahagiri shrine at the bottom of the rock outcropping are several small *cafes* with Bamar food. No beef or pork is served.

Getting There & Away

Mt Popa is about 50km from Bagan or 10km from the railhead at Kyaukpadaung. You can visit Mt Popa by day-tripping from Bagan, or as a stop-off between Bagan and Thazi or Mandalay. Getting there by public transport is time-consuming. One bus leaves Nyaung U daily at 8 am for K160. From Kyaukpadaung, pickups packed with pilgrims leave frequently for Mt Popa for K60.

With private car charters, more travellers are managing to fit Mt Popa into their itinerary between Bagan and Thazi or Inle. To hire a car and driver for the day to Mt Popa, expect to pay around US$20 from Bagan.

KYAUKPADAUNG

If you're travelling around Myanmar by public bus, you stand a chance of eventually ending up in the junction town of Kyaukpadaung at midnight on your way to Bagan, Salay, Mandalay or Pyay. If so, look for *Pho Pargyi Restaurant* (☎ 061-50402). In local parlance, it's two furlongs (about 400m) north of the town junction. The owners are experienced in finding either local accommodation (very basic), or a 'salon' taxi that will take you to Bagan for about US$15 to US$20.

MEIKTILA

Only a short distance west of Thazi, Meiktila is the town where the Bagan-Taunggyi and Yangon-Mandalay roads intersect, just as Thazi is the place where the equivalent train lines intersect. It's an important and prosperous trade centre that also draws revenue from a nearby air force base and training facility. Although there's nothing of particular historical interest here (a bad fire in 1991 almost destroyed the entire town), Meiktila does offer the opportunity to savour the atmosphere of a mid-sized town that until recently has seen very few foreigners.

The town sits on the banks of huge Lake Meiktila, bridged by the road from Nyaung U. From one end of this bridge, a wooden pier extends out over the lake to small **Antaka Yele Paya**, a cool spot to rest on warm evenings. The municipality has recently added a promenade around the lake.

Shwebontha Kyaung is a monastery with huge lions out the front – you can't miss this main street landmark while passing through town. Just north of town, by the airfield, there's a WWII Spitfire on display in remarkably good condition.

Places to Stay

Honey Hotel (☎ 064-21588), a converted mansion on Pan Chan Lan next to the lake, offers large rooms with high ceilings, air-con, private hot showers and good mattresses for US$15/25 a single/double, or similar rooms with shared bath and air-con for US$10/15. An evening breeze often catches

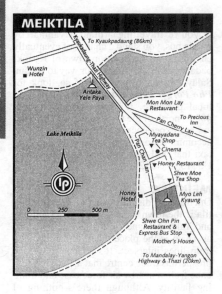

MEIKTILA

To Kyaukpadaung (86km)

Wunzin
■ Hotel

Kyaukpadaung-Thazi Highway

Antaka
Yele Paya

Mon Mon Lay
▼ Restaurant

To Precious
Inn

Pan Cherry Lan

Lake Meiktila

Myayadana
Tea Shop

Pan Chan Lan

● Cinema

▼ Honey Restaurant

Shwe Moe
Tea Shop

Honey ■
Hotel

Myo Leh
Kyaung

0   250   500 m

Shwe Ohn Pin
Restaurant & ▼
Express Bus Stop ▼
Mother's House

To Mandalay-Yangon
Highway & Thazi (20km)

the rooms facing the lake. Breakfast is available for US$1, or kyat equivalent.

Near the market in the bowels of the town, the *Precious Inn (☎ 064-21818, 131 Butar Houng Lan)* offers bleak rooms with fan and shared facilities in a three storey, concrete-and-wood box for US$5/8. Two air-con rooms with attached bath cost US$10/18. A busy cafe downstairs serves Chinese and Bamar food.

On the northern edge of the lake, the friendly *Wunzin Hotel (☎ 064-21848)* has a variety of rooms in a long two storey wooden building. Fairly clean standard rooms have concrete floors, mosquito nets, satellite TV, air-con and attached hot-water bath for US$36/42 a night. An extra bed is US$10. A separate wooden building out the back contains a set of economy rooms with ceiling fans and attached large hot-water showers. For these the hotel charges US$18 for a single, plus US$6 for each additional person. The best thing about the economy section is that, unlike the main building, it faces the lake and thus catches the cool evening breezes. The dining room is quite

decent, if rather expensive, by Burmese standards (breakfast US$1, lunch and dinner US$3 each), and the lakeside grounds are pleasant.

The *Meiktila Hotel (☎ 064-21892)* sits near the Yangon-Mandalay highway north of town and offers 24 clean rooms in chalet-style buildings. All rooms have air-con and attached toilet and hot-water shower; rates are US$30/36, including breakfast.

Places to Eat

Meiktila has much better food than the typical Burmese town. Most famous of the local restaurants is *Shwe Ohn Pin restaurant* on the main road (Thazi-Kyaukpadaung Hwy). A couple of the major express buses from Mandalay and Yangon stop here. One of the house specialities is a delicious curd curry, with big hunks of *hlan no kei* (Indian-style cheese) mixed with cauliflower and okra in a thick and spicy sauce. You can order Chinese dishes from the English-language menu or point at the curry pots for Bamar food. All Bamar meals come with a complimentary dahl stocked with lots of okra and turnips.

A block behind this restaurant, then two blocks north-east of the Honey Hotel (and under the same ownership), is the *Honey Restaurant* near the lake. This small, humble wooden restaurant serves decent Chinese food.

Next door to the Shwe Ohn Pin, a snack shop called *Mother's House* stocks soft drinks, Mars bars, Pringles and cold beer, along with traveller requisites such as mosquito repellent, shampoo and film. There are a few tables and chairs out the front. The English-speaking father of the owner drops by occasionally to share his English poems with visitors.

At the south-eastern end of the lake's bridge, where the road forks, check out *Mon Mon Lay Restaurant*, a small, reliable Bamar restaurant run by an Indian family. For tea and snacks, the *Myayadana Tea Shop* near the cinema is a popular spot any time of the day. Nearby is the *Shwe Moe* (Gold Ring), a good teashop.

Getting There & Away

The public bus stop for Thazi (K30), Mandalay (K180), Pyinmana (K120), Taunggyi (K700) and Yangon (K1000) is located at the Highway Gate bus station. You can also catch buses to Mandalay near the clock tower – this is the stop for buses and pickups west to Kyaukpadaung (K80) and Nyaung U (K120).

Sein Kabar (Diamond World) Express and Hnin Thu Wai Express will pick up passengers at the Shwe Ohn Pin on the way to Yangon or Taunggyi.

Getting Around

Horsecarts serve the western side of town; many of them park near the south-eastern end of the lake's bridge. Trishaws cruise the main streets. A trip from the Honey Restaurant to the Wunzin Hotel costs around K100 by horsecart; from the Honey Hotel to Shwe Ohn Pin by trishaw costs around K40.

PAKOKKU

As the region continues to open up, a trickle of travellers are stopping off in Pakokku on the way to Bagan – either by river from Mandalay, or more commonly by private car. A bustling tobacco trading centre, the town itself has little to see, but 20km northeast of Pakokku are the remains of **Pakhangyi**, a 19th century town with old city walls, an archaeological museum and one of the oldest surviving wooden kyaungs in Upper Myanmar. The latter is supported by 254 teak pillars. Further west is Myanmar's largest wooden kyaung, a 19th century structure with 332 teak pillars called **Pakhanngeh Kyaung**.

Besides tobacco, which is cultivated in the surrounding Ayeyarwady floodplain, Pakokku is famous for jaggery (palm sugar), *thanakha (Linoria acidissima)* logs, *longyis* (sarongs), and *saun* (checked blankets) made from cotton and wool. Vendors selling these items line up along the pontoon landing whenever a ferry arrives at Pakokku.

One of the town's biggest festivals, Thihoshin, is held from the 8th waxing day to the 8th waning day of Nayon (May/June).

The festival is famous for its *pwes* (shows/festivals), both human and marionette.

Places to Stay & Eat

The friendly *Mya Yatanar Inn (☎ 062-21457)* rents very simple rooms for K500 per person; someone from the inn usually meets arriving passengers at the pier. The inn can also arrange meals, or direct you to one of several *rice and noodle restaurants* and *cafes* around town. A trishaw from the pier to the inn costs about K60. Less favourable accommodation is available at the *Tha Pye Nyo Guest House No 1* for K300 per person.

Getting There & Away

The most convenient way to reach Pakokku is by bus or pickup from Mandalay. These cost around K250 to K300 per person and leave the central/main bus centre at 7 am and 11 am, a schedule timed with the Chindwin River ferry crossings at 11 am and 3 pm. Another crossing is to the north at Monywa, which is a scenic route if travelling by car.

Another way to reach Pakokku is via the Mandalay-Bagan ferry – see the Getting There & Away section at the start of this chapter for details.

MYINGYAN

This Bamar-majority township of 260,000 sits on a flat plain along the Ayeyarwady River about midway between Mandalay and Nyaung U. Roads to Mandalay, Nyaung U and Meikila all intersect there, and long-distance ferries stop there as well. To top it off, a rail line links Myingyan to Mandalay, Thazi and Nyaung U, so the township is a busy transport junction. A modern, two storey central market indicates that trade is an important byproduct of the town's transport function. **Yan Aung Myin Paya**, a standard bulb-tipped, bell-bottomed gilded stupa, is the town's only pride and joy after the market. The townspeople might also boast about the town's tidy green-and-white train station, one of the better kept stations in Upper Myanmar.

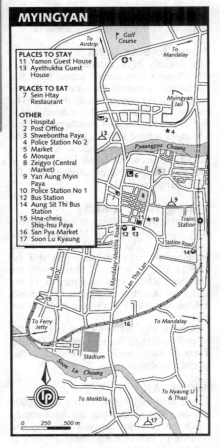

MYINGYAN

PLACES TO STAY
11 Yamon Guest House
13 Ayethukha Guest House

PLACES TO EAT
7 Sein Htay Restaurant

OTHER
1 Hospital
2 Post Office
3 Shwebontha Paya
4 Police Station No 2
5 Market
6 Mosque
8 Zeigyo (Central Market)
9 Yan Aung Myin Paya
10 Police Station No 1
12 Bus Station
14 Aung Sit Thi Bus Station
15 Hna-cheiq Shiq-hsu Paya
16 San Pya Market
17 Soon Lu Kyaung

To Airstrip
Golf Course
To Mandalay
Myingyan Jail
Pyaungpya Chaung
Mandalay-Meiktila Road
Lan Thit Lan
Train Station
Station Road
To Ferry Jetty
To Mandalay
Stadium
Soon Lu Chaung
To Meiktila
To Nyaung U & Thazi

0 250 500 m

In the southern part of town at **Soon Lu Kyaung**, the remains of the well known Soon Lu Sayadaw are draped in monastic robes and on display in an ornate gilded funerary dais. The sayadaw died 50 years ago; though desiccated, his body is remarkably well preserved.

Places to Stay & Eat

The Ministry of Hotels & Tourism's (MHT) licencing division hasn't gotten around to Myingyan yet, but foreigners are occasion-

ally accepted at the *Ayethukha Guest House* or the *Yamon Guest House* opposite one another on Station Rd. Both offer spartan rooms for K400 per person, plus a couple of air-con rooms for around K900. There are other less palatable places to stay as well.

There are several basic *rice-and-noodle shops* (Burmese signs) opposite the train station and the bus station near the guest-houses. *Sein Htay Restaurant* is a few blocks north of the bus station on the Mandalay-Meiktila road.

Getting There & Away

Around a dozen intercity transport services run buses and pickups to Magwe (four hours, K350), Mandalay (three hours, K300), Nyaung U (three hours, K300), Meiktila (four hours, K400) and Yangon (15 hours, K1000). The main bus station is in the centre of town, near the Ayethukha Guest House.

Myingyan is linked by rail with Thazi, the junction for the Mandalay-Yangon express trains. The train station is on the east side of town. One train per day makes the six hour journey to Thazi. Although the train fare is cheap, buses do the same route (with a change in Meiktila) in around four hours. A newer train line connects Myingyan to Nyaung U and Bagan. The Bagan-Mandalay train stops in Myingyan around noon.

Ferries between Mandalay and points south also stop off in Myingyan. The ferry landing is located west of town.

Getting Around

Trishaws, horsecarts and motorised three-wheelers ply the streets of Myingyan. At K30 per kilometre, trishaws are the cheapest option, while motorised three-wheelers and horsecarts cost about K50 to K60 per kilometre.

MAGWE

Capital of Magwe Division, this mid-size town on the eastern bank of the Ayeyarwady River is 850km north of Yangon and 152km south-west of Nyaung U. The town has an estimated 99% Bamar majority and, like the

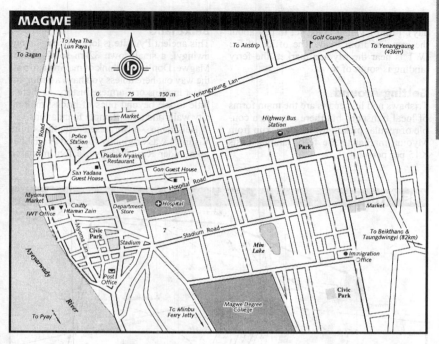

MAGWE

rest of the area surrounding Bagan, it's very hot and dry from April to May.

There's very little to interest tourists in the town, although the locals will try to send you out to see the famous 1929-vintage **Mya Tha Lun Paya**, a typical Burmese stupa north-west of town on the river. Magwe's main value to the traveller is as a lunch or dinner stopover on long road trips between Pyay and Bagan.

There is considerable boat traffic between Magwe and Minbu, just across the river.

Places to Stay & Eat

After a K60 trishaw ride from Magwe's Highway bus station in the north-east part of town, *Gon Guest House* has very good rooms with air-con for K1000. The more basic *San Yadana Guest House* near Myoma market offers passable rooms for K500. Of course, neither of these are licensed for for-

eigners, but in out-of-the-way Magwe no one seems to mind the occasional foreign visitor.

Both guesthouses have attached *cafes* that aren't too bad. A block east of the police station, *Padauk Myaing Restaurant* serves decent Chinese and Bamar food, while the *Chitty Htamin Zain* (Rice Shop) near Myoma market does very inexpensive Indian meals.

Getting There & Away

Bus & Pickup The main bus station is in the north-eastern part of town; from there you can catch pickups and buses to Pyay, Kyaukpadaung and Bagan.

Boat Ferries from Pyay arrive on Tuesday, Wednesday and Saturday, and cost K86 (deck class) and K172 (upper class). However, it makes more sense to travel in the faster downriver direction on the intervening days (Sunday, Monday, Thursday and Friday). From Nyaung U expect to pay about the same as from Pyay. The office of the IWT is near the Myoma market; the ferry landing is south of town.

Getting Around

Trishaws and horsecarts are the main forms of local transport, but there are also a couple of regular pickup routes. A pickup from Myoma market to the ferry landing costs K15 per person.

AROUND MAGWE
Beikthano

This ancient Pyu site is located near Taung-dwingyi, a small town 82km south-east of Magwe. Don't even think of making a trip all the way out here unless you have a strong interest in ruins or Burmese history, as there's little to see beyond piles of bricks, melting city walls and a few temple foundations.

Beikthano – a Burmese corruption of the Vishnu – was originally founded as Vishnu-loka under King Pyinbya, a Pyu monarch

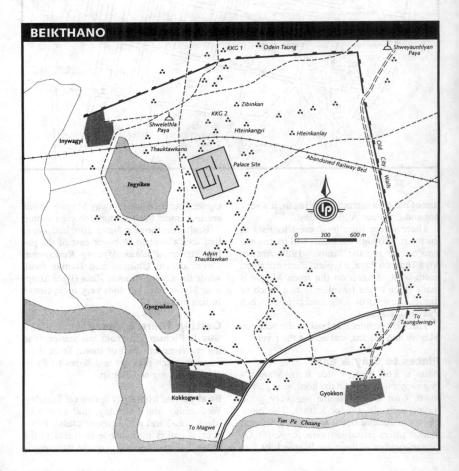

BEIKTHANO

who may have been part Indian. Excavations among the ruins have uncovered beads, terracotta votives, stone and metal art objects, skeletal remains, stucco relief fragments, silver coins, potshards and burial urns. The design of these items and their Pyu inscriptions indicate links with the Pyu principalities of Thayekhittaya and Hanlin, but little else is known about the city-state. A number of these artefacts are on display in a museum in Taungdwingyi.

With their wheel and swastika-shaped bases, the building plans of some of the structures bear a strong resemblance to Buddhist monuments found at Nagarjunakonda in South India. Since *dhammachakkas* (dharma wheels) and other Buddhist symbols (but no likenesses of the Buddha himself) were found here, one theory is that the settlement may have been started by Nagarjunakonda missionaries. If true, this would indicate that Beikthano had 3rd-century origins, a period when Buddhists didn't permit the sculpture or worship of Buddha images. Most scholars agree that Beikthano predates Thayekhittaya by about four centuries and that it was destroyed by fire in the 4th to 5th century.

Getting to Beikthano is difficult without wheels. The road to Taungdwingyi is paved, but not in very good condition. During the dry season, there is usually one pickup per day between Magwe's Myoma market and Taungdwingyi. The ruins lie just north of Kokkogwa, a village 19km to the west of Taungdwingyi; you should get off just before Kokkogwa when you see the city walls, which are bisected by the Magwe-Taungdwingyi road.

Beikthano is contained within the old walls a short walk north-east of this point and is spread over nine sq km. The old palace site sits a little north-west of the centre of the rectangle formed by the city walls. Just west of the old palace is a large pond called **Ingyikan**, an ancient reservoir still used by the villagers of Inywagyi, to the immediate north-west. Less than 500m from the north-eastern corner of the old city is a famous stupa called **Shweyaunhlyan Paya**.

One of the only written English-language sources on the ruins is the 1969 archaeological survey *Report on the Excavations at Beikthano* by Aung Thaw, sometimes available in Yangon.

PYINMANA

One of the major towns along the Yangon-Mandalay train and road routes, Pyinmana is a very leafy place with plenty of trees and many thatched-roof homes at the edge of Shan Lake – a welcome change after visiting the 'dry zone' around Mandalay and Bagan. Overall, it has a more colourful and interesting feel than Taungoo to the south, even though it's of less historic interest. Coconut palms are planted along the Ngalaik River, which passes through town, and you can see the Shan Yoma and Aleh Yoma (mountain ranges) to the east and west. The surrounding valley is carpeted with rice fields, many of which yield two crops a year.

The **Yezin Forest Research Institute**, 15km north of town, is an important facility for the study of Burmese hardwoods. Like Taungoo further south, a fair amount of Myanmar's teak trade is centred here. Korea, Japan, China, Taiwan and Singapore are the major players involved.

The town's diverse population supports three **mosques** as well as **St Michael's Catholic Church**, a small brick edifice near the river. You may notice more propaganda signs in Pyinmana – they're erected to scare visiting undercover rebels. Insurgent territory begins just 30km east of town: the Kayin (Karen), Kayah and Shan states intersect around 80km south-east of Pyinmana.

Places to Stay

The boxy, four storey *Phoenix (Zar Mani) Motel* (☎ 067-21646, 183 Bulet Yar Lan) is close to the central market. A group of economy rooms enclose a large central lobby where the TV is on until about midnight. These rooms cost US$7/12 a single/double. Upstairs, quieter standard rooms with air-con and cold-water shower cost US$12/18. Superior rooms are similar but have a TV, and cost US$18/24. A meagre breakfast is included.

The friendly *Mingala Kanthaw* (☎ 067-21226) is a government-owned guesthouse over a large auditorium on the eastern side of the main north-south road through town. Very basic rooms with thin mattresses, fan and mosquito nets cost US$3 per person. Cleaner and quieter is the *Shwe Tharapu (Golden Crown) Guest House* (☎ 067-21186, 175 Bo Tar Yar Lan), a two-storey house in the central district. Air-con rooms with attached cold-water bath cost US$6 to US$7 (or kyat equivalent) per person. Although neither of these guesthouses has a licence to do so, the staff welcome foreigners.

One other unlicensed to stay is *Thukhamyaing Motel* (also known as Pyinmana Co-op Motel) (☎ 067-21094), on the main street farther south. It's not particularly clean, but for K600 you get a thin mattress, mosquito net and cup of tea in the morning. Bath and toilet are separate.

Places to Eat

There are several very good eateries in Pyinmana. One of the better places is the popular *Yan Naing Restaurant (1813 Bo Tauk Htain Lan)* on the main street. The menu includes Bamar and Chinese food. There are several other small, rustic *restaurants* nearby,

as this is where most buses stop on their way north or south.

Nearby, *Aye Zin Aung Restaurant (125 Bogyoke Lan)* and *Shwe Nadimyit Restaurant (2 Bogyoke Lan)* both serve excellent Chinese and Bamar food.

Getting There & Away

Pyinmana lies close to the southern end of Mandalay Division, just north of the Bago Division border, 303km south of Mandalay and 393km north of Yangon.

From a point near the central market, pickups leave frequently for Taungoo for K150. Pickups depart throughout the day for Meiktila for K150 (K300 front seat).

Two bus companies make the Yangon trip for around K1000. Sein Kabar Express Bus and Mahar Express Bus depart for Yangon at 9.30 pm for a 7 am arrival at the Highway bus station.

Mandalay-bound buses (K350) cruise the main north-south street for passengers a couple of times each day. The Yangon-Mandalay air-con express buses stop near the Yan Naing Restaurant for meals and to pick up passengers if necessary, but this is not as reliable a stop as Taungoo or Meiktila. Enquire at the Yan Naing for arrival and departure times.

North-Eastern Myanmar

Shan State

Nearly a quarter of Myanmar's geographic area is occupied by the Shan State. Before 1989 the area was broken into several administrative divisions collectively known as the Shan States. It's the most mountainous state in the country, divided down the middle by the huge north-south Thanlwin (Salween) River. To the west of the river lies the 1000m-high Shan Plateau, to the east a jumble of north-south mountain ranges and international borders with China, Laos and Thailand.

About half the people living in the Shan State are ethnic Shan, who for the most part live in valleys formed by the Thanlwin River and its tributaries. The traditional Shan ruling system revolves around the *sao pha loang* (*sawbwagyi* in Burmese, or Great Sky Lord, a hereditary, feudal leadership position) installed in each of the original nine Shan states. Under the British, a system of indirect rule created 37 administrative divisions, with a sao pha in charge of the largest ones. After independence, the Shan leadership signed away their hereditary rights in the 1947 Panglong Agreement, which guaranteed a cooperative, semiautonomous administration of the Shan States. Much of the current conflict in the state dates from this time: Shan commoners were appointed to government positions after the formation of the Union of Burma, much to the dismay of the sao pha, who expected the appointments; and from the perspective of most Shan, the degree of expected autonomy never materialised.

In addition to the Shan, the state's major ethnic groups include the Palaung in the mountainous north-western corner, the Kachin in the far north, the Kaw (Akha) and Lahu (Musoe) in the far east and north-east, the Kokang and Wa in the north-eastern mountains, and the Padaung and Taungthu in the south-west. Dozens of smaller groups

HIGHLIGHTS

- Serene waters of Inle Lake and its floating gardens.
- Inle's Holy temple of Phaung Daw U, site of a distinctive Shan festival.
- Golden Triangle centre of Kengtung with its diverse hill tribes and colourful markets.
- Hiking to hill tribe villages in the Shan State.
- Regional capital of Myitkyina, home of the Kachin people.
- Myit-son and the confluence of the Mehka and Malihka Rivers, the beginning of the great Ayeyarwady River.

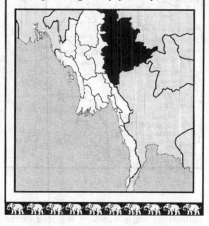

also inhabit various parts of the state, particularly the mountainous areas.

Because of its elevation, most of the Shan State – even the river valleys – is ill-suited for the cultivation of lowland crops, such as rice. One crop that flourishes even at high elevations is *Papaver somniferum*, the opium poppy, which is the state's main source of income. Although the opium trade

NORTH-EASTERN MYANMAR

347

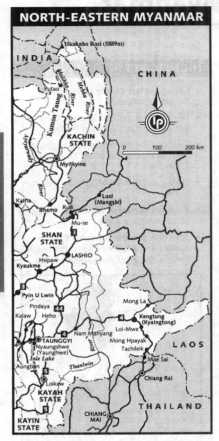

NORTH-EASTERN MYANMAR

corridor between Pyin U Lwin (Maymyo) and Lashio north-east of Mandalay, and the isolated township of Kengtung (Kyaing-tong), in the far east of the state.

THAZI

Although Thazi is located about 65km west of the Shan State border in the Mandalay Division, most visitors begin or end their journey into Shan territory in this rail-junction town. It's little more than a place where people embark or disembark from the train when travelling to/from Bagan (Pagan) or Inle Lake.

Places to Stay & Eat

The only licensed lodging is the *Moon-Light Rest House* (☎ *Thazi 56*) on the top floor of the *Red Star Restaurant*, on the main Thazi-Taunggyi road, run by the same friendly family. Clean, simple rooms with two beds, mosquito nets and shared shower and toilet cost US$3 per person, without breakfast. Two larger rooms with air-con and attached shower cost US$8/15 a single/double, breakfast included. The busy dining room downstairs serves very good Chinese, Bamar and Indian Muslim food, including fresh yoghurt. The proprietors also invite travellers to bathe and rest upstairs while waiting for a train.

There is also a decent *snackbar* on the platform of the train station, with good food and service.

Getting There & Away

Bus The Thazi bus stop is a couple of hundred metres from the train station – just an empty building and a patch of dirt. Pickups to Kalaw and Taunggyi will only leave when they get 20 passengers or when some impatient traveller pays the difference in fare for any number less. Thazi to Kalaw costs K500 for a seat in the back, K700 up the front; there's usually only one departure a day at around 7 am.

Since a new bypass road was built in 1998, it's now possible to skip Meiktila when travelling between Thazi and Mandalay. Nevertheless, there are more buses

extends to most parts of the state, poppy cultivation and processing is concentrated in the far north and south-east. Not coincidentally, these are the areas where Shan and Pa-O rebel armies and Wa and Chinese opium warlords operate, hence travel to these areas is restricted by the government. The areas most accessible at the time of writing include the highway/railway corridor between Kalaw and Taunggyi and the Inle Lake area, which extends east from Thazi in the Mandalay Division, a similar going through Meiktila bound for Mandalay. The simple solution is to get to Meiktila by pickup, then wait for a bus to Mandalay (see the Meiktila section in the Bagan Region chapter for information on buses to Mandalay). The riskier choice is to wait for a Taunggyi-Mandalay bus to come through Thazi and hope you can get on. A passenger pickup between Meiktila and Thazi costs around K50.

Train See the Getting Around chapter at the start of this book for details on train travel to/from Thazi. Some travellers from Thazi have managed to get ordinary class seats to Yangon (Rangoon) for US$9, or to Mandalay for US$5. It's more likely, however, that you'll have to buy upper class tickets.

For information on the train to Shwenyaung, for Inle Lake, see the Inle Lake section later in this chapter.

Car Ask at the Red Star Restaurant about arranging a car tour of Upper Myanmar. The going rate is about US$30 per day (or kyat equivalent), depending on the condi-

tion of the vehicle. It's hard to get the lower rental rates available around Mandalay or Bagan, simply because the steep winding roads of the Shan State require more vehicle upkeep.

KALAW

Situated 70km west of Taunggyi, about half-way along the Thazi-Taunggyi road, Kalaw sits high on the western edge of the Shan Plateau. This was a popular hill station in the British days, and it's still a peaceful and quiet place with an atmosphere reminiscent of the colonial era. At an altitude of 1320m, it's pleasantly cool and a good place for hiking amid gnarled pines, bamboo groves and rugged mountain scenery. There is good accommodation, and you can make interesting excursions around Kalaw and treks into the surrounding mountains.

The small population is a mix of Shan, Indian Muslims, Bamar and Nepalis (Gurkhas retired from British military service), many of whom are missionary-educated. As recently as the 1970s, there were still American missionaries teaching in the local

NORTH-EASTERN MYANMAR

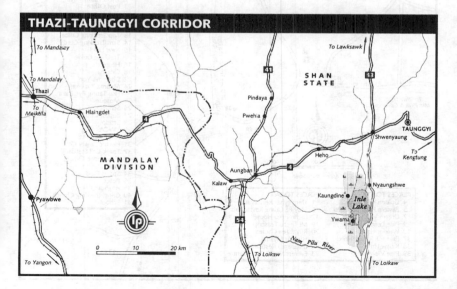

THAZI-TAUNGGYI CORRIDOR

To Mandalay

To Lawksawk

To Mandalay

Thazi

SHAN STATE

To Meiktila

Hlaingdet

Pindaya

Pweha

TAUNGGYI

Shwenyaung

MANDALAY DIVISION

Heho

To Kengtung

Aungban

Kalaw

Pyawbwe

Kaungdine

Nyaungshwe

Inle Lake

Ywama

0   10   20 km

Nam Pilu River

To Yangon

To Loikaw

To Loikaw

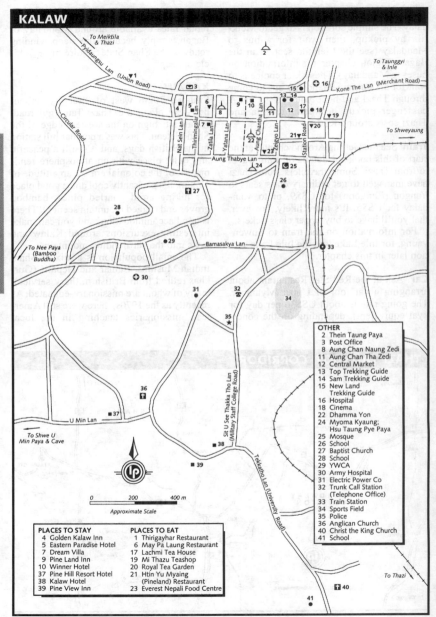

KALAW

To Meiktila & Thazi

Pyidaungsu Lan (Union Road)

To Taunggyi & Inle

Kone The Lan (Merchant Road)

To Shweyaung

Circular Road

Nat Sein Lan
Thirimingalar Lan
Zatila Lan
Yatana Lan
Aung Thabye Lan
Aung Chantha Lan
Beigyo Lan
Station Road

Bamasakya Lan

To Nee Paya (Bamboo Buddha)

To Shwe U Min Paya & Cave

U Min Lan

Sit U See Thakka Tho Lan (Military Staff College Road)

Tekkatho Lan (University Road)

To Thazi

0   200   400 m
Approximate Scale

OTHER
2 Thein Taung Paya
3 Post Office
8 Aung Chan Naung Zedi
11 Aung Chan Tha Zedi
12 Central Market
13 Top Trekking Guide
14 Sam Trekking Guide
15 New Land
   Trekking Guide
16 Hospital
18 Cinema
22 Dhamma Yon
24 Myoma Kyaung;
   Hsu Taung Pye Paya
25 Mosque
26 School
27 Baptist Church
28 School
29 YWCA
30 Army Hospital
31 Electric Power Co
32 Trunk Call Station
   (Telephone Office)
33 Train Station
34 Sports Field
35 Police
36 Anglican Church
40 Christ the King Church
41 School

PLACES TO STAY
4 Golden Kalaw Inn
5 Eastern Paradise Hotel
7 Dream Villa
9 Pine Land Inn
10 Winner Hotel
37 Pine Hill Resort Hotel
38 Kalaw Hotel
39 Pine View Inn

PLACES TO EAT
1 Thirigayhar Restaurant
6 May Pa Laung Restaurant
17 Lachmi Tea House
19 Mi Thazu Teashop
20 Royal Tea Garden
21 Htin Yu Myaing
   (Pineland) Restaurant
23 Everest Nepali Food Centre

NORTH-EASTERN MYANMAR

schools. Because of the British colonial and missionary heritage, many people speak English. About 20,000 people live in and around Kalaw.

Information

To make cheap domestic or international phone calls from Kalaw, go to the Trunk Call Station half-way between the market and the Kalaw Hotel. It's the usual business of placing the call, then waiting about 20 minutes for a call back. A five minute call to Thailand is K300, anywhere else in the world is K800. A window is open daily from 8 am to 8 pm. Some hotels in Kalaw allow you to make similar calls, although they're not as cheap.

Kalaw shares the same telephone code as nearby Taunggyi (081).

Things to See & Do

There are three rather interesting temples to see in town. Perched on the hill overlooking the Thazi-Taunggyi road is the **Thein Taung Paya**. In the town centre is a glittering *stupa* (Buddhist religious monument), covered in gold-coloured mosaics, called **Aung Chang Tha Zedi**. Just across the street is the dilapidated **Dhamma Yon**, a two storey temple; it's not particularly interesting in itself, but from upstairs you can get fair views of the town, Dhamma Yanthi Paya and the ruins of the **Hsu Taung Pye Paya**, now a field of crumbling stupas behind the Dhamma Yon towards the Kalaw Hotel. Just west of town, **Nee Paya** (also called Hnin Paya) features a gold lacquered bamboo Buddha. It's about 20 minutes away by car, but during festival time, you can catch a ride in a pickup with other pilgrims.

Near the Kalaw Hotel is **Christ the King Church**, a brick Catholic church under the supervision of the Burmese Father Paul, and the Italian Father Angelo Di Meo, who has been in Myanmar since 1931 – despite Japanese suspicion of his possible British sympathies during WWII, British suspicion after the war and the State Peace & Development Council (SPDC) suspicion today. The Christ figure over the altar came from

Italy, and Father Angelo painted the mural background. A stone grotto built behind the church is reputed to have curative powers. Mass is held daily at 6.30 am; and at 8 am and 4 pm on Sunday.

Places to Stay

In Kalaw there are several places to stay on or close to the main road, and several more on the outskirts of town. The main road goes by several names, including Pyidaungsu Lan (Union Rd) and Thazi-Taunggyi Hwy.

The friendly *Golden Kalaw Hotel* offers clean (if spartan) rooms with common bath for US$3 per person. Larger rooms with bath cost US$5. The *Eastern Paradise Motel*, on a quiet street, has large clean rooms with private bath for US$8/14 a single/double, breakfast included. The well managed *Winner Hotel* (☎ 081-50025), on the main road, is good value, with clean rooms with bath and TV for US$15/18. Five economy basement single rooms with common bath go for US$5 per person. This is a good place to ask about local treks.

The cheapest place to stay in town is the *Pine Land Inn* (☎ Kalaw 99), a rambling and shabby two storey guesthouse, right on the main road through Kalaw. Very basic two-bed rooms with shared hot-water shower and toilet cost US$1 per person. Similar rooms with attached bath are US$3 per person. Breakfast is not included.

The *Pine View Inn* (☎ 081-50185) on quiet Tekkatho Lan (University Rd) is good value. Spacious rooms with desks, plenty of light and attached hot-water shower cost US$15/20. A tasty Bamar or western breakfast is included, along with a good view.

Though not as historic as the Kalaw Hotel, the 30 room *Pine Hill Resort Hotel* (☎ 081-50078, 101 U Min Lan) is probably the nicest place to stay in Kalaw. Well appointed bungalow-style rooms overlooking the surrounding hills cost US$30/36, and have fridge, TV and hot-water bath, with breakfast included. Four deluxe larger two-room chalets cost US$46/54. The hotel restaurant serves very good Bamar and Indian-flavoured dishes.

NORTH-EASTERN MYANMAR

The historic *Kalaw Hotel (☎ 081-50039, 84 University Rd)* looks like a cross between a Tudor mansion and a hunting lodge, with rattan furniture and satellite TV. The hotel was built between 1903 and 1906 and served as resort quarters for British officers. The Japanese used it as a hospital during WWII, after which it became a private hotel until 1984, when the government took it over. In 1994 it was privatised (ie a 'joint venture') once again. The hotel offers accommodation in the standard wing for US$25/36, including private bath and breakfast. In the middle and new wings attached to the foyer and reception area, larger superior rooms with high ceilings, fridge and private bath cost US$36/45. All rooms have hot water. Set well behind the town, it's a very quiet and peaceful place to stay. The hotel is famous for its restaurant service but, unfortunately, not its food.

The *Dream Villa (☎ 081-50144)*, on Zatila Lan, has decent and airy rooms with hot water for US$18/24, breakfast included. During the low season (May to October), prices may drop by 50%. There is one large family suite with a balcony that costs US$36. As with most hotels in cool Kalaw, there is no air-con.

Places to Eat

As in most hill stations in Myanmar, many Kalaw restaurants have an Indian or Nepali touch. One of our favourites is the clean and modest *Everest Nepali Food Centre*, two blocks from the main road on Aung Chantha Lan. Tasty and reasonably priced curries, fresh juice and dry *chapatis* (flat, unleavened bread) are available daily from 6.30 am to 9 pm.

Thirigayhar Restaurant (Seven Sisters) is a popular and very good Shan-Chinese-Indian eatery on the main road.

A block south of the central market, *Htin Yu Myaing Restaurant* (Pineland) serves good Chinese and Bamar fare.

The Shan-owned *May Pa Laung Restaurant* near Aung Chang Naung Zedi (four blocks west of the market) offers some of the best Bamar and Shan dishes in town; the cooks can also prepare delicious Indian food with advance notice.

For a splurge, the dining room at the *Kalaw Hotel* is recommended for lovers of British cuisine and high tea. The hotel prepares Bamar, Chinese and European dishes, but the kitchen's reputation is a leftover from better days. Decent Australian wine is usually available by the bottle, at reasonable prices.

There are quite a few teashops in Kalaw, but they're nothing fancy. The *Royal Tea Garden*, near the cinema, is large and popular. Across the street the tiny Nepali-operated *Lachmi Tea House* serves very good tea, chapatis and curry, and is open from 5 am till around 9 pm, longer than any of the other places. Around the corner is a larger Nepali teashop, *Mi Thazu*, where chapatis, tea and *raksi* (Nepali-style moonshine) are available.

Getting There & Away

From Thazi, pickups for Kalaw leave in the morning for around K100 per person. Taunggyi-bound buses from either Meiktila or Bagan pass through Kalaw, though you may have to pay the full Taunggyi fare. Travel time is about three hours. From Taunggyi to Kalaw by pickup, it's K100 for the two to three hour trip. To charter a vehicle to either Thazi or Taunggyi will cost around US$20 to US$25. For Aungban and Pindaya, see the later Pindaya section.

It's possible to take the train from Thazi or Shwenyaung; it takes around 4½ hours from Thazi, about half that time from Shwenyaung. Either way, it's a scenic, if slow, trip. If you can pay in kyat, the fare for ordinary class is about K100. The fare will run as high as US$4 for 1st class.

To return to Yangon, it's possible to book a seat through the Winner Hotel, Kalaw Hotel or Top Trekking Guide Service for one of the Taunggyi-Yangon air-con express buses for about K1500. To Mandalay, expect to pay about K1200; to Bagan about K1400. In Yangon, check with Eastern State Express. There's also the usual Mandalay-Yangon train connection via Thazi.

AROUND KALAW
Visiting Nearby Villages

Trekking around Kalaw can vary from a one-day hike to five-day treks into the surrounding hills. The plateau near Kalaw is inhabited by people of the Palaung and Pa-O (or Black Karen) tribes. Intha, Shan, Taungthu, Taung-yo, Danu, Kayah, Danaw and Bamar people occupy the mountains to the north and east.

Palaung women wear colourful blue-and-red costumes and families often live in 'long houses'. One of their main sources of income is the cultivation of *thanaq-hpeq* (a large leaf used to wrap Burmese cigars). The Pa-O wear more sombre dark blue or indigo costumes, and are regarded as good businesspeople. Tribespeople come into town on Kalaw's market day, which comes around every five days. On the way home, their woven backpack baskets may be filled

with *cheroots* (Burmese cigars), candles and treats for the children.

Several nearby villages can be visited in half-day or whole-day hikes. Some guides are beginning to lead multiday trips. Licensed guides in Kalaw generally charge about US$4 to US$5 for a day hike, and US$5 to US$7 per day for overnight treks. The cost generally includes food and lodging. Expect to hike for at least six hours a day and cover about 15km.

One advantage of overnight treks is that by evening time people are back home in the village after spending a day tending to the fields. Lodging is usually in long houses, occasionally in *kyaungs* (monasteries). Be prepared for the lingering smoke of longhouse cooking fires. On the plus side, it keeps mosquitoes at a minimum.

Because most villagers do not yet know what food foreigners like, long house meals

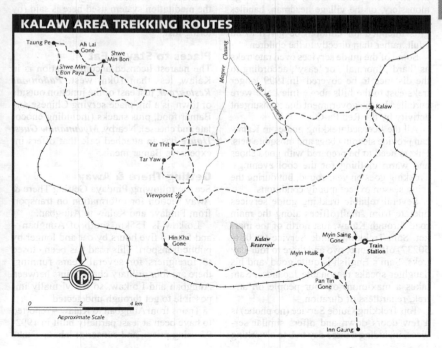

KALAW AREA TREKKING ROUTES

Taung Pe
Ah Lai Gone
Shwe Min Bon
Shwe Min Bon Paya
Magwe Chaung
Nge Mat Chaung
Kalaw
Yar Thit
Tar Yaw
Viewpoint
Hin Kha Gone
Kalaw Reservoir
Myin Saing Gone
Myin Htaik
Train Station
Pan Tin Gone
Inn Gaung

0   2   4 km
Approximate Scale

are quite authentic. On the other hand, the presence of foreigners has not gone unnoticed; a small canteen at one of the lookouts we came upon sported a sign in English offering 'water, soft drinks, beer, snacks'.

Trekking Services

If you want to trek to nearby villages, there are several sources of information. Many of the hotels (the Winner, the Eastern Paradise) and restaurants (May Pa Laung and Everest Nepali) can offer guide assistance. Father Paul at Christ the King Church is also quite helpful (see the previous Kalaw section for contact details).

When visiting the villages, it's better to contribute cash gifts to the village health fund rather than hand out medicines, toys or food. Pencils, paper notebooks and ballpoint pens are also welcome. Your guide should know what's appropriate and what's not. Usually the *sayadaw* (chief abbot) of the village monastery, or the village headman, handles such donations. Village elders prefer that any gifts intended for children be given to an adult, rather than directly to the children.

Some of the guide services even rate treks as 'hard', 'normal', or 'easy', according to the distance to be covered. In 1999 longer treks east to the hills above Inle Lake were curtailed by the government due to insurgent activity by the Red Pa-O.

All the licensed trekking guides in Kalaw can provide sleeping bags and mosquito nets. Hikers need to be prepared with good shoes and warm clothing for the cool evenings. Trekking goes on year-round, but during the rainy season expect muddy conditions.

Several reliable trekking guide services operate from small offices along the main road through Kalaw, just north of the market. Sam Trekking Guide Service (☎ 081-50237) offers one, two and three to four-day treks. Sam's English is quite good, and his daughter speaks reasonable Japanese. Sam takes a maximum of four people on any trek, regardless of duration.

Top Trekking Guide Service (no phone) is a few doors down and offers similar services, including a three day trek to a working elephant camp west of Kalaw. New Land Trekking (☎ 081-50150) is just across the road, and offers similar services, including longer treks north to the Pindaya caves.

AUNGBAN

This small highway town is an important transport junction for cargo and passengers moving between Thazi and Taunggyi, north to Pindaya or south to Loikaw, the capital of Kayah State. As such, Aungban's main function is to feed and fuel; among Shan State truck drivers it's also infamous for its brothels. As elsewhere in Myanmar, AIDS is on the rise.

There is little of substance to the town itself, except when the five day **market** is held. For seekers of Buddhist wisdom, the **Taungpulu Meditation Monastery**, a little east of town off the highway, has been an important waystation for many years. Founded by the late Taungpulu Sayadaw, the meditation system used here is said (by locals) to be particularly effective in countering lust.

Places to Stay & Eat

The nearest licensed accommodation is in Kalaw, less than 10km west. *Padonmar Restaurant*, just east of the junction outside of town, is a big place serving Chinese and Bamar food, plus snacks (including chocolate and cheese). Nearby, *Myatmanaw Guest House* has an attached cafe that offers inexpensive Bamar meals.

Getting There & Away

See the following Pindaya Getting There & Away section for information on transport from Pindaya and Kalaw to Aungban.

Loikaw is 155km south of Aungban – and four to five hours by car and longer by public transport. This road has been closed to foreigners for several years running; there are four military checkpoints between Aungban and Loikaw, so it's virtually impossible to get through undetected.

Trains from Aungban to Kalaw – reported to have been at least partially built in 1992-93 using prison and conscript labour – take about 10 hours to cover the distance. The fare is K100. For more information, see the Loikaw section at the end of this chapter.

PINDAYA

About 40km north of Aungban is the town of Pindaya, noted for its extensive limestone caves and picturesque Boutaloke Lake. The scenic Aungban-Pindaya road passes through the Pa-O and Danu villages of Pwehla and Ji-Chanzi. There are fields of dry-cultivated mountain rice along the way and potato fields where the tuber is grown in red mud mounds.

Pindaya itself is a centre for the Burmese-speaking Taung-yo people. Local handicrafts include Shan paper and parasols made from mulberry bark. The town's symbol is a *pin-gu* (spider). According to legend, seven princesses bathing in the lake took refuge in the caves during a storm where they were imprisoned by a giant spider.

It is possible to begin short treks to surrounding Danu, Pa-O, Palaung and Taung-yo villages. Inquire at Diamond Eagle Guest House or Myit Phyar Zaw Gyi Hotel for more information (see Places to Stay & Eat in this section for details).

Pindaya Caves

The famous Pindaya Caves (officially Pindaya Natural Cave Museum) are ensconced in a limestone ridge overlooking the lake. It's a long walk from the lake to the foot of the cliff containing the caves; if you've chartered a jeep or car from Kalaw or Taunggyi, make sure that you're driven all the way up to the cliff. Travel from town to the foot of the cliffs costs K100 by horsecart. A 200 step stairway leads to the cave entrance – leave your shoes at the bottom or carry them with you in a bag. Foreigners are charged a US$3 admission fee.

Inside the cavern there are more than 8000 Buddha images – made from alabaster, teak, marble, brick, lacquer and cement – which have been put there over the centuries and arranged in such a way as to form a labyrinth throughout the various cave chambers. Some of the smaller side cham-

The 31 Stages of Being

The people of Myanmar are highly religious, and predominantly Buddhist. Children routinely go through ceremonies to become novice monks and nuns for periods of time. At the Pindaya Caves, there are more than 8000 Buddha images at last count, most of them donated by devout Buddhists.

To put this life in perspective, a small signboard inside the entrance hall reminds pilgrims and other visitors of the 31 Bhumis (Stages of Being), plus a final word of wisdom:

Mind Only	4
Mind & Matter	15
Matter Only	1
Devas (Spirit Beings)	6
Human Beings	1
Apaya (Lower Worlds)	4
	= 31

'Nibbana (Nirvana) is not situated in any bhumis, nor is it a sort of heaven. It is a state which is dependent on ourselves.'
Michael Clark

bers are only accessible on hands and knees, and in these you may come across lay people practising meditation.

Among the more unusual features in the cave is a set of stalagmites that can be struck with large wooden mallets to produce 'gong' tones. In one corner of the cave stand three 'perspiring Buddhas', sitting images that stay wet because of condensation in the damp cave. Burmese worshippers believe they will gain good fortune and beauty by rubbing the drops of 'sweat' on their faces.

Although many areas within the caves are illuminated by electric lights, power has been known to fail and a torch would help make out the darker corners. Take care on the slippery paths.

From a temple complex built along the front of the ridge you can view the nearby lake and the ruins of **Shwe U Min Paya**, a cluster of low stupas just below the ridge. Beginning on the full moon of Tabaung (February/March), Pindaya hosts a colourful *paya pwe* (pagoda festival) at Shwe U Min.

Padah-Lin Caves

North-west of Pindaya, and near the village of Ye-Ngan is the most important prehistoric site in Myanmar, the Padah-Lin Caves (also known as Badalin, or Badut Hlaing which mean Chameleon Cave). The interior of one of the caves is decorated with the remains of very old paintings of animal and human subjects, not unlike Neolithic cave paintings in Europe. To get here you will have to charter a 4WD – this can be added on to a Pindaya trip from either Kalaw or Taunggyi for about an extra K1500 per vehicle. From Ye-Ngan, a rough track leads several kilometres south-west to Yebok village. The two caves are a little over a kilometre west of Yebok on a footpath.

Places to Stay & Eat

Pindaya is growing as a tourist destination, and there are already six places to stay between Boutaloke Lake and the caves, including the *Pindaya Hotel (Taunggyi ☎ 081-22409)*, a clean and comfortable two storey place about half-way between the town and the caves. Standard rooms with fan and attached shower and toilet cost US$12/16 a single/double. Slightly bigger superior rooms with fridge and balcony views of the lake cost US$20/25. The hotel restaurant serves very decent Chinese and Shan dishes.

The nearby, friendly *Golden Cave Hotel (Pindaya ☎ 66, Taunggyi ☎ 081-23471)* has simple and clean two-bed rooms with attached hot-water shower for US$14/18, breakfast included.

The three storey *Myin Phyar Zaw Gyi Hotel (☎ Pindaya 92, Taunggyi ☎ 081-22158)* has 16 standard rooms with attached hot-water bath for US$12/20, and five larger superior rooms with fridge for US$15/25, breakfast included. Its dining room serves mostly Chinese food.

Entering Pindaya from the south, you'll see the quiet *Inle Inn (Pindaya ☎ 29, Taunggyi ☎ 081-21347)*, set in a bamboo grove. All rooms have hot water and a veranda. Standard rooms cost US$25/30, including breakfast. Larger superior rooms cost US$35/40. There are no fridges, and no TVs.

The *Conqueror Hotel (Taunggyi ☎ 081-23257)* is more expensive and caters largely to tour groups. During the low season, it often drops its prices by at least 20%. Standards rooms cost US$30/36; larger, superior rooms cost US$39/48. All rooms are duplex bungalows, and come with attached hot-water bath, satellite TV, fridge and fireplace.

A good and cheap Pindaya alternative is the friendly *Diamond Eagle Guest House (Pindaya ☎ 30)*, next to the lake. Clean rooms with common bath cost US$6 per person (no breakfast), and even offer a view of the lake.

In addition to the standard hotel dining rooms mentioned, good food can be found in the market area in town – the best is at *U Aseik*, where you can get a delicious full Bamar meal for around K60. *Teik Sein Restaurant* serves delicious Shan food, and nearby *Kyanlite Restaurant* has an English menu featuring Chinese fare. At the cave temple, as well as in the market (between December and March), you can buy delicious local avocados (*tawpaq-thi* in Burmese, meaning Butter Fruit).

Getting There & Away

From Kalaw it costs K50 to Aungban and another K120 to Pindaya by public transport. It can be difficult to find buses or pickups later in the day, especially between Aungban and Pindaya, so leave early in the morning and allow a whole day for the trip. The first pickup from Pindaya to Aungban leaves from the market area at 6 am. From Taunggyi, there's one bus per day at 2 pm for K160; the same bus travels in the opposite direction at 6 am the next day.

You can also hire a car and driver in Kalaw to make the day trip to Pindaya and back for about US$15 to US$20. If you don't want to stay in Pindaya, you could hire a car to take you from Kalaw to Pindaya, have it wait for a couple of hours while you take in the caves and have lunch in town, and then take you on to Nyaungshwe (also called Yaunghwe) for Inle Lake. This should cost about US$30 or the kyat equivalent for the whole day – it's better to pay in US dollars than kyat. One pickup can take four or five passengers with baggage. The actual road time is about two hours for the 50km from Kalaw to Pindaya and three hours or more for the 93km from Pindaya to Nyaungshwe (Yaunghwe). Add waiting time (which can be considerable) in Aungban and Shwenyaung if you go by public transport.

HEHO

Another highway town, Heho is about half-way between Aungban and Shwenyaung, which is the junction for the road south to Nyaungshwe and Inle Lake. North of the town is an airstrip that fields Air Mandalay (AM), Yangon Airways (YA) and Myanma Airways (MA) flights from Yangon and Mandalay (see the Inle Lake Getting There & Away section for details).

Heho has a dusty market area just off the highway that hosts the largest of the five-day markets in the southern area of the Shan State. The several *guesthouses* in town admit locals only. On the highway near the market area are a couple of decent places to eat, including the *Oasis Café* (tea snacks), *San San Restaurant* (Chinese food) and *Island Restaurant* (Chinese and Bamar meals). There is a small *snack bar* at the airport.

SHWENYAUNG

Few people stop off in Shwenyaung, except to change from a Thazi-Taunggyi pickup or bus going to Nyaungshwe. Should you find yourself needing overnight accommodation, there is one good choice; in fact it may be good enough to warrant an intentional stopover for those seeking something away from the lake scene.

The two storey, L-shaped *Remember Inn*, near the crossroads, has budget singles with shared facilities for US$3, standard rooms with air-con, fridge and attached toilet and bath for US$15 a single/double, or superior

---

Five Day Market

In the Shan State, community markets are held on a traditional rotating basis, in which each town or village within a given area hosts a market every five days. Hence a five day market held on Saturday in Pindaya will come around five days later, not every Saturday.

The schedule in the Kalaw-Inle Lake corridor is as follows:

Day 1	Phaung Daw U Monastery (Inle Lake), Kalaw, Shwenyaung
Day 2	Pindaya, Nyaungshwe
Day 3	Heho, Kyoung (on the way to Pindaya)
Day 4	Ywama, Taunggyi, Aungban
Day 5	Pwehla (on the way to Pindaya)

Joe Cummings

---

rooms with TV for US$20. All rooms are spacious and there's a rooftop terrace with umbrellas and chairs. The proprietors lead treks to local Shan and Pa-O villages.

Getting There & Away

You can get all the way to Shwenyaung by train, but it's time consuming. From Yangon or Mandalay, the program would be to take one of the Yangon-Mandalay express trains and disembark at Thazi. See the Getting Around chapter at the start of this book for timetable details.

The train from Thazi to Shwenyaung is rather slow – the average speed must be around 10km/h with occasional sprints of 15km/h – but the route is very picturesque and having the run of a carriage can be more comfortable than sitting in the back of a cramped pickup on mountain curves. It's a spectacular eight to nine-hour journey through the Shan mountains and local villages, partially on a zigzag railway. Stations en route have masses of fruit, snacks and flowers for sale. From Thazi the No 141 Up leaves at 9 am and arrives in Shwenyaung between 5 and 6 pm. From Shwenyaung to

Thazi the No 142 Down leaves at 8.30 am and arrives around 6 pm, in plenty of time to connect with the Mandalay-Yangon train, which is scheduled to depart from Thazi around 8.30 pm but usually doesn't leave till around 9 pm.

If you can manage to pay in kyat, the fare between Thazi and Shwenyaung is around K50 in ordinary class. Lately, the ticket-sellers in Shwenyaung have been charging foreigners US$4 in ordinary class or US$9 in 1st class (which is often unavailable).

INLE LAKE

Inle Lake is 22km long, roughly 11km wide, 875m above sea level and outrageously beautiful – it has very calm waters dotted with patches of floating vegetation and busy fishing canoes. High hills rim the lake on both sides; the lakeshore and lake islands bear 17 villages on stilts, mostly inhabited by the Intha people. Culturally and linguistically separate from their Shan neighbours, the Inthas are thought to have migrated to this area from Dawei (Tavoy) on the Tanintharyi (Tenasserim) peninsula in Southern Myanmar. The Intha dialect is related to standard Burmese but also shows similarities with the Mon-influenced Dawei dialect. The Burmese 'th' sound becomes an 's' in Intha, so that the Burmese *'beh-thwa-ma-lay?'* ('Where are you going?') becomes *'beh-swa-ma-lay?'* among the Intha.

According to one story, two brothers from Dawei came to Nyaungshwe in 1359 to serve a Nyaungshwe sawbwa. The latter was so pleased with the hard-working demeanour of the Dawei brothers that he asked them to invite 36 more families from Dawei; purportedly, all the Intha around Inle Lake are descended from these migrant families. Another theory says they migrated from the Mon region in the 18th century to avoid wars between the Thais and Bamar. Like the Shan, Mon and Bamar, the Intha are Buddhist; there are around 100 Buddhist kyaungs around the lake and perhaps 1000 stupas. The Inle style of religious architecture and Buddhist sculpture is strongly Shan-influenced.

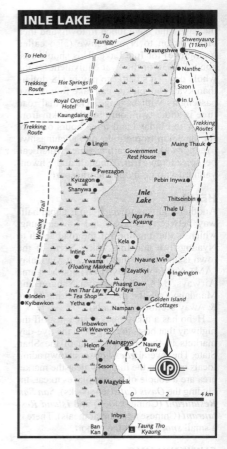

The hard-working Intha are famous for propelling their flat-bottomed boats by standing at the stern on one leg and wrapping the other leg around the oar. This strange leg-rowing technique offers relief to the arms – which are also used for rowing – during the long paddles from one end of the lake to another. It also enables the rower to better see the floating islands *(kyun myaw)* and water hyacinth *(beda)*. It's sometimes necessary to stand up to plot a path around the obstacles – and to spot fish. Although outboard motors are used for cross-lake ferries and for carrying tourists to the islands and lakeshore villages, most people still use oars and paddles, thus avoiding petrol shortages, saving money and precluding the hassle of hyacinth-tangled propellers.

The entire lake area is contained in the township of Nyaungshwe and supports a population of 130,000 people that consists of Intha, Shan, Taungthu (Pa-O), Taung-yo, Danu, Kayah, Danaw and Bamar people. The township seat of the same name sits north of the lake and is approached by road from Shwenyaung or from the lake to the south via a long, narrow channel. Around 70,000 people live on the shores and islands of the lake.

In the hills east of town, some Pa-O insurgents are still active despite the signing of a truce with the Yangon government in 1992. The White Pa-O, led by Aung Khamti, are keeping to the ceasefire and have established the Golden Island Cottages Hotel as a source of income for local development and training for the Pa-O people. But the Red (communist) Pa-O, with whom they split in 1974, are still fighting both them and the SPDC, from their base in Hsiseng, south of Taunggyi.

The industrious villagers inhabiting the lake region support themselves by growing a wide variety of flowers, vegetables and fruits year-round, including tomatoes, beans, cauliflowers, cabbages, eggplants, garlic, onions, betel vine, melons, papayas and bananas. They also grow rice, especially at the northern end of the lake around Nyaungshwe. Many of these crops are cultivated on floating islands, where marsh, soil and water hyacinth have combined to form incredibly fertile solid masses that are staked to the lake bottom with bamboo poles. Between the islands and peninsulas thus formed is a network of canals that are the main avenues of transportation for the Intha. Tall lattices of betel vine line the canals in some of the villages, providing a curtain of privacy and another source of income. Ywama is known as the floating village since it has *chaungs* (canals) for streets, and much of

the day-to-day village activity, including marketing, is carried about from canoes.

Using cone-shaped nets stretched tautly over wood and bamboo frames, Intha fishermen harvest *nga-hpein* (a type of carp) and other kinds of freshwater fish. Women in the villages (especially Ywama and Heya at the southern end of Inle Lake) weave Shan-style shoulder bags and silk *Zinme* (Chiang Mai-style) *longyis* (sarong-style garments) on wooden handlooms. Using raw silk from China, these weavers produce more silk garments than anywhere in the country, after Amarapura.

When they aren't busy with fishing or farming, the men of Inle produce silver and brassware, as well as pottery and lacquerware. The area around Kaungdaing, on the western shore, is famous for the production of noodles, tofu and other soybean products that end up in kitchens all over Myanmar.

The lake itself is very shallow and clear – a swim looks inviting and the **Inleh Bo Teh** is a good place to have one. Inleh means middle of, Bo is officer, or official, and Teh is house, so the Inleh Bo Teh is literally an official's house in the middle of the lake. It's no longer used as such, but makes a good place to stop for a mid-lake picnic or swim.

During January and February, the nights and mornings around the lake area are cold, so you should bring socks and a sweater. Hotels and guesthouses have adequate blankets.

Information

To enter the Inle Lake zone, tourists are required to pay a US$3 entry fee at the Myanmar Travels & Tours (MTT) office on Strand Rd or, more commonly, at one of the hotels or guesthouses around town. You can arrange a boat tour at your guesthouse, or from a couple of places near the canal leading to the lake.

Special Events

One of the best times of the year to visit Inle Lake is during September and October. The ceremonial Phaung Daw U festival, which lasts for almost three weeks, is closely followed by the Thadingyut festival, when the

Inthas and Shan dress in new clothes and fervently celebrate the end of Waso (Buddhist Lent). They are so religious that it's not unusual for families to spend all of their meagre savings during this one annual event.

Around the Lake

To really experience Inle Lake culture you need to get out onto the lake itself. MTT no longer has a monopoly on lake tours and you can hire watercraft from just about anyone who has a boat. The exact price per person or per boat depends on two things: the price of petrol and the distance travelled. Most trips around the lake cost K1600 to K2000.

The typical motorboat trip is not bad – you will see the floating gardens, leg-rowers, fishermen, Phaung Daw U Paya (see its entry later in this section) and whatever lake commerce is going on. Ywama market day has become a bit too famous for its own good. The sizeable floating market is jammed with both real shoppers and merchants in canoes, but when a boat of tourists arrives, all the attention seems to swing their way – not a pretty sight if you're caught in the middle of a dozen souvenir boats.

The lake itself is rich in wildlife, especially various waterfowl. All avifauna on the lake and adjoining wetlands is reportedly protected by law, as Inle Lake has been an official bird sanctuary since 1985. Egrets fly in formation over the lake every day, about an hour before sunset. The boat trips usually include stops at souvenir shops near Phaung Daw U Paya. The selection isn't bad at these shops, but prices are lower at the five day floating market or at the paya – at all these places you'll see Shan shoulder bags, embroidered shirts and longyis, tapestries, pottery, jewellery and all the other souvenirs.

Canoe Trips With all the package tours heading to the southern end of the lake by noisy powerboats nowadays, a quiet canoe paddle through the villages along the lake channel has become an attractive alternative. Unfortunately, canoes are no longer allowed onto the lake itself. But several people in town do shorter canoe trips on the canals branching from the lake and along the Nyaungshwe shore of the lake for rates of about K400 per two or three hour paddle. Although you won't get to see the more famous lake sights, life along the canals is itself fascinating and the villagers are friendly. Slow moving canoes are also better for photography.

One place that can only be visited by canoe is the large **nat shrine** in the middle of a swampy banyan tree jungle opposite Nanthe village on the main channel. No one dares cut the trees for fear of the *nats'* (spirits) wrath, so it's a good place to see unfettered nature, including plenty of waterfowl. The house-sized, wooden nat shrine sits on stilts and contains a rustic altar.

Trekking Extended walks to the north or south of Nyaungshwe pass among extensive rice paddies dotted with Shan stupa ruins. Trails into the hills east of town lead to Pa-O villages and panoramic views of the lake area. A good and rugged all-day trek is to the monastery of **Koun Soun Taungbo** and nearby **Ta-Eh Gu** (Cave). You pass through two Pa-O villages on the way. Further away, and currently off-limits, are the ruins of Kekku.

Guided day hikes can be arranged through any guesthouse or hotel in town or at Golden Island Cottages on the lake (see Places to Stay – Top End in this section for details); guides typically charge US$3 to US$4 a day. Multiple-day trips are not currently allowed. It's a good idea to bring some bottled water on any day trek.

Nyaungshwe

Nyaungshwe (Golden Banyan Tree, also called Yaunghwe) is the small town 3.5km from the northern end of the lake. There are a number of places to stay and eat, and boats run out onto the lake from the wide channel that runs along the western side of town. At first it appears there's not a lot to do around town, but between the lake itself, the nearby villages, countryside walks and historic ruins, there's actually enough to occupy an active visitor for a week or more.

Shan Palace Museum Also known as Yaunghwe Haw Museum, and housed in a large teak and brick mansion in the north-eastern part of town, this was the *haw* (palace) of the 33rd and last Shan sawbwa, Sao Shwe Thaike. Thaike, who became the first president of Myanmar in 1948, was imprisoned when Ne Win came to power and died in jail. Overall the collection of Shan regalia and photos is not particularly interesting, but the building itself is worth a visit as it's the best surviving example of a Shan haw since the demolition of the *haw sao pha* (Shan lord's palace) in Kengtung in 1991.

For years, much of the two storey building, laid out in a double cruciform floor plan, remained in a state of disrepair. Some recent renovations have slightly improved things, but it will be a long project. An upstairs room displays original woodcarvings that once decorated the exterior of the palace. A small room to the side contains a royal bed and throne. Most impressive is the huge teak-floored throne-and-audience hall in the north wing, behind the front building. Admission is US$2.

Shrines, Monasteries & Stupas The oldest temple in town, **Yadana Man Aung Paya**, is worth visiting for its unique step-spired stupa. Look for the 'you will be old' and 'you will be sick' figures in glass cases, in one of the shrine buildings.

There are several good-sized monasteries in the centre and south-eastern parts of town, including **Kan Gyi Kyaung, Shwe Gu Kyaung** and **Yangon Kyaung**. On the south-eastern outskirts of town, the ruin of an old Shan monastery called **Nigyon Taungyon Kyaung** – originally built by the Nyaung-shwe sawbwa – features a set of slender whitewashed Shan stupas and some very old plinths with surviving stucco relief. Under the supervision of an old monk, the complex is being transformed into a *kam-mahtan kyaung* (meditation monastery). A new shrine hall on the grounds contains two alabaster sitting Buddhas in the Mandalay style, and there are a few thatched huts for meditators.

Less than 1km north of the town entrance, an old 18th or 19th century monastery called **Shwe Yaunghwe Kyaung** features a venerable wooden *thein* (consecration hall) with unique oval windows. A long, low, rectangular brick-and-stucco *pahto* (shrine) on the premises bears slender Shan *zedis* (bell-shaped stupas) on top and Buddha images of various ages inside.

A short walk south of town along the eastern side of the main channel leads to the small but atmospheric ruins of **Kyaukhpyu-gyi (Big White Stone) Paya** next to the Intha village of Nanthe. Surrounded by brick-and-stucco *devas* (Pali: spirit beings), lions and stupas is a huge sitting Buddha, said to be 700 years old. The cloister around the image is lined with intact stucco reliefs, while the stupas behind the main shrine are topped with surrealistically bent and twisted metal *htis* (decorative umbrellas).

Mingala Zei The main municipal *zei* (market) near the town's northern entrance is busiest in the morning, when vendors congregate to sell their wares. In addition to mountains of fresh produce, Shan noodles and other local products, there are a few stalls selling pottery and textiles.

Ywama

Regular boats run from Nyaungshwe to the village of Ywama – to see the famed floating market, you must calculate the day according to the local five day market scheme. Unfortunately, you must also take into account what has happened to this once-interesting local event. On market day, Ywama floating market is a traffic jam of tourist boats and souvenir hawkers, with a few local farmers trying to sell their vegetables to a few local buyers. On nonmarket days, it's almost worse because it's only souvenir and tourist boats (at a ratio of about five to one!); of course, the smart vegetable farmers are already at another five day market. Arriving early won't help; the action is in full swing by 8.30 am, and it's downhill from there.

But don't despair. We think you can enjoy a floating market without fighting the crowds – and without adding to the already crazy atmosphere of Ywama. Simply check out the five day market schedule around Inle (see boxed text on page 357), and choose a market that is convenient in terms of location and your schedule. Any guesthouse or hotel in Nyaungshwe will have the current schedule. A secondary five day circuit that rotates among the lake villages of Kaungdaing, Mainthauk, Nanpan, Indein and Thandaung is worth checking out.

The approach to Ywama is quite beautiful, despite the market scene. And after the morning rush hour (and before the late afternoon one) it's a lovely place to see. You pass through floating fields where the Intha people grow everything from vegetables to flowers. The fields make an unusual and picturesque sight.

Just north of Ywama, you can stop at **Nga Phe Kyaung**, a wooden monastery built on stilts over the lake four years before the construction of Mandalay Palace. It's known among the package-tour crowd as the Jumping Cat Monastery because the monks there have trained a few cats to leap through small hoops. But a better reason to visit is to see the modest collection of Buddha images in Shan, Tibetan, Bagan and Inwa styles. Just as impressive as the Buddhas themselves are the tall, highly ornate, wood-and-mosaic pedestals and cases built for the images. Such pedestals are a speciality of Shan and Northern Thai Buddhist art and those at the monastery are over 100 years old. Many of the original Shan images they once contained have been sold or stolen, so the cases mostly contain newer images. A

Phaung Daw U Festival

The biggest event in the southern area of Shan State takes place at Phaung Daw U Paya, one of the state's holiest sites, from the first day of the waxing moon to the third day after the full moon of Thadingyut (September/October). The focus of the large two storey sanctuary is five goldleaf-covered statues, of which three are said to be Buddha images, while the remaining two are reportedly Arahats (historical disciples of the Buddha). The goldleaf on the figures has become so thick that it's hard to tell what the figures represent; they look a bit like short, squat bowling pins or lopsided dumbbells.

The statues were reportedly fashioned during the reign of King Alaungsithu (1112-67). The gold lumps are so holy that pilgrims rub red strips of cloth against them, then tie the cloth strips to their bikes, cars and trucks to create protective spiritual forcefields around themselves and their vehicles.

During the 20 days of the festival, a ceremonial barge carries four of the five Phaung Daw U images around the lake, from village to village, to bless the village monasteries. The smallest of the five figures stays at Phaung Daw U to act as 'guardian' of the temple, following an incident that happened many years ago when the procession used to carry all five images around the lake. About 8km from Phaung Daw U, in the middle of the lake, you can see a pillar mounted by a *shwe hintha* (golden swan figure – actually a *hamsa*, a swan-like creature from Indian mythology). This monument marks the spot where the ceremonial barge once capsized. Only four of the five figures were immediately recovered, but when the stunned crew returned to Phaung Daw U they found the fifth sitting on its pedestal, covered with lake weeds. Ever since the legendary incident, that image has never left the monastery.

Hundreds of other vessels travel in the entourage in a general celebratory atmosphere. Thousands of people from around the Shan State attend this most holy of Shan celebrations.

Joe Cummings

few 150-year-old Shan images are uncere-moniously kept off to the side on a smaller altar; crafted by Intha artisans, the gilded wood images feature crowns and royal attire decorated with mosaics.

If your tolerance for souvenir hawkers is low, make it clear to your boat pilot or guide that you'd prefer to spend more time at other lake sights. Public ferries make the trip a couple of times in the early morning from the public boat landing in Nyaung-shwe, for K100 per person.

Phaung Daw U Paya The main landing at Ywama stands in front of Phaung Daw U Paya, the holiest religious site in the southern area of the Shan State.

Stalls on the ground floor of the shrine and nearby sell brightly coloured cotton Shan shoulder bags, other local crafts and 'antiques'. Silk and cotton fabrics are a local speciality; there are over 200 handlooms in Ywama. A shady *khamauk* (conical bamboo hat) is another popular purchase here.

Kaungdaing

Also spelt Kaungdine, this Intha village on the north-western shore of the lake is known for the production of soybean cakes and noodles. It's easy to wander around the village and observe the methods used, as just about every other household is involved in this cottage industry. Potting and weaving can also be seen. Just outside the village are some interesting Shan temple ruins featuring brick-and-stucco zedis, pahtos and *chinthes* (half-lion/half-dragon guardians); the villagers use some of the pahtos for storing straw or hay.

A little north of Kaungdaing is a hot spring, which is open daily from 7 am to 5 pm. You can bathe in communal baths for a few kyat, but be sure to bring a longyi to wear in the bath. Private rooms are also available for US$1. The water is very hot and is said to be cleanest between May and August. Kaungdaing and the hot springs are a 1½ hour drive from Nyaungshwe around the top of the lake via Shwenyaung on the Heho road or about 30 minutes across the lake by

boat. A boat charter costs K800 (each way) to Kaungdaing. There are a couple of hotels near Kaungdaing; see the following Places to Stay section.

Places to Stay – Budget

Nyaungshwe has around 30 hotels and guesthouses, plus a few on or around the lake itself. With the increase in hotels and guesthouses in Nyaungshwe, you can expect low-season discounts of 10% to 20%.

The *Four Sisters Inn* used to be a well known dining spot. The sisters have expanded it into a quiet guesthouse between the canal and a large rice paddy, about 1km south of the main village. Rooms with fan, hot-water shower and good beds cost US$7/12 a single/double. Like most places in town, they can help arrange boat tours and rent bicycles.

The *Gypsy Inn* (☎ 84) on Chaung Lan (Strand Rd), along the canal, is one of the brighter budget spots. Spacious, if simple, rooms with fan cost US$3 per person, breakfast included. Because it's next to the canal, you'll hear the early morning canal boats going by. The *Nawng Khan (Little Inn)*, on Phaundawpyan Lan opposite Shwe Zali Paya, has bright clean rooms with fan and hot-water shower for US$6/10, breakfast included.

The cheapest place in Nyaungshwe is the friendly but shabby *Mingalar Hotel* with small rooms at US$2 a person, including breakfast. The *Teakwood Guest House*, three blocks east of the canal, offers good budget lodgings. Large wooden rooms with attached hot-water showers and fan cost US$3 per person.

Another good budget place is the friendly *May Guest House* (☎ 081-21416) on Mya-wady Lan opposite Hlaing Gu Kyaung (monastery). Clean linoleum-floor rooms with hot-water shower and small veranda cost US$5 per person, Bamar breakfast included.

Facing the lake access canal on the western edge of town, the friendly *Shwe Hintha Guest House* (☎ Nyaungshwe 62, 48 Strand Rd) offers a variety of rooms in a rambling converted house. Economy rooms with common hot-water shower and toilet cost

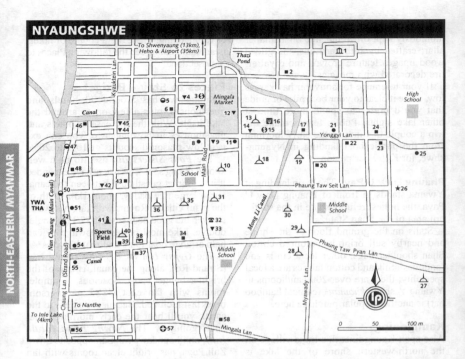

NYAUNGSHWE

PLACES TO STAY
- 2 Paradise Hotel & Restaurant
- 6 Hu Pin Hotel
- 17 Evergreen Hotel
- 20 May Guest House
- 22 Nanda Wunn Hotel
- 23 Remember Inn
- 24 Inle Inn
- 34 Mingalar Hotel
- 37 Pyi Guest House
- 39 Nawng Khan (Little Inn)
- 43 Teakwood Guest House
- 46 Joy Hotel
- 48 Shwe Hintha Guest House
- 53 Gypsy Inn
- 56 Four Sisters Inn
- 58 Primrosen Hotel

PLACES TO EAT
- 4 Hu Pin Restaurant
- 7 Shwe Inlay Bakery
- 9 Thukha Cafe

- 12 Teashop
- 14 Nam-Bya Shop
- 33 Shwe Pye Soe Restaurant
- 42 Daw Nyunt Yee Restaurant
- 44 Chow Su Ma Restaurant
- 45 Shanland Restaurant
- 49 Big Drum Restaurant

OTHER
- 1 Shan Palace Museum
- 3 Bank
- 5 Bus/pickup Stop
- 8 Comet Travel
- 10 Monastery
- 11 Longyi Shop
- 13 Stupa
- 15 Money Changer (foreign exchange)
- 16 Sri Jagdish Hindu Temple
- 18 Yangon Kyaung
- 19 Hlaing Gu Kyaung
- 21 Puppet Theatre

- 25 Township Office
- 26 Police
- 27 Nigyon Taungyon Kyaung
- 28 Monastery
- 29 Kan Gyi Kyaung
- 30 Shwe Gu Kyaung
- 31 Stupas
- 32 Telephone Office (Myanmar only; no overseas calls)
- 35 Yadana Man Aung Paya
- 36 Stupas
- 38 Post Office
- 40 Shwe Zali Paya
- 41 Independence Monument
- 47 Boat Landing
- 50 Boat Landing
- 51 Moe Ma Kha Boat Hire
- 52 MTT Office
- 54 Handicrafts
- 55 Moe Moe Boat & Bicycle
- 57 Hospital

US$5/10, while standard rooms with attached cold-water shower and toilet are US$12. All rates include breakfast. Some of the economy rooms upstairs have balconies overlooking the canal; there is also a small canal-view terrace where anyone can sit.

Further north on a narrower, quieter canal, *Joy Hotel (☎ Nyaungshwe 83)* has 12 basic, but clean, rooms in a two storey house, plus five newer rooms in an adjacent building. The cheapest rooms are in the old building and cost US$2 per person with shared bath. A few more cost US$3 per person and include bath and fan. For US$6/10, you get a larger, newer room with shared hot-water shower and toilet. And there's one huge triple with a seating area, desk, tub and closet for a flat rate of US$15. Breakfast is included. A small sitting area overlooks the canal.

The *Pyi Guest House*, in the southern part of town, three blocks east of the main canal, is a big thatched-roof building with very spartan cubicles for US$5 per person, toilet and shower outside. There is also one nicer room with attached shower for US$18. As at the Inle Inn (see Places to Stay – Mid Range), the proprietors sometimes arrange dinner shows with Shan food, music and dancing.

East of Mingala Market on a stream that runs through town is the long, two storey *Evergreen Hotel (☎ Nyaungshwe 79)*. Basic economy rooms with common toilet and hot-water shower cost US$5 per person. Slightly larger standard rooms with softer mattresses and attached hot-water shower and toilet cost US$12/20.

Places to Stay – Mid-Range

The *Primrose Hotel (Taunggyi ☎ 081-22709, 40 Mingala Lan)* is in the south part of town near the Mong Li canal. It's quiet and the service is good. Clean attractive rooms with bath, fan and fridge cost US$18/24 a single/double, including breakfast.

On the east side of town, the well run and quiet *Inle Inn (☎ Nyaungshwe 16, Taunggyi ☎ 081-21347)* is one of the oldest privately owned inns in the country. Rooms in the main building and in a new wing to the side come with attached toilet and hot-water shower for US$15/22/30 a single/double/triple, including breakfast, with *mohinga* (pronounced mounhinga, a dish of noodles, fish and eggs) available upon request. There is a pleasant garden sitting area out the back. Good food is available; a Shan dinner and puppet show is offered nightly.

The *Nanda Wunn Hotel (Taunggyi ☎ 081-22513)* is on Youngyi Lan, a few blocks east of the market in a quiet compound. Attractive duplex bungalows with hot water, fridge and TV cost US$24/30 for a single/double and US$30/36 for a similar room with a larger bed.

Places to Stay – Top End
Nyaungshwe The top end in Nyaungshwe isn't luxurious but it is comfortable enough for people who desire softer beds, service foyers and more attractive decor.

Of the few places that fit this category, the best value is *Paradise Hotel & Restaurant (Taunggyi ☎ 081-22009, 40 3rd St)*, east of the main road as you come into town and near the Shan Palace Museum. Standard bungalow-style rooms cost US$30/36 a single/double. Hot-water shower, fridge, TV and air-con are included, as well as breakfast. The staff are quite helpful with travel and air ticket arrangements.

Easily the most picturesque hotel is the 30 room *Golden Island Cottages (Taunggyi ☎ 081-23136)* run as a Pa-O collective and located on the lake near Nampan. Individual bamboo and hardwood cottages on stilts, each with a private balcony, seem to float on the lake surface. Rooms cost US$35/46 and reservations are required during the high season (November to February). The restaurant specialises in Chinese cuisine; Shan and Pa-O dishes are available upon request.

A block west of Mingala Market, the modern four storey *Hu Pin Hotel (☎ Nyaungshwe 23, ☎ Taunggyi 081-21374)* is owned by the famed nearby restaurant of the same name. Ordinary rooms with attached hot-water shower cost US$25/30, add TV and fridge for US$30/36, or pay US$45/60 for a

NORTH-EASTERN MYANMAR

larger room with bathtub, fridge and TV. All rates include breakfast at the rooftop restaurant or around the corner at the Hu Pin Restaurant. Although Hu Pin has its own generator, electric power is still erratic.

Near Kaungdaing on the north-west part of the lake, the quiet and relaxing *Royal Orchid Hotel & Restaurant (Taunggyi ☎ 081-23182)* sits about 50m from the lake bank. It offers 20 spacious bungalow rooms with private facilities and serene views. Room rates vary from US$24/30 to US$40/48, depending on room size and view.

South of Kaungdaing in the middle of the lake, *Dak Bungalows* is a small wooden resort on stilts. It's strictly for government VIPs only, but boats often stop there to enjoy the view.

Places to Eat

Vegetarians will find Inle Lake a fine place to eat because of the year-round variety of vegetables, fruits and soy products. Mingala Market is a good place to shop for local produce; there are also plenty of Shan *hkauq-sweh* (noodle soup) *vendors* at the market every morning. Another local delicacy is *maung jeut* (round, flat rice crisps).

A *teashop* on the outside, north-eastern corner of the market sells good *nam-bya* (flat bread similar to nan) with bean dip. Another *nam-bya shop* can be found next to the ruined stupa near the Evergreen Hotel.

In the centre of town near the market, the popular *Thukha Café* serves a variety of Burmese teashop snacks. On the opposite side of the street, further north, *Shwe Inlay Bakery* bakes tasty Chinese and European-inspired pastries; it's open daily from around 5 am to 6 pm.

The *Hu Pin Restaurant* is said to be Nyaungshwe's best Chinese restaurant and is also the cleanest place in town. The English menu is divided into three sections: chicken, fish and pork. The Hu Pin closes around 8 pm – late for a town that is almost completely closed by 7 pm.

On the lake near Phaung Daw U, *Inn Thar Lay Tea Shop* is really more of a Chinese restaurant and makes a nice lunch stop.

Two popular restaurants near the Joy Hotel are *Chow Su Ma Restaurant* for good Chinese, and *Shanland Restaurant* for tasty Shan cuisine. Both are reasonably priced.

For very good Bamar fare, try the cosy *Shwe Pye Soe Restaurant* near Yadana Man Aung Paya. *Daw Nyunt Yee Restaurant* near the canal on the east-west Phaungdaw Seiq Lan is a good Chinese/Bamar eatery.

At the friendly *Big Drum Restaurant*, a set of thatched A-frame shelters on the western bank of the canal opposite Shwe Hintha Guest House, a Shan dinner of fish curry, bean soup, fried peanuts, rice and maung jeut costs K400. Chinese food is also available.

For excellent Shan home-style cooking, try the *Four Sisters Inn*. The Intha family that live here serve dinner to guests by advance arrangement; there's no set charge for the meal but donations are gladly collected. Some nights the sisters dance and sing as well as cook. One of the four sisters is living in Germany now, but the remaining three, plus their brother, carry on the tradition. They also arrange canoe and motorboat trips (see Places to Stay – Budget also).

The *Chinese restaurants* are the only places in town that serve beer (and Mandalay Rum), although some smaller shops sell *ayeq hpyu* (white liquor) by the shot, which mixes well with lemon-lime soda.

Getting There & Away

Apart from flying, all the routes to the Inle Lake area are time-consuming, but there are several options to consider that can save you much time and trouble getting to the lake. First of all, there is no need to go to Taunggyi, the main town in the area and the location of the main MTT office. If you want to simply go to the lake, you'll save a couple of hours by skipping Taunggyi.

Air AM, YA and MA fly to Heho, which is 30km west of Shwenyaung, from where it's a further 11km to Nyaungshwe or 20km to Taunggyi. The airstrip at Heho is only 12.5m wide; according to AM this is the smallest ATR landing in the world. There are a couple of small restaurants situated behind the terminal.

AM provides the most comfortable and most punctual service, and has direct flights from Yangon to Heho four times weekly and flights via Mandalay on the same day (Monday, Wednesday, Friday, Saturday). YA provides very similar service on the alternate days. During the high season, you can count on at least one flight per day from Heho with either of these reliable carriers, but during other times of the year, service is often curtailed to every other day. The Yangon-Heho fare is the same on both flights: US$80. From Mandalay the fare is US$45.

For the foolhardy, MA flies from Yangon to Heho daily, except Thursday, for US$75 by F-27 (US$85 by F-28), and from Mandalay four times weekly for US$35 by F-27 (US$40 by F-28). MA's F-27s (or what's left of them) have been involved in nine fatal crashes since 1989, so avoid them.

From Heho, each airline flies daily to Bagan with a stopover in Mandalay. Aboard AM or YA, a ticket for this leg costs US$80; on MA it's US$70.

Taxis from Heho to Nyaungshwe cost US$13 to US$15. If you wait for a pickup, you can get a ride as far as the Shwenyaung junction for K200; from Shwenyaung, another pickup goes to Nyaungshwe for K40. If you're continuing to Taunggyi, it's K60 straight through.

Bus, Pickup & Car By road, most people travel to Inle Lake from Bagan, Thazi or Mandalay. Around January the trip over the mountains from the plains to Inle Lake can be very cold in an open truck – make sure you have some warm clothes.

You can hire a private taxi from Nyaungshwe to Bagan for around US$40. Inquire at Comet Travel at 27 Youngyi Lan (south-west of the market), or at one of the hotels.

Thazi & Meiktila The road between Thazi and Taunggyi has improved considerably over the last few years, but it's still a stiff ride of around six hours by public transport, five hours if you have your own vehicle.

The fare for the better Thazi-Taunggyi trucks varies from K200 to K350, depending on the type of vehicle and number of passengers. The less expensive trucks don't leave till there are passengers hanging off every protrusion on the truck; the better trucks have more leg room and fewer passengers. Most trucks depart from either town at 9 and 11 am. If you're heading for Inle Lake, get off at the Shwenyaung junction and catch one of the frequent pickups (from 6 am to 6 pm only) to Nyaungshwe, which is 11km south, for K60. Share taxis do the same trip for K200 per person.

There are also a couple of trucks per day between Shwenyaung and Meiktila for K300.

The staging area for most public transport to/from Nyaungshwe is the street that runs south of the Hu Pin Hotel, one block west of Mingala Market.

Mandalay Pickups between Mandalay and the lake area cost around K600 to K700 per person, depending on the company; all leave between 4 and 6 am and arrive at the other end in 10 to 12 hours. Two of the more reliable express bus companies, Tiger Head (Kya Hkaung) and Lion King (Chinthe Min), depart for Taunggyi at 5 am. The cost is K1500. Both companies also do central district pickups near the north-east corner of 82nd and 23rd Sts in Mandalay. As usual, go to Shwenyaung and catch a public pickup to Nyaungshwe for K60.

Most hotels and guesthouses in Nyaungshwe can help make bus reservations, so you can be picked up at the Shwenyaung junction when the bus from Taunggyi comes through. Comet Travel, near Mingala Market, is very good at arranging Shwenyaung junction bus connections, as well as handling flight reservations.

Bagan Generally, an overland trip from Bagan entails getting to Meiktila or Thazi, then changing to a Nyaungshwe, Shwenyaung or Taunggyi-bound bus or pickup. See the Bagan chapter for more information.

Tiger Head Express operates a bus from Bagan Myothit (New Bagan) to Taunggyi for K1500 that leaves at 4 am; as usual, get off at Shwenyaung and continue to Nyaungshwe by public pickup for K60.

Taunggyi A pickup to Taunggyi costs K50. See Getting There & Away in the following Taunggyi section for more information.

Yangon Several companies run buses between Yangon and Taunggyi; see the following Taunggyi Getting There & Away section for details. Two Yangon-bound buses stop briefly in Shwenyaung at around 1 pm daily. Shan Mintha Express costs K1800, and Eastern State Express costs K1600. Both arrive the next morning at Yangon's Highway bus station.

TAUNGGYI

At 1430m, the pine-clad hill station of Taunggyi provides a cool break from the heat of the plains. There are some pleasant walks if you're in the mood, but basically it's a growing trade centre for the southwestern area of Shan State.

Taunggyi is the official end of the line for eastern-bound foreigners in Myanmar – at least for those travelling by road. Beyond Taunggyi lies a world of black-marketeers, ruby miners, insurgent armies and opium and methamphetamine warlords. The town was once a place of respite for the perspiring British, although all that remains of the colonial era is an overgrown graveyard, a stone church, a line of cherry trees and a handful of timbered cottages, all on the fringes of town. The main street is strictly 'socialist realism', with signs done in raised concrete letters, just like China (Myanmar's current benefactor).

Because it functions as a conduit for smuggled goods from Thailand, China and India, and a base for trips to the Maing Shu (Mong Hsu) gem tract to the east, this is one of Myanmar's most prosperous and enterprising towns. Long-haired smugglers in army fatigues saunter down the street alongside turbaned hill tribe people and sleek-suited Chinese businesspeople. An abundance of black-market consumer goods is dis-

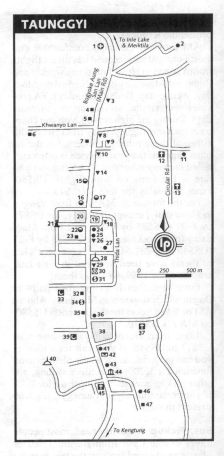

TAUNGGYI

played in the Taunggyi market, which is located at the edge of a Chinese enclave, whose residents include many illegal immigrants. The remainder of the population of 100,000 people includes tribespeople, Shan, Bamar, Sikhs, Punjabis and retired Gurkhas, who once fought for the British. Along Taunggyi's main streets you'll see various temples, mosques and churches.

There's a fairly ordinary temple on the hill, with views over the plains, Inle Lake and Taunggyi, and the walk itself is pleasant.

TAUNGGYI

PLACES TO STAY		OTHER			
4	Hotel Heart Hom	1	Hospital	28	Myoe Le Dhamma
5	Eastern Hotel	2	Gem Market		Yon Paya
6	Paradise Hotel	11	Myanma Airways	30	Sikh Temple
7	Khemarat Guest House	12	St George Church	31	Myanmar Economic Bank
23	May Khu Guest House	13	First Union Baptist Church		(MEB) (foreign exchange)
32	Saween Hotel	15	Eastern State	33	Mosque
35	Maw Thi Ri Guest House		Express Bus	34	Mayflower Bank (foreign
47	Taunggyi Hotel	16	Taxis, pickups to Inle		exchange)
		17	Buses to Yangon,	36	Yangon Airways
PLACES TO EAT			Mandalay, Bagan	37	St Joseph Catholic Church
3	Maxim's Restaurant	19	Old Market	38	Bogyoke Park
8	Coca Cola Restaurant	20	New Market	39	Mosque
9	Maw Kan Restaurant	21	Clock Tower	40	Yat Taw Me Paya
10	Shan Noocles (Burmese sign)	22	Taxis, Pickups &	41	YMCA
14	Sein (Diamond) Restaurant		Local Buses	42	Post & Telephone Office
18	Htun Restaurant	24	Asian Light Supermarket	43	Shan State Library
26	Lyan Yu Hotel Restaurant	25	Myoma Cinema	44	Shan State Museum
29	Brother Hotel Restaurant	27	Cheroot Factory	45	St George Anglican Church
				46	Township Offices

NORTH-EASTERN MYANMAR

Information

Find information on the street and at the MTT office (☎ 081-21303) located in the Taunggyi Hotel (see Places to Stay). At the post office near the hotel you can make long-distance calls to Yangon and other parts of Myanmar, as well as trunk calls overseas. International Direct Dial (IDD) phone service is available from the Taunggyi Hotel. The mail is said to be reliable in Taunggyi.

Special Events

In November, to coincide with the full-moon festival of Tazaungmon (also Tazaung-daing), the city hosts a hot-air, or fire balloon, festival.

Things to See & Do

Taunggyi has an interesting central market area in the centre of town where you're likely to see colourful hill tribe people – there's a daily market, plus one that comes to town every five days. From Taunggyi, the market moves to Pwehla (on the way to Pindaya), then to Kalaw on the third day, and from there (in turn) to Pindaya, Heho and back to Taunggyi. Basket making is a popular local handicraft.

There is also a daily gem market in the north-eastern part of town where jade, rubies and sapphires are bought and sold from noor to 4 pm. While it doesn't really compare with the gem markets of Mogok, the well informed may be able to ferret out a deal or two.

For those interested in the Shan State's cultures, the modest Shan State Museum and Shan State Library, near the Taunggyi Hotel, are worth a visit. Although only a relatively small number of items are labelled in English, you can look at items that include local native costume, musical instruments, ceramics and weapons. If nothing else, you may begin sorting out hill tribe names: Kaw for Akha, Tai for Shan, Jin-Phaw (Jinghpaw) for Kachin, Lahta and Yanglai for different Karen groups; and identifying kinds of dress for the 35 different ethnic groups officially recognised in the state. There's also a display of royal Shan regalia and an exhibit of religious art that includes Buddhist sculpture in Shan and Mandalay styles, Shan *jatakas* (life stories of the Buddha) paintings, *pitaka* (Buddhist scripture) chests, *kammawas* (Buddhist lacquered scriptures), *parabaik* (folding manuscripts) and ornate votive tablets.

One upstairs room is devoted to the Panglong Agreement of 1947, in which Shan,

Kachin and Chin leaders signed a document promising cooperation in the proposed Union of Burma. Admission to the museum is US$2 and English-speaking lecturers are available to lead visitors around.

The Pa-O have established a **cultural centre** near the market at 98 Merchant St. The small but well laid-out museum contains musical instruments, including a typical Pa-O accordian, banknotes and costumes.

There's a cheroot factory called **Flying Tiger Mashua** on a side street south of the Myoma cinema. The handrolling technique is impressive, and cheroot bundlers are able to bunch 50 cheroots in bundles without counting the individual cigars – they judge simply by feel.

Places to Stay

An old standby in Taunggyi, the *May Khu Guest House* (☎ 081-21431) is a rambling, dark and shabby wooden structure on Bogyoke Aung San Lan (the main road), with foreigner rates of US$2 to US$3 per person in stark two-bed rooms with common bath.

The newer, cleaner *Khemarat Guest House* (☎ 081-22464, 48 Bogyoke Aung San Lan) has economy rooms with shared bath for US$8/10 a single/double plus rooms with attached bath for US$15/20. Overall, this hotel, owned by Maing Shu gem traders, is the best value in town.

The *Paradise Hotel* (☎ 081-22009, 157 Khwanyo Lan), a few blocks west from the Khemarat, is a new four storey (no elevator), modern Chinese-style place. Well appointed but noisy rooms with good mattresses, hot-water showers, polished wood floors and TV cost US$24/30. Slightly nicer rooms with fridge cost US$36/42. There are plush sitting rooms at the end of each floor.

The *Salween Hotel* (☎ 081-22605, 289 Bogyoke Aung San Lan) is similar in price and quality.

The privatised and somewhat efficient 56 room *Taunggyi Hotel* (☎ 081-21127) sprawls over landscaped grounds near the southern end of town. Spacious rooms with attached hot-water bath cost US$30 to US$40. The old Ministry of Hotels & Tourism (MHT)-

style bar and restaurant attract a mix of well-heeled businesspeople and military types. Perched on a hillside, the hotel is a short stroll from the town centre and is one of the more comfortable older hotels in Myanmar.

The other places in Taunggyi are all quite central and fairly similar – small and basic. The *Maw Thi Ri Guest House*, at 134 Bogyoke Lan, is an old standby, but is currently off-limits to foreigners. Two new hotels that have applied for foreign licenses are the *Eastern Hotel* (☎ 081-22243, 27A Bogyoke Aung San Lan) and the *Hotel Heart Hom* (☎ 081-22604, 9(4) Bogyoke Aung San Lan). Prices should be in the US$20 to US$30 range.

Places to Eat

A row of small *food stalls* in the market serve decent Chinese and Shan dishes. Very little English is spoken here, however, so brush up on your Burmese and/or point-to-order technique. The unassuming *Maw Kan Restaurant* (also known as Maokham) serves very good Shan and Chinese fare from 10 am to 8 pm; walk east from the main street down the road near the Shwe Innlay Guest House, make an immediate left and it's the unmarked wooden building on the right (Burmese sign).

Maxim's Restaurant, on the way out of town toward Inle, serves decent Chinese and European dishes, though it's on the expensive side. On Bogyoke Aung San Lan, in the same area, the *Coca-Cola Restaurant* has an all-Chinese menu; it's nothing great, but it's popular.

The *Lyan Yu Hotel Restaurant* prepares good noodle dishes, and also shows them off in a picturesque window display. Sometimes Australian wine is available for around K600 per bottle. A block south is the *Brother Hotel Restaurant*, which serves decent Chinese meals.

Two Bamar/Shan restaurants are worth checking out. *Sein (Diamond) Restaurant* (Burmese sign) is on the main road, north of the market, and a favourite for out-of-town Shan visitors. Equally popular with the Shan crowd is *Htun Restaurant*, behind the old

Smokin'

Kipling immortalised the Burmese cheroot with his poem dedicated to a 'Burma girl a-settin' … a-smokin' of a whackin' white cheroot'. Such large *cheroots* (originally from the Tamil *curuttu*, meaning roll, and later the Hindi-Urdu *charut* meaning cigar/cigarette), wrapped in the paper-thin bark of the betel palm *(kun-thi-hpeq-hse-leiq)*, are very rarely seen nowadays, but their smaller green cousins are more commonly smoked than regular cigarettes in Myanmar. This mild *hse-baw-leiq* – similar to the Indian *bidi* but about twice the size – contains a mixture of Virginia-style tobacco leaves and stems that may have been sweetened with tamarind pulp and jaggery before drying and shredding, along with a sprinkling of wood chips to mellow the smoke and enhance steady burning. The narrow end of the gently cone-shaped hse-baw-leiq holds a filter made of corn husks wrapped tightly in newspaper pages (adding new meaning to the *New Light of Myanmar*).

Tobacco is cultivated in Myanmar's dry central plains, particularly in the sandy soils around Pakokku and Myingyan. Planters sow tobacco seeds in September, and the plants are harvested and sun-dried in March. The outer wrapper of the modern cheroot, a large leaf called *thanaq-hpeq* that grows well on the mountain slopes of the Shan State, is one of the main cash crops for the Pa-O and Palaung ethnic groups. In lowland Myanmar, rural women still occasionally wrap market tobacco in a white maize husk that resembles the betel-bark wrapper of a hundred years ago. But for most of the country, the slim thanaq hpeq-wrapped hse-baw-leiq is the norm.

In Taunggyi, widely regarded as the source of Myanmar's finest smokes, a hse-baw-leiq factory will employ up to 100 women, each of whom may hand-roll up to 1000 cheroots per day. Elsewhere in the Shan State, women take in the raw ingredients – tobacco, wrappers, labels, filters and glue – and roll a few 50-cheroot bundles in their spare time. Although the hse-baw-leiq remains the predominant nicotine delivery device in Myanmar, the more expensive western-style cigarette is rapidly becoming a status symbol, particularly for young men. Smoking Marlboro, 555 or Benson & Hedges cigarettes at K300 per packet signifies wealth and an imagined cosmopolitanism. Many urbanites can afford only Chinese or Burmese brands, such as Polo Nine, London or Duya, which sell for less than K100 per pack. Even at these prices, Burmese smokers typically buy only one cigarette at a time or, if feeling flush, a *hse-leiq tabwe* (bowl) of five cigarettes.

Vicky Bowman

---

market in the middle of town. Just south of the Khemarat Guest House is a very good *Shan noodle shop* (Burmese sign).

Between the Sikh temple and the cinema on the main road are a number of decent *teashops* and *small eateries* that specialise in an extensive variety of pastries and tea snacks, including basic *dan bauk* (biryani).

Getting There & Away

Air There are daily flights from Yangon, Bagan and Mandalay to Heho, 35km west

of Taunggyi. A taxi to Taunggyi costs around US$10 or the kyat equivalent.

Bus & Pickup Public pickup trucks to Taunggyi from Inle Lake charge K60 and leave frequently from the Nyaungshwe market area between 7 am and 5 pm for the 45 minute trip. A taxi along the same route costs around US$10 or kyat equivalent.

There's one pickup per day from Taunggyi to Pindaya at 2 pm, arriving at 5.30 pm and costing K150 to K200. There are frequent pickups to Pindaya from the Shwenyaung junction, starting at 6 am.

From Mandalay, pickups cost K600 to K700 per person and take seven or eight hours to reach Taunggyi. A minibus from Bagan costs K1300, a Tiger Head pickup costs K1000.

Several buses depart for Yangon around noon from a point near the Taunggyi market. Eastern State Express (K1600) and Shan Mintha Express (K1800) are reliable and fairy comfortable, arriving in Yangon around 6 am the next morning. Tickets can be bought in the office on the main road, near the Sun Minn Hotel.

HOPONG

Although few foreigners have seen it, the valley around Hopong, just 20km east of Taunggyi, is the start of a beautiful stretch of forested hills that continue more or less all the way to Kengtung in the extreme eastern end of Shan State.

From Hopong, a decent sealed road leads 155km south to Loikaw, the capital of Kayah State. Wanyin, 65km south of Hopong and surrounded by 2400m peaks, is a centre for the Taungthu and Padaung people, who outnumber the Shan by two to one in this area.

Hopong is officially closed to foreigners, and anyone tempted to make the day trip from Taunggyi will be turned away at army checkpoints. Along the way, the hills are dotted with Shan-style stupas, and in Hopong itself there's an interesting paya trimmed with hundreds of bells and chimes.

Around 16km east of Taunggyi and equally off-limits, a spring-fed pool is a popular local spot for picnicking and swimming.

KENGTUNG (KYAINGTONG)

Tucked away in a far eastern corner of the Shan State, 456km north-east of Taunggyi, 163km north of the border town of Tachileik (opposite Mae Sai, Thailand) and 787m above sea level, is Kengtung, the sleepy but historic centre for the state's Khün culture, surrounded by Wa, Shan, Akha and Lahu villages. Built around a small lake, and dotted with ageing Buddhist temples and crum-

bling British colonial architecture, Kengtung is probably the most scenic town in the Shan State.

Its opening to foreign visitors in January 1993 came as a complete surprise considering this was – and still is – one the most remote inhabited mountain valleys in Myanmar. Access is difficult and restricted to YA flights from Myanmar's interior or a rough overland road trip from Tachileik/Mae Sai. It is also a strategic Myanmar government stronghold in the middle of the shifting seas of Shan and Wa insurgency and the opium trade. Its position is doubly strategic considering the area is a crossroads with outlets in four different countries – Myanmar, China, Thailand and Laos. As such, it is a critical linchpin in the country's defence. During WWII the town was occupied by Japanese and Thai soldiers because it was 160km equidistant from three international borders.

Although Kengtung lies about mid-way between the Thanlwin and Mekong river valleys, it is more or less cut off from the former by a series of north-south mountain ranges. Hence, culturally, the area has more of an affinity for the nearby cultures of the Mekong – Laos, Xishuangbanna (southeastern Yunnan Province) and Thailand – than for the Shan and Bamar cultures west of the Thanlwin.

The Khün speak a Northern Thai language related to Shan and Thai Lü and use a writing script similar to the ancient Lanna script of Chiang Mai in northern Thailand. The original Khün people are said to have been 13th-century migrants from Chiang Mai, and their rulers claim to be descendants of the Lanna (or Lan Na Thai, for Million Thai Rice-Fields) dynasty.

Before the Khün began paying tribute to the Bamar under King Anawrahta, they had their own independent kingdom, variously called Muang Tamilap, Muang Ong Puu, Muang Sanlawachilakam, Muang Khemmaratungkburi (or Khemarattha, as *khema* means blissful in Pali and *rattha* means state, or country) and Tungkalasi before settling on Kengtung, which means Walled City of Tung. Tung is a reference to the kingdom's mythical founder, a hermit named Tungka-lasi, who used his magic staff to draw two channels to drain a lake of near-sea proportions, leaving behind the current town lake and the Nam Lap and Nam Khon streams. Remains of the original city walls and gates can still be seen. Today the Thais know the city as Chiang Tung, while in Burmese it is Kyaingtong.

Traditional Khün dress consists of a horizontally striped longyi and Shan-style jacket with a crossover front that ties on the side. Nowadays most Khün dress similarly to their counterparts in neighbouring countries. About 80% of the township population of 180,000 people are Khün; roughly 15% are Shan-Chinese and the remainder is a mix of other ethnicities from around the Shan State and beyond. About half the population is Buddhist, another 17% Christian and the rest belong to various spirit cults.

About 70% of all foreign visitors to Kengtung are Thais seeking a glimpse of ancient Lanna. Few westerners are seen around town, save for contract employees working for the United Nations Drug Control Project (UNDCP), whose sizeable expenditures lead many of the locals to believe all western arrivals are similarly rich.

Crossing the Border from Mae Sai

Foreigners are ordinarily permitted to cross the bridge over the Sai River into Tachileik, and to continue by air or road the 163km to Kengtung for two weeks, upon payment of a US$18 fee and the exchange of US$100 for 100 foreign exchange certificates (FECs), the phony money Myanmar's government uses to dampen black-market currency exchange. You can use the FEC to pay for hotel rooms and plane tickets, but that's about all – or change them for kyat at the going black-market rate. Your two week tourist visa can be extended for up to two months (two weeks at a time) at a cost of US$36 at the immigration office in Kengtung.

In May 1994 Khun Sa's Mong Tai Army (MTA) bombed the Tachileik dike, draining the reservoir that supplied the town with water. The border was closed to foreigners for several weeks, then reopened, but other incidents in April 1995 closed the border. Although Khun Sa did a deal with the SPDC in 1996, the Shan State Army continues to be active near the border, and there are also skirmishes between the drug trafficking United Wa State Army (UWSA), the Shan State Army (SSA) and Thai forces.

Hence, if you're contemplating an overland trip to Kengtung from Thailand, you'll simply have to take your chances on finding the border crossing open or closed – more often than not it has been open.

Foreigners are not at direct risk from the fighting, although the possibility of getting caught in the crossfire somewhere along the road between Tachileik and Kengtung can't be ruled out. Kengtung itself seems relatively safe; the MTA hasn't attacked the town since the 1980s. See the Tachileik section later in this chapter for more information on border crossings.

Things to See & Do

When the British settled into Kengtung, they centred the town around a large, natural lake. Decaying colonial-style buildings, taken over by the Burmese government or by squatters, are reminiscent of British colonial provincial architecture found elsewhere in Myanmar and India. The faded colonial air, along with the pagoda spires of over 30 local temples, the surrounding green hills and narrow, winding streets combine to create something of a Burmese counterpart to Luang Prabang (Laos).

Kengtung's many well-kept monasteries – called *wats* rather than kyaungs by the Khün – reflect Shan, Siamese, Burmese and Chinese influences.

The most impressive is **Wat Jong Kham (Zom Kham)**, which features a tall gilded zedi topped by a gold hti inlaid with silver, rubies, diamonds, sapphires and jade, and hung with tiny gold bells. The interior walls bear older gold-leaf-on-lacquer jatakas, as well as modern painted jatakas, sparkling mirrored pillars and a dozen or so Buddha images on an altar draped with gilded cloth.

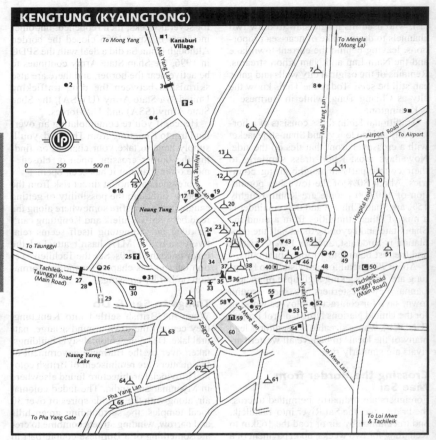

KENGTUNG (KYAINGTONG)

Much intricate tinwork outlines the gables and plinths of the temple. Legend says Jong Kham dates to a visit by Gautama Buddha and that the zedi contains six strands of his hair. Most likely the site dates to the 13th century Chiang Mai migration. The temple was substantially renovated in 1906 and 1936, when the height of the stupa rose to 38m. The zedi was regilded in 1988 and 1989. Wat Jong Kham is located north of the town centre.

Right in the centre of town are a couple

of busy and visually striking 19th-century temples, **Wat Pha Jao Lung** (which gets its Burmese name Maha Myat Muni from a 1920 replica of the Mandalay Maha Myat Muni image) and **Wat Ho Kong**.

On a hill to the south of town, **Wat Pha That Jom Mon** features an older wood-and-plaster sanctuary with good tinwork. Further up the hill behind the monastery are some very tall dipterocarp trees and two picturesque white stupas. The surrounding hillside provides good views of the town below.

KENGTUNG (KYAINGTONG)

PLACES TO STAY	10	Wat Naung Kham	35	Independence Monument
1 Harry's Guest House &	11	Mangala Kyaung	37	Maung Ming Kyaung
Trekking		(Wat Tamawtaya)	38	Maung Mai Kyaung
9 Win Guest House	12	Wat Jong Kham	39	Kengtung Cinema
18 Noi Yee Hotel		(Zom Kham)	40	Tomb of Princes
24 Kyaingtong Hotel	13	Wat In	41	Wat Chiang Jan
36 Barami Motel	14	Wat Noi Naw		(Keng San)
44 Kyi Lin Star Guest House	15	Wat Chiang Ing (Keng Ing)	42	Tai Khun Silverworks
54 Hsam Yweat Guest House	16	Jail	45	Wat Ho Kat
	19	Immigration Office	47	Buses to Tachileik
PLACES TO EAT	20	Wat Chiang Ying	48	Paleng Gate
17 Keng House Restaurant		(Keng Yun)	49	Hospital
43 Tai Khun Restaurant	21	Wat Pha Jao Lung	50	Mosque
46 Golden Banyan		(Maha Myat Muni)	51	Wat Jom Mai
Restaurant	22	Wat Ho Kong	52	Chinese Clan House
55 Lauo Tien Lu	23	Wat Pha Kaew	53	Regional Offices
Restaurant	25	St Mary's Convent	56	Khemarat Cinema
58 Honey Teashop	26	Buses to Taunggyi	57	Thai Flying Service
	27	Yang Kham Gate	59	Town Hall
OTHER	28	Water Buffalo Market	60	Central Market
2 Chinese School	29	Roman Catholic Mission &	61	Wat Pha That Jom Mon
3 Naung Pha Gate		Immaculate Heart Cathedral	62	Wat Tuya
4 UNDCP Office	30	Fax & Telegram Office	63	Wat Chiang Khom
5 American Baptist Church	31	Myanma Airways		(Keng Khom)
6 Wat Kae Min	32	Wat Asok	64	Wat Si Naw
7 Wat Yang Kon	33	Police	65	Wat Mahabodhi Vipassana
8 Pottery Works	34	Sports Field		(Kamathan Kyaung)

In the same area is the modest **Wat Mahabodhi Vipassana**, a forest-style monastery where monks practice intensive meditation.

On the road leading west out of town toward Taunggyi, the British-era **Roman Catholic Mission** (RCM) and the 12-year-old **Immaculate Heart Cathedral** are still thriving on a hillside where the original town was founded 1000 years ago. Visitors are welcome. The mission cares for nearly 100 orphaned boys, many from Shan State hill tribes.

One of the great sights in Kengtung is the large **Haw Sao Pha Kengtung**, considered the most outstanding example of Shan-style palace architecture in Myanmar. The stucco-and-teak structure combined Buddhist temple-style pavilions with Islamic-looking domes, said to have been inspired by the suggestions of a visiting Muslim Indian prince. Despite a protest mounted by a group of monks and Khün residents who appealed to the local army commander to pre-

serve the building, the Burmese government demolished the palace in 1991 to make way for a hotel that remains unbuilt. Reportedly there are two other smaller royal residences surviving in town – **Haw Sao Pha Yong Huay** and **Haw Sai Paa Si Paw Lae**.

The **central market** draws people from all over Kengtung District, including a variety of hill tribe people. Fresh produce and household goods are the market's main emphases, but some handicrafts are also available. Look for Kengtung-style lacquerware, which, like that found in Kyaukka in the Sagaing Division, doesn't employ the polychromatic incising techniques found in Bagan, but rather two-colour lacquer-moulding reliefs.

A **water buffalo market** convenes daily on the southern side of the road to Taunggyi on the western outskirts of town; visitors are welcome to wander around and observe the negotiations. It's like touring a used-car lot, with peddlers extolling the virtues of their animals while buyers point out their flaws until finally a price is agreed upon, money changes hands and the new owners walk off leading their buffaloes by the nose.

The lake in the centre of town, **Naung Tung** (Naung is the Shan word for small lake), is a popular spot for morning and evening strolls.

Places to Stay

Blackouts are common in Kengtung, so be sure to bring along a torch. *Harry's Guest House & Trekking (☎ Kengtung 21418, 132 Mai Yang lan, Kanaburi)*, 500m north of the Naung Pha gate at the northern edge of town, has basic rooms in a large house for US$5 per person. Harry is an English-speaking Kengtung native who spent many years as a trekking guide in Chiang Mai.

The *Noi Yee Hotel (☎ Kengtung 21298, 5 Myaing Yaung Lan)*, near the centre of town, charges US$5 for economy rooms with cold-water common shower. Larger multibed rooms with mosquito nets, high ceilings, and attached hot-water bathrooms cost US$10/15 a single/double per night.

MTT tries to steer tourists toward the more expensive, government-run *Kyainge Tong Hotel*, where rooms with air-con and hot water cost US$36/42 in the A and B sections; similar rooms without air-con or hot water are US$30/36 in the C and D sections, and cheaper rooms in the E section cost US$15. The management has been known to deny the existence of the latter. At night the hotel dining room is converted into a 'taxi dancing' parlour; a Shan ensemble plays live music while male patrons dance with women dressed in traditional garb, each dance timed by a matron armed with a whistle.

The *Win Guest House*, on the road to the airport north-east of town, offers decent rooms in a modern-looking house for US$25/30, each with private toilet and cold-water shower. Although it's a bit removed from the town centre, it's quiet.

The *Hsam Yweat Guest House (☎ Kengtung 21235, 21643, 21 Kyainge Lan)* has decent rooms for US$10/15, and hopes to open another place for foreigners in the Naung Kham quarter.

Other places in town that are poised to accept foreigners, if and when they receive licences, include the *Barami Motel (☎ Kengtung 21089, 3 Loimwe Lan)* and *Kyi Lin Star Guest House*, near Paleng gate. Both plan to ask US$10 to US$15 per person.

Places to Eat

Two Chinese restaurants a few blocks southeast of the central market get more than their share of regular clientele. The longest-running and most reliable is *Lauo Tien Lu Restaurant* (also known as Lawt Tin Lu), a branch of a restaurant owned by the same family in Thailand's Chiang Khong. It's a simple open-sided restaurant with good Southern Chinese food. The second is *Golden Banyan Restaurant* (also called Shwe Nyaung Bin or Ton Pho), near Wat Chiang Jan (Keng San) and opposite Kyi Lin Star Guest House. The main feature of this restaurant is outdoor tables beneath a huge banyan tree.

On the eastern shore of Naung Tung is *Keng House Restaurant* a pleasant, open-air spot with an extensive Chinese menu; hotpot is a house speciality. *Tai Khun Restaurant*, east of Kengtung Cinema, serves authentic Shan/Khün food.

The *Honey Teashop*, next to the central market, is one of the best places in town for morning *samosas* (fried triangular-shaped pastries stuffed with vegetables) and *palata* (fried flatbread).

Getting There & Away

The road between Kengtung and Taunggyi is still firmly off-limits to foreigners. At the moment only Burmese citizens are permitted to use this road, and they travel in convoy as it is rife with robbery. Rumour has it that some bus companies accept protection money from bandits/rebels in return for allowing them to rob passengers. Fighting between the Yangon government and the Shan and Pa-O insurgents also makes the Kengtung-Taunggyi journey potentially hazardous.

The drive from Taunggyi takes two long days (sometimes four or five days in wet weather) over a narrow and winding road.

The main overnight stops are **Loilem**, **Kunhing** and **Mong Ping**, each of which has rustic guesthouses and rudimentary cafes.

Air The airport at Kengtung is subject to the occasional closure, so the information in this section is especially vulnerable. Both YA and MA fly between Tachileik and Kengtung. YA currently schedules three flights a week (Monday, Tuesday and Sunday), but you must buy a one way ticket for each segment the day before you intend to fly. MA flies once a week (usually Saturday). The cost for the 30 minute flight is US$30 with either YA or MA, though we think it's always safer to avoid MA.

Mae Sai/Tachileik The cheapest form of transport to Kengtung is the pickup truck for 60B (only baht (Thai currency) are accepted) that leaves each morning from Tachileik. Lately we've heard that Myanmar authorities forbid foreigners to ride the public trucks, but we know visitors have done it.

You can rent pickups on either side of the border, but Thai vehicles with a capacity of five or fewer passengers are charged a flat US$50 customs fee; it's US$100 for vehicles with a capacity of over five. The nearest car rental agencies on the Thai side are in Chiang Rai; some agencies won't allow their cars to be taken into Myanmar, while others require a substantial deposit.

Car rental is more expensive (about 2000B or US$80) and requires the use of a driver, although of course you save on the customs fee. Whatever form of transport you use, count on at least six to 10 gruelling hours to cover the twisting, pot-holed and rutted stretch of road between the border and Kengtung. Until this road is sealed, it should be avoided during the monsoon season (June to September).

The unsealed road passes through steep narrow river valleys and past numerous Akha, Wa and Shan villages. Along the way the main rest stops are **Talay**, a small town with interesting Shan temples and an army post, and **Mong Hpayak**, the most popular food stop.

The road is being slowly improved and reportedly will eventually be sealed all the way to the Chinese border 100km beyond Kengtung.

AROUND KENGTUNG
Hot Springs
Just south of town on the road to Tachileik is a large public hot springs spa. Entry to one of the gender-segregated bathhouses costs K25 per person. Shampoo and soap are available for sale, so this is a great spot to clean up if you're staying at one of the cold-water guesthouses in town during the cool season. Vendors on the grounds sell noodles and other snacks, so you could easily spend an entire afternoon here. The spa is busiest on weekends.

Hiking
Hiking to nearby Lahu (Musoe), Akha (Kaw), Shan and Wa villages is permitted in the company of a licensed guide, available at the Kyainge Tong Hotel or Harry's Guest House & Trekking for around US$5 a day per person (see Places to Stay in the previous Kentung section for details). The private Khemarat Tour Guide Centre at 14 Zaydangyi Lan, just south of the traffic circle and Wat Pha Jao Long in Kentung, can also provide guides. Overnighting in the villages is not officially permitted.

Yang Kong
On the northern outskirts of town in the village of Yang Kong, on the road to Mong Ma, you can visit pottery works where roof tiles, utilitarian bowls and other ceramic items are made.

Loi-mwe
Although it lies a little outside the permitted radius, no one seems to care if you visit Loi-mwe, 33km south-east of Kengtung. Located at over 1600m, this 'hill station' features a number of old colonial buildings and a century-old Catholic church. The main attraction, though, is the scenery on the ascent to Loi-mwe, which passes through forests, terraced rice fields and a lake. You'll

NORTH-EASTERN MYANMAR

Opium, Khun Sa & The Golden Triangle

The opium poppy, *Papaver somniferum*, has been cultivated and its resins extracted for use as a narcotic since (at least) the time of the early Greek empire. The Chinese were introduced to the drug by Arab traders during the time of Kublai Khan (1279-94). It was so highly valued for its medicinal properties that hill tribe minorities in Southern China began cultivating the opium poppy in order to raise money to pay taxes to their Han Chinese rulers. Easy to grow, opium became a way for the nomadic hill tribes to raise what cash they needed in transactions – willing and unwilling – with the lowland world.

Many of the hill tribes that migrated to Myanmar in the post-WWII era, in order to avoid persecution in China, took with them their one cash crop – the poppy. The poppy is well suited to hillside cultivation as it flourishes on steep slopes and in nutrient-poor soils. However, large tracts of land are needed for the crop; it takes the sap of 3000 poppies to produce one *joi* (1.6kg), the standard unit of weight in the opium trade.

For many hill tribes, opium plays an important role in traditional medicine. Among some ethnic groups, such as the Lolo, raw opium sap (which in small amounts is nonintoxicating) is also a significant element of their daily food intake. In the lowlands, opium poppyseeds are the main flavouring in *bei moq* (opium cake).

Because of all the money earned via opium trafficking in the region where Myanmar, Laos and Thailand meet, the area has been dubbed 'the Golden Triangle'. The term might more accurately be expanded to 'the Golden Quadrangle', in order to include South-Western China, a major location for the refining and smuggling of illicit opiates.

One of the region's most colourful figures is Khun Sa (also known as Chang Chi-Fu, or Sao Mong Khawn) a half-Chinese, half-Shan opium warlord. Born in Lashio District in 1934, Khun Sa started out in the 1950s and 1960s working for the Kuomintang (KMT) – Chiang Kai Shek's nationalist Chinese troops who had fled to Myanmar. The KMT were continuing military operations against the Chinese communists along the Myanmar-China border, financed by the smuggling of opium (with CIA protection). They employed Khun Sa as one of their prime local supporters/advisors. Khun Sa broke with the KMT in the early 1960s, after establishing his own opium-smuggling business, with heroin refineries located in Northern Thailand.

From that time forward, the history of heroin smuggling in the Golden Triangle was intertwined with the exploits of Khun Sa. In 1966 the Burmese government deputised Khun Sa as head of 'village defence forces' against the Burmese Communist Party (BCP), which was at maximum strength at this time and fully involved in opium trade. Khun Sa cleverly used his government backing to consolidate power and build up his own militia, by developing the Shan United Army (SUA), an antigovernment insurgent group heavily involved in opium throughout the Golden Triangle, in competition with the BCP and KMT.

Beginning in the late 1970s, Khun Sa's armies continued to buy opium from the Shan, Kokang, Wa and hill tribe cultivators in Myanmar, Laos and Thailand, transporting and selling the product to Yunnanese-operated heroin refineries in China, Laos and Thailand, who in turn sold to ethnic Chinese syndicates who control access to world markets via Thailand and Yunnan.

Turning points in Khun Sa's fortunes occurred in 1982 and 1983 when the Thais launched a full-scale attack on his Ban Hin Taek stronghold, forcing him to flee to the mountains of the Kok River valley, across the border in Ho Mong, Myanmar, where he directed his independent

Opium, Khun Sa & The Golden Triangle

empire from a fortified network of underground tunnels. This move led to the fragmentation of opium and heroin production in much of North-Western Thailand.

The SUA merged with several other Shan armies to form the Mong Tai Army (MTA), led by the Shan State Restoration Council. The MTA reached an estimated strength of 25,000, the largest and best-equipped ethnic army in Myanmar – before Khun Sa's surprise surrender to Yangon on 1 January 1996.

Khun Sa's retirement, first to an island off the coast of Myanmar and more recently to a villa in Yangon, smacks of collusion with the Yangon-based military. He reportedly made a deal with the government to give up drug trafficking in exchange for the right to pursue legal businesses in road construction and transport. However, members of his family remain in Laos and along the Thai border, and it's widely believed that his links with the drug trade remain. In Yangon it is rumoured that Khun Sa's Yangon-Taunggyi bus line transports more than passengers and luggage. The US government has offered a US$2 million reward for information leading to his capture and conviction in the USA. The Myanmar government refuses to extradite him.

Meanwhile, the 20,000-strong United Wa State Army (UWSA) has entered the vacuum left by Khun Sa's departure and a weakening MTA. For years, the Wa had fought Khun Sa's forces for control of heroin and opium smuggling routes in the eastern and northern Shan State – first as foot soldiers for the BCP and then, following their 1989 truce with the Myanmar government, as Yangon surrogates. The UWSA have expanded their wares to include methamphetamine, produced in jungle refineries primarily for the Chinese and Thai markets. As many as 10 speed factories controlled by the Wa are thought to exist within a 10km radius of Tachileik.

As for opium, production has dipped in recent years, from a peak of 2300 tonnes in 1997 to 1990 tonnes in 1998, thanks to a drought, as well as the relatively greater profitability of speed production. Despite the clear decline, Myanmar remains the world's largest opium and heroin producer.

Meanwhile, power shifts from warlord to warlord, while the hill tribe and Shan cultivators continue as unwilling pawns in the opium-heroin cycle. The planting of the poppy and the sale of its collected resins has never been a simple moral issue. Cultivators who have been farming poppies for centuries, and heroin addicts who consume the end product, have both been exploited by governments and crime syndicates, who trade in opium for the advancement of their own interests. Because of the complexities involved, opium production in the Golden Triangle must be dealt with as a political, social, cultural and economic problem, and not simply as a conventional law enforcement matter.

There is an end of joy and sorrow
Peace all day long, all night, all morrow
But never a time to laugh or weep.
Their end is more than joy or anguish,
Than lives that laugh or lives that languish,
The end of all the poppied sleep.
Charles Swinburne (1837-1909)

Joe Cummings

ire a car or motorcycle as there
eem to be any regular public trans-
po..   veen Kengtung and Loi-mwe.

Mengla

Eighty-five kilometres north of Kengtung
lies the border district of Mengla (or Mong
La as it's sometimes spelt). Although Mengla is mainly a Thai Lü district, in a deal
worked out with the Myanmar military, it's
currently controlled by ethnic Wa, who once
fought against Yangon troops but now enjoy
peaceful relations with Yangon (in return
for a sizeable share in the Wa's thriving
opium trade, it is suspected). The district receives lots of Chinese tourists, who come to
peruse Mengla's well known wildlife market and to gamble in the district's several
casinos. The largest and plushest, the Myanmar Royal Casino, is an Australian-Chinese
joint venture. Inside are the usual Chinese
and western games of chance with the setup
typically seen in Macau, the Genting Highlands (Malaysia) and on cruise ships in the
South China Sea. There are also plenty of
karaoke, discos (including a thriving gay
and transvestite scene) and other staples of
modern Chinese entertainment life. The
main currency used in town is Chinese
yuan. Many of the payas in Mengla have
been built in the past 10 years as part of the
SPDC's drive to convert the border areas to
Buddhism. In 1997 a Drug Eradication Museum was opened by U Sai Lin, a local
Wa/Chinese drug-trafficker turned establishment figure and head of the Eastern
Shan State Army (ESSA), who declared, to
widespread disbelief, that the area around
Mengla was henceforth an 'opium-free
zone'. As in much of the Shan State, AIDS
is a serious problem.

When you pass through the southern gate
into Wa territory, a charge of 80 yuan is collected for each four wheeled vehicle, 10
yuan for a motorcycle, plus five yuan per
person. Rooms at the *Mengla Hotel* are
available for 270 yuan (about US$32), an
astounding figure given the fact the hotel
doesn't have running water. You can also
stay with the district headman in his Thai

Lü-style house for around 30 yuan – a much
better deal and a more interesting experience.

In order to proceed to Mengla from Kengtung, you must first register at the Kengtung
immigration office. The staff at the Noi Yee
Hotel or Harry's Guest House & Trekking
can help you accomplish this.

The obvious question is, can you cross the
border from Mengla into Daluo, China? The
simple answer is we haven't tried, and we
don't know anyone else who has done it at
the time of writing. But it seems reasonable
that if you have a valid China visa in your
passport, there should be no legal impedi-
ment to doing so – unless Myanmar immigration officials won't allow it. However,
leaving Myanmar from Tachileik, if you have
arrived from Yangon, is expressly forbidden.

Crossing the Border to Laos

About 19km north-east of Tachileik on the
Tachileik-Kengtung road, a smaller road
branches off from Nam Manyang and heads
east-south-east to the Mekong River, the
border between Laos and Myanmar. At the
small town here, Wan Pasak, you can get a
boat across the river to Xieng Kok in Laos.
From Xieng Kok there's a dirt road north-
east of Muang Sing in Laos, which connects
with roads to Luang Nam Tha and Udomxai.
You *might* be permitted to cross into Laos
here if you already possess a valid Lao visa.
Then again you might not! Much depends
on the local political situation, obviously, as
well as the mood of local officials. It is not
a legal international border crossing, yet
plenty of Burmese and Lao do use the crossing. Sooner or later, however, this could become an official crossing for all nationalities.

TACHILEIK

Most travellers head straight for Kengtung
to the north rather than linger at the border,
but it's also possible to arrange a one day
pass for Tachileik. Besides shopping for
Shan handicrafts (about the same price as
on the Thai side, and everyone accepts baht)
and eating Shan/Bamar food, there's little to
do in Tachileik. About 3000 to 4000 people
cross the bridge to Tachileik daily, most of

them Thais who shop for dried mushrooms, herbal medicines, cigarettes and other cheap imports from China.

Border Crossings

A day pass for Tachileik costs US$5, paid to Myanmar immigration officials at the border crossing. There is no FEC exchange requirement as there is for longer stays. If you hold a day pass, you're restricted to a radius of 5km. See the Kengtung section earlier for information on longer permits.

The Mae Sai-Tachileik border is usually open from 6 am to 6 pm weekdays, and until 9 pm on weekends and holidays. This early closing time on weekdays can be a problem if you're driving back from Kengtung, given the unpredictability of road conditions between Kengtung and Tachileik.

Should you find yourself stranded in Tachileik after the border has closed you have two choices. One option is to check in at the A-frame bungalows strung with coloured lights on the Tachileik riverbank west of the town centre, where adequate rooms facing the river cost US$8 to US$14 a night. This is the only foreigner-licensed lodging in town. Alternatively you can check in with the immigration office near the western side of the bridge on the Myanmar side, where an immigration officer will undoubtedly escort you to the bridge and show you how to climb over the border gate at the Thai end. If you have a Thai vehicle, you can leave it parked at the immigration office and pick it up the next morning; ask for a note from Myanmar immigration that will allow you back into Tachileik without obtaining a new permit.

PYIN U LWIN TO LASHIO
Gokteik Viaduct

The unusual Gokteik railway viaduct is 55km out of Pyin U Lwin, en route to Lashio. When, on behalf of the British, the Pennsylvania Steel Co built the Gokteik Bridge over the deep gorge 100 years ago, it was the second-highest railway bridge in the world. A British insurance policy expired just 20 years ago and until then the Burmese

Gokteik Viaduct

In 1899 Burma Railways solicited bids for the construction of a railway viaduct over the Gokteik gorge, a geographic obstacle that for all intents and purposes cut off North-Eastern Myanmar from the country's centre. It was an engineering problem of immense proportions for that day and age, and one that drew world attention. Pennsylvania Steel Co vied with several British engineering outfits for the project, coming in with a bid far below that of their competitors in price and scheduling and, according to a 1901 engineering magazine, with a design 'much superior to anything else submitted'.

Work on the bridge began in February 1900. The crew of Americans, British, Germans and Burmese – including 'a North Carolina negro who spoke Hindustani' – drove the last rivet in December of the same year. Considered the greatest railway viaduct in the world at the time, Gokteik was the only American-built span in the British Raj.

Joe Cummings

government didn't service it much; however, it was recently renovated. Its age shows; even today Burmese trains slow to a crawl when crossing the viaduct, in order to lessen undue stress on the structure.

If you go by train, get off at the station before the bridge to get the best view. You're not permitted to go under the bridge since there's a military camp there. In fact, you should be careful wandering around the bridge as land mines are reputed to be planted in some areas – to fend off insurgents who might want to destroy the span. You'll only have a few minutes before you must get back on the train – if you're continuing on to Hsipaw or Lashio. Be cautious with a camera; the military forbids taking pictures from the bridge.

Getting There & Away From Pyin U Lwin, catch the Mandalay-Lashio train between 7 and 8 am for the two hour journey to Gokteik; the fare is US$4 (1st class only, unless you can wrangle a kyat ticket). Or start at Mandalay aboard the 4.45 am train.

You can also go by car or bus to Gokteik via the Mandalay-Lashio road – see the Lashio section later in this chapter for details. The road itself, with a ribbon of hairpin bends descending into the gorge, is impressive, but the railway viaduct is only visible in the far distance.

Kyaukme

The market towns between Gokteik and Lashio are in many ways more interesting and atmospheric than Lashio. Unlike Lashio, which has a large Chinese and Bamar population, Kyaukme and Hsipaw are Shan-majority towns with small numbers of Chinese and Indian traders. Both towns are located on the road and rail routes between Mandalay and Lashio, the main China-Myanmar trade route. Kyaukme is also joined by road with Mogok to the northwest, so it sees a steady stream of gem traders. Several colonial-era buildings are adjacent to the bustling Kyaukme market.

Hsipaw

Hsipaw (called Thibaw in Burmese) was once the centre of a small Shan state of its own and is becoming a popular hangout for travellers, thanks to its cool climate and relaxed atmosphere.

A haw sao pha (sawbwa haw in Burmese), or Shan Palace, still stands at the northern end of Hsipaw – see it before it disappears. The last sao pha was arrested in 1962 and hasn't been heard from since. This story about vanquished royalty is the topic of *Twilight over Burma: My Life as a Shan Princess*, a recent memoir by American Inge Sargent who became the popular Mahadevi of Hsipaw in the 1950s, until the military takeover in 1962. The prince's niece and nephew take care of the palace, which was built in 1924, and welcome foreign visitors. It's a K200 trishaw ride from the clock tower in the centre of town, or about 20 minutes walk, past the old town jail.

One of the busiest religious sites in Hsipaw is **Mahamyatmuni Paya** at the southern outskirts of town. A shrine in the compound contains a large Buddha image inspired by its Mandalay namesake, Mahamuni Paya.

Eight kilometres south-west of town off the Mandalay-Lashio road is the Shan-style **Bawgyo Paya**. This is the most revered paya in northern Shan State – equivalent to Inle Lake's Phaung Daw U Paya in the southern half of the state. It is said that the sagawa tree growing by the paya bends over at the top in deference to the paya. It lost much of its charm following hamfisted renovations in 1995, but its situation by the river still gives it some appeal. The paya contains four gold Buddha images.

One of the oldest and largest Shan festivals, the Bawgyo Paya Pwe, is held here from the 10th waxing day to the first day after the full moon of Tabaung (February/March). Shan pwes traditionally served as important economic and administrative, as well as social, events since this was when the sawbwa collected taxes and reviewed the accounts of his lieutenants and subjects. The Bawgyo pwe still draws a large encampment of traders and festival-goers who pay tribute, in spirit if not in cash, to the old Shan ways. *Zat pwe* (costumed dance-drama based on jataka stories) is performed nightly. Before dawn on the full moon day, hundreds of Palaung pilgrims who come from miles around offer rice to the images. Although the government has officially clamped down on the gambling that used to be the sawbwa's big money earner, you may be able to find a dice game of 36 animals, which is still sceretly played in parts of Shan State.

On a hill to the left, just as you enter the city limits of Hsipaw from Bawgyo, is the overgrown and ruined mausoleum of the sawbwas of Hsipaw.

Hsipaw's large **market** is best in the morning when Shan and other tribal people from nearby villages come to trade. The Dokhtawady River (also called the Myitngeh

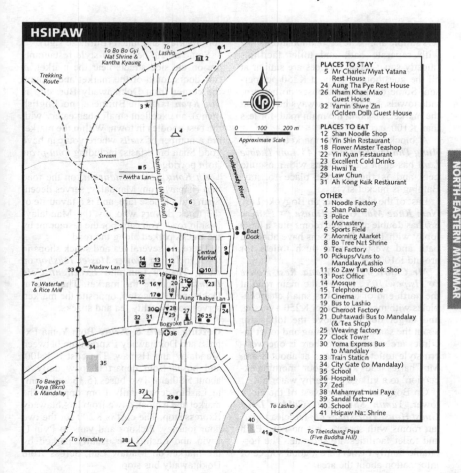

HSIPAW

PLACES TO STAY
5 Mr Charles/Myat Yatana Rest House
24 Aung Tha Pye Rest House
26 Nham Khae Mao Guest House
32 Yamin Shwe Zin (Golden Doll) Guest House

PLACES TO EAT
12 Shan Noodle Shop
16 Yin Shin Restaurant
18 Flower Master Teashop
22 Yin Kyan Restaurant
23 Excellent Cold Drinks
28 Hwai Ta
29 Law Chun
31 Ah Kong Kaik Restaurant

OTHER
1 Noodle Factory
2 Shan Palace
3 Police
4 Monastery
6 Sports Field
7 Morning Market
8 Bo Tree Nat Shrine
9 Tea Factory
10 Pickups/Vans to Mandalay/Lashio
11 Ko Zaw Tun Book Shop
13 Post Office
14 Mosque
15 Telephone Office
17 Cinema
19 Bus to Lashio
20 Cheroot Factory
21 Duhtawadi Bus to Mandalay (& Tea Shop)
25 Weaving factory
27 Clock Tower
30 Yoma Express Bus to Mandalay
33 Train Station
34 City Gate (to Mandalay)
35 School
36 Hospital
37 Zedi
38 Mahamyatmuni Paya
39 Sandal factory
40 School
41 Hsipaw Nat Shrine

NORTH-EASTERN MYANMAR

or Namtu), just east of the market, is cool and clear. According to local saying, if you drink the river's water, you will return. Alternatively, you can do as the locals do and use the river as an impromptu car wash.

To catch a great **sunset** in Hsipaw, walk to either Five Buddha Hill or Nine Buddha Hill. First cross the bridge on the Lashio road, and go about 200m. On your right, look for a path which leads to both small hills.

There are walking tours and boat trips to nearby villages, a sandal factory that recycles

old tires and a cheroot/cigar factory near the market. Visit the hospitable and well informed bookseller Ko Zaw Tun (known as Mr Book to many travellers) on the main road for reliable advice on moving around Hsipaw.

A sign in some guesthouse lobbies warns tourists not to visit SSA occupied areas. Although officially off-limits, the few SSA folk we encountered were exceedingly friendly – apparently a problem in the eyes of government officials of Hsipaw.

Places to Stay This small Shan town offers simple and basic accommodation, most with separate bath and toilet facilities (mostly squat toilets). Prices are similar at all the guesthouses – about K250 per person. Some of the guesthouses do not provide towels, but you can always buy one at the market, or along the main road, for less than K100.

A block south of the market, friendly *Aung Tha Pye Rest House (43 Aung Thabye Lan)* has eight clean rooms with mosquito nets and is the quietest place to stay. Bathing is bucket-style.

East of the clock tower on Bogyoke Lan, *Nam Khae Mao Guest House (☎ Hsipaw 88)* has double and triple rooms plus a large lobby with TV. A few rooms have attached bath and western-style flush toilets for around K1000.

Mr Charles/Myat Yatana Rest House (☎ Hsipaw 105), just off the main road at the north end of town, has small clean cubicles with mosquito net for K250 a person, and larger doubles above the lobby for about the same price. Bathing and toilet facilities are separate, and there is one western-style toilet. Most days at about 8 am, Mr Charles leads a three hour 'morning excursion' to a village or nearby waterfall.

On Bogyoke Lan and west of the clock tower, *Yamin Shwe Zin (Golden Doll) Guest House (☎ Hsipaw 66)* has clean spartan rooms with screens, but no nets. Bath and toilet facilities are separate. The hospitable family owners are a good source of information about the area.

Places to Eat Good Shan-style restaurants and tea shops are common in Hsipaw. There are several very good Shan and Chinese restaurants along the main road (Namtu Lan) near the cinema and across the street from the Yoma bus stop. *Hwai Ta* and *Law Chun* both serve good rice, curry and noodle dishes. Fresh fish is available at both.

Across the road near the cinema, *Yin Shin Restaurant* serves decent Chinese food. Half a block north on the north-east corner of the main road and Lan Madaw is a very tasty *Shan noodle shop* that's open for breakfast and lunch (Burmese sign).

Some of the best Shan-style restaurants are on the side streets near the market. A few doors south of the market and around the corner from Dokhtawady Bus stop is *Yin Kyan* (sign in Burmese, no English menu), an excellent small Shan eatery with the best noodles in town. Within the market are a number of *stalls* where you can have good Shan breakfasts, including *tohu-pyaw* (tofu porridge).

Ah Kong Kaik Restaurant, on the road into Hsipaw from Mandalay, serves decent Shan and Chinese fare, and is a favourite of the truck drivers who ply the Mandalay-Lashio road. You can spot the restaurant by the trucks parked along the road.

There are several tea and snack shops in town, including *Flower Master Teashop* on Aung Thabye Lan and *Excellent Cold Drinks* opposite the market. The *cafe* at Dokhtawady bus stop, opposite the market, serves good quality tea and snacks.

Getting There & Away Both Yoma Express and Dokhtawady Express run between Mandalay and Hsipaw. The cost is K400, and buses from depart Hsipaw daily at about 5.30 am. Two buses (5.15 and 6 am) to Lashio depart daily from opposite the market and a block down from Dokhtawady Express stop. The cost is K200 for the two hour journey. Pickups and vans to Pyin U Lwin and Lashio are usually parked by the market on Madaw Lan, across from Dokhtawady bus stop.

The city gate to Hsipaw from the Lashio side closes at 6 pm – a custom representing both the warlord legacy, and possible threat from Shan rebels to the north and east.

Buses and pickups come and go from stands along Namtu Rd in the centre of town near the market. Pickups cost K100 to Lashio (72km north-east) or K300 to Mandalay (209km south-west) and leave once or twice a day early in the morning. See the Mandalay chapter for information on other public vehicles to Lashio, all of which make stops in Hsipaw.

Train The Mandalay-Lashio train departs from Mandalay at 4.45 am and arrives in Hsipaw at 3 pm (with any luck). Ordinary class costs US$4; 1st class (a step down from upper) is US$9. Tickets must be purchased at least a day before at the Mandalay train station between 6 am and 4 pm. The same train leaves Hsipaw at about 3.30 pm, arriving in Lashio at 7.30 pm.

Getting Around Bicycles are available for rent at most guesthouses. Rates are about K30 per hour, or K250 for the day. Most places are within easy walking distance. The only public transport around town are trishaws, which cost around K10 to K15 per person per kilometre.

Namhsan

A few travellers have made it from Hsipaw as far as Namhsan, although you are likely to be told that this is not allowed. The 80km journey, on a road barely maintained since colonial times, takes at least six hours, and if it is blocked by trucks it can take days. Namhsan was the capital of the former Shan State of Tawngpeng. It clings to a 1600m-high narrow ridge, surrounded by valleys and mountains which rise to 2000m. The area is stunningly beautiful, and nicknamed the Switzerland of Myanmar. Most of the inhabitants are Shwe (Golden) Palaung and make a living from tea, although opium poppies are never far away. In Namhsan and nearby Payagyi are a number of tea factories where tea is roasted, boiled or pickled. The tea harvest runs from April to August, and during the monsoon, overloaded trucks heading for Mandalay are a particular hazard, sometimes blocking the road for hours, sometimes days.

From Hsipaw, the road passes through the lowland Shan villages of Konzaleik, Mo-te and Mali, before crossing a bridge over the Dokhtawady and climbing to Panglong (Big Village), a dull market town on the junction with the road to the mines at Namtu, 43km away. The road then descends to the river again at the small village of Loilu, where there are a few teashops with an army checkpoint, before skirting the mountainside through tea plantations that run all the way to Namhsan.

The sawbwa's haw, or Tawngpeng Palace, is unimpressive. It dates from 1931, but was partially rebuilt following bomb damage. Khun Pan Sing, the sawbwa, designed it as a long rectangle to fit the narrow ridge and provide a long veranda for pushing prams in rainy weather. His children 'donated' it to the government in 1974, and it is now a hospital. On a nearby hill is a monastery, with good views.

A cobbled track leads up behind the town, past typical wooden carved houses that cling to the steep hillside, to a couple of payas, a monastery and the green, shady reservoir that supplies Namhsan with water. It is possible to make day treks to Shan and Palaung villages nearby.

Places to Stay & Eat Namhsan has no guesthouses, but *Daw Aye Wun (Patsy)* has been given permission to put foreigners up for a few hundred kyat a night in the attic of her house at A115 Mingala Quarter, next to the three way junction at the far end of town. She will register you with immigration.

There are several *Chinese restaurants* along the narrow main street. Like the rest of the town, they close early (about 9 pm). There are a limited number of *noodle stalls* for breakfast.

Getting There & Away Pickups leave Hsipaw and return from Namhsan at about 6 am. Tickets cost about K500. Breakdowns are common and you may be better off trying to hire a pickup in Hsipaw. The old road from Namhsan to Kyaukme is not passable by car.

LASHIO

This township of mostly Shan-Chinese and Chinese inhabitants is located at the southern end of the infamous Burma Road. Until the early 1990s Lashio was off-limits to foreigners because of its proximity to China – and the hated Chinese communists – and to ethnic insurgent territory. Since the 1950s, the

NORTH-EASTERN MYANMAR

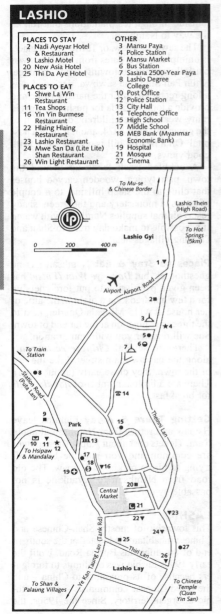

LASHIO

PLACES TO STAY
2 Nadi Ayeyar Hotel
   & Restaurant
9 Lashio Motel
20 New Asia Hotel
25 Thi Da Aye Hotel

PLACES TO EAT
1 Shwe La Win
   Restaurant
11 Tea Shops
16 Yin Yin Burmese
    Restaurant
22 Hlaing Hlaing
    Restaurant
23 Lashio Restaurant
24 Mwe San Da (Lite Lite)
    Shan Restaurant
26 Win Light Restaurant

OTHER
3 Mansu Paya
4 Police Station
5 Mansu Market
6 Bus Station
7 Sasana 2500-Year Paya
8 Lashio Degree
   College
10 Post Office
12 Police Station
13 City Hall
14 Telephone Office
15 High School
17 Middle School
18 MEB Bank (Myanmar
    Economic Bank)
19 Hospital
21 Mosque
27 Cinema

To Mu-se
& Chinese Border

Lashio Thein
(High Road)

To Hot
Springs
(5km)

Lashio Gyi

0   200   400 m

Airport   Airport Road

To Train
Station

Station Road
(Puta Lan)

To Hsipaw
& Mandalay

Park

Theinni Lan

Central
Market

Ye Kan Taung Lan (Tank Rd)

Thin Lan

Lashio Lay

To Shan &
Palaung Villages

To Chinese
Temple
(Quan
Yin San)

town has been flanked by the SSA to the west and south, the Kachin Independence Army (KIA) to the north and the Wa fighters of the Burmese Communist Party (BCP) to the east. Since 1989 fragile truces with most of these groups, along with the tremendous boost in trade with China, led to an announcement in 1992 that the town of Lashio – and the town only – would be open to foreign visitors.

Shan insurgents are still around, and you're not likely to be allowed beyond the military checkpoints at the north-eastern edge of town without special permission from the regional army command. Although the Myanmar government allows foreigners to travel from China to Lashio with permits obtained at the consulate in Kunming, it doesn't sanction travel in the opposite direction (see the Getting There & Away chapter and Mu-se in the Around Lashio section later in this chapter).

Lashio is in a mountain basin at 855m – clouds may form and deliver rain at almost any time of the year. It is divided into two main districts, Lashio Lay (Little Lashio) and Lashio Gyi (Big Lashio), connected by Theinni Lan. Lashio Lay is the newer and bigger of the two districts.

Information
The main post office is opposite the Lashio Motel on Mandalay-Lashio road at the corner of Puta Lan (Station Rd). Telephone and telegraph services are available at the Lashio telephone office on the main road between Lashio Lay and Lashio Gyi. Although direct dialling is only possible within the city (you can direct dial *to* Lashio from other places), overseas and trunk calls may be made through the operator, or at the Lashio Motel and Nadi Ayeyar Hotel (see Places to Stay in this section).

Things to See & Do
Mansu Paya stands between Lashio Lay and Lashio Gyi on a hill to the western side of Theinni Lan, and is said to be over 250 years old. It is unremarkable, except for the fact that it has no planetary post for Monday; the Monday-born pay homage to the main

Buddha image instead. More impressive is the **Sasana 2500-Year (Pyi Lon Chantha) Paya**, reportedly built by the last Shan sawbwa in the area, Sao Hon Phan. One of the shrines in the paya complex contains a Bagan-era Buddha image. A second stupa of similar name, **New Pyi Lon Chantha Paya**, sits on Mya Kantha Hill in the northern part of town and offers good views of the city. The latter is also known as Kyaw Hein's Paya because the famous Burmese film actor of the same name paid for its construction.

More interesting than any of the Buddhist shrines in town is the large and busy **Quan Yin San Temple** in Lashio Lay. Built around 40 years ago, it's the main Chinese temple in Lashio and possibly the largest in Myanmar; the steady traffic here bears testimony to Lashio's heavily Chinese population. Nearby is a popular new paya, **Hsu Taung Pye**.

Markets include the larger main market in central Lashio Lay and a smaller one called Mansu Market on Theinni Lan (Hsenwi Rd) closer to Lashio Gyi. The central market has just about everything, while Mansu Market focuses on fresh produce and foodstuffs. Some visitors to Lashio expect its markets to be very exotic and colourful – if you want to see people from various ethnic groups participating, you're better off in Hsipaw, Kyaukme or Kengtung.

Places to Stay

Once, just about any hotel or guesthouse in Lashio seemed prepared to accept foreign guests. Things are more regulated now, but it's still worth asking. Rates quoted vary between kyat and US dollars, or are sometimes quoted in both.

The quiet *Nadi Ayeyar Hotel & Restaurant* (☎ 082-23725, 21725), on Theinni Lan in Lashio Gyi, 1km from the town centre, has clean but small rooms with carpet and good mattresses for US$10/15 a single/double. Toilet and bath facilities are attached; hot water is available from 5 to 10 pm. A good Bamar or western breakfast is included. The friendly owner, Moira Yang, speaks English.

The unlicensed *Mo Shwe Li Guest House*, near the bus station and Mansu Market, charges K600 for a simple single with shared facilities, K1000 for a double or K2000 with attached hot-water shower. Some visitors have been charged US$5 for the latter room.

The *New Asia Hotel* (☎ 082-23622), just east of the central market on San Khaung Lan, is a modern four storey place that has simple rooms with attached bath for K1000/1500. A few dark single rooms with common bath cost K800 per person.

The three storey *Lashio Motel* (☎ 082-21702, 22763), at the intersection of the Mandalay-Lashio road and Station Rd, charges US$20 (for one or two people) for a clean, spacious and quiet rooms with a view of the hills. All rooms come with aircon, TV, fridge, toilet and hot-water shower. The price includes breakfast. Favoured by visiting Chinese businesspeople, the motel features an attached karaoke lounge and an expensive restaurant.

The two storey *Thida Aye Hotel* (☎ 082-22166, 218 Thiri Lan), in Lashio Lay, has clean and spacious single or double rooms for US$10, and economy rooms for US$4 per person. The US$10 rooms have a fan, attached hot-water shower and toilet, plus a nice view of the surrounding hills. A Chinese restaurant is next to the foyer. Some rooms face a nearby mosque, where the call to prayer begins at 4 am.

Places to Eat

Chinese and Shan eateries are abundant in Lashio Lay. The famous *Lashio Restaurant*, on Theinni Lan just east of New Asia Hotel, is one of the most reliable for both kinds of cuisine. Another good restaurant serving Shan and Chinese meals is *Mwe San Da (Lite Lite) Shan Restaurant*, near the New Asia Hotel on Chinese Temple St. The nearby *Hlaing Hlaing Restaurant* is similar.

For Yunnanese Muslim (look for the number 786) cuisine, the *Win Light Restaurant*, near the cinema, is inexpensive and good. *Yin Yin Burmese Restaurant*, behind the Myanmar Economic Bank building north of the central market, is the best place for Bamar food – there are also a few Shan and Chinese dishes available.

There are also many **Shan restaurants**, large and small, near the central market on Ye Kan Lan (Tank Rd), and a row of good **teashops** between the post office and the nearby police station.

There are fewer restaurants in Lashio Gyi, but **Shwe La Win Restaurant** is very good for Chinese/Shan dishes.

Getting There & Away

Air Although Lashio has an airport and MA allegedly flies there twice weekly (Monday and Thursday) from Yangon (US$100 by F-27) and Heho (US$50), it's not worth the risk of flying with them, particularly when the train trip is quite comfortable. YA no longer flies to Lashio.

The airport is north of Lashio Gyi. A taxi pickup from the airport into town costs around K500.

Bus From Mandalay there are buses to Lashio for around K600 that operate from the central/main bus centre near the corner of 26th and 82nd Sts. Both Yoma Express and Dokhtawady Express buses depart at around 6 am. Buy tickets at least one day before to get a seat. A slightly cheaper alternative, though officially illegal, is to take a bus from the Shan neighbourhood around 23rd and 82nd Sts. To be safe, check both places and reserve a seat a day in advance as this seems to change depending on the season (or perhaps on bribes paid). In either direction, the 220km ride between Mandalay and Lashio takes a slow 10 hours (on a rough road). To break up the trip, it's a good idea to schedule at least a day's stopover in Pyin U Lwin or Hsipaw along the way. The main bus station in Lashio stands on Theinni Lan south of Mansu Paya and near the Mansu Market.

Pickup In Mandalay, pickups to Lashio are available from the central/main bus centre near the corner of 26th and 82nd Sts. The cost to Lashio is K800. Because they climb the escarpment to Pyin U Lwin more easily, pickups are a good hour faster than the bus.

Van & Car From Mandalay, small air-con vans (Toyota Super-roofs) are also available for K2000 in the rear seats, K2500 at the front; these deliver their passengers door-to-door, but they fill up fast. You can also hire your own car and driver in Mandalay to make the one way trip for about US$40. A three or four-day round trip between Mandalay and Lashio costs about US$30 to US$40 per day. Inquire at the Mandalay Royal Hotel, the Royal Guest House or the ET Hotel. As usual, rates vary according to the price of petrol.

The road entrances to Lashio from Mandalay and from Mu-se close at 6 pm, so don't count on any night-time travel in/out of town.

Train Although it's expensive and sometimes takes longer, travel to Lashio by train is definitely more comfortable than by pickup. The No 131 Up leaves Mandalay at 4.45 am and arrives in Lashio around 7 pm – when it's not delayed by track conditions (late arrivals aren't unusual). Along the way you'll crawl across the famous Gokteik Bridge and wind around four monumental switchbacks. This route was long known as the black-market train among the Burmese because of all the contraband goods smuggled on board in both directions. Today, more and more of the trade consists of medicine, TVs and other taxable items from China.

The Mandalay to Lashio fare costs US$5 for ordinary class, US$13 in the only 1st class (a step down from upper) coach on the train. From Pyin U Lwin the fare drops to US$10. (Officially, ordinary class isn't available for foreigners, but if 1st class is full, it's worth asking. In a pinch, you can just board the train and wait for the ticket collector to come by.) Tickets for this route can be bought from one to seven days ahead of time, and they sell out very quickly. In Lashio, the train station lies 3km north-west of the centre of Lashio Lay. The Lashio train departs for Mandalay at 4 am, and is very cold in the wee hours of the morning during the cool season.

Getting Around

Pickups circulate between the train station, Lashio Lay and Lashio Gyi for K20 per person.

Small vans and taxi pickups with black numbered plates park at the Lashio Motel and central market in Lashio Lay, as well as at the train station and airfield. The drivers charge K500 per hour for either vehicle, with a one hour minimum rental.

AROUND LASHIO

If you want to leave town via the northern entrance (toward Mu-se), you must have a permit from the regional military headquarters. Taxi drivers or staff at the Nadi Ayeyar, New Asia Hotel and Lashio Motel in Lashio can sometimes help to arrange these.

Hot Springs & Caves

The **Lashio Hot Spa** is a hot spring about 10km north-east of Lashio Gyi via Theinni Lan. If you've come by road from Mandalay or Pyin U Lwin you might want to head straight there to wash all the dust off! It's open till 8 pm and there's a US$3 fee which gives you up to 30 minutes of bath time. There are also outdoor pools. Vendors on the premises sell Chinese and Shan snacks.

Although you're not officially allowed to visit them, **Peiqchinmyaing Caves**, 72km north-east of Lashio, features Buddha-filled caverns up to 793m deep.

Mu-se

The Shweli River forms the border between Myanmar's Shan State and China's Yunnan Province at Mu-se. Although it extends all the way to Lashio (and to some degree beyond), the Chinese influence is of course stronger here than elsewhere in the Shan State. You're not likely to be allowed to visit Mu-se from the south. However, package tours entering from China have received permission to enter Myanmar at Mu-se, and travel south to Lashio.

Such permission is best obtained through private travel agencies in Kunming. You will need three photos, your passport and US$18 for the permits. It should be noted

that we haven't yet met or heard from anyone who has actually done this trip, although according to the Myanmar government this is the procedure. As Mu-se continues to prosper, the situation may open up for foreign independent travellers (FITs).

Anyone entering Myanmar for the first time via Mu-se might easily think the country was in the midst of an economic boom. Unlike the rest of the country, the city is prospering as a trade centre. In 10 years the population has rocketed from 10,000 to over 100,000 people, with no end in sight.

The once sleepy frontier-town atmosphere has been swept away by the bustling border trade with China. The town's electricity is supplied by China, so the power cuts common around the country are unheard of. Chinese tourists flock to Mu-se to shop, keeping the moneychangers busy.

Trucks from Myanmar cross to China with dried fish, rattan, fresh beans and fruit – including tamarind, which is then processed into a soft drink and sold back to Myanmar at a tidy profit. On the return trip from China, the same trucks carry electrical goods and spare parts, cement and other building components. Smuggled goods include teak, cigarettes and alcohol.

The territory surrounding Mu-se is one of the primary pipelines for opium and heroin smuggling from the Shan State to Yunnan Province, and from Yunnan to Hong Kong. East of Mu-se, along the border, there are reportedly several major heroin refineries and some amphetamine labs. This area to the east is strictly off-limits to foreigners.

The area around Mu-se is thought to have been the centre of one of the first consolidated Shan kingdoms – called Kawsumpi, or Mong Mao – as early as the 7th century. From this point the Shan dispersed to other river valleys to the west, east and south.

Cut by the Shweli River, the verdant **Namkham Valley**, south-west of Mu-se is a beautiful patchwork of bamboo and rice paddies. Most of the people living off the land in this area are Shan and other Thai ethnic groups. **Namkham** itself is renowned as the WWII-era location of Dr Gordon

Seagrave's American Medical Center. Doctor Seagrave renounced his associations with the American Baptist Mission in order to offer medical service free of Christian proselytisation; people from all over the northern frontier states emerged from his medical centre trained as doctors and nurses. He and his staff tended to wounded soldiers around the clock during the Allies' siege of Myitkyina in 1944. In 1951 Seagrave was briefly imprisoned by the post-independence Burmese government for his alleged associations with Kachin rebels. After his release he remained in Namkham till his death in 1965.

Places to Stay & Eat

If you cross from China, the most popular place to stay is the privatised 40 room *Muse Hotel*, with rooms for US$10/15 a single/double.

Indicative of the boom in Mu-se is a new complex currently under construction by the Chinese. When completed the Silver Elephant Hotel should have 80 rooms and more than 20 shops and restaurants.

There are cheaper places to stay on the Chinese side, including the *Ruili Guest House* and *Mingrui Hotel* at the budget end, *Yongchang Hotel* and *Nanyang Hotel* at the top end.

Getting There & Away

From Mu-se it's four or five hours by pickup or car along the famed Burma Road to Lashio, a distance of 176km. With the increased traffic between Mu-se and Mandalay, the road to Lashio has livened up with businesses catering to the truck drivers. Pickups start at about 6 am in either direction, costing K500 per person. Air-con shared taxis – Toyota hatchbacks – are available for K1200 to K1600 per person. Hitching is possible, but any driver who picks you up will probably want some money for fuel plus a little extra for stopping.

Since 1992 there has been a bridge over the Shweli River (called Ruili River on the Chinese side), which you'll be permitted to cross from China – if you've brought the

proper paperwork from Kunming. There are also one-day border passes available to foreigners for US$10, but you'd have to be pretty twisted to go all the way to China to spend one day in Mu-se.

From Kunming, Ruili can be reached by air (50 minutes, Y350) or by bus (24 hours, Y155 for a sleeper).

Kachin State

Myanmar's northernmost state borders India and China to the north and east, the Sagaing Division to the west and the Shan State to the south. Major rivers flowing north to south – the Malihka, Mehka, Tanainghka and Ayeyarwady (Irrawaddy) – form fertile upland valleys where most of the state's meagre population lives. Above these valleys stand the nation's highest mountain peaks, part of the southern edge of the Himalaya.

Most people living in the Kachin State are of Tibeto-Burman origin, representing four main language groups: the Jinghpaw, Maru, Yawyin and Lisu. The Jinghpaw, who are generally known as Kachin, are the majority, and since their language can be written (using a Roman alphabet system devised by 19th-century Christian missionaries), Jinghpaw has become a lingua franca for the state.

Although many Kachin people nowadays are nominally Christian or Buddhist, some of the old beliefs are practised syncretically. Under the British and today, to a much lesser degree, under the SPDC, the Kachin tribes have continued to practice their own form of semidemocratic civil administration, *gumlao-gumsa*. One of the distinctions of this system is that the youngest in the family – rather than the eldest – is the legal heir when a parent dies.

Until the early 1990s, the Kachin Independence Organisation (KIO) and its tactical arm, the KIA, operated with near impunity throughout the state. Following the 1993 signing of a truce with the Yangon government, the KIA have ceased active insurgency. The Burmese government, however, still considers the state a sensitive area and the movements of both foreigners and Burmese are strictly curtailed.

The jade trade may also have something to do with travel restrictions in the state. During the Konbaung era, roughly 75% of all Kachin jade ended up in China. The Chinese are still the biggest market for Burmese jadeite, which is preferred over China's nephrite, although both minerals can be called jade.

The Manao

Traditionally, the Jinghpaw are animists who recognise a spirit world presided over by Karai Kasang, a supreme deity who requires animal sacrifice. *Duwa* (hereditary chieftains) maintain ceremonial and cultural leadership, especially with regard to the *manao* (also spelt manau or manaw, important festivals held periodically to placate or pay homage to the Jinghpaw nats). There are several types of manao depending on the region and time of year. One of the most common types, the *sup manao*, looks toward the future, insuring good weather for farming and serving to ward off danger and general ill fortune; a *padang manao*, on the other hand, celebrates a past victory or success.

A typical manao involves the sacrifice of 29 cows and/or buffaloes, one for each of the 28 Jinghpaw nats plus one dedicated to all of them. Participants dance to music played on a large doubled-headed drum, brass gong, cymbals and buffalo-horn oboe. These festivities are centred around *manao-taing* (brightly painted totems strung with banners of red, black and white) whose colours are considered most attractive to the nats. Dancers often carry fans in imitation of bird feathers; the lead dancer wears a headdress designed to resemble the head and beak of a great hornbill. Other dances mimic the movements of horse-riding, fishing and cattle herding. There is much drinking of local *churu* (rice beer) and feasting on *shat kada* (special meal packets).

On 10 January – Kachin State Day – a major manao in Myitkyina draws Kachin groups from all over the state and beyond.

MYITKYINA

Set in a flat valley that is extremely hot in the dry season and very rainy during the monsoon, Myitkyina (By The Big River) itself is not very interesting. However, since the lifting of the 25km radius travel restriction, the town now holds the possibility of being the starting point for visits to the many Kachin villages in the area. Kachin men living in the lowlands wear dark blue and green longyis, while those from the mountains wear trousers. The women wear distinctive red and black headdresses, but the most colourful fashions are reserved for weddings and festivals, events that would make any village visit much more compelling. In a Kachin wedding the groom presents his bride with a silver sword and a shoulder bag to symbolise the offering of protection and material support.

The enduring pride of Myitkyina, indeed the entire state, is the abundance of fruits available in the local markets, especially in the cooler months. The chief produce is pineapples, lychees, watermelons, star apples and mustard oil plants. In addition to the large variety of fruit, many local hill tribe people can be seen haggling over produce and consumer goods in the **central market**. *Khat cho* (rice produced in this valley) is considered the best in Myanmar; highly valued for its delicate texture and fine fragrance, khat cho is scarce and expensive outside the Kachin State. The most popular souvenir among visitors is, of course, the dark indigo and green Kachin longyi, which has become something of a pro-democracy symbol among many Burmese.

Hsu Taung Pye Zedidaw is a pretty, gilded, 'wish-fulfilling' stupa on the banks of the Ayeyarwady River. The larger **Andawshin Paya** boasts a silver-plated zedi said to contain tooth relics and a Buddha footprint; there are a couple of adjacent monasteries. Other religious structures of interest in town include the **Sri Saraswati Gurkha Hindu Temple**, **Ja-me Mosque** and a Taoist-Buddhist **Chinese Temple**.

Most of the Kachin people living in and around Myitkyina have been missionised and there are now around 15 churches in town – mostly Baptist with a few Methodist and Catholic churches sprinkled in. About 14km north is **Praying Mountain**, a sacred site for Kachin and Lisu Baptists and location of a bible school and seminary. The town is also home to a small Nepali community.

Many older Kachin people speak English since they were educated in mission schools. There are also a few elderly WWII veterans around who like to talk about Merrill's Marauders and the various campaigns fought in the region.

Only a handful of visitors have visted the **Kachin State Cultural Museum** on Youngyi Lan since it was built in 1994. On display is the usual collection of costumes and Kachin and Shan artefacts, such as pipes, baskets, fishing nets, looms and musical instruments. Upstairs are the conch, chests and a homemade cannon belonging to the former sawbwa of Hkamti Long (Putao). Most labels are in Burmese. It's open daily, except Monday, from 10 am to 3 pm. Admission is US$2.

Myit-son

Myit-son, the confluence of the Mehka and Malihka rivers, 43km north of Myitkyina, forms the beginning of the great Ayeyarwady River. A government rest house overlooking the water was burned to the ground by Kachin insurgents in the 1960s; a new hotel to replace it has been planned for years. The return trip taxi fare is K3000. It's an hour each way.

Another spot formerly off-limits is the jade mining centre of **Hpakan**, 148km west of Myitkyina. Permission is required and can usually be arranged by any hotel in Myitkyina. The first 80km to Kamaing is via a sealed road, the rest is an unsealed dryweather road. If you're only interested in buying jade, however, there's plenty in Myitkyina. South-west of Kamaing is the huge and serene **Indawgyi Lake**.

Places to Stay & Eat

Hotel and restaurant infrastructure in Myitkyina is behind that found in more touristed regions of the country, and rates are high.

The *Popa Hotel (☎ 074-21746)* at the train station charges US$8/14 a single/double for simple rooms with a fan and a common bath. The nearby and friendly *YMCA* is quieter and charges US$5 per person for a clean, simple room with fan and common bath. The *White House Rest House* is not officially licensed, but you might find a room there for around K1000.

An expensive government hotel, *Sumpra Hotel & Restaurant (☎ 074-22298)*, on the riverbank, caters to tour groups. It charges US$40/50.

Most of the restaurants in town serve Chinese and Kachin food. One of the best is *Shwe Ainsi (Ein Zay)*, which doesn't look like much but serves quite reasonable food. Its owned by the proprietor of a Hpakan jade mine and is favoured by gem dealers. Also good is the *Chili Restaurant*, owned by an Indian Gurka family.

Getting There & Away

You can reach Myitkyina by air, train or boat – although there are drawbacks to each method of travel, and its inaccessibility, combined with the limited number of sights, mean that few visitors bother. Officially, you can't arrive by car.

Air MA flies to Myitkyina from Mandalay on Monday and Friday; the flight takes 50 minutes and costs US$80 by F-28. On Monday and Tuesday, MA makes the flight to Myitkyina via Bhamo on an F-27 for US$70. The 25 minute flight from Bhamo costs US$30. Until YA resumes its currently suspended service to Myitkyina as planned, risky MA is the only choice by air. It often doesn't fly according to schedule, and tickets are difficult to obtain. There is an MA office in town.

Train The No 57 Up train from Mandalay leaves daily at 3 pm and is supposed to take 25 hours to reach Myitkyina. In everyday practice it often takes longer – up to 40 hours due to the poor condition of the railbed. In early 1995 a derailment at the railway bridge near Mohnyin killed over

100 passengers. The fare is US$27 for an upper-class sleeping berth, and US$9 for a seat. Tickets should be purchased at least three days in advance.

Two private companies run somewhat better trains to Myitkyina on certain days of the week. The problem is that they use the same track, and are therefore subject to the same delays.

Malihka Railways departs from Mandalay on Monday and Friday at 4.40 pm, arriving in Myitkyina around 24 hours later – usually. A seat costs US$30 for foreigners, or you can get a sleeper for US$60. If you can manage to buy an ordinary class seat in kyat, the fare is only K500. The Malihka ticket office is at the southern end of the train station in Mandalay. Malihka trains return to Mandalay on Sunday and Wednesday.

Across the street, Santhawta Co charges US$30 for a seat and US$60 for a sleeper with dining car. This train runs on Wednesday and Sunday at 4 pm and arrives at Myitkyina around 6 pm the next day; it returns to Mandalay on Friday and Tuesday. Santhawta is more likely to have berths available, as it has three sleeper carriages with a total of 60 berths; Malihka has two carriages totalling 40 berths. In the seat cars, both lines feature 40 seats per carriage.

Road There are no regular public transport services along the road between Mogok and Myitkyina, as road conditions are quite bad between Mogok and Bhamo.

The 188km road between Bhamo and Myitkyina, which runs parallel to the China-Myanmar border, is passable in all weather. Strictly speaking, you're not supposed to arrive in Myitkyina by road. This may change as 'security' improves. Reportedly, the fare for the four to five hour trip is K1500 per passenger. We know of a couple of travellers who tried to make the trip from Mandalay by car via Moehnyin, only to be turned back and put on the train, less than 160km from Myitkyina.

Boat & Road You could try to catch a ferry north from Mandalay, as far as Bhamo, and

then continue to Myitkyina by road. The ferry trip is fairly straightforward (see the following Bhamo section for details).

Boat & Train Another alternative is to travel by train as far as Khataw (about two-thirds of the way between Mandalay and Myitkyina) and continue by boat from there. This breaks up the long train trip, and gives you the most scenic views of the river.

If you end up in Khataw, the police are helpful in finding a guesthouse. Your choices are either the basic *Friendship Hotel* (K500 per person) or the also basic *Shwe Naga (Golden Dragon) Hotel* (K300 per person). There are good *noodle vendors* in the market.

Getting Around

Trishaws and Mazda taxis are easy to hire in Myitkyina, and the YMCA will lend bicycles. Taxis are available from the airport and opposite the market. For trips further afield, eg to Indawgyi, you will need to arrange an excursion with a registered tour guide and the necessary permission. The local military commander is very strict about travel beyond the Myitkyina-Myitson corridor.

BHAMO

Those who have been there say Bhamo, 186km south of Myitkyina, is more interesting than the latter. The **daily market** draws Lisu, Kachin and Shan participants from the surrounding countryside. The overgrown city walls of **Sampanago**, an old Shan kingdom, can be seen around 5km east of town. **Theindawgyi Paya**, in the town centre, features an older stupa.

Places to Stay & Eat

The *Friendship Hotel* has decent and clean rooms with common bath for K500 per person, and a few larger rooms with attached bath and fan for K1000. The *Golden Dragon Hotel* accepts foreigners for K300 per person. The hotel – really more of a guesthouse – can provide a guide to nearby Kachin villages such as Aungtha.

Decent Chinese food is available from the *Sein Sein Restaurant*.

NORTH-EASTERN MYANMAR

NORTH-EASTERN MYANMAR

Ledo-Bhamo-Burma Road

The so-called Burma Road – actually a network of three major routes – came about during WWII, when Japanese invasion forces closed in on Myanmar from the north via China, and from the south via Thailand. In what was known as the China-Burma-India (CBI) Theatre, Allied supplies for the ground war fought in Lower Myanmar were easily flown or shipped in from India. Supplying the China front, however, required dangerous flights over 'The Hump', a series of high Himalayan peaks that separate Myanmar and China.

Over 1000 airmen died flying this route, prompting the Allies to look for a new way to supply Chiang Kai-shek's nationalist Kuomintang (KMT) army, who were fighting the Japanese in Western China. The Yunnanese themselves built the original Burma Road from Kunming to Wanting, China, between 1937 and 1939. They then laid an extension into Myanmar from Wanting to Lashio in 1940, for a total length of 1200km. Early in the war, this Lashio-Kunming route served as the main supply line for the KMT, but as Japanese pressure from the south increased, the Allies looked for an alternate route from India.

American General Joseph 'Vinegar Joe' Stilwell proposed the construction of an all-weather, two lane road from India to China via Northern Myanmar. The plan was to link up not with the original Lashio-Kunming route, but with a rough dry-weather track developed by the Chinese between Bhamo in southern Chin State and Yunchang, Yunnan. British army engineers, using a trail created by war refugees fleeing to India from Upper Myanmar, began building the 800km Ledo road from Ledo, Assam, to the Bhamo terminus of the Bhamo road in 1942. Although the engineers originally had 5000 labourers at their disposal, progress was slow and work on the Ledo road was abandoned in May 1942.

A huge contingent of American engineers took over in November 1942, and assembled 35,000 Burmese, Indian, British and Chinese troops to tackle the enormous task of cutting through thick jungle, upgrading the Bhamo track, and spanning 10 major rivers and 155 secondary streams between Ledo and Wanting. So many men were lost along the way that the builders sardonically dubbed the route the 'man-a-mile road'.

Completed in May 1945, the Ledo road – also known as the Stilwell road – was maintained until a year later, when all Allied units were withdrawn from the CBI Theatre. The Myitkyina Bridge, which spanned the Ayeryarwady (Irrawaddy) River south of Myitkyina and was the longest pontoon bridge in the world, was deemed an obstacle to river traffic and was dismantled in 1947. One of the chief postwar effects of the Bhamo-Myanmar road network was the opening up of the Kachin State remains of the Ledo road, which quickly fell into disuse.

The main Lashio-Kunming route, though in poor condition nowadays, sees much traffic as a major smuggling route to China for opium, heroin, gems, jade and teak. In the reverse direction, traders bring finished goods, such as auto parts, pharmaceuticals, processed foods, clothing and homewares. The Yangon government has made such trade – legal and illegal – much easier than in the past by making the border crossing at Mu-se a legal overland port of entry from China.

Joe Cummings

Getting There & Away

Air MA flies to Bhamo from Mandalay on Monday and Tuesday; the flight costs US$50 in an F-27, and takes one hour. This flight originates in Yangon – the fare all the way from Yangon to Bhamo via Mandalay is US$130. It then continues to Myitkyina (US$30 from Bhamo).

Boat A double decker public ferry plies the

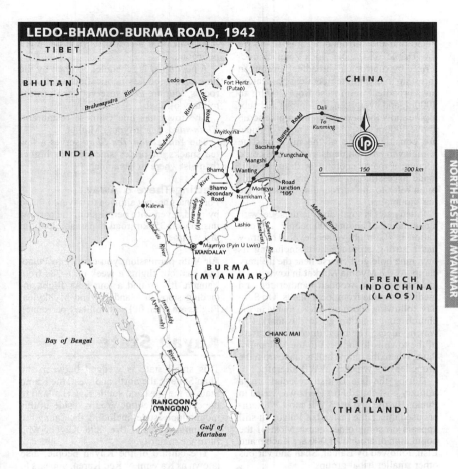

LEDO-BHAMO-BURMA ROAD, 1942

Ayeyarwady River between Mandalay and Bhamo twice weekly. When the water level is optimum, the upriver journey takes 1½ days, but when the river's low it can take as long as 2½ days. The overcrowded boat stops along the way in Kyaukmyaung and Katha. The foreigner fare is US$50 for a stuffy, smelly cabin, US$27 for a lower deck cabin that is cleaner and more comfortable, and US$9 for upper-deck class – which is fine if you can sleep in a deck chair. There's a nice lounge, but don't ex-

pect to see it – it's a hangout for the crew. The lower deck features open cooking fires and a shower. Some foreigners have reported having better luck paying in kyat from Kyaukmyaung, which is a short road journey east of Shwebo.

The scenery along the upper reaches of the Ayeyarwady is supposed to be very fine, especially north of Kyaukmyaung, where the riverbanks are lush with bamboo and other flora and the boat passes through steep rock gorges.

PUTAO

Putao and the surrounding area lie above the Tropic of Cancer, in a zone characterised by subtropical, broadleaf, evergreen forest up to 2000m; temperate, semideciduous, broadleaf rainforest from 2000m to 3000m; and evergreen, coniferous and subalpine snow forest passing into alpine scrub above 3000m. The highlands north of Putao are considered one of the most pristine Himalayan environments in Asia and could become a major ecotourism destination if made accessible to foreigners. The locals often refer to the surrounding peaks as the Ice Mountains.

Putao itself is small and picturesque, with a population of about 6000 people. The elevation is 402m above sea level. The army has a strong presence here, including its own nine hole golf course near the military camp. At the **Myoma Market** in town, there are bamboo and wooden handicrafts, and medicines made from local plants. On Sunday following morning mass, many in the church congregation go to the market to watch videos. The most interesting feature of the town is found next to the Mahamuni Paya, where the chime bell is made from the propeller of a wrecked WWII aircraft.

During the late British colonial era, a military post called Fort Hertz was based in Putao. By the end of WWII most westerners used this name instead of Putao – it still appears on some older maps. Most of the population of around 10,000 are Kachin and Lisu, followed by Bamar, Shan and various other smaller tribal groups.

Hkakabo Razi stands 5889m high and is, as its name suggests, snowcapped year-round. Satellite peaks in adjoining massifs include **Namni-Lka** (4664m) in the Adung Valley and **Diphuk-Ha** (4360m) in the Seingku Valley. A protected 'trans-frontier reserve' has been proposed by neighbouring countries.

Places to Stay & Eat

Until recently, most foreigners who travelled to Putao ended up staying and dining at the government guesthouse (officially known as *No 46 Light Infantry Division Rest House*) at a cost of US$20 per night per room.

A new *hotel* is scheduled to open by the time of this book's publication. Of the 21 rooms, four are to be reserved for Burmese military officials.

The town has one Chinese restaurant, *Khamsuko*, near Myoma Market.

The *Yadanapon Tea Shop* serves a few tea snacks, at prices significantly higher than elsewhere in Myanmar.

Getting There & Away

Foreigners are not allowed to travel to Putao by road. Even with permission, the narrow, unsurfaced 356km road is passable only in dry weather.

Air With permission, you can fly to Putao. MA has four flights a week on F-28s from Yangon. It's around a four hour flight, including stops in Mandalay and Myitkyina. Flights are often full with military personnel.

Kayah State

This small state is wedged between the Shan State to the north and west, the Karen State to the west and south, and Thailand to the east. Eight ethnic groups reside in this mountainous state, including the Taungthu, Padaung, Yinbaw, Bre, and Kayah, who form the majority.

The culture of the Kayah people, also known as Karenni or Red Karen, appears to the outsider to be a blend of Kayin (Karen) and Shan influences. Hereditary chieftains called *saopya* have obvious similarities with the sao pha of the Shan, while bronze frog drums are used ceremonially as in the Kayin culture. Most of the Kayah are animist, although there are significant numbers of Christians and Buddhists as well. Animists, Buddhists and Christians alike participate in the annual Kuhtobo festival in May, which pays homage to the rain spirits.

Most known outside Myanmar are the minority Padaung, whose women traditionally stack up to 22kg of brass rings around their necks. The rings depress the collarbone, making it look as if their necks have been unnaturally stretched. No one knows for sure how the ring custom got started; one theory says it was to make the women's appearance strange enough that men from other tribes wouldn't pursue them. The Padaung also wear thin hoops, made of cane or lacquered cord, in bunches around their knees and calves.

Until the early 1990s, Kayah rebel groups controlled much of the eastern half of the state. The Myanmar government has concentrated on securing the capital, Loikaw, and the very important hydroelectric plant at nearby Lawpita. The recent ceasefire has allowed the government to build a railway between Aungban and Loikaw.

LOIKAW

The Kayah State is open by permit only, and permits have yet to be given for the state capital, Loikaw – located near the state's northern tip at an elevation of just over 1200m.

Loikaw's colourful **Thirimingala Market** sees participants from several tribal groups, including the Padaung. Naungyar, towards the northern quarter of town, is inhabited by mostly Kayah people; now that a ceasefire with the insurgents is in effect, it's not unusual to see Kayah rebel soldiers in this area. Two small lakes and a stream add visual interest to the town. Visit the **Taungkwe Zedi** on Taungkwe, a twin-peaked mountain on the edge of town, for Loikaw vistas.

Twenty kilometres south-east of Loikaw is a huge hydroelectric facility built by the Japanese as war reparation. A dam impounds the Bilu Chaung, which flows from Inle Lake 120km to the north. The facility supplies most of the power in the national grid system and so is highly strategic. Nearby, **Lawpita Falls** is said to be beautiful; it's in insurgent territory, so you're unlikely to be permitted to visit, despite the ceasefire.

Pinlaung, roughly half-way between Aungban and Loikaw, is the highest point on the road/railway route, at over 1500m. It's inhabited mainly by Pa-O and it can be quite cold in winter.

Places to Stay

The *Garden Hotel* reportedly provides economy rooms for US$10/15 a single/double and standard rooms for US$15/20.

Getting There & Away

At the time of writing, travel to Loikaw for foreigners was not permitted.

MA flies to Loikaw from Yangon on Tuesday, Wednesday and Saturday. The flight takes 70 minutes and costs US$55 in an F-27.

The new railway between Aungban and Loikaw takes six to 10 hours, but it isn't open to foreigners (at the time of writing). Locals pay K100 for the ride.

The road trip from Aungban takes four to five hours by car, longer by public transport. Officially this road is strictly off-limits to foreigners; there are four military checkpoints between Aungban and Loikaw.

South-Eastern Myanmar

Mon State

The homeland of the Mon wraps around the eastern coast of the Gulf of Mottama (Martaban) from the mouth of the Sittoung (Sittang) River to the northern end of Tanintharyi Yoma (Tenasserim Range). Once native to a broad region stretching from Lower Myanmar to Cambodia, the Mon have been absorbed – sometimes willingly, sometimes unwillingly – by the more powerful Bamar and Thai cultures in Myanmar and Thailand over the last thousand years or so. The absorption has been so effective that their own history and culture have received little attention by scholars, even though vestiges of the Mon culture and language clearly survive in both countries.

Though no one knows for sure, the Mon may be descended from a group of Indian immigrants from Kalinga, an ancient kingdom overlapping the boundaries of the modern Indian states of Orissa and Andhra Pradesh. They are responsible for much of the early maintenance and transmission of Theravada Buddhism in mainland South-East Asia even though Sri Lankan monks may have initially introduced the *Tripitaka* (the 'three baskets'; the classic Buddhist scriptures) and ordination lineage. In the case of Myanmar, the Bagan kingdom forcefully captured these elements, while in Thailand it was the peaceful interest of King Rama IV that led to the growth of Mon Buddhism.

Since 1949 the eastern hills of the state (as well as mountains farther south in Tanintharyi Division) have been a refuge for the New Mon State Party (NMSP) and its tactical arm, the Mon National Liberation Front (MNLF), whose objective has been self-rule for the Mon State. In addition to harassing the Burmese government, the Mon have occasionally fought the Kayin over control of the remote border crossings along the Thai border. With growing gov-

HIGHLIGHTS

- Sacred and extraordinary gold-leafed Kyaiktiyo boulder-temple, delicately balanced on a cliff.
- Post colonial tropical atmosphere of seaport town Mawlamyaing.
- Thanbyuzayat, western terminus of the infamous Burma Railway.
- Historic port of Myeik with colonial architecture, and sleepy Dawei with its sacred monuments.
- Tropical beaches and islands of the remote Tanintharyi Peninsula.
- Excellent diving in the Myeik Archipelago.
- Frontier state of Kayin.

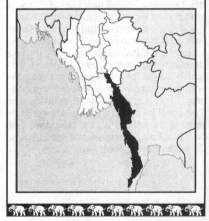

ernment influence along this section of border – and following a string of Kayin defeats – the situation has cooled. In 1995 the NMSP signed a cease-fire with the Burmese government.

Despite these events, the lower half of the state south of Mudon is still a 'brown area'

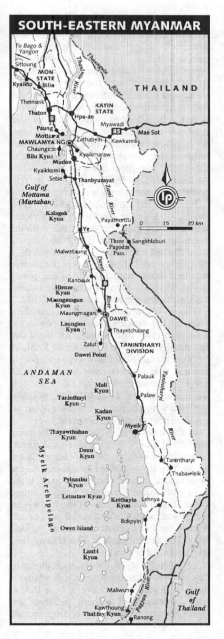

SOUTH-EASTERN MYANMAR

where road travel is considered unsafe. Highway robberies have been common, even in broad daylight. Regardless of claims on either side, it's very unclear whether these assaults are politically motivated or whether the robbers are simple *dacoits* (highwaymen). For political reasons the government tends to lump both kinds of attacks together as 'insurgent activity'. A new source of tension in the area is provided by the ongoing construction of a heavily guarded pipeline from the Andaman Sea (near Dawei) to Thailand. For the traveller, the upshot is that it can be difficult to get permission for travel outside the main towns.

KYAIKTIYO

One of the most interesting, formerly off-limits, trips is to the incredible balancing boulder *stupa* (*zedi*, a traditional religious Buddhist monument) at Kyaiktiyo. It's about 20km from the small town of Kyaikto, which in turn is midway between Bago (Pegu) and Thaton. The small stupa, just 7.3m high, sits atop the Gold Rock, a massive, goldleafed boulder delicately balanced on the edge of a cliff at the top of Mt Kyaikto. Like Shwedagon Paya in Yangon (Rangoon) or Mahamuni Paya in Mandalay, Kyaiktiyo is one of the most sacred Buddhist sites in Myanmar.

Legend says that the boulder maintains its precarious balance due to a precisely placed Buddha hair in the stupa. Apparently King Tissa received the Buddha hair in the 11th century from a hermit who had secreted the hair in his own topknot. The hermit instructed the king to search for a boulder whose shape resembled the hermit's head, then enshrine the hair in a stupa on top. The king, who inherited supernatural powers as a result of his birth to a *zawgyi* (an accomplished alchemist) father and *naga* (dragon serpent) princess, found the rock at the bottom of the sea. Upon its miraculous arrival on the mountaintop, the boat used to transport the rock then turned to stone. This stone can be seen approximately 300m from the main boulder – it's known as the Kyaukthanban (Stone Boat Stupa).

SOUTH-EASTERN MYANMAR

The atmosphere surrounding Kyaiktiyo during the height of the pilgrimage season (from November to March) is charged with magic and devotion, especially when the glinting boulder is bathed in the purple, sometimes misty, light of dawn. Pilgrims chant, light candles and meditate all through the night. Men are permitted to walk along a short causeway and over a bridge spanning a chasm to the boulder and affix gold-leaf squares on the rock's surface. It's also said that if you wedge a short piece of wood or bamboo into the space between the bottom of the boulder and the cliff on which it rests, you can watch it flex as the boulder gently rocks back and forth.

A new terrace allows devotees to view the boulder from below. There are several other stupas and shrines scattered along the ridge at the top of Mt Kyaikto; though none is as impressive as Kyaiktiyo. The interconnecting trails, however, sometimes lead to unexpected views of the valleys below.

Kinpun, about 9km in from the highway and Kyaikto, lies at the base of the mountain. This is the starting point for either beginning the four hour hike up or catching one of the frequent trucks-with-benches up the winding road. The charge is K150 per person each way. Vehicles are not permitted near the top, so you still have about a 45 minute walk up to the stupa area. Along the way, you pass through an array of village vendors.

Although permits are no longer required, there is now a US$6 entrance fee to the stupa area, payable at the tourist office (open daily from 6 am to 6 pm) opposite the pilgrim truck-loading area. There is a table-and-chair checkpoint near the top, where you can also pay. By the way, your permit is valid for 30 days, so you may visit again without paying the government another US$6.

Places to Stay

Although Kyaiktiyo can be visited as a day trip from Bago, the advantage of staying at the top is that you can catch sunset and sunrise – the most magical times for viewing the boulder shrine.

Along the ridge at the top of Mt Kyaikto,

the well situated and government-owned *Kyaikto Hotel* features a couple of long wooden buildings overlooking the valley below. Standard rooms with attached bath cost US$36/44 a single/double. 'Economy' rooms with two beds and two buckets of water cost US$15/24. Some travellers have had to politely insist they wanted an economy room. All rates include the standard toast-and-egg breakfast. Compared to other accommodations in the area, rooms here are rather shabby. Its appeal is its proximity to the stupa,. The hotel has a booking office (☎ 01-551563) at 69 Theingyi Lan in Yangon if you want to book a room in advance.

Prices at the new *Golden Rock Hotel* (☎ 035-70174) are similar to the Kyaikto Hotel, but are much better value – with the exception that the hotel is just up the path from the last truck stop – in other words, a 40 minute walk from the top. Attractive standard rooms with TV, fridge and phone cost US$36/48. Smaller economy rooms, also with attached bath, cost US$24/30.

The new *Mountain View Motel* is the best value of the upscale places. It's closer to Kyaiktiyo town than Kinpun, although you can usually get a free lift to either location. Very comfortable bungalow-type rooms with fan and cold-water shower are US$15/20. Larger 'superior' rooms with a desk and hot-water shower cost US$30/40. Breakfast is included with all rooms, and there is an attractive indoor/outdoor restaurant.

In the town of Kyaikto along the main road from Bago, there are several guesthouses; none of them very appealing. Of the lot, the two storey *Nilar Guesthouse*, on the main road at the corner of Hospital St, is the most conveniently located; Yangon-bound buses leave from in front of the hotel. Cubicle rooms with fan cost K400 per person. Bucket bath and toilets are on the ground floor. The nearby *La Min Tha Guesthouse* on Station Rd is similar.

Closer to the stupa, the cheapest places to stay are in Kinpun, the base village. Many of the new guesthouses have a here-today-gone-tomorrow feel to them, but three are worth looking for. Each has separate shower

Intha fishermen on Inle Lake, Shan State.

SARA-JANE CLELAND

Fresh produce at Mingala Market, Nyaungshwe.

GLENN BEANLAND

Women at Shin Pyu festival in He Ho, Shan State.

BERNARD NAPTHINE

Young monks in residence at a *kyaung* (monastery), near Nyaungshwe, Shan State.

MARK KIRBY

RICHARD I'ANSON

Worshippers at beautiful Kyaiktiyo, near Kyaikto, South-Eastern Myanmar.

and toilet facilities. The best value is the well managed **Pann Myo Thu Guest House**. The rooms are clean and light and cost US$5/6. The friendly **Htet Yar Zar Guest House** is the cheapest of the lot so far, with rooms for one or two people at K600. **Sea Sar Guesthouse** is behind the popular Sea Sar Restaurant & Bar. Rooms are very basic, with wooden slats and mosquito nets. The cost is US$4/5 per room.

Foreigners aren't permitted to stay in the *zayat* (rest shelters) for pilgrims, nor are they permitted to camp in wooded areas on the mountain.

Places to Eat
Because Kinpun is the starting point for this popular Burmese site, there are a number of good **Chinese and Bamar restaurants** up and down the main street. In addition to the **food stalls** at the Kinpun base camp and along the footpaths, there's a decent **teashop** opposite the front entrance of the Kyaikto Hotel at the summit. As well as serving the usual teashop snacks, the tiny kitchen can make fried noodles and fried rice.

If you're coming by road from Bago, **Yadana Oo Restaurant**, just north-west of the town of Waw (35km from Bago), serves good Bamar food in clean surroundings.

Getting There & Away
For individual travellers, Bago makes a better starting point for road trips to Kyaiktiyo than Yangon, since hotel staff there are adept at arranging inexpensive alternatives. A guide and driver to Mt Kyaiktiyo can be hired through any of the central Bago hotels for around US$40. The same tour booked in Yangon costs US$80.

Bus & Pickup Big air-con buses straight from Yangon to Kyaikto cost K350 from the Highway Bus Centre; smaller air-con minibuses leave from Yangon's Hsimmalaik bus station for K300. If you start from Bago, a large bus costs K250. Pickups from Bago to Kyaikto cost K150 and take five hours.

For travellers wanting to visit Kyaiktiyo, pickups bound for Kinpun (12km from Kyaikto at the base of Mt Kyaiktiyo) leave from a spot near the Kyaikto train station every half-hour or so between 6 am and 4 pm, depending on the number of passengers. The fare for the 20 minute ride is K30 per person.

Train A direct train from Bago to Kyaikto leaves daily at 4.30 am, supposedly arriving three hours later, though many travellers report the trip can take six hours or more. The train from Mottama (Martaban) arrives in Kyaikto around 5 pm, sometimes later if the train is delayed. The foreigner fare is US$7 per seat.

Car If you're coming to Kyaikto by car, keep in mind that the Sittoung Bridge closes at 6 pm.

AROUND KYAIKTO TO MAWLAMYAING
South-east of Kyaikto is **Bilin**, a dusty town of wooden buildings and a favoured stop for truckers making the Yangon-Mawlamyaing (Moulmein) haul. Among the mechanic shops that line the main road through town are a couple of cheap but quite decent **Bamar restaurants**. A few kilometres south-east of town there's a toll bridge over the Bilin River.

Taunzaung Paya, another large and interesting old zedi, can be found at Zokthok village, slightly south of Bilin. The most famous of the many hillside stupas is **Myathabeiq Paya** (Emerald Alms-Bowl Stupa), which can be reached by road and offers good views of town.

Thaton
Long before the rise of Bagan (Pagan), Thaton was an important centre for a Mon kingdom that stretched from the Ayeyarwady River delta to similar river deltas in Thailand, and possibly as far east as Cambodia. Early on it may have been known as Suvannabhumi, the 'Golden Land' – legend says Asoka, the great Indian Buddhist emperor, sent a mission there in the 3rd century BC – and later as Dvaravati when it reached

Visiting the Boulder Stupa of Kyaiktiyo

There are four names to keep in mind in the Kyaiktiyo area: Kyaikto is the town on the highway, Kyaiktiyo is the name of the shrine which is located on Mt Kyaikto, and Kinpun is the pilgrims' village (often called the basecamp) between Kyaikto and Kyaiktiyo. It serves as a staging area for continuing up the mountain, either on foot or by truck. There are also buses to Bago or Yangon.

At Kinpun, 12km from Kyaikto, you'll find several decent restaurants and foodstalls, half a dozen guesthouses, souvenir shops, and a tourist office with restrooms and a washbasin.

From Kinpun, there are two ways to reach the summit. The most time-consuming, but meritorious for Burmese Buddhists, is a strenuous 13km climb along a winding footpath. This hike takes around four hours to reach the boulder shrine itself; it's a pretty hike once you get into the wooded uplands, and there are around 30 rest stops along the way. Foodstalls serve Bamar and Chinese food, water, tea and fruit. As the mountain is flush with bamboo, many souvenir vendors along the path hawk items made from the sturdy grass, including huge toy machine guns labelled Rambo!

You certainly won't be alone on the hike; a trip to the top accumulates considerable merit and there is a steady stream of pilgrims making the ascent during the dry months (November to April). On full moon days, the number swells to the thousands.

The path ascends about 1000m from base to summit, and it's impossible to miss – just follow the crowds. In addition to the various rest stops at the side of the path, there are shrines which relate the legend of the temple's creation.

The quicker, less meritorious way to reach the summit is to catch one of the large trucks that carry pilgrims most of the way up. After a 30 minute, white-knuckle ride around precipitous hairpin curves, the trucks stop at a point that's within a 45 minute hike of the top along a winding footpath. Like the main trail (which it eventually joins), this one's lined with snack and souvenir stalls. The ride costs K125 each way. However, late in the day, the trucks drive all the way to the top (K145), so people can catch the last truck back. From the upper station, if you can't physically make the 45 minute hike, you can hire a *palanquin* (sedan chair) and four bearers to carry you to the top for US$4 or the kyat equivalent. When descending this trail back to the truck stop, be sure to bear right at the first fork; the left fork leads to the long way down – a four hour journey, instead of 45 minutes.

Note that it is only really possible to get to the top when the pilgrimage season commences, at the end of the rainy season in late October. Fewer pilgrims come in April or May, as the weather is so hot that the climb becomes very trying, and the haze from local slash-and-burn agriculture obscures views from the summit. Once the rainy season starts in June, the whole mountain more or less closes for four or five months; both the original footpath and the truck road become virtually impassable. There is some discussion about sealing the truck road and cementing the steps in the final 45 minute climb to allow all-weather travel.

Joe Cummings

its dynastic peak between the 6th and 10th centuries AD. The thriving port carried on trade with the south of India and Sri Lanka. Shin Aran, a monk from Thaton, carried Theravada Buddhism north to the Burmese kingdom of Bagan, and in 1057 Thaton was conquered by King Anawrahta of Bagan.

Today Thaton sits on the main road and rail line that stretches from Bago to Mottama. Little of ancient Thaton is visible, as the modern town has been built over the old sites; piles of brick here and there are all that remain of the massive city walls. The town's core is a leafy place, lining each side of the highway with colonial mansions and thatched-roof homes, and a few older stupas on hillsides surrounding town. A picturesque canal network irrigates rice paddies and fruit orchards.

Shwe Zayan Paya, on the northern side of the road just beyond the clock tower, features a nice set of monastery buildings and a large stupa supposedly built during the early Mon era. A famous 10th century standing Buddha stele found at this paya was sculpted in the classic Mon style and shows strong similarities with Dvaravati-period Buddhas from central Thailand.

Places to Stay & Eat An overnight rest stop in Thaton might be worthwhile if you're travelling between Yangon and Mawlamyaing without any other stops. A large, two storey, no-name *guesthouse* (☎ *Thaton 186)*, off the northern side of the main street through town, has clean and comfortable rooms with shared facilities for K500 per double. The friendly staff report that although the guesthouse isn't likely to be officially licensed to accept foreigners, they can arrange permission for overnight stays at the police station on a case-by-case basis.

There are several *teashops* and basic *Bamar-style restaurants* along the busy main street.

Mottama (Martaban)

Double-decker passenger ferries cross the Thanlwin River to Mawlamyaing from the Mottama landing every half hour from 7.15 am to 6.45 pm. The fare is K5 and the trip takes 20 to 30 minutes, depending on tides.

Less frequent vehicle ferries from Mottama to Mawlamyaing cost K100 per passenger plus K300 per car or van, more for trucks and buses. Departures depend on the tides; the last boat leaves just before sunset and the crossing takes about half an hour.

If you don't feel like waiting for a ferry you can charter a passenger boat across the river for around K1000. If you arrive by train, just get in one of the faster 25 seat long-tail boats, which cost K30 per person.

See the Getting There & Away entry in the Mawlamyaing section for details on bus and rail transport to Mottama.

MAWLAMYAING (MOULMEIN)

The atmosphere of post-colonial decay is more palpable here than in fast-developing Yangon or Mandalay; it's also an attractive, leafy, tropical town with a ridge of stupa-capped hills on one side and the sea on the other. George Orwell (author of *Burmese Days)* was stationed here for a time in the 1920s during his service with the Indian Imperial Police.

Mawlamyaing served as capital of British Burma from 1827 to 1852, during which time it developed as a major teak port. Much coastal shipping still goes on, although Pathein (Bassein) and Yangon have superseded it as Myanmar's most important ports. Today it's Myanmar's fourth largest city with a population of around 300,000 people, composed roughly of 75% Mon or some mixture of Mon, plus Kayin, Bamar, Indian, Chinese and other ethnicities.

Orientation

The city's main north-south thoroughfares begin with North Bogyoke Lan, which runs east-west from the vehicle ferry landing at the northern end of Mawlamyaing and links with Htet Lan Magyi (Upper Main Rd) in the centre of town. Htet Lan Magyi continues south past several government buildings to the main bus station at the southern end of town, then connects with the highway southward to Ye. Along the western side of town, South Bogyoke Lan (Lower Main Rd) connects through the market and commercial districts. Another block west, Strand Rd hugs the waterfront and offers access to various local and long-distance passenger ferry jetties. From Strand Rd, Kyaik-than Lan runs from west to east and terminates at Kyaikthanlan Paya.

The main west-east avenue is Dawei Jetty Rd, which leads from the Dawei jetty,

SOUTH-EASTERN MYANMAR

on the coast across town, to the southern end of the ridge, where most of the city's famous temples and shrines are located. On the eastern side of the ridge stand several grand colonial-era mansions that have been converted to government offices.

Taungwaing Lan cuts diagonally from near the bus station south-east to the airport and Mawlamyaing University, terminating near Taungwaing Paya.

Mon Cultural Museum

This two storey building at the north-eastern corner of Baho Lan (formerly Dalhousie St) and Dawei Jetty Rd is dedicated to the Mon history of the region. Exhibits are displayed downstairs, while upstairs are reading rooms and toilets.

The museum's modest collection includes: stelae with Mon inscriptions; 100-year-old wooden sculptures depicting old age and sickness (used as *dhamma*-teaching devices in monasteries); ceramics; *thanakha* grinding stones; silver betel boxes; an English-language letter, dated 22 December 1945, from Bogyoke Aung San to Mo Chit Hlaing, a famous Mon leader; lacquerware; *parabaik* (folding manuscripts); royal funerary urns; Mon musical instruments; and wooden Buddha altars.

In front of the museum is a British cannon dated 1826, plus a huge Burmese gong. Some labels are printed in English though most are in Burmese only.

The museum is open Tuesday to Sunday from 9.30 am to 4 pm. Admission is free.

Religious Monuments

In the city's east, a hilly north-south ridge is topped with five separate monasteries and shrines. At the northern end is **Mahamuni Paya**, the largest temple complex in Mawlamyaing. It's built in the typical Mon style with covered brick walkways linking various square shrine buildings. The main image is a replica of its namesake in Mandalay (see the Mahamuni Paya section in the Mandalay chapter for more information) – without the thick goldleaf. Another difference is that women may enter the main Buddha

chamber here. Tilework on the chamber walls includes colourful peacock representations. In the outer cloister several well executed paintings depict local scenes from the 1920s and 1930s.

Farther south along the ridge stands **Kyaikthanlan Paya**, the city's tallest and most visible stupa. It was probably here that Rudyard Kipling's poetic 'Burma girl' was 'a-settin' ...' in the opening lines of *Mandalay*: 'By the old Moulmein Pagoda, lookin' lazy at the sea'.

For K5 you can take a lift to the main platform surrounding the 40m stupa, which offers fine views over the city and harbour. You can also see the plains to the east towards Kyaikmaraw and the coconut tree-shrouded islands in the mouth of the Sittoung River. The zedi's name comes from the Mon word for stupa, *kyaik*, while *than-lan* is thought to mean Siamese-defeating (than=shan=siam). The defeat refers to the Mon effort in building the highest stupa in the region, rather than a military manoeuvre. A large bell at the shrine's western entry dates to 1855 and weighs 600 *viss* (960kg).

Below Kyaikthanlan is the 100-year-old **Seindon Mibaya Kyaung**, a monastery where King Mindon Min's queen, Seindon, sought refuge after Myanmar's last monarch, King Thibaw Min, took power. On the next rise south stands the isolated silver-and-gold-plated **Aung Theikdi Zedi**.

Farther south, on the western side of the ridge, a view looks out over the city and is a favoured spot for catching sunsets and evening sea breezes. Just beyond the viewpoint stands **U Khanti Paya**, built to commemorate the hermit of Mandalay Hill fame; supposedly U Khanti spent some time on this hill as well. It's a rustic, airy sort of place centred around a large Buddha image. Various bells and gongs are suspended by ropes from the steel supports of the sanctuary's ceiling.

U Zina Paya, on the southern spur of the ridge, was named after a former monk who dreamt of finding gems at this spot, then dug them up and used the proceeds to build a temple on the site. One of the shrine buildings contains a very curvy, sensual-looking

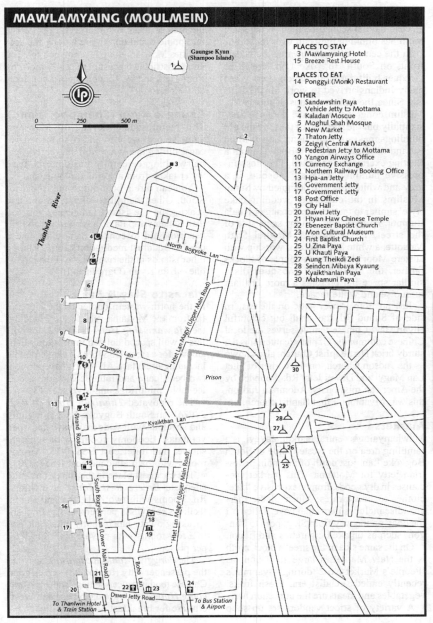

MAWLAMYAING (MOULMEIN)

Gaungse Kyun
(Shampoo Island)

Thanlwin River

0   250   500 m

North Bogyoke Lan

Htet Lan Magyi (Upper Main Road)

Zaymyin Lan

Prison

Strand Road

Kyaikthan Lan

South Bogyoke Lan (Lower Main Road)

Htet Lan Magyi (Upper Main Road)

Boho Lan

Dawei Jetty Road

To Thanlwin Hotel
& Train Station

To Bus Station
& Airport

PLACES TO STAY
3 Mawlamyaing Hotel
15 Breeze Rest House

PLACES TO EAT
14 Ponggyi (Monk) Restaurant

OTHER
1 Sandawshin Paya
2 Vehicle Jetty to Mottama
4 Kaladan Mosque
5 Moghul Shah Mosque
6 New Market
7 Thaton Jetty
8 Zeigyi (Central Market)
9 Pedestrian Jetty to Mottama
10 Yangon Airways Office
11 Currency Exchange
12 Northern Railway Booking Office
13 Hpa-an Jetty
16 Government Jetty
17 Government Jetty
18 Post Office
19 City Hall
20 Dawei Jetty
21 Htyan Haw Chinese Temple
22 Ebenezer Baptist Church
23 Mon Cultural Museum
24 First Baptist Church
25 U Zina Paya
26 U Khauti Paya
27 Aung Theikdi Zedi
28 Seindon Mibaya Kyaung
29 Kyaikthanlan Paya
30 Mahamuni Paya

reclining Buddha topped with a blinking electric halo; a second recliner in the same room has blinking lights all over its body.

In the centre of town towards the waterfront, on South Bogyoke Lan, are three mosques built during the colonial era when many Indians arrived to work for the British. Since the Indian exodus of the 1970s, Muslim congregations have declined substantially but the survival of these grand old buildings makes a walk along Lower Main Rd and its extension South Bogyoke Lan a fleeting exercise in nostalgia. The most impressive building, **Kaladan Mosque**, is a grey and white structure designed by Sunni Muslims in the elaborate 'wedding-cake style' similar to that seen in Penang or Kuala Lumpur. Farther south, on the same side of the street, is the smaller **Moghul Shah Mosque**, a white Shia place of worship with austere Moorish arches. A couple of blocks farther, the Sunni **Sulati Mosque** fills a similar space but presents a more brilliant turquoise and white facade.

Just up from Dawei jetty, on the eastern side of Strand Rd, the small but colourful **Htyan Haw** Chinese temple serves the local Chinese community. Of historic interest is the sturdy brick **First Baptist Church**, also known as the Judson Church, on the corner of Htet Lan Magyi and Dawei Jetty Rd. Founded by the American missionary, Adoniram Judson, this was Myanmar's first Baptist church.

Markets

Mawlamyaing's central market, **Zaygyi**, is a rambling area on the western side of South Bogyoke Lan, just north of the main pedestrian jetty for Mottama. This market specialises in dry goods, from inexpensive 'bale' clothes to housewares. Much of the merchandise includes items that have 'fallen off the boat' on the way from Singapore to Yangon, such as untaxed cigarettes and liquor.

On the same side of the street a block north is the **New Market**, a large shed built as 'People's Market No 2' during Myanmar's recently ended socialist era. Fresh fruits, vegetables and meats are the attraction here.

A variety of street vendors set up shop along both sides of South Bogyoke Lan in the area of these two markets. Fresh areca nut, pomelo and durian are among the specialities Mawlamyaing is renowned for. The entire district is busiest in the early morning from 7 to 8 am; by 9 am business is considerably slower.

Gaungse Kyun (Shampoo Island)

This picturesque little isle off Mawlamyaing's north-western end is so named because during the Ava period the yearly royal hairwashing ceremony customarily used water taken from a spring on the island.

You can hire a boat out to the island for K500. Other than just walking around and soaking up the island ambience, you can visit Sandawshin Paya, a whitewash and silver zedi said to contain hair relics, and a nearby Buddhist meditation centre. Among other islands in the river, there is the largest one – Bilu Kyun (Ogre Island).

Places to Stay & Eat

In the north-western corner of the city, not far from the Mottama vehicle ferry landing, the *Mawlamyaing Hotel* (☎ 032-22560) offers a well spaced collection of roomy bungalows for a steep US$36/48 a single/double including breakfast. All rooms have air-con, two beds, cane and rattan chairs, desk, coffee table, minifridge and Myanmar TV.

The renovated *Thanlwin Hotel* (☎ 032-21976), on South Bogyoke Lan, is friendly and spacious with wide stairways and open verandas. Economy rooms with separate shower and toilet cost US$10/15. Air-con rooms with bath attached cost US$15/20.

The cheapest place is the funky but quite adequate *Breeze Rest House* at 6 Strand Rd. Rooms with two beds, fan and shared facilities cost US$5 per person. The English-speaking owner has recently added air-con to a few rooms with private bath for US$7 per person.

The *Ponggyi (Monk) Restaurant*, opposite the passenger jetty (to Hpa-an) serves good Chinese food in a clean setting. The *Mawlamyaing Hotel* serves good Chinese and Western fare for breakfast, lunch and dinner.

Getting There & Away

Air Unfortunately, Yangon Airways (YA) has not yet made Mawlamyaing a regular part of its South-Eastern Myanmar route. Recently we have seen flights scheduled during peak tourist times, only to be cancelled during off-peak times. Nevertheless, YA continues to maintain an office in town, next to the bank by the passenger ferry jetty.

That only leaves always-risky Myanma Airways (MA), which flies direct from Yangon to Mawlamyaing on Wednesday, and via Dawei (Tavoy) on Saturday. For the latter flight, an overnight in Dawei is necessary since seats from Dawei to Mawlamyaing can only be reserved in Dawei, not in Yangon. From Yangon to Mawlamyaing the fare for the 35 minute flight is US$50 by F-27, US$55 by F-28. From Dawei, an hour away, the fare is US$50/55. There is an additional flight from Dawei to Yangon on Wednesday.

Bus & Pickup Several overnight buses costing K800 to K1000 leave Yangon for Mawlamyaing at 8 pm, and arrive at Mottama at about 6 am. From there, you take a ferry (K5) or much faster 25 passenger outboard motorboat (K30) across the river to Mawlamyaing. Bus tickets can be purchased from offices opposite the central train station, and most companies provide free shuttles to the Highway bus station. The fare costs K800 to K1000.

Pickups leave from west Yangon's Hsimmalaik bus station in the morning for K500.

Recently, permits have been sometimes required to proceed south by road into Tanintharyi Division. However, since travel has been opening up in nearby Mon State and elsewhere, it may be possible to go overland despite vague official restrictions. Mawlamyaing's main station for southbound buses or pickups is near the southern end of town off the road to Ye-U, where public vehicles go to Thanbyuzayat, Kyaikkami, Setse, Dawei, or Payathonzu on the Thai border (opposite Three Pagodas Pass).

Train Two express trains run from Yangon to Mottama daily, the No 81 Up at 8 am and the No 89 Up at 10 pm. Both trains make brief stops in Bago and Thaton. When the trains are running on time the trip takes nine hours – similar to the bus. The foreigner price for an upper-class seat is US$17. Ordinary-class seats cost K200, although they aren't officially available to foreigners. Tickets can be purchased at the train station.

In the reverse direction, the No 82 Down leaves Mottama at 7 pm and is scheduled to arrive in Yangon at 4.30 am; the No 90 Down leaves at 9 am and arrives in Yangon at 6 pm. In Mawlamyaing tickets may be purchased one day in advance at the Northern Railway Booking Office, which stands between Strand Rd and South Bogyoke Lan, just north of the Hpa-an jetty.

A separate southern railway line begins at the southern end of the city and terminates at Ye-U. From Ye-U, another local train continues to Dawei. Foreigners have not been allowed to travel on these rail lines for some time, due to a lack of security farther south. With the military presence surrounding a pipeline being built near Dawei, this situation is unlikely to change soon.

Boat See the earlier Mottama section for details on the Thanlwin River ferry crossings to Mawlamyaing. There are two main jetties on the Mawlamyaing side for ferries to/from Mottama: the vehicle jetty at the northern end of town and the pedestrian jetty just south of the central market off Strand Rd. Double-decker passenger ferries depart for Mottama across the Thanlwin River every half hour; the fare is K5 and the trip takes 20 to 30 minutes. Faster 25-seat outboards cross the river for K30 per person.

The next jetty south of the Mottama pedestrian jetty handles boats to Hpa-an in the Kayin (Karen) State. See the Getting There & Away entry in the Hpa-an section later in this chapter for details on twice-daily ferries to Hpa-an from Mawlamyaing.

Next south are two jetties reserved for government boats only, followed by the larger Dawei jetty for boats to Dawei and Myeik (Mergui). It can be quite difficult for foreigners to arrange passage on any of

SOUTH-EASTERN MYANMAR

these boats, if only because local officials are not yet aware of newer and often more relaxed regulations. In such cases it may pay to inquire in Yangon at the Myanma Five Star Line (MFSL) office.

Getting Around
Motorised *thoun bein* (three wheelers) are the main form of public transport around the city. The highest concentration of three wheelers is found on South Bogyoke Lan in front of the Zeigyi market. The going rate is K50 to K60 for a short hop within the centre of town and as much as K150 or K200 for a ride up the ridge to Kyaikthanlan. You can also rent or sometimes borrow bikes from one of the hotels.

AROUND MAWLAMYAING
The authorities often frown upon foreigners travelling south of Mawlamyaing, even though the local tourist brochures are flush with photos of Thanbyuzayat, Kyaikkami and Setse. We have heard from travellers who have gone south without a problem, and from others who were turned back at the bus station. However, **Mudon**, 29km south of the city, is considered a 'white area' and there are no checkpoints on the way. Verdant mountains to the east are a source of 'jungle food' – deer, snake and other wild forest species – for restaurants in Mudon. The town is also known for cotton weaving.

Just north of Mudon is a turn-off east to **Azin Dam**, a water storage and flood control facility that's also used to irrigate local rubber plantations. A tidy recreation area at **Kandawgyi** – a lake formed by the dam – is a favourite picnic spot; bring your own snacks or rely on the vendors who gather here on weekends and holidays. At the northern end of the lake stands the gilded stupa of **Kandawgyi Paya**.

Just off the road between Mawlamyaing and Mudon are two interesting hilltop shrines at **Kyauktalon Taung** and **Yadana Taung**. The former is a flat-topped limestone crag crowned with stupas. On the opposite side of the road is a similar but smaller outcropping surmounted by a Hindu

temple. On Yadana Taung, local Buddhists are constructing a huge reclining Buddha, which when completed will reportedly measure around 160m in length, making it the largest such image in the world. Many other stupas and standing Buddhas dot the countryside around the reclining image.

South of Mudon begins a 'brown area'. Most locals will warn against travelling along the roads here after 3 pm. The government attributes road attacks in this area to Mon or Kayin insurgents, but since the attacks don't discriminate between government and private vehicles, and since the motive always seems to be robbery, it's hard to conceive that the perpetrators are anything other than common highway bandits. One of the methods used is to roll a log across the road to force vehicles to stop, at which time armed men appear and demand money from drivers and passengers. Incidents between 8 am and 2 pm are apparently quite rare because that's when most people travel – increased traffic means increased safety. Public transport – buses or pickups – are comparatively safer from attack than private vehicles.

Kyaikmaraw
This small, charming town 24km south-east of Mawlamyaing is accessible via a sealed road. For the most part, Kyaikmaraw is considered a 'white area' although insurgents or bandits have been known to rob rubber plantations along the road to Mawlamyaing.

Hugging the banks of the Ataran River, a branch of the Thanlwin River, the town consists of mostly wooden homes with thatched-palm or corrugated metal roofs.

Kyaikmaraw Paya The pride of the town is this temple built by Queen Shin Saw Pu in 1455 in the late Mon regional style. Among the temple's many outstanding features are multicoloured glass windows set in the outside walls of the main sanctuary, an inner colonnade decorated in mirrored tiles, and beautiful ceramic tile floors. Painted reliefs appear on the exterior of several auxiliary buildings; one wall of the *thein* (ordination hall) bears a large relief of

Myei Sountmatham, the Hindu-Buddhist earth goddess (Ma Dharani in Pali), twisting her wet hair to create a flood to wash away Mara the tempter.

Covered brick walkways lead to and around the main square sanctuary in typical 15th century Mon style. The huge main Buddha image sits in a 'European pose', with the legs hanging down as if sitting on a chair rather than in the much more common crosslegged manner. The Burmese call this the 'going to leave' pose, a transition between the canonical sitting and standing/walking postures. A number of smaller crosslegged Buddhas surround the main image, and behind it are two reclining Buddhas, one with eyes open, one with eyes closed. The robes of all the Buddha figures in the main sanctuary are gilded; some are encrusted with semiprecious stones. Another impressive feature is the carved and painted wooden ceiling.

A side room to the inner sanctuary contains sculptures depicting the Buddha in various stages of illness and death – other than the traditional *parinibbana* reclining posture, these are unusual motifs for Buddhist temples. Two images show the Buddha lying on his back with hands folded on his abdomen; another depicts an ill Buddha stooping over slightly with one hand clasped to his chest, the other hand against the wall as his disciples reach out to assist him. Another elaborate sculpture display features *devas* (spirit beings) dividing the Buddha's remains to serve as relics while his monastic disciples watch.

Next to the main sanctuary is a small museum with Buddha images, donated by the faithful, on the upper floor; other artefacts from the area are on the lower floor. Some of these objects are over 500 years old.

Getting There & Away Two kinds of trucks frequently ply the Kyaikmaraw road from Mawlamyaing; bright green Chevy trucks with wooden door panels and wooden passenger compartments cost K30 per person and take about 45 minutes, while smaller white Japanese pickups cost K50 per person

and take 30 minutes. Lined with toddy palms and rubber plantations, the road passes through eight villages before ending at the riverbank in Kyaikmaraw.

Thanbyuzayat

South of Mudon, little traffic is seen and the hills to the east grow more densely forested. Thanbyuzayat (Tin Shelter), 30km south of Mawlamyaing, was the western terminus of the infamous Burma-Siam Railway, dubbed the 'Death Railway' by the thousands of Allied prisoners of war (POWs) and Asian coolies who were forced by the Japanese military to build it. It was here that the Japanese broke into Myanmar after marching over the rugged mountain range separating Myanmar from Tak in Thailand via Three Pagodas Pass.

The strategic objective of the railway was to secure an alternative supply route for the Japanese conquest of Myanmar and other Asian countries to the west. Construction on the railway began on 16 September 1942 at existing terminals in Thanbyuzayat and Nong Pladuk, Thailand. At the time, Japanese engineers estimated that it would take five years to link Thailand and Burma by rail, but the Japanese army forced the POWs to complete the 415km, 1m-gauge railway, of which roughly two-thirds ran through Thailand, in 16 months. Much of the railway was built in difficult terrain that required high bridges and deep mountain cuttings. The rails were finally joined 37km south of the town of Payathonzu (Three Pagodas Pass); a Japanese brothel train inaugurated the line. The railway was in use for 20 months before the Allies bombed it in 1945.

An estimated 16,000 POWs died as a result of brutal treatment by their captors, a story chronicled by Pierre Boulle's book *Bridge on the River Kwai* and popularised by a movie based on the book. The notorious bridge itself still stands in Kanchanaburi, Thailand. Only one POW is known to have escaped, a Briton who took refuge among pro-British Kayin guerrillas.

Although the statistics of the number of POWs who died during the Japanese occupation are horrifying, the figures for the labourers, many from Myanmar, Thailand, Malaysia and Indonesia, are even worse. It is thought that 90,000 to 100,000 coolies died in the area.

A clock tower in the centre of Thanbyuzayat stands at a road junction; the road south leads to Ye-U while the road west goes to Kyaikkami and Setse. About 1.5km south of the clock tower, a locomotive and piece of track commemorating the Burma-Siam Railway are on display. A kilometre west of the clock tower, in the direction of Kyaikkami, on the south side of the road, lies the **Htaukkyant War Cemetery**, which contains 3771 graves of Allied POWs who died building the railway. Maintained by the Commonwealth War Graves Commission, the landscaped cemetery is reminiscent of, but much smaller than, the Taukkyan War Cemetery near Yangon. Most of those buried were British, but there are also markers for American, Dutch and Australian soldiers.

Thanbyuzayat is easily reached by public pickup from the Mawlamyaing bus station; there are six departures, all before noon, for K150 per person. As there is no legal lodging in Thanbyuzayat, start early so that you can catch the last pickup back to Mawlamyaing at around 2 pm.

Kyaikkami

Located 9km north-east of Thanbyuzayat, Kyaikkami was a small coastal resort and missionary centre known as Amherst during the British era. Adoniram Judson (1788-1850), an American missionary and linguist who has practically attained sainthood among Burmese Baptists, was sailing to India with his wife when their ship was blown off course, forcing them to land at Kyaikkami. Judson stayed on and established his first mission here; the original site is now a Catholic school on a small lane off the main road.

Among other accomplishments, Judson developed the first Burmese-English dictionary in 1849 and was the first person to translate the Bible into Burmese. He was buried at sea, but the grave of his wife, Anne Judson, can still be see in Kyaikkami,

a couple of hundred metres off the main road near the school.

However, the main focus of Kyaikkami is **Yele Paya**, a metal-roofed Buddhist shrine complex perched over the sea and reached via a long two level causeway; the lower level is submerged during high tide. Along with 11 Buddha hair relics, the shrine chamber beneath Yele Paya reportedly contains a Buddha image that supposedly floated here on a raft from Sri Lanka in ancient times. According to legend, a gifted Sinhalese sculptor fashioned four different Buddha images using pieces from the original Bodhi Tree mixed with a cement composite. He then placed them on four wooden rafts and set the rafts adrift on the ocean; the other three landed near Pathein, Kyaikto and Dawei. A display of 21 Mandalay-style Buddha statues sit over the spot where the Sinhalese image is supposedly buried. Some of the seashells for sale on the premises have been fashioned into religious charms.

During the early half of the day there are occasional pickups to Kyaikkami from Thanbyuzayat for K70 per person. You can also charter a car for around K1200.

Setse

This low-key Gulf of Martaban beach lies about half way between Kyaikkami and Thanbyuzayat. It's a very wide, brown-sand beach that tends towards tidal flats when the shallow surf-line recedes at low tide. The beach is lined by waving casuarina trees.

A recently built guesthouse on the beach is licensed for foreigners – perhaps an indication that the region will continue to open up. The privately owned *A Htou She Guest House* has four rooms with attached bath for K1800 per room, and two rooms with common bath for K1200. It's on the beach, along with several bungalows for Burmese citizens. *Vendors* sell fresh young coconuts, and a few modest *restaurants* offer fresh seafood. The biggest, *Mya Annawa* (Emerald Sea), serves delicious lobster and prawns.

There is no public transport to Setse as yet; from Thanbyuzayat you can charter a taxi for K2000.

Kayin State

Many districts in Kayin State and Tanintharyi Division (which both share borders with Thailand) are very much off-limits to foreign visitors travelling from Yangon, but things are changing. The Kayin State, homeland to around a million Kayin, has probably received more foreign visitors who have crossed over – unofficially – from Thailand than from any other direction. Many international volunteers have ventured into the frontier area to assist with refugee concerns.

Ever since Myanmar attained independence from the British in 1948, the Kayin have been embroiled in a fight for autonomy. The main insurgent body, the Karen National Union (KNU), controls much of the northern and eastern parts of the state, although recent Yangon military victories have left the KNU and its military component, the Karen National Liberation Army (KNLA), without a permanent headquarters. A split between Christian and Buddhist factions has also weakened the KNU, which had become the de facto centre of the Democratic Alliance of Burma (DAB); an alliance of a dozen rebel groups fighting for regional autonomy. KNU headquarters was also the seat of the National Coalition Government of the Union of Burma (NCGUB), a 'parallel government' established by a group of disaffected National League for Democracy (NLD) members who won parliamentary seats in the ill-fated May 1990 national elections. Much of the state remains a potential battleground as sporadic fighting between Burmese troops and the KNLA continues.

HPA-AN

Hpa-an, capital of Kayin State, was recently removed from the restricted list of travel destinations. It's now possible to reach it by road from Yangon across a new bridge over the Thanlwin River, west of the town, or by river ferry from Mawlamyaing – a very scenic trip. Another new bridge across the

Gyaing River at Zathabyin, east of Mawlamyaing, links Hpa-an with Mawlamyaing by road. The trip by car takes an hour.

Even though Hpa-an is a small but busy commerce centre, it still has something of a village atmosphere. Away from the jetty, which is crowded with trucks and motorcycles, you can see farmers coming to town in horsecarts, or trishaws stacked with baskets or mats to sell in the market. The townspeople are a mixture of Mon, Bamar and Muslim. Burmese is the primary language, but Kayin is spoken by many. The mosque seems to be the town hub, and there are numerous teashops around, along with pickups to Thaton and Kyaikto.

Hpa-an is famous among Burmese for the Buddhist village at **Thamanyat Kuang** and the highly respected monk U Winaya, whose solid support of democracy leader Aung San Suu Kyi is well known throughout Myanmar. Thamanyat monastery is about 40km south-east of Hpa-an, and there is a daily flow of small buses to this busy religious site. The fare by bus from Hpa-an is K70.

Places to Stay & Eat

So far there are only two places worth staying at in Hpa-an. Near the jetty is the *Royal Guesthouse*, managed by the ever-helpful Mr Robin. The rooms are adequate, with separate shower and toilet, and cost US$3 per person. Slightly better value is the friendly *Parami Hotel*, a few blocks away. Rooms with fan, mosquito net and common bath cost US$4 per person. There are a few rooms with attached bath and toilet for US$7.

Khit-Thit Restaurant (New Age Restaurant) and *Dream Restaurant* are near the guesthouses, although the food is quite ordinary.

Getting There & Away

Bus & Pickup Shwe Chin The (Golden Lion) buses depart from Yangon's Hsimmalaik bus station at 8 pm and arrive at about 7 am. The fare is K600. Pickups from Hpa-an to Kyaiktiyo depart from in front of the green mosque and cost around K400 or K500 for a front seat. Pickups from Thaton

SOUTH-EASTERN MYANMAR

cost about K200. Buses depart from near the Parami Hotel at about 6 pm for Kyaiktiyo and Bago.

Boat Double-decker ferries leave from the Hpa-an jetty in Mawlamyaing daily at 7 am and noon for the four hour trip up the Thanlwin River to Hpa-an on the river's eastern bank. The fare for foreigners is US$2 for upper-deck class, and US$12 for a stuffy cabin. There's a Chinese restaurant across from the loading dock in Mawlamyaing.

From Hpa-an a rutted, unsurfaced road heads 143km south-east to Myawadi, a town controlled by the Tatmadaw (armed forces) on the western bank of the Thaungyin River (known as Moei River to the Thais) opposite the northern Thai town of Mae Sot. As many as 100,000 Kayin refugees fleeing KNLA-Tatmadaw battles are encamped on the Thai side of the border in this area. In late 1994 the Burmese and Thai governments agreed to span the river with a vehicle bridge but construction was halted in mid-1995 because of disputes over the repatriation of refugees. Yangon is demanding that the Thais send the refugees back; so far the Thai government has refused, on humanitarian grounds.

Although it's possible to drive from Hpa-an (or Mawlamyaing) to Myawadi in six or seven hours, the final 64km between Kawkareik and Myawadi is considered unsafe due to fighting in the area. There are several military checkpoints along the way and it's highly unlikely any foreigner would be permitted to make this trip.

Tourist brochures printed in Yangon sometimes mention that Myawadi is open to day visits from the Thai side but in practice the border situation is often so tense that this is rarely allowed.

PAYATHONZU (THREE PAGODAS)
Another Yangon-controlled town on the Thai-Burmese border, Payathonzu is around 110km south-east of Thanbyuzayat via an unsurfaced road. Three small zedis mark a mountain pass used for many centuries as a route for overland trade as well as military

invasion. The zedis today stand on Thai turf, 12m from the Burmese border crossing. Control of the Burmese side of the border once vacillated between the KNU and the MNLF, as Payathonzu was one of several 'toll gates' along the Thai-Burmese border where insurgent armies collected a 5% tax on all merchandise passing through.

The Kayin also conduct a huge multi-million dollar business in illegal mining and logging, the products of which are smuggled into Thailand by the truckload under cover of night – not without the 'palms-up' cooperation of the Thai police, of course. Pressure for control of these border points has increased since the Thai government enacted a ban on all logging in Thailand in 1989, which has led to an increase in teak smuggling.

In late 1988 heavy fighting broke out between the Kayin and the Mon for control of the 'toll gate' here. Since this is the only place for hundreds of kilometres in either direction where a border crossing is geographically convenient, this is where the Mon army (who traditionally have controlled this area) have customarily collected the 5% tax on smuggling. The Kayin insurgents do the same at other points north along the Thai-Burmese border. Burmese government pressure on the Kayin farther north led to a conflict between the Kayin and Mon over Three Pagodas trade, and the village on the Burmese side was virtually burnt to the ground in the 1988 skirmishes.

In 1989 the Yangon government wrested control of the town from both the Kayin and Mon, and the Burmese seem firmly established at the border for the time being. The town has been entirely rebuilt and filled with shops catering to an odd mix of occupation troops and Thai tourists.

Foreigners are allowed to cross the border here for day trips upon payment of 130B (baht – Thai currency) or US$5 cash. Payathonzu lies 470km by road from Yangon but is considered '75% safe' by the Burmese military. Insurgent Kayin forces are still in the area, and there are occasional firefights. Payathonzu has three teashops, a cinema, several mercantile shops with *longyis* (sarong-style garments), cheroots, jade, clothes and a few souvenir shops with Mon/Kayin/Bamar handicrafts. Bargaining is necessary but, in general, goods are well priced. About 20 Thai merchants operate in town – the Burmese government offers them free rent to open shops. A new temple, given the Thai name **Wat Suwankhiri**, sits on a bluff near the town.

Kloeng Thaw Falls, located 12km from the border, takes a couple of hours by motorcycle to reach from Payathonzu. The road to the falls is only open in the dry season – reportedly the Kayin control the waterfall area during the rainy season. Even in good weather, the two-rut track is very rugged – not recommended for motorcycle novices. Like other sites in the region, this one is subject to closure. Lately, the falls area has been closed more often than it has been open.

The border is open daily from 7 am to 6 pm.

Getting There & Away

Only military vehicles or commercial vehicles under armed guard use the road from Thanbyuzayat. For the time being, foreigners are only permitted to visit Payathonzu from the Thai side; the nearest Thai town of any size is Sangkhlaburi, where lodging and food are readily available.

On the Thai side, a 19km-long paved road to Three Pagodas Pass begins 4km before you reach Sangkhlaburi off Thailand's Highway 323. At this intersection a Thai police checkpoint may stop you for minor interrogation, depending on recent events in the Three Pagodas Pass area. Along the way you'll pass a couple of villages inhabited entirely by Mon or Kayin; at one time there was a branch of the All Burma Students Democratic Front (ABSDF), where self-exiled Yangon students had set up an opposition movement with the intention of ousting the Ne Win government from Myanmar. The students have since moved north, to Thailand's Tak Province.

Pickups to Three Pagodas Pass leave about every 50 minutes between 6 am and 5 pm from Sangkhlaburi's central market area. The fare is 40B; the last pickup back to Sangkhlaburi leaves Three Pagodas Pass at around 4.30 pm.

Tanintharyi (Tenasserim) Division

Known to the outside world as Tenasserim until 1989, Tanintharyi has a long history of trade with India (especially Coromandel) and the Middle East. Because it's joined with Thailand to a relatively slender length of land separating the Andaman Sea/Indian Ocean from the Gulf of Thailand, this trade link included Siam and other nations east of Myanmar's eastern mountain ranges. Routes through Dawei and Myeik were especially important, and for many years, before the arrival of the British in the late 19th century, the Siamese either controlled the state or received annual tributes from its inhabitants.

Most of the people living in the division are of Bamar ethnicity, although splitting hairs one can easily identify Dawei and Myeik subgroups of the Bamar who enjoy their own dialect, cuisine and so on. Large numbers of Mon also live in the division, and in or near the larger towns you'll find Kayin (often Christian) and Indian (often Muslim) residents.

The Tatmadaw have pushed the KNLA and its Mon equivalent, the MNLF, south from their states into rural or forested areas of the Tanintharyi Division. Hence much of the eastern portion towards Thailand – and parts of the southern extent between Myeik and Kawthoung – is considered 'black territory' by Yangon. Road banditry is not uncommon along the main roads in the interior.

Although permits are no longer required for visits to Dawei, Myeik or Kawthoung, only Dawei is accessible by land. To reach Myeik you must fly from Yangon, Dawei or Kawthoung. The latter is easily reached by boat from Ranong, Thailand.

DAWEI (TAVOY)

The area near the mouth of the Dawei River has been inhabited for five centuries or more, mostly by Mon and Thai mariners. English trader Ralph Fitch mentions a stop at Tavi during his 1586 sea journey between Bago and Melaka in a written account stating that tin from the area 'serves all India'. The present town dates to 1751 when it was a minor 'back door' port for the Ayuthaya empire in Thailand (then Siam). From this point it bounced back and forth between Bamar and Siamese rule until British annexation in 1826.

Still a port of medium importance, Dawei today is a sleepy, tropical seaside town, only recently connected to the rest of Myanmar by road and rail. Areas to the west and north of town are planted in rice, while to the east lie patches of jungle. Some of the architecture in town is quite impressive, with many old wooden houses in the two storey vernacular, with hipped rooflines and plenty of temple-like carved wood ornamentation. Mixed in are more modest thatch-roofed bungalows and a few colonial-style brick-and-stucco mansions. Tall, slender sugar palms, coco palms, banana and other fruit trees, along with heliconia and lots of hanging orchids, are interspersed throughout – it's a very green town due to the abundant annual rain that falls on the southern half of Tanintharyi Division. In spite of its remote location – or perhaps because of it – Dawei has become a significant Burmese Buddhist centre.

Dawei's sleepy, laid-back demeanour is threatened by the development of a new Ye-U-Dawei railway, which was largely built using locally conscripted labour. Hundreds of Tanintharyi Division residents fled to Thailand rather than work on the railway under conditions – if refugee reports are to be believed – that almost rival those described in chronicles of the Japanese army's 'Death Railway'. According to Amnesty International, one of the camps of refugee labourers at the Thai border was attacked by a battalion of Myanmar's 62nd Infantry and some of the refugees were forcefully repatriated.

Dawei is also near the starting point of the massive Yadana gas pipeline project. When operational, the 700km pipeline will carry natural gas from natural gas fields in the Gulf of Mottama to Ratchaburi Province in Thailand. About 400km of its length runs through the Mon State and Tanintharyi Division, the remainder through Thailand. Reportedly, the Myanmar government relocated villages originally in the pipeline's path with little or no compensation for the villagers. A second pipeline, leading from the Yetagun gas field south of the Yadana field, began construction in 1998 and will eventually join the existing Yadana line in delivering natural gas to Thailand. Low demand in Thailand – due to the economic crunch of 1997-98 – has thus far meant that the actual delivery of gas will have to wait till the Thai economy recovers substantially.

Because of the pipeline's perceived strategic importance, there is a fairly heavy military presence around Dawei.

A steady trade in marine products (mostly dried fish), rubber, cashews and wolfram (tungsten) has made Dawei a relatively prosperous town for Myanmar though not as prosperous as Myeik, farther south. Under Thai supervision and consulting, tin mining may soon start up again.

Special Events

During the annual Thingyan festival in April, Dawei's male residents don huge, 4m bamboo-frame effigies and dance down the streets to the beat of the *kalakodaun*, an Indian long drum. The origin of this custom, peculiar to Dawei, seems to be a mystery but it's most likely linked to a similar custom brought by Indian immigrants many decades ago.

Theinwa Kyaung (Payagyi)

The main Buddhist monastery in town, usually referred to simply as Payagyi (Big Pagoda), contains a complex of sizeable Mon-style *viharas* (glittering cubes of reflective mosaics filled with gilded Buddhas). A sculpture of Dharani, the earth goddess, standing in the corner of one of the main thein is a much venerated object of worship among the people of Dawei, who rub her breasts, thighs and shoulders for good luck.

The best time to visit Theinwa Kyaung is in the early evening, just after sunset, when hordes of local residents come to make offerings and to meditate for an hour or two. To find it, head north-west along Yodaya Lan, past the Royal Guest House on your right, until you come to a large fork in the road. Bear right at the fork, follow the road another 200m and you'll come to the paya on your right.

Shwethalyaung Daw Mu

Completed in 1931, the largest reclining Buddha in the country – 74m long, 21m high – can be seen at the edge of town (about 5km from the central Strand Rd market). Although not as beautiful an image as the Shwethalyaung in Bago, its sheer scale is indeed impressive.

Shinmokhti Paya

About 5km beyond Shwethalyaung Daw Mu on the same road, this paya is the most sacred of local religious monuments. Reportedly constructed in 1438, it's one of four shrines in the country housing a Sinhalese Buddha image supposedly made with a composite of cement and pieces of the original bodhi tree – see the Shwemokhtaw Paya entry in the Pathein section in the Around Yangon chapter, or the Kyaikkami entry in the Around Mawlamyaing section earlier in this chapter for an account of the legend. During religious festivals this is one of the most lively spots in the district.

Municipal Market

The main municipal market can be found in the centre of town on Strand Rd. Enclosed by brick walls dating to the British colonial era, it's divided into two main sections; there's a spacious open-sided shelter where fresh produce is sold, and an equally voluminous enclosed shed where dry goods, cosmetics, longyis and ready-made clothes are displayed.

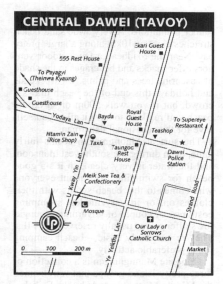

CENTRAL DAWEI (TAVOY)

Ekari Guest House
555 Rest House
To Payagyi (Theinwa Kyaung)
Guesthouse
Guesthouse
Yodaya Lan
Bayda
Royal Guest House
To Supereye Restaurant
Teashop
Htamin Zain (Rice Shop)
Taxis
U Kway Yin Lan
Taungoc Rest House
Dawei Police Station
Meik Swe Tea & Confectionery
Mosque
Ye Yeiktha Lan
Our Lady of Sorrows Catholic Church
Strand Road
Market
0   100   200 m

American Baptist Sites

The American Baptists had a long and active history in Myeik (altogether there are 45 Kayin Baptist churches in the district), and the **Karen Baptist Church**, founded by an American evangelist in 1957, is still in use in the Shan Malei Swe Quarter. The original *padauk* flooring and pews are in good condition; foreign visitors are welcome.

Impressive, thick-walled **Morrow Karen High School** is now Dawei College. Like most other colleges and universities in the country, it's now closed to students for fear of rebellions against the government. Although the teaching staff dutifully show up for work each school day, the college has sadly decayed. The equally impressive former **American Baptist Mission** is now No 3 State High School.

Beaches & Islands

Few foreigners have been permitted to visit coastal areas around Dawei so details are still sketchy. The best local beach, **Maungmagan** (also spelt Maungmakan) is around 18km west of Dawei via a narrow, winding, patched blacktop road over a high ridge and through rubber plantations. A very wide sand beach stretches eight or 10km along a large, pretty bay. Near the roadhead a few outdoor vendors offer snacks and beverages in the shade of casuarina trees and palms. On weekends and holidays this end of the beach draws a crowd, but if you walk 500m or so up the beach you're likely to have it all to yourself, save for the occasional fisherman.

The surf at Maungmagan seems fairly tame, even during the south-west monsoon, and the water is very clean, so it's a good beach for swimming. Just about everyone who comes to this beach swims with their clothes on, or in very modest swimming costumes. A couple of government bungalows offer rooms usually reserved for VIPs. They're extremely basic – beach camping looks preferable actually.

Opposite Maungmagan is a collection of three pretty island groups that were named the Middle Moscos Islands by the British – they are now known as **Maungmagan, Henze** and **Launglon** (or collectively as the Maungmagan Islands). Due to a natural profusion of wild boar, barking deer, sambar and swiftlets (sea swallows), these islands belong to Myanmar's only marine sanctuary – established by the British in 1927 and still officially protected.

A long peninsula ending in **Dawei A-Ngu** (Dawei Point), about 60km south of Dawei, creates a vast estuarine bay dotted with islands. Because the waters of the lengthy bay are to some degree protected from strong ocean currents, these islands may be more easily accessible by boat than the Maungmagan Islands. **Zalut**, a small town near the tip of Dawei A-Ngu, offers basic services.

Local taxi trucks from the Strand Rd market go to the beach at Maungmagan or to Zalut for about K500 and K1200 per person, or you can charter a truck for around K1000 per hour.

Places to Stay

Most visitors to Dawei come on business – traders involved in oil, marine products, rubber, wolfram, tin or cashews – so the guesthouses in town are not used to tourists. The cleanest and best run place is *Ekari Guest House* (☎ 036-21980, 21780, 52 Ye Yeiqtha Lan), a two storey wood hostelry in the Myauq Ywa Quarter. All rooms contain two twin beds, a fan and a few sticks of furniture; clean toilets and cold-water showers are at the back of the building. Although locals pay only a pittance to stay here, foreigners (this includes visiting Thais) must pay US$10 per person. The Ekari is also the Dawei representative for YA. Electricity is available from 5.30 pm to about 5.30 am. Some English is spoken by the staff. Besides being the cleanest place in town, the Ekari is in a relatively quiet neighbourhood.

On a corner of one of the main four-way intersections in the centre of town, *Royal Guest House* occupies a well restored, two storey, colonial-era former company office on Yodaya Lan (so called because this road heads east to Thailand, known in Burmese as Yodaya or Ayuthaya). Rooms are similar to those at the Ekari but not nearly as well kept, and there is some ambient street noise. Room charges are the same, US$10 per person for foreigners.

Right across the street from the Royal, *Taungoo Rest House* (☎ 036-21951) is another big, two storey colonial building. It's run by an Indian Muslim family, most of whom speak not one word of English. There is a semi-outdoor cafe downstairs. At the time of writing, the Taungoo hadn't got onto the dollar kick, and you could readily get a room with shared bath for just K400 a night. How long this will last is anyone's guess.

The same room rates apply at *555 Guest House*, on U Kyaw Yin Lan, nearby. For your K400 all you get is a tiny and very basic cubicle with walls open at the top.

Places to Eat

Neither the Ekari nor the Royal offer food service, but the ground floor *htamin zain* (rice shop) at *Taungoo Rest House* serves good, inexpensive Bamar food. Two curries – a choice of beef or chicken – and a couple of vegetable dishes plus *peh-hin-ye* (dahl) and rice cost around K200.

Along Yodaya Lan, one of the main thoroughfares through town, are several small *htamin zain* and *teashops*. One of the better htamin zain is a small, simple affair on the corner of Yodaya Lan and U Kyaw Yin Lan, where chicken curry and a few tasty vegetable side dishes are served with good quality rice for K150. *Supereye*, on Strand Rd, offers an extensive English-language menu of Chinese and Dawei-style Bamar cuisine, much of it seafood-based. It's relatively clean and the food is good, if expensive by Myanmar standards. Count on spending around K1500 for three or four dishes, plus rice and a large bottle of beer.

The best teashop in town, *Meik Swe Tea & Confectionery*, is attached to a mosque on U Kyaw Yin Lan, not far from the Taungoo and Royal guesthouses. It's extremely popular and tends to be semifull all day. In addition to good quality Burmese tea, Meik Swe serves a small but changing menu of Indian-style tea snacks – perhaps *puris* (potato curry) with curry dip one day, *tohsay* (dosa) the next.

About 75m north-east of Royal Guest House is a Chinese-style teashop called *Beda* (no sign in English) that's also very popular.

Getting There & Away

Air YA fields three direct flights per week from Yangon to Dawei aboard an ATR-72 for US$70 per person. Since ticket brokers – rather than the airline – control the price, it can fluctuate up or down according to market demand. The flight takes one hour and 10 minutes. MA also flies this route three days per week, for US$65 aboard an F-27, US$75 on an F-28.

There are also flights from Myeik twice a week aboard YA (40 minutes) and once a week with MA (55 minutes). From Kawthoung, each airlines flies three times weekly, and the fare varies from US$35 on one of MA's F-27s to as much as US$70 with YA (though the 'listed' fare is only US$30).

Bus Various private bus companies now operate buses from Yangon's Highway bus station all the way to Dawei, beginning at around 7 pm for K2000 per person. It's a 24 hour trip; along the way passengers spend a night somewhere near Mawlamyaing, usually at the Mottama side of the ferry crossing.

A more reasonable overland approach would be to start out from Mawlamyaing. The 317km trip takes 12 hours and costs K1200. From either end the buses tend to leave around 3 am to make sure the main portion of the trip takes place during daylight hours – due to road hazards and possible bandit attacks. Even during supposed 'safe hours', dacoits and KNLA/MNLF regulars sometimes collect a 'road tax' from drivers along the way. The tropical, mountainous scenery between Ye-U and Dawei – a 160km stretch – is superb.

Boat MFSL sails between Yangon, Dawei, Myeik and Kawthoung several times a month, but travel is slow It takes two days and two nights between Yangon and Dawei, and possibly up to a week in the rainy season.

MYEIK (MERGUI)

The Tanintharyi coast, in the extreme south of Myanmar where Myanmar and Thailand share the narrow peninsula, is bounded by the beautiful islands of the Mergui Archipelago. Myeik – known to the colonials as Mergui and locally as Beik (Myeik is the written rather than the spoken form) – sits on a peninsula that juts out into the Andaman Sea. Because of the safe harbour offered by the peninsula and facing islands, Myeik became an important port over 500 years ago.

Hindus from the Indian kingdom of Coromandel ruled this area during the latter half of the 15th century, trading with merchants from Siam, Ceylon, China, Malaya and the Arabian Peninsula. A Bolognese named Ludovico di Varthema visited the port in 1506, noting the trade with India and remarking favourably of the inhabitants: 'Their writing is on paper like ours, not on the leaves of a tree like that of Calcutta.'

The original Mon inhabitants called their town, at the confluence of the Tanintharyi and Kyaukpaya rivers, Maw-reik, but the locale was known by several other names as well. A 1545 Portuguese expeditionary chronicle refers to Tanancarim, somewhere along the north-west coast of the Thai-Malay Peninsula, and this Portuguese rendering became Tenasserim in later European records in reference to both Myeik and a town farther upriver now known by that name. The current name for the Tanintharyi Division is the Burmese pronunciation of this name. Myeik, the Burmese mispronunciation of the Mon name Maw-reik, was officially applied to the port by Bamar rulers in 1770.

As for Mergui – the most common British colonial name for the port – no one today seems to be able to figure out where the word hailed from. Some European maps drawn between the late 16th and late 19th centuries spot Merguim, Mergen, Merguay, Mergee or Merguy. Simon de La Loubère, a chevalier in the French mission to Ayuthaya, wrote in 1688, 'The Port of Merguy ... is the most lovely in all India'. In the 18th century Mergui served as a port for Thailand's Ayuthaya empire. Ocean-going visitors from the west would land here and continue up the Tanintharyi River on smaller boats to Tenasserim (today Tanintharyi), then finish the trip by road to Ayuthaya via Dan Singkon (in present-day Prachuap Khiri Khan Province, Thailand). As Myeik became an important trade entrepôt, many European traders and envoys in the employ of the Ayuthaya court settled in the area. The most infamous of these, Samuel White, used his position as harbourmaster of both Mergui (which he called Mergen) and Tenasserim to plunder visiting ships at will and to tax the local population for every shilling he could squeeze.

The British occupied the region following the First Anglo-Burmese War in 1826, so that along with Sittwe, Myeik became one of the first cities in Myanmar to become part of 'the Raj'. The Japanese invaded in 1941, but by 1945 Myeik was back in British hands, until independence was achieved in 1948.

The area inland from Myeik is a major smuggling route into Thailand as well as a

'brown area' from the military perspective, but at the time of writing the port of Myeik was open to foreign visitors. Despite the opening, one sees very few foreign visitors wandering around town.

Along with rubber and coconuts, marine products are a major source of livelihood for Myeik residents, and the *ngapi* (fermented fish or shrimp paste) made here is renowned throughout Myanmar. Another local product is the swiftlet's nest, collected and exported as the main ingredient in the 'bird's-nest soup' favoured by Chinese throughout Asia. A steady stream of marine traffic carries these and other products into world shipping lanes, while other seacraft stop to offload electronic goods, machinery and other manufactured goods.

Today Myeik is one of the most picturesque coastal cities in Myanmar. A wide range of traditional colonial and vernacular architectural styles line the streets, which lie flat towards the waterfront but wind upward into a hilly section to the east. Viewed at a distance from this hilly ridge, the city and island-studded harbour look much as they must have 100 years ago.

Things to See & Do

The city's most venerated Buddhist temple, **Theindawgyi Paya**, sits on a ridge overlooking the city and harbour. A beautiful, Mon-style ordination hall of wood, brick and stucco contains an impressive painted and carved ceiling, a 'European pose' Buddha towards the front entry, 28 smaller Buddhas (representing different historical Buddhas) along its two sides, a large meditation Buddha in the centre and a sizeable reclining Buddha at the back. A mirrored mosaic decorates the lower interior walls and columns. A tall gilded stupa stands on a broad platform with excellent views of the city below and islands in the distance.

Pataw Padet Island, a five minute boat ride (K100 shared, K800 chartered) from the harbour, is named for two prominent hills at either end of the island. Several religious buildings, stupas and sculptures have been constructed on the island. A large, hollow reclining Buddha, **Atula Shwe-thalyaung** lies at the foot of rocky, jungle-covered Padet Hill to the south. At 66m it's the third longest reclining Buddha in Myanmar – but with a twist: it's a hollow cement form with an interior walkway lined with comic-strip-like *jatakas* (life story of the Buddha) as yet unfinished.

Payagyi Lan (Big Pagoda Rd) is a wide street lined with Buddhist monasteries, including Theinwa Kyaung, Atulawka Marrazein (architecturally inspired by the Kuthodaw Paya in Mandalay), Palaw, Nyaung Yeiktha, Shwetaung, Kantha and San, all with separate compounds. Walking or driving down this street one can't help but be impressed with local piety – it's like a mini-Sagaing without the hills.

At the edge of town, **Kuthein-nayon Kyaung** features square shrine buildings in the regional Mon style. One of the shrines contains scenes of the sick-and-dying Buddha, reminiscent of Kyaikmaraw Paya near Mawlamyaing. The name of the monastery, in fact, is the Burmese pronunciation of Kusinara, the place in India where the historical Buddha is supposed to have died. Also displayed at the monastery are a few Buddha images made in Thailand, possibly dating to the era when Myeik was a Siamese territory.

The **harbour front** is worth a stroll to watch stevedores loading and offloading cargo from ships big and small. Towards the south end of the waterfront, on the east side of the street, you may notice what appears to be a large stone-slab box on the footpath. This is the **tomb of Mary Povey White**, the wife of the notorious Siamese-employed harbourmaster Samuel White. White and Povey met and fell in love aboard a ship sailing from Great Britain to Madras in 1675. At the time she was betrothed to someone in Madras, whom she married upon arrival in that city. Shortly thereafter she divorced, married White in 1676 and moved to Mergui. Povey died of cholera in 1682 and was entombed on the waterfront. Hardly anyone gives the tomb any notice anymore. The city has grown around it and the uninformed

would be excused for thinking it enclosed a fire plug, public well or something similar.

Not far from Theindawgyi Paya there's a **Muslim quarter** with two mosques and lots of teashops. The larger of the two, **Lamat Tin Mosque**, is said to be over 50 years old and is quite Arabic-looking. There are seven other mosques in the city.

Sibinthaya Zei (Municipal Market), near the harbour, is a very large and colourful collection of enclosed stalls covering a city block. It's open daily from 6 am to 5 pm except Sunday and gazetted holidays.

Myeik Archipelago

Far beyond the value of any local product – rubber, marine products or swiftlet's nests – is the Myeik Archipelago's huge, almost completely untapped potential in the beach-going and ecotourist market. The Burmese say there are over 4000 islands in the archipelago, though British surveyors recognised only 804. Most are uninhabited, though a few are home to 'sea gypsies', a nomadic seafaring people who sail from island to island, stopping off to repair their boats or fishing nets. Known as Salon to the Burmese, *chao naam* to the Thais, *orang laut* or *orang basin* to the Malays and *Moken* or *Maw Ken* (sea-drowned) among themselves, this may have been the first ethnic group to have lived in what is today Myanmar. With stones tied to their waists as ballast, a Moken diver can reportedly descend to a depth of 60m while breathing through an air hose held above the water surface.

Mayanpin Kyun, known to the British as King Island (and locally known both as Kadan Kyun and Kyunsu, the latter the name of the island district's capital), lies a good distance offshore. In spite of its size and geographic variation – at 44,000 hectares it's the largest island in the archipelago – reports say there are no good beaches on the island. A government guesthouse accommodates visitors to a hydroelectric power station – reportedly built with forced labour – on the island. All the power goes to a navy base on the island, while Myeik's civilians rely on part-time diesel generators.

White Gold

Many of the nests that go into making the Chinese delicacy 'bird's-nest soup' come from islands in the Myeik Archipelago. Sea swallows (*Collocalia esculenta*, also known as 'edible-nest swiftlets') like to build their nests high in limestone caves, in rocky hollows which can be very difficult to reach. Agile collectors build vine-and-bamboo scaffolding to get at the nests, but are occasionally injured or killed in falls. Before ascending the scaffolds, the collectors pray and make offerings of tobacco, incense and liquor to the cavern *nats* (spirits). The collectors sell the nests to intermediaries who then sell them to Chinese restaurants abroad. Known as 'white gold', premium teacup-sized birdnests sell for US$2000 per kilo – Hong Kong alone imports US$25 million worth every year.

The translucent nests are made of saliva which the birds secrete – the saliva hardens when exposed to the air. Cooked in chicken broth, the bird's nests soften and separate and look like bean thread noodles. The Chinese value the expensive bird secretions highly, believing them to be a medicinal food that imparts vigour.

Joe Cummings

Boats to nearby islands can be chartered for US$60 per day from Myeik's harbour. See the Diving & Snorkelling section under Activities in the Facts for the Visitor chapter for details on dive sites and tour companies that operate overnight archipelago trips. The August/September 1998 issue of *Action Asia* magazine contains a very good article on Myeik island diving.

Places to Stay

The place to stay (if you can get a room) is the one storey, five room, wooden *Annawa Guest House*, high on a ridge near Theindawgyi Paya, overlooking the harbour. Large rooms with two beds, mosquito nets, fan and shared facilities cost US$20. One end room with private toilet and shower is also occasionally available for US$25. Rates include breakfast. Electric power is supplied only from 5.30 pm to 5.30 am. A very pleasant sitting terrace extends along the entire back of the guesthouse, offering rattan lounge furniture and views of the city and harbour. For its proximity to Theindawgyi, the Muslim quarter, the market and the harbour, this is arguably the best location in town. The house of Maurice Collis, former deputy commissioner of Mergui under the British, and author of *Siamese White*, can be seen farther south along the ridge. One can imagine that Samuel White's house must have been located in the same vicinity. Reservations aren't accepted for foreigners, so it's best to simply turn up and try your luck.

At the time of writing there were two other choices in town. *Myeik Golden Pearl (Myeik Shwe Palei) Guest House* on Pyitawtha Lan, near the waterfront, is a modern, two storey place over a shophouse. The musty rooms contain damp carpet, a couple of beds, and attached shower and toilet. It's very much a second choice at US$20 per room. As at Annawa, electric power comes on at night only.

Opposite the Myeik airport and adjacent to the Myeik Golf Club, the *Palemon Resort* (☎ 021-21841) has large, plain rooms with comfortable beds, air-con, minifridge, TV and private cold-water shower for US$20/30 single/double. It has its own generator, so it has power 24 hours a day. Recently privatised, it's sometimes referred to as the 'government guesthouse' because it was originally owned and managed by the government. Nonetheless it's popular with Tatmadaw officers, who play golf next door.

The old colonial-era Hotel Mergui on High School No 1 St in Myint Nun Quarter, near a small lake in the middle of the city, was recently taken over by Asian Adventures, a dive operation based in Phuket. When we visited, an American was busy restoring the thick-walled architectural beauty, with plans to re-open the hotel as the diving-oriented *Adventure Inn* (☎ 021-21527, email info@asian-adventures.com) by the time of this book's publication. Room rates for walk-in guests are expected to run at US$55 a night, possibly more if meals are included. Most guests will initially arrive to participate in diving/kayaking/hiking tours.

Places to Eat

When it comes to local cuisine, Myeik can be a real delight. Seafood is abundantly available and inexpensive. One local speciality is *kat gyi kai* (scissor-cut noodles): wheat noodles that have been cut into short strips and stir-fried with seafood and various spices. It's a delicious meal, usually eaten for breakfast or lunch. One of the best places to try kat gyi kai is *Meik Set*, a decade-old wood and thatch teashop/restaurant with a dirt floor and open front on U Myat Lay Lan, Kan Paya Quarter. Other treats available here include *hkauq hnyin kin* (sticky rice steamed with coconut milk in little banana-leaf packets). It's open from 6 am to 5 pm.

On the same street, *Sakura Food & Drinks* is a much nicer-looking place with an air-con dining room decorated with wood and thatch, plus an outdoor area with umbrella tables. The chef/owner worked in Singapore for a number of years and has created a unique and very good menu of South-East Asian seafood dishes, barbecued satay, burgers, omelettes and sandwiches. Considering the high quality of the food and service, it's not expensive, and hence it's very popular with locals who have hitherto never had access to a local restaurant quite this good.

Pan Myint Zu, on Payakozu Lan in the Kan Paya Quarter, is a quiet and semi-rustic, thatched-roof restaurant with good Chinese dishes and seafood. It's open daily from 7 am to 10 pm.

For traditional Bamar cuisine with a local flair, you can do no better than *Shwe Mon Family Restaurant* near the waterfront in the Seik Nge Quarter. Highlights include delicious *bei hin* (egg-and-potato curry), and *balachaung* (chutney-like spices) made with peanuts. It's open daily from 7 am to 8 pm.

On the same street, closer to the harbour, *Point Restaurant* is more of a night-time place, with Chinese and seafood dishes, and

tables covered with tablecloths. It's not a bad place to down a beer or two and eat appetisers. Later in the evening there's karaoke.

In the same quarter, on Bogyoke Lan, south of the YA office, *Myeik Restaurant* occupies a historic building and serves a mixed menu of Chinese, Bamar and seafood.

Between the two mosques in the Muslim quarter, *Pearl World Bakery House* does decent, light pastries.

Behind the Palemon Resort, a small *restaurant* serves good Chinese and Bamar food.

Getting There & Away

Air YA flies to Myeik three times weekly with a stopover in Dawei for US$70 to US$100, depending on demand. These flights take a total of two hours and 10 minutes to reach Myeik. MA drops in six days a week from Yangon for US$100 on an F-28, and these flights take one hour and five minutes.

MA also flies an F27 from Mawlamyaing every Wednesday for US$75 for foreigners; the flight takes one hour and 50 minutes. To/from Dawei, you can choose between MA (Sunday only, F27, US$35, 55 minutes) or YA (three days a week, US$40 to US$70, 40 minutes). For flights to/from Kawthoung, there's a choice: MA (Sunday, F27, US$50, one hour) or YA (three times a week, US$45 to US$70, 50 minutes).

In Myeik, the YA representative (☎ 021-21160) has an office at 115 Bogyoke Lan near Sitinthaya Zei (Municipal Market). The MA office is next door to Sakura Food & Drinks on U Myat Lay Lan.

Bus There are daily buses and pickups from Dawei, 249km north, but it's highly unlikely foreigners will be permitted to travel by bus to Myeik. The road is so bad – and plagued by bandit attacks – that the trip sometimes requires an overnight stop at Palaw, 73km north of Myeik. Also, there are four ferry crossings, one each at Palauk Chaung, Pyicha Chaung, Palaw River and Tomok River.

Boat MFSL sails, on average, twice a month between Yangon, Dawei, Myeik and Kawthoung, but travel is very slow.

SOUTH-EASTERN MYANMAR

KAWTHOUNG

This small port at the southernmost tip of Tanintharyi Division – and the southernmost point of mainland Myanmar (800km from Yangon and 2000km from the country's northern tip) – is only separated from Thailand by a broad estuary in the Pakchan River. To the British it was known as Victoria Point and to the Thais it's known as Ko Sawng (Second Island). The Burmese name, Kawthoung (also spelt Kawthaung), is a mispronunciation of the latter.

The main business here is trade with Thailand, followed by fishing, rubber and cashews. Among Burmese, Kawthoung is most known for producing some of the country's outstanding kickboxers. Most Kawthoung residents are bilingual in Thai and Burmese. Many residents born and raised in Kawthoung, especially Muslims, also speak Pashu, a dialect that mixes the Thai, Malay and Burmese languages.

Kawthoung's bustling **waterfront** is lined with teashops, moneychangers and shops selling Thai construction materials. Touts stroll up and down the pier area, arranging boat charters to Thailand for visitors and traders. A huge **duty-free market** was built in pseudo-Bamar style in 1997, next to the harbour, but so far it stands completely empty. Along one side of the harbour lies **Cape Bayinnaung**, named for King Bayinnaung, a Bamar monarch who invaded Thailand several times between 1548 and 1569. A bronze statue of Bayinnaung – outfitted in full battle gear and brandishing a sword pointed at Thailand, not exactly a welcoming sight for visiting Thais, stands at the crest of a hill on the cape.

Five kilometres north of town, the fishing village of **Thirimyaing Lan** is known for its hilltop Third Mile Pagoda, with good sea and island views. Thirimyaing Lan also boasts good local seafood restaurants along its waterfront. Another 11km on is **Paker Beach**, reportedly the best nearby mainland beach.

Islands

The Mergui Archipelago continues south to Kawthoung and many islands lie tantalisingly offshore in this area. Unfortunately, there is no regular transport to any of these islands, except to the closest ones, and boat charters are expensive.

Nearby islands are inhabited by bands of nomadic Moken or sea gypsies. Opposite Kawthoung's harbour the southernmost island in the Myeik Archipelago, **Mwedaw Kyun**, is mounted by two gilded zedis.

Thahtay Kyun or Thahtay Island (Rich Man Island, known as Pulau Ru to the Moken), one of the closest isles, sports a large resort owned by Thailand's Dusit chain. Known variously as *Andaman Club* and *Andaman Club Resort (☎ 01-956 4354, radio phone in Ranong)*, the resort's main features include a casino, duty-free shops and a golf course – an arrangement obviously designed to appeal to rich Thais and Singaporeans. There are no beaches to speak of on the island, but the resort offers trips to beaches on Zadetgale Kyun (St Luke's Island) or Zadetgyi Khun (St Matthew's Island), each about 45 minutes away by speedboat.

A more interesting nearby island known as **Salon Island** (Sea Gypsy Island; or Pulau Besin) is heavily wooded and boasts a lagoon in its centre and sand beaches on its shores. A Malaysian company started constructing a few bungalows here but quit after a year. A Yangon company had plans for two developments here, *Yadana Beach Resort* and *Suwanna Bhumi Resort*, but these have yet to materialise.

Farther offshore, **Lampi Kyun**, possibly one of the least disturbed island habitats in South-East Asia, has been designated as a national park. Extending about 90km long and 8km wide, this rugged landmass features a forested, mountainous interior and two year-round rivers that flow into the sea from the island's western shore. According to *Action Asia* magazine, known wildlife on the island includes white-bellied sea eagles, Brahminy kites, parakeets, hornbills, gibbons, crab-eating macaques, flying lemurs, civets, tigers, leopard cats, boar, barking deer, sea otters, crocodiles and fruit bats. Some naturalists speculate the interior of Lampi might harbour hitherto undiscovered animal species, or species thought to be extinct elsewhere in South-East Asia, such as the Sumatran rhinoceros or kouprey. At least five Phuket-based tour companies operate hiking and river excursions on Lampi – see Diving & Snorkelling under the Activities section in the Facts for the Visitor chapter for a list of outfitters.

Organised Tours

Jansom Thara Hotel (in Ranong, Thailand, ☎ 077-821511, fax 821821), offers Kawthoung and island tours aboard four boats with capacities ranging from 15 to 200 people. A half-day tour costing 750B per person (minimum of 10) sails from Ranong, visits a couple of pagodas in Victoria Point and returns to Ranong around 11 am. The full-day tour costing 1000B goes to Pulau Besin for beach swimming and lunch, and returns at 2 pm. Rates include immigration procedures on both sides, plus guide and boat transport; lunch costs extra.

Places to Stay

So far there are only two places in Kawthoung approved to accept foreigners. On the waterfront about 150m from Myoma jetty (the main landing for boats to/from Ranong), the modern and friendly *Honey Bear Hotel* (☎ 01-229 6190) offers 24 hour power and 39 clean rooms with air-con, satellite TV and cold-water shower for 700B – not a great deal by Thai standards but it's a comfortable hotel.

The other option is the mouldy *Kawthoung Motel* (☎ 09-22611, 01-272723), about 300m beyond the main immigration office and about 500m from the jetty. For simple double rooms with private cold-water shower, including breakfast, foreigners pay US\$25 or 1000B.

On nearby 700 hectare Thahtay Kyun, well heeled Thai and Singaporean gamblers shack up at the *Andaman Club Resort* (☎ 01-956 4354, Bangkok ☎ 02-856 4047, fax 285 6408), a huge five star hotel complex sporting a casino and a Jack Nicklaus-designed 18 hole golf course. All 191 rooms come with sea views and start at US\$200 –

unless you happen to be a regular high roller, in which case the casino will pick up your room tab. Guests with reservations are able to take a 250B boat direct from Jansom Thara Resort on Hat Chandamri, about 10km north-west of Ranong. If you're already in Kawthoung, you can catch a five minute boat ride out to the island from the Kawthoung jetty for 100B.

Places to Eat

Li Li Flower Restaurant, an air-con place attached to the Honey Bear Hotel, serves good Thai, Bamar and Chinese food along with well chilled beer. Around the corner from the hotel is a plain, no-name *Thai restaurant* – look for a glass case out the front filled with pans containing Thai curries.

Smile Restaurant, a Chinese-run place up the hill from the jetty near the Kawthoung Motel, is one of the few places besides the Li Li Flower offering cold drinks all day. The English-language menu offers several seafood dishes including a delicious crab curry.

Getting There & Away

It is now legal to travel from Kawthoung into the interior of Myanmar – eg to Dawei or Yangon – by plane or by ship. Road travel north of Kawthoung, however, is forbidden by the Myanmar government due to security concerns.

Air Flights between Yangon and Kawthoung cost US\$130 on YA or MA. All flights stop in Myeik and Dawei. See the Getting There & Away entries in the Dawei and Myeik sections earlier in this chapter for details on these individual flight segments.

Bus Buses run between Kawthoung and Myeik, but road conditions are bad and robbery is not uncommon. Hence foreigners are unlikely to be permitted to travel this route.

In 1993 the government began constructing a new Myeik-Kawthoung road that passes through Tanintharyi and Bokpyin. Because there are so many streams and rivers along the way, engineers must design

SOUTH-EASTERN MYANMAR

and construct 358 bridges to complete this 486km route. Given current economic circumstances, it's unlikely the road will be finished before 2001.

Boat Boats to Kawthoung leave the Saphan Pla pier in Ranong regularly from around 7 am till 6 pm for 40B to 50B per person. You can charter a boat for 200B to 400B, depending on the size of the boat and your bargaining skills. Once the boat trip is underway, there's an initial stop at Thai immigration, where your passport is stamped. Then upon arrival at the Kawthoung jetty (Myoma jetty), again before leaving the boat, there's a stop at Myanmar immigration. At this point you must inform immigration authorities whether you're a day visitor – in which case you must pay a fee of US$5 for a day permit. If you have a valid Myanmar visa in your passport, you'll be permitted to stay up to 28 days, but also be required to buy US$300 worth of foreign exchange certificates (FECs).

See the Getting There & Away entries in the Dawei and Myeik sections earlier in this chapter for information on ship travel along the coast to/from Yangon.

Western Myanmar

The Rakhaing Yoma (Arakan Range) separates the Rakhaing and Chin states from the central Ayeyarwady (Irrawaddy) River plains. Isolated from the Bamar heartland, in many ways the inhabitants of both states have more in common with the peoples of eastern India and Bangladesh.

The Rakhaing

Rakhaing ethnicity is a controversial topic – are the Rakhaing actually Bamar (Burmans) with Indian blood, Indians with Bamar characteristics, or a separate race (as is claimed by the Rohingya insurgents)? Although the first inhabitants of the region were a dark-skinned Negrito tribe known as the Bilu, later migrants from the eastern Indian subcontinent developed the first Hindu-Buddhist kingdoms in Myanmar before the first Christian millennium. These kingdoms flourished before the invasion of the Tibeto-Burmans from the north and east in the 9th and 18th centuries. The current inhabitants of the state may thus be mixed descendants of all three groups, Bilu, Bengali and Bamar.

The Burmese government denies the existence of a Rohingya minority, a group of around three million people who distinguish themselves from the Rakhaing majority by their Islamic faith. Many Rakhaing Muslims – or Rohingyas as they prefer to be called – have fled to neighbouring Bangladesh and India to escape Bamar persecution.

The Chin

The Chin State, to the immediate north of Rakhaing, is hilly and sparsely populated. The people and culture exhibit a mixture of native, Bengali and Indian influences similar to that found among the Rakhaing, with a much lower Burman presence. As in the Rakhaing State, there have been clear governmental efforts in recent years to promote Burmese culture at the expense of Chin culture, and many Chin have fled west to Bangladesh and India.

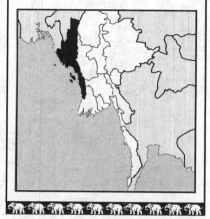

Of Tibeto-Burman ancestry, the Chin call themselves Zo-mi or Lai-mi (both terms mean mountain people), and share a culture, food and language with the Zo of the adjacent state of Mizoram in India. Outsiders name the different subgroups around the state according to the district in which they live: eg Tidam Chins, Falam Chins, Haka Chins etc.

Traditionally the Chin practice *swidden* (slash-and-burn) agriculture. They are also skilled hunters, and animal sacrifice plays a role in important animistic ceremonies. Currently, Chin State has the largest proportion of animists of any state in Myanmar, but the Zo culture is fast disappearing in the face of

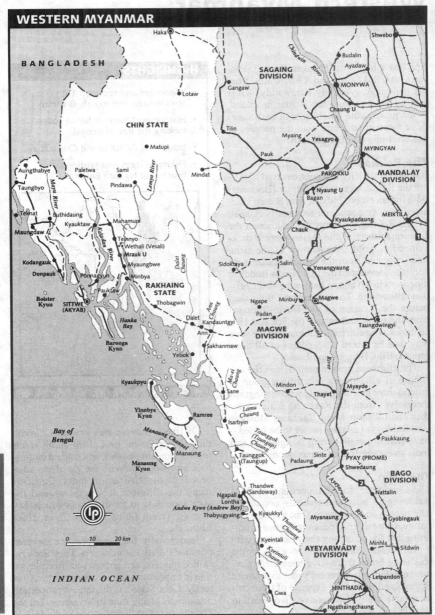

WESTERN MYANMAR

BANGLADESH

SAGAING DIVISION

CHIN STATE

MANDALAY DIVISION

PAKOKKU

MEIKTILA

RAKHAING STATE

MAGWE DIVISION

Bay of Bengal

BAGO DIVISION

AYEYARWADY DIVISION

HINTHADA

INDIAN OCEAN

Haka
Shwebo
Budalin
Ayadaw
MONYWA
Chindwin River
Gangaw
Chaung U
Lotaw
Tilin
Myaing
Yesagyo
MYINGYAN
Matupi
Pauk
Mindat
Nyaung U
Bagan
Kyaukpadaung
Aungthabye
Paletwa
Sami
Pindawa
Lemyo River
Taungbyo
Chauk
Mahamuni
Buthidaung
Kyauktaw
Teknat
Teinnyo
Wethali (Vesali)
Maungdaw
Mrauk U
Sidoktaya
Salin
Yenangyaung
Myaungbwe
Dalet Chaung
Kodangauk
Minbya
Donpauk
Ponnagyun
Pauktaw
Ngape
Minbu
Magwe
Boister Kyun
SITTWE (AKYAB)
Thobagwin
Padan
Taungdwingyi
Hanka Bay
Dalet
Kandauntgyi
Ann Chaung
Baronga Kyun
Ann
MAGWE DIVISION
Sakhanmaw
Yebok
Kyaukpyu
Ma-ei Chaung
Mindon
Thayet
Myayde
Yinnbye Kyun
Ramree
Lamu Chaung
Isarbyin
Paukkaung
Manaung Channel
Taunggok (Taungup) Chaung
Sane
Sinte
PYAY (PROME)
Manaung Kyun
Manaung
Taunggok (Taungup)
Padaung
Shwedaung
BAGO DIVISION
Nattalin
Thandwe (Sandoway)
Myanaung
Gyobingauk
Ngapali
Lontha
Andwe Kywe (Andrew Bay)
Thabyugyaing
Kyaukkyi
Thandwe Chaung
Minhla
Sitdwin
Kyeintali
Kyeintali Chaung
AYEYARWADY DIVISION
Letpandon
Gwa
HINTHADA
Ngathaingchaung

Moyu River
Kaladan River
Ayeyarwady River

0   10   20 km

Christian and Buddhist missionary influences. Some Chin follow the Pau Chin Hau religion, which is based on the worship of a deity called Pasian and named after Pau China Hau, a spiritual leader from the Tidam District, who lived from 1859 to 1948. Hau also devised the written Chin language and is at least partially responsible for resurgent Chin nationalism.

The more traditional Zo or Chin groups live in the south near the Rakhaing State border. Chin Christians from the north have bombarded the area with a project called Chin Christianity in One Century (CCOC), the goal of which is to convert all Chin to the 'one true faith'. The Yangon government, on the other hand, has its own Buddhist missions in the area and is pushing against both the animists and Christians in a battle for the Chin soul.

The Chin National Front, a nonviolent nationalist movement active on both sides of the India-Myanmar border, would like to create a sovereign 'Chinland' divided into the states of East Zoram (the current Chin State, Myanmar), West Zoram (part of south-eastern Bangladesh plus Tripura, India), Central Zoram (the state of Mizoram, India), and North Zoram (Manipur, India) – a unified area before the British came along.

SITTWE (AKYAB)

Known to the Bengalis as Akyab and to the Rakhaing as Saitway, this port city of the Rakhaing State sits at the mouth of the Kaladan River where it empties into the Bay of Bengal. Offshore delta islands form a wide protected channel that has served as an important harbour for many centuries. Sittwe has at least a 2000 year history of habitation, though in its modern form the city started as a trading port around 200 years ago and further developed after the British occupation of 1826.

During the British era, international trade along the coast bloomed. Each day, two huge cargo steamers plied back and forth between Calcutta and Sittwe; old-timers in Sittwe and Mrauk U still wistfully recall the huge Indian mangoes and creamy Bengali

halvah that arrived on the ships. Among British colonials, Sittwe had a reputation for malaria and cholera epidemics, although historical records don't seem to support that image – nor is Sittwe a particularly swampy place compared to places farther south in the Delta. A historical footnote: Scottish short-story writer and novelist Hector Hugh Munro, known by his pen name Saki, was born here in 1870.

For both Buddhists and Muslims in Sittwe, there is a distinctive Rakhaing twist on standard Burmese culture that includes the enjoyment of much spicier foods and brighter-coloured clothing. For example, Rakhaing women tend to wear blouses and *longyis* (sarong-style garments) that are pink, orange or red, colours that are somewhat uncommon elsewhere in Myanmar except in conjunction with Buddhist monastic robes.

Information

The main post office sits on the riverfront towards the southern end of town. There is a branch post office one block west of the Prince Guest House, on the same side of the street. Mail is said to be fairly reliable here, and phone calls to Yangon and abroad can be arranged.

During the monsoon season (July to October), it can rain often and heavily in Sittwe. As in other larger cities in Myanmar, electric power rotates from quarter to quarter, but even when up and running, it's generally available from 6 to 11 pm only.

Payagyi

This temple (full name: Atulamarazei Pyeloun Chantha Payagyi) is located near the Prince Hotel and features a large plain shed supported by pillars decorated with glass mosaic. A large sitting image beneath the shelter was cast in 1900 in the Rakhaing style – minus the 'royal attire' (crown and jewelled chestpiece) common to many Rakhaing images. The face of the figure shines with gold, while the rest of the body is bronze. It weighs a reported 5425 *viss* (8680kg). Next door, the **Kyayouq Kyaung** features both a Sinhalese and a Burmese-style stupa.

Buddhistic Museum

Housed in a colonial-style building on the grounds of Mahakuthala Kyaungdawgyi (Large Monastery of Great Merit), about three blocks east of the *chaung* (canal) that runs through town, this modest two storey museum is the best place in Myanmar to view Rakhaing-style Buddha images. Maintained by resident monks, the collection here represents a rare instance of historical preservation in a country where older Buddhas are stolen, bought and sold with frequency – partly due to the dire need for foreign exchange, partly because the Burmese generally associate older Buddhas with karmic accumulations that they would rather not contend with.

Most of the images are under 1m in height and feature the royal attire common to Rakhaing Buddhas. The majority date to the Mrauk U period, although a few date as far back as the Wethali era, and are made of bronze, silver, nickel, quartz or alabaster. Unique motifs include Buddhas seated on pedestals, which are in turn supported by the backs of elephants that stand in a circle. In glass cases are numerous small saucers filled with white pebbles, deemed to be bone relics of the Buddha.

There are also some Indian Buddhas and Hindu deities on display: a few Thai and Japanese Buddhas; silver coins from the Mrauk U era; clay pipes; terracotta votive tablets; and engraved astrological charts. Entry is free, though donations are gratefully accepted. The *sayadaw* (chief abbot) in charge insists his is the only museum of its kind in the world, even when told similar Buddhist museums exist in neighbouring countries.

Rakhine State Cultural Museum

The government's spacious new museum on the main road is worth a look, even though there is little Rakhaing culture on view. The museum is largely a collection of Wethali and Mrauk U period artefacts and a number of more contemporary exhibits. Visitors to Mrauk U will get a quick lesson in the history of the period, starting with a Pali-inscribed

slab that reads (in translation): 'Out of all the laws, the law of cause is the origin.' Nearby, a famous regional author, U Ottama, is described as: 'the first person who infused political consciousness and the spirit of independence into the hearts of the sleeping South-East Asians, including Myanmar.'

Other exhibits include dioramas of ancient cities, replicas of a crocodile xylophone and a coconut shell violin, local school children's sketches of Mrauk U pictographs, and the famous '64 Kinds of Coiffures of the Mrauk U Period', which adorn a row of mannequin heads in a glass case on the museum's upper floor.

The museum is open Monday to Saturday from 10 am to 4 pm. The helpful curator, U Tin Aung Soe, told us that visitors should come to the side door if they find the museum closed for any reason! Admission is US$2.

Around Town

An old steel **clock tower** topped with a weathervane in the centre of town was erected by the Dutch in the 18th century. As a counter-symbol of Burmese nationalism, the State Law & Order Restoration Council (SLORC) built the more ornate white clock tower on Main Rd in 1991.

The tomb of **Babagyi**, a local Muslim saint who lived 200 years ago in Sittwe, can be seen near the mosque, in the town's heavily Bengali Bodawma Quarter – this quarter is also where Sittwe's oldest mosque and oldest Hindu temple are found.

Waterfront

As a seaside town, Sittwe has plenty of waterfront action. As in many other British-influenced towns in Myanmar, the road along the river is called The Strand; a new promenade along the river towards the southern end of town provides a nice walking route between the centre of town and The Point.

The Point is a land projection at the confluence of the Kaladan River and the Bay of Bengal. A large terrace constructed over the flat, shale and sandstone point is a good spot to catch the breeze and cool off on hot afternoons. A former lighthouse tower now serves

SITTWE (AKYAB)

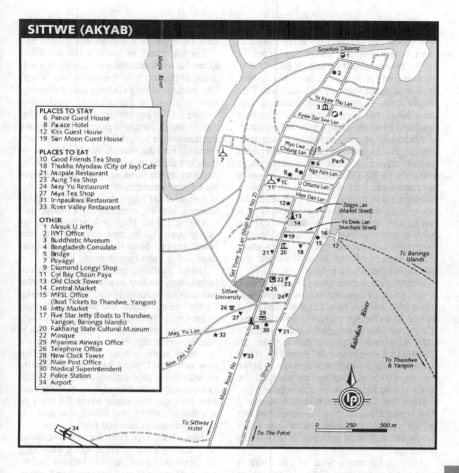

PLACES TO STAY
6 Prince Guest House
8 Palace Hotel
12 Kiss Guest House
19 Sun Moon Guest House

PLACES TO EAT
10 Good Friends Tea Shop
18 Thukha Myodaw (City of Joy) Café
21 Mopale Restaurant
23 Aung Tea Shop
24 May Yu Restaurant
27 Mya Tea Shop
31 Innpaukwa Restaurant
33 River Valley Restaurant

OTHER
1 Mrauk U Jetty
2 IWT Office
3 Buddhistic Museum
4 Bangladesh Consulate
5 Bridge
7 Payagyi
9 Diamond Longyi Shop
11 Cyi Bay Chaun Paya
13 Old Clock Tower
14 Central Market
15 MFSL Office
  (Boat Tickets to Thandwe, Yangon)
16 Jetty Market
17 Five Star Jetty (Boats to Thandwe,
  Yangon, Baronga Islands)
20 Fakhaung State Cultural Museum
22 Mosque
25 Myanma Airways Office
26 Telephone Office
28 New Clock Tower
29 Main Post Office
30 Medical Superintendent
32 Police Station
34 Airport

as a viewing platform. There are picnic tables available for public use, and a snack bar at one end is open from sunrise to sunset. Fresh coconut juice is available from vendors. Admission to The Point costs K20 per pedestrian, K70 for trishaws, K300 for cars.

South-west of The Point is a beach area with grey-brown sand. Trucks drive onto the beach to collect sand for construction use but overall, it's okay for swimming, especially if you move farther west away from The Point, towards the new Sittwe

Hotel. The main beach hazard is probably hotel guests practicing golf.

About halfway up the shore side of town, heading north, is an inlet where fishing boats moor. During low tide the boats rest on mudflats, and the fishermen retire to a group of huts on shore. Just north of the inlet is the harbour proper, where ocean-going vessels dock – including oil tankers operated by Myanma Electric Power Enterprise (MPPE) and cargo and passenger ships run by Myanma Five Star Line (MFSL).

Places to Stay

At the time of writing, only three places in town were licensed to accept foreigners.

The **Prince Guest House** (☎ 043-21395, 27 Main Rd) is in the centre of town, next door to a small, century-old mosque. This simple three storey wooden building features basic but clean rooms with ceiling fans, and a bathroom down the hall at a cost of US$5 per person. One huge room with air-con, fridge, private bath and beds with decent mattresses and mosquito nets is available for US$12. Since electric power is only available from 6 to 11 pm, the air-con and fridge don't mean much; even when the power is on there's rarely enough voltage to run an air-con unit! However, as it's at the back of the building, this room is quieter than those at the front. There is also a small sitting terrace off the third floor and the family staff are quite helpful.

Nearby is the three storey **Palace Hotel**, which offers large rooms with attached cold-water bath and overhead fan that shuts off at 11 pm. Even though the rooms have screens, it's a good idea to accept the management's offer of a mosquito net. Room rates are US$10/15 a single/double. Breakfast is not included, but the staff will arrange to serve *mohinga* (rice noodles in fish soup) in the lobby if you request it the day before.

Both the **Sun Moon Guest House** and **Kiss Guest House** are on the main road, but do not yet accept foreigners. If they do in the future, we found both places to be clean and friendly.

About a kilometre west of The Point is the government's new **Sittwe Hotel**, which sits on a large compound spread along the beach. Large rooms with air-con (evening hours only) cost US$35/40, plus the usual government tax and service charge. There are several other very nice-looking government guesthouses in the area.

Places to Eat

Seafood and spicy Rakhaing curries are what Sittwe kitchens do best. If you can manage to find it, order *kagadit*, a delicious white-fleshed fish caught off the coast of Sittwe, best lightly fried whole and served with a tasty lime-garlic-chili sauce *(chin ngan za)*.

The top place in town is the attractive **River Valley Restaurant** on the main road, about 200m south of the new clock tower. The menu is mostly Chinese and Rakhaing-style seafood; a multicourse meal costs around K1000 per person. A close second is the all-wood, brightly painted **Innpaukwa Restaurant** on Strand Rd, opposite the main post office on the waterfront. Service can be slow but the food is good. You can dine indoors or on the terrace, which juts out over the adjacent mangrove swamp.

Just north of Innpaukwa is **May Yu Restaurant**, serving a variety of Chinese and Rakhaing dishes. **Mopale Restaurant**, diagonally opposite the new state cultural museum, serves both Rakhaing and Bamar food and is open from 9 am to 10 pm.

Hotter Rakhaing curries can also be obtained from various **street vendors** and **htamin zain** (rice shops) around town, especially on the street behind the new culture museum. One of Sittwe's specialities is *moundi*, a Rakhaing version of mohinga. Moundi is usually served dry, but is sometimes served in a light broth, instead of the thicker fish stew native to Central Myanmar. It usually comes with grilled onions and garlic, chili sauce and crumbled dried fish. At night **vendors** light candles along Main Rd No 1 to sell peanut brittle, and sticky rice and coconut steamed in bamboo joints.

Aung Tea Shop, near the mosque, opens early and by 7 am is full of locals savouring the shop's delicious *chapati* (flatbread), *nambya* (nan), *palata* (fried flatbread) and potato curry. The **Thukha Myodaw Café** (City of Joy), in the same general vicinity, serves decent *hsi htamin* (turmeric-coloured sticky rice) and *bei palata* (stuffed palata), and what look to be slabs of thick French toast – bread fried in egg batter with banana essence.

Mya Tea Shop, just opposite Sittwe University, serves tasty curries and bei palata. Around the corner from the Palace Hotel is the popular **May Shwe Gaung Tea Shop**, serving spicy Rakhaing curries and a variety of snacks.

Things to Buy

At the **central market**, or at one of the few **longyi shops** in town, you can purchase the famous Rakhaing-style longyis. These garments feature a supplementary-weft weaving technique that creates dense, geometric patterns with a shimmering patina. Check out Diamond Longgyi Shop, located on U Ottama Lan, for a good selection of fine Rakhaing cloth.

Getting There & Away

Air Air Mandalay (AM) makes the Yangon to Sittwe flight on Wednesday and Sunday. The fare is US$80. Myanma Airways (MA) offers direct flights from Yangon on Tuesday and Friday. The fare is US$60 on F-27s, US$70 on F-28s. Sittwe's airstrip is only 10 minutes from town. A government MA flight crashed in January 1998 at Sittwe, killing several passengers.

It costs K800 to charter a pickup for this short ride, or around K100 per person in a shared pickup. A small taxi costs K400 and can be arranged from your hotel. Three small shops next to the airport serve fried rice, moundi, tea, coffee, soft drinks, and beer. Check-in is chaotic; don't forget to clear immigration and customs, for which there are no English signs.

Boat The Inland Water Transport (IWT) office is near the government Mrauk U jetty, which sits on Sayokya Chaung, a tributary of the Mayu River, which in turn, runs north-west off Kaladan River. See the Mrauk U section later in this chapter for details on ferries to Mrauk U.

MFSL ships take two days to reach Sittwe from Yangon, with an overnight at Kyaukpyu. Check the MFSL office in Yangon, or the MFSL office near the Five Star jetty in Sittwe, for shipping dates. There is no English sign at the Sittwe office, but it's at the top of a stairway next to the number 1956 in green relief (indicating the building's construction date). The friendly staff speak only a little English. Ship schedules are posted for Sittwe and Calcutta, Thandwe, Taunggok (Taungup), Yangon and Kawthaung.

There are two boats a week to Thandwe, at a cost of K1879 for upper class (cabin with toilet) and K1206 for ordinary class. The same vessels continue to Yangon at a cost of K1696/2592 for ordinary/upper class.

The staff appear willing to sell foreigners ordinary class tickets upon request. See the Getting Around chapter at the beginning of this book for a description of MFSL booking procedures.

Getting Around

Trishaw is the main form of public transport for getting around Sittwe. A ride from Mrauk U jetty to the Prince Guest House costs K50 per person, one way.

AROUND SITTWE
Baronga Islands

Also spelt Phaynoka, Bayonga and Bayonka, these three islands just offshore, near the mouth of the Kaladan River, could make an interesting day excursion. Hand-dug, privately owned oil wells are a major source of livelihood on the island of East Baronga. The hereditary owners of the wells, called *twin-zar* (literally, well-eater), typically employ five worker-partners to operate the well, each of whom receives an equal share of the daily production. Simple tripod pumps extract the crude product, which is sold to local agents who refine the petroleum into diesel, kerosene and wax for local distribution. Although the island oil deposits tapped by the twin-zars are generally too small for industrial purposes, foreign oil companies have recently begun offshore explorations in the area.

Fishermen and coconut farmers live on Middle and West Baronga. The fishing is said to be especially good in the channel between Middle and East Baronga, and there are some decent beaches on the western side of West Baronga and along the south-western shore of East Baronga. Regular boats to East Baronga leave from the Mrauk U jetty (also called Sayokya jetty) twice a week, but foreigners are supposedly required to gain permission from the regional army command to make this trip. One boat stops at a jetty on the eastern side of the island, while a larger boat operated by Myanma Oil & Gas Enterprises stops on the western side before continuing to Yangon. You can also charter a boat to the islands for a return trip costing US$100 to US$200, depending on the boat.

MRAUK U

Once a centre for one of Myanmar's most powerful kingdoms, Mrauk U straddles the banks of Aungdat Chaung, a tributary of the Kaladan River, 72km from the coast. The surrounding rice paddies are well watered by the annual monsoon, which brings up to 508cm of rain per annum. Also cultivated in the region are coconut, banana, jackfruit, mango, areca nut, citrus, lychee and a variety of vegetables.

The Rakhaing king Minzawmun founded Mrauk U (pronounced Myauk U by the Burmese) in 1433, though in the common practice of the times, dynastic legends endowed the kingdom with a make-believe 3000 year history. A network of chaungs allowed access by large boats, even ocean-going vessels.

In the next century, the city became a free port that traded with the Middle East, Asia, Holland, Portugal and Spain; elephants were one of the main commodities supplied from the Rakhaing region. A Dutchman who visited Mrauk U in the 16th century described it as one of the richest cities in Asia, and compared it with Amsterdam and London in size and prosperity. The remains of a European quarter called Daingri Kan can still be seen south-west of town.

The Mrauk U dynasty, which lasted 352 years, was much feared by the peoples of the Indian subcontinent and Central Myanmar, who called the Rakhaing warlords Magh (the origins of this name are lost). Mrauk U kings even hired Japanese samurai as bodyguards against assassination. At Mrauk U's peak, King Minbin (1531-53) created a naval fleet of some 10,000 warboats that dominated the Bay of Bengal and Gulf of Martaban.

Mrauk U was a successor to two earlier kingdoms in the area: Dhanyawady (circa 1st to 6th centuries AD) and Wethali (3rd to 10th centuries AD), the remains of which are still visible to the north. All three kingdoms blended elements of Theravada and Mahayana Buddhism with Hinduism and Islam. In the late 18th century, the Konbaung dynasty asserted its power over the region and Mrauk U was integrated into the Bamar kingdoms centred around Mandalay.

After the First Anglo-Burmese War (1824-26), the British Raj annexed Rakhaing and set up its administrative headquarters in Sittwe, thus turning Mrauk U into a political backwater virtually overnight. The Burmese name gradually changed to Myohaung (Old City), though the Rakhaing continued to call the town Mrauk U.

Today, the original city lies in ruins and a small, poor town with simple buildings of brick, wood and thatch has grown up adjacent to the old city site. It's the kind of town where every man, woman and child seems to chew betel and smoke cheroots. The town is intersected by several chaung, the main source of transport and water. Much daily activity seems to be taken up with water trips to and from the chaung. Instead of the usual clay pots or rectangular oil cans employed in most of the rest of Myanmar, Mrauk U residents are seen carrying shiny aluminium waterpots (imported from India) on their hips with one arm crooked around the pot's neck.

One of the best times – or worst times, depending on your tastes – to visit Mrauk U is during the huge *paya pwe* (pagoda festival) held in mid-May. Centred on the large grassy open area to the southern side of Dukkanthein, the festival lasts about a week and features the usual menu of fortune-tellers; craft vendors; seriocomic theatre; music; and food.

Temples of Mrauk U

See the following special section for a full description of the history and architectural styles of the temples of old Mrauk U. This section also incorporates the map of the general Mrauk U area.

TEMPLES OF MRAUK U

Temples of Mrauk U

BERNARD NAPTHINE

BERNARD NAPTHINE

BERNARD NAPTHINE

Title Page: Gold-faced Buddha (Photograph by Bernard Napthine).

Top: View from Shittaung to Andaw Paya.

Middle: A pet bird finds a friendly perch.

Bottom: A line of Buddha statues.

TEMPLES OF MRAUK U

Unlike Bagan (Pagan), where temple ruins are strewn over a vast plain, the ruins of Mrauk U sit on or against bluffs in hilly terrain interlaced with streams and leafy trees. Overall this lends an intimate, friendly feeling to the place. In addition to the major sites located one or 2km north-east of town, there are lots of crumbling stupas next to the town itself, especially on hillocks along the stream at the southern end of town – a very nice area for sunrise or sunset strolls.

Altogether, there are around 70 named temple, stupa or city wall sites around Mrauk U, plus dozens of other unnamed sites. Only the more significant temple and stupa sites are described below. Most of the city walls are found to the eastern side of town, since the west, north and south provided natural defences in the form of hills and streams. The walls were built to fill in the gaps in these natural barriers, so they appear intermittently.

Palace Ruins & Museum

Walls and gateways of sandstone blocks and earth are all that's left of the Mrauk U royal palace, constructed in 1430 according to some sources; as late as 1553 according to others. A Portuguese monk and envoy to Mrauk U described the palace as it appeared during his visit in the 1630s:

> The royal palaces ... have massive wooden columns of such extraordinary length and straightness that one wonders there are trees so tall and so straight. The inside columns are entirely gilt, without any admixture of other materials. In the same palace there is a hall gilt from top to bottom which they call the 'Golden House' because it has a vine of the purest gold which occupies the whole roof of the hall, with a hundred and odd gourds of the same pure gold. There are also in that very rich house seven idols of gold, each of the size and proportions of an average man. These idols are adorned on the forehead, breast, arms and waist with many fine precious stones, rubies, emeralds and sapphires, and also with some brilliant old rock diamonds of more than ordinary size.

Unfortunately, the palace buildings were lost to fire long ago. A museum within the old palace walls contains a good collection of religious sculpture and other artefacts unearthed around Mrauk U. In the yard out the front, there are several sandstone figures, including a Hindu *yoni* (a vagina-shaped pedestal designed to support a Shiva *lingam*, or phallus), headless Buddhas, Vishnu figures and various inscribed stelae.

Inside is a collection of Wethali, Mrauk U and Konbaung period Buddhas and bodhisattvas, votive tablets, small bronze stupas, Krishna statuettes, Buddha heads, musical instruments, sandstone lintels from 15th century monuments, some broken pieces of painted frescoes

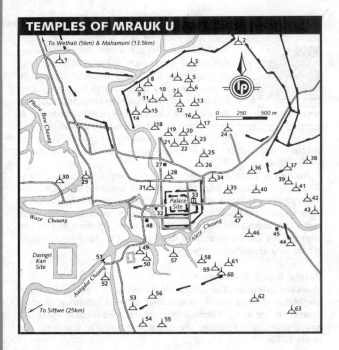

TEMPLES OF MRAUK U

To Wethali (5km) & Mahamuni (13.5km)

Phara Baw Chaung

Waze Chaung

Daingri Kan Site

Aungdat Chaung

To Sittwe (25km)

Palace Site

Alex Chaung

0   250   500 m

from the Shittaung temple, painted ceramics, one large 4th century relief from Kyauktaw depicting the Buddha teaching one of his disciples, *dvarapalas* (gate guardians) from the 14th century Mrauk U palace and ornate 16th century Portuguese headstone slabs bearing astrological runes. Among the more historically interesting artefacts are a set of stelae dating between the 8th and 16th centuries and inscribed with several different scripts, including Arabic. Some of the Mrauk U Buddhas on display are exquisite in design.

Opening hours for the museum don't seem to be regular – in fact it's often locked; however, it's well worth seeking out the caretaker to get in. Some items are labelled in English, though most appear in Burmese only. Admission is free.

Shittaung

The most complex and well preserved of the surviving Mrauk U temples, Shittaung (Sittaung to the Burmese) was constructed in 1535 by King Minbin, the most powerful of the Rakhaing kings. The name means 'Shrine of the 80,000 Images'; a reference to the number of holy images found inside. A maze-like floor plan – which vaguely resembles a square-cornered pinwheel – suggests the shrine was originally used for Tantric-like initiation rituals. A walk through each of the

TEMPLES OF MRAUK U

PLACES TO STAY
27 Mrauk U Hotel
45 Prince Hotel

PLACES TO EAT
32 Moe Cherry
    Restaurant

OTHER
33 Museum
48 Market
51 Jetty

TEMPLE RUINS
1   Ngwetaung
    Fortress
2   Yenla Fortress
3   Ahmyinttaung
    Fortress
4   Pitaka Taik
5   Anoma
    Shwekhyatheing
6   Alaisaita
7   Htuparyon
8   Shantaung
9   Tayzayamo
10 Thoropavata

11 Mokseiktaw
12 Laungbanpyauk
    Paya
13 Mahabodhi
    Shwegu
14 Parahla
15 Myatanzaung
16 Ratanasanraway
17 Ratanamhankin
18 Laymyetnha
19 Dukkanthein
20 Yadanapon
    Paya
21 Shittaung
22 Andaw Paya
23 Ratanc Thinkha
24 Ratanamanaung
25 Ngapithema
26 U Myawa
28 Haritaung
29 Lokamanaung
30 Parabow
31 Yokkhataung
34 Shwegutaung
35 Htintawmu
36 Sakyamanaung
37 Neikbuzar (Main)
38 Paranyinaung

39 Neikbuzar
    (Middle)
40 Wuntnattaung
41 Neikbuzar (Lower)
42 Paraoke
43 Minkhaung
    Shwegu
44 Ponnomyaung
    Fortress
46 Shwetaung
47 Myawtawmu
49 Sankartaung
50 Pannzeemyaung
52 Naretsa
53 Aungminggala
    Fortress
54 Laytanknan
55 Kaenawin
56 Pagan taung
57 Wuthaie Image
58 Tinamanaung
59 Sakka Thila
60 Minkhamaung
61 Kalamya
62 Myataung
    Fortress
63 Laythataung
    Fortress

interior passages exposed the initiate to different sets of formulaic Buddhist messages carved in sandstone on the walls. With its thick walls, tiny windows and commanding views of the surrounding area, the temple may have also served as a royal fortress during times of attack.

Shittaung sits on a bluff known as Phokhaung Taung and presents a layered quadrangle studded with straight-sided stupas that curve gently at the top where they are joined to their *sikharas* (temple finial). Though much fewer in number, the stupas are very reminiscent of Indonesia's Borobudur in shape, general absence of ornamentation and in the way they rise platform to platform. The large central and topmost stupa is flanked by 33 smaller stupas lined up in flaring angles to the northern and southern walls, while two significant sandstone stupas sit on the lowest platform – the circular Nay Win Paya (Sunset Paya) and octagonal Nay Htwet Paya (Sunrise Stupa).

The entire monument features a mortarless assembly of laterite and sandstone blocks, carried to Mrauk U by boat along local rivers and streams. At the northern entrance to the complex stands the Shittaung Pillar, a 3m, four sided obelisk brought from Wethali to Mrauk U by King Minbin in 1535. Three sides of the pillar are inscribed in Sanskrit; the earliest inscription, facing east, is for the most part illegible but has been dated to between the 3rd and 6th centuries, ie the middle of the Dhanyawady era. The western face dates to the early 8th century and displays a list of Rakhaing kings, while the northern face is ascribed to King Minrazagyi in 1593.

A walking tour of the monument takes you through four separate passages, five if you include the reliefs on the exterior walls. The latter are difficult to see unless you climb out onto the crumbling ledges in front of the reliefs. The reliefs appear to represent figures from Hindu-Buddhist mythologies – considered *nats* (spirits) by the Burmese today – who are both protecting and paying homage to the temple interior. Many of these reliefs have decayed into an unrecognisable state and some are missing altogether.

The first outer chamber inside Shittaung features arched passages along the outside wall with pairs of Buddha images sitting back-to-back. The inner wall of the 94m passage features sandstone slabs with high relief cut into six tiers. The lowest tier depicts people in Rakhaing dress engaged in festival-oriented activities – boxing, dancing, drama, wrestling – plus work-related activities using elephants, water buffaloes and oxen. On the middle four tiers, over 1000 separate sculptures chronicle 550 *jatakas* (scenes from the Buddha's life). Along the top layer of reliefs, male and female figures participate in devotional activities. The teaching impetus of the reliefs perhaps implies that festival-going and making a living are lower sorts of human activities; learning about the history of the Buddha represents a step up, and then actually taking an active role in the religion is the highest level. Some of the reliefs bear paint remnants. Small depressions along lower ledges were designed to hold oil for illumination. Nowadays the temple caretakers request a small donation to turn on electric lights in the concentric passageways.

The two inner galleries display hundreds of Buddha images in niches, while a Buddha footprint is the terminal point of the innermost passage, taking the visitor from an appreciation for the serenity and wisdom of the Buddha to the knowledge that he actually walked on this spot – or so it is said – during his postenlightenment travels. The route set by the first three

Below: King Minbin's fortress-like Shittaung or 'Shrine of the 80,000 Images', built in 1535.

passages moves in the traditional clockwise direction, but when you come to the Buddha footprint you're forced to double back counterclockwise through the smallest and darkest chamber – a twist perhaps further indicative of Tantric influence. Due to the insulating quality of the surrounding laterite substructure, each passageway feels cooler than the last – a perfect sensual metaphor for the psychologically 'cooling' effect of the Buddhist teachings.

The best of the Buddha sculptures are reserved for the innermost sanctuary and for the large prayer hall added to the eastern side of the temple where there was once a courtyard. Throughout the monument the images represent typical Rakhaing style, though most have been restored and many are badly painted. Several images were gathered from other monuments in the region, including the Wethali and Dhanyawady sites. One Wethali image we couldn't identify looked like it had worms crawling out of its ears.

The prayer hall itself features an impressively carved and painted

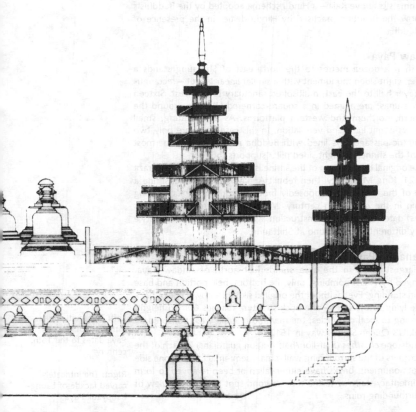

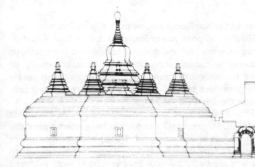

wooden ceiling. A lintel around the large portico into the main chamber has been restored in the original style. A *Kala* (Hindu god of Time and Death) head over this entry is surrounded by *devas* (Pali: deities), and a Brahma sits above Kala – a Hindu schema adopted by the Buddhists to show the devotion practised by Hindu deities in the presence of the Buddha.

Andaw Paya

Less than a dozen metres to the north-east of Shittaung stands a smaller, eight sided monument with a similar linear layout – rectangular prayer hall to the east, multispired sanctuary to the west. Sixteen *zedis* (stupas) are aligned in a square-cornered U-shape around the southern, northern and western platforms. As at Shittaung, small windows admit light and ventilation. In this case there are only two concentric passageways lined with Buddha niches; at the innermost core of the shrine, an eight sided pillar supports the roof.

The original construction of the shrine is ascribed to King Minhlaraza in 1521. King Minrazagyi then rebuilt Andaw in 1596 to enshrine a piece of the tooth relic supposedly brought from Sri Lanka by King Minbin in the early 16th century. Most likely the roofline *sikharas* (spires) date to his later reconstruction, as their slender, terraced style is very different to that found at Shittaung.

Yadanapon Paya

The largest stupa in the area stands just north of Andaw Paya. Damaged by WWII bombing, only the bottom 'bell' portion and base remain standing. Even without the original sikhara – now a pile of brick rubble lying to the sides – the brick structure reaches 60m in height. According to local chronicles, the mammoth stupa was sponsored by Mrauk U's Queen Shin Htway in 1612.

Sandstone *chinthes* (half-lion/half-dragon guardians) at each of the four corners of the surrounding wall remain semi-intact. Along one side of the monument, bricks have either fallen or been removed to form a rudimentary stairway to the top – a good spot for a sunset view of the surrounding ruins.

Left: The multi-spired sanctuary of Andaw Paya dates to the 16th century.

Right: The intricately carved facade of Laungbanpyauk Paya.

Dukkanthein

Said to have been constructed by order of King Minphalaung in 1571, Dukkanthein stands on a bluff 100m opposite and to the north-west of Shittaung. A loose translation of the name is 'ordination hall that spiritually reinforces the town', and it certainly looks like a huge bunker from the outside. Although the overall structure is relatively intact, a closer inspection shows it to be in a state of disrepair, with weeds and plants sprouting from cracks between the laterite and sandstone bricks.

Wide stone stairways lead up the eastern and southern sides of the tall base. Simple dome-shaped stupas, similar to those at Shittaung, stand atop receding terraces over a large, slope-sided sanctuary. Two inner cloisters form a U shape around the central rectangular sanctum in which a series of steps ascend to an egg-shaped Buddha chamber. The cloisters are lined with 146 Buddha niches, along with sandstone reliefs depicting 64 different types of hairstyles for the wives of Mrauk U nobility. A tall entranceway on the east side admits light into this interior chamber.

Pitaka Taik

This compact, highly ornate building is now surrounded by rice paddies in a secluded site accessible by a narrow path around 300m north-east of Dukkanthein. It was built in 1591 under King Minphalaung as a repository for the *Tripitaka* (Buddhist canon), and is one of the few 48-such Mrauk U-period libraries that have survived. Originally, it is said to have contained 30 pitaka sets brought from Sri Lanka in the mid-17th century, though at the moment it contains nothing but a pile of brick rubble.

The rectangular structure stands only 2.75m high, with a floor plan that measures 4m by 3m. The monument's most distinguishing features are its five-tiered roofline and beautifully decorated east-facing entranceway.

Laungbanpyauk Paya

Built in 1525 by order of King Minkhaungraza, this zedi stands roughly midway between Yadanapon Paya and Pitaka Taik. Locally it's known as the Plate Pagoda because a wall in front of the structure is embedded with plate-like tiles in bright yellow, red, white, celadon and blue. Not all the tiles are intact though; many broken pieces lie strewn on the ground.

Stylistically, the octagonal stupa somewhat resembles the sikharas atop Andaw Paya, with a receding terrace effect from the base to halfway up each side, followed by a smoothly rising bell shape topped by a lotus-bud sikhara that's only half-intact. Before the latter toppled, the zedi is reputed to have reached 37m in height; today it measures only 23m. Sixteen Buddha niches surround the base of the zedi; unfortunately, thieves have emptied some entirely and taken the heads of the remaining figures. However, the carved lintels over the niches are still impressive.

Sakyamanaung Paya

Situated approximately 1km north-east of the old palace walls, this graceful zedi was erected in 1629 under King Thirithudhammaraza. At this point in the development of Mrauk U architecture, the stupa had been modified into a more vertical and highly ornate form, an obvious absorption of Bamar, and especially Shan, styles, by way of Bagan and Ava.

The lower half of the well preserved, 85m zedi features a multi-tiered octagonal profile as at Laungbanpyauk Paya, but beyond this the bell reverts to a layered circular shape which is mounted by a decorative *hti* (umbrella-like top). The western gate into the surrounding compound is guarded by a pair of half-kneeling, half-squatting *yakka* (giants).

The source for the illustrations in this section is A Guide to Mrauk-U *(Sittway Degree College, Sittwe, 1992) by Tun Shwe Khine.*

Places to Stay & Eat

At the time of writing there were only two places in Mrauk U that accepted foreigners. The friendly but basic *Prince Hotel* is a funkier version of the Prince in Sittwe. Rooms are on the shabby side, and you should request a mosquito net from the staff. Rooms with cold-water shower and bath cost US$5 per person.

The new *Mrauk U Hotel* is the government hotel, and it's quite comfortable. Like most state-sponsored hotels, it's spread across a large landscaped compound. Large rooms with air-con, TV, fridge and attached hot-water bath cost US$30/45 a single/double. Breakfast is included. A small *restaurant* serves decent Chinese fare.

The best food in the village is served by *Moe Cherry Restaurant*. The Rakhaing menu features several tasty curries and appetizers, and they serve cold Mandalay beer. A large meal for one, including beer, costs about K1200. When we visited, the owners were enjoying a Charlie Chaplin video. The restaurant is open from 7 am to 11 pm, and like most establishments in town, the electricity is on from 6.30 to 11 pm. Moe Cherry will also prepare a lunch box for you to take on either an excursion around Mrauk U or for the ferry ride back to Sittwe.

An *unnamed restaurant*, opposite Khite San Tailor on the main street, serves fried rice, noodles, soup, fried vegetables and noodle soup. The *Dhanyawady Tea & Cold Drink Shop* (no English sign) opposite the market isn't bad. It has the usual teashop snacks and is especially good for breakfast, when *kyet-u palata* (egg palatas) with onions and chillies are served.

U Kyaw Taw, the English-speaking owner of *U Yebaw Rice Mill*, may be able to provide very good Rakhaing food if you give him a day's notice.

Getting There & Away

Both government and private ferries make the river trip between Sittwe and Mrauk U. The boats are old double-decker Irrawaddy Flotilla craft that carry at least twice the number of passengers they were designed to

carry. The lower steel deck is chaotic, while the upper deck is also quite crowded, but has a limited number of sling chairs, plus a salon cabin. The fare for foreigners is US$4 each way. You can rent a sling chair for K50, but do so immediately upon boarding because they go fast.

The salon cabin has 10 or so wooden chairs and a table and seems to be reserved for VIPs. It's the coolest part of boat since it gets direct breezes through windows, and it has an attached toilet room. However, we've yet to see a foreigner gain admission to this area.

You can buy your ticket at the jetty; it's quite informal, but give yourself an extra 20 minutes to fill out a form at a table amid coils of rope, wooden crates and thick stacks of tattered forms wrapped in brown paper.

The ferries leave daily from the Mrauk U jetty on Sayokya Chaung at the northern end of Sittwe. Departure times depend on the tide, but boats usually leave in the early morning on the way upriver; early afternoon on the way down. On the way the boat stops at the town of Ponnagyun (Brahman Island) on the 26km-long island of the same name. On a hill nearby you can see the stupa of U Yit Taung Paya, supposedly erected in 993 AD and renovated in 1521, 1641 and 1688. The lower half of the large bell shape is whitewashed, the upper half gilded. Vendors standing on the pier extend bamboo poles holding plastic bags of curry and rice to passengers on the boat. Other stops include Satha and Pade. It takes about 4½ hours to reach Mrauk U.

For about US$60 (or kyat equivalent) you can charter a private boat to Mrauk U. You can also take the ferry one way, and a private boat the other way (starting at either Mrauk U or Sittwe). Most types of boats take about 4½ hours to Mrauk U, five hours back. The boats we saw could hold about six people comfortably. (Inquire at jetty or at any Sittwe hotel, or at Moe Cherry Restaurant in Mrauk U for charter boat information.) For part of the way the boats move against the current on the Kaladan River, then they turn east onto the Theinganadi

River and go with the current before turning upriver again on the Henyakaw River. The government boat terminates in Kyauktaw, another four hours north of Mrauk U on the Kaladan River, connected to Mrauk U by the Theinganadi River.

Coming back, the government boat arrives from Kyauktaw on the way to Sittwe at around 11.30 am, depending on tide and season. This is usually the most crowded direction because people from the villages up-country are carrying goods to sell in Sittwe.

Getting Around

There is a US$5 'zone fee' that is collected at the hotels that accept foreigners.

Mrauk U is small enough that you can get around most of the town easily on foot. A trishaw costs K50 to K60 anywhere in town, about double that if you want to be taken out to the major ruins or to the ferry jetty.

Old jeeps (usually without windows) can be hired through Moe Cherry Restaurant or the Mrauk U Hotel for about US$10 for a half-day tour of the area.

AROUND MRAUK U
Wethali

Just under 10km north of Mrauk U are the remains of the Wethali, or Vesali (Waithali in the local parlance), kingdom. According to Rakhaing chronicles, Wethali was founded in 327 AD by King Mahataing Chandra. Archaeologists believe that this kingdom lasted until the 8th century. Of the oval-shaped city boundaries that remain, only parts of the moat and walls are still visible amid the rice paddies. Many of the hillocks around this area are actually overgrown stupas. A central palace site – whose walls are relatively well preserved – measures about 500m by 300m. The palace prayer hall is now used as an irrigation tank during the rainy season.

Other than these meagre, unexcavated ruins, there is but one other sight worth seeing in Wethali. The **Great Image of Hsu Taung Pre (Pye)** sits in the base of a large *pahto* (temple) that is missing all of its superstructure. Now covered with a corrugated metal roof, the 5m, Rakhaing-style sitting Buddha and its pedestal are said to be made from the one piece of solid stone and date to 327 AD. The highly revered image is swathed in embroidered red holy cloth and attended by monks and nuns; an umbrella painted with runes stands over the figure. Pilgrims are starting to gild the image from the top down by handing gold-leaf squares to an attendant who climbs a bamboo scaffold to affix the gold to the head of the image.

Regular public transport to Wethali from Mrauk U is scarce, but you can arrange to charter a jeep or pickup through Moe Cherry Restaurant for US$10 to US$15 for a return trip. The once or twice-daily pickup north to Mahamuni and Kyauktaw passes Wethali. Hitching might be possible, though traffic on this road is light.

Mahamuni

The **Mahamuni Paya**, located 40km north of Mrauk U and about 10km east of the farm town of Kyauktaw, sits at the northeastern corner of the old Dhanyawady city site. This was the original site for Mandalay's famous Mahamuni Buddha, a huge and very old bronze image, which Rakhaing kings believed provided supernatural protection for their successive kingdoms. When the Bamar under King Bodawpaya invaded Rakhaing in 1784, they dismantled the image into three pieces and hauled it over the Rakhaing Yoma to Amarapura to further legitimise the Konbaung dynasty.

Some Rakhaing say the Bamar unknowingly took a counterfeit figure and that the true Mahamuni image lies hidden somewhere in the jungle. Nowadays, three smaller stone images sit on the pedestal where the Mahamuni image once sat. A famous sandstone stele found there depicts a Gupta-style Buddha dating from 400 to 500 AD.

The current Konbaung-style shrine buildings date to the 18th or 19th centuries, as the earlier ones were destroyed by fire. One of the infamous *yadaya* bells used by Rakhaing rulers to keep invaders at bay was once displayed here but has disappeared in recent years.

You can reach the town of Mahamuni by

taking a boat to Kyauktaw (four hours from Mrauk U) and from there catching a pickup east to Mahamuni. It's quicker to go to Kyauktaw by road from Mrauk U (50km, about three hours) but this would involve a vehicle charter.

NGAPALI BEACH

Of the beach resorts most accessible to Myanmar visitors, Ngapali is easily the prettiest. The origin of the name is something of a mystery, though the most popular story says a homesick Italian who lived here for a while told everyone the beach reminded him of beaches near Naples. The Burmese name does have a meaning of its own – roughly, Inveigling Fish. It's the kind of name that should come with a story, but no one in the area seems to know one, so perhaps the meaning has been grafted to the Burmese pronunciation.

Backed by swaying palms and casuarinas, the Ngapali area is a good place to relax and take a break from the rigours of Myanmar road travel. The very broad, pristine stretch of sand known as Ngapali Beach reaches over 3km, and is separated from several more beaches by small, easily negotiated rocky headlands. Surfing is possible during the monsoon season (mid-May through to mid-September). With the opening of several new hotels and guesthouses, it is now possible to find a room at Ngapali year-round. In the past, the few beach hotels tended to close down because of the heavy rains. Malaria precautions should be taken.

There's more to do around Ngapali than just sit on the white sand and splash around in the sea, though for many people that's reason enough to go. Even the beach in front of the main hotel is a centre of activity. Fishermen begin setting and drawing drift nets before dawn and continue into the late morning, when they load their catches in baskets. Women carry baskets of the fish on foot to nearby villages, then return with lunch for the men; everyone breaks to eat at noon, then some pack up while others continue fishing till early evening. Before sunset, a group of fishermen often turn their

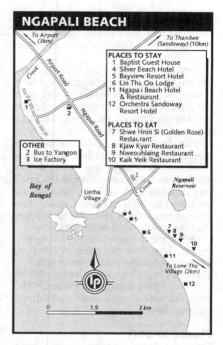

NGAPALI BEACH

To Airport (3km)

To Thandwe (Sandoway) (10km)

Airport Road

Ngapali Road

Creek

PLACES TO STAY
1 Baptist Guest House
4 Silver Eeach Hotel
5 Bayview Resort Hotel
6 Lin Tha Oo Lodge
11 Ngapa i Beach Hotel & Restaurant
12 Orchestra Sandoway Resort Hotel

PLACES TO EAT
7 Shwe Hnin Si (Golden Rose) Restaurant
8 Kjaw Kyar Restaurant
9 Nweoohlaing Restaurant
10 Kaik Yeik Restaurant

OTHER
2 Bus to Yangon
3 Ice Factory

Bay of Bengal

Lintha Village

Creek

Ngapali Reservoir

4
5
7
8 9
6
10
11
To Lone Tha Village (2km)
12

0   1.5   3 km

attention to an impromptu game of soccer near the creek at the north end of the beach.

With a bicycle, you can tour several of the villages. Just north of Ngapali Beach are the small villages of **Ngapali** and **Lintha**, both supported by the area's bounteous harvest of fish, coconuts and rice. **Myabyin**, to the immediate south of Ngapali Beach, is similar, followed by **Kyiktaw**, a larger and more interesting village with a market, a couple of teashops, monasteries and a government rice-storage facility. If you choose to walk along the beach to these villages, rather than cycle along the paved road opposite the beach, you'll pass large areas of the beach where the villagers sun-dry fish, shrimp and coconut on cane mats spread over the sand. Just offshore, near these villages, are several small, rocky islets reachable during low tide, and a bit farther south there's a mangrove swamp. Farther offshore are the larger islands of **Balet** and **Kayi**; a two hour boat trip to these islands can be arranged at any of the hotels or guesthouses for K3000.

Even farther south is the village of **Lontha** and an inlet of the same name backed by a sweeping curve of mangrove and sand. It's prettiest at high tide; during low tide the bay becomes muddy and rocky. There's a pier here, and the inlet is used heavily by smaller fishing boats, since it's the most protected harbour in this area. The inlet is connected to a larger bay called **Andwe Kywe** on recent government maps, Andrew Bay on older colonial maps (and still the term used by most Burmese). All of these villages are connected by a sealed, two lane road that ends at the Lontha jetty.

On the other side of the bay (accessible only by boat from this point, or by taking another road farther inland) is the village of **Thabyugyine**. This village has an MFSL jetty used by big fishing trawlers and MFSL ships, as well as by a large seafood processing plant nearby.

Places to Stay

Since AM started a weekly service to nearby Thandwe, the beach area has continued to sprout new accommodation. For years, only the **Ngapali Beach Hotel & Restaurant** (☎ Thandwe 28) was licensed to accept foreign visitors. This unusually well managed, state-owned hotel has two-room wooden bungalows with louvred walls and shaded verandas, fan, cold-water shower and mosquito nets, for US$20/25 a single/double. Larger superior rooms with a partition on the veranda for more privacy, along with a desk and four beds cost US$30/35. There are two large junior suites with hot-water showers for US$40/50. Electricity is available from about 6 to 11 pm. Trees and palm-thatch umbrellas on the beach provide shade. Treehouse-like platforms built into the banyan trees on the beach are a nice place to read or nap while catching a breeze.

Two new resort hotels have recently opened. The **Bayview Resort Hotel**, at the north end of the beach, is a Burmese-German joint venture with large air-con rooms, shaded verandas and hot-water showers, with rooms going for US$40/60. At the opposite end of the beach is another joint venture (Burmese-Italian), known as the **Orchestra/Sandoway Resort Hotel**, with similar rates and facilities. Both resort hotels have very good restaurants, with a mix of international and Myanmar cuisine.

Silver Beach Hotel (☎ Ngapali 25, Yangon office ☎ 01-294587) sits in a shaded compound along the beach. Two-bed bungalows with a small veranda cost US$30/36, with standard toast-and-eggs breakfast included. Prices may be lower outside the popular November-March season. Each room has a fan (electricity from 6 to 11 pm only) and attached cold-water bath. There are two large screened windows for a breeze. The management like to come by around sunset to blast each room with bug spray. If this isn't your idea of enjoying sunset on the veranda, you may request that they skip your room.

Linn Thar Oo Lodge (☎ Ngapali, 10 Yangon office ☎ 01-229928) is the only place on the beach with rooms at various prices. They have several four room wooden bungalows with common bath for US$5 per person, and several standard rooms with cold-water shower and small veranda for US$10/15. Two larger and brighter rooms with large private veranda cost US$20/25. Prices include breakfast. The dining room is quite good.

The **Baptist Guest House** is a popular budget place to stay. It's also the only place that's removed from the larger hotels and resorts springing up along the main beach. Comfortable and basic bungalow rooms with separate bath cost US$5 per person. The family owners prepare excellent and reasonably priced meals. You only need to alert them to when you'll be staying around for lunch or dinner.

Places to Eat

The Ngapali Beach Hotel has an open-air beachside restaurant with very good Chinese and Bamar dishes that are reasonably priced (kyats acceptable). Sunset views are a bonus.

Almost opposite the Ngapali Beach Hotel

section is *Kaik Yeik Restaurant*, a small, friendly, family-run place with fresh seafood plus Bamar and Chinese dishes – and an English-language menu.

Several other family-run restaurants that specialize in fresh seafood are across the road, just north of the Ngapali Beach Hotel. Our favourites include *Shwe Hnin Si (Golden Rose) Restaurant*, *Kjaw Kyar Restaurant* and *Nweoohlaing Restaurant*. Prices are very reasonable at each.

Getting There & Away
See Getting There & Away in the Thandwe section for details on air and road travel to Thandwe, the transport hub for the region.

Getting Around
A pickup from Thandwe or Thandwe airport to the Ngapali Beach Hotel costs K150 person. If you have a reservation, most of the hotels will give you a free lift. Thandwe, Kyiktaw, Myabyin, Lintha and Lontha are all linked by narrow sealed roads and can be visited by bicycle. At night, you'll need a torch to walk around Ngapali. It's probably easiest to walk along the beach at night, as every lodging or restaurant fronts the bay.

Bikes can be rented from any of the hotels or guesthouses at K50 per hour.

THANDWE (SANDOWAY)
Located around 9.5km north-east of Ngapali Beach, Thandwe (also spelt Thantwe) is the seat of a township by the same name with a population of approximately 80,000. Around 25% of the population is Muslim, most of whom live in the small township and attend the five mosques located there. For the most part, the surrounding villages are Buddhist.

Thandwe has been a key Rakhaing centre for many centuries and may originally have been an independent principality with the Sanskrit name of Dvaravati (roughly translated as Gated Kingdom, a name borrowed from India's *Ramayana* epic). Thandwe (Iron-Fastened) may in fact be a Burmese variation of this name. When the British stationed a garrison here around the

turn of the century, they twisted the name into Sandoway.

The town boasts a network of sealed and unsealed streets lined with two storey buildings that range from 50 to 100 years of age, constructed of masonry on the ground floors and wood on the upper floors. Away from the centre of town, virtually all houses are made of thatch. A former British jail in the centre of town is now used as a market where vendors sell medicinal herbs, clothes, textiles, hardware and free-market consumer goods. Among the many small shops surrounding the market are a number of gold shops, which suggests that the area is marked by some wealth.

Along the road between Thandwe and Ngapali you'll see a number of rubber plantations, including terraced ones – a deviation from the usual flat groves seen in most parts of the world. Rice and coconuts are also heavily farmed in the area. A battalion from the Tatmadaw's 55th Regiment has replaced the old British garrison outside town – so it's not unusual to see trucks overflowing with men in green on the roads.

Three stupas perched on hillsides at the edge of town are of mild interest. **Sandaw Paya**, reportedly built in 784 AD by the Rakhaing king Minyokin to house a Buddha hair relic and rebuilt by the Burmese in 1876, is a fairly ordinary stupa that affords good views of the town, river and surrounding hill. **Nandaw Paya**, on a higher hill opposite, was supposedly erected in 761 by King Minbra to enshrine a rib or piece of a rib of the Buddha. **Andaw Paya**, on a lower hill, claims a molar relic and a dating of 763. Outside one of the shrine buildings at Nandaw stands an old sculpture of a Rakhaing king that reportedly dates to the 6th century. A stone niche, inscribed in the Pali language using Rakhaing script, says the king reigned from 525 to 575 AD.

Places to Stay & Eat
San Yeik Nyein Guest House, a set of bare but adequate wooden rooms with shared facilities set over a video house a block south of the market, charges K200 per person. This

guesthouse was not accepting foreigners when we came along, but it may be worth a try. However, with the increase in the number of rooms available at nearby Ngapali, this situation is unlikely to change soon.

Thandwe has little in the way of restaurants despite its apparent relative prosperity. Next to the market and opposite a large mosque is a very good teashop called *The Point*, which offers whitewashed chairs instead of the usual tiny stools. Sticky rice and palatas are available here, as well as *nam bya* (flat bread), which is cooked in an outdoor oval oven painted like a soccer ball. The quality of the tea is very good here, but if you want it less sweet, remember to not stir it. You can also use the ever-present Chinese tea to thin it. On the same block, *Chit Khoung* serves a variety of mostly sweet snacks and ice cream.

There are several other *tea and cold drink shops* in this area, and in the market itself there are a few rather questionable-looking *noodle vendors*. On the next street south, a few blocks west of the San Yeik Nyein Guest House, *Jupiter Food & Drink* serves a mix of Chinese and Indian pastries, including *paug-si* (steamed buns), *ei-kya-kwe* (long fried pastries), and samosas.

Getting There & Away
Air AM flies from Yangon to Thandwe and back on Wednesday, Friday and Saturday. The flight takes 50 minutes and costs US$80.

MA also flies between Thandwe and Yangon on Tuesday and Friday. For this route MA usually employs an F-27. The fare from Yangon is US$55. On the same days, and with the same aircraft, MA flies from Sittwe via Kyaukpyu for US$50. The flight segment from Thandwe to Kyaukpyu costs US$30. An MA flight crashed at Thandwe in 1998.

MA doesn't usually fly to Thandwe during the rainy season (mid-May through to mid-September). AM usually cuts back flights outside the November to April high season, but with new hotels recently opening in nearby Ngapali Beach, expect regular if limited service year-round.

MA maintains a ticket office in the centre of Thandwe. AM has no office in Thandwe as yet; eventually it may establish a local office, most likely at one of the hotels. Until then, the only time you can speak with a representative is when there's an AM plane on the runway at Thandwe airport – the rep accompanies each flight from Yangon, spends about an hour taking care of business at the airport, then boards the return flight to Yangon. If you want to buy or confirm a ticket out of Thandwe, be sure to turn up at the airport around 5 pm on days when the AM flights are scheduled to arrive.

Bus A variety of buses, pickups and taxis operate regionally out of Thandwe. A private bus, Mihara Express, operates between Thandwe and Yangon's highway bus terminal and costs K1500. Departure is at 3 pm, and the trip usually takes 17 or 18 hours one way, with breaks at Taunggok and Pyay. The Taunggok Pass in the Rakhaing Yoma was only breached in 1960. Thandwe's bus station sits at the side of the road that leads to Andaw Paya on the edge of town, but if you make a reservation, the bus will pick you up at any Ngapali Beach hotel or guesthouse. There is a Mihara ticket counter in the Emerald Tea Shop at the airport junction, midway between Ngapali Beach and the airport.

Taunggok A government bus departs from Pyay at noon, arriving in Taunggok (86km south of Thandwe) at 7 pm. The fare is K1100. In Taunggok, there is one *guesthouse*, next to the bus station, that costs K500 per person. They don't have a licence for foreigners, but it doesn't seem to matter in out-of-the-way Taunggok. A decent *restaurant* with an English sign (Restaurant) is nearby.

A longer and more scenic bus route to Thandwe starts in the delta region at Pathein and takes you up the coast. Many of the roads are unsealed and subject to flooding. A bus from Pathein north-west to Ngathaingchaung costs K150 and takes around four or five hours. Buses continue along a decent road from Ngathaingchaung to Gwa (mornings only), on the coast, for K300; this leg takes six hours or more. From Gwa, one bus per day heads straight north to Thandwe on a dusty, unsealed road, a nine hour trip that costs K200. Much of the trade on this route is cargo, rather than passengers.

Car You can accomplish the same routes described above by private vehicle, depending on the time of year and possible flooding along many coastal roads. Cars can be hired at a cost of about US$40 in Pyay to make the trip to Thandwe. A set of new roads under construction will allow continued road travel north of Taunggok as far as Sittwe and beyond to Taungbyo on the Bangladesh border. By the time you read this the entire route from Ngathaingchaung to Sittwe – about 840km – should be driveable.

Boat There are a few boat options to/from Thandwe:

Passenger Boat MFSL sails from Yangon to Thabyugyine jetty, south of Thandwe, once or twice a week on their way to Sittwe. MFSL maintains an office in Thandwe right around the corner from the MA office. Dates for voyages to Yangon are posted on a chalkboard. At least one of the government vessels is an express ship, making the trip between Taunggok and Sittwe in a day and a half, with an overnight stay in a village along the way. The fare is US$9 for the boat, and another K150 to stay in the village.

Chartered boats go from the Thabyugyine jetty to the Lontha jetty for K1200. From Lontha, regular buses to Thandwe cost K20.

Cargo Boat It may be difficult to find a cargo boat in Yangon, but not in Taunggok. There is usually some kind of boat going north or south every day. In Taunggok, you need to go to the jetty and ask about departure times. For example, a cargo boat to Sittwe should cost about K1500 for a two night/three day trip. You sleep on the deck with potato and onion sacks, but the crew does cook for you.

Getting Around
Most of Thandwe is easily seen on foot. Trishaws for short trips around town cost K50.

Local minibuses, as well as pickups, cruise several times a day from Thandwe to Lontha for K20; you can get off at Ngapali Beach along the way.

Sometimes you can ride for free to Thandwe from Ngapali with one of the hotel drivers on their way to the morning market to buy food for the hotel restaurant.

KANTHAYA (THAYA BEACH)
The Rakhaing coast's latest beach resort is 26km north of Gwa, a small town on the coast just north of the Ayeyarwady Division border, and 130km south of Thandwe. Kanthaya extends a sandy 5km, but few people know about the place yet, partly because access is very limited and partly because Chaungtha Beach to the south and Ngapali Beach to the north are drawing more and more visitors.

Nevertheless, the bungalow-style *Kanthaya Beach Resort* should be open by the time you read this. As elsewhere in Myanmar, more accommodation may come along as demand grows.

It's about six to seven hours by car from Yangon via Ngathaingchaung, about four to five hours from Pathein, or five hours from Ngapali. See the Getting There & Away section under Thandwe for details on public transport to Gwa from Ngathaingchaung and Thandwe.

An old airfield outside Gwa may eventually be renovated for use by AM/MA flights.

EXCURSIONS INTO SOUTHERN CHIN STATE
Although it's possible to visit the northern part of the Chin State by road from Kalewa in the Sagaing Division, the true heart of traditional Chin culture is found in the south. **Paletwa**, just over the state line from the Rakhaing State, can be reached via boat along the Kaladan River from Sittwe or Kyauktaw. A new road under construction between Mahamuni and Paletwa will also allow vehicles to travel direct from Mrauk U when completed.

In the Chin Hills some women still tattoo their faces, though it's a custom that's fading fast. At higher elevations they wear thick, striped cotton blankets draped over the body, and ornaments of copper and bronze. Among the Khamui, a subtribe that inhabits the lower elevations of southern Chin State, unmarried women wear short skirts and little else. The Chin men tend to wear simple western-style dress such as shirts and trousers.

Although the Chin State is currently off-limits to independent travellers, the Ministry of Hotels & Tourism (MHT) has recently started to issue sporadic permits to visitors on package tours. As in other formerly off-limit parts of Myanmar, this is usually the government's first step in loosening travel restrictions. We met an experienced traveller in Mandalay who had managed to get as far as Paletwa on his own, only to be told at the bus station that he had '10 minutes to leave the state'. If you're able to stay longer, there's a lot to see.

Language

Pronunciation

The Burmese pronunciation in this language guide follows that used in the textbooks by Okell, the most up-to-date Burmese course available.

Vowels

Burmese vowel sounds occur in open, nasalised and stopped forms. Nasalisation of vowels is like that in French; speakers of English or other languages can approximate this by putting a weak 'n' at the end of such a syllable. In this guide the nasalisation is indicated by *n* after the vowel, as in *ein* (house).

non-nasalised

i	as the 'e' in 'be'
e	as the 'a' in 'bay'
eh	as the first 'e' in 'elephant'
a	as in 'father'
aw	as the British pronounce 'law'
o	as in 'go'
u	as the 'oo' in 'too'

nasalised / stopped

nasalised		stopped	
in	as in 'sin'	iq	as in 'sit'
ein	as in 'lane'	eiq	as in 'late'
		eq	as in 'bet'
an	as in 'man'	aq	as in 'mat'
oun	as in 'bone'	ouq	as in 'boat'
un	as in German *Bund*	uq	as in 'foot'
ain	as in German *mein*	aiq	as in the English 'might'
aun	as in 'brown'	auq	as in 'out'

Consonants

Consonants only occur at the beginning of a syllable; there are no consonants that occur after the vowel. The consonants **b, d, j, g, m, n, ng, s, sh, h, z, w, l, y** are pronounced as in English; the 'w' sound can occur on its own, or in combination with other consonants. The following may cause confusion:

th – as in 'thin'

dh – as in 'the' or 'their'

ny – similar to the consonants at the beginning of the British 'new'

hm, hn, hny, hng, hl – made with a puff of air just before the nasal or **l** sound

p', t', s', c', k' – aspirated

p, t, c, k – unaspirated

Aspirated Consonants

The aspirated sounds are made with a puff of air; this is the way the letters 'p', 't', 'k' are pronounced in English at the beginning of a word. When these sounds are unaspirated they sound like the 'p', 't', 'k' after an 's', as in 'spin', 'stir' and 'skin'.

The unaspirated **c** and aspirated **c'** are similar to the 'ch' in 'church'. Remember that **sh** as in 'ship', **s** as in 'sip' and the aspirated **s'** are three different sounds. Another difficulty is in saying the **ng** at the beginning of a syllable; try saying 'hang on', then leave off the 'ha' to get an idea of the sound.

Tones

Burmese tones are largely a matter of relative stress between adjoining syllables. There are three tones, plus two other possibilities.

Creaky High Tone

This is made with the voice tense, producing a high-pitched and relatively short, creaky sound, such as occurs with the English words 'heart' and 'squeak'. It is indicated by an acute accent above the vowel, for example *ká* (dance).

Plain High Tone

The pitch of the voice starts quite high, then falls for a fairly long time, similar to the pronunciation of words like 'squeal', 'car' and 'way'. It is indicated by a grave accent above the vowel, for example *kà* which, conveniently, is also the Burmese word for 'car'.

Low Tone

The voice is relaxed, stays at a low pitch for a fairly long time, and does not rise or fall in pitch. It is indicated by no accent above the vowel, for example *ka* (shield).

Stopped Syllable

This is a very short and high-pitched syllable, on a high pitch, cut off at the end by a sharp catch in the voice (a glottal stop); it's similar to the 'non' sound in the middle of the exclamation, 'oh-oh', or the Cockney pronunciation of 't' in a word like 'bottle'. It is indicated in this book by a 'q' after the vowel, for example *kaq* (join). However, the 'q' is not pronounced.

Reduced (Weak) Syllable

This is a shortened syllable, usually the first of a two-syllable word, which is said without stress, like the first syllable of 'again' in English. Only the vowel 'a', sometimes preceded by a consonant, occurs in a reduced syllable; this is indicated by a small 'v'-like symbol above the vowel, eg *ălouq* (work). Any syllable except the last in a word can be reduced.

Transliteration

In Burmese writing, **c, c', j** are written using the letters for **k, k', g** plus **y** or **r**; so anglicised forms of Burmese often represent them as **ky, gy** and so on. One example of this is the unit of currency, *caq*, which is usually written 'kyat' in the Roman alphabet. Aspirated consonants (**k', s', t'** and **p'**) may be spelt with an 'h' before or after the consonant. A creaky tone may be indicated by a final **t**, eg Hpakant (in Kachin State).

Various combinations of letters may be used to represent the same vowel sound: **e** and **eh** are both often transliterated as 'ay'; **ain** may be represented as 'aing', **auq** as 'auk' and so on.

There is no 'r' in Burmese but the sound appears in some foreign words such as *re-di-yo* (radio), or *da-reiq-s'an* (animal) (Pali). Sometimes it is substituted with a **y**. Similarly there is no 'f' or 'v' in Burmese; loan words containing these consonants often use **p'** and **b** respectively.

In the transliteration system used in this guide, transliterated syllables (with the exception of the reduced syllable **ă**) have been separated by hyphens, and breaks between

words, or groups of words, by spaces. This is intended to make it easier for the learner. However, native speakers often do not speak with a clear division between words or syllables.

The aspirated sounds are made with a puff of air after the sound; this is the way English 'p', 't', 'k' are pronounced at the beginning of a word. The unaspirated sounds are without this puff of air, as in English 'p', 't', 'k' after an 's', as in 'spin', 'stir' and 'skin' respectively.

Greetings & Civilities

Hello. (lit. It's a blessing)
min-gălà-ba
မင်္ဂလာပါ။

How are you/Are you well?
k'ămyà (m)/*shin* (f) *ne-kaùn-yéh-là?*
ခင်ဗျား/ရှင် နေကောင်းရဲ့လား။

(I) am well.
ne-kaùn-ba-deh
နေကောင်းပါတယ်။

Have you eaten?
t'ămìn sà-pì-bi-là?
ထမင်းစားပြီးပြီလား။

(I) have eaten.
sà-pì-ba-bi
စားပြီးပါပြီ။

Where are you going?
beh thwà-măló-lèh?
ဘယ်သွားမလို့လဲ။

To this, a general, non-specific reply is *di-nà-lè-bèh*, ဒီနားလေးပဲ (literally 'Just around here'). However, you could say:

I'm going back to my hotel.
ho-teh-go pyan-táw-meh
ဟိုတယ်ကို ပြန်တော့မယ်။

I'm leaving now. (Goodbye)
thwà-ba-oùn-meh
သွားပါဦးမယ်။

While a smile is often enough, it's always appreciated if you say 'thank you' in Burmese.

Thanks.
cè-zù-bèh
ကျေးဇူးပဲ။

Thank you.
  cè-zù tin-ba-deh
  ကျေးဇူးတင်ပါတယ်॥
You're welcome. (It's nothing)
  keiq-sá măshi-ba-bù
  ကိစ္စမရှိပါဘူး॥

Language Difficulties

Do you understand?
  nà-leh-dhălà?
  နားလည်သလား॥
I understand.
  nà-leh-ba-deh
  နားလည်ပါတယ်॥
(I) don't understand.
  nà-măleh-ba-bù
  နားမလည်ပါဘူး॥
Please say it again.
  pyan-pyàw-ba-oùn
  ပြန်ပြောပါအုံး॥
I can't speak Burmese.
  băma-zăgà lo măpyàw-daq-bù
  ဗမာစကား လို့ မပြောတတ်ဘူး॥
I speak English.
  ìn-găleiq-zăgà lo pyàw-daq-teh
  အင်္ဂလိပ်စကား လို့ ပြောတတ်တယ်॥
Can you speak English?
  k'ămyà (m)/*shin* (f) *ìn-găleiq-zăgà lo
  pyàw-daq-thălà?*
  ခင်များ/ရှင် အင်္ဂလိပ်စကား လို့ ပြောတတ်သလား॥
What do you call this in Burmese?
  da băma-lo beh-lo k'aw-dhălèh?
  ဒါ ဗမာလို ဘယ်လိုခေါ်သလဲ॥

Small Talk

What's your name?
  k'ămyá (m)/*shin* (f) *na-meh beh-lo
  k'aw-dhălèh?*
  ခင်များ/ရှင် နာမည် ဘယ်လို ခေါ်သလဲ၊
My name is ...
  cănáw (m)/*cămá* (f) ... *ló k'aw-ba-deh*
  ကျွန်တော့်/ကျွန်မ ... လို့. ခေါ်ပါတယ်॥
I'm glad to meet you.
  k'ămyà (m)/*shin* (f) *-néh*
  ခင်များ/ရှင်နဲ့.
Yes.
  houq-kéh   ဟုတ်ကဲ့॥
No.
  măhouq-p'ù   မဟုတ်ပါဘူး॥

Getting Around

Where is the ...?
  ... beh-hma-lèh?
  ... ဘယ်မှာလဲ॥
airport
  le-zeiq   လေဆိပ်
railway carriage
  mì-yăt'à-dwèh   မီးရထားတွဲ
train station
  bu-da-youn   ဘူတာရုံ
bus station
  baq-săkà-geiq   ဘတ်စ်ကားဂိတ်
riverboat jetty
  thìn-bàw-zeiq   သင်္ဘောဆိပ်

When will the ... leave?
  ... beh-ăc'ein t'weq-mă!èh?
  ... ဘယ်အချိန်ထွက်မလဲ॥
plane
  le-yin-byan   လေယာဉ်ပျံ
train
  mì-yăt'à   မီးရထား
express train
  ămyan-yăt'à   အမြန်ရထား
local train
  law-keh-yăt'à   လော်ကယ်ရထား
bus
  baq-săkà   ဘတ်စ်ကား
riverboat
  thìn-bàw   သင်္ဘော
jeep
  jiq-kà   ဂျစ်ကား

I'd like ...
  cănaw (m)/*cămá* (f) ... *lo-jin-ba-deh*
  ကျွန်တော်/ကျွန်မ ... လိုချင်ပါတယ်॥
one ticket
  leq-hmaq-dăzaun   လက်မှတ်တစ်စောင်
two tickets
  leq-hmaq hnăsaun လက်မှတ်နှစ်စောင်

Where does this bus go?
  ăi baq-săkà beh-go thwà-dhălèh?
  ဒီဘတ်စ်ကား ဘယ်ကိုသွားသလဲ॥
Where should I get off?
  beh-hma s'ìn-yá-mălèh?
  ဘယ်မှာဆင်းရမလဲ॥
What time does the boat leave?
  thìn-bàw beh-ăc'ein t'weq-mălèh?
  သင်္ဘော ဘယ်အချိန်ထွက်မလဲ॥

Can I get on board now?
ăk'ú teq-ló yá-dhălà?
အခု တက်လို့ရသလား။

bicycle	*seq-beìn*	စက်ဘီး
motorcycle	*mo-ta s'ain-keh*	မော်တော်ဆိုင်ကယ်
rickshaw/sidecar	*s'aiq-kà*	ဆိုက်ကား
taxi	*ăhngà-kà*	အငှါးကား

Can I get there by ...?
... néh thwà-ló yá-mălà?
... နဲ့ သွားလို့ရမလား။

bicycle	*seq-beìn*	စက်ဘီး
bus	*baq-săkà*	ဘတ်စကား
taxi	*ăhngà-kà*	အငှါးကား

Please go slowly.
pyè-pyè thwà-ba
ဖြည်းဖြည်းသွားပါ။
Please wait for me.
cănaw (m)/*cămá* (f)*-go saún-ne-ba*
ကျွန်တော်/ကျွန်မကိုစောင့်နေပါ။
Stop here.
di-hma yaq-pa
ဒီမှာ ရပ်ပါ။

Directions

What ... is this?
da ba ... lèh?
ဒါ ဘာ ...လဲ။

town	*myó*	မြို့
street	*làn*	လမ်း
bus	*baq-săkà*	ဘတ်စကား

Is this the way to ...?
di-làn ... thwà-déh-làn-là?
ဒီလမ်း ... သွားတဲ့လမ်းလား။
How do I get to ...?
... ko beh-lo thwà-yá- dhălèh?
... ကို ဘယ်လိုသွားရသလဲ။
Can I walk there?
làn-shauq-yin yá-mălà?
လမ်းလျှောက်ရင် ရမလား။
Is it nearby?
di-nà-hma-là? ဒီနားမှာလား။

Signs

ENTRANCE	အဝင်
EXIT	အထွက်
NO ENTRY	မဝင်ရ
TELEPHONE	တယ်လီဖုန်း
TOILETS	အိမ်သာ
NO SMOKING	ဆေးလိပ် မသောက်ရ
NO PHOTOGRAPHS	ဓါတ်ပုံ မရိုက်ရ
DANGER	ရှိသည်
STOP	ရပ်
WOMEN FORBIDDEN	အမျိုးသမီးများ မဝင်ရ

Is it far?	
wè-dhălà?	ဝေးသလား။
left	
beh-beq	ဘယ်ဘက်
right	
nya-beq	ညာဘက်
straight (ahead)	
téh-déh	တည့်တည့်
very far away	
theiq wè-deh	သိပ်ဝေးတယ်။
not so far away	
theiq măwè-bù	သိပ်မဝေးဘူး။
north	
myauq-p'eq	မြောက်ဘက်
south	
taun-beq	တောင်ဘက်
east	
ăshé-beq	အရှေ့ ဘက်
west	
ănauq-p'eq	အနောက်ဘက်

Around Town

Where is the ...?
... beh-hma-lèh?
... ဘယ်မှာလဲ။

bank	*ban-daiq*	ဘဏ်တိုက်
market	*zè*	ဈေး
museum	*pyá-daiq*	ပြတိုက်
post office	*sa-daiq*	စာတိုက်

I'd like to make a call.
p'oùn-s'eq-c'in-deh
ဖုန်းဆက်ချင်တယ်။

Can I send a fax?
fax pó-ló yá-dhàlà?
ဖက်စ်ပို့လို့ ရလား။

I want to change ...
... *lèh-jin-ba-deh*
... လဲချင်ပါတယ်။
dollars
daw-la ဒေါ်လာ
pounds
paun ပေါင်
foreign currency
nain-ngan-gyà နိုင်ငံခြားငွေ
ngwe
money
paiq-s'an ပိုက်ဆံ
travellers cheques
k'ăyì-c'eq-leq- ခရီးချက်လက်မှတ်
hmaq

How many kyat to a dollar?
tădawla beh-hnăcaq-lèh?
တစ်ဒေါ်လာ ဘယ်နှစ်ကျပ်လဲ။
Please give me smaller change.
ăkywe-ănouq lèh-pè-ba
အကြွေအနုပ်လဲပေးပါ

Accommodation
Is there a ... near here?
... *di-nà-hma shí-dhălà?*
... ဒီနားမှာရှိသလား။
hotel *ho-teh* ဟော်တယ်
guesthouse *tèh-k'o-gàn* တည်းခိုခန်း

Can foreigners stay here?
nain-ngan-gyà-thà di-hma tèh-ló
yá-dhălà?
နိုင်ငံခြားသား ဒီမှာတည်းလို့ရသလား။
May I see the room?
ăk'àn cí-bayá-ze?
အခန်း ကြည့်ပါရစေ
This room is good.
di ăk'àn kaùn-deh
ဒီအခန်း ကောင်းတယ်။
Is breakfast included in the price?
ăk'àn-k'á-dèh-hma măneq-sa pa-dhălà?
အခန်းခထဲမှာ မနက်စာ ပါသလား။
Can I pay in kyats?
caq-néh pè-ló yá-là?
ကျပ်နဲ့ ပေးလို့ရလား။

I will stay for two nights.
hnăyeq ı̀'èh-meh
နှစ်ရက်တည်းမယ်။

How much is ...?
... *beh-lauq-lèh?*
... ဘယ်လောက်လဲ။
one night
tăyeq တစ်ရက်
two nights
hnăyeq နှစ်ရက်
a single room
tăyauq-k'an တစ်ယောက်ခန်း
a double room
hnăyauq-k'an နှစ်ယောက်ခန်း

clean	*thán-deh*	သန့်တယ်
dirty	*nyiq-paq-deh*	ညစ်ပတ်တယ်
fan (electric)	*pan-ka*	ပန်ကာ
noisy	*s'u-nyan-deh*	ဆူညံတယ်
pillow	*gaùn-oùn*	ခေါင်းအုံး

Shopping
Where is the ..?
... *beh-hma-lèh?*
... ဘယ်မှာလဲ။

bookshop	*sa-ouq-s'ain*	စာအုပ်ဆိုင်
chemist/	*s'è-zain*	ဆေးဆိုင်
pharmacy		
market	*zè*	ဈေး
shop	*s'ain*	ဆိုင်

Where can I buy ...?
... *beh-hma weh-yá-mălèh?*
... ဘယ်မှာဝယ်ရမလဲ။
Do you have ... ?
... *shí-là*
... ရှိလား။
How much is ...?
... *beh-lauq-lèh?*
... ဘယ်လောက်လဲ။

lacquerware	*yùn-deh*	ယွန်းထည်
matches	*mì-jiq*	မီးခြစ်
shampoo	*gaùn-shaw-ye*	ခေါင်းလျှော်ရည်
soap	*s'aq-pya*	ဆပ်ပြာ
toilet paper	*ein-dha-thoùn-*	အိမ်သာသုံးစက္ကူ။
	seq-ku	
toothbrush	*dhăbuq-tan*	သွားပွတ်တံ
toothpaste	*thwà-taiq-s'è*	သွားတိုက်ဆေး

Do you have a cheaper one?
da-t'eq zè po-pàw-dé tăk'ú shí-dhălà?
ဒါထက် ဈေးပိုပေါတဲ့တစ်ခု ရှိသလား။
OK. (lit. 'good')
Kàun-ba-bi　ကောင်းပါပြီ။
cheap
zè-pàw-deh　ဈေးပေါတယ်
expensive
zè-cì-deh　ဈေးကြီးတယ်

Geographical Features

beach	*kàn-byin*	ကမ်းပြင်
countryside	*tàw*	တော
field (irrigated)	*leh*	လယ်
hill	*taun/koùn*	တောင်/ကုန်း
island	*cùn*	ကျွန်း
lake	*ain*	အိုင်
lake (small/ artificial)	*kan*	ကန်
map	*mye-boun*	မြေပုံ
river	*myiq*	မြစ်
sea	*pin-leh*	ပင်လယ်
town	*myó*	မြို့
track/trail	*làn-jaùn*	လမ်းကြောင်း
village	*ywa*	ရွာ
waterfall	*ye-dăgun*	ရေတံခွန်

Time & Date

What time is it?
beh-ăc'ein shí-bi-lèh?
ဘယ်အချိန်ရှိပြီလဲ။
At what time?
beh-ăc'ein-hma-lèh?
ဘယ်အချိန်မှာလဲ။

7 am
măneq k'ú-hnăna-yi
မနက် ခုနစ်နာရီ
1 pm
né-leh tăna-yi
နေ့လည် တစ်နာရီ
4.30 pm
nyá-ne lè-na-yi-gwèh
ညနေ လေးနာရီခွဲ
10.15 pm
nyá s'eh-na-yi s'éh-ngà-măniq
ည ဆယ်နာရီဆယ့်ငါးမိနစ်

hour	*na-yi*	နာရီ
minute	*măniq*	မိနစ်

Emergencies

Help!	*keh-ba!*	ကယ်ပါ။
Watch out!	*dhădí t'à-ba!*	သတိထားပါ။
Go away!	*thwà-zàn!*	သွားဆင်း။
Stop!	*yaq!*	ရပ်။
Thief!	*thăk'ò!*	သူခိုး။

Call a doctor!
s'ăya-wun-go k'aw-pè-ba!
ဆရာဝန်ကို ခေါ်ပေးပါ။
Call an ambulance!
lu-na-din-gà k'aw-pè-ba!
လူနာတင်ကားခေါ်ပေးပါ။
I'm ill.
ne-măkàun-bù
နေမကောင်းဘူး။
I'm lost.
làn pyauq-thwà-bi
လမ်းပျောက်သွားပြီ။
I've been raped.
mú-dèin cín-k'an-yá-deh
မုဒိမ်းကျင့်ခံရတယ်။
I've been robbed.
ăk'ò-k'an-yá-deh
အခိုးခံရတယ်။

morning (6 am to midday)
măneq　မနက်
midday (noon to 3 pm)
né-leh　နေ့လည်
afternoon/evening (3 to 7 pm)
nyá-ne　ညနေ
night (7 pm to 6 am)
nyá　ည
today
di-né　ဒီနေ့
tomorrow
măneq-p'yan　မနက်ဖြန်
day after tomorrow
dhăbeq-k'a　သဘက်ခါ
next week
nauq ăpaq　နောက် အပတ်
yesterday
măné-gá　မနေ့က

Sunday
tănìn-gănwe-né　တနင်္ဂနွေနေ့

Monday
tănìn-la-né တနင်္လာနေ့
Tuesday
in-ga-né အင်္ဂါနေ့
Wednesday
bouq-dăhù-né ဗုဒ္ဓဟူးနေ့
Thursday
ca-dhăbădè-né ကြာသပတေးနေ့
Friday
thauq-ca-né သောကြာနေ့
Saturday
săne-né စနေနေ့

Numbers

1	၁	*tiq/tă*	တစ်/တ
2	၂	*hniq/hnă*	နှစ်/နှ
3	၃	*thòun*	သုံး
4	၄	*lè*	လေး
5	၅	*ngà*	ငါး
6	၆	*c'auq*	ခြောက်
7	၇	*k'ú-hniq/ k'ú-hnă*	ခုနှစ်/ခုနှ
8	၈	*shiq*	ရှစ်
9	၉	*kò*	ကိုး
10	၁၀	*(tă)s'eh*	တစ်ဆယ်
11	၁၁	*s'éh-tiq*	ဆယ့်တစ်
12	၁၂	*s'éh-hniq*	ဆယ့်နှစ်
20	၂၀	*hnăs'eh*	နှစ်ဆယ်
35	၃၅	*thòun-zéh-ngà*	သုံးဆယ့်ငါး
100	၁၀၀	*tăya*	တစ်ရာ
1000	၁၀၀၀	*(tă)t'aun*	တစ်ထောင်
10,000	၁၀၀၀၀	*(tă)thàun*	တစ်သောင်း
100,000	၁၀၀၀၀၀	*(tă)thèin*	တစ်သိန်း
one million	၁၀၀၀၀၀၀	*(tă)thàn*	တစ်သန်း

Note that 100,000 is often called *lakh*.

Health

Where is the ...?
... *beh-hma-lèh?*
... ဘယ်မှာလဲ။

chemist/pharmacy	*s'è-zain*	ဆေးဆိုင်
doctor	*s'ăya-wun*	ဆရာဝန်
dentist	*thwà-s'ăya-wun*	သွားဆရာဝန်
hospital	*s'è-youn*	ဆေးရုံ

Please call a doctor.
s'ăya-wun kaw-pè-ba
ဆရာဝန် ခေါ်ပေးပါ။
I'm allergic to penicillin.
cănaw (m)/*cămá* (f)
pănăsălin-néh mătéh-bù
ကျွန်တော်/ကျွန်မ ပင်နီစလင်နဲ့ မတည့်ဘူး။
I'm pregnant.
baiq cì-deh/ko-wun shí-deh
ဗိုက်ကြီးတယ်/ကိုယ်ဝန်ရှိတယ်။
It hurts here.
di-hma na-deh
ဒီမှာ နာတယ်။
I vomit often.
k'ăná-k'ăná an-deh
ခဏခဏ အန်တယ်။
I feel faint.
mù-lèh-deh
မူးလဲတယ်။

asthma
(pàn-na-)yin-caq s'ì-jo-yàw-ga
ပန်းနာရင်ကျပ် ဒိဗတောစေ ဆီးချိုရောဂါ
have diarrhoea
wùn-shàw-deh/wùn-thwà-ne-deh
ဝမ်းလျှောတယ်/ဝမ်းသွားနေတယ်
have a fever
p'yà-deh
ဖျားတယ်
have a headache
gàun kaiq-ne-deh
ခေါင်းကိုက်နေတယ်
have a stomachache
baiq na-deh
ဗိုက်နာတယ်
have a toothache
thwà kaiq-teh
သွားကိုက်တယ်

aspirin	*eq-săpărin*	အက်စပရင်
bandage	*paq-tì*	ပတ်တီး

FOOD

Is there a ... near here?
... *di-nà-hma shí-dhălà?*
... ဒီနားမှာရှိသလား။

Shan noodle stall
shàn-k'auk-swèh- zain
ရှမ်းခေါက်ဆွဲဆိုင်

Chinese restaurant
   tăyouq-s'ain   တရုတ်ဆိုင်
food stall
   sà-thauq-s'ain   စားသောက်ဆိုင်
restaurant
   sà-daw-s'eq   စားတော်ဆက်
breakfast
   măneq-sa   မနက်စာ
lunch
   né-leh-za   နေ့လည်စာ
dinner
   nyá-za   ညစာ
snack/small meal
   móun/thăye-za   မုန့်/သရေစာ
food ('edibles')
   sà-zăya   စားစရာ

At the Restaurant
Please bring (a) ...
   ... *yu-pè-ba*   ... ယူပေးပါ။

chopsticks	*tu*	တူ
fork	*k'ăyìn*	ခက်ရင်း
spoon	*zùn*	ဇွန်း
knife	*dà*	ဓါး
glass	*p'an-gweq*	ဖန်ခွက်
plate	*băgan-byà*	ပန်းကန်ပြား
bowl	*băgan-loùn*	ပန်းကန်လုံး
cup	*k'weq*	ခွက်

I can't eat meat.
   ăthà măsà-nain-bù
   အသား မစားနိုင်ဘူး။
Do you have any drinking water?
   thauq-ye shi-dhălà?
   သောက်ရေရှိသလား။
What's the best dish to eat today?
   di-né ba-hìn ăkaùn-zoùn-lèh?
   ဒီနေ့ဘာဟင်းအကောင်းဆုံးလဲ။
I didn't order this.
   da măhma-bù
   ဒါ မမှာဘူး။

Typical Bamar Dishes
clear soup
   hìn-jo   ဟင်းချို
sizzling rice soup
   s'an-hlaw-hìn-jo   ဆန်လှော်ဟင်းချို
'12-taste' soup
   s'eh-hnămyò-hìn-jo   ဆယ်နှစ်မျိုးဟင်းချို

mohinga (rice vermicelli in fish sauce)
   móun-hìn-gà   မုန့်ဟင်းခါး
Mandalay moun-ti (noodles & chicken/fish)
   móun-di   မုန့်တီ
coconut noodles with chicken and egg
   oùn-nó-k'auk-swèh   အုန်းနို့ခေါက်ဆွဲ
coconut rice
   oùn-t'ămìn   အုန်းထမင်း
fried rice
   t'ămìn-gyaw   ထမင်းကြော်
beef in gravy
   ămèh-hnaq   အမဲနှပ်
chicken curry
   ceq-thà-hìn   ကြက်သားဟင်း
fried chicken
   ceq-thà-jaw   ကြက်သားကြော်
fried spicy chicken
   ceq-thà-ăsaq-ceq   ကြက်သားအစပ်ချက်
grilled chicken (satay)
   ceq-thà-gin   ကြက်သားကင်
pork curry
   weq-thà-hìn   ဝက်သားဟင်း
pork curry in thick sauce
   weq-thà s'i-byan   ဝက်သားဆီပြန်
red pork
   weq-thà-ni   ဝက်သားနီ
sweet chicken
   ceq-thà-ăc'o-jeq   ကြက်သားအချိုချက်
fish salad
   ngà-dhouq   ငါးသုပ်
prawn/shrimp curry
   băzun-hìn   ပုစွန်ဟင်း
steamed fish in banana leaves
   ngà-baùn-douq   ငါးပေါင်းထုပ်
packet/bamboo section of sticky rice
   kauk-hnyìn-baùn ămèh-dhà-hìn
   ကောက်ညှင်းပေါင်း ဗမော ၇ရရယ အမဲသားဟင်း
vegetable curry
   hìn-dhì-hìn-yweq-hìn/thì-zoun-hìn
   ဟင်းသီးဟင်းရွက်ဟင်း/သီးစုံဟင်း

sago/tapioca in syrup
   tha-gu-móun   သာဂူမုန့်
sticky rice cake with jaggery
   móun-zàn   မုန့်ဆန်း
sweet fried rice pancakes
   móun-s'i-jaw   မုန့်ဆီကြော်
toddy palm sugar cake
   t'àn-thì-móun   ထန်းသီးမုန့်

Meat

beef	ămèh-dhà	အမဲ
chicken	ceq-thà	ကြက်သား:
pork	weq-thà	ဝက်သား:

Seafood

catfish	ngăk'u	ငါးခူ
eel	ngăshín	ငါးရှဉ့်
fish	ngà	ငါး
seafood	pin-leh-za/	ပင်လယ်စာ/
	ye-thaq-tăwa	ရေသတ္တဝါ
shellfish	k'ăyú	ခရု
squid	pyi-jì-ngà	ပြည်ကြီးငါး:
steamed carp	ngà-thălauq-	ငါးသလောက်–
	paùn	ကပေါင်း:
steamed fish	ngà-baùn	ငါးပေါင်း:

Vegetables

banana flower		
hngăpyàw-bù	ငှက်ပျောဖူး:
beans		
pèh-dhì	ပဲသီး:
cabbage		
gaw-bi-douq	ဂေါ်ဖီထုပ်
carrot		
moun-la-ú-wa	မုန်လာဥဝါ
cauliflower		
pàn–gaw-p'i	ပန်းဂေါ်ဖီ
chick peas		
kălăbèh	ကုလားပဲ
corn (cob)		
pyaùn-bù	ပြောင်းဖူး:
cucumber		
thăk'wà-dhì	သခွားသီး:
eggplant/aubergine		
k'ăyàn-dhì	ခရမ်းသီး:
mushrooms		
hmɔ	မှို
onion		
ceq-thun-ni	ကြက်သွန်နီ
pumpkin		
p'ăyoun-dhì	ဖရုံသီး:
tomato		
k'ăyàn-jin-dhì	ခရမ်းချဉ်သီး:
vegetables		
hìn-dhì-hìn-yweq	ဟင်းသီးဟင်းရွက်
white radish		
moun-la-ú-p'yu	မုန်လာဥဖြူ
zucchini/gourd		
bù-dhì	ဘူးသီး:

Fruit

fruit		
thiq-thì	သစ်သီး:
apple ('flower-fruit')		
pàn-dhì	ပန်းသီး:
avocado ('butter-fruit')		
t'àw-baq-thì	ထောပတ်သီး:
banana		
ngăpyàw-dhì	ငှက်ပျောသီး:
breadfruit		
paun-móun-dhì	ပေါင်မုန့်သီး:
coconut		
oùn-dhì	အုန်းသီး:
custard apple ('influence-fruit')		
àw-za-thì	ဩဇာသီး:
durian		
dù-yìn-dhì	ဒူးရင်းသီး:
lemon		
shauq-thì	ရှောက်သီး:
lime		
than-băya-dhì	သံပရာသီး:
lychee		
lain-c ì-dhì	လိုင်ချီးသီး:
mango		
thăyeq-dhì	သရက်သီး:
orange		
lein-maw-dhì	လိမ္မော်သီး:
papaya ('boat-shaped fruit')		
thìn-bàw-dhì	သင်္ဘောသီး:
peach		
meq-mun-dhì	မက်မွန်သီး:
pear		
thiq-taw-dhì	သစ်တော်သီး:
pineapple		
na-naq-thì	နာနတ်သီး:
plum (damson)		
meq-màn-dhì	မက်မန်းသီး:
jujube plum		
zì-dhì	ဆီးသီး:
pomelo		
cwèh-gàw-dhì	ကျွဲကောသီး:
rambutan ('cockscomb fruit')		
ceq-mauq-thì	ကြက်မောက်သီး:
tamarind		
măjì-dhì	မန်ကျည်းသီး:
watermelon		
p'ăyèh-dhì	ဖရဲသီး:

Spices & Condiments

| betel quid | | |
| kùn-ya | ကွမ်းယာ |

butter
  t'àw-baq ထောပတ်
cardamon
  p'a-la-zé ဖါလာစေ့
cashews
  thi-ho-zí သီဟိုစေ့
chilli sauce
  ngăyouq-ye ငရုတ်ရည်
chilli
  ngăyouq-thì ငရုတ်သီး
coriander
  nan-nan-bin နံနံပင်
coconut cream
  oùn-nó အုန်းနို့
fish sauce
  ngan-pya-ye ငံပြာရည်
galangal (white ginger-like root)
  meiq-thălin မိတ်သလင်
garlic
  ceq-thun-byu ကြက်သွန်ဖြူ
ghee
  kalà t'àw-baq ကုလားထောပတ်
ginger
  gyìn ဂျင်း
honey
  pyà-ye ပျားရည်
lemongrass
  zăbălin စပါးလင်
lime (for betel)
  t'oùn ထုံး
peanuts
  mye-bèh မြေပဲ
fried peanuts
  mye-bèh-jaw မြေပဲကြော်
raisins
  zăbyiq-thì-jauq စပျစ်သီးခြောက်
rose syrup
  hnìn-ye နှင်းရည်
sago/tapioca
  tha-gu သာဂူ
salt
  s'à ဆား
sesame
  hnàn နှမ်း
soy sauce
  pèh-ngan-pya-ye ပဲငံပြာရည်
sugar
  thăjà သကြား
tofu/beancurd
  to-hù တိုဟူး

turmeric
  s'ănwìn ဆနွင်း
vinegar
  sha-lăka-ye ရှာလကာရည်

DRINKS
Cold Drinks
alcohol
  ăyeq အရက်
beer
  bi-ya ဘီယာ
coconut juice
  oùn-ye အုန်းရည်
lime juice
  than-băya-ye သံပရာရည်
milk
  nwà-nó နွားနို့
orange juice
  lein-maw-ye လိမ္မော်ရည်
soda water
  s'o-da ဆိုဒါ
soft drink
  bí-laq-ye/p'yaw-ye ဘီလပ်ရည်/ဖျော်ရည်
sugarcane juice
  can-ye ကြံရည်
toddy
  t'àn-ye ထန်းရည်
water
  ye ရေ
boiled cold water
  ye-jeq-è ရေချက်အေး
bottled water ('clean water')
  thán-ye သန့်ရေ
cold water
  ye-è ရေအေး
hot water
  ye-nwè ရေနွေး
wine
  wain ဝိုင်

Hot Drinks
plain green tea
  lăp'eq-ye-jàn/- လက်ဖက်ရည်ကြမ်း/
  ye nwè-jàn ရေနွေးကြမ်း
coffee
  kaw-fi ကော်ဖီ
Indian tea
  leq-p'eq-ye လက်ဖက်ရည်

with milk
  nwà-nó-néh နွားနို့နဲ့.
with condensed milk
  nó-s i-néh နို့ဆီနဲ့.
with lime
  than-băya-dhì-néh သံပရာသီးနဲ့.
with sugar
  dhăjà-néh သကြားနဲ့.

GAZETTEER
Place and other names in Myanmar have conventional English versions, which may appear on signs and in guidebooks. In some cases these are rather different from the pronunciation of these places.

Amarapura
  ămárá-pu-rá အမရပူရ
Aungban
  aun-bàn အောင်ပန်း
Ayeyarwady Division
  e-ya-wădi-dain ဧရာဝတီတိုင်း
Ayeyarwady River
  e-ya-wădi myiq ဧရာဝတီမြစ်
Bagan (Pagan)
  băgan ပုဂံ
New Bagan
  băgan myó-thiq ပုဂံမြို့သစ်
Old Bagan
  băgan myó-haùn ပုဂံမြို့ဟောင်း
Bago (Pegu)
  băgò ပဲခူး
Bago Division
  băgò-dain ပဲခူးတိုင်း
Bhamo
  bămaw ဗန်းမော်
Chaungtha Beach
  c'aùn-tha kàn-je ချောင်းသာ ကမ်းခြေ
Chin State
  c'in-pyi-neh ချင်းပြည်နယ်
Chindwin River
  c'in-dwin myiq ချင်းတင်းမြစ်
Dawei (Tavoy)
  dăweh ထားဝယ်
Gokteik
  gouq-t'eiq ဂုတ်ထိပ်
Heho
  hèh-hò ဟဲဟိုး

Hopong
  ho-poùn ဟိုပုံး
Hpa-an
  p'à-an ဘားအံ
Hsipaw (Thibaw)
  thi-bàw သီပေါ
Htaukkyant
  t'auq-cán ထောက်ကြံ့
Indawgyi Lake
  in-daw-jì ain အင်းတော်ကြီးအိုင်
Inle Lake
  in-lè ain အင်းလေးအိုင်
Inwa (Ava)
  in-wá အင်းဝ
Kachin State
  kăc'in-pyi-neh ကချင်ပြည်နယ်
Kaladan River
  kălădan myiq ကုလားတန်မြစ်
Kalaw
  kălàw ကလော
Kanthaya (Thaya Beach)
  kàn-tha-ya ကမ်းသာယာ
Kawthoung
  káw-thaùn ကော့သောင်း
Kayah State (Karenni State)
  kăyà-pyi-neh ကယားပြည်နယ်
Kayin State (Karen State)
  kăyin-pyi-neh ကရင်ပြည်နယ်
Kyaikkami (Amherst)
  caiq-k'a-mi ကျိုက္ခမီ
Kyaiktiyo
  caiq-t'i-yò ကျိုက်ထီးရိုး
Kengtung (Kyaingtong)
  cain-toun ကျိုင်းတုံ
Kyaukme
  cauq-mèh ကျောက်မဲ
Kyaukpadaung
  cauq-pădaùn ကျောက်ပန်းတောင်း
Kyauktan
  cauq-tàn ကျောက်တန်း
Lashio
  là-shò လားရှိုး
Letkhokkon (Beach)
  leq-k'ouq-kòn လက်ခုပ်ကုန်း
Loikaw
  loi-kaw လွိုင်ကော်
Magwe (Magway)
  măgwè မကွေး

Magwe Division
măgwè-dain မကွေးတိုင်း

Mandalay
màn-dălè မန္တလေး

Mandalay Division
màn-dălè-dain မန္တလေးတိုင်း

Maungmakan (Beach)
maùn-măgan မောင်းမကန်

Mawlamyaing (Moulmein)
maw-lămyain မော်လမြိုင်

Meiktila
meiq-t'i-la မိတ္ထီလာ

Mingun
mìn-gùn မင်းကန်း

Minnanthu
mìn-nan-thu မင်းနန်သူ

Mogok
mò-gouq မိုးကုတ်

Mon State
mun-pyi-neh မွန်ပြည်နယ်

Monywa
mon-ywa မုံရွာ

Mrauk U (Myohaung)
mrauq-ù မြောက်ဦး

Myeik (Mergui)
beiq မြိတ်

Myingyan
myìn-jan မြင်းခြံ

Myinkaba
myìn-ká-ba မြင်းကပါ

Myitkyina
myit-cì-nà မြစ်ကြီးနား

Ngapali (Beach)
ngăpăli ငပလီ

Nyaung U
nyaun-ù ညောင်ဦး

Nyaungshwe (Yaunghwe)
nyaun-shwe ညောင်ရွှေ

Pakokku
păk'ouq-ku ပခုက္ကူ

Pathein (Bassein)
păthein ပုသိမ်

Payathonzu Taunggya (Three Pagodas Pass)
p'ăyà-thoùn-zu ဘုရားသုံးဆူတောင်ကြား
taun-jà

Pindaya
pìn-dăyá ပင်းတယ

(Mt) Popa
pouq-pà-taun ပုပ္ပါးတောင်

Putao (Fort Hertz)
pu-ta-o ပူတာအို

Pwasaw
pwà-zàw ဖားစော

Pyay (Prome)
pye ပြည်

Pyinmana
pyìn-mănà ပျဉ်းမနား

Pyin-U-Lwin (Maymyo)
pyin-ù-lwin ပြင်ဦးလွင်

Rakhaing State (Arakan State)
răk'ain-pyi-neh ရခိုင်ပြည်နယ်

Sagaing
zăgain စစ်ကိုင်း

Sagaing Division
zăgain-dain စစ်ကိုင်းတိုင်း

Salay
săle စလေ

Setse (Beach)
seq-sèh စက်စဲ

Shan State
shàn-pyi-neh ရှမ်းပြည်နယ်

Shwebo
shwe-bo ရွှေဘို

Shwenyaung
shwe-nyaun ရွှေညောင်

Sittoung River (Sittang)
sit-taùn myiq စစ်တောင်းမြစ်

Sittwe (Akyab)
sit-twe စစ်တွေ

Tachileik
ta-c'i-leiq တာချီလိတ်

Tanintharyi Division (Tenasserim)
tănin-tha-yi-dain တနသ်ာရီတိုင်း

Taunggyi
taun-jì တောင်ကြီး

Taungoo
taun-ngu တောင်ငူ

Thanbyuzayat
than-byu-zăyaq သံဖြူဇရပ်

Thandwe (Sandoway)
than-dwèh သံတွဲ

Thanlwin River (Salween)
than-lwin myiq သံလွင်မြစ်

Thanlyin (Syriam)
tănyin သန်လျင်

Thazi
tha-zi သာစည်

Thiripyitsaya
thi-ri-pyiq-săya သီရိပစ္ဆယာ
Twante
tun-tè တံတေး
Union of Myanmar (Burma)
pyi-daun-zú myăma nain-gan-daw
ပြည်ထောင်စုမြန်မာနိုင်ငံတော်

Wetkyi-in
weq-cì-in ဝက်ကြီးအင်း
Yangon (Rangoon)
yan-goun ရန်ကုန်
Yangon Division
yan-goun-dain ရန်ကုန်တိုင်း

Glossary

acheiq longyi – *longyi* woven with intricate patterns and worn on ceremonial occasions

a-nyeint pwe – traditional variety *pwe*

ayeq hpyu – 'white liquor', a strong alcoholic beverage distilled from rice or palm sap

Bamar – Burman ethnic group

bedin-saya – astrologer; very important person in Myanmar, where important ceremonies, eg weddings and funerals, must be take place on auspicious days

bei moq – Burmese 'opium' cake, made with poppyseeds

betel – the nut of the areca palm which is chewed as a mild intoxicant throughout Asia

Bodhi tree – the sacred banyan tree under which the Buddha gained enlightenment; also 'bo tree'

bo gyi – literally 'big leader'

Brahman – pertaining to Brahma or to early Hindu religion (not to be confused with 'brahmin', a Hindu caste)

Buddha footprints – large, flat, stylised sculptures that represent the Buddha's feet, distinguished by 108 identifying marks; footprint shrines mark places where the Buddha himself is reputed to have walked

cantonment – the part of a colonial town occupied by the military, a carry-over from the British days

chaung, **gyaung** – stream or canal; often only seasonal

cheroots – Burmese cigars; ranging from slim to massive, but very mild as they contain only a small amount of tobacco mixed with other leaves, roots and herbs

Chindits – the 'behind enemy lines' Allied forces who harried the Japanese during WWII

chinlon – an extremely popular Burmese sport in which a circle of up to six players attempts to keep a rattan ball in the air with any part of the body except the arms and hands

chinthe – half lion/half dragon mythical beast that guards *paya* entrances

dacoit – a Hindi-Urdu term for robbers who specialise in roadside assaults

dah – long-bladed knife, part of the traditional dress for the Shan and several hill tribes

deva – Pali-Sanskrit word for spirit beings

dhamma – Pali word for the Buddhist teachings; called *dharma* in Sanskrit

dobat – rural musical instrument; a small, two-faced drum worn around the neck

eingyi – traditional long-sleeved shirt worn by Burmese men

flat – covered pontoon used to carry cargo on the river, often up to 30m long

furlong – obsolete British unit of distance still used in Myanmar; one-eighth of a mile

gaung baung – formal turban-like hat made of silk over a wicker framework, for men

gyo-daing – 'planetary post', a small shrine near the base of a zedi containing a Buddha image to which worshippers make offerings according to the day of the week they were born; there are usually eight posts, one for each day of the Burmese week (Wednesday is divided into two days)

haw – Shan word for 'palace', a reference to the large mansions used by the hereditary Shan *sawbwas*

hintha – mythical, swan-like bird; *hamsa* in Pali-Sanskrit

hka – stream or river in Kachin State

hkauq sweh – noodles

hneh – a wind instrument like an oboe; part of the Burmese orchestra

hsinbyudaw – royal white elephant

hsingaung – head elephant man, above an *oozi*

htamin zain – rice shop

htan, **tan** – sugar palm

htan ye – palm toddy, a slightly alcoholic drink made from the sap of the sugar palm

hti – umbrella-like decorated top of a stupa

htwa – half a *taung*

in – lake; eg Inle means little lake

Jataka – life stories of the Buddha; a common theme for temple paintings and reliefs

kalaga – embroidered tapestries
kamma – Pali word for the law of cause and effect; called *karma* in Sanskrit
kammahtan – meditation; *kammahtan kyaung* is a meditation monastery
kammawa – lacquered scriptures
kan, gan – beach; can also mean a tank or reservoir
Karaweik – the royal bird-mount of Vishnu (Garuda in Sanskrit); also the royal barge on Inle Lake
kon, gon – hill
kutho – merit, what you acquire through doing good; from the Pali *kusala*
kyaik – Mon word for paya
kyauk – rock
kyaung, gyaung – Burmese Buddhist monastery; pronounced chown
kye waing – circle of gongs used in a Burmese orchestra
kyi, gyi – big; eg Taunggyi means big mountain
kyun, gyun – island

lay, le, galay – small
lin gwin – cymbals in a Burmese orchestra
Lokanat – Avalokitesvara, a future Buddha and guardian spirit of the world
longyi – the Burmese unisex sarong-style lower garment, sensible wear in a tropical climate; unlike men in most other South-East Asian countries, few Burmese men have taken to western trousers

Manuthiha – half-lion/half-human mythical creature; visible around Shwedagon Paya
maya ngeh – 'lesser wife', a man's second wife
mohinga – traditional and very popular dish found at many street stalls (pronounced moun-hinga); it consists of rice noodles, fish and eggs
Myanma let-hwei – Burmese kickboxing
myit – river

myo – town; hence Maymyo (after Colonel May), Allanmyo (Major Allen) or even Bernardmyo
myothit – 'new town', usually a planned new suburb built since the 1960s

Naga – multiheaded dragon-serpent from mythology, often seen sheltering or protecting the Buddha
nam-bya – flat bread cooked in a clay oven, similar to *nan* in South Asia
nat – spirit being with the power to either protect or harm humans; Myanmar's syncretic Buddhism
nat-gadaw – spirit medium (literally 'spirit bride'), embraces a wide variety of nats
nat pwe – dance performance designed to entice a nat or nats to possess a spirit medium or *nat-gadaw*
ngapi – fermented fish or shrimp paste, an all-purpose Burmese flavouring
ngwe – silver

o-zi – a long-bodied, goblet-shaped, one-faced drum used for accompanying folk music in the country

pagoda – generic English term for zedis or stupas as well as temples; see also *paya*
pahso – *longyi* for men
pahto – Burmese word for temple, shrine or other religious structure with a hollow interior
Pali – language in which original Buddhist texts were written; the 'Latin' of Theravada Buddhism
paq-ma – Burmese bass drum
parabaik – folding Buddhist palmleaf manuscripts
pattala – bamboo xylophone used in the Burmese orchestra
paya – a generic Burmese term meaning holy one; often applied to Buddha figures, zedis and other religious monuments
pin, bin – banyan tree
pi ze – traditional tattooing, believed to make the wearer invulnerable to sword or gun
pongyi, hpongyi – Buddhist monk
pongyi-byan – cremation ceremony for an important monk

pongyikyaung – monastery; see also *kyaung*

pwe – generic Burmese word for festival, feast, celebration, ceremony or gathering; also refers to public performances of Burmese song and dance, often all-night (and all-day) affairs

pyatthat – wooden, multiroofed pavilion, usually turret-like on palace walls, as at Mandalay Palace

Pyithu Hluttaw – Peoples' Congress or parliament, now defunct

ro-ro – 'roll on, roll off', a ferryboat that carries vehicles; see also *zed craft*

saing waing – circle of drums used in a Burmese orchestra

Sanskrit – very ancient Indian language and source of many words in the Burmese vocabulary, particularly those having to do with religion, art and government

saung gauq – 13-stringed, boat-shaped harp

sawbwa – Burmese corruption of the Shan word *sao pha* or 'sky lord', the hereditary chieftains of the Shan people

sayadaw – 'master teacher', usually the chief abbot of a Buddhist monastery

shinpyu – ceremonies conducted when young boys from seven to 20 years old upwards enter a monastery for a short period of time, required of every young Buddhist male; girls have their ears pierced in a similar ceremony

shwe – golden

shwe leinmaw – orange brandy distilled in the Shan State

sikhara – Indian-style, corncob-like temple finial, found on many temples in the Bagan area

sima – see *thein*

soon – alms food offered to monks

stupa – see *zedi*

tatmadaw – Myanmar's armed forces

taung, **daung** – mountain, eg Taunggyi means 'big mountain'

taw, **daw** – a common suffix, meaning sacred, holy or royal; it can also mean forest or plantation

tazaung – shrine building, usually found around *zedis*

thabeiq – monk's food bowl; also a traditional element of stupa architecture

thanakha – yellow sandalwood-like paste, worn by many Burmese women on their faces as a combination of skin conditioner, sunblock and makeup

thein – ordination hall; called *sima* in Pali

The Thirty – the '30 comrades' of Bogyoke Aung San who joined the Japanese during WWII and eventually led Burma (Myanmar) to independence

thilashin – nun

Tripitaka – the 'three baskets'; the classic Buddhist scriptures consisting of the Vinaya (monastic discipline), the Sutta (discourses of the Buddha) and Abhidhamma (Buddhist philosophy)

twin, **dwin** – well, hole, mine

u-min, **ohn-min** – cave, usually artificial and part of a temple

u-zi – elephant handler or *mahout*

vihara – Pali-Sanskrit word for sanctuary or chapel for Buddha images

viss – Burmese unit of weight, equal to 1.6kg

votive tablet – inscribed offering tablet, usually with images of the Buddha

wa – mouth or river or lake; Inwa means 'mouth of the lake'

wa leq-hkouq – bamboo clapper, part of the Burmese orchestra

yagwin – small cymbals

Yama pwe – Burmese classical dancing based on the Indian epic *Ramayana*

ye – water, liquid

yediya – the superstitious belief that fate can be averted by carrying out certain, sometimes contradictory, activities

yoma – mountain range

youq-the pwe – Burmese marionette theatre

ywa – village; a common suffix in place names such as Monywa

zat pwe – Burmese classical dance-drama based on *Jataka* stories

zawgyi – an alchemist who has successfully achieved immortality through the ingestion of special compounds made from
base metals

zayat – an open-sided shelter or resthouse
associated with a *zedi*

zed craft – large vehicle ferry

zedi – stupa, a traditional Buddhist religious monument consisting of a solid hemispherical or gently tapering cylindrical cone,
and topped with a variety of metal and
jewel finials; zedis are often said to contain
Buddha relics

zei, **zay** – market

ACRONYMS
AM – Air Mandalay
FEC – Foreign Exchange Certificate
IWT – Inland Water Transport
MA – Myanma Airways
MAI – Myanma Airways International
MFSL – Myanma Five Star Line
MHT – Ministry of Hotels & Tourism
MTT – Myanmar Travels & Tours
NLD – National League for Democracy
SPDC – State Peace & Development Council
SLORC – State Law & Order Restoration
Council
YA – Yangon Airways

Acknowledgments

THANKS

Many thanks to the travellers who used the last edition and wrote to us with helpful hints, useful advice and interesting anecdotes:

Masud Akhtar Zaman, Alfons Akutowicz, Brett W Alcock, Dalen Alexander, Dr Rita Aloni, Paola Alzetta, Raymond Ang, Sascha Apitius, Cedric Arnaud-Battandier, Guy & Lior Backner, Chris Bain, Pochi Balladelli, David Barnett, Maria Bartolini, Alexis Berry, Ewan Best, Andrea Bianchi, John Birkett, Dennis Blackmore, David JH Blake, Oda Bogger, Anne-Marie Bouvron, JHF Bown, FJ Brannigan, Sandy Brayshaw, Frank Breiting, Edwin Briels, Robert Bryce, Cormac Bryne, Jennifer Buckle, Joy Budd, Denis Cambier, Amy Canning, Ronald Carlson, Eliane Cavalcante de Almeida, Ross Chalmers, Sewin Chan, Jaques & Liliane Chapon, Samuel Charache MD, Ethel Chicharra, Bernard Citroen, Samantha Colclough, B Campbell Cole, Teri Conti, Christopher Cook, Earl Cooper, Sylvie Corbett, A Corcoran, Geoff Cordell, Tui Cordemans, Terry Cormier, Iago & Caroline Cornelius-Jones, Cris & Ary, Anke Cruse, Alain Cuzin, Matar & Claudia Dakhil, Chris Dale, David & Sandra, Harris De Cruz, Anja de Graaf, John Deacon, Albert G Dempster, Francis Dix, Ulrike Dorrie, Marah Dorris, Olivier Doual, Lorie Downey, Francois Dufour, Nicky Dunnington-Jefferson, Michael Eckert, Venot Emmanuel, MT Erwich, Matthijs Erwich, David & Karen Eubank, Gaynor M Evans.

Salvati Fabio, Donna Ferguson, Justin Foster, Simon Fox, Ludek Frybort, Kevin Furuta, Natalie Garfield, JJ Gaudel, Ruth Gerson, Christina Gerth, Mr & Mrs Giulj, Steven F Goddard, Steve Golden, Eugen Goldfracht, Martin Gray, Matthew Gubb, Nigel Hall, Christopher Hargett, Craig Harris, Ashley Heath, Ladina Heath, Ray Hegarty, Dan Hegland, Dr Dagmar Heller, Emma Hetherington, Victor Heyde, Lucy Hill, Curtis Hinson, Evelyn Hirsch, Larry Hlebechuk, Airell Hodgkinson, Robrecht Hoet, David Hogarth, David J H Hogarth, Mark Holloway, Maciej Janowski, Gerda Jansen, Sigrid Janssen, Phillip Jeffries, Jim & Renzo, Maria Johnson, S Johnston, Rosanne Jones, Hakan Jonsson, Roger Joyner.

Louis Kalogiannidis, Khoo Kay Young, T Kelleher, Jane King, Nick Kluding, Heidi Kluender, Bo Koolen, Joachim Koster, Steffi & Rainer Krenzke, Robert Krichenbauer, Ko Ku, David Kulka, Raymond Lae, David Lai, MK Lee, TA Lee, Jurgen Leitzke, Gerry Leteve, Keith Liker, Arlene Lindbichler, Cofe Linsbauer, Chong Sau Long, Joan Longley, Gabriel Loos, Rod MacLeod, Ng Man Fei, Carl Mandabach, David Mandel, Robert & Lorraine Mann, Karen Marien, Phillip Martin, Robert Mayhew, Rick McCharles, Sunil S Mehta, Joyce Meijer, M Meijer, Frank Milla, Don Miller, Iris Miller, Ron Miller, Doris Mitsch, Linda Moldauer, Lynda Moldauer, Ana Moore, Anita Morav, J Morris, Werner Mulder, Werner R Mulder, Christine Muler, Liz Mulqueen, Hla Myaing, Jonathan Newton, Mark Nicholls, Masaki Norizuki, Alexandra Norrish, Sachiko Osada, Len Outram.

Samir Patel, Robert Patterson, Sharon Peake, Sebastian Pearson, Sabine Pensel, David Perlstein, Peter & Helen, Michael Pfeiffer, Lorenzo Piccardi, Bruce Pickering, Yoel Pinchevsky, Olaf Prawitt, Annette Primero, Low Puay Hwa Roger, Milan Rajtmajer, Sarah Ramsden, Andrew & Helen Randall, Helen Ranger, Helen Ranger, Edwin Reavley, Jules Reinhart, Miro Reverby, Ted Rheingold, John Richards, Bryan Roche, John Rolfe, Chris Rowe, Mrs Ruiter, Herb Russell, T Sagawa, Johannes Sailer, Lou Samson, Jerome Sastre, Patricia Savola, Philip Scheir, Martin Schmidt, Jutta Schutte, Sebastien, Eric Seed, Ronald Seegers, Andrew Selth, Yeo Seng Chong, Bruce Seymour, Betty Sheets, Atsuko Shinno, Yum Shoen Liang, Stans Slaats, J Slikker, Andrea Smith, Les Smith, Robert J Smits, Neil & Diana Sowaards, Sara Stahl, Marilyn Staib, David Steinke, Franco Stibiel, Amanda Stock, Nathalie Stroobant, Caroline Stuart, Yvette Stumpf, Timothy Syrota, Charles Taylor, Chris Thomas, Roslyn Thurn, Phil Ting, Norman Tod, Claudio Tomba, Lois & Steve Tonnison, Adriana Totonelli, Shelby Tucker.

Aldo Valerio, Peter Van Aernam, Christine Van den Winckel, Connie Van Der Hulst, Sandra Ann Van Dijk, JWJ van Dorp, Veronique van Gool, Jeffrey van Hout, Paul van Roekel, Joeke van Waesberghe, Piet Vanasten, Margaret Vannan, CA Vearnncombe, NH & Rene Voyer, Leonard Vum Ko Hau, Ulli Waas, Reto Wagner, Wong Wai Cheung, Susanne Wanner, Dick Warren, Hugh Waters, Emma & Gavin Watson, Jennifer West, Bob Wheatley, Claudia Wieser, Debbie Williams, John Winward, Arne Wolfart, Ken Wong, Hanspeter Worni, Patrick Wtterwulghe, Pierre Wursch, Bill Wyeth, C-h Yee, W-b Yee, Kin Yuen Ng, Zhenhui, Maarten Zonjee.

LONELY PLANET

Phrasebooks

Lonely Planet phrasebooks are packed with essential words and phrases to help travellers communicate with the locals. With colour tabs for quick reference, an extensive vocabulary and use of script, these handy pocket-sized language guides cover day-to-day travel situations.

- handy pocket-sized books
- easy to understand Pronunciation chapter
- clear & comprehensive Grammar chapter
- romanisation alongside script to allow ease of pronunciation
- script throughout so users can point to phrases for every situation
- full of cultural information and tips for the traveller

'...vital for a real DIY spirit and attitude in language learning'
– Backpacker

'the phrasebooks have good cultural backgrounders and offer solid advice for challenging situations in remote locations'
– San Francisco Examiner

Arabic (Egyptian) • Arabic (Moroccan) • Australian *(Australian English, Aboriginal and Torres Strait languages)* • Baltic States *(Estonian, Latvian, Lithuanian)* • Bengali • Brazilian • British • Burmese • Cantonese • Central Asia • Central Europe *(Czech, French, German, Hungarian, Italian, Slovak)* • Eastern Europe *(Bulgarian, Czech, Hungarian, Polish, Romanian, Slovak)* • Ethiopian (Amharic) • Fijian • French • German • Greek • Hebrew phrasebook • Hill Tribes • Hindi/Urdu • Indonesian • Italian • Japanese • Korean • Lao • Latin American Spanish • Malay • Mandarin • Mediterranean Europe *(Albanian, Croatian, Greek, Italian, Macedonian, Maltese, Serbian, Slovene)* • Mongolian • Nepali • Papua New Guinea • Pilipino (Tagalóg) • Quechua • Russian • Scandinavian Europe *(Danish, Finnish, Icelandic, Norwegian, Swedish)* • South-East Asia *(Burmese, Indonesian, Khmer, Lao, Malay, Tagalog Pilipino, Thai, Vietnamese)* • South Pacific Languages • Spanish (Castilian) *(also includes Catalan, Galician and Basque)* • Sri Lanka • Swahili • Thai • Tibetan • Turkish • Ukrainian • USA *(US English, Vernacular, Native American languages, Hawaiian)* • Vietnamese • Western Europe *(Basque, Catalan, Dutch, French, German, Greek, Irish)*

LONELY PLANET

Lonely Planet Journeys

JOURNEYS is a unique collection of travel writing – published by the company that understands travel better than anyone else. It is a series for anyone who has ever experienced – or dreamed of – the magical moment when they encountered a strange culture or saw a place for the first time. They are tales to read while you're planning a trip, while you're on the road or while you're in an armchair in front of a fire.

These outstanding titles explore our planet through the eyes of a diverse group of international writers. JOURNEYS books catch the spirit of a place, illuminate a culture, recount a crazy adventure or introduce a fascinating way of life. They always entertain, and always enrich the experience of travel.

IN RAJASTHAN
Royina Grewal
As she writes of her travels through Rajasthan, Indian writer Royina Grewal takes us behind the exotic facade of this fabled destination: here is an insider's perceptive account of India's most colourful state, conveying the excitement and challenges of a region in transition.

SHOPPING FOR BUDDHAS
Jeff Greenwald
In his obsessive search for the perfect Buddha statue in the backstreets of Kathmandu, Jeff Greenwald discovers more than he bargained for ... and his souvenir-hunting turns into an ironic metaphor for the clash between spiritual riches and material greed. Politics, religion and serious shopping collide in this witty account of an enlightening visit to Nepal.

BRIEF ENCOUNTERS
Stories of Love, Sex & Travel
edited by Michelle de Kretser
Love affairs on the road, passionate holiday flings, disastrous pick-ups, erotic encounters ... In this seductive collection of stories, 22 authors from around the world write about travel romances. A tourist in Peru falls for her handsome guide; a writer explores the ambiguities of his relationship with a Japanese woman; a beautiful young man on a train proposes marriage ... Combining fiction and reportage, *Brief Encounters* is must-have reading – for everyone who has dreamt of escape with that perfect stranger.

Includes stories by Pico Iyer, Mary Morris, Emily Perkins, Mona Simpson, Lisa St Aubin de Terán, Paul Theroux and Sara Wheeler.

LONELY PLANET

Lonely Planet Travel Atlases

onely Planet has long been famous for the number and quality of its guidebook maps. Now we've gone one step further and produced a handy companion series: Lonely Planet travel atlases – maps of a country produced in book form.

Unlike other maps, which look good but lead travellers astray, our travel atlases have been researched on the road by Lonely Planet's experienced team of writers. All details are carefully checked to ensure the atlas corresponds with the equivalent Lonely Planet guidebook.

- full-colour throughout
- maps researched and checked by Lonely Planet authors
- place names correspond with Lonely Planet guidebooks
- no confusing spelling differences
- legend and travelling information in English, French, German, Japanese and Spanish
- size: 230 x 160 mm

Available now: Chile & Easter Island • Egypt • India & Bangladesh • Israel & the Palestinian Territories • Jordan, Syria & Lebanon • Kenya • Laos • Portugal • South Africa, Lesotho & Swaziland • Thailand • Turkey • Vietnam • Zimbabwe, Botswana & Namibia

Lonely Planet TV Series & Videos

onely Planet travel guides have been brought to life on television screens around the world. Like our guides, the programs are based on the joy of independent travel, and look honestly at some of the most exciting, picturesque and frustrating places in the world. Each show is presented by one of three travellers from Australia, England or the USA and combines an innovative mixture of video, Super-8 film, atmospheric soundscapes and original music.

Videos of each episode – containing additional footage not shown on television – are available from good book and video shops, but the availability of individual videos varies with regional screening schedules.

Video destinations include: Alaska • American Rockies • Australia – The South-East • Baja California & the Copper Canyon • Brazil • Central Asia • Chile & Easter Island • Corsica, Sicily & Sardinia – The Mediterranean Islands • East Africa (Tanzania & Zanzibar) • Ecuador & the Galapagos Islands • Greenland & Iceland • Indonesia • Israel & the Sinai Desert • Jamaica • Japan • La Ruta Maya • Morocco • New York • North India • Pacific Islands (Fiji, Solomon Islands & Vanuatu) • South India • South West China • Turkey • Vietnam • West Africa • Zimbabwe, Botswana & Namibia

The Lonely Planet TV series is produced by: Pilot Productions
The Old Studio
18 Middle Row
London W10 5AT, UK

LONELY PLANET

Guides by Region

Lonely Planet is known worldwide for publishing practical, reliable and no-nonsense travel information in our guides and on our Web site. The Lonely Planet list covers just about every accessible part of the world. Currently there are nine series: travel guides, shoestring guides, walking guides, city guides, phrasebooks, audio packs, travel atlases, diving and snorkeling guides and travel literature.

AFRICA Africa – the South • Africa on a shoestring • Arabic (Egyptian) phrasebook • Arabic (Moroccan) phrasebook • Cairo • Cape Town • Central Africa • East Africa • Egypt • Egypt travel atlas • Ethiopian (Amharic) phrasebook • The Gambia & Senegal • Healthy Travel Africa • Kenya • Kenya travel atlas • Malawi, Mozambique & Zambia • Morocco • North Africa • South Africa, Lesotho & Swaziland • South Africa, Lesotho & Swaziland travel atlas • Swahili phrasebook • Tanzania, Zanzibar & Pemba • Trekking in East Africa • Tunisia • West Africa • Zimbabwe, Botswana & Namibia • Zimbabwe, Botswana & Namibia travel atlas
Travel Literature: The Rainbird: A Central African Journey • Songs to an African Sunset: A Zimbabwean Story • Mali Blues: Traveling to an African Beat

AUSTRALIA & THE PACIFIC Australia • Australian phrasebook • Bushwalking in Australia • Bushwalking in Papua New Guinea • Fiji • Fijian phrasebook • Islands of Australia's Great Barrier Reef • Melbourne • Micronesia • New Caledonia • New South Wales & the ACT • New Zealand • Northern Territory • Outback Australia • Papua New Guinea • Papua New Guinea (Pidgin) phrasebook • Queensland • Rarotonga & the Cook Islands • Samoa • Solomon Islands • South Australia • South Pacific Languages phrasebook • Sydney • Tahiti & French Polynesia • Tasmania • Tonga • Tramping in New Zealand • Vanuatu • Victoria • Western Australia
Travel Literature: Islands in the Clouds • Kiwi Tracks • Sean & David's Long Drive

CENTRAL AMERICA & THE CARIBBEAN Bahamas and Turks & Caicos • Barcelona • Bermuda • Central America on a shoestring • Costa Rica • Cuba • Dominican Republic & Haiti • Eastern Caribbean • Guatemala, Belize & Yucatán: La Ruta Maya • Jamaica • Mexico • Mexico City • Panama
Travel Literature: Green Dreams: Travels in Central America

EUROPE Amsterdam • Andalucía • Austria • Baltic States phrasebook • Barcelona • Berlin • Britain • British phrasebook • Brussels, Bruges & Antwerp • Canary Islands • Central Europe • Central Europe phrasebook • Corsica • Croatia • Czech & Slovak Republics • Denmark • Dublin • Eastern Europe • Eastern Europe phrasebook • Edinburgh • Estonia, Latvia & Lithuania • Europe • Finland • France • French phrasebook • Germany • German phrasebook • Greece • Greek phrasebook • Hungary • Iceland, Greenland & the Faroe Islands • Ireland • Italian phrasebook • Italy • Lisbon • London • Mediterranean Europe • Mediterranean Europe phrasebook • Norway • Paris • Poland • Portugal • Portugal travel atlas • Prague • Provence & the Côte d'Azur • Romania & Moldova • Rome • Russia, Ukraine & Belarus • Russian phrasebook • Scandinavian & Baltic Europe • Scandinavian Europe phrasebook • Scotland • Slovenia • Spain • Spanish phrasebook • St Petersburg • Switzerland • Trekking in Spain • Ukrainian phrasebook • Vienna • Walking in Britain • Walking in Italy • Walking in Ireland • Walking in Switzerland • Western Europe • Western Europe phrasebook
Travel Literature: The Olive Grove: Travels in Greece

INDIAN SUBCONTINENT Bangladesh • Bengali phrasebook • Bhutan • Delhi • Goa • Hindi/Urdu phrasebook • India • India & Bangladesh travel atlas • Indian Himalaya • Karakoram Highway • Mumbai • Nepal • Nepali phrasebook • Pakistan • Rajasthan • South India • Sri Lanka • Sri Lanka phrasebook • Trekking in the Indian Himalaya • Trekking in the Karakoram & Hindukush • Trekking in the Nepal Himalaya
Travel Literature: In Rajasthan • Shopping for Buddhas

LONELY PLANET

Mail Order

Lonely Planet products are distributed worldwide. They are also available by mail order from Lonely Planet, so if you have difficulty finding a title please write to us. North and South American residents should write to 150 Linden St, Oakland, CA 94607, USA; European and African residents should write to 10a Spring Place, London NW5 3BH, UK; and residents of other countries to PO Box 617, Hawthorn, Victoria 3122, Australia.

ISLANDS OF THE INDIAN OCEAN Madagascar & Comoros • Maldives • Mauritius, Réunion & Seychelles

MIDDLE EAST & CENTRAL ASIA Arab Gulf States • Central Asia • Central Asia phrasebook • Hebrew phrasebook • Iran • Israel & the Palestinian Territories • Israel & the Pa estinian Territories travel atlas • Istanbul • Jerusalem • Jordan & Syria • Jordan, Syria & Lebanon travel atlas • Lebanon • Middle East on a shoestring • Syria • Turkey • Turkish phrasebook • Turkey travel atlas • Yemen
Travel Literature: The Gates of Damascus • Kingdom of the Film Stars: Journey into Jordan

NORTH AMERICA Alaska • Backpacking in Alaska • Baja California • California & Nevada • Canada • Chicago • Florida • Hawaii • Honolulu • Los Angeles • Louisiana • Miami • New England USA • New Orleans • New York City • New York, New Jersey & Pennsylvania • Pacific Northwest USA • Puerto Rico • Rocky Mountain States • San Francisco • Seattle • Southwest USA • Texas • USA • USA phrasebook • Vancouver • Washington, DC & the Capital Region
Travel Literature: Drive Thru America

NORTH-EAST ASIA Beijing • Cantonese phrasebook • China • Hong Kong • Hong Kong, Macau & Guangzhou • Japan • Japanese phrasebook • Japanese audio pack • Korea • Korean phrasebook • Kyoto • Mandarin phrasebook • Mongolia • Mongolian phrasebook • North-East Asia on a shoestring • Seoul • South-West China • Taiwan • Tibet • Tibetan phrasebook • Tokyo
Travel Literature: Lost Japan

SOUTH AMERICA Argentina, Uruguay & Paraguay • Bolivia • Brazil • Brazilian phrasebook • Buenos Aires • Chile & Easter Island • Chile & Easter Island travel atlas • Colombia • Ecuador & the Galapagos Islands • Latin American Spanish phrasebook • Peru • Quechua phrasebook • Rio de Janeiro • South America on a shoestring • Trekking in the Patagorian Andes • Venezuela
Travel Literature: Full Circle: A South American Journey

SOUTH-EAST ASIA Bali & Lombok • Bangkok • Burmese phrasebook • Cambodia • Hanoi • Healthy Travel Asia & India • Hill Tribes phrasebook • Ho Chi Minh City • Indonesia • Indonesia's Eastern Islands • Indonesian phrasebook • Indonesian audio pack • Jakarta • Java • Laos • Lao phrasebook • Laos travel atlas • Malay phrasebook • Malaysia, Singapore & Brunei • Myanmar (Burma) • Philippines • Pilipino (Tagalog) phrasebook • Singapore • South-East Asia on a shoestring • South-East Asia phrasebook • Thailand • Thailand's Islands & Beaches • Thailand travel atlas • Thai phrasebook • Thai audio pack • Vietnam • Vietnamese phrasebook • Vietnam travel atlas

ALSO AVAILABLE: Antarctica • Brief Encounters: Stories of Love, Sex & Travel • Chasing Rickshaws • Lonely Planet Unpacked • Not the Only Planet: Travel Stories from Science Fiction • Sacred India • Travel with Children • Traveller's Tales

LONELY PLANET

Lonely Planet On-line

Whether you've just begun planning your next trip, or you're chasing down specific info on currency regulations or visa requirements, check out Lonely Planet On-line for up-to-the minute travel information.

As well as mini guides to more than 250 destinations, you'll find maps, photos, travel news, health and visa updates, travel advisories, and discussion of the ecological and political issues you need to be aware of as you travel. You'll also find timely upgrades to popular guidebooks which you can print out and stick in the back of your book.

There's also an on-line travellers' forum where you can share your experience of life on the road, meet travel companions and ask other travellers for their recommendations and advice.

And of course we have a complete and up-to-date list of all Lonely Planet travel products including travel guides, diving and snorkeling guides, phrasebooks, atlases, travel literature and videos, and a simple on-line ordering facility if you can't find the book you want elsewhere.

Lonely Planet Diving & Snorkeling Guides

Beautifully illustrated with full-colour photos throughout, Lonely Planet's Pisces Books explore the world's best diving and snorkeling areas and prepare divers for what to expect when they get there, both topside and underwater.

Dive sites are described in detail with specifics on depths, visibility, level of difficulty, special conditions, underwater photography tips and common and unusual marine life present. You'll also find practical logistical information and coverage on topside activities and attractions, sections on diving health and safety, plus listings for diving services, live-aboards, dive resorts and tourist offices.

FREE Lonely Planet Newsletters

We love hearing from you and think you'd like to hear from us.

Planet Talk

Our FREE quarterly printed newsletter is full of tips from travellers and anecdotes from Lonely Planet guidebook authors. Every issue is packed with up-to-date travel news and advice, and includes:

- a postcard from Lonely Planet co-founder Tony Wheeler
- a swag of mail from travellers
- a look at life on the road through the eyes of a Lonely Planet author
- topical health advice
- prizes for the best travel yarn
- news about forthcoming Lonely Planet events
- a complete list of Lonely Planet books and other titles

To join our mailing list, residents of the UK, Europe and Africa can email us at go@lonelyplanet.co.uk; residents of North and South America can email us at info@lonelyplanet.com; the rest of the world can email us at talk2us@lonelyplanet.com.au, or contact any Lonely Planet office.

Comet

Our FREE monthly email newsletter brings you all the latest travel news, features, interviews, competitions, destination ideas, travellers' tips & tales, Q&As, raging debates and related links. Find out what's new on the Lonely Planet Web site and which books are about to hit the shelves.

Subscribe from your desktop: www.lonelyplanet.com/comet

Index

Bold indicates maps.

Bold indicates maps.

xed Text

MAP LEGEND

BOUNDARIES

─··─··─··─	International
─··─··─··─	State
─ ─ ─ ─	Disputed

HYDROGRAPHY

	Coastline
	River, Creek
	Lake
	Intermittent Lake
	Salt Lake
	Canal
⊚ ──➤──	Spring, Rapids
─∦─	Waterfalls
▲ ▲ ▲	Swamp

○	**CAPITAL**	National Capital
◉	**CAPITAL**	State Capital
●	**CITY**	City
●	**Town**	Town
●	**Village**	Village
○		Point of Interest
■		Place to Stay
⋏		Camping Ground
⌗		Caravan Park
⌂		Hut or Chalet
▼		Place to Eat
▮		Pub or Bar

ROUTES & TRANSPORT

	Freeway
	Highway
	Major Road
	Minor Road
══════	Unsealed Road
	City Freeway
	City Highway
	City Road
	City Street, Lane

	Pedestrian Mall
⟩══⟨	Tunnel
├─┼─┼─●─┼─	Train Route & Station
─ ─ ─Ⓜ─	Metro & Station
	Tramway
─⊩─⊩─⊩─⊩─	Cable Car or Chairlift
─ ─ ─ ─ ─	Walking Track
· · · · · · · ·	Walking Tour
─ ─ ─ ─ ─	Ferry Route

AREA FEATURES

	Building
✿	Park, Gardens
+ + × ×	Cemetery

	Market
	Beach, Desert
	Urban Area

MAP SYMBOLS

✈	Airport		🏛	Museum
	Ancient or City Wall		🜨	National Park
∴	Archaeological Site		)(	Pass
🏃	Beach		★	Police Station
⌒	Cave		✉	Post Office
🏛	City Hall		▭	Swimming Pool
✚	Church		✡	Synagogue
	Cliff or Escarpment		卐	Temple (Hindu)
🗼	Clocktower, Monument		卍	Temple (Other)
◒ ✚	Embassy, Hospital		☬	Temple (Sikh)
⚑	Golf Course		⊡	Tomb
❄	Lookout		❶	Tourist Information
☪ ⊿	Mosque, Paya		⊖	Transport
▲	Mountain or Hill		🐾	Zoo

Note: not all symbols displayed above appear in this book

LONELY PLANET OFFICES

Australia
PO Box 617, Hawthorn, Victoria 3122
☎ 03 9819 1877 fax 03 9819 6459
email: talk2us@lonelyplanet.com.au

USA
150 Linden St, Oakland, CA 94607
☎ 510 893 8555 TOLL FREE: 800 275 8555
fax 510 893 8572
email: info@lonelyplanet.com

UK
10a Spring Place, London NW5 3BH
☎ 020 7428 4800 fax 020 7428 4828
email: go@lonelyplanet.co.uk

France
1 rue du Dahomey, 75011 Paris
☎ 01 55 25 33 00 fax 01 55 25 33 01
email: bip@lonelyplanet.fr
minitel: 3615 lonelyplanet *(1,29 F TTC/min)*

World Wide Web: www.lonelyplanet.com *or* AOL keyword: lp
Lonely Planet Images: lpi@lonelyplanet.com.au